sandiṭṭhiko akāliko ehipassiko opaneyyiko
paccattaṁ veditabbo viññūhī'ti

Well-revealed by the world-honoured one, the Law
Is immediately perceptible; unpostponed; inviting one to come and see; applicable;
To be discovered by any wise person, by himself or herself.[1]

{ BUDDHA }

chos-kyi sku-la byams-sdang mi-mnga' yang, srid-gsum gdug-pa ma-lus 'dul-bai phyir,
thugs-rje thabs-kyis khrod-rgyal skur bstan-pa, 'jigs-byed gshin-rje gshed-la phyag-'ts'al-lo

Homage to the fearful deathlord-butcherer, revealed by gracious ways as the king of wrath,
To tame all ill of the triple world, but none, tho' no love nor hate holds in the Body of Truth![2]

{ SANGHA }

sarvasattvaniḥsvabhāvāt tadhi sarvasattvamaṇḍam

Understanding all beings lack independent reality, all beings are the seat of awakening.[3]

---

[1] These are the canonical praises of the Dharma or the Laws the Buddha discovered, as stated for example in the *Cloth Simile Discourse,* no. 7 of the Medium-length Discourses of the Theravāda canon. Listen to the Pali at:
http://www.buddhanet.net/filelib/mp3/06-chant-06.mp3

[2] These lines are from a Tibetan meditation manual derived from *The Tantra of Thunderbolt Great Terror (Vajramahābhairava)*, an esoteric tradition of Indo-Tibetan Buddhism.

[3] From The Discourse Delivered by Immaculate Renown (Vimalakīrti), a teaching for the Career of Awakening Beings.

Kālāmā Sutta
Rediscovery of Conscience

Saber Uddiyan

Vajra Publications
www.vajrabooks.com.np

Published by

Vajra Publications

Jyatha, Thamel, Kathmandu, Nepal

Tel.: 977-1-4220562, Fax: 977-1-4246536

e-mail: bidur_la@mos.com.np

www.vajrabooks.com.np; www.vajrabookshop.com

Distributed by

Vajra Book Shop

Kathmandu, Nepal

ISBN No. 978-9937-506-50-2

Printed in Nepal

Contents

Preface

Here we present two books:

Book One is the original Pali text and a new English translation of the Kālāmā Sutta. I have taken as authoritative the Pali text from the Chaṭṭha Saṅgāyana (the Sixth Council of the Elders' School, which took place at Kaba Aye, in Yangon, Myanmar in 1954) as avaliable at the website[4] of the Vipassana Research Institute at Igatpuri, India, which includes variant readings. I have compared previous complete translations by F. L. Woodward[5], Thannisaro Bhikkhu[6], Soma Thera[7] and partial translations by Hari Shankar Prasad[8] and Saya U Chit Tin[9]. Translation rationales are given in an appendix[10].

Book Two is my detailed commentary on, and reflection on the implications of, the discourse. Its main purpose is to demonstrate the urgent relevance of the discourse to our situation in the world today. It will be noted that I have taken the scope of the Buddha's advice to be very broad. Such an approach has been criticised[11] by some members of the Elders' School. However, I believe that I have sufficiently justified this choice of scope in the course of the commentary.

A few of the points made are original, most not. Some of the latter are expressed in what will seem novel ways. This is partly because of my lack of familiarity with many of the disciplines the Buddha's advice touches on, but also partly out of a sense that not only need one not frame points in particular jargon, but also those wisdoms in danger of neglect deserve expressing again and again in fresh language.

While I have aimed for even-handedness and meticulousness, there is behind the points I attemt to elucidate what the Buddha would probably disparage as 'sārambha', which means getting into a temper and becoming haughty, a term applied especially in a situation of mutual grappling. It is my

---

4 (The Pḷali Tipiṭaka)

5 (Hare & Woodward, 1932/2006)

6(Bhikkhu, 2009)

7 (Thera S. , 2009)

8 (Prasad, 2007)

9 (Tin, 1982)

10 Appendix Two: Translation rationales, p. 528.

11 See Introduction, p. vii.

regretful conviction that, original or not, these are all points which should be remembered again and again if we are to remain sane on this earth. The commentary is presented therefore with something of a sense of urgency which I do not claim always to have repressed.

I have drawn on my little knowledge of Buddhist, Islāmic and Christian teachings, which I owe entirely to my teachers, and for any distortions of which, unwittingly wrought due to the limitations of my understanding, I apologise. Because the commentary is so far-ranging it touches on a great number of academic fields in which I have insufficient experience to contextualise my points or frame them in language workers in those fields would find familiar. I beg their patience in this matter and hope I have not trodden on too many toes.

The commentary will, I hope, be found insightful, no matter from what background the reader comes. It is most emphatically not intended for Buddhists alone: the points apply to a diversity of practices and beliefs. A great deal of discussion of Islām and Christianity is made, for example, and I hope adherents of those faiths will read it carefully and seriously, for although challenges are made to elements in those faiths (as to elements in Buddhism) they are made carefully and seriously. But its most urgent message addresses not these religions' doctrines but certain seldom questioned characteristics found among them and their adherents *and more importantly beyond them*, in secular society as much as in the religious, characteristics which drag us all towards catastrophe and require remedial measures.

The Kālāmā Sutta, whether or not it stands as the vindication of free inquiry the rationalist enthusiasts would like it to be, presents, I am quite persuaded, a trenchant critique of these ominous characteristics, and offers radical and surprising solutions to them.

I hope and pray that, through the circumstance of her or his intelligence, meeting the discourse and considering, with the aid of the commentary, its implications, the reader will feel encouraged and empowered to contribute to realising these solutions.

Introduction

The Kālāmā Sutta: a minor scripture of Theravāda Buddhism?

The scriptures known as the 'Pali canon' ('Pali' referring to the language of these scriptures, and meaning 'scriptural') of the Theravāda or 'Elders' School' of Buddhism were first published in their entirety in Burma in 1900 CE and the oldest surviving manuscripts are (incomplete and) from the 15th century. However the school's tradition maintains that the scriptures have been copied in writing continuously since the 1st century BCE and between the Buddha's lifetime and then that they were transmitted perfectly orally.

Among them the Kālāmā Sutta does not stand out as being particularly important, at least if we judge by how it has been classified. Fig. 1 shows the Pali canon's divisions. Within the 'Three Boxes' or Tipiṭaka it is in the Discourse Box, the Sutta Piṭaka, meaning that it is a record of a discourse given by the Buddha or one of the major disciples (in this case by the Buddha) on the Laws of Reality, Dhammā, rather than regulations of monastic discipline, Vināya, or the classified 'Higher Teaching', Abhidhamma. Among the Discourses it is classified as one of the Numerical Section, the Aṅguttara Nikāya, because it was felt that some numbered list of phenomena in it was its most defining feature. Among these it is placed in the Threes Section, Tika Nipāta, since in this case it is a list of three phenomena which is included in the discourse. Among these it is placed in the fifth or Minor Group, Cūlavagga, and within that, in the second or Large Group, Mahāvagga. Within that it is the fifth discourse.

Most scholars concur on the unlikelihood of these texts recording what the Buddha said, though the texts themselves make that claim, but also on the probability that a lot of what the Buddha did teach is likely to be in the texts somewhere, though with a lot of later material added, and with a great many adjustments for the sake of memorising the texts for oral transmission: they contain a great deal of formalised chunks which are repeated pretty much unchanged throughout the texts, and this discourse includes several. Much of the material in this discourse is repeated verbatim in the next one, delivered not by the Buddha but by the disciple Nandaka, to Sālha, and in another discourse to the Licchavi Bhaddiya.

However many people today who have never practised Buddhism in any tradition, and who certainly are not Pali scholars delving into the further nooks and crannies of the Three Baskets, have heard of the Kālāmā Sutta. It has gained a certain notoriety, and as we shall see this is not by accident, for its contents speak to us directly across the millennia, and seem if anything more relevant today than they were when first delivered.

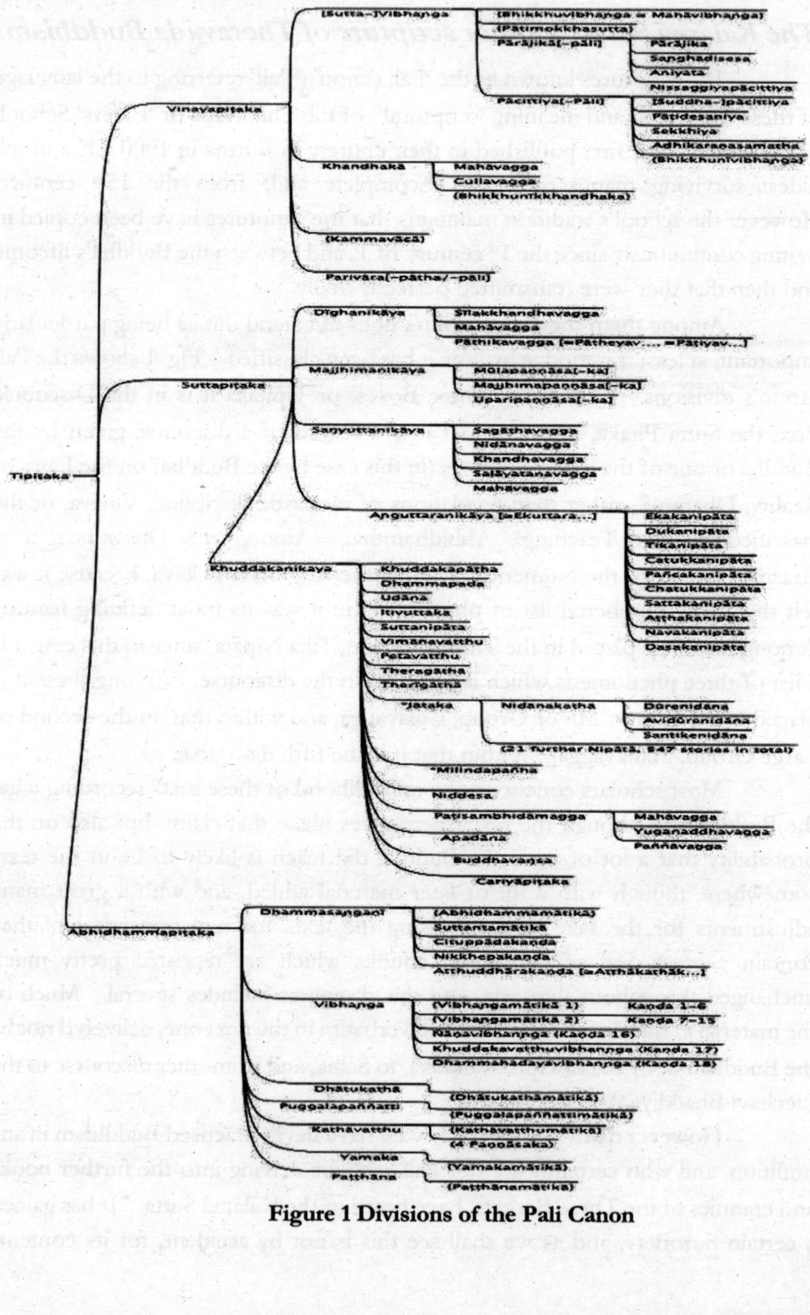

Figure 1 Divisions of the Pali Canon

The Kālāmā Sutta: The Buddha's Charter of Free Inquiry?

In stark contrast to this lowly status in the canon, was the exalting appreciation of the discourse which quickly developed in post-Christian countries, by which I mean those countries which, in the last century or so, have seen an explosion of interest in religion or 'spiritual approaches' other that the Christianity which had previously dominated them. In these countries science had become the new authority, and religious faith a private, and for some even embarrassing, matter.

For them the novelty of Buddhism as it was being 'discovered' (in the same sense, if sense is the word, as America had been) was exciting. Here was a religion which needed no Creator God, but emphasised the spiritual path as something to be worked out by the individual. Its frequent insistence on direct experience and its deconstruction or even disregard of metaphysics had an obvious resonance with the scientific method that excessively metaphysical Christianity conspicuously lacked. Schopenhauer and others were convinced that this new contact (with Buddhism and Hinduism) would lead to a much-needed revolution in European thought. Since then a great deal has been written on the parallels between Buddhism and science[12], Buddhism or Hinduism or Taoism and quantum physics[13], Buddhism and psychoanalysis[14], etc. And the Kālāmā Sutta has become perhaps the most quoted scripture in Buddhism[15].

However, as they suffered from afar this extraordinary spectacle, some doctors in its 'more native' lands were not amused, as is exemplified by various articles they wrote in which they showed themselves highly critical of it.

There is at present a view, widely prevalent especially among

---

12 See the excellent surveys by B. Alan Wallace (Contemplative Science: Where Buddhism and Neuroscience Converge (Columbia Series in Science and Religion), 2009) (Embracing Mind: The Common Ground of Science and Spirituality, 2008) (Hidden Dimensions: The Unification of Physics and Consciousness (Columbia Series in Science and Religion), 2009).

13 Starting with Capra (The Tao of Physics: An Exploration of the Parallels Between Modern Physics and Eastern Mysticism, 1975) which has provoked various criticisms (Scerri, 1989).

14 Such as a pioneer work (Suzuki, Fromm, & De Martino, 1970) which has the privilege of being one of the handful of books on Buddhism translated into Arabic, and now a swathe of modern works such as Safran (2003).

15 A Google search throws up 80,000 hits as compared to 75,000 for *The Diamond Sutra*, with *The Lotus Sutra* and *The Heart Sutra* at about 150,000 each.

> the educated Buddhists, that Buddhism is a rationalist teaching based on scientifically verifiable evidence. Much has been written to substantiate this view-point and, undoubtedly, such writings have immensely contributed to the further strengthening and spreading of this view. Most of the proponents of this view cite the Kālāmā Sutta of the Anguttara-nikaya as providing unassailable evidence to prove that Buddhism is a rationalistic teaching with an absolutely scientific basis, and that the Buddha advocated a rationalistic approach as the sole method of understanding all his teachings.
>
> It is no exaggeration to say that it is Western scholarship that highlighted the importance of the Kālāmā Sutta as some kind of 'Charter of Free Inquiry'. This 'new finding' was enthusiastically taken up and strongly supported by the predominantly Western-trained Buddhist scholarship of the time to bring to light that the Buddha denounced adherence to blind faith and dogmatism and instead encouraged free inquiry and investigation. In further support of such a position, these writers cited the Buddha's rejection of the belief in a divine creator, his acceptance of free will, his anthropocentric approach to the human predicament, his acceptance of the superiority of man, his invitation to the followers to inquire about the Dhamma as well as his own claim to enlightenment and so on.[16]

There was lively concern that the Buddha was being misrepresented:

> On the basis of a single passage, quoted out of context, the Buddha has been made out to be a pragmatic empiricist who dismisses all doctrine and faith, and whose Dhamma is simply a freethinker's kit to truth which invites each one to accept and reject whatever he [sic] likes. But does the Kālāmā Sutta really justify such views? Or do we meet in these claims just another set of variations on that egregious old tendency to interpret the Dhamma according to whatever notions are congenial to oneself – or to those to whom one is preaching? [...] Partly in reaction to dogmatic religion, partly in subservience to the reigning paradigm of objective scientific knowledge, it has become fashionable to hold, by appeal to the Kālāmā Sutta, that the Buddha's teaching

[16] The voice from Sri Lanka: Sanath Nanayakkara writing in the Kandy-based periodical Bodhi Leaves (Nanayakkara, 2002).

> dispenses with faith and formulated doctrine and asks us to accept only what we can personally verify.[17]

The discourse passage in question, so often quoted, 'out of context', is a list of widely accepted sources of knowledge or authorities, each of which the Buddha advises should not be relied on for certainty in the matter of deciding what practices to adopt and what practices to abandon. The new converts, carried away by their rationalist enthusiasm (as it were), were perceived to have extended the scope of the Buddha's advice too far.

> …they concluded that the Kālāmā Sutta advocates the use of free, independent thinking as the only valid means of deciding what is right and wrong with regard to all matters, religious as well as otherwise. […] The Sutta itself does not provide any justification to expand the ambit of its application, either to cover all matters pertaining to the Dhamma, or in general to all matters. This second assumption is obviously very far-fetched.
>
> There are many matters that we all cannot understand and know for ourselves. Yet, we accept them and take them for granted reposing 'faith' on the competence of those who pronounce views on them. We would not be able to conduct even affairs of day to day life if we ourselves try to understand and know all issues and problems that we have to face. This is why we seek the help, and advice of those who are more knowledgeable, and possessing expertise in different areas.
>
> Even the first assumption is questionable. The Buddha made this admonition to an ordinary set of people. Therefore, it is apparent that he did not expect them to use any expertise or super-knowledge in deciding on the issues concerned.[18]

In other words, the scope of the advice should be recognised: as to the Kālāmā people and those like them, asking the same questions they were asking. If it were advocating free inquiry at all, it would be into an ordinary person's confusion at the beginning of the spiritual training only, and not beyond.

However, as we shall see, the Kālāmā people were not the only people to be advised with this critique of sources of knowledge, and it is debatable how

[17] (Bodhi, 2009)

[18] (Nanayakkara, 2002)

easily we, even dressed in robes, can escape the epithet 'mere ordinary people'. The pronouncements of the elders have not been unanimous:

> 'The Buddha's Charter of Free Inquiry' [...] The instruction of the Kālāmās (Kālāma Sutta) is justly famous for its encouragement of free inquiry; the spirit of the sutta signifies a teaching that is exempt from fanaticism, bigotry, dogmatism, and intolerance.
>
> The reasonableness of the Dhamma, the Buddha's teaching, is chiefly evident in its *welcoming careful examination at all stages of the path to enlightenment.*[19]

[19] (Thera S. , Kalama Sutta: The Buddha's Charter of Free Inquiry, 1987) Italics mine: notice the contradiction with the earlier commentator's assertion that the critique does not even apply to all aspects of the Dhamma.

BOOK ONE: the KALAMA SUTTA

The Discourse
to the Kālāmā People

Chapter One: THE SETTING

Evaṁ me sutaṁ – ekaṁ samayaṁ bhagavā kosalesu cārikaṁ caramāno mahatā bhikkhusaṅghena saddhiṁ yena kesaputtaṁ[20] nāma kālāmānaṁ nigamo tadavasari. Assosuṁ kho kesaputtiyā kālāmā – 'samaṇo khalu, bho, gotamo sakyaputto sakyakulā pabbajito kesaputtaṁ anuppatto. Taṁ kho pana bhavantaṁ gotamaṁ evaṁ kalyāṇo kittisaddo abbhuggato – itipi so bhagavā arahaṁ sammāsambuddho vijjācaraṇasampanno sugato lokavidū anuttaro purisadammasārathi satthā devamanussānaṁ buddho bhagavā. So imaṁ lokaṁ sadevakaṁ samārakaṁ sabrahmakaṁ sassamaṇabrāhmaṇiṁ pajaṁ sadevamanussaṁ sayaṁ abhiññā sacchikatvā pavedeti. So dhammaṁ deseti ādikalyāṇaṁ majjhekalyāṇaṁ pariyosānakalyāṇaṁ sātthaṁ sabyañjanaṁ kevalaparipuṇṇaṁ parisuddhaṁ brahmacariyaṁ pakāseti. Sādhu kho pana tathārūpānaṁ arahataṁ dassanaṁ hotī'ti.

Thus have I heard – that once the worthful one[21], on a tour among the Kosalans with a large community of almsfolk, reached Kesaputta, the town of the Kālāmās. Now these Kālāmās of Kesaputta heard of this: 'Gotama the ascetic – scion of the Sakya, who went forth as a wanderer from the Sakyan clan – has reached Kesaputta. And of the master Gotama this fine repute has spread: They say he is a worthful one – a saint, rightly and fully awakened, consummate in knowledge and conduct, that he has reached wellbeing, and is a knower of the cosmos, an unexcelled trainer of people yet untamed, a teacher of human and divine beings, awakened – full of such worth; they say he has understood this world with its divine and demonic beings, its creator gods, its generations with their ascetics and divines, their rulers and the common people, having with super-sense seen with his own eyes; has explained the Law good in the beginning, good in the middle, good in the end; and has shed light on what wholly and totally complete, totally pure holy life is, in the spirit and in the letter. It would be good to see such a saint.'

---

[20] Some versions have Kesamutta.

[21] i.e. the Buddha – 'worthful' (bhagavat) is his commonest epithet in the discourses. In the culture of the time it was applied principally to divine beings and saints.

Chapter Two: THE PREDICAMENT

Atha kho kesamuttiyā kālāmā yena bhagavā tenupasaṅkamiṁsu; upasaṅkamitvā appekacce bhagavantaṁ abhivādetvā ekamantaṁ nisīdiṁsu, appekacce bhagavatā saddhiṁ sammodiṁsu, sammodanīyaṁ kathaṁ sāraṇīyaṁ vītisāretvā ekamantaṁ nisīdiṁsu, appekacce yena bhagavā tenañjaliṁ paṇāmetvā ekamantaṁ nisīdiṁsu, appekacce nāmagottaṁ sāvetvā ekamantaṁ nisīdiṁsu, appekacce tuṇhībhūtā ekamantaṁ nisīdiṁsu. Ekamantaṁ nisinnā kho te kesamuttiyā kālāmā bhagavantaṁ etadavocuṁ –

'Santi, bhante, eke samaṇabrāhmaṇā kesamuttaṁ āgacchanti. Te sakaṁyeva vādaṁ dīpenti jotenti, parappavādaṁ pana khuṁsenti vambhenti paribhavanti omakkhiṁ [22] karonti. Aparepi, bhante, eke samaṇabrāhmaṇā kesamuttaṁ āgacchanti. Tepi sakaṁyeva vādaṁ dīpenti jotenti, parappavādaṁ pana khuṁsenti vambhenti paribhavanti omakkhiṁ karonti. Tesaṁ no, bhante, amhākaṁ hoteva kaṅkhā hoti vicikicchā – ko su nāma imesaṁ bhavataṁ samaṇabrāhmaṇānaṁ saccaṁ āha, ko musā'ti

So the Kālāmās of Kesaputta went to the worthful one. Having arrived, some saluted the worthful one and sat to one side; some exchanged courteous greetings with the worthful one and, after the exchange of friendly greetings and courtesies, sat to one side; some raised their joined palms to the worthful one and sat to one side; some announced their name and clan, and sat to one side; and some without saying anything sat to one side.

Sitting to the side thus, the Kālāmas of Kesaputta said to the worthful one, 'Sir, certain ascetics and divines come to Kesaputta. They proclaim their own doctrines and expound them in full, but as for the doctrines of others, they deprecate them, revile them, show contempt for them, and disparage them[23]. And then, sir, other ascetics and divines come to Kesaputta. They proclaim their own doctrines and expound them in full, but as for the doctrines of others, they deprecate them, revile them, show contempt for them, and disparage them. They leave us doubting and wavering about which of these venerable ascetics and divines speak the truth, and which speak falsely.'

---

[22] Some versions read opakkhiṁ, some opapakkhiṁ, some omakkhikaṁ.

[23] Or 'deprive them of their wings'.

Chapter Three: THE MAIN POINT

'Alañhi vo, kālāmā, kaṅkhituṁ alaṁ vicikicchituṁ. Kaṅkhanīyeva pana vo ṭhāne vicikicchā uppannā

'Yes, Kālāmās, you may well doubt! You may well waver! What has given rise in you to wavering is indeed something deserving of doubt.

Chapter Four: THE TEN IRRELEVANCIES & THE CRITERION FOR REJECTION

'Etha tumhe, kālāmā, mā anussavena, mā paramparāya, mā itikirāya, mā piṭakasampadānena, mā takkahetu, mā nayahetu, mā ākāraparivitakkena, mā diṭṭhinijjhānakkhantiyā, mā bhabbarūpatāya, mā samaṇo no garūti. Yadā tumhe, kālāmā, attanāva jāneyyātha – "ime dhammā akusalā, ime dhammā sāvajjā, ime dhammā viññugarahitā, ime dhammā samattā samādinnā[24] ahitāya dukkhāya saṁvattantī"ti, atha tumhe, kālāmā, pajaheyyātha.

'Look, Kālāmās, it is not by recitation, nor by tradition, nor by report, nor by scriptural authority, nor by reason of philosophy, nor by reason of inference, nor by thinking ideas through, nor by favouring views, nor by (others') seeming capability, nor insofar as a particular ascetic is your teacher, but rather when you know *for yourselves,* – that particular things are unskilful; that these things are censurable; that these things are scorned by the wise; and that these things, when adopted and carried out, convert into loss and suffering – that you should abandon them.

---

[24] Some versions have samādiṇṇā.

Chapter Five: WHAT TO REJECT

'Taṁ kiṁ maññatha, kālāmā, lobho purisassa ajjhattaṁ uppajjamāno uppajjati hitāya vā ahitāya vā'ti

'Ahitāya, bhante.'

'Luddho panāyaṁ, kālāmā, purisapuggalo lobhena abhibhūto pariyādinnacitto pāṇampi hanati, adinnampi ādiyati, paradārampi gacchati, musāpi bhaṇati, parampi tathattāya[25] samādapeti, yaṁ sa[26] hoti dīgharattaṁ ahitāya dukkhāyā'ti.

'Evaṁ, bhante.'

'What do you think, Kālāmās? When wanting arises within a person, does it arise to their profit or loss?'

'To their loss, sir.'

'And thus wanting, Kālāmās, does not a person overcome by wanting, with their mind possessed by it, kill a living being, or take what is not given, or go after another person's spouse, or tell lies, or induce others to do such things, such that there will long be loss and suffering?'

'Yes, sir.'

'Taṁ kiṁ maññatha, kālāmā, doso purisassa ajjhattaṁ uppajjamāno uppajjati hitāya vā ahitāya vā'ti

'Ahitāya, bhante.'

'Duṭṭho panāyaṁ, kālāmā, purisapuggalo dosena abhibhūto pariyādinnacitto pāṇampi hanati[27], adinnampi ādiyati, paradārampi gacchati, musāpi bhaṇati, parampi tathattāya samādapeti, yaṁ sa hoti dīgharattaṁ ahitāya dukkhāyā'ti.

'Evaṁ, bhante.'

'What do you think, Kālāmās? When disliking arises within a person, does it arise to their profit or loss?'

---

25 Some versions have tadatthāya.

26 Some versions have yaṁ tassa and the equivalent passage in the next discourse is yaṁ' sa.

27 Some have hanti.

'To their loss, sir.'

'And thus disliking, Kālāmās, does not a person overcome by disliking, with their mind possessed by it, kill a living being, or take what is not given, or go after another person's spouse, or tell lies, or induce others to do such things, such that there will long be loss and suffering?'

'Yes, sir.'

'Taṁ kiṁ maññatha, kālāmā, moho purisassa ajjhattaṁ uppajjamāno uppajjati hitāya vā ahitāya vā'ti

'Ahitāya, bhante.'

'Mūḷho panāyaṁ, kālāmā, purisapuggalo mohena abhibhūto pariyādinnacitto pāṇampi hanati, adinnampi ādiyati, paradārampi gacchati, musāpi bhaṇati, parampi tathattāya samādapeti, yaṁ sa hoti dīgharattaṁ ahitāya dukkhāyā'ti.

'Evaṁ, bhante.'

'What do you think, Kālāmās? When delusion arises within a person, does it arise to their profit or loss?'

'To their loss, sir.'

'And thus being deluded, Kālāmās, does not a person overcome by delusion, with their mind possessed by it, kill a living being, or take what is not given, or go after another person's spouse, or tell lies, or induce others to do such things, such that there will long be loss and suffering?'

'Yes, sir.'

'Taṁ kiṁ maññatha, kālāmā, ime dhammā kusalā vā akusalā vā'ti

'Akusalā, bhante.'

'Sāvajjā vā anavajjā vā'ti

'Sāvajjā, bhante.'

'Viññugarahitā vā viññuppasatthā vā'ti

'Viññugarahitā, bhante.'

'Samattā samādinnā ahitāya dukkhāya saṁvattanti, no vā? Kathaṁ vā ettha hotī'ti?

'Samattā, bhante, samādinnā ahitāya dukkhāya saṁvattantīti. Evaṁ no ettha hotī'ti.

'So what do you think, Kālāmās: Are these things skilful or unskilful?'

'Unskilful, sir'

'Censurable or uncensurable?'

'Censurable, sir.'

'Scorned by the wise or praised by the wise?'

'Scorned by the wise, sir.'

'When adopted and carried out, do they convert into loss and suffering, or not? How does it appear to you?'

'When adopted, sir, and carried out, they convert into loss and suffering. That is how it appears to us.'

'Iti kho, kālāmā, yam̊ tam̊ avocumhā[28] – "etha tumhe, kālāmā! Mā anussavena, mā paramparāya, mā itikirāya, mā piṭakasampadānena, mā takkahetu, mā nayahetu, mā ākāraparivitakkena, mā diṭṭhinijjhānakkhantiyā, mā bhabbarūpatāya, mā samaṇo no garūti. Yadā tumhe kālāmā attanāva jāneyyātha – 'ime dhammā akusalā, ime dhammā sāvajjā, ime dhammā viññugarahitā, ime dhammā samattā samādinnā ahitāya dukkhāya sam̊vattantīti, atha tumhe, kālāmā, pajaheyyāthā'ti," iti yam̊ tam̊ vuttam̊, idametam̊ paṭicca vuttam̊.

'So, then, Kālāmās, as for what I just said – "Look, Kālāmās, it is not by recitation, nor by tradition, nor by report, nor by scriptural authority, nor by reason of philosophy, nor by reason of inference, nor by thinking ideas through, nor by favouring views, nor by (others') seeming capability, nor insofar as a particular ascetic is your teacher, but rather when you know *for yourselves,* – that particular things are unskilful; that these things are censurable; that these things are scorned by the wise; and that these things, when adopted and carried out, convert into loss and suffering – that you should abandon them." – This is what I said, and that is why I said it.

---

28 Some versions and Ang. Nik. 4, 193 have avocumha.

Chapter Six: THE TEN IRRELEVANCIES & THE CRITERION FOR ACCEPTANCE

'Etha tumhe, kālāmā, mā anussavena, mā paramparāya, mā itikirāya, mā piṭakasampadānena, mā takkahetu, mā nayahetu, mā ākāraparivitakkena, mā diṭṭhinijjhānakkhantiyā, mā bhabbarūpatāya, mā samaṇo no garūti. Yadā tumhe, kālāmā, attanāva jāneyyātha – "ime dhammā kusalā, ime dhammā anavajjā, ime dhammā viññuppasatthā, ime dhammā samattā samādinnā hitāya sukhāya saṁvattantī"ti, atha tumhe, kālāmā, upasampajja vihareyyātha.

And look, Kālāmās, neither is it by recitation, nor by tradition, nor by report, nor by scriptural authority, nor by reason of philosophy, nor by reason of inference, nor by thinking ideas through, nor by favouring views, nor by (others') seeming capability, nor insofar as a particular ascetic is your teacher, but again rather when you know for yourselves, – that particular things are *skilful*; that these things are *un*censurable; that these things are *praised* by the wise; and that these things, when adopted and carried out, convert into *profit* and *bliss* – that you should *undertake* and *abide* by them.

Chapter Seven: WHAT TO ACCEPT

'Taṁ kiṁ maññatha, kālāmā, alobho purisassa ajjhattaṁ uppajjamāno uppajjati hitāya vā ahitāya vā'ti

'Hitāya, bhante.'

'Aluddho panāyaṁ, kālāmā, purisapuggalo lobhena anabhibhūto apariyādinnacitto neva pāṇaṁ hanati, na adinnaṁ ādiyati, na paradāraṁ gacchati, na musā bhaṇati, na parampi tathattāya samādapeti , yaṁ sa hoti dīgharattaṁ hitāya sukhāyā'ti.

'Evaṁ, bhante.'

'What do you think, Kālāmās? When freedom from wanting arises within a person, does it arise to their profit or loss?'

'To their profit, sir.'

'And thus free from wanting, Kālāmās, does not a person who is undominated by wanting, and whose mind is not possessed by it, *refrain* from killing a living being, or from taking what is not given, or from going after another person's spouse, or from telling lies, or from inducing others to do such things, such that there will long be *profit* and *bliss*?'

'Yes, sir.'

'Taṁ kiṁ maññatha, kālāmā, adoso purisassa ajjhattaṁ uppajjamāno uppajjati hitāya vā ahitāya vā'ti?

'Hitāya, bhante.'

'Aduṭṭho panāyaṁ, kālāmā, purisapuggalo dosena anabhibhūto apariyādinnacitto neva pāṇaṁ hanati, na adinnaṁ ādiyati, na paradāraṁ gacchati, na musā bhaṇati, na parampi tathattāya samādapeti , yaṁ sa hoti dīgharattaṁ hitāya sukhāyā'ti.

Evam, bhante.'

'What do you think, Kālāmās? When freedom from disliking arises within a person, does it arise to their profit or loss?'

'To their profit, sir.'

'And thus free from disliking, Kālāmās, does not a person who is undominated by disliking, and whose mind is not possessed by it, *refrain* from killing a living being, or from taking what is not given, or from going after another person's spouse, or from telling lies, or from inducing others to do such things, such that there will long be *profit* and *bliss*?'

'Yes, sir.'

'Taṁ kiṁ maññatha, kālāmā, amoho purisassa ajjhattaṁ uppajjamāno uppajjati hitāya vā ahitāya vā'ti

'Hitāya, bhante.'

'Amūḷho panāyaṁ, kālāmā, purisapuggalo mohena anabhibhūto apariyādinnacitto neva pāṇaṁ hanati, na adinnaṁ ādiyati, na paradāraṁ gacchati, na musā bhaṇati, na parampi tathattāya samādapeti, yaṁ sa hoti dīgharattaṁ hitāya sukhāyā'ti

'Evam, bhante.'

'What do you think, Kālāmās? When freedom from being deluded arises within a person, does it arise to their profit or loss?'

'To their profit, sir.'

'And thus free from being deluded, Kālāmās, does not a person who is undominated by delusion, and whose mind is not possessed by it, *refrain* from killing a living being, or from taking what is not given, or from going after another person's spouse, or from telling lies, or from inducing others to do such things, such that there will long be *profit* and *bliss*?'

'Yes, sir.'

'Taṁ kiṁ maññatha, kālāmā, ime dhammā kusalā vā akusalā vā'ti

'Kusalā , bhante.'

Savajjā vā anavajjā vā'ti

'Anavajjā, bhante.'

'Viññugarahitā vā viññuppasatthā vā'ti

'Viññuppasatthā, bhante.'

'Samattā samādinnā hitāya sukhāya saṁvattanti no vā? Kathaṁ vā ettha hotī'ti

'Samattā, bhante, samādinnā hitāya sukhāya saṁvattanti. Evaṁ no ettha hotī'ti.

'So what do you think, Kālāmās: Are these things skilful or unskilful?'

'Skilful, sir.'

'Censurable or uncensurable?'

'Uncensurable, sir.'

'Scorned by the wise or praised by the wise?'

'Praised by the wise, sir.'

'When adopted and carried out, do they convert into profit and bliss, or not? How does it appear to you?'

'When adopted, sir, and carried out, they convert into profit and bliss. That is how it appears to us.'

'Iti kho, kālāmā, yaṁ taṁ avocumhā – "etha tumhe, kālāmā! Mā anussavena, mā paramparāya, mā itikirāya, mā piṭakasampadānena, mā takkahetu, mā nayahetu, mā ākāraparivitakkena, mā diṭṭhinijjhānakkhantiyā, mā bhabbarūpatāya, mā samaṇo no garūti. Yadā tumhe, kālāmā, attanāva jāneyyātha – ime dhammā kusalā, ime dhammā anavajjā, ime dhammā viññuppasatthā, ime dhammā samattā samādinnā hitāya sukhāya saṁvattantīti, atha tumhe, kālāmā, upasampajja vihareyyāthā"ti, iti yaṁ taṁ vuttaṁ idametaṁ paṭicca vuttaṁ.

'So, then, Kālāmās, as for what I just said – "And look, Kālāmās, neither is it by recitation, nor by tradition, nor by report, nor by scriptural authority, nor by reason of philosophy, nor by reason of inference, nor by thinking ideas through, nor by favouring views, nor by (others') seeming capability, nor insofar as a particular ascetic is your teacher, but again rather when you know for yourselves, – that particular things are *skilful*; that these things are *un*censurable; that these things are *praised* by the wise; and that these things, when adopted and carried out, convert into *profit* and *bliss* – that you should *undertake* and *abide* by them." – This is what I said, and that is why I said it.

Chapter Eight: THE MEDITATION

'Sa kho so[29], kālāmā, ariyasāvako evaṁ vigatābhijjho vigatabyāpādo asammụlho sampajāno patissato[30] mettāsahagatena cetasā ekaṁ disaṁ pharitvā viharati, tathā dutiyaṁ, tathā tatiyaṁ, tathā catutthaṁ, iti uddhamadho tiriyaṁ sabbadhi sabbattatāya sabbāvantaṁ lokaṁ mettāsahagatena cetasā vipulena mahaggatena appamāṇena averena abyāpajjhena pharitvā viharati.

'Now, Kālāmās, one who is a disciple of the noble, and thus devoid of envy, devoid of ill will, unbewildered, conscientious and aware, rests suffusing one quarter [the east], and likewise the second, and likewise the third, and likewise the fourth, with a spirit of amity, and in the same way rests suffusing the all-encompassing universe upwards, downwards, all around, everywhere and in every way with an abundant, expansive, immeasurable spirit of amity, free from aversion and free from ill will,

karuṇāsahagatena cetasā ekaṁ disaṁ pharitvā viharati, tathā dutiyaṁ, tathā tatiyaṁ, tathā catutthaṁ, iti uddhamadho tiriyaṁ sabbadhi sabbattatāya sabbāvantaṁ lokaṁ karuṇāsahagatena cetasā vipulena mahaggatena appamāṇena averena abyāpajjhena pharitvā viharati.

and rests suffusing one quarter [the east], and likewise the second, and likewise the third, and likewise the fourth, with a spirit of *caring*, and in the same way rests suffusing the all-encompassing universe upwards, downwards, all around, everywhere and in every way with an abundant, expansive, immeasurable spirit of *caring*, free from aversion and free from ill will,

muditāsahagatena cetasā ekaṁ disaṁ pharitvā viharati, tathā dutiyaṁ, tathā tatiyaṁ, tathā catutthaṁ, iti uddhamadho tiriyaṁ sabbadhi sabbattatāya sabbāvantaṁ lokaṁ muditāsahagatena cetasā vipulena mahaggatena appamāṇena averena abyāpajjhena pharitvā viharati.

and rests suffusing one quarter [the east], and likewise the second, and

---

29 Or yo kho.

30 Or sato.

likewise the third, and likewise the fourth, with a spirit of *sharing joy*, and in the same way rests suffusing the all-encompassing universe upwards, downwards, all around, everywhere and in every way with an abundant, expansive, immeasurable spirit of *sharing joy*, free from aversion and free from ill will,

upekkhāsahagatena cetasā ekaṁ disaṁ pharitvā viharati, tathā dutiyaṁ, tathā tatiyaṁ, tathā catutthaṁ, iti uddhamadho tiriyaṁ sabbadhi sabbattatāya sabbāvantaṁ lokaṁ upekkhāsahagatena cetasā vipulena mahaggatena appamāṇena averena abyāpajjhena pharitvā viharati.

and rests suffusing one quarter [the east], and likewise the second, and likewise the third, and likewise the fourth, with a spirit endowed with *perspective*, and in the same way rests suffusing the all-encompassing universe upwards, downwards, all around, everywhere and in every way with an abundant, expansive, immeasurable spirit endowed with *perspective*, free from aversion and free from ill will.

Chapter Nine: THE BENEFITS

'Sa[31] kho so, kālāmā, ariyasāvako evaṁ averacitto evaṁ abyāpajjhacitto evaṁ asaṁkiliṭṭhacitto evaṁ visuddhacitto. Tassa diṭṭheva dhamme cattāro assāsā adhigatā honti. "Sace kho pana atthi paro loko, atthi sukatadukkaṭānaṁ[32] kammānaṁ phalaṁ vipāko, athāhaṁ[33] kāyassa bhedā paraṁ maraṇā sugatiṁ saggaṁ lokaṁ upapajjissāmī"ti, ayamassa paṭhamo assāso adhigato hoti.

'Now, Kālāmās, one who is a disciple of the noble, whose spirit is thus free from hostility, whose spirit is thus free from ill will, whose spirit is thus free from affliction, and whose spirit is thus in all ways pure, realises four things here and now that let them breathe easily:

' "If there is a world beyond, and fruits that ripen from deeds done well or badly, (then) I, body rotting, after death, shall be reborn in a happy fate, a heaven world." This is the first thing they realise that lets them breathe easily.

' "Sace kho pana natthi paro loko, natthi sukatadukkaṭānaṁ kammānaṁ phalaṁ vipāko, athāhaṁ[34] diṭṭheva dhamme averaṁ abyāpajjhaṁ anīghaṁ sukhiṁ[35] attānaṁ pariharāmī"ti, ayamassa dutiyo assāso adhigato hoti.

' "But if there is no world beyond, and no fruits that ripen from deeds done well or badly, then here and now I am keeping myself free from aversion, free from ill will, free from trouble, and blissful." This is the second thing they realise that lets them breathe easily.

' "Sace kho pana karoto karīyati pāpaṁ, na kho panāhaṁ kassaci pāpaṁ cetemi. Akarontaṁ kho pana maṁ pāpakammaṁ kuto dukkhaṁ phusissatī"ti, ayamassa tatiyo assāso adhigato hoti.

' "Even if certain acts when done consitute evil, I do not even intend evil for anyone, so from where will suffering for evil deeds touch me who have not

---

[31] Or sace

[32] Or sukaṭadukkaṭānaṁ

[33] Or ṭhānamahaṁ, or ṭhānametaṁ yenāhaṁ

[34] Or idhāhaṁ

[35] Or sukhaṁ, or sukhī

done any?"[36] This is the third thing they realise that lets them breathe easily.

' "Sace kho pana karoto na karīyati pāpaṁ, athāhaṁ ubhayeneva visuddhaṁ attānaṁ samanupassāmī'ti, ayamassa catuttho assāso adhigato hoti.

' "But even if acts when done might not constitute evil, then I could assume myself pure in both cases anyway." This is the fourth thing they realise that lets them breathe easily.

'Sa kho so, kālāmā, ariyasāvako evaṁ averacitto evaṁ abyāpajjhacitto evaṁ asaṁkiliṭṭhacitto evaṁ visuddhacitto. Tassa diṭṭheva dhamme ime cattāro assāsā adhigatā hontī'ti.

'So, Kālāmās, one who is a disciple of the noble, whose spirit is thus free from hostility, whose spirit is thus free from ill will, whose spirit is thus free from affliction, and whose spirit is thus in all ways pure, realises these four things here and now that let them breathe easily.'

'Evametaṁ, bhagavā, evametaṁ, sugata! Sa kho so, bhante, ariyasāvako evaṁ averacitto evaṁ abyāpajjhacitto evaṁ asaṁkiliṭṭhacitto evaṁ visuddhacitto. Tassa diṭṭheva dhamme cattāro assāsā adhigatā honti. "Sace kho pana atthi paro loko, atthi sukatadukkaṭānaṁ kammānaṁ phalaṁ vipāko, athāhaṁ kāyassa bhedā paraṁ maraṇā sugatiṁ saggaṁ lokaṁ upapajjissāmī"ti, ayamassa paṭhamo assāso adhigato hoti.

'So it is, worthful one. So it is, reacher of well-being. One who is a disciple of the noble, whose spirit is thus free from hostility, whose spirit is thus free from ill will, whose spirit is thus free from affliction, and whose spirit is thus in all ways pure, does indeed realise four things here and now that let them breathe easily:

' "If there is a world beyond, and fruits that ripen from deeds done well or badly, (then) I, body rotting, after death, shall be reborn in a happy fate, a

---

36 Woodward (Hare & Woodward, 1932/2006, p. 175 (ii)) has, 'Though, as a result of action, ill be done by me, yet do I plan no ill to anyone. And if I do no ill [sic], how can sorrow touch me?' By over-emphasising the intention/action dichotomy he has created a non-sequitur which is not there in the Pali.

heaven world." This indeed is the first thing they realise that lets them breathe easily.

' "Sace kho pana natthi paro loko, natthi sukatadukkaṭānaṁ kammānaṁ phalaṁ vipāko, athāhaṁ diṭṭheva dhamme averaṁ abyāpajjhaṁ anīghaṁ sukhiṁ attānaṁ pariharāmī"ti, ayamassa dutiyo assāso adhigato hoti.

' "But if there is no world beyond, and no fruits that ripen from deeds done well or badly, then here and now I am keeping myself free from aversion, free from ill will, free from trouble, and blissful." This indeed is the second thing they realise that lets them breathe easily.

' "Sace kho pana karoto karīyati pāpaṁ, na kho panāhaṁ – kassaci pāpaṁ cetemi, akarontaṁ kho pana maṁ pāpakammaṁ kuto dukkhaṁ phusissatī"ti, ayamassa tatiyo assāso adhigato hoti.

' "Even if certain acts when done consitute evil, I do not even intend evil for anyone, so from where will suffering for evil deeds touch me who have not done any?" This indeed is the third thing they realise that lets them breathe easily.

' "Sace kho pana karoto na karīyati pāpaṁ, athāhaṁ ubhayeneva visuddhaṁ attānaṁ samanupassāmī"ti, ayamassa catuttho assāso adhigato hoti.

' "But even if acts when done might not constitute evil, then I could assume myself pure in both cases anyway." This indeed is the fourth thing they realise that lets them breathe easily.

'Sa kho so, bhante, ariyasāvako evaṁ averacitto evaṁ abyāpajjhacitto evaṁ asaṁkiliṭṭhacitto evaṁ visuddhacitto. Tassa diṭṭheva dhamme ime cattāro assāsā adhigatā honti.'

'So, sir, one who is a disciple of the noble, whose spirit is thus free from hostility, whose spirit is thus free from ill will, whose spirit is thus free from affliction, and whose spirit is thus in all ways pure, does indeed realise these four things here and now that let them breathe easily.'

Chapter Ten: THE RESPONSE OF THE PEOPLE

'Abhikkantaṁ, bhante, abhikkantaṁ, bhante. Seyyathāpi, bhante, nikkujjitaṁ vā ukkujjeyya, paṭicchannaṁ vā vivareyya, mūḷhassa vā maggaṁ ācikkheyya, andhakāre vā telapajjotaṁ dhāreyya – "cakkhumanto rūpāni dakkhantī"ti, evamevaṁ bhagavatā anekapariyāyena dhammo pakāsito. Ete mayaṁ mayaṁ, bhante, bhagavantaṁ saraṇaṁ gacchāma dhammañca bhikkhusaṅghañca. Upāsake no, bhante, bhagavā dhāretu ajjatagge pāṇupete saraṇaṁ gate'ti.

'Magnificent, sir! Magnificent, sir! Just as if, sir, he were to have set right what was overturned, to have revealed what was veiled, to have shown the path to one who was lost, or to have carried a lamp into the dark such that those with eyes could make forms out, in the same way has the worthful one by means of several demonstrations shed light on the Law. We refer ourselves to the worthful one, and to the Law, and to the community of almsfolk. May the worthful one hold us to be companions who refer themselves to him, from this day forward, for life.'

-o-

BOOK TWO: REDISCOVERY of CONSCIENCE, KALAMA SUTTA VYAKHYA

An Elaborate Commentary On the Discourse to the Kālāmā People

The commentary is three parts:

Part I: The Predicament

I will consider:

- the predicament of the Kālāmā people, and then
- our predicament (p. 41).

Consideration 1: The Kālāmās' Predicament

I consider here four points:

- who the Kālāmās were,
- who had been visiting them (p. 26),
- what the visitors taught (p. 27), and
- the origin of the difficulties the Kālāmās experienced in consequence (p. 40).

Who were the Kālāmā people?

> Thus have I heard – that once the worthful one, on a tour among the Kosalans with a large community of almsfolk, reached Kesaputta, the town of the Kālāmās.

Their township: Kesaputta

The settlement referred to in the extant texts of the discour**23** | P a g e se as Kesaputta (and in some recensions as Kesamutta) has been identified with the modern Kesariya (26.365°N, 84.873°E) in the East (Purba) Champaran of India's northern state Bihar bordering Nepal.

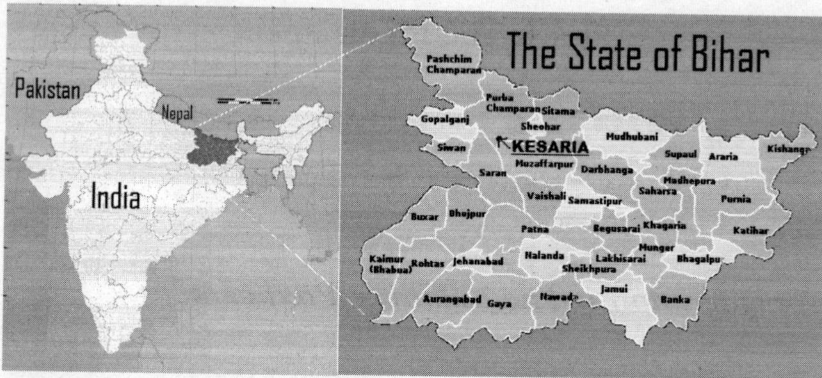

Figure 2 Maps showing the location of modern-day Kesaria in the State of Bihar in North India

The only evidence that the Kālāmā people once lived here is an enormous Buddhist monument or 'stupa' commemorating the fact that the Buddha gave discourse here. At the time of writing the area is in a state of neglect, and this year an article appeared in a Bihar newspaper bemoaning the lack of development of the area for pilgrims and encouraging the Bihar government to remedy this. However, the accounts of many visitors suggest that this neglect does not in fact damage the ambience of wondrousness about the place.

Like many such monuments, the Kesaria stupa is supposed by many to have been built by King Ashoka, but it could date back to anywhere between 200 and 500 CE. It is in the form of a vast 'maṇḍala' (radially organized sacred precinct) over 1000ft in circumference, with six tiers or plinths. At intervals around the plinths are niches containing large statues of the Buddha, in various stages of ruin. (One of these provides the cover of the book.) It is considered to be the tallest stupa in the world, taller at over 104 feet even than the famous stupa at Borobudur, Java (and previous to an earthquake Bihar suffered in 1934 it seems to have stood almost 170ft high, although reports vary).

Figure 3 the Kesariya Stupa marking the site at which the Buddha gave the discourse to the Kālāmā people.

The Kālāmā people

No other discourses recorded in the Pali canon were delivered at this place, to the Kālāmā people, so we cannot glean any information about them from that source.

It may be, however, that the first of Siddhārtha Gautama's two teachers was from among them. His name was Alāra (Sanskrit Arāda) Kālāmā and although some reports say he lived in Rājagrha (about 200km away from Kesariya), others situate him 'near Vaisali'[37], and Vaisali only 40km from Kesariya. He impressed the Buddha by saying that everything he taught he had realised for himself, that he had needed to rely on no-one, which is very much in the spirit of what the Buddha would later say to the Kālāmā people. Under his guidance the Buddha matched him in gaining facility in the four states of successively refined absorption, and the subsequent four states of formlessness, concluding in the state named 'nothingness', and was credited with such and offered half of his

37 Soka Gakkai *Dictionary of Buddhism* http://www.sgilibrary.org/

students, but the Buddha soon moved on, dissatisfied with what he saw would just lead to aeons in a state of quiescence but not destroy the root of future suffering.[38]

Who had been visiting them?

> Sitting to the side thus, the Kālāmās of Kesaputta said to the worthful one, 'Sir, certain ascetics and divines come to Kesaputta.

Two kinds of people had been visiting the Kālāmās: 'divines' and 'ascetics'.

The word translated as divines, brāhmaṇa, was used at the Buddha's time as now in so-called Hindu society principally to refer to one of the four hereditary and genetically isolated social castes – that responsible for sacrifices to the gods and for successful performance of other rituals essential for the correct functioning of society. (The other three castes are the rulers including the military, the traders and the servants.) Strictly speaking, there were various kinds of such divines, and only those who had trained in memorizing and reciting the Veda ('Wisdom'), the ancient mantras or praises which formed the most authoritative source of knowledge for the community, were entitled to the title brāhmaṇa. Nevertheless it was frequently used in the more general sense.

At the time of the Buddha it could also refer even more generally to any holy person, and as is well known the Buddha seems to have encouraged the shift in the sense of the word in this, less genetic and more spiritual, direction.

Etymologically, the word derives from the ancient Vedic language where it referred to those who were able to use the brahmaṇ, the basic energy of existence, which was also the breath by which the self-sounding Veda or Wisdom came to our ordinary ears. The most revered humans were those who 'heard' this sound: called ṛsi, they were what we would call prophets, seers and poets. Later on this creative energy was personified as a deity, and instead of the grammatically neuter brahmaṇ, the masculine Brahmā was used to represent this deity, depicted with four heads each looking in one of the cardinal directions, and credited as being, of the principal trinity (the others being Viṣṇu and Śiva), the deity responsible for creation of the world: the root of the word, bṛh, means 'grow' and 'strengthen'.

---

[38] See for example *The Long Discourse to Saccaka*, no. 36 in the Middle-Length Collection.

The word translated as 'ascetic', sāmāṇa, literally means those engaging in spiritual exercises. In the Buddha's time the word was used for those spiritual seekers who went into the wilderness to pursue their quest beyond the sphere of the sophisticated rigidities of the ritual-dominated institutional religion of mainstream society. Although the community around the Buddha used the term of themselves, it applied equally to all such individuals who sought or discovered truths beyond the rituals and doctrines of the organised religion of the priests, including such important spiritual communities of the time as the Jains.

It is important for our later discussion to realise also that the Buddha spoke of abilities or distinctions belonging to such people which we would consider the distinguishing marks of *a prophet*: seeing the hidden world, knowing the past and the future, delivering messages from deities, rousing the masses to higher ethics, speaking of moral consequences of actions and so on, as we shall see. The term certainly is not restricted to 'spiritual seekers working out their own salvation and therefore denied the grace of the deity' as some people would like to think.

Incidentally the word is the probable origin of the Siberian word 'shaman'.

These two terms together cover pretty much all varieties of religious teacher likely to be encountered in those lands at that time or in other lands at other times.

What did they teach?

'They proclaim their own doctrines and expound them in full, but as for the doctrines of others, they deprecate them, revile them, show contempt for them, and disparage them.

There is plenty of information in the canonical literature of Theravada Buddhism about what such divines and ascetics as the Buddha encountered or knew of taught. The first long discourse of the canonical Pali collection, *the Discourse of the Net of Brahma*, has a long list of the kind of religious teachings scholars nowadays associate with the forest-dwelling ascetics, the origin of the texts which have come down to us through Hindu lineages as the Upaniṣads.[39] In it we find a staggering variety of religion, irreligion and 'religious philosophy' being taught, a variety which should once and for all put paid to the infamous notion that religious thought was 'simply not as sophisticated then as it is now'.

---

39 (Prasad, 2007)

The context in which the doctrines are presented in the Brahma Net Discourse is the question of the grounds on which the Buddha (and the Laws he discovered and revealed, and anyone of his religious community) could be praised. The basis of the discourse is a furious row between one Suppiya and his pupil, the former disparaging the Buddha, his teachings and his community, and the latter praising these. Angered monks report overhearing this to the Buddha who takes them severely to task for being thus needlessly and harmfully angry at the dispraise, and furthermore tells them that it is also harmful for them to be pleased by the praise. Instead they should recognize when the praise is apt and point this out. And when is that?

Ethics

In his exposition of when praise is apt he first considers various forms of ethical behavior by which he abides. Parts of this list have quite a mind-flattening flood of detail so I have simplified the Buddha's presentation somewhat here, classing similar elements together.

General Good Behaviour

Firstly he considers behavior which all agree on, because it is so basic. He does not compare himself with other religious teachers, the priests or the ascetics, on the basis of this first set of behavioural codes, so we can assume that in general they too accepted it, abided by it and taught it to those who would listen, such as the Kālāmā people. (We might soberly reflect on what this says about the religious leaders of the Buddha's day compared to those of our own, especially in the matter of speech.)

One should:

- abstain from taking another creature's life, and using weapons or violence,
- abstain from taking things which have not been not offered,
- live soberly, piously, and honestly,
- abstain from illegal and unjust sexual relationships,
- abstain from speaking falsehoods,
- speak only the truth, in a believable and reliable way, and not contradict oneself,
- abstain from slander,
- promote, speak for, and enjoy unity and not division (and conflict),

- abstain from rough, insulting words,
- say polite, likeable, accurate, well chosen words that will make people's hearts joyful, and not waste time in idle gossip,
- discuss the religious laws and the behavior code at the appropriate times, and
- discuss in clear, detailed, and understandable words.

Rather specific good behaviour

Secondly there is a group of activities, on the basis of his abstention from which the Buddha contrasts himself favourably with other religious teachers, priests and ascetics, who live off the alms of the faithful. This indicates that these ethical codes were not universally accepted – i.e. that they all probably contributed to the various contentions about which the Kālāmās became so confused.

The points of contention are whether, if one is living off the alms of the faithful, one should abstain from:

- damaging seeds, vegetation, roots, and branches, and from cheating, trading, slavery, forgery, bribery, and criminal conduct,
- hoarding food, drink, clothing, bedding, perfume, spices, and other accessories,
- taking food more than once a day,
- watching shows (dances, exhibitions, matches, music performances, parades, etc),
- playing games (card games, board games, dice games, games of chance, racing games, acrobatics, word games, etc),
- using luxurious furniture and bedding,
- using cosmetics, make-up, and fancy or luxurious clothing,
- discussing people, politicians, criminals, terrors, food and beverages, clothing, places, families, cities, wars and battles, heroes, ghosts, street rumors, speculation on how the world is created, or about existence and non-existence,
- accusing, denying, goading or challenging others
- being the courier or messenger of politicians or higher administrations, and
- deceiving lay people by uttering spells to exorcise demons or make

someone's fortune, acting like a holy person by reciting mantras.

Livelihood

Finally there is a third group called the 'great' ethics, a list of livelihoods on the basis of his abstention from which again the Buddha contrasts himself favourably to other religious teachers, priests and ascetics, who live off the alms of the faithful. They give some idea of the kinds of activities religious teachers used to make money even while they were accepting alms.

The points of contention for an almsman were whether one should abstain from these methods of livelihood:

- fortune telling;
- interpreting dreams, or physiognomy, or signs;
- worshipping fire and divine entities;
- politics and making predictions about rulers and their wars;
- magic, mediumship and exorcism;
- medicine, dentistry, healthcare;
- astrology;
- meteorology;
- mathematics;
- teaching controversional treatises;
- match-making and dealing with divorce cases;
- economics;

Involvement in the world

Looking beyond the Buddhist scriptures at the other traditions' own, we find that the Vedic religion of the time was in the process of developing the four-stage system of the perfect dutiful life. In particular, the fourth stage was added – saṁnyāsin, literally the completely (saṁ-) no longer (ny-) is (ās-) person (-in), the recluse whose aim is liberation – seemingly in response to the challenge presented by the forest ascetics' spiritual practices to the worldly system of the Veda, which stressed family, society, and balance, making the perfect dutify life thus: chastity and study, followed by making a family, followed by forest life, and finally the life of the recluse.[40]

---

40 (Prasad, 2007, pp. 126-9)

Beliefs

At the end of the section on ethics in the *Brahma's Net Discourse*, the Buddha changes gear and says that since such ethical codes are trifling matters in comparison to wisdom, he should *more aptly* be praised not in terms of his ethics but in terms of *the Laws (Forms) of reality he discovered.* This discovery, he goes on to say, included the realization that a vast swathe of beliefs currently being propounded by priests and ascetics, were *too shallow*: that there was a deeper understanding of reality than that which they represented, namely that expressed in the aforementioned Laws.

The Buddha goes on to classify the kinds of these shallow beliefs, in each case giving a series of explanations of how the beliefs are likely to have come about – a series which in each case he declares to be exhaustive[41]. While these explanations are fascinating, I will consider them later as their relevance becomes more clear to our discussion, and for now limit myself to summarizing the Buddha's classification of the beliefs.

Incidentally, the word for belief here is diṭṭhi (the Sanskrit equivalent being dṛṣṭi) generally closer in meaning to 'view'. But since without exception these specific 'views' depend on excluding certain rival 'views', and given that, as the Buddha eventually points out, this exclusion is a kind of tension, based on being seized by craving and longing, the modern use of the word 'belief', with all its connotations of hope for a particular outcome, is quite apposite.

Beliefs about Time Until Now and Cosmology

The Eternal Self and Its Eternal Place (Cosmos)

The Buddha classifies proponents of such beliefs by just how far into the past they claim to be able to see, but the consequences of their claim are the same: they conclude from their experience that there is an eternal self or soul and that the cosmos it inhabits is also eternal. Commentaries add that the self is variously defined, but the basic distinction is between the experiencer and the experienced. And both are believed to go on forever.

[41] Some modern translations I have seen consider the Pali to mean that they held these beliefs and rejected others, but this does not strike me as correct: instead the phrase seems to mean that in each category, the types of belief the Buddha lists are found and no others.

The Creation by the Eternal Creator of Transient Creation

This group includes any belief that in a past existence in a divine realm an 'Eternal Being' willed the creation of other beings, and that as a consequence these other beings, creatures, not eternal but transient, came into existence, and were less beautiful and less magnificent that the 'First Being'. The doctrine in this world of the existence of this 'Creator', the Buddha says, is considered by its proponents to be a reflection of the relation which was more obvious in the previous, divine, existence.[42]

The Fall from Grace

The beliefs grouped here are in addition to, or specific examples of, the belief in the 'Creator'. The Buddha mentions two kinds: the belief that we have reached this fallen state as a punishment for greed and zeal in that previous, divine existence, and the belief that it was a punishment for envy.

Communion with God

Several other discourses, notably *The Discourse on the Threefold Wisdom*,[43] make reference to members of the orthodox religion who follow teachers who tell them that by following certain observances it is possible to gain communion with the 'Divine Creator'. They also report that there was bitter dispute about which teacher's system was best or whether they were all different paths leading to the same goal.

Holy Water

Various discourses, among them *The Cloth Simile Discourse*, mention prevalent beliefs that water from particular sources was sacred and had the power to purify bad deeds.

Praying and praising at funerals

In *The Connected Sayings*[44] reference is made to orthodox beliefs that the bad deeds of someone who had passed away could be rectified or palliated by praying and praising the deity as part of the funeral rites.

---

42 This view, having become, thanks to the spread of Christian and Islamic systems that include it, the single most dominant religious view on earth, we consider in more detail under the Buddha's questioning of 'logic' (naya).

43 Number 13 of the Long Discourse Collection.

44 In volume IV.

Eternal Mind observes Transient Objects

The Buddha goes on in *The Net* to note that some believe that while the mind which experiences reality is eternal, what it experiences changes.

The Finite Cosmos

Similar beliefs classified a little further on make it clear that the finiteness in question is spatial not temporal: that is to say, the universe has a spatial limit in all directions.

The Infinite Cosmos

And some hold this opposite view, that there are no spatial limits to the universe.

The Infinite Heavens

The Buddha adds that some believe that while the earth is horizontally limited, there is no vertical limit: the heavens are infinite.

The Cosmos Beyond such Descriptions

Some believe for whatever reason that it is impossible to declare a finite or infinite cosmos, or one where there is a limit in one sense and infinity in another, and that instead one the only reasonable belief is that it is neither finite nor infinite.

The Necessity for 'Agnosticism'

The Buddha is often said to be an agnostic in religious matters. This, I suspect, has less to do with the records of what he taught that have come down to us than a wish to make the Buddha appear less challenging to religious doctrine. What will startle those who make this claim is that the Buddha did not spare 'agnostics' from the accusation of shallow beliefs! He describes those who have concluded with agnosticism, for whatever reasons, rather unflatteringly as 'wriggling eels'. The depiction of their manner of speaking (whose dizzying phrases I have actually simplified in English here) is, one imagines, intended to provoke a smile:

> If I were asked whether or not there is another world, or whether or not there both is and is not another world, or whether or not there is such a thing as nongenetic birth of beings, or whether or not there both is and

> is not nongenetic birth of beings, or whether or not there are consequences to action depending on its goodness or badness, or whether or not there both are and are not consequences to action depending on its goodness or badness, or whether or not there is life after death, or whether or not there is both life as well as no life after death, and if I understood [say] that it is not that there is both life as well as no life after death, then I should indeed answer : 'It is not that there is both life as well as no life after death.' *But I do not speak in this way, that way, or the other way; neither do I speak against this way, that way, or the other way; nor do I speak otherwise.*

Another discourse[45] gives the name of a teacher of this kind of eelish wriggling, Sañjaya Belatthaputta. We will explore the notion of agnosticism and its relation to the Kesaputta discourse and to our society in more detail when we consider our predicament, and in particular the transmutation of faith.

A Universe without Reason

Some believe, the Buddha continues in *The Net*, that the universe has arisen without any reason, spontaneously, absurdly we might say, and of these the Buddha mentions one class that believes that they exist now but did not exist before, and that they came into existence randomly and meaninglessly.

Beliefs About the Future and Eschatology

The Bodily Afterlife

As for what happens after death, some hold that there will be an afterlife, we shall be aware, and we shall have bodies, which do not degenerate of course.

The Afterlife of Ethereal Souls

On the other hand, some deny that we could be bodies, at least bodies as we ordinarily conceive of them, in the afterlife.

The Afterlife of Souls which are Embodied but also Disembodied

This category would include the belief that although our soul will be

---

[45] *The Discourse of the Fruits of Ascesis* (the second of the long discourse collection).

embodied, we shall enjoy some freedom to move out of the body; as well as the belief that although we shall have a body, it will be so far from what we ordinarily think of as a body, we might as well say it is not a body too, as would be the case, for example, with a so-called 'astral' body.

The Afterlife of Souls about whose Embodiment or otherwise one Cannot Speak

Then come the beliefs of those who for one reason or another have decided that it is inappropriate to refer to souls in terms of whether they are embodied or not.

Individual Souls

Now the Buddha goes on to describe what beliefs were held about the nature of souls with respect to each other. First, there are the beliefs that souls will be delimited, or separately defineable.

Infinite Soul

And in contrast to that here we have the belief that as souls we shall merge into an Infinite Oneness, the Great Soul. As with agnosticism, it is worth highlighting that the Buddha is here accusing of shallowness a belief which has very frequently been ascribed to him, especially by Hindu commentators.

Individual Souls Partaking of the Infinite

The paradoxical beliefs of this group are attempts to preserve the qualities of both the individual soul, with personal identity and experience, and the glorious merging into the Infinite One, impersonal and without separable identities.

Souls whose Delimitedness or Otherwise Cannot be Expressed

This case is as for the question of the soul's embodiment or not, *mutatis mutandis*.

Souls Thinking Singly

Some believe that we shall each have a singular 'consciousness' (the word used in Pali is sanna, equivalent to the Sanskrit saṃjña, generally referring to ordinary thought and thinking).

Multitasking Souls

In contrast, some believe that we shall be conscious of several things at the same time.

Souls of Circumscribed Consciousness

Here are classified any beliefs that our souls will have limited consciousness, which is not to say that this limit need be small.

Souls with Cosmic Consciousness

And in contrast there is the belief that we shall be conscious of anything and everything simultaneously.

Heaven

In this group are all beliefs that as souls we shall be able to experience, and that there will be a state of bliss after death.

Hell

And in contrast to those, the beliefs that there will be no bliss, only suffering.

Heaven and Hell

And then the more familiar belief that both states will be possible.

Divine judge

Turning to non-Buddhist sources, we find that at least one deity, named Varuṇa, was worshipped as a gracious judge of ethics in the Vedic religion, and called 'king of kings'.[46] The word 'mercy' shares its root with the word used for this deity's grace in Vedic Sanskrit. Some scholars emphasise that the Vedic religion (at the time of the Buddha) did not teach reincarnation, such that Varuṇa would have been presiding over a single judgment occasion post death for every soul.

Souls in Peace and Equanimity

The Net continues with beliefs of those who have concluded that we shall

[46] (Panikkar, 1977, pp. 148, 150, 482)

not experience either bliss or suffering, at least as they are ordinarily conceived, because we shall be totally free and our equanimity invincible.

Organisms Without Mind

This rather bizarre group of beliefs have in common the notion that the awareness will not persist after death but that a non-degenerating body will.

A Subtle Mind Passing On

Here the Buddha mentions variations on the core belief that something of the consciousness will pass on to another life: at the moment of conception it cannot be said to be the same mind as previously, but at the same time cannot be denied completely since even in early development there is some kind of subtle awareness.

This Life Only

The Buddha then mentions a series of beliefs, which differ in the kinds of self they allow to exist, but share the idea that at the end of only one life the self will become nothing. In this group we find the familiar belief that the self is embodied, or identical with the body, and that the body's death ends the self, leaving the material of the body to rot. Included in this group are also less familiar beliefs in the existence of various invisible divine beings, who will also meet their end in extinction. The Buddha also mentions the belief that extremely subtle entities arising from the development of absorption of the mind into formless states similarly will become nothing in the end.

Radical Hedonism

Some believe that nirvāṇa, the 'blowing-out' of the fires of suffering, is the experience of unsurpassed enjoyment of the pleasures of the five senses. Delightfully, the chaste monastic commentators generally point out that this is not the nirvāṇa the Buddha taught!

The Liberation of Meditative States

Here we begin to recognise some of the Buddha's own teachers. The Buddha mentions the belief that the extinction of suffering lies in achieving such control over one's own mind that the hindrances associated with the unreliable (because changing) objects of sensual enjoyment and the suffering they cause no longer arise. The ability to make distinctions and investigate remains, and one experiences bliss and delight. Others contend that one should further refine concentration such that only bliss and delight remain. There are even those who declare that the elation of delight detracts from liberation so further refinement is in order, and even those who declare that any positive experience, like bliss, detracts from liberation such that true 'blowing out' of suffering is only achieved by eliminating bliss, again by refining concentration.

Ethical beliefs

In other discourses[47] some detail is gone into about what contemporary spiritual leaders had to say about the ethical status of actions of body, speech and mind. Ethical beliefs are especially relevant to our discussion because the Buddha later in the discourse takes them as case studies in his invitation to free inquiry, as we shall see.

Amoral souls

The teacher referred to in the discourses as Pūraṇa Kassapa taught that sin and merit were false concepts. The same actions which the Buddha considers later in our discourse – killing the life of others, taking what has not been given, resorting to others' spouses, speaking untruths, and encouraging others to do these – bring, Kassapa teaches, no punitive consequences, and conversely conventionally meritorious behaviour such as giving, performing sacrifices, and encouraging others to do these, bring, he says, no merit. This is because the soul is not involved in action in any way, i.e. it is not a moral agent.

Total predestination

The teacher referred to as Makkhali Gosāla taught that although people had an idea that through their chosen deeds and own efforts they could purify themselves and achieve deliverance, in fact this was erroneous, and rather everything was pre-ordained by God. They would continue to arise and die in successive states in a process similar to biological evolution, until, like a ball of string finally unwinds, their pre-ordained wandering would come to an end.

Materialism

The teacher referred to as Ajita Kesakambalin taught that the this-life/after-life dichotomy was empty chatter and that existence referred to

[47] Such as *The Fruits of Ascesis*.

senses' embodiment in the elements. At physical death, these elements united with the environmental elements and the sense faculties dissolved in space. For that reason, he said, to teach generosity and so on as bringing future rewards was idiotic.

Non-interrelation of elements

The teacher referred to as Pakudha Kaccayana taught that in reality seven elements – the usual four plus pleasure, pain and the soul – were all uncreated, eternal, solid and not interrelated. Ideas of agents and experiencers were illusory: there were in reality no killers and no killed individuals, instead (for example) a sword passing through the elements.

Four-fold restraint

The teacher referred to as Nigantha Nataputta, considered by most scholars to be identical to the founder of the Jain religion, otherwise known as Mahāvīra, upheld the doctrine of moral causation – the experience of unpleasant consequences after evil actions, and pleasant ones after good actions. In *Ascesis' Fruits* it is noted that he claimed that to be restrained in four ways – denied, conjoined with, cleansed by and suffused with all 'waters' – is to be self-perfected, self-controlled and self-established. These four restraints, presented in these peculiar water similes, have led some scholars to suggest that it might not be a fair presentation of Mahāvīra's teaching at all but instead a sarcastic imitation of his manner of speaking! However, Kamta Prasad Jain has argued[48] persuasively that they refer to the Jain ascetic's famous restraints, as mentioned in Śri Samantabhadra Swāmi's 17- or 18-century-old *Ratnakarnadaka* – firstly, nirāmbha, denied all traffic with the world (including taking cold water); secondly, viśayasāvasatitā, conjoined with purity (as of water) so 'not resting in the objects of the senses'; thirdly, aparigraha, 'cleansed' (as if by water) of grasping, at external and internal objects; and fourthly, suffused (as though by water) of the 'jewel penance', jñānadhyāna, mental absorption in knowing. In terms of actions' moral repercussions, Mahāvīra held that all actions, even good and neutral ones, had the consequence of binding the agent, such that spiritual exercise involved refraining from all actions and exhausting previous ones.

---

48 (Jain, 1926)

The nature of the Kālāmās' consequent difficulties

> 'They leave us doubting and wavering about which of these venerable ascetics and divines speak the truth, and which speak falsely.'

From the way they speak it is clear that the Kālāmās are not concerned about losing their own traditions, for example, or defending the symbols of their community or the honour of their ancestors, or by the very fact that people expressing such diverse opinions are still alive on this earth, or by the reckless atmosphere of liberality such expressions of diverse opinions suggest! The fact that they are apparently coolly ready to take on novel ethics and beliefs we should keep in mind as we turn to modern society and its particular discontents.

Consideration 2: OUR PREDICAMENT

My presentation will deal with:

- the similarities between the Kālāmās' predicament and ours,
- the differences (p. 45), and
- the consequences of those differences for our understanding of the intent of the discourse (p. 52).

The Similarities between the Kālāmās' predicament and ours

Since the parallels between the ethics and beliefs of the Buddha's time and ours are so extensive and so obvious I hardly need to drag the honoured reader through them. Instead I want to mention some salient points which will become more important later on in our discussion.

Most of us are taught what is right and wrong, in the most mundane matters just as in the most world-transcending matters, by proponents of mutually exclusive belief systems. Even if our formal teaching was consistent, we are exposed to many other kinds of belief than those we ourselves have concluded on. This is as much to do with communications technology and travel than with inconsistent education.

Furthermore it is clear, as we survey the categories of ethics and beliefs the Buddha encountered, that almost all of them are still with us. Just to mention a few of the most popular beliefs: belief in the 'Creator God', or in a cosmos that arose meaninglessly, or in the 'Fall from Grace', or in 'the eternal soul', or in the annihilation of the self at bodily death, or in 'the afterlife', or in 'the consequences there of our good and bad actions', or in lack of such consequences.

Most relevantly to our intent in this discussion, we can see that, in our age just as then, proponents of each system glorify their own and denigrate others' systems.

Although in our times the sources of various teachings about ethical practices and beliefs often come from more massive and more solidified systems, many of the quandaries that result are the closely equivalent to those the Kālāmās faced. Let us consider some examples of 'culture clashes' that throw up dilemmas for the modern global village, noting in passing that all of these questions are relevant to everyone, not just to the community most associated with them. In each case, I ask the question as though from the community's majority point of view – as a positive question if the issue is answered by the majority in the negative, and *vice versa* – as though they were rhetorically challenging someone who held the dissenting view.

Issues associated with Islām

Shouldn't we make sacrificial slaughters to obey the deity and honour the prophet? Shouldn't we tax communities who do not share our religious identity? Shouldn't people who share our religious identity pay regular tribute to demonstrate their allegiance? Should interest be charged on loans? Shouldn't a man's sexual activity be restricted to his wives and slaves? Shouldn't there be slavery? Shouldn't a woman's sexual activity be restricted to her single husband? Shouldn't a man marry as many as four women if he has the capacity? Should anyone be celibate for life? Shouldn't pubescent girls get married even though they be young? Shouldn't all of the female body and the trunk of the male body be covered? Should there be co-education of both sexes? Should we drink alcohol? Should we eat pork? Shouldn't we smoke if we like? Shouldn't we conceal elements of our religious tradition in order to spread it? *Shouldn't we publicly distinguish between our religious identity and others*, praising and rewarding the former and condemning and penalising the latter? Shouldn't women be responsible for ensuring that men whom they do not want to marry do not get aroused by looking at them? Shouldn't other religious traditions' infrastructure be dismantled or appropriated by our religious tradition? Should we criticise our religion and our rulers? Should we change religion if we are not convinced by our adopted one? Shouldn't we execute others who leave our religion and refuse to recant? Should women be religious leaders? And for each of these issues, shouldn't the decision be imposed by the authorities?

And as for belief, isn't there only one deity? Aren't other so-called deities in fact devils, or at best mere imagination? Aren't other scriptures deceiving? Does the deity still need to send messages to us? Is Arabic not the language of heaven? Can adherents of other traditions enter paradise when they reject Muḥammad's prophethood? Is it not possible to identify an unbeliever? Can someone reject Muḥammad and be a believer?

Issues associated with Christianity

Shouldn't we spread the Good News is whatever way we can, including by means of financial incentives and concessions to local beliefs? Shouldn't we sacrifice sensual pleasures to please God and obtain transcendent pleasure in the hereafter? Shouldn't we be celibate if possible, but if not, at least only marry one person and restrict all sexual pleasure to that relation? Should we ever fight back? Should we be rich? Should we use contraception? Shouldn't abortion be abhorred, even if a pregnancy is unwanted or dangerous for the mother or the child? Shouldn't we prevent homosexuality? Should priests not be male? Shouldn't we enjoy food animals as part of God's creation for our benefit? Should we trust in God and the Kingdom to come or try to create the Kingdom on earth?

Is not Jesus the only way? Isn't deeply appreciating His sacrifice the only means within God's plan that we sinners can be redeemed? Aren't non-Christians, who refuse to make such appreciation, damned forever? Isn't love of God more important than worldly love?

Issues associated with Buddhism

Should we kill animals or not? Should we not meditate rather than do premature charity work? Shouldn't there be almsfolk (religious mendicants) even in the modern age? Should members of the religious community qualify for state benefits or not? Should monasteries own wealth and land or not? Should we participate in the monetary system or not? Shouldn't at least some religious people be celibate? Should we masturbate or have oral or anal sex or not? Should tantra be seen as the royal path or as perversion and superstition? Should we drink alcohol, take drugs, or smoke? Should we swear or insult people? Should we express afflictive emotions in catharsis? Should we point out others' faults? Should formal respect be shown to the ordained? Should we criticise our teacher? Should we tell people we are Buddhist when we do not practise? *Shouldn't we have individual freedom to choose these things?*

Should we believe that there are past lives and potential future ones or not? Should nirvana be seen as supreme bliss or nihilistic super-suicide? Should we believe that the Buddha could see all things, past, present and future, or not?

General and 'secular' issues

How should we live? How should we make a living? What constitutes an unethical livelihood? How important are money, status, property, reputation, etc.? Should we have private property or not? To what extent should property be shared by communities? How should we relate to the media? How should we relate to the government? How much or little constraint should be put on sexual relations? How much should we socialise? How should we balance work and entertainment? How do we known when it is appropriate to launch protests and demonstrations? To what degree should we put up with rulers' decisions even when they clash with our convictions? To what extent and how should religions which clash with democracy be tolerated? To what extent and how should religious doctrines be taught in schools and at home to children? What ethical position is demanded by being a citizen of a country which profits from international economic discrepancies and how should people from those countries and people excluded from them deal with that ethical position? How much control should the state exert in the lives and loves of its citizens?

Does life have any meaning or not? Are ethics important or not? Is democracy, or each alternative system of government, viable or not, good or not? Should there be states, and nationalities, and passports? Is free-market capitalism, or each alternative system, viable or not, good or not? Etc. etc.

Of course the list can be extended very greatly, but to do so here would serve no great purpose. We can all quickly come up with issues we feel are particulary challenging.

What distinguishes us from them

There are some fundamental differences between us and the Kālāmās. In these comparisons I advisedly *idealise* the Kālāmās. I am not so interested in what the Kālāmā people, or the inhabitants of the surrounding lands, were like beyond the descriptions in this discourse, which would be a historical anthropological investigation detracting from our main intent. Instead it will be instructive, in terms of throwing up otherwise overlooked characteristics, to take the Kālāmās as they appear here as a kind of mythical archetype, the light of which might throw us, today, into instructive relief.

Crudity and Violence

In our societies now disputes between proponents of different systems frequently turn violent. In such conflicts most stick to their native or chosen faith unless they are dressed in orange and on their knees, with a butcher's knife at their throat, or electrodes attached to their genitals. Just how far mankind has progressed in the matter of allaying such conflicts is demonstrated in newspapers every day[49].

Transmutation of Faith

All religions teach that 'faith' is the doorway to the benefits. But a

---

[49] For example, at the time of writing Malaysians Muslims are burning churches because the supreme court of the country has ruled that the Christians may now use the Arabic-derived word Allāh in their writings to refer to their deity, which the arsonists, for some reason best known to themselves and quite unknown to Arabic-speakers who include millions of Christians using this word, believe insults or is a danger to Islam. And today there has been attempted arson on two mosques. In the last few days hundreds of people in Nigeria have been killed in violence between the Muslim and Christian communities there. A few days ago the government of Thailand declared a state of emergency to clamp down on the almost entirely Muslim southern provinces, whose inhabitants are protesting against what they consider to be religion-based discrimination. And this is not an unusual week. Rarely has an uneventful week passed in this glorious decade, decorated with such stripes as of the 'new Crusaders' killing tens of thousands of civilians to occupy Iraq and Afghanistan under the banner of democracy and the internecine jihad they provoked and continue to stoke, edifying side-shows such as the Beslan school massacre by a group named in Arabic after the Practices of the Righteous (the said righteous being the companions of the Prophet Muḥammad), and breath-taking entertainment such as the World Trade Centre attack, to name but a few.

cursory acquaintance with the massive religions and their history demonstrates what is meant by 'faith' has varied a great deal. Here we will consider some of the implications of the word in modern times, and how far the mentality of 'the faithful' therefore is from the Kālāmās' as described in this discourse. We will have much more to say about faith later, when the Buddha addresses it directly.

Non-admission of not knowing

Whereas the Kālāmās did confess to being in doubt, we generally do not. For us it is a sort of shame on us to admit that we doubt – it deserves stigma. It has not always and everywhere been like this. In the course of history, and in the minds of the people who make it, a perversion has taken place: lack of experience has changed from being a reason for doubting *into a reason for declaring 'certainty'*. Either that or the cultures within which lack of experience establishes 'certainty' came to predominate.

It is hard to resist ascribing this perversion in European culture to Christianity's influence: the notion of the so-called 'leap of faith' the virtue of which became a necessity in proportion to advancing scientific knowledge. Yet the tendency seems to be much older than this notion, usually ascribed to Kierkegaard, who in fact wrote of a 'leap *to* faith' – and much more widespread than European culture.

In Islāmic cultures we need look no further than the Qur'ān for the origin of the tendency. It states that mankind is superior to the angels because Allāh taught Adam the names of everything in creation. This is an equation of nomenclature with information[50]. The Qur'ān's many declarations that Allāh is 'The Wise' (in Arabic, al-ḥakīm), 'The Knower' (al-`ālim), 'The Most Knowing' (al-`alīm) and the source of all knowledge for mankind are interpreted to mean that the Qur'ān is the only source of religious knowledge by the vast majority of Muslims (other scriptures being declared tampered with or entirely made up by humans), and for a sizeable proportion, *all* knowledge[51]. In religious matters at least, then, to know the Quran, then, is *to know*. The word used by it for the

---

[50] This seems to be equivalent to the intuition of essences according to Aristotle which Popper (1945; 5th edition 1966) demolishes logically and tries with being a source of the anti-rationalism he so despises in European culture.

[51] It is nothing abnormal to consider that *all* knowledge can be found in the Qur'ān. See, for example, the reading of all modern astronomical observations into the Qur'ān by various Muslim authors.

entirety of mankind before it 'descended'[52] is 'The Ignorant' and their times and cultures as 'The Ignorance' (in Arabic, al-jāhiliyya). In such an overheated system it becomes quite impossible for those who do accept the Qur'ān to admit, on any matter treated by it, to not knowing.

Whatever its origin, this sly switch of certainty and doubt[53] leaves us in a much more lamentable state than the Kālāmās. We do not admit to not being certain; indeed instead we frequently and hopelessly confuse the ignorant affectation of 'certain knowledge' with certain knowledge, and conversely the certain knowledge of the extent of our ignorance with ignorance. It is a matter of dignity. They were confused, but we dare not be.

Incidentally, some might raise the objection that believers at least in the Christian versions of God do not make such a false declaration of certainty, and they might cite such ideas as 'the numinous' (a neologism based on another Latin word for god, sought one presumes for a much-needed sense of freshness in the matter), and the *mysterium tremendum et fascinans*, in the experience of the divine.[54] If the divine is experienced as a mystery, they might object, how can there be the conceit of certainty? Well, this experience is common to all humanity without the aid of scriptures and sermons, as many non-Christian intensely religious people and intensely irreligious people have pointed out; but then a subset of that humanity have declared that we can know nothing more of this mysterium because it is beyond us. What that subset are saying is that they themselves have known all that is possible – which is hardly a humble admission of ignorance. This kind of enthralment by the superfice of concepts (such that they can confuse a declaration of final knowing with an admission of ignorance), as we shall see, is

---

[52] and by extremist thinkers such as Sayyid Qutb for all non-Muslims and even 'nominal' Muslims not accepting the total theocracy they consider the Qur'ān established: For these thinkers knowledge comes exclusively by means of utter acceptance of the Qur'ān together with its truth claims rather than by 'merely' hearing or understanding it.

[53] This is, as far as I understand him, what the contemporary religious thinker James Carse refers to as a change from infinite game to finite game, from horizons to boundaries, from admitted ignorance to unadmitted ignorance (belief). These salutory realisations are presented in his excellent books *The Religious Case Against Belief* (Carse, 2008) and *Finite and Infinite Games: A Vision of Life as Play and Possibility* (Carse, 1998).

[54] These terms all come from the works of the enormously influential German Lutheran theologian Rudolf Otto (1869-1937), especially *Das Heilige* (Otto, Das Heilige - Über das Irrationale in der Idee des Göttlichen und sein Verhältnis zum Rationalen, 1917) translated into English as *The Idea of the Holy* (Otto, 1923). We shall have more to say about Otto's ideas when we come to consider the danger of analogies.

quite a characteristic temptation within massive religious and ideological traditions. The problem is this very satisfaction, which is a closure, a stupefied and stupefying resistance to subsequent reality as it unfolds.

> Always apply yourself with both hands to seeking
> – for search is an excellent guide on the way.
> Lame and limping, bent in figure and unmannerly
> – ever creep towards Him and be in quest of Him.
>
> Rumi, *Couplets*, III, 979-

Immunity to inquiry

In our times 'faith' has come to mean, effectively, the supreme excuse to cut off communication with those who do not share our beliefs, tantamount to a declaration of immunity to enquiry, even within oneself. One's 'faith' is unassailable: by definition it is without proof, a personal choice, a private matter. In common modern usage, 'faith', 'belief' and 'creed' all mean this.

That this arrogant fideism might be unacceptable in a communicative world is sometimes, though rarely, admitted even within Christian theological discourse:

> Even the belief that faith is immune from [sic] critical examination and must be either accepted or rejected on other grounds must itself be rationally explained.[55]

(We will consider some of the 'rational explanations' that the faiths' thinkers have come up with later.) However the prevalence nowadays of the idea that there is no fault in so declaring immunity is exemplified by its ratification in modern theology. Proudfoot[56], to take a typical example, argues that description of belief and explanation of it *must* be different. What this implies is that the explanation, which is reasonable, would always destroy the belief, which therefore must be unreasonable. The fact that a belief is immune to inquiry or debate is therefore taken for granted.

This is how low our notion of belief has sunk – not because of such philosophers of religion (who are simply pointing something out or scrabbling to dignify it) but because of an long history of *people who did not deign to communicate.*

---

55 (Peterson, Hasker, Reichenbach, & Basinger, 2008)
56 (Proudfoot, 1985)

Allegiance with the tribe

Unless it occur to the reader to question the contention that faith is for most people built upon lack of experience, she need only bring to mind all the billions of people in the world and recognize the grim statistical fact that for almost all of them, with a relatively vanishing and negligible number of exceptions, the faith they will profess as an adult is simply determined by the faith into which they were born.

This has uncomfortable implications which are almost as frequently shouted down as they are pointed out. If truth (even the truth of a particular person's 'prophetship') is universal, as all the universal religions obviously claim, this must mean that, whatever is experienced of reality by these conformists, it is not sufficient for determining their decision about what is true in it. (If it were, then for example the decision as to whether or not to accept Islām would be based on experience which anyone can access, that is, it would be possible for everyone to experience the truth or otherwise of 'the prophetship of Muḥammad', and everyone would be converted immediately into or out of Islām.) So anyone who adopts the faith of the community in which they are born is deceiving themselves and lying if they assert that the 'truths' of their faith are universal.

It is not like adopting local belief about, for example, whether a particular style of dress being respectable. With notable exceptions most people are aware that this is a locally determined ethic, such that one's experience of what is respectable and what is not respectable really is different in different localities. (This is the only way nudist beaches can survive!) In contrast, the choices these religions call on one to make relate to truths and falsehoods which are claimed by necessity (since these religions aim to proselytize the universe) to be universal. So unless the truth in question is a Person with a cruel sense of humour, the experience of it should not be locally determined.

What one is doing, effectively, then, when one chooses along with the overwhelming majority of humankind to profess the faith of one's local community and to hold that this faith embodies universal truths, is declaring that the decision, which the faith declares to be based on experience, is *not* based on experience. Almost all of us are thus hypocrites, and obvious hypocrites at that.

Almost four thousand million people worldwide today ally themselves with two most massive faiths, Christianity and Islām. The nature of these religions means that for the vast majority of these people we can say with confidence that they have almost identical beliefs, in doctrines of 'the eternal Creator God', 'the previous divine existence of mankind with the Creator', and 'the fall from Grace due to desire'; and that a great many of them accept the same faiths' doctrines that 'the soul' lives on after death, and is aware after death, and undergoes the consequences of previous good and bad actions, rewards or punishments in 'the afterlife in heaven or hell' respectively after 'the Day of Judgment'. In addition we can say that the vast majority of Muslims believe that the soul will be bodily resurrected after death.

Whilst all of these beliefs are reported by the Buddha to have been taught by various religious teachers of his time, the Kālāmā people were clearly more open to hearing of and adopting or rejecting these and alternative doctrines individually than we *can* be now. These two religions, Christianity and Islām, quickly came to prohibit heresy (choice), and this prohibition is again an intrusion of violent power authority into authority for truth. We are so thoroughly habituated to the idea of faith as a community which we should defend, religion surveys of our times refer to 'adherents' of the various community faiths – literally those who *stick to* them. In the record of the discourse to the Kālāmās there is not even a hint that the Kālāmās might resist considering new beliefs because of their identity as a community, a 'faith', or because they fear being punished, much less burnt alive or decapitated, for making a choice. Taking the Pali canon as a whole there is very little evidence that anyone adopted doctrines merely to follow their parents or community-wide edicts. On the contrary a very great number of people in the Buddha's time were making strenuous efforts to discover the truth, even if it meant (as it did for the Buddha himself) leaving their family, their family's religion and their homeland. Furthermore, as we shall see, the Buddha displayed an almost callous disapproval of people wanting to 'stick' to him. However, although Buddhism was the most populous religion on earth half a century ago, the massive population explosion of Christianity and Islām have caused a tide change in the consensus on what constitutes religion, such that 'sticking' and 'God' have come to be seen as the defining features of religion.

When contrasted with this herd mentality of modern faith, the capacity to consider ethical practices and beliefs each in their own terms therefore begins to look rather noble. And the Kālāmās clearly possessed this nobility, this integrity, that we, by and large, and very much to our own detriment, seem to lack.

Case: secular faiths

What is harder to see is how the same mentality informs most other sectors of our cultures too. In academic knowledge, political systems, the market, and even in entertainment, fashion and taste, we herd around identities. Just as much as is (or for some, used to be) true for the objects of religious belief of our societies, the objects of post-religious belief, i.e. our authorities, are delimited, closed, and thereby dissociated from evolving truth.

In recent decades the tendency to rally around identity has much increased. For instance, the historian Ed Wilson argues that the cult of identity in Britain which seemed to consume everyone in the 80s was the natural consequence of Margaret Thatcher's drive to promote economic freedom (in the market) at the expense of civil liberties there: under her government participation in government was severely restricted leaving Britain with the lowest number of elected officials *per capita* in the democratic world. 'Why does this matter if we are left in freedom to pursue our individual aims?' he asks.

> The history of the late twentieth and early twenty-first century supplies the answer. In this time old solidarity and concepts of citizenship declined, replaced in many cases by single-issue campaigns, identity politics, multiculturalism and other rights-based claims which put personal interests above the idea of civic virtue and fellow-feeling. Those who saw the outcome of economic freedom as – for good or ill – extreme individualism failed to realise that people would create new forms of association. In most cases this is harmless, but bundles of competing groups, often claiming rights at the expense of others, have the potential to cause great harm. Those who call upon the state to give special protection to their culture, their religion, their preferences or their sense of decency are motivated by something very different from the ideals of citizenship when these rights are claimed without regard to the impact on others. The emergence of this type of politics, even these habits of mind, constitutes a grave danger to liberty in the modern state.[57]

We will consider the mechanism and consequences of this tendency later in our analysis of 'authority projection' (under 'Not by seeming capability').

Uniformity in some communties and reaction to diversity

There are, as a result of this transmutation of faith, many countries where the pervading views are so close to uniform and so unspoilt by troublesome exceptions as to give the impression of certainty, which clearly was not the case with the Kālāmās.

---

57 From chapter 13 of What Price Liberty? (Wilson, 2009, pp. 301, 2).

Such certainty might be thought difficult to sustain in our world, because of travel or exposure to other countries' culture via other means, principally the internet. But although these things may undermine certainty, this is not to say that the views will be abandoned! – often one finds that under such seige conditions people cling all the more stubbornly to their views or even react violently against the new ones to which they have been exposed.[58]

The implications for our understanding of the discourse

One might imagine this chasm between the Kālāmas' open-mindedness and our compromised mentality has grave implications for our reading of the discourse, for given our natural disposition, actually opposite to the Kālāmas', this discourse is *not meant for people like us.* Without exception, all traditions of Buddhism assert that the dharma, the 'Law' or 'good form', taught by the Buddha, was geared very carefully to the listeners, to address their capacity as effectively as possible. Most of us clearly do not possess the capacity of the Kālāmā people: we are too strongly identified with a particular community's system of beliefs to consider adopting alternatives (what about 1 billion of us call apostasy and millions more call 'weakness of faith') and we are not able to be honest with ourselves about the lack of experiential foundation for radical decisions we have made.

Perhaps the best course of action then would be to lay the Kālāmā Sutta aside and turn to discourses in which the audience more closely parallels our own disposition.

However, since it is my contention that there is much of benefit *for us* in how the Buddha answered the Kālāmas' petition, I will press on, with a very important proviso:

The Buddha is famously supposed to have declared,

---

58 A major brain in the early think-tank of the currently banned Islamist group the Muslim Brotherhood in Egypt, Sa`īd Qutb, is said to have developed his radical ideas after visiting the West, for example. Having tasted for himself the education there, and recognised its potential, he returned to Egypt and wrote such books as *Ma`ālim fī l-tarīq, Milestones* (Quṭb, 1964) for which he is famous and which has been described as one of the most influential Islamist tracts ever written, a long and startling diatribe invoking Islamic scriptural authorities to formulate total prohibitions on Muslims' study of psychology, sociology, evolutionary biology, comparative religion, etc. etc.

'The world contends with me,
But I do not contend with the world.'

This claim is borne out by a careful reading of the discourses and dialogues as they have come down to us: the Buddha seems to have been inordinately careful about how he spoke to people, and indeed the various traditions have noted this and tried in various ways to classify the elements that went to make up this extraordinary way of speaking. It seems therefore unlikely to me that, had the Buddha been confronted, not with a soul-searching, open-minded townsfolk, but with children of modernity who are, no matter what he might have to say thank you very much, 'certain', committed *a priori* to their particular herd's beliefs, he would have delivered the same discourse or indeed one even resembling it.

For, as we shall see, his answer to the Kālāmās' quandary is very much a celebration of qualities they already have. Whilst there is some shock there, some shunting around, the vehicle for the journey these townsfolk are encouraged to make is nevertheless a rather comfortable carriage padded with praises of their natural qualities.

But these unfortunately are the very qualities that we, in the modern world, lack. They all relate to this basic tendency to conclude from doubtful matters that we are uncertain rather than to conclude from doubtful matters that we are 'certain'. So for us, disgruntled teenagers and drop-outs aside, the journey is rather rougher and tougher – as it were, without a vehicle, barefoot over rocky ground, and beaten back at every step with a stick.

There are of course those among us of course who do not choose belief systems according to our community. And these people, if they are not already devotees of this scripture, will find the journey the Buddha encourages a very pleasant, vindicating, ride. *But that is not to say that these people are the intended audience of the discourse or that the Buddha would have spoken thus to them either!* For, as is often the case in such matters, it is those who are in reaction against their community's belief system who are the most strongly governed within themselves by that very same tendency, to turn doubtful matters into certainty, which produces the results in their fellows they most object to. To oppose an authority because of the perceived constraint on one's freedom is a type of 'cognitive bias', meaning a distortion of one's ability to decide, and it is referred to technically as 'reactance' – the problem being, of course, that the reaction itself is preventing one from making a free choice.

So, for one thing, I make the same proviso for the rebels among us as I do for the conformers: that they should constantly bear in mind that these words were not intended for people such as them. And for the rebels I make an additional proviso: that they pay doubly careful attention to the intent of the Buddha's answer. For if complacent they will miss the intent completely, and it addresses very directly the roots of a disease infecting them, even while they might fondly be imagining it only to infect someone else.

Having made that proviso, let us turn to the Buddha's answer to the Kālāmās' questions, for I believe it addresses with almost alarming alacrity our own situation too.

Part II: The Buddha's Solution

My commentary on the solution is in five stages:

Stage 1: The Profound Main Point

> 'Yes, Kālāmās, you may well doubt! You may well waver! What has given rise in you to wavering is indeed something deserving of doubt.

My presentation here has two parts:

- the peculiarities of the Buddha's answer, and
- a demonstration of the relation of those peculiarities to the nature of reality (p. 58).

The Peculiarities of the Buddha's Answer

He answers a different question to the one asked

The Buddha gives a rather troubling answer. He does not directly address the question they asked, namely, how to tell which preachers' words are true and which are false: in this sense the questioners are not given immediate satisfaction.

He provides no advocacy or refutation

Despite their wish, he does not authoritatively choose from among the various doctrines of the visiting preachers, perhaps advocating some here or refuting others there. He does not even refer to the content of what they have said. We can assume that some of the doctrines the preachers expounded were similar to doctrines the Buddha himself had expounded, but he makes no reference to this.

He changes their view of their own situation

They wanted him to guide them in one or other of the directions previous preachers have urged, but he implies that their willingness to be led in this way, without which the preachers would not have bothered to glorify their own doctrines and denigrate others', is a fault.

He demonstrates that conceiving of external authorities is, at root, error

Instead of rescuing the questioners from their irritating doubt, he exclaims that they *should doubt*, that it is *natural* that they should doubt. That is to say, in their current circumstances, it would be *improper to be 'certain'*, or rather improper to *affect certainty*, that any particular preachers' words were right, or that another's were wrong.

Why might that be? Was it the case that the Kālāmās did not yet have enough information about the preachers to come to a decisive conclusion about the respective authority of their words, that the Buddha was recommending they spend more time listening to what the preachers had to say, or that they clarify doctrinal points better so as better to decide between them? No: we do not read that the Buddha asked them to call the preachers back. And we do not read that he encouraged the Kālāmās to debate more on the points the preachers had raised.

The Buddha goes on to detail the various circumstances under which in general it is similarly improper to affect certainty, so we can assume that this first statement is his brief assertion of this impropriety.

And thus the Buddha throws down the most spectacular gauntlet to defy what has become our custom almost without exception today: to accept *authority*.

Showing the Relation of the Peculiarities to the Nature of Reality

Questioning is based on desire which if satisfied directly plants harmful seeds

The Buddha's intent is liberation from suffering. The manner in which he answers questions reflects a discipline in speaking in order to avoid adding fuel to the fire of the afflictve emotions, which later on in the discourse become the main subject for a meditative inquiry. In many discourses the Buddha is on record as having made statements to the effect that it is not enough for speech to be truthful or beneficial: it should be *both* truthful *and* beneficial. And presumably he did not imply by this that although you should not invent false calumnies and spread them by speaking, it is acceptable to write them down and publish them! So 'speech' includes all verbal communication.

We are accustomed, by and large, to underrate the importance of speech, even in this general sense, but a moment's reflection prompts otherwise. We know that identity-based conflicts and the violence they bring dominate humanity, and indeed like language have been considered often as the defining feature of humanity which sets it apart from other species on our planet. It is no coincidence that these two, language and identity-based conflict, come together:

for what else defines identity than language? Even if the identity in question is recognizable without language, as is the case with many ethnic conflicts and as becomes the case in large-scale wars when a distinct way of dress (uniform) is necessary to advertise who should not be killed, what is it which allows news of 'atrocities' and 'injustices' perpetrated by the 'enemy' to stoke the fires of hatred of only one group of people based on their identity, if it is not language?

Moreover, if we consider for a moment the nature of the transmission of ideas, such as the idea of the deity-determined superiority of a particular community, or the necessity to wage war against the wealthy class to lay rightful claim to what they have stolen from us, we can see that 'speech' in the general sense is the only vehicle of transmission. It is the 'reproductive act' of multiplying ideas, in the same way that sex and conception are the reproductive act of multiplying genes. So in the same way that tampering with sexual reproduction is a way to influence all of the next generation directly, tampering with speech is a way to influence all of the next generation of ideas directly, and by extension all future conflicts.

Evil is easy:
A cutting word will outlive the world,
Will intoxicate all but the clearest minds...
It will let loose Hell.

Consider well,
You who know how they make an enemy of you,
And craft your decision
In elegant verse.

Know those you curse -
Both the party you slight
And leave no way out for,
And the party who get you,
Given new cause to fight for,
In whom sin resides.

Wisdom divides.
Compassion and faith must respectively bless the two sides.

For evil is easy,

And wise ones will make fools of those who don't know.

Fools need relief,
And the wise must reach out,
Else wisdom is woe:
The future will show.[59]

'Authority' always deceives

What kind of authority?

First of all we need to clear up a linguistic confusion based on the English word 'authority', which includes two senses, one of which is roundly counselled against in the Buddha's answer as we shall see, and the other totally re-appreciated.

The regrettable fact is that our current idea of authority is a conflation of two very different significations: that to which recourse is made for physical power ('the authorities', the government, the police and the military, do not try to persuade us of the correctness of their view), and that to which recourse is made for truth ('an authority on Plato' does not use a truncheon to cow us into accepting his line on the Greek philosopher). The Kālāmās were attracted to the latter only in the question of what to abandon and what to adopt and practice (they did not ask what they should adopt in order not to be arrested by their king), and so should we be[60], but in the course of our discussion we will see that a great deal of the difficulty the modern mind has with this call to free inquiry is related to muddling up power and truth, and of course our history (not to mention our religion) sometimes seems like an elaborate exposition of how one has masqueraded as, or blithely supplanted, the other.

As a recent example of such conflation, the Bush administration's

---

[59] 'To Poet Prophets', Cairo, 18.11.05.

[60] It is more regrettable that today even this assertion may for some require justification. (While it is generally recognised that for long periods of its history mankind has considered fear a disgrace, submission to power cowardice and sacrifice of pragmatic security in the defence of truth noble, the faculty which makes this recognition is, most spectacularly in the USA and Europe, currently being eroded on a massive scale. I am troubled by the conviction that in my short lifetime an unprecedented catastrophe to the nobility of mankind has occurred.) This discourse however highights a subtle but penetrating justification for asserting that power authority should not be allowed to interefere in truth authority in its treatment of the afflictive processes (such as fear) and freedom from them.

effective invention of convenient intelligence to justify invading Iraq and Afghanistan, invasions which have led directly to the killing of, at a minimal estimate, tens of thousands of civilians, has been attributed [61] to its 'neo-conservative' think-tank who could write such wisdom as:

> 'Truth is not the goal [of intelligence operations] but instead victory.'[62]

In the act of deciding on an authority as part of the quest for truth, who is deciding, and how? A decision should be an act of clear judgment with clear evidence. In this act it could be that we have a good basis in experience to choose; or it could be that we do not have a good basis in experience. But whatever experience we have, we are the judge.

If the judgment is made under restriction of any kind from outside (as opposed to an enrichment of experience from outside about what is true), it is crucial to recognize that *this restriction is the interference of power, circumventing the recourse to truth.*

For example, if I choose a scientific authority on the basis of her reputation, then I am relying on consensus with the group, in exactly the same way children take sides on the school playground to seek 'safety' (i.e. violent power) in numbers. The common excuse, that by assuming all these other scientists are reliable we save time because we don't need to establish for ourselves that the candidate for authority in question is reliable, quite blithely and stupidly overlooks the fact that the reliability of all the supporting scientists is never any less in question than that of the supported candidate, so the assumption of their reliability might as well be made of the candidate, without recourse to their support!

Take another example, that of the modern idea of religious faith, the perversion (which we discussed in the context of considering how much worse our predicament is than the Kālāmā people's) of uncertainty about a doubtful matter into 'certainty' about the same doubtful matter. Here too it is we who choose to make this step.

The most 'intelligent' defence of it in the Christian tradition is that the choice to be certain about this version of God (i.e. one of the multifarious Christian versions) is 'not absurd because God has in His grace bestowed the gift of faith upon me'. Again, in exactly the same way, it is crucial to recognize that

---

[61] For example by John Gray (Gray, 2007)

[62] (Schmitt & Shulsky, 1991)

what this means is that the freedom of choice has been restricted, such that *power has subverted a recourse to truth*: you, the believer, were not free to choose to believe, because the private revelation to you by His grace was overwhelming.

If you object that this accusation of subversion lacks one essential extra piece of information, namely that 'God is truth [because he said so]', then the onus is upon you to demonstrate by what experiential knowledge you judge this information to be reliable, beyond the very same 'grace of God' you are attempting to rescue from doubt. Since you must then declare that the experiential knowledge is only available to you because of (i.e. as a reward for) your own choice to accept 'God's authority' (and this is a sinister partiality indeed that you are ascribing to your deity), then it only remains to return to the initial question: on what experiential knowledge did you make it?

(That itself is a complete refutation. We might nevertheless also decry that divine partiality, the other consequence of this defence, impressively appalling as it is. In your view then the universal deity is doing a very dirty business, withholding the 'truth' from those who do not pay the price of submitting and revealing 'the truth' to those that submit – the submission in question being necessarily made in the state of not knowing this 'truth', i.e. it is necessarily an absurd choice (in the sense of being made without reason), since the 'truth' is only ever revealed *consequent* to the choice. In effect you are accusing your own deity of an all too human and rather ludicrous capriciousness. This might lead you to question such a deity's reliability for truthfulness in the first place! The doubt should remain even if you nevertheless submit pragmatically out of fear of the deity's violence, or craving for its favour.)[63]

Incidentally this idea of our faith being chosen for us can be equated on the basis of its form with the Hegelian idea that the way we think is dependent upon our place in the unfolding of the grand scheme of history, and condemned with it on the basis of its psychological and social consequences:

> …the idea that we 'think with our race' may perhaps be replaced by the idea of elect or inspired souls who 'think by God's grace'. I refuse, on moral grounds, to be impressed by these differences; for the decisive

63 It is common nowadays to read apologists for such 'logical defences' of faith as the chosenness argument attack critics with the accusation that the latter 'have not studied theology sufficiently'. This accusation must still apply to me because nothing in the long tracts of such 'theology' through which I have dutifully dragged myself has refuted the critique of authority I am explaining here. If any of my respected readers *has* studied 'theology' *sufficiently* to refute this critique I look forward to hearing from them.

similarity between all these intellectually immodest views is that they do not judge a thought on its own merits. By thus abandoning reason, *they split mankind into friends and foes*, into the few who share reason with the gods, and the many who don't (as Plato says) [...] Once we have done this, political equalitarianism becomes practically impossible.

Now the adoption of an anti-equalitarian attitude [...] I call criminal. For it offers a justification [...] that different categories of people have different rights; that the master has the right to enslave the slave [...] Ultimately, it will be used, as in Plato, to justify murder.[64]

If we are not prepared to answer for the conceit of awarding ourselves a partial deity's suspiciously convenient favours, then we have no alternative but to answer the charges levelled by reason. We should not be cowed by the immensity of what is at stake.

> Should free enquiry lead to the destruction of Christianity itself, it ought not, on that account, to be discontinued; for we can only wish for the prevalence of Christianity on the supposition of its being true; and if it fall before the influence of free enquiry, it can only do so in consequence of its not being true.[65]

It is worth pointing out that this notion of some version of deity choosing to grace only a part of its human creation with a literally absurd tendency towards faith in it is a dressed up version of the earlier arrival in the history of totalitarianism, the Jewish claim to being the race chosen by the deity Yahweh. In Islām and some versions of Christianity it is believed that the deity has chosen an 'elect' that includes *all* humanity, and the awkward absence of the appropriate faith in the majority of them is then described as their 'rejection of' and 'lying about' God's offer. This rejection, it is recognised, could not be allowed to be a *reasonable* decision (i.e. based on grounds) without casting their own decision to accept into painful relief (since they would clearly be ignoring these grounds), so such inappropriate disbelief *must be* ascribed to *unreasonableness* or even ignorance. Such grounds can be found, however, so if the challenge is pursued, the nature of the 'unreasonableness' or 'ignorance' will be seen to become more and more

---

64 (italics mine) from chapter 24, III of *The Open Society and Its Enemies* (Popper, 1945; 5th edition 1966).

65 This 250-year-old remark comes from Joseph Priestley, one of the most famous proponents of political liberty in British history (Priestley, 1785).

mysterious, revealing at length the same basic premise in the believer: that the deity has selected the proper believer and condemned the other to her blindness.

So, to return to our earlier point, that authority involves two very different processes, power and truth, we can ask ourselves how to separate the two. The Buddha is not the only religious teacher to have recognized the importance of this. Many martyrs of the Christian tradition were attempting to assert this distinction, by defying the orders of power authorities (whom they often sought out) to give up their belief. Certain great masters of the Sufist traditions of Islām have declared that in a quest for what is right we must separate one kind of authority, the violently powerful, from the other, 'the truthful', and to point out that while we might have pragmatic recourse to the former, we should recognize that the latter do not exist, *even if God does*: the Islāmic mystic Manṣūr al-Ḥallāj is famously recorded to have announced:

ana al-ḥaqq

I am the truth.

And he was famously condemned and executed for it – not by other 'mystics', but by the power authorities, the Islāmic scholars allied with the government of Baghdād. We might even credit with such psychological profundity, rather than with mere political pragmatism, Jesus of Nazareth's 'render unto caesar…' This also seems to be what Sartre is getting at with his insistence on perfect and total freedom and the *mauvaise foi* of using it to affect a surrender of freedom. But we might ask what exactly is the probem with letting power 'influence' our choices? Is it not simply practical?

If we are *not* the freely acting assessors of the factors distinguishing a variety of potential sources of true knowledge, then power has impinged on truth and we cannot any longer trust in our own decision among them at all: we might as well have walked through a mirror into Wonderland. This is not avoidable by seeking help: if we go on to decide on particular 'reliable' authorities in that restricted state, how can trust in the authorities we have decided to rely on thus?! It is like laying tiles on uneven ground and expecting them to become flat.

What about the implication of Hallāj's pronouncement, that there is no external authority for truth anyway?

There is no external authority for truth

> Sustained liberty [...] is rather to be sought within than without.
> -Milton, The Second Defence of the English People[66]

A rather dramatic way of stressing the necessity to recognize that all 'authority decisions' are judgments made by a free (unrestricted) subject, is to say that the final authority must always be the subject, i.e. 'internal', or even to declare that 'external authorities' *do not exist* for truth, because they are by nature deceptive. What could that mean?

The ordinary person *believes* that what he knows, and accepts as true, is either by his own knowledge or by accepting 'external authority'. In reality, as we have seen, it is *always* on one's own authority that one accords others theirs. This has been stated and restated in a dazzling variety of ways in various cultures, but the majority still proceed in blissful oblivion.

> Whatever authority we accept, it is we who accept it. We only deceive ourselves if we do not realise this simple point.[67]

This rather embarrassing fact is covered up more or less skilfully in all fields of knowledge, but nowhere as deviously as in religious discourse.

The fact that we shirk authority cuts very, very deep. As the popular mind experiment has it we could all be brains in jars being subjected to the experiments of a mad scientist: we cannot even prove that there is anything external. If you disagree, ask yourself, what (including other people reporting their experience) have I ever experienced which was not mediated by my mind? And when you have brought that little meditation to its inexorable conclusion, reflect on the power in the dream state for the mind's images to fool us completely. This conundrum has been exploited in popular culture in films such as 'The Matrix', where 'reality' turns out to be a computer programme-generated pattern of stimulation to keep our minds happy while our actually immobilised bodies are used as batteries by those computers; and 'The Island', where our childhood memories turn out to have been implanted by computer to conceal the fact that we were not born but cloned as near-adults under accelerated growth conditions to provide spare organs for our rich 'originals'. Whether one accepts

---

66 (Milton, 1654)

67 From chapter 5, part V of *The Open Society and Its Enemies* (Popper, 1945; 5th edition 1966)

that the technology is available for such feats is clearly beside the point since our entire reality – including what year it is and what state technology has advanced to – are thrown into question by these diverting interpretational possibilities.

> Is all that we see or seem
> But a dream within a dream?[68]

To perform the imaginative feat of entertaining the reinterpretation that what appears to us is not what is, as such movies and poems powerfully suggest, is indeed highly diverting; but it is also arguably a component of all religions, and in Buddhism and some others taken very seriously and applied with thoroughness and diligence as a powerful means of attaining profound insights. The very opening of the famous Dhammapada (*The Steps or Words of the Law of Reality*) declares:

> Mano pubbāṅgamā dhammā mano seṭṭhā mano mayā

> With mind at their prior edge are phenomena, mind is their chief, and they are made of/by mind.

In the same text it is said:

> Attā hi attano nātho ko hi nātho paro siyā
> Attanā hi sudantena nāthaṁ labhati dullabhaṁ

> One is indeed one's own lord, for what other lord could there be?
> By dominating oneself well one obtains a lord difficult to find.[69]

It is interesting to note that what philosopher of science Popper calls 'a simple point' the Buddha says is difficult to obtain: *we are not talking about exchanging opinions easily* but discovering something about ourselves which is not immediately obvious. It could be the simplest thing, but for that very reason it is very difficult for our complex mental patterns to discern. So if you read the previous description of authority wondering what on earth it was talking about, you are not alone!

---

68 Edgar Allan Poe, 'A Dream Within A Dream' Boston, 1849.
69 XII, 4.

The Buddha is recorded in the famous *Diamond-Cutter Discourse* to have said that a presentation of reality can be called 'a complete presentation' only if it says:

> tārakā timiraṁ dīpo māyāvaśyāya budbudam|
> svapnaṁ ca vidyudabhraṁ ca evaṁ draṣtavya saṁskṛtam||

> As a star by night, or a lamp, or a seduction by illusion, or a bubble,
> or a dream, or a flash of lightning in cloud, so view "concrete" things![70]

The Lanka Visitation Discourse says:

> There is no outside form,
> For such is just a projection of the mind itself.

We shall have occasion to consider external authority in a great deal more detail later, under 'Not by seeming capability'.

Doubts should never be stifled

In the very instant that a single doubt is stifled, we have in that same moment lost all integrity and conscience. The English mathematician W. K. Clifford (1845-1879) spoke well when he said:

> It is never lawful to stifle a doubt; for either it can be honestly answered by means of the inquiry already made, or else it proves that the inquiry was not complete.[71]

---

70 This is one of very few versed sections of the discourse and occurs near the end.

71 (Clifford, 1970, pp. 159-60)

Stage 2: The Buddha's Condemnations of Certainty

> 'Look, Kālāmās, it is not by recitation, nor by tradition, nor by report, nor by scriptural authority, nor by reason of philosophy, nor by reason of inference, nor by thinking ideas through, nor by favouring views, nor by (others') seeming capability, nor insofar as a particular ascetic is your teacher, …'

Here my presentation pursues:

- a brief overview of the ten condemnations to introduce their general characteristics, and then
- a detailed treatment, one by one (p. 87).

General Characteristics

Non-rhetorical

To introduce them as a whole, I first of all want to draw attention to what they are not: assertions intended to persuade us.

Aristotle in a treatise wrote, introducing and justifying its subject, rhetoric, or verbal means of persuasion, that –

> Rhetoric is useful, [...] for argument based on knowledge implies instruction, and *there are people whom one cannot instruct.* [...] If it be objected that one who uses such power of speech unjustly might do great harm, that is a charge which may be made in common against all good things except virtue, and above all against the things that are the most useful, as strength, health, wealth, generalship. A man can confer the greatest of benefits by a right use of these, and inflict the greatest of injuries by using them wrongly.[72]

This rather ungenerous view of humanity, as needing rhetoric (persuasion in addition to or instead of a presentation of truth) for guidance, might strike some as quite justified from a casual acquaintance with our species. And there is a lingering reverence for rhetoric (in politics) in those cultures which hark back to Greece as the cradle of civilisation, and (in religious discourse) in those cultures which hark back to Makkah as its cradle.

Rhetoric is an example of that very conflation of power and truth in the Christian-Islāmic notion of authority that we have discussed, and its ongoing prestige reflects a preponderance of the respect for power over that for truth which arguably explains a lot about that aspect of history traditionally termed Christian and Islāmic 'civilisation'. As Locke drily put it,

> There is reason to think, that if men were better instructed themselves, they would be less imposing on others.[73]

It is a noteworthy quality of the Buddha, incidentally, that unlike Aristotle by his own admission, he dismissed no-one as inferior to instruction in

---

72 (My italics.) From the introduction to *Rhetoric* (Aristotle, c. 350 BCE).

73 *Essay Concerning Human Understanding,* book IV, chapter xvi, section 4 (Locke, 1690).

truth, even serial killers[74] never mind people of blind faith. So, even though we have compared ourselves unfavourably with the Kālāmās, we can take heart from this readiness to accept all comers.

Conferring rhetoric-immunity

Logically enough, then, the Buddha did not make recourse to rhetoric, and the next part of the Buddha's advice includes a systematic dismantling of the mental apparatus which allows rhetoric to sway us, and carefully undergoing this will leave even those previously most gullible in a position to begin to see things as they are, at least without interference from verbally intimated power authority. The ten 'authorities' that the Buddha declares to be irrelevant to certain knowledge cover pretty much every rhetorical strategy in the book, those ways of arguing a point which are considered a mark of eloquence or skilfulness in speaking, so we have a kind of anti-Aristotelian manual in our hands.

For this reason a portion of the commentary is an exploration of these rhetorical methods and how to recognise them.

Conferring immunity to other intrusions of power into truth

Rhetoric is only one way we are duped rather than instructed. Modern advertising and political propaganda is well aware of other, much less obvious ways, that an audience can be deceived while thinking they are informed, deploying the full arsenal of the latest knowledge about information cascade in societies and psychology, The Buddha's critique pulls the carpet from under such dubious enterprises.

Instructive

Furthermore, with Aristotle's supposed concern that speech be 'beneficial' even if it is false, we can compare the Buddha's recommendation that speech be both beneficial *and true*. Moreover Aristotle's idea of what is beneficial to the masses is by his own admission to guide or goad them, since he cannot, he says, instruct them. Aristotle in the quoted passage was warming up to drive his listeners like sheep into the correct camp. He claims in the same treatise that once people had been thus hustled (as we may say) by rhetoric, they would somehow be in a position better to recognise the truth to which they had been hustled. We will consider whether this is possible, and the nature of this hustling

---

[74] The at the time notorious 'Finger-Necklace', Angulimala.

tendency, which would become pervasive in cultures dominated by monotheism, in the course of the commentary. For now let us note simply that the Buddha here does not want to shepherd the Kālāmā people into his own pen, but on the contrary to draw their attention to how we are ordinarily hustled *away from* what we want and equip them with the wherewithal to overcome such deception.

Not directed at tribal thinking

We notice here a parallel between, on the one hand, the difference between the 'Buddhic' and Aristotelian means in speech, and, on the other, the previously noted difference between the Kālāmās and ourselves in terms of open-mindedness and sincerity. After all, those very people Aristotle claims not to be able to instruct sound like the 'opiners *en masse*', the massive faiths, the massive ideological parties and schools Popper accuses of tribal inclinations. The seeming parallel will be strengthened by a cursory examination of the history of rhetoric in European Christianity and the Islāmic world, both primarily influenced by the Greeks. The appeal to *logic*, which one might in naivety assume to be generally considered essential to get to conceptual truth, is in the classical art of persuasion demoted to the same status as Aristotle's other two so-called artistic proofs, namely the appeal to *ethics* and the appeal to *pathos*. This is tangible in the accounts of the teaching in Europe of Christianity: the preachers clearly felt they faced either a population or a doctrine (I leave it to the reader to surmise which) whose logical acumen was deemed inadequate for the one to persuade the other. Hence proponents' (and more pertinently opponents') reputations and the population's passions were brought in, *ethos* and *pathos* to support a limping *logos*. And it was further East, of course, where the Muslim philosophers preserved for us such Greek 'philosophy' in Arabic translations.

(This during those dark years of Europe when, having employed it successfully to persuade *us*, the European Church was burning all the records of it which might arm potential rebels among us with the wherewithal to re-persuade *the Church*. As is now, thanks to the demise of the Church's power, widely known, the European Renaissance, in which interest in the Greeks astonishingly revived and flourished, is a misnomer, since the interest had just migrated back out of the Arabic translations: more of a Homecoming than a Renaissance.)

Little wonder then that so many of the old ways of rhetoric persist in the arguments of Christians and Muslims to 'defend' their beliefs.

Something of the same difference seems to have persisted even up to colonial times, meaning of course the time of European countries' colonisation of other countries. Much shallow calumny was levelled by European colonists against the people of the Indian subcontinent and other colonisable areas, for example that they were 'apathetic' and 'lacked the active individual spirit', (a spirit which is often, so it seems, assumed to have been conferred by Christ on the whites[75]), and indeed still is. However some experience of living in a variety of cultures in both areas affords rather the insight that it is *the Europeans* who seem to lack individualism. What the Europeans seem to have in abundance is instead *identification*, be it with religious alignment, political party, class, school of art, or whatever, as we saw when considering what distinguishes us from the Kālāmās.

Furthermore it is clear from their own admissions that the colonists' efforts to shepherd the 'benighted apathetic natives' of 'the East' invariably ended in disaster, simply because the said natives were in general so unaccustomed to the herd formation which is so familiar in European society it goes practically unnoticed. [76]

---

[75] John Stuart Mill said that the Chinese 'have become stationary [...] and if they are ever to be improved it must be by foreigners.' (Mill, 1998) Kant writes, 'The Negroes of Africa have by nature no feeling that rises above the trivial.' (Kant, 1764) Even equalitarian John Locke says of the Native Americans that they forfeited their right to property and freedom by 'some Act that deserves Death' (opposing the European). See *What Price Liberty?* (Wilson, 2009) pp. 84-5. Hegel writes in his *Lectures on the Philosophy of History* (1830), 'The distinguishing feature of the negroes' contempt for humanity is not so much their contempt for death as their lack of respect for life. They set as little value on life as they do on human beings as such, for life is only valuable in so far as there is a higher value in man... They give no thought to the preservation of life, or to death itself. The great courage of the negroes, reinforced by their great physical strength, must also be ascribed to this lack of respect for life; for they allow themselves to be shot down in thousands in their wars with the Europeans. In the war between the Ashanti and the English, the natives persisted in running straight up to the mouths of the cannon, although they were invariably shot down fifty at a time. In fact, life is of no value unless it has a worthy object.' Clearly the Europeans were innocently firing these weapons (at passing wildebeest, one presumes) and one is reassured that this accident positioned them well to teach the blacks *respect for life.* Hegel however seems inexplicably to lack this generous spirit: 'The Negro [...] exhibits the natural man [sic] in his completely wild and unnatural state. We must lay aside all thought of reverence and morality — all that we call feeling — if we would rightly comprehend him. There is nothing harmonious with humanity to be found in this kind of character.'

[76] I cannot resist quoting Rudyard Kipling here:

> Now it is not good for the Christian's health
> To hustle the Aryan brown,
> For the Christian riles and the Aryan smiles,
> And it weareth the Christian down.

Against uncritical propagation

Having noted that the Buddha's answer is not designed to persuade but instead to sensitise us to potentially deluding rhetoric, propaganda, manipulation and misinformation, we should add that the Buddha's recommendations go much further than this. Investigating this discourse as we are about to, we could be forgiven for concluding that almost everything we have until now considered reliable is brought into question. For it was not just mere intentional manipulation that the Buddha saw as leading people away from the truth and away from happiness. His critique also highlights a 'natural' degeneration of culture in how it interprets reality.

Such a degeneration from truth is possible, for example, because of what we might call 'carrying mechanisms', akin to the way a virus can survive to infect future generations (our virus being accumulated error), and we can identify a huge number and variety of such mechanisms. For example, to make a quick survey, mimicking elders in their deployment of the religious symbols is a great carrier mechanism; as are traditions and customs passed on, say, out of a sense of necessity, frequently neurotic fear of supernaturally originating repercussions to not passing them on; reporting stories you hear credulously or incredulously is another; fixing of the patterns which express meaning, religious or otherwise, which as we shall see is a precursor to their spectacular degeneration, is perhaps the most important; it is always aided by their codification in an 'eternal scripture'; while there will always be awkward awareness at least among some members of the community that such degeneration is taking place, if the complaints of such people are dealt with by clever befuddling reasoning and fallacious but effective rhetoric, this will make sure the rallying power of the symbols is not lost such that they continue to be passed out and down; developing a sense of certainty as we as a community become familiar with a certain expression of symbols, and developing a sense that rejecting strange ones out of hand is acceptable, because that's what everyone else is doing, foster a conclusion of conviction which we have highlighted as one of our especial ills today, and which leaves people nothing else to pass on; associating the patterns of expression with authoritative figures

---

And the end of the fight
Is a tombstone white
With the name of the late deceased
And the epitaph drear: 'A fool lies here
who tried to hustle the East.'

This is from Chapter 5 of *Naulahka* (Kipling, 1892).

and honourable persons and communities will help tremendously in the degeneration we have described because the human heart so much more willingly and more energetically, nay with bottomless energy, loves *people* than it loves *patterns*, and so will come when threatened to defend, vociferously and to the death, the both together.

As we shall see, this entire apparatus, in response to a seemingly innocuous plea for guidance, the Buddha in ten succinct exhortations dismantles once and for all, if only we have ears to listen.

Against distortion by the afflictive emotions

Many of these manipulations and carrying mechanisms depend on partiality and so on, what we might call 'dangerous' emotion or 'destabilising' psychological processes. Not only whether error is carried on but also whether it dupes us successfully is influenced by such emotions and processes. Later on in the discourse the Buddha simplifies their complexity into a three-fold classification, but they include our natural inclination towards making recourse to the security afforded by physical power, as well as more obvious partialities. What might not be so obvious is the involvement of distorting anger in much so-called 'rational thought': in stark contrast to the Greek rescue of 'thought' from what they considered the pollutions of the emotions, the Buddha reveals how such rational thought is itself a kind of emotion or afflictive process. Readers unfamiliar with Buddhism might also be surprised to see that even basic confusion about reality is classed as an afflictive process in Buddhism, as we shall see.

Against heteronomy

To put it succinctly, we can say that all the Buddha's exhortations are to refuse heteronomy (identifying the locus of our freedom to decide the truth with, or defining the locus of our freedom as, 'another', or in other words taking some external source, or internal constraining system, of knowledge as a decisive authority) so that only autonomy (the unrestricted choice of the individual, self-determination) is left to us.[77]

---

[77] Philosophers should note that I am not using the terms autonomy and heteronomy in the rather unintuitive sense Kant did: here heteronomy refers to according external authority for any reason, not (as Kant meant) being under the domination of desires, although later we shall see that the two ways of using these terms might not be so different as they appear.

As we shall see, it is not a matter of rejecting a potentially viable kind of heteronomy, of arbitrarily adopting an autonomous attitude, out of some desire (for example) to be seen to be the member of a particular philosophical school – it is a matter of investigating reality carefully enough to discover that what have until now appeared to us to be sources of certainty are not at all viable as such, and thus to realise that *we have been deceived.* This renewed clarity of vision, seeing what is actually there rather than behaving according to principles derived from the imagination, is aptly described by the Latin term conscientia, which originally meant 'being conscious of what was present'. In effect the Buddha is making a call for us to waken this conscientia, this supremely valuable conscience. Rather than a dereliction of responsibility to idol-like certainties, we are being exhorted to rediscover 'prohairesis', the faculty of choice over our impressions first adverted to in Greek philosophy by Aristotle (in the 'Nicomachean' Ethics) and developed by Epictetus.

Against the delusion of certainty

Now let us turn to those 'idol-like' certainties. Whilst we might not be quite up to the standard of open-mindedness displayed by the Kālāmās, there are examples of our type, that is to say, frankly, the more bigoted variety, in the Pali canon, and one extraordinary example suits our purpose very well, since the Buddha challenges an almost identical list of sources of 'certainty' (as we shall see), the only difference being that for our type he tellingly adds two extra sources to the beginning of the list – faith and relishing – and the extra instruction that, while they are all useful to an extent in safeguarding truth, it is inappropriate to *reach a decisive conclusion* on the basis of any of them. The examplary bigot I am referring to appears in *The Caṇkī Discourse*[78]: a young priest of the orthodox religion of the time (i.e. a Brāhmaṇa) who is greatly honoured by his fellows for his learning. He asks the Buddha rather provocatively:

> 'Yadidaṁ, bho gotama, brāhmaṇānaṁ porāṇaṁ mantapadaṁ itihitiha paramparāya piṭakasampadāya, tattha ca brāhmaṇā ekaṁsena niṭṭhaṁ gacchanti – "Idameva saccaṁ, moghamañña"nti. Idha bhavaṁ gotamo kimāhā'ti?

78 This lively exchange is classified as the fifth of the section on divines in the middle section of the middle-length discourses.

'Master Gotama, the divines' ancient hymns, which are recited as tradition and included in their canon, and about which the divines have come to the definite conclusion that only they are true and all else is vain, what does Master Gotama have to say about this?'

The Buddha replies by asking him a question:

'Kiṁ pana, bhāradvāja, atthi koci brāhmaṇānaṁ ekabrāhmaṇopi […] ekācariyopi , ekācariyapācariyopi, yāva sattamā ācariyamahayugāpi, […] te brāhmaṇānaṁ pubbakā isayo mantānaṁ kattāro mantānaṁ pavattāro yesamidaṁ etarahi brāhmaṇā porāṇaṁ mantapadaṁ gītaṁ pavuttaṁ samihitaṁ tadanugāyanti tadanubhāsanti bhāsitamanubhāsanti vācitamanuvācenti seyyathidaṁ – aṭṭhakovāmako vāmadevo vessāmitto yamataggi aṅgīraso bhāradvājo vāseṭṭho kassapo bhagu, tepi evamāhaṁsu – "mayametaṁ jānāma, mayametaṁ passāma. Idameva saccaṁ, moghamañña'"nti?

'Tell me, Bhāradvāja, is there among the divines even one divine […] even one teacher or teacher's teacher back through seven generations […] among the divine prophets of the past, the creators of the hymns, the composers of the hymns, (the divines' ancient hymns, which were sung, repeated, and collected, and which they still sing, which they chant on with, chanting what has been chanted, voicing what has been voiced,) Aṭṭhaka, Vāmaka, Vāmadeva, Vessāmitta, Yamataggi, Angīrasa, Bhāradvāja, Vāseṭṭha, Kassapa, Bhagu… was there even one of these who said, "This we know; this we see; only this is true, all else is vain?"'

'No hidaṁ, bho gotama.'

'No, Master Gotama.'

Since none of them has this confidence, then the system of education into the traditions is compared by the Buddha to the blind leading the blind:

'Iti kira, bhāradvāja, natthi koci brāhmaṇānaṁ ekabrāhmaṇopi […] Seyyathāpi, bhāradvāja, andhaveṇi paramparā

> saṁsattā purimopi na passati majjhimopi na passati pacchimopi na passati; evameva kho, bhāradvāja, andhaveṇūpamaṁ maññe brāhmaṇānaṁ bhāsitaṁ sampajjati – purimopi na passati majjhimopi na passati pacchimopi na passati. Taṁ kiṁ maññasi, bhāradvāja , nanu evaṁ sante brāhmaṇānaṁ amūlikā saddhā sampajjatī'ti?

> 'So then, Bhāradvāja, it seems that there isn't among the divines even one [such…] Suppose there were a row of blind men, each holding on to the one in front of him: the first one doesn't see, the middle one doesn't see, the last one doesn't see. In the same way, the statement of the divines turns out to be a row of blind men, as it were: the first one doesn't see, the middle one doesn't see, the last one doesn't see. So what do you think, Bhāradvāja: this being the case, doesn't the faith of the brahmans turn out to be groundless?'

In a move from personal autonomy to 'external authority' which is absolutely characteristic of people under such a challenge, and directly relevant to the Kālāmā discourse, the boy priest says:

> 'Na khvettha, bho gotama, brāhmaṇā saddhāyeva payirupāsanti, anussavāpettha brāhmaṇā payirupāsantī'ti.

> 'It's not only out of faith, Master Gotama, that the divines honor this. They also honor it as a tradition passed down.'

First the Buddha draws the boy's attention to what he has done[79]:

> 'Pubbeva kho tvaṁ, bhāradvāja, saddhaṁ agamāsi, anussavaṁ idāni vadesi.'

> 'Bhāradvāja, first you went on faith. Now you speak of tradition.'

The Buddha then launches into a challenge of the validity of relying on these two sources of knowledge, faith and tradition, and others, the very same ones he challenges in our discourse. The challenge is that, in each case, there are two potential consequences to each kind of source.

---

79 It is a manner of argument called antiptosis.

> 'Pañca kho ime, bhāradvāja, dhammā diṭṭheva dhamme dvedhā vipākā. Katame pañca? Saddhā, ruci, anussavo, ākāraparivitakko, diṭṭhinijjhānakkhanti…'

> 'There are five things by means of whose viewpoint there can be a double consequence. Which five? Faith, relishing, recited tradition, thinking ideas through and satisfaction with a view.'

And he goes on to describe what these two unwanted consequences are:

> 'Api ca, bhāradvāja, susaddahitam̊yeva hoti [surucitam̊yeva hoti…pe… svānussutam̊yeva hoti…pe… suparivitakkitam̊yeva hoti…pe… sunijjhāyitam̊yeva hoti], tañca hoti rittam̊ tuccham̊ musā; no cepi susaddahitam̊ hoti [pe…], tañca hoti bhūtam̊ taccham̊ anaññathā.'

> 'Now some things are firmly held in faith [or thoroughly relished… or recited in a particular tradition… or well-thought-through[80]… or clearly demand no more meditation[81]] and yet empty, trifling and false. Conversely some things are *not* firmly held in faith [or thoroughly relished etc…], and yet they are genuine, factual, and unmistaken.'

What should our conclusion from this be? That certainty is inappropriate:

> 'Saccamanurakkhatā, bhāradvāja, viññunā purisena nālamettha ekam̊sena niṭṭham̊ gantum̊ – "idameva saccam̊, moghamañña"'nti.

> 'To safeguard the truth, in these cases it isn't proper for a wise person to come to the definite conclusion that only something is true, and all else vain.'

Since the boy priest's resembles the modern mentality rather more closely than the Kālāmās', we have added the two extra sources of 'certainty', faith and relishing, to the commentary, as applying particularly to ourselves.

---

80 Referring to ideas.

81 Referring to beliefs.

Drawing attention to deification

It is, ironically, a charge frequently levelled at ancient religions and beliefs that they were so primitive that they deified natural phenomena, such as the sun's light and warmth. Much scorn is poured on such notions, by people who consider themselves to have transcended such superstition.

However, this discourse turns the scorners' laughter around and directs it back to them. It draws attention to the way we all inadvertently or otherwise deify natural phenomena, including ways of thought. Since this might not seem in the least justifiable at first, it's worth spending some time reflecting on how it could be.

Deification means 'making a god' out of what is not, investing phenomena with power or truth beyond our experience of them, and often even attributing to them awareness, such that the phenomena gain teleological significance (i.e. occurrences are considered to unfold according to some grand scheme). A merely casual investigation of our species immediately reveals that this psychological tendency is alive and well in all societies, including the most self-professedly 'modern'.

For deification is exactly what has happened in the case of these sources of knowledge (tradition, reason, authority figures, etc.), if they are taken as sources of *certainty*: their reliability has been exaggerated (just as the sun's was by ancient cultures) and they have come to be seen as somehow aiming for something rather than a natural development of human culture. This process of deification has been taken to staggering degree and complexity in the 'monotheistic' systems, something the 'mystics' of those traditions have long recognised and fought against, and so their adherents might well reflect carefully on the reformulation of their deities' anti-idolatry injunctions by these 'mystics'. As K. Venkata Ramanan explains, in the context of an exposition on extreme misappropriation of experiences as having ultimate essence or 'being in themselves', in his magisterial exploration of Nāgārjuna's Mahā Prajñāpāramita Śāstra:

> This is an imagination of ultimacy in regard to that which is in fact determinate. This is the error of misplaced absoluteness carried to its completion. Strictly it is [...] the complete form of satkāyadṛṣṭi, the false sense of self, the error which is the root of all errors. It is a dṛṣṭi (view) in which the complex, conditioned entity (kāya) is imagined to be absolute and unconditioned (sat) and in which this imagination is

extended to everything that differentiating intellect seizes hold of.[82]

We will examine the roots of absolutism in the afflictive processes based on misappropriating experience as personal self in the course of the Buddha's discourse later, but for now let the popular Islāmic mystic Rumi anticipate us:

مادر بتها بت نفس شماست... زانک آن بت مار و این بت اژدهاست
آهن و سنگست نفس و بت شرار... آن شرار از آب می‌گیرد قرار
سنگ و آهن زآب کی ساکن شود... آدمی با این دو کی ایمن بود
بت سیاهابه‌ست در کوزه نهان... نفس مر آب سیه را چشمه دان
آن بت منحوت چون سیل سیاه... نفس بتگر چشمه‌ای بر آب راه
صد سبو را بشکند یکپاره سنگ... و آب چشمه می‌زهاند بی‌درنگ
بت‌شکستن سهل باشد نیک سهل... سهل دیدن نفس را جهلست جهل
صورت نفس ار بجویی ای پسر... قصه‌ی دوزخ بخوان با هفت در
هر نفس مکری و در هر مکر زان... غرقه صد فرعون با فرعونیان

The idol of your self is the mother of idols
– because those idols are only snakes but this idol is a dragon.
The self is iron and stone while the idol is sparks
– those sparks are quieted by water.
How should the stone and iron be quieted by water
– how should man, having these twain, be secure?
The idol is black water in a jug
– the self is a fountain of the black water.
That sculpted idol is like the black jet
– the idol-making self is a fountain full of water for it.
A single piece of stone will break a hundred pitchers
– but the fountain is jetting forth water incessantly.
'Tis easy to break an idol, very easy
– to regard the self as easy is folly, folly.
O son, if you seek to know the form of the self
– read the story of Hell with its seven gates.
Every moment an act of deceit, and in every one of those deceits
– a hundred Pharaohs are drowned together with their followers.[83]

---

[82] (Ramanan, 1966/2002, p. 102)

[83] Verses 772- of Volume I of Rumi (602-673 h.)'s *Meaningful Couplets* (Rumi J. u.-D., 662-672 h. (1260 CE)), translation after Nicholson (Rumi & Nicholson, 1925-1940).

The fact that the monotheistic systems encourage this deifying, awareness-imbuing tendency is easy to see. For example, take the uproar about the term 'selfish gene' as popularised by Richard Dawkins[84], who has always stressed that he did not mean to invest the genes with teleology: it was just that the phenomenon of natural selection (a term itself misunderstood in the same way) at the level of genes led to patterns, for example of transmission, which one could predict by *imagining* that the genes *were* each a selfish person with a purpose.[85] However, his audience were not as subtle as he might have hoped, and the term, like 'natural selection', has been consistently misunderstood throughout its history as implying purpose – in the case of the selfish genes, not only that the genes, like microscopic Satans, are indeed selfish, but that they make us, the 'sinners' we might say, selfish too. It should hardly surprise us that this kind of deificatory thinking has originated in certain communities of thinkers who are inured to 'one-level teleologising', due to doctrinal commitments. Amid the variety of humankind, those with the strongest teleologising inclinations will be drawn to the teleologising systems. The notion of 'God's plan' is, as it were, a powerful temptation.

In the course of our justification of the Buddha's critique of such absolutism, of this attribution of reliability and purpose to, or deification of, various sources of knowledge, we will not only object to traditional and overt deification: we shall unmask, scrutinise, and perhaps poke fun at, a fair number of 'modern' gods – justice, morality, the free market, logic, security and grievance, to name but a few – and we will find that taboos on even questioning them, never mind mocking them, are if anything even more vociferous than those on questioning and mocking the old deities.

Incidentally, the word Nicholson translates as 'folly' is not an original Persian word but the Arabic (and therefore Islām-associated) word for ignorance, jahl, which has a connotation of pre-Islamic beliefs (Islām being considered to bring knowledge): the strong connotation is that those who consider the idol of the self to be easy to break are like the ignorants (or 'pagans') that Islām was revealed among.

84 Originally in his book *The Selfish Gene* (Dawkins R. , The Selfish Gene, 1976).

85 His attempt to remedy this confusion by drawing (in a way strongly reminiscent of Nagarjuna) the analogy between such teleological language and the optical illusion famous as the Necker Cube (the 2D line-drawing of a cube from an oblique angle which simultaneously represents two difference perspectives) in his *The Extended Phenotype* (Dawkins R. , The Extended Phenotype: The Long Reach of the Gene, 1982) has seemingly fallen on deaf ears.

Suitability for a variety of mentalities

These challenges to ten sources of certainty in the Kālāmā Discourse are taught on two other occasions according to the Pali canon, once[86] by the Venerable Nandaka, one of the Buddha's students, and once by the Buddha.

> Ekaṁ samayaṁ āyasmā nandako sāvatthiyaṁ viharati pubbārāme migāramātupāsāde. Atha kho sāḷho ca migāranattā sāṇo ca sekhuniyanattā [87] yenāyasmā nandako tenupasaṅkamiṁsu; upasaṅkamitvā āyasmantaṁ nandakaṁ abhivādetvā ekamantaṁ nisīdiṁsu. Ekamantaṁ nisinnaṁ kho sāḷhaṁ migāranattāraṁ āyasmā nandako etadavoca…
>
> Once the venerable Nandaka was living at Sāvatthi in the Eastern Monastery, Migāra's Mother's Palace. Then Migāra's grandson, Sāḷha,[88] went to the venerable Nandaka, and after salutation sat down at one side. After having sat, Migāra's grandson Salha was addressed by the venerable Nandaka…

And exactly the same challenge is made, this time unprompted, to the same ten sources of certainty challenged in the Kālāmā Discourse. If Rohana and Sāḷha responded, their response was not recorded.

The other occasion the Buddha himself made the same tenfold challenge was to a very different audience indeed. While staying in the Great Sāl Forest at Kūṭāgāra (Peak House) near Vaiśali the Buddha received a rather contentious visitor:

> Atha kho bhaddiyo licchavi yena bhagavā tenupasaṅkami; upasaṅkamitvā bhagavantaṁ abhivādetvā ekamantaṁ nisīdi. Ekamantaṁ nisinno kho bhaddiyo licchavi bhagavantaṁ etadavoca: 'Sutaṁ metaṁ, bhante: "māyāvī samaṇo gotamo āvaṭṭaniṁ māyaṁ[89] jānāti yāya aññatitthiyānaṁ sāvake āvaṭṭetī"ti. Ye te, bhante,

---

[86] *The Discourse to Sāḷha* is the arranged directly after *The Kālāmā Discourse* in the canon.

[87] Some recensions add: rohaṇo ca pekhuṇiyanattā

[88] Some add: and Pekhuniya's grandson, Rohana.

[89] Or āvaṭṭanīmāyaṁ, or āvaṭṭanimāyaṁ.

> evamāham̊su: “māyāvī samaṇo gotamo āvaṭṭanim̊ māyam̊ jānāti yāya aññatitthiyānam̊ sāvake āvaṭṭetī”ti, kacci te, bhante, bhagavato vuttavādino, na ca bhagavantam̊ abhūtena abbhācikkhanti, dhammassa ca anudhammam̊ byākaronti, na ca koci sahadhammiko vādānupāto gārayham̊ .thānam̊ āgacchati, anabbhakkhātukāmā hi mayam̊, bhante, bhagavanta”nti
>
> Bhaddiya of the Licchavi came to see the worthful one. Having arrived, he saluted the worthful one and sat to one side. Sitting at the side, he addressed the worthful one thus: ‘I hear, sir, that the illusionist ascetic Gotama knows an enticing illusion with which he entices students away from other systems of salvation.[90] Now, sir, as to those who say so, that the illusionist ascetic Gotama knows an enticing illusion with which he entices students away from other systems of salvation, pray sir do they express the views of the worthful one and not accuse the worthful one of being what he is not? Do they speak of the Law in accordance with the Law, and is it not that someone who falls in line with his Law comes to a state to be scorned? I would, sir, not misrepresent the worthful one.’

The Buddha’s reply was immediately the tenfold challenge, just as to the Kālāmās.

Those of us with some familiarity with the Buddha’s teaching, in particular those of us who have encountered them outside of a living tradition of practice, may well harbour such doubts. Is it not actually accurate to say that the Buddha weaves seductive words, and that the end result is that the audience is duped into abandoning their cherished beliefs? Is he not just a sophist, picking clever holes in everyone else’s arguments, but failing to provide alternatives of his own? And is it not a dangerous exercise, indeed, since important beliefs are demolished, beliefs which provide succour to many, and that he thus bereaves them of their comforts, and since practical systems are undermined, systems on which society depends to run if we are not all to adopt beggary and parasitism? Is his teaching not casuistry, verbal and intellectual spells cast by a master enchanter, which superficially challenge noble systems of thought and belief, and are at root cynical, as derisive of those who are persuaded to doubt as much as

---

90 Systems of salvation is literally ‘ways of fording’ – namely the river of existence. ‘Fording’ in the Buddhist texts usually has a connotation of erroneous ways to cross, which lead instead to drowning in cyclic existence’s suffering.

those who are not, if not more so?

This is what Bhaddiya has heard, and this is what he has come to suspect. The next section of our discourse is word for word what the Buddha said in answer to Bhaddiya's challenge, so let us see for ourselves what kind of illusionist the Buddha might be.

Detailed Presentation

In each case what is being exhorted is the recognition that a particular widely-accepted source of certainty does not afford certainty. For each source, my treatment will involve three main considerations:

- the meaning in English, or what the Pali phrase refers to,
- some examples of it, old and new
- an investigation of why the Buddha declared such things irrelevant to practice, in terms of a refutation of its being a source of certain knowledge, applying the refutation to the examples.

These are treated in order thus:

Sutta[91] C	K	MANNER OF CERTAINTY CONDEMNED	Page
1		Not by faith	89
2		Not by relishing	95
3	1	Not by recited tradition, ma anussavena	103
	2	Not by traditions, ma paramparāya	110
	3	Not by reports, ma itikirāya	129
	4	Not by what scriptures impart, ma piṭakasampadānena	149
	5	Not by reason of philosophy, ma takkahetu	159
	6	Not by reason of logic, ma nayahetu	185
4	7	Not by thinking ideas through, ma ākāraparivitakkena	219
5	8	Not by intuitive acceptance of views, ma diṭṭhinijjhānakkhantiyā	283
	9	Not by (others') seeming capability, ma bhabbarūpatāya	327
	10	Not by 'This ascetic is our teacher', ma samaṇo no garūti	349

91 In this column figures at the left-hand side (K) refer to the order in which the source of knowledge is mentioned in *The Discourses to the Kalama People, Sālha* and *Bhaddiya the Licchavi*; those on the right (C) to the order in *The Caṅkī Discourse*.

Not by faith

'Api ca, bhāradvāja, susaddahitaṁyeva hoti, tañca hoti rittaṁ tucchaṁ musā; no cepi susaddahitaṁ hoti, tañca hoti bhūtaṁ tacchaṁ anaññathā… *Saccamanurakkhatā, bhāradvāja, viññunā purisena nālamettha ekaṁsena niṭṭhaṁ gantuṁ – "idameva saccaṁ, moghamañña"'nti.*

'Now some things are firmly held in faith, and yet empty, trivial and false. Some things are not firmly held in faith, and yet they are genuine, factual and unmistaken. *To safeguard the truth, in such cases [as faith] it isn't proper for a wise person to come to the definite conclusion that something is true and all else is vain.*''

The Buddha[92]

Croyex ceux qui cherchent la vérité, doutez de ceux qui la trouvent.

Andre Gide (1869-1951)[93]

The meaning of faith

The state of mind referred to in Pali as saddhā and in Sanskrit śraddhā is taught in all the Buddhist traditions a crucial member of the 37 supports for awakening (the usual way of surveying the entire spiritual path). The authoritative 4th century CE *Compendium of the Higher Teaching* of the Universal Career says:

What is skilful by nature? The eleven mental qualities beginning with śraddhā.[94]

And it is also important in various religions under the umbrella of so-called Hinduism.

What does this term, routinely translated as 'faith', mean? śraddhā

---

92 In *The Caṅkī Discourse.*

93 'Believe those who are seeking the truth; doubt those who find it.' (Gide, 1952, p. 174).

94 The remaining ten are integrity (hrī), modesty (apatrāpya), absence of wanting (alobha), absence of dislike (adveṣa), absence of delusion (amoha), vigor (vīrya), serenity (praśrabdhi), diligence (apramāda), perspective (upekṣa) and harmlessness (avihiṁsā). (Boin-Webb, Rahula, & Asanga)

breaks down to śrat and dhā. The first part is recorded in a 2500-year-old dictionary of synonyms (the Naighantuka of Yaska) to be a synonym of satya, meaning 'truth' or 'genuineness'. Together with the second part (meaning 'do' or 'hold') a verb is formed whose meanings are various according to the cases of the nouns used with it: with the accusative of a thing it means to hold that thing to be true, or to expect the thing, or to consent to or welcome the thing, or to wish for the thing; with the dative or genitive of something or someone it means to be true to the thing or person; with the locative of a place it means to trust in that place. Although the word *can* be used with a referent, such as 'trickster', to mean belief in the trickster ('s truthfulness), it *need not* be used with an object[95], and when it is not, holding something *particular* as true is not implied. That is to say, the translation 'faith' is rather inadequate or even misleading for the broader meaning of this word.

Another word from Buddhist and Hindu traditions routinely translated as 'faith', sometimes as 'clear faith', is the Sanskrit prasāda (Pali pasāda), which is an intense form of sāda, 'sitting/settling', and means 'clearness', 'brightness', 'calmness', 'serenity', 'good humour', 'graciousness', 'kindness', 'gift', and 'well-being'. It is related to verbs meaning 'acceptance' and 'be pleasant'.

The Universal Career's *Compendium of the Higher Teachings* defines śraddha in terms of prasāda thus:

> What is śraddhā? It is full and firm conviction (abhisampratyaya) with regard to existence (astitva), serene joy (prasāda) relating to good qualities (guṇavattva), and eagerness (abhilāṣa) for the potential (sakyatva). Its function consists in giving a basis to will.[96]

Notice the term astitva – existence, or more literally *is-ness.* In neither of these terms śraddhā and prasāda do we see any sense of unquestionable adherence to any *being* or *doctrine.* Rather they imply sticking to genuineness; clarity and the calm and goodness these bring; and an open-minded questing. The clarity implies a heightened awareness, to whatever there might be arising in one's experience. And the good humour and acceptance imply that

---

[95] There is a possibility of concealing particularity of belief by establishing by linguistic convention that a particular object is implied by the verb even without the object. We consider this under the Buddha's warning not to take language as absolute (under 'Not by thinking ideas through').

[96] (Boin-Webb, Rahula, & Asanga)

whatever is realized is welcome. Similarly the Higher Teachings of the Elders' School compare the clearing, brightening and calming action (sam̊pasādana) to a magic crystal which when thrown in muddy water causes all turbidity to settle and so clears the water.[97]

The words 'faith', 'belief' and 'creed' in English and their equivalents in other European languages have never meant this however. It would be an interesting but almost inconceivably vast project to study religious texts and commentaries over the centuries in detail to see how the usage of the words evolved and of course many attempts at it have been made. Here we consider an unusual but revealing method to get at the intentions behind these word symbols at various stages of their history, using Sanskrit.

Sanskrit is an uncommonly conservative language because (like Arabic and Hebrew in their respective cultures) it was considered a divine language, but also because it was (unlike Arabic and Hebrew) largely artificial: its grammar was codified over 2000 years ago, 2500-year-old world lists exist, some of which refer explicitly to meanings of previous millennia, and spoken dialects diverged from it without very much affecting it. It also happens to parallel closely and pretty much comprehensively the so-called Proto-indoeuropean, the hypothesised root of most European, Central Asian and Indian languages backwards-extrapolated from them by etymologists.

This peculiar framework affords us an unusually reliable direct access to the meaning of any word branch in a natural European, Central Asian or Indian language at the time of its branching from Proto-indoeuropean.

Turning to our first case, we learn that 'faith' (like French 'foi' etc.) is derived from fide in Latin or pistis in Greek. Going deeper, one finds that these both have the Proto-indoeuropean root bheid[98], its Sanskrit equivalent vidh, which means 'to worship and honour a deity' and is the root of words relating to ritual.

What about 'belief'? Well, that (along with love and libido) derives from Proto-indoeuropean leubh[99], its Sanskrit equivalent lubh, meaning 'to long for', 'to be confused by', 'to be interested in or enticed by' and 'to care for'. Incidentally, the noun of this verb, lobha, is the first of the three afflictive processes the Buddha mentions later in this discourse. The be- prefix, found in many Germanic verbs, is a contracted form sharing its origin in Indo-European with the Latin prefix ambi-, meaning on both sides, and the Sanskrit prefix

---

[97] (Thera N. , 1956/1979, p. 123)

[98] (The American Heritage Dictionary of the English Language, 2004)

[99] (The American Heritage Dictionary of the English Language, 2004)

abhi-. In Sanskrit abhilubh is a verb meaning to entice or allure.

And finally, what about 'creed' and its relatives? The Proto-indoeuropean root is kerd- whence then Sanskrit hṛd meaning 'heart' (like the Latin derivatives in cord-). One theory is that the word 'creed' arose from kerd-dha, meaning 'place or hold in the heart'. Another theory links it to śraddhā (via a supposed craddha)[100], but we can be sure that if the Latin equivalents lack, as they do, the meanings of the Sanskrit term other than 'holding *as* true', the English derivatives of the Latin can hardly be considered to include them.

It should be noticed straight away that if these terms bore a similar sense to their equivalents in the conserved vocabulary of Sanskrit, they are quite unlike the Buddhist and Hindu terms for 'faith' in that they all require an object. Who or what is one honouring, longing for, and holding in his or her heart? Of course in theistic traditions it is some version of the deity, 'God', who is the object of these verbs. We might wonder if the word 'God' (shorn of doctrinal considerations) had some older sense of authenticity or truth or is-ness.

The conclusion of faith

A cursory exploration suggests that neither the word 'God' nor its Germanic equivalents (or the cognate Old Persian khuda) has its origins in anything like authenticity or truth. Etymologists locate their origin in the Proto-indoeuropean root gheu[101], which exists in Sanskrit as hu, with the past participle huta, meaning 'that to which oblation is offered' or 'that by which the oblation is offered' (the fire in the Vedic ritual) and as the root hve meaning 'summon'. Tellingly in Sanskrit (as distinct from in Persian, the Germanic languages and English) these words have complete inflections (incomplete inflections of a word being circumstantial evidence of its having been recently borrowed from another language), including the active form hoṭṛ which refers to the person offering the oblation or the oblation itself, and the noun homa, meaning the act of offering the oblation.

In the Christian tradition 'God' was chosen in the 6th century after Christ to translate the Greek theos and Latin deus which both derive from Indo-European div, a word which means 'belonging to the light' (compare the Hindu festival of lights, Divali) and is also the origin of our words 'devil' and 'divine'. Theos and deus were in turn were translating earlier biblical terms for gods – NW Semitic El (cognate with Arabic Ilāh, the supposed root of the proper

---

100 (Monier-Williams, 2008)

101 (The American Heritage Dictionary of the English Language, 2004)

name Allāh), its plural Elohim and the proper name Yahweh, which some link to 'he is that he is' after the revelation 'I am that I am'. The Semitic El may have meant power. Perhaps coincidentally (although some scholars have argued for a connection) the root iḷa is present in old Sanskrit as 'the one to whom a flow of glorification should be addressed', and relates to a root meaning 'flow', and īḷa simply means 'to glorify'. (Some scholars have also argued for a connection between Sanskrit īśu meaning 'lord' and the name Jesus, and between the Sanskrit aśūra meaning 'an almighty being'[102] or the morphologically related īśvara meaning 'almight god' and various Semitic deities, including (unsurprisingly) the Assyrian god of gods Ashur, and via the s>h slide[103] the Zoroastrian god Ahura and the Jewish god Yahweh.) It is interesting to note that in only the opening line of the Ṛg Veda ('Versed Wisdom', the oldest division of the Veda, dating say the scholars from at 1500BC but including astronomical and geographical references that some claim date it millennia earlier) –

> agnim **īḷe** purohitam̊ yajñasya **devam** ṛtvijam **hotāram̊** ratnadhātamam

> Fire I glorify, the foremost-placed (i.e. a divine intermediary), belonging to sacrifice, the divine, the truth-generated, the oblation-offerer, the richness-holder!

– we can see all these parallel terms for the Christian and Islāmic god words in the context of 'oblation to the oblation-worthy' via the fire: El, Deus, God.

Clearly such concepts even in their naïve form involve particularization of spiritual experience (at the very least as power or praise, light, and the object of oblation respectively), and clearly receptivity to spiritual experience did not begin with the first revelations of these particular forms, so we can say that the

---

102 The aśūra in ancient Indian myths were the enemies of the deva (more familiar 'Hindu' gods such as Indra, beings made of light), their wars frequently being related to their envy of the riches enjoyed by the gods, (symbolised strikingly by the so-called Tree of Heaven, which, though its roots were in the aśūra realm, bore fruit in the deva realms) and so frequently get translated into English as 'jealous gods'. This aśūra/deva opposition is present in the Zoroastrian religion as Ahura/deva, with the crucial difference that the good/evil polarity is reversed: for them Ahura was the great God of good, and the deva were the enemy. From this derives our tradition of 'devils' as the enemy of God.

103 The same slide that had Arabs and Persians refer to Sind (a river basin mainly in what is now Pakistan) as 'Hind' and thus give us the words Hindu and Hindi.

particularization was a development in time.[104]

Irrelevancy as a source of certainty

So the problem is not with faith when it is refers to receptivity to and serene delight in the authentic, but with *particular objects faith.* These are ideas, and the dismal consequences of cogitating on ideas as real (metaphysics) the Buddha turns to later.

> 'Saddhā cepi, bhāradvāja, purisassa hoti; "evaṁ me saddhā"ti – iti vadaṁ saccamanurakkhati [105], *natveva tāva ekaṁsena niṭṭhaṁ gacchati – "idameva saccaṁ, moghamaññā"nti.* Ettāvatā kho, bhāradvāja, saccānurakkhaṇā hoti, ettāvatā saccamanurakkhati, ettāvatā ca mayaṁ saccānurakkhaṇaṁ paññapema; *na tveva tāva saccānubodho hotī'ti.*

> 'Bhāradvāja, a person with faith saying, "This is my faith," safeguards the truth.[106] *But he or she doesn't yet come to the definite conclusion that only something is true and all else is vain.* To this extent, Bhāradvāja, there is safeguarding of the truth. To this extent he or she safeguards the truth. I describe this as the safeguarding of the truth. *But it is not yet an awakening to the truth.*'[107]

---

[104] The history of language has other telling clues. The word 'bigot' was first used against the Normans and derives from their perceived overuse of the expression 'by God'.

[105] Or evameva sijjhatīti iti vā, taṁ saccamanurakkhati

[106] Or [saying] "In this way availing myself [of faith]," he or she safeguards the truth.

[107] In *The Caṅkī Discourse.*

Not by relishing

> 'Api ca, bhāradvāja, surucitaṁyeva hoti, tañca hoti rittaṁ tucchaṁ musā; no cepi surucitaṁ hoti, tañca hoti bhūtaṁ tacchaṁ anaññathā. Saccamanurakkhatā, bhāradvāja, viññunā purisena nālamettha ekaṁsena niṭṭhaṁ gantuṁ – "idameva saccaṁ, moghamañña"'nti.
>
> 'Now some things are thoroughly relished and yet empty, trivial and false. Some things are not relished, and yet they are genuine, factual and unmistaken. To safeguard the truth, in such cases [as relishing] it isn't proper for a wise person to come to the definite conclusion that only something is true, and all else is foolish.'
>
> The Buddha[108]

Meaning

The word ruci was originally associated with illumination. It came to mean the enjoyment of particular tastes. In devotional Hinduism this 'taste' refers to a particular stage of devotion. More generally it can refer to any enjoyment of a particular experience.

Examples

The 'first glow' and further visionary experiences from meditation or prayer; the pleasure derived from ritual practices and observances relating to a particular tradition; the relief of siding with dogma or identification with noble tradition; exultation at beautiful and tremendous world-views.

Irrelevancy as sources of certainty

It might seem unnecessary to refute pleasure as a source of certainty. After all, one imagines that very few people would try to argue that you can rely on pleasure to guide you to any benefit, never mind to 'certain truth'. Sugar leads to obesity and diabetes, not to mention desensitisation to sweetness, and meat fat to heart disease.

The fact that this refutation is addressed not to sensualists but to a group of priests of the most socially respected religion of the Buddha's time and place should help us realise what kind of pleasure is being referred to here: relish

108 In *The Caṅkī Discourse.*

of the religious life itself, including all its traditions, doctrines, observances, practices and rituals, both individual and social. People involved in such activities are not likely to admit so easily that they choose among sources of knowledge on the basis of pleasure. That is a good reason for drawing their attention to the possibility, though, that nevertheless, *they do.* The point is not that we need to be made aware that deriving certainty from pleasure is ludicrous, but that we need to recognise when this ludicrous step is taking place.

Being converted between religious identities

Some people are able quite blithely to say, 'I would love to be Buddhist, but I couldn't give up bacon.' Or, 'I wish I could be a Christian, but the idea of loving your enemy is just beyond the pale.' Or again, 'I'd much rather be a Muslim than a Christian: at least you get some sex in heaven.' In speaking thus they are betraying the fact that identity has come to seem more important to them than the doctrines taken as the object of their identification. It is as if there is an additional burden upon Buddhists which is not a burden upon anyone else – the karma of eating meat – or that loving one's enemy is an additional burden one assumes if one converts to Christianity, or that by choosing a particular religious identity such as Islām one thereby creates for oneself its limited set of options in the afterlife.

These might seem like silly examples, but we should not be too quick to congratulate ourselves as immune to such flippant reasoning. It has led to serious misunderstandings, for example, in the interpretation by Christians of Buddhism's teachings on suffering, misunderstandings which still, sad to say, turn people away from the dharma in its entirety and percolate through to highest Christian authorities, not the least of which is someone we presumably should not accuse of flippancy, the last pope of the Catholic Church. The Buddha and all the other great teachers of the various traditions of Buddhism of course do not say that to be a Buddhist you have to recognise that the nature of all life is suffering, that that is the entry price as it were, and that you need not pay if you do not enter: it says that anyone who examines life carefully will find that its nature is suffering, such that everyone must pay, whether you want to enter or not – and indeed the entrance is the way ultimately *not* to pay, since the Laws discovered by these teachers claim to offer the means to eliminate this suffering for all living beings.[109]

---

[109] Many more such absurdities arise because of the root tendency to conceive of systems of different teachers or founders as somehow unrelated – a phenomenon to

We have become so inured to shopping, I sometimes think, that we look at the various wisdom traditions and what they claim, and make our choice by inclination or taste (ruci). Oh yes, I like that idea of the afterlife, but, oh no, that's a nasty rule, I won't bother with that one… etc. And after the shopping, the parading of ourselves with our new purchase: look at my new meekness, and I'm smiling at you even though I pity you – yes, I've decided to become a practising Christian; or, excuse me, it's the time for the sunset prayer, and did you notice my beard – yes, I have been persuaded after long reflection that Islām is the truth; or, I think you have noticed how radiant I look, and tonight I confess I won't be able to make squash as I will be at the meditation centre… Somehow, somewhere, amid all of this furious drive to appropriate identity and display it, the notion that any of these traditions might carry means by which we might finally know reality nakedly, and be of uncontaminated benefit in the world to ourselves and others, seems to get lost.

Debauched piety

This is not just about religion. The same tendency characterises our societies much more widely. In the course of our analysis we will consider religious and ideological examples. Few of us are unaware of *the pleasure* of 'taking a stance' on some issue, of 'sticking by' our principles, or enjoying the moral high-ground (as it seems to us at least) for some reason or another. Sanctimonious vegetarianism and sexual puritanism spring to mind, and a little more reflection unmasks US-style election campaigning, and the glorification of victim status that underpins grievance culture.

It is surprisingly easy to confuse the pleasure of displaying piety before one's peers, and the conviction that that piety is well-founded. It is that mistake which is unmasked by exposure to piety based on stances in others that contrast with one's own – which in turn explains a lot of what constitutes 'spiritual jealousy', the inability to bear piety in other traditions. That this jealousy is made an attribute of the 'deity' in the massive religions builds a formidable obstacle to recognising the potential error of the pious stance. With this potential natural check (seeing alternative piousness as valid) removed, what we might call '*debauched piety*', the totally exulting intoxication with one's own righteousness, is the result, with all the familiar consequences.[110]

---

which the Buddha draws attention later (see 'Not by "this ascetic is our teacher"').

110 In the course of the commentary we shall have a great deal to say about related problems in the 'monotheistic' systems.

Wanton myth

We have been called the myth-making species. It is difficult to find any culture, including modern ones, who do not frame their existence in terms of myths which appear to lend immediate significance to them. If we ask whether a myth is more appealling because it is closer to the truth, we will quickly concede that it is the psychological resonance of elements of myths which make them appealling, whether or not they are true.[111]

However this recognition is rarely extended to one's own cherished myth, even by those whose profession is to study mythology. For example, so-called 'western academia' considers itself to be founded in, and indeed takes its name from, Ancient Greece, and tangibly defends that story on all fronts. Few philosophical, mathematical or scientific ideas are not traced to Plato and Aristotle, and dictionaries until recently gave one the impression, by ending all etymologies at Greek and Latin, that these two languages had descended from celestial realms fully formed. Formidable resistance arises to tracing influences elsewhere – what a certain popular UK philosophy professor calls 'keeping the elephants out of London'. Now that Christianity has receded, the foundation of Ancient Greece has assumed new solidity, and it is with some justice that recent Arabic literary scholarship compares the position of Homer's epics in western civilisation with that of the Qur'ān in the Islāmic one.

The pleasure of thus belonging to a tradition, with such awesome treasures of wisdom and resonant significance, is intense. To abandon oneself wantonly to such pleasure within one's own myths obscures that character of all myths, invention, which seems so obvious in others'.

Lusting religious observance

Even those who deny Freud's claim that religious observance provides the same comfort and relief to the religious as compulsive behaviour does to the neurotic, cannot deny that there is some kind of pleasure involved in following religious observance, and that it is intense.

Beauty has been embodied in the observances of the massive religions to a startling degree. The very places of worship are extraordinarily pleasing to see and be in, displaying as they do the most affecting qualities we have been able to devise in buildings, from the tremendousness and aching magnificence of

---

111 Modern cognitive science has made great inroads into understanding why our minds are likely to have particular seeming inclinations. We consider a brief survey of these when the Buddha deals with 'intuitive truths'.

cathedrals and grand mosques, to the mind-clarifying simplicity of a village chapel. This is without going into the spine-chilling beauty of the Islāmic call to prayer echoing across a cityscape, or the transport of organ tones shuddering through a vast, dark, empty cathedral, or the breath-taking sight of millions of white-clad people prostrating in unison, or the exquisite tension in the sudden silence over a Sikh temple's pond before the principle prayer is begun or in an Islamic city before the sunset breakfast in Ramaḍān, or the thrilling combination of terrifying horns, cymbals and drums and other-worldly nay demonic bass chanting of a Tibetan tantric ritual, or the hypnotic exchanges between priest and congegration, clad in mysterious harmonies and clouds of incense, of the Catholic and Orthodox mass, or – well, of course, the examples are endless. That this was considered an especial temptation in the Buddhist traditions is evident in the numerous instances of singling out 'holding observances as supreme' in even basic lists of potential faults in practice.

No-one would claim that the more beautiful religion must therefore be the truest or most beneficial. But it is a fact that a great deal of the attachment we feel to our own tradition stems from the recognition of beauty in its culture and observances, beauty we somehow feel we should honour. This arousal by and involvement in beauty is a species of lust and gives rise subsequently to similar defensiveness, jealousy and miserliness that other species of it do. Since this lustful feeling might well *detract* from truth and benefit, the Buddha draws attention to it. This is perhaps even more true in modern times, when the pervasive suspicion that all the religions are false has led to a trivialisation of their doctrines and a heightening in the tendency to judge them solely on such superficial criteria as beauty. Given the treacherousness of the beauty of festivals too, it is perhaps a blessing in disguise that in the modern world they are all being commercialised so thoroughly as totally to separate them from the religious traditions that gave birth to them – a blessing since in this way the doctrines are left 'naked', to fend for themselves as it were without the crutch of beauty.

Voracious virtue

Even morality can be sensual enjoyment. As Hume pointed out, to the consternation of many,

> To have a sense of virtue, is nothing but to *feel* a satisfaction of a particular kind from the contemplation of a character. [...] We do not infer a character to be virtuous, because it pleases: But in feeling that it pleases after such a particular manner, we in effect feel that it is virtuous.

> The case is the same as in our judgments concerning all kinds of beauty, and tastes, and sensations.[112]

Virtue is attractive. Since Hume wrote this much has been unmasked by psychology and other disciplines which help us to understand *why* it might be attractive to us, and we will consider a fair number of examples in the course of the commentary, but for now we advert to the bare fact that the lust for virtue is merely another lust, as liable to mislead us as any other. Indeed those lusts we more readily admit as such frequently combine with this one inextricably and unluckily, as in the case of the veneration of virgin females, which walks hand-in-hand with the stimulating fantasy of deflowering them and thus claiming them as an eternal possession, in backward patriarchal societies.

The delectable, exquisite, intoxicating beauty of systems

There is perhaps one case where people really do knowingly derive certainty from beauty, and that is in the case of mathematics, and in ideologies heavily dependent upon mathematics such as certain traditions of economics.

One of the most vigorous modern religions is that of total unrestrained capitalism as the economic system which will automatically benefit the world. Its most notorious branch, currently dominating the ideology behind the kind of government which has turned some parts of the world into a living hell, can be traced to the so-called Chicago School. We have occasion later to examine the Christian origins of this extraordinary doctrine machine. In his autobiography, Milton Freidman, its most influential ideologue, reports the epiphany he had at school which set him on his later course: his teacher had introduced the theorem of Pythagorus and, in consequent awe at its elegance, had quoted Keats' 'Ode on a Grecian urn':

> 'Beauty is truth, truth beauty,' – that is all
> Ye know on earth, and all you need to know.

Given that this equation, exactly the error we are addressing here, was Friedman's 'epiphany' it is little wonder that his school turned into one of the major contributors to the world's ills. Klein reports[113] that one of the Chicago School's founders, Frank Knight, used to inculcate in his students the notion that

---

[112] Book III, Part I, Section II of *A Treatise of Human Nature* (Hume, 1888).
[113] (Klein, 2007, p. 50)

elements of economic systems were not debatable hypotheses but 'sacred elements' of the system.[114] Despite (or rather because of) the fact that there had never been a situation where perfectly unrestrained capitalism could be tested, it was believed with unassailable faith that if there were a test-case, it would demonstrate a perfect balance of the 'natural forces' of supply, demand, inflation, unemployment, and so on, like an exquisitely beautiful jewelled clockwork mechanism.[115] Aside from the interested propagation of this system by the very few among the economic élite who profit from it (and they profit in financial terms very heavily) its relishers have done their fair share of promoting it, and their refusal of the reality of its failure to bring happiness, extraordinary defensiveness, and adulation of particular figures in its history, are elements we will see in the more traditional religious traditions.

Infatuating meditation

As we mentioned, in Hinduism this word ruci is used for a stage of attainment in the type of religious system known as bhakti, meaning 'loving devotion to the deity', and originally it was related to 'illumination'. Now, most people who have more than a passing acquaintance with meditative training will know how immensely pleasurable it can be. The two main teachers of the Buddha both trained him in methods of mental absorption (the Pali jhāna, Sanskrit dhyāna – transliterated in Japanese as Zen) whose early discoveries included intense 'bliss' and 'rapture' and these discoveries can be made again by anyone who cares to make the effort. In some discourses the Buddha employs similes for these discoveries which accentuate their pleasurableness – relating to a cooling spring feeding the water of a lake and the feel of one's wet clothes drying on the skin when one emerges, and so on. However, it is crucial that one's attitude to them not slip into attachment, and for this reason there are many injunctions against infatuation with meditative experiences in the Buddha's teachings.[116]

In the massive religions, however, these pleasures, which are likely to arise through the minimal mental absorption required for traditional prayer, are not warned about but celebrated. As we shall see for many other dangers within

114 (Knight, 1932)

115 (Bell, 1981)

116 Injunctions which seem to go unnoticed among certain very fashionable meditation communities these days, one suspects because that very pleasure is, very regrettably, part of their (conscious or automatic) advertising.

these systems, it takes so-called *mystics* from within them to advert to the risk. For example, for Islām, the Persian Sufi master Farīd ud-Dīn `Aṭṭār warns[117] that, having found jewels in the path, one should not stoop to pick them up, but walk on.

In this case, as in the case of all of the sources of truth and benefit he challenges, it is not that the Buddha is saying that enjoyment of or pleasure in these things *always* deceives or misleads. Quite the contrary, intense involvement provoked by sensual stimuli can bring one to degrees of awareness which could not be achieved otherwise except with great effort or skilfulness, a fact which is heavily relied upon in the Buddhist tantric systems for example. Nevertheless, and perhaps it hardly needs stating, to be ruled by such lust, be it for myth, piety, observances, virtue, or even meditative rapture would be a grave mistake.

> 'Ruci cepi, bhāradvāja, purisassa hoti; "evaṁ me ruci"ti – iti vadaṁ saccamanurakkhati , *natveva tāva ekaṁsena niṭṭhaṁ gacchati* – "idameva saccaṁ, moghamañña"nti. Ettāvatā kho, bhāradvāja, saccānurakkhaṇā hoti, ettāvatā saccamanurakkhati, ettāvatā ca mayaṁ saccānurakkhaṇaṁ paññapema; *na tveva tāva saccānubodho hotī'ti.*

> 'Bhāradvāja, a person with something to relish saying, "This is my inclination," safeguards the truth. *But he or she doesn't yet come to the definite conclusion that only something is true and all else is foolish.* To this extent, Bhāradvāja, there is safeguarding of the truth. To this extent he or she safeguards the truth. I describe this as the safeguarding of the truth. *But it is not yet an awakening to the truth.*'[118]

---

[117] From Manṭiq al-Ṭayr, translated as *The Conference of the Birds* (`Attar, 1974)

[118] In *The Caṅkī Discourse.*

Not by recited tradition, ma anussavena

'Api ca, bhāradvāja, svānussutaṁyeva hoti, tañca hoti rittaṁ tucchaṁ musā; no cepi svānussutaṁ hoti, tañca hoti bhūtaṁ tacchaṁ anaññathā. *Saccamanurakkhatā, bhāradvāja, viññunā purisena nālamettha ekaṁsena niṭṭhaṁ gantuṁ – "idameva saccaṁ, moghamaññā"*'nti.

'Now some things are a particular recited tradition, and yet empty, trivial and false. Some things are not a particular recited tradition, and yet they are genuine, factual and unmistaken. *To safeguard the truth, in such cases [as recited traditions] it isn't proper for a wise person to come to the definite conclusion that only something is true, and all else is worthless.'*

The Buddha[119]

The devil said to Jesus, 'Say, "There is no god but Allāh."'
Jesus answered, 'That is true, but *I shall not repeat it after you.*'

al-Ghazāli (450-505 h.)

Meaning

Anu- carries the sense (as a prefix to verbs and nouns) of after, along, alongside, lengthwise, near to, under, subordinate to, with, and (when prefixed to nouns, especially in adverbial compounds), according to, severally, each by each, orderly, methodically, one after another, repeatedly; -ssava (equivalent to Sanskrit śrava) means 'hearing' (noun) and the morphologically related sota (Sanskrit śrota) means 'stream'.[120] Hence the full word means something like 'oral tradition', and the Latinate word 'recite' gets to the same core matter. The Sanskrit anuśrava refers particularly to one oral tradition, the Veda or 'Wisdom', the holy recitations of the orthodox religion of the Buddha's time, and of today's Hinduism, and indeed the Buddha often described his teachings as paṭisotagāmī, 'going against the stream', as opposed to 'anusotagāmī', going with the stream. It could be that the Buddha meant to refer especially to the 'stream', or the oral tradition, of the Veda, but given the other recommendations he makes in the discourse it seems likely he meant here any such tradition.

---

119 In *The Caṅkī Discourse.*

120 The English words 'stream', 'rheum' and 'maelstrom' all share their Proto-Indo-European root with śrota ('maelstrom' is a 'milling stream', i.e. a 'grinding current' – a whirlpool.)

Examples

The recited sections of the Pali canon and certain central treatises (śāstra) of the Indo-Tibetan Buddhist tradition; the Qur'ān and the main collections of reports (aḥādīth) about the Prophet as traditionaly learnt; the Veda; the information presented to children and adults to be 'learnt' in the context of 'education' by rote learning, such as the times tables, spelling rules and mnemonic rhymes about the months, the alphabet, etc. and tongue-twisters; non-improvised music; bed-time stories, nursery rhymes and lullabies. These examples are very much 'remnants of a bygone age': in general, of course, modern cultures have veered away from recitation for transmission of information towards concrete records such as writings and digital storage. This, it is worth noting, is often seen as a great loss to cultural life.

Irrelevancy as sources of certainty

We should remind ourselves from the outset that the Buddha did not mean that these things were irrelevant to any purpose and so he did not mean that they should be rejected wholesale. Clearly music is not irrelevant to enjoyment or even spiritual transport and lullabies are not irrelevant to stopping a child from crying and encouraging it to sleep; tongue-twisters are not irrelevant to developing elocution and playing; the Qur'ān is not irrelevant to performing the prayer to the deity Allāh according to Islāmic custom; and the Pali canon is not irrelevant to knowing what the Buddha taught or indeed to writing this book!

To appreciate, on the other hand, why it might be that the Buddha declared that all recitals are irrelevant as sources of certainty, we will survey the characteristics that they all share and see what the danger might be in terms of truthfulness and benefit.

Lies and harm can be imitated

If people act as copying machines, listening to reciters and imitating what they hear such that others can listen to their recitation in the same way, then anything that is embodied in produceable sound can be transmitted, from the beneficial to the harmful, from the truthful to the erroneous. A copying machine has no discretion. This might seem like an obvious point, but a subtle point is being made: that this form, no matter how impressive, *in itself* guarantees nothing in terms of truthfulness or benefit.

Much is made, for example, of the perfection of the copying of the Qur'ān in recitation, for example, and how much more accurate the transmission of it has been than of the Bible, as if this in itself guarantees the Qur'ān's greater accuracy as a source of certainty. It does not.

It is easy to confuse impressiveness with importance

It might be that such recitation is no longer the central means of tradition but this docs not mean that in some modern cultures it is not very highly valued still. In most Islāmic countries even today someone who has memorised the entire Qur'ān is called Ḥāfiẓ (a Safeguarder) and it is common to find such people provoke nothing short of awe in their fellows. In the Elders' School of Buddhism how much of the Pali canon one has memorised is similarly a badge of status. Indeed the fact that memorisation is no longer necessary means those who achieve it provoke even greater awe than they would have done in pre-literate times.

It is natural for us to conclude from such impressive feats that their content must be important. This is mainly because of our psychological tendency to single out seeming causes and overlook other causes, which the Buddha considers later.[121] We neglect to examine the psychological state and circumstances of the reciter, and attribute the motivation for memorising solely to the content of the recital. This leads us to confuse the impressiveness of the feat of recital with the importance of what is recited: the content gains a false extra kudos through the feat's impressiveness.

The point is not that, for example, the Qur'ān or the Pali canon recitations have valueless content, but to underline the fact that included in their kudos is much which is independent of their content.

Identification by forms not meaning, and overvaluation of forms

Furthermore we are not talking about acting as generalist copying machines. There are certain criteria for the copying. In all cases the copier conceptually identifies certain things patterns as deserving of copying, neglecting others, not based on their truthfulness or benefit but simply on whether they are what is supposed to be recited.

For example, when reciting the words of the deity in the mosque the imam will not launch into an arguably relevant recitation of the Torah in Hebrew even though he might be unusually educated and accord authenticity to certain parts of it, for the pattern he recognizes as worthy of transmission is a well-defined selection of sentences in a certain kind of Arabic, sung in a certain

121 See 'Not by logic'.

way – the Qur'ān.

This is intimately related to the idea of authoritative scriptures and authoritative figures, which we will consider in more detail later.[122] For now we just need to recognise that we naturally accord authority to certain external sources, and that this can lead to fallacious reasoning. We can identify, in particular, *the founder fallacy*, which is to assume that all the teachings of a tradition originate in a particular person and that what is attributed to them must be perfect. Clearly this is the situation with the 'final revelation' of Muḥammad in Islām or the 'crucial' incarnation of Christ in Christianity. It is important to realise that independent of the truth of these claims, unless there is some evidence beyond the claim itself, to accept the authority is to commit this fallacy.

It has implications for traditions' understanding of each other. For example consider typical expositions of 'Buddhism' from outside practising communities. Although such expositions use the term 'Buddha', an epithet applied within such communities as a recognition of a special quality of 'total awakening' such that there are no longer any veils to what *is*, the expositors almost never accept those comminities' application of the same epithet to figures after Śakyamuni Gautama. Indeed these later figures are usually completely overlooked. This is the reflection of the founder fallacy informing their outlook, and what is called 'confirmation bias' informing their interpretation of the traditions.

Another example of the effect of the fallacy is in a particular expression of 'concern for historicity', the insistence on 'authenticity'. This makes sense in the context of the revelation-for-all-time, but in no other situation. To question whether a particular teaching was actually spoken by the founder is of crucial importance only when the founder's authority is prioritised above all others. Otherwise this kind of 'historicity' should be of relatively minor concern – historicity should rather recognise in addition that the realisations and teachings of others in the 'founder' 's community are also relevant, for example – to do otherwise would be effectively to say that the very best a member of that community can be is a transmitter of the 'founder' 's word. And here we see why the Buddha draws attention especially to oral traditions: because it can happen that we inadvertently come to see that word and its tradition as more important than actual realisation and understanding. It is an easy mistake to make.

Furthermore, given that the fallacy is the result of a universal human tendency, a truly 'historical' account should presumably recognise the potential

---

122 See 'Not by scripture' and 'Not by seeming authority' respectively.

for the very same fallacy even among the community contemporary with the founder. Advocates of rival teachings, including those actually originating in the realisations of people other than the founder, would be expected to compete for the claim of the founder having spoken them, if they realise that their audience is under the sway of the founder fallacy. Unfortunately even in expositions which claim to be meticulously historical such finesse of treatment is almost never found.

It is debatable whether the 'revelation' interpretation is appropriate even for the 'back from the mountain' event which catalyses the authority of the prophet for the valley folk, because the assumption is that not one of the listeners in the valley have equivalent insight or knowledge to the one returning from the mysterious mountain experience, and we shall see later how this actually destroys the very grounds on which that authority is claimed for later generations. However, it is not merely inappropriate, but preposterous, to apply such an interpretation to a situation (as was the case around Gautama the Buddha) where an entire community is seeking in the way the hypothesised founder sought. (Unlike the early Muslims, who did not expect to become prophets, or the early Christians[123], who did not expect to become christs, the community around the Buddha *did* expect to attain nirvāna.)

This inappropriacy is like, after a girl goes missing, organising a search party to hunt for her in a forest, but then refusing to listen to a claim that she has been found because it comes from the wrong person. Only one person in the search party is credited with the ability to discover her, even though everyone is searching. The claims of another to have discovered her is dismissed as 'inauthentic' (because only the 'founder' has authority), 'heretical' (because it is forbidden to depart by choice from this oral tradition of the founder), 'innovation' (because the oral tradition carries eternal truth which could therefore never change, such that no message will ever superceded it) or even 'counterfeit' (accusing the claimant not only of the other errors but also of the crime of attempting to capitalise on the kudos of the claim to authenticity). All of these dismissal methods are used in authoritative Christianity and Islām and the words used to refer to them reek of opprobium.

It could be that someone is a vessel of a form-preserved oral tradition. But this does not mean that they have understood the message better than someone who is a vessel of a form-evolving oral tradition. The information being transmitted is by definition a fixed pattern of symbols (letters, words,

123 Including Christ, one suspects.

sounds). What it refers to is not. Furthermore it is only by consensus that the fixed pattern 'refers' to a particular phenomenon. We will consider later the inherent danger in these forms or symbols to degenerate and the mechanism by which this occurs.

Use of repetition to foster acceptance

Repetition has the psychological effect of making us more likely to accept what is being repeated. This is used in declamatory speech and writing, of course. A common tactic in religious discourse is a strengthening effect achieved by repeating a word or a few words. In the Greek art of persuasion, at the start of sentences this was called *antistrophe* or *anaphora.* At the end it was called *epistrophe.*

Repetition is a staple of the religions, of course. Many striking examples of repeated verses occur in the Qur'ān, where for example in the intense and poetic al-Raḥmān chapter, one line,

> Fa bi 'ayyi 'ālā'i rabbikumā tukadhdhibāni

> And about which of your Lord's bounties will you and you lie (by denying them)?

is repeated thirty times, between vivid descriptions of heaven and hell. The Pali canon, includes an astonishing degree of repetition: the fact that its purpose is to aid memorisation should not deflect our attention from the fact that it also fosters acceptance.

The Islāmic prayer includes a great deal of repetition. In the system of the most populous sect, the Sunnite, the opening of the Qur'ān is repeated every bowing cycle, of which there are a total of 2, 4, 4, 3 and 4, in the respective prayer rituals of dawn, noon, midafternoon, sunset and twilight; and for each bowing cycle, there are three repetitions of 'Allāhu akbar – Allāh is greater' (in addition to the one which begins the entire ritual), at the bow and at the two subsequent five-point prostrations with one 'Sami` allāhu li man ḥamidah – Allāh hears whoever praises him' for each cycle, as one rights oneself after the bow. In the special all-morning prayers of the Festival of the Sacrificial Victim, the so-called Enlarging ('Allāh is greater') and Unification ('There is no deity except Allāh') are repeated along with other prayers, including prayers for Muḥammad and his family and companions, many more times.

Repetition is taken to extremes in the 'mystical' traditions. Each Sufi order uses the repetition of particular formulae (called awrād), such as the names of Allāh, excerpts from the Qur'ān and prayers, in ceremonial rehearsal (dhikr in Arabic) and in ascetic retreats. Vajrayāna Buddhists deploy sentences in Sanskrit or Prakrit called mind-guards (mantra in Sanskrit) whose repetition is considered to bring special powers – and the number of repetitions can prescribed in the hundreds of thousands for preliminary retreats and millions for subsequent training. The prayers of the rosary, extremely popular among Catholics despite fierce criticism from other sects of Christianity, involve repetition of prayers for the 'holy family' – the father, the mother and the son.

There is no denying that such practice has strong effects on the mind, and these may be useful. But the point being made here is that nothing about the form of the practice in itsef, repeating, guarantees this benefit. Later on, as we shall see, the Buddha stresses that we should be especially careful about our susceptibility to accept more easily what seems intuitively correct – a conviction which can be fostered simply by such repetition.

> 'Anussavo cepi, bhāradvāja, purisassa hoti; "evaṁ me anussava"ti – iti vadaṁ saccamanurakkhati, *natveva tāva ekaṁsena niṭṭhaṁ gacchati* – "idameva saccaṁ, moghamañña"nti. Ettāvatā kho, bhāradvāja, saccānurakkhaṇā hoti, ettāvatā saccamanurakkhati, ettāvatā ca mayaṁ saccānurakkhaṇaṁ paññapema; *na tveva tāva saccānubodho hotī'ti.*

> 'Bhāradvāja, a person with an oral tradition saying, "This is my oral tradition," safeguards the truth. *But he or she doesn't yet come to the definite conclusion that only something is true, and all else is foolish.* To this extent, Bhāradvāja, there is safeguarding of the truth. To this extent he or she safeguards the truth. I describe this as the safeguarding of the truth. *But it is not yet an awakening to the truth.*'[124]

Now, though, the Buddha goes on to expand his focus from oral tradition to tradition in general. This gives a kind of society-wide perspective. He then focuses on the more personal and less formal version, reporting. All of these first three sources of knowledge are quite similar, and we will find that many of the criticisms which apply to one can be applied equally to the other two.

---

124 In *The Caṅkī Discourse.*

Not by traditions, ma paramparāya

> 'Seyyathāpi, bhāradvāja, andhaveṇi paramparā saṁsattā purimopi na passati majjhimopi na passati pacchimopi na passati; evameva kho, bhāradvāja, andhaveṇūpamaṁ maññe brāhmaṇānaṁ bhāsitaṁ sampajjati – purimopi na passati majjhimopi na passati pacchimopi na passati. Taṁ kiṁ maññasi, bhāradvāja , nanu evaṁ sante brāhmaṇānaṁ amūlikā saddhā sampajjatī'ti?
>
> 'Like a train of blind men, clinging one to the other [*or* 'in a tradition'] the first one of whom doesn't see, the middle of whom one doesn't see, and the last one of whom doesn't see, the statement of the priests turns out to be a train of blind men, the first one of whom doesn't see, the middle of whom one doesn't see, and the last one of whom doesn't see. So what do you think, Bhāradvāja: this being the case, doesn't the faith of the divines turn out to be unfounded?'
>
> The Buddha[125]

> Of all the offspring of Time, Error is the most ancient, and is so old and familiar an acquaintance, that Truth, when discovered, comes upon most of us like an intruder, and meets the intruder's welcome.
>
> Charles Mackay[126]

Meaning

Para means 'other', 'former' or 'later', so this is literally 'a series in which one follows after another', i.e. a 'succession' or 'continuation of a chain'. More specifically and idiomatically it refers to 'tradition' and 'traditions'. It can also have the sense of 'mediation', and focus on the idea of what we might call 'second-hand truth', what experiential knowledge is passed from one to another, i.e. what one learns *about* experience rather than what one directly experiences.

Examples

Social customs and conventions; the commandments from God revealed by the prophets; the laws of reality discovered by the Buddhas; social

---

125 In *The Caṅkī Discourse.*

126 (Mackay, Extraordinary Popular Delusions and the Madness of Crowds, 1841)

norms passed from generation to generation; laws, decrees, orders, etc.; scientific and technological knowledge passed down; advice; the information accepted by academic authorities and religious authorities.

Irrelevancy as sources of certainty

Again it is probably wise to emphasise that none of these are being declared totally irrelevant. The prophets' message is clearly relevant to the prophet-followers' purpose of 'knowing what God wants of us', and scientific knowledge about genetic inheritance is clearly relevant to the purpose of producing more vigorous strains of staple crops. The laws the Buddhas discovered are not irrelevant to discovering the truth.

The point the Buddha is making is that *in itself* this form of knowledge cannot guarantee certainty, that is to say, the question of its truthfulness or otherwise cannot be decided simply by reference to the knowledge itself, not that the knowledge should be rejected outright as false. The philosopher of science Karl Popper concurs:

> Tradition, more especially, which both the intellectualists (Descartes) and the empiricists (Bacon) tended to reject, can be admitted by us as one of the most important 'sources', since almost all that we learn (from our elders, in school, from books) stems from it. I therefore hold that anti-traditionalism must be rejected as futile. Yet traditionalism – which stresses the authority of traditions – must be rejected too; not as futile, but as mistaken…[127]

In my treatment of why this is so, I will consider first order disqualifications from certainty, but also have to go deeper, because of the devices which we inherit along with the traditions themselves and which act as protecting mechanisms and propagating mechanisms: the second order disqualifications apply to these mechanisms.

First order disqualification: logical fallacy

Deferring to tradition of course forms the basis of the vast majority of so-called religion, as well as most people's beliefs about everything. This deference is very persuasive for uncritical minds, and is often considered perfectly

[127] From addendum I, 9 of *The Open Society and Its Enemies* (Popper, 1945; 5th edition 1966)

reasonable. When it is invoked as a justification for doing, saying or thinking something without any other defence (for example a defence of why this was done/said/thought before and a defence of the unchangingness of justifying context between then and now) then it is the logical fallacy called *argumentum ad antiquitatem* meaning 'argument from oldness'. It is most frequently found as confusion between what is and what ought to be.

Case: marriage

For example, consider the almost universal common belief that it is good to marry. Unquestionably in the context of a society in which this belief is pervasive, it is indeed good to marry, because not doing so and what is worse indulging in alternative sexual arrangements are frowned upon and sometimes illegal, such that detractors from the belief are likely to be stigmatised or even punished. The system is very old indeed, of course, and almost never questioned, because one feels it need not be: it seems always to have been in place. This is an example of what the Buddha will deal with later, the tendency to accept views because they seem to be untuitively right even without needing any thought. But if the system is questioned, then the 'proof by antiquity' is very commonly brought in.

Its neglect of circumstances' change

The easily overlooked loophole in the argument is that conditions have changed since the times of those figures, no matter how great they were. We can hypothesize that there were logical reasons for these norms, and in fact even their strictest adherents frequently do invoke reasonableness to defend them. So we need to investigate whether the logical reasons which applied when the revered figures enounced the norms still apply now.

Case: protecting children by the prohibition of extra-marital sex

For example, the commonest logical reason invoked for the institution (in place in most territories of the world till now) of marriage as *a legal requirement* for sex is the protection of the children, which result from sex. Is this still a valid reason?

Now the condom has been with some of us (the rich) for about 400 years and generally available (even to the poor) for more than 100. Until recently (and sometimes until now), unwanted conception was considered the woman's problem and of course alternatives to condoms are much less attractive, especially the one most commonly resorted to – abortion. Furthermore the condom's main *raison d'être* was initially to deal with a problem the men could not send away: syphilis ('the Europeans' disease' as it is known in the Sanskrit texts). Condoms could not in any case be relied upon for contraception until way into the last century with the development of rubber and especially latex. Freud for example was dead against all contraceptive use *on the grounds that their failure rates were too high*. (He also singled out the condom for especial blame as lessening the pleasure of sex.)

Our situation today is of course that sex and reproduction can be completely separated by contraceptive use. Avoiding the kind of conflation of arguments (as we shall discuss under second order disqualifications) frequently invoked at this point, since the conditions could hardly be more different, indeed since there are *no children* with contraceptive sex, what strength does the children-protecting argument have for contraceptive sex?

Case: the prohibition of particular meats

Muslims defending the traditional prohibition on eating pork often point out that this was a logical counsel because pigs ate disgusting food and lived in disgusting conditions. Is this still true?

Well, while it might be said to be true for factory-farmed pigs or pigs allowed to roam near cities (i.e. on their rubbish dumps and sewage disposal sites), it cannot be said about organic free-range pigs, for example. And of course the appalling conditions in factory farms are not reserved for pigs but apply to many other animals, and as much if not more to chickens. This information is clearly more nuanced than and established independently of the Jewish/Muslim tradition.

Case: the law

Our legal systems suffer throughout from this fallacy. The fact that laws are (generally!) updated regularly does not alter the fact that it is always a danger that every new law which is promulgated is suitable for conditions at that time, but may become years later very unsuitable. One of the most distressing consequences of this is that governments very frequently gain unwarranted intrusion into the lives of civilians in peacetime by means of emergency laws devised under crisis.

Churchill's government, for example, employed WWII legislation after the war to muzzle anti-government satire in the press. The same manoeuvre we have seen deployed with dismaying regularity by the British and American governments over the last decade, and in consequence repressive measures introduced by the governments of such countries as Belarus, Malaysia and Sri Lanka were done so with a justification framed in terms of an appeal to the British precedents.[128]

Exploitation

Each of these examples is also a vivid demonstration of how interested parties might encourage others in their fallacious tradition-following to further their own benefit to the detriment of the followers, and whether or not we allow traditions to be great sources of certain knowledge, we can form some reasoned judgment about the kind of damage done in their name.

The point that religious traditions become useful to irreligious powers hardly needs elaborate justification. The most ardent supporters of the Catholic Church cannot excuse its history, and the most pious Sunnite reads the career of caliphs such Mu`awiyya (even though he was a 'companion') flinching. The fact that, whether or not we believe it was his deity's intention, Muḥammad used the piety of his followers to spur them to fight battles, is proven by the verses in the Qur'ān castigating those who refused to fight, and in Hinduism the Veda also codifies the exploitation of religious feeling for political purposes in the jarring (and – as scholars now agree – later) hymns in which the divines' power as intermediaries in ritual swells to such proportions that they have total control over the deities, and these latter begin, according to these hymns, to worship the divines.

It need not be conscious

The appeal to tradition need not be recognised as such. It happens very often that we learn a strategy in one situation, and then fail to recognise that the situation changes to a degree which renders the strategy redundant or even counter-productive. The very failure to recognise the change, a belief that because a situation used to be 'like this' it still is, is clearly an unstated appeal to antiquity.

This has potentially catastrophic ramifications in policy. It has been argued, for example, that the foreign policy initiatives of the neo-conservatives of the Bush administration were the result of applying habits of thought acquired during the Cold War era to the very different conditions that prevailed while they were in power, as though conditions had not changed.[129]

---

128 (Johnson B. , 2006)

129 From Chapter 4, subsection 'The Possessed' in Gray, 2007

Second order disqualifications: carrier mechanisms

> When we look at religion from a meme's eye view we can understand why they have been so successful.
>
> Susan Blackmore[130]

It is by thinking not of what is true or false, good or bad, in tradition, but of what makes traditional notions, discourse and behaviours *fit or unfit* to survive, quite independent of their truth or goodness, that we will find a thorough-going explanation for how tradition can mislead, and for example why religion, despite being immensely popular, is the most potent force that we know, as Nobel laureate Steven Weinberg said, to cause 'good people to do evil'.

> Or, must the lyre on which my spirit lingers
> Soon pause in silence, ne'er to sound again,
> Though it might shake the Anarch Custom's reign…?[131]

We are here going to use 'fitness' in its biological sense. What lasts is what is *good at lasting* in ('fit' for) certain conditions, not what is merely good, beautiful or perfect (even in those conditions, much less unchangingly); and it is crucial to recognise that just because something is good, beautiful or perfect doesn't mean that it will last. What is fit to survive is not necessarily what helps. Since the term fitness first came into general use in biology as denoting the likelihood to survive, especially in successive generations, it has been consistently misunderstood as something positive, as indeed the general use of the word 'fitness' does imply, especially in our era of obsession with personal health. As Darwin pointed out:

> Nor ought we to marvel if all the contrivances in nature be not, as far as we can judge, absolutely perfect; and if some of them be abhorrent to our ideas of fitness.[132]

---

130 Just as genes survive or die out according to their fitness to certain conditions, so do patterns of ideas ('memes'): this was Richard Dawkins' contention, developed by Susan Blackmore in *The Meme Machine* (Blackmore, 1999), and popularised more recently by the creator of Microsoft Richard Brodie in *Virus of The Mind* (Brodie, 2009).

131 From the dedication (verse X) of Shelley's *The Revolt of Islam.*

132 From chapter 14 of *On the Origin of Species* (Darwin, 1859).

Despite such usage even by the 'founder' of evolutionary theory, the word fitness came to represent exactly those contrivances' power to survive, or to have survived until now – i.e. to those contrivances which still exist.

We might imagine that traditions which have proved to be true and useful are likely to persist. However with more care we can see that, with time, just as happens to genes, fixed patterns of information ('memes') that are transmitted more than others will by this outcompeting come to predominate across cultures. So their predominance does not develop necessarily on the basis of their truthfulness or benefit but simply on the basis of more transmission having been done: 'these memes are fitter'.

This totally undermines the possibility which many believe in, if unconsciously, that, with the accumulation of information, what is passed down, taken as a whole, gradually improves, i.e. that there is *necessarily* progress in truth or benefit in what is transmitted. This is simply not the case. Many factors do determine the nature of transmission, but regrettably truthfulness and benefit are rarely among them, as we shall see.

When teaching history in an English classroom, for example, there is a great deal of information relevant to her purpose that the teacher simply will not consider – namely any narrative which lacks the Eurocentric focus which she recognizes as a mark of 'reliable history'.

We can identify a series of characteristics which favour the transmission of a particular tradition to future generations independent of its truthfulness or benefit, or rather in addition to what it might deserve because of its truthfulness or benefit: for this reason we will make reference to traditions being 'over-transmitted', i.e. transmitted in excess of their deserts. In effect what we are saying is that any tradition which possesses these characteristics is thrown into question because it *could be* both false and harmful but transmitted nevertheless. Again let us stress that this does not mean we are saying such traditions are inescapably either false or harmful! The intent is to be clear about why certain traditions really stay with humanity. Nevertheless, in the case of extremely over-transmitted traditions, we might go beyond this basic doubt, and ask, if these traditions are being transmitted by conscious organisms, which one hopes humans are, and these organisms were able to and *consider each other able to* judge the truthfulness and benefit of the traditions, why the 'carrying mechanisms', the means of over-transmission, were ever considered necessary, and why many people make active efforts to strengthen them and even invent new ones, such as chain e-mails.

Preaching

The most obvious carrying mechanism is the injunction to preach to others. Clearly any tradition associated with this injunction will get over-transmitted. And clearly Islām and Christianity both make it.

Punishment and reward

These can apply to preaching the tradition, believing it, or following it. Thomas Jefferson once wrote that punishments and rewards in the attempt to impose ideology

> tend only to beget habits of hypocrisy and meanness.[133]

This may be true, but the ideology associated with them will proliferate much faster than without them.

If the necessity of transmission is associated with avoiding terrible consequences, either directly ('tell the people or else') or indirectly by associating the content of the tradition and its availability with such avoidance, then the tradition will be over-transmitted.

Case: heaven and hell

The threat of damnation in Hell is the most obvious example of this in religion. It is essential to realise that any traditions associated with avoiding damnation will be over-transmitted, *whether or not the threat is real.* That is to say, if someone challenges the claim that there has been such over-transmission by reporting 'the way things really are', i.e. that Hell really exists, and this is true, this does not alter the fact that the traditions are over-transmitted!

Case: punishing heresy and apostasy

Clearly 'in this world' the same principle applies to doctrines associated with worldly bodies such as Church authorities which periodically effected public punishment upon heretics, or such as Muslim communities which periodically effect public punishments upon apostates. We will develop this later in the context of control and extreme punishment of sexual pleasure.

---

133 (Jefferson, 1904, p. 438)

Case: the terrorist threat

In modern society there are many less obvious but arguably more important manifestations of this. For example, there has arisen a tradition in the USA, now much more widespread in countries populated mainly by certain ethnic groups ('Caucasians'), of suspecting certain other ethnic groups (Arabs and anyone else considered to look like them) of being terrorists or likely to be terrorists[134], and so interrogating them more vociferously (if you belong to the authorities), shunning them (if you don't), etc. This behaviour, rightly or wrongly, is associated thanks to media attention and certain politicians' hysterical pronouncements with the idea that if we do not do so, then a terrorist attack is more likely to happen.[135] Thus it is currently being over-transmitted. Again, if it is objected that the behaviour is useful, in that it significantly increases efficiency of uncovering real terrorists, this does nothing to refute the over-transmission of the behaviour.

Assertion of eternality

Another such mechanism is by means of the claim that the forms being transmitted by the tradition are an eternally valid. This is usually done by claiming that the traditional form originated from and still represents an unchanging edict from an omniscient god, but modern gods such as 'justice' can bring similar and sufficient kudos to carry off the claim to eternal veracity. To see how it becomes a protection for fallacies, let us consider the case of successions of religions.

Case: closure of revelation, the god's silence, and the all-trumping final message

Frequently, when there arises an inconvenient succession of religious figures each proclaiming truth which is asserted as universal but which differs from the others' proclamations, it is argued that later ones must supercede earlier ones. Christians and their books assert that Christ's incarnation supercedes many Mosaic laws deriving from the Jewish religion's prophets. Muslims and their books assert that Muḥammad's message (including denial of the Christian atonement) supercedes all extant bibles. Bahā'is and their books assert that

---

[134] What nowadays go by the name of a 'suspected terrorist' – a beautiful and horrifying modern example of vocabulary engineering to conceal evil, which we consider later: see 'Not by thinking ideas through'.

[135] We consider the psychological foibles which facilitate such distortions later: see 'Not by intuitive acceptance of views'.

Bahā'ullah's message supercedes the Qur'ān, for example in asserting that jihād in the sense of fighting unbelievers is no longer valid..

Unless there is independent argument supporting the correlation between time and quality, these are examples of the logical fallacy called *argumentum ad novitatem*, meaning 'proof by novelty'.

It is with depressing frequency that one encounters among adherents to religions the blithe combination of the *argumentum ad antiquitatem* to dismiss new-fangled religions (in that these have broken with tradition), and the *argumentum ad novitatem* to dismiss earlier religions (in that theirs was newer and therefore truer). Such a combination can only be logical if the time of the revelation of that religion marked a change in the deity from which the revelation was received, from delivering messages every now and again, to silence, like a jilted lover who finally gives up on the SMSs. I.e., this time must mark the closure of revelation. Without wishing to be flippant, it is hard to find a deity which is not silent. This silence of the deity ringing in the ears of the believers is therefore used as evidence for the revelation having been closed, at the time of the inception of their own religion. This is certainly more comfortable than the arguably more straightforward interpretation that the deity is not there. And if the said deity is omnipotent and desirous to guide us to a glorious future, as is the case in the beliefs of the massive religions, then he must include everything which is necessary for that guidance in that final message. This is what makes the notion of an unchanging law so appealling: it deflects logical attacks on this paradoxical situation by slyly allowing the closure of revelation (which the combination of the two proofs, by antiquity and novelty, requires) to become evidence for that revelation being eternal and the deity still being there. In effect, it makes the deity's ensuing silence *speak*, nay eloquently, as testimony to that revelation having been the last, and therefore necessarily the eternal one. Whether or not any such claims are true, again we stress, the point is that this would work as a sleight of hand even if they were not. We will consider similar sleights of hand in our discussion of the Buddha's questioning of intricate philosophy later.[136]

Interpenetration with driving forces

The last 200 years have seen great revelations in psychology of the power certain forces have within us to drive us. If a tradition associates itself with them, then the tradition itself can become driven with the same impetus.

---

136 See 'Not by philosophy'.

Case: bridling pleasure and normalising the family

One extraordinarily effective transmission mechanism for a tradition is to get linked with a restriction of orgasmic pleasure to those particular patterns of a particular lifestyle that best propagate it. It is particularly noticeable that extreme doctrines, such as absolution by mutilation or execution, are especially closely associated with this kind of transmission mechanisms. Sometimes the libidinous impulse is channelled explicitly into propagation of traditions. For example, in Vedic Hinduism, under the caste- and stage-based laws (in Sanskrit, varnāśramadharma) the first of the four stages of the novice priest's life involves living the 'pure career' (brahmacārya) with his teacher, learning the Veda, and the law books say explicitly that he makes a sacrifice of sexual activity for the sake of this learning. However the restriction of sexual pleasure to activities involving propagation and transmission of traditions occurs most commonly in the form of 'the family' and its normalisation, because this norm is itself a severe limitation of orgasmic activity to the multiplication of tradition-indoctrinable offspring. (In Hinduism this forms the second of the four obligatory stages, and the law books point out that in this case sex is made into an offering to the ancestors, 'repaying' their gift of life by the furtherance of the bloodline.)

There are doubters of the importance of this restriction, who might object, 'Have we not enjoyed the sexual revolution? Are we not free of primitive superstitions about sex?' On the contrary, in today's world, most societies are in the thrall of an ongoing (if fluctuating) anathemisation of orgasmic pleasure, and even those who supposedly went through a sexual revolution are still very heavily stamped by traces of this anathema, and in their commercialisation of de-restricted pleasure still must engage pragmatically with restrictions.

Mainstream cinema affords insight into widespread contemporary values. So what is the lesson from cinema in this matter? While violent killing earns a film universality more or less in proportion to the number of deaths shown, sex, if shown at all, even once, earns it illegality in most countries – supposedly for moral reasons. This issue has been obfuscated by focus on 'real' versus 'faked' action. We might quibble that killing in films is always simulated, so less realistic. But actually it is indistinguishable from real killing, and much more closely observed, often in slow motion, whereas hardcore sex in *cartoons* is illegal: realism is clearly not the problem. We are not talking about the morality of the act in the studio, but about that of the act as it appears on screen, and modern technology makes the discussion of 'real' or 'faked' there perfectly redundant, as we can quickly verify to ourselves if we imagine the kind of rating a fantasy film populated by computer-generated beings would get if their alien genitals were shown *in copula.*[137] We are allowed to see knives enter flesh or bullets shatter skulls and splatter brains in countless mainstream films. The number in which we can see penises pumping vaginas let alone anything else, however, is practically zero.

It is hard to avoid the conclusion that the screening of explicit murder is considered more morally uplifting than the screening of explicit sex. This bizarre discrepancy was rammed home beautifully in a cinema-hall presentation I happened to attend of the horror film *Urban Legend.* Though the censorship I will describe occurred in a 'traditional' country, it could equally have occurred in 'family-time' TV elsewhere. The film includes two parallel scenes. In the first scene the heroine, a student, comes back to her room to find her goth room-mate having noisy sex with a man picked up through the internet, and in response to being berated for the interruption, the heroine meekly goes to her bed and does her best to ignore the orgasmic screams and get to sleep. In the later, and parallel, scene, she comes back to her room and is met by much the same images and sounds, and having learnt her lesson does not interrupt but goes meekly straight to bed, ignoring the orgasmic screams. What the viewer knows but she does not is that in the second scene these are not orgasmic screams, and the room-mate is not having sex with a man she has picked up, but is being murdered by the bad guy of the film. In the 'respectable' cinema presentation I attended the first scene was almost completely cut, because of the moral inadmissability of the sex, but *the second scene was left in uncut*, despite almost identical images and sounds, because, I presume, murder appearing to be sex was deemed to lack the moral danger of sex. This is just a particularly startling example via censorship of a well-recognised tendency in classic post-60s horror films aimed at teenagers *encoded in the script*, for sex only to be presented explicitly when it is coupled with terrible violence, a tendency which copious studies have concluded is linked to our enjoyment of the apparent moral retribution.[138]

Noble efforts such as DH Lawrence's to undo the outrage concomitant with reading and hearing words such as 'cock' and 'cunt' clearly have not yet paid off, unless one considers the transition made in certain strata of certain societies to being bored with such words – still recognising their uniqueness though – as an improvement. *Lady Chatterley's Lover* is still hawked on the basis of its naughtiness, I notice. Filmed sex cannot be shown in cinemas till today in the vast majority of countries of the world and even simulated sex cannot be shown in

---

137 Of course, aliens never *have* genitals in the first place, outside of William Burroughs adaptations.

138 (Dika, 1990), (Williams, 1996)

many. The first time most cinema audiences saw an erection in a film there was when it was cut off and thrown to a dog to be eaten (in *Hostel 2*). Can anyone argue that such absurdities speak nothing of superstition infecting our treatment of sex? We are just too inured to them to notice, or care.

The normal family required in the most persistent traditions will be found to maximise their faultless transmission to the children, by minimising the number of parents, maximising the number of children, and prescribing indoctrination of the children. These are the conditions to which all orgasmic pleasure must be restricted, so that the undeniably immense drive to such pleasure is bridled and directed exclusively to the propagation and transmission of the traditions with which this restriction is associated. This means, incidentally, that unless the positive feedback is countered by other forces, restrictions on orgasmic pleasure over time will naturally get stricter and stricter, *independent of the nature of the other traditions.* That is where the Sixties went.

As young children we blindly obey our parents – a matter of survival of physically weak organisms in a potentially hostile world – so the upbringing situation is the ideal locus for such transmission. It hardly needs mentioning that each massive religions stipulates that children be indoctrinated in it and not another. This is particularly nasty in Islām, in which parents are required to beat their children until they perform the ritual prayer (in the form prescribed by Muḥammad of course). This violation of children is perhaps the most pernicious aspect of 'religious tradition' and the sin accrues as much to those few irreligious ideologies, such as Communism, that make equivalent stipulations of course.

The ideal family context for such transmission to the next generation is first of all, of course, one which at the very least generates a new generation, preferably a voluminous one! (Childless families will not be smiled upon by persistent and successful religions.) Since adoption from an early age is difficult this generally means biological procreation is a must. In turn this, of course, requires at least one male and one female from the current generation – or at least it did until the advent of insemination technology – so we would expect persistent traditions to be associated with prescription of procreative copulation. Of course, they are.

Furthermore, for ideal transmission of any one tradition, the number of potentially conflicting traditions in the parents must be minimised, so out with Aldous Huxley and the hippies with their 'over-sensible' and 'more civilised' multi-parent families. Even two is a potential hazard since the other parent could carry a different tradition, so we should expect persistent traditions to prescribe that even if only one parent is a follower, the children must still be raised as followers. This law is found expressly in Islām, where a Muslim man who marries a non-Muslim woman must raise the children as Muslims, and where a Muslim woman cannot even marry a non-Muslim man.

The ideal family for transmission of a tradition would maximise the number of children. Even in our grossly over-populated world Islām and Catholicism still advocate huge families [139], and dominate the world – an undeniable success in terms of numbers of adherents if nothing else.

Ethical developments more recent than the 'revelation', such as the current environmental emergency, which threaten the hallowed 'go forth and multiply' we would expect to be interpreted away. This is of course the case. The Pope's recent setting of sperm injection on a higher priority than HIV exclusion for African Catholics is a pretty enough demonstration. In a recent book which claims to be offering revolutionary Islāmic solutions to the world's ills we are edified by the argument that, since the prophet Muḥammad according to some traditions mercifully allowed his horny conquering army to relax their self-imposed duty of *coitus interruptus* with women they had just 'captured' from the enemy and enjoy instead the *non interruptus* variety (I hastily pass over consideration of the ethical status of the 'captures' themselves) by reminding them of the happy fact that Allāh had already created souls to pop into the resulting bairns, for that reason (so argues our 'revolutionary' author) it is an eternal law that not using contraception is good in Allāh's eyes – and after an alarmist description of the benighted western families with their dwindling numbers of offspring, disdain is poured on their *stinginess*, no mention being made of such exotica as environmental concerns.

Aside from the environmental consequences, there are more vivid, bodily ones. It is a fact with tragic consequence that such a bipolar parental system, while it might be the optimal for transmitting traditions (i.e. persistent traditions are more likely to be associated with it), is not the most physically or psychologically pleasant one we might happen across or devise if following such traditions were not such a central concern. As the poet put it so justly,

Thy wisdom speaks in me, and bids me dare
Beacon the rocks on which high hearts are wrecked.
I never was attached to that great sect,
Whose doctrine is, that each one should select

139 A euphemistic Egyptian invitation to have sex currently doing the rounds is, '*Yalla nigīb islām* – Let's bring [forth] Islām!'

> Out of the crowd a mistress or a friend,
> And all the rest, though fair and wise, commend
> To cold oblivion, though it is in the code
> Of modern morals, and the beaten road
> Which those poor slaves with weary footsteps tread,
> Who travel to their home among the dead
> By the broad highway of the world, and so
> With one chained friend, perhaps a jealous foe,
> The dreariest and the longest journey go.
> …Narrow
> The heart that loves, the brain that contemplates,
> The life that wears, the spirit that creates
> One object, and one form, and builds thereby
> A sepulchre for its eternity.[140]

All pleasures which disincline humans to form this tradition-transmission-maximising system will be forbidden, and the more intensely they are forbidden, the more persistent the tradition which forbids them will be.

Pleasure of the bodily, especially the orgasmic, kind is undeniably intense, and likely, without other considerations, to discourage one from sacrificing it in the interests of stabilising the system which happens (without our being too aware of it) best to transmit those beliefs we happen to hold which are not beneficial or truthful enough not to be threatened by our experience. Such pleasure presents, then, a direct threat to the transmission. If I may be permitted a little of that poetic licence which gets twisted into a claim of teleology by adventurous readers, if traditions were living things, what a terrifying enemy the prostate would seem to them!

> Homosexual behaviour occurs in more than 450 different kinds of animals worldwide, and is found in every major geographical region and every major animal group.[141]

Lust and lasciviousness, you might imagine, are among the timeless vices. Yet their etymology tells another story, a story of the hijacking of symbols. For they all derive from Proto-Indo-European las which exists in Sanskrit as a number of words relating not to the dangers of the orgasm as its

---

140 Shelley, from *Epipsychidion.*

141 (Bagemihl, 1999)

current incarnations in Germanic and Latin languages suggest but to spontaneity, sport, playing, dance, freedom and ease.[142]

Case: extreme punishment for human nature

What could have favoured this death of play, this summoning of opprobrium? Consider a pool of competing traditions carrying absurd doctrines. (And every adherent of the massive and other-refuting religions must consider our situation in the world to be just that, at least until the 'Day of Glory' comes.) After centuries upon centuries of transmission, the more robust among these traditions will be those whose prescription of the sacrifice of orgasmic pleasure on the altar of this most particular version of family is most intense. In other words: measure a tradition's potential to delude by the intensity of its prohibition of pleasure.

Prosecutors of religious law and those who side with them should take note: what this means is that every 'moral' high-ground one might take on pleasure could effectively be heaped up of the muck of traditions which need be neither beneficial nor true. The higher they pile, the more those wise enough to see this should smirk up to such pious souls, knowing how far these may have parted from the cleanliness of truth, knowing them slaves of the traditions' transmission mechanisms, ejaculators of the absurd, doctors of the over-transmitted. Every stone thrown at adulterers they have wrapped in sheets [143] speaks of their tradition's potential departure from benefit and truth. Every noose they hang buggers from to death is a hieroglyphic sign, which in the language of the wise reads, 'To save tradition.'

It might be doubted that extreme punishments themselves can have the effect of assuring better transmission of *any* attached doctrines. Well, some fascinating mathematical models of the evolution of culture in human society incorporating moralistic punishment and run on game theoretical lines have recent been developed and analysed extensively. For example, in 2005 in an

---

142 I find it ironic but symptomatic that the word in Sanskrit that referred to exactly the Buddha's free spontaneous acts in the world, lalita, from the root lal = laḍ = las (which all mean play, sport, or frolic), turns out to be the equivalent of the origin of the English word 'lust', frequently chosen in our Christianised culture to translate what the Buddha cited as a fetter to cyclic existence and its inevitable suffering (namely in Sanskrit *tṛṣṇā*, actually English's 'thirst')!

143 In Iran and Saudi Arabia, following what they call Islamic law, it is customary to wrap the orgasm-offenders, those who dared to burst the sacred bubble of legal marriage, in white sheets before burying them to their knees and stoning them to death.

article[144] entitled 'Punishment Allows the Evolution of Cooperation (or Anything Else) in Sizable Groups' an environmental scientist and policy analyst and an anthropologist reported the results of analysing a model they had developed in which they supposed groups of individuals of a particular size from a larger population form by the repeated interaction among their members. Each interaction consisted of a chance to cooperate or defect, followed by a stage when defectors were punished. The model resembled a special case of the so-called 'prisoner's dilemma' which had been used in economic and political science to model provision of public goods and the linear model of social interaction used in most treatments of kin selection in evolutionary biology. The addition of the chance to punish was assumed to be at a particular cost to the punisher, and at a particular cost to the punished individual, in terms of fitness. Individuals were characterised according to an inherited strategy based on their experience till then, such as, 'Never cooperate and never punish non-cooperators,' or, 'Always cooperate and always punish non-cooperators'. They allowed for individual fallibility, such as defecting by mistake. They assumed strategies to be inherited as haploid sexual traits, or in close approximation to that.

Although the results of their analysis are fascinating and diverse, what concerns me here is that they discovered that, in such a system, moralistic strategies, such as, 'Always cooperate, and punish those who are not in good standing i.e. who have behaved like me since they were last punished,' do not only, as was expected, stabilise behaviour beneficial to the group but costly to the individual: they also stabilise any behaviour, *even behaviour costly both to the group and the individual, i.e. beneficial to no-one.* There mere possibility of this should make us turn to reflect anew on the doctrines transmitted by the highly punitive Christian and Islāmic traditions.

It should be obvious that models comparing various ethical systems would yield fascinating results.

As we alluded to befor, misunderstanding of evolutionary theory aside, it has long been recognised that what is 'fit', i.e. successful at getting transmitted to later generations, is not necessarily what is 'good', i.e. beneficial – to the individual or the group. The Buddhist tradition encapsulates causes of misery in the Sanskrit term āsrava, meaning that which flows on or that which causes the flow's continuation. We can see that success in persistence can often mean failure in goodness or in truthfulness. This adds much needed irony to pronouncements such as:

---

144 (Richerson, 2004)

Verily have the believers succeeded.[145]

'Trapped' belief

Many transmission mechanisms reach a degree of fixation because they foster conditions in which they appear necessary, conditions which otherwise would not occur. Since this is an example of mis-identification of causes, or faulty logic, we discuss it under this topic later.

Aggravating circumstances

The fallacious appeal to tradition is aggravated by various other phenomena, such as the tendency towards polarisation of arguments for example because of politicisation, and the tendency to imagine that associated ideas refer to associated realities for example by linking traditions to people associated with them.

Disputes which address the *argumentum ad antiquitatem* fallacy of any particular norm are almost always politicised as being between on the one hand those who favour the preservation of the *status quo* and on the other those who want reform, revolution, or anarchy. The membership of the second category by habitually disdained sectors of society and the exaggeration of positions towards extremes suggested by the polarity allows the fallacy upon which the comfortableness of the status quo depends to be conveniently or even accidentally forgotten.

Although a vast swathe of sexual, dietary and social restrictions are almost always justified, at least psychologically, by this fallacious appeal to tradition alone, in the sphere of religion and sometimes even in academia, its temptation is aggravated by the belief that particular figures important in the establishment of the tradition knew more than we do and either instituted or supported its details. We will consider this contention later with the Buddha's questioning of the relevance of the seeming ability of others. For now we can note that these two beliefs, that we should do as we always have, and that our religious figures, scientists, or whoever, knew better than we do, combine to make an argument so persuasive it seems almost perverse to question it.

---

145 This is the opening of the chapter of the Qur'ān called *The Believers*.

Not by reports, ma itikirāya

Meaning

The particle iti in Pali and Sanskrit has the sense of 'as was just said' and so is used most frequently where we would use a closing inverted comma to show the end of a verbatim quote or direct representation of a concept as one thinks of it. The word 'kira', also a particle related to speaking, and equivalent to the Sanskrit 'kila', means that one is reporting something, and it adds emphasis in a way very similar to how we use, often after a dramatic pause and sliding of eyes to ensure a privy ear, 'Apparently...' – i.e. it implies some particular feeling (e.g. remarkableness or probability or reasonableness or even dislike) about what was said, which is likely to be shared between reporter and listener.

Examples

The 'ḥadīth' (report) literature of Islām; the collected 'Word' of the Buddha which begins, 'Thus have I heard, that once...'; the 'gospel' (good news) of Christianity; gossip; the news as reported in the media; history; reputation and honour.

Irrelevancy as a source of certainty

Once again we should first of all remind ourselves that the point here is not that these are not relevant to any purpose. If we want to know what information is available to us about historic figures who died before we were born, most of us cannot travel through time to meet them, so there is nothing better than reports about them. Similarly if we prefer not to be in the war zone while we have breakfast, we will have to rely on the newspaper we read over it to tell us what the latest state of play is for the home troops.

Nevertheless, these cannot *in themselves* guarantee certainty. While this point is probably uncontroversial in the way we approach the newspaper or the television news since the triumph of corporate-controlled media, it causes stiff resistance of course in the matter of religious accounts, and as any famous actor or actress knows, once a rumour spreads generally it can be pretty much incontrovertible such that the truth, sometimes including one's entire personality, becomes irrelevant and eventually seems itself untrue.

A report is just that. Even a report about an undeceiving ruler of the universe in whose hands your fate lies is still a report. This means that it is the speech of a reporter, about whose speech one can be no more or less certain than if he or she had been reporting the results of yesterday's football match or the visitation by UFOs to a nearby village.

Let us consider all the ways reports come down to us for reasons *other than* that they are true.

First-order disqualifications: the generation of the report

This is hardly controversial. We are all too familiar with the fact that people report lies and mistakes. They also unwittingly misreport, i.e. unwittingly create new reports, as the game Chinese whispers demonstrates. The only specific case of this which seems to need stating in the context of our survey is the astonishing and demoralising resurgence of respect in an activity which had, one imagined, become so disreputable that it could never again be admitted to.

Extraction of reports under torture

Not so long ago, scholars generally acknowledge pre-16th century, torture attracted no ethical opprobium and was considered necessary to prevent crime. However in that century a movement of revolt began against the use of torture to extract confessions, and in 1776 Austria became the first country to ban it. The entire revolt movement was motivated by the overwhelming evidence that such confessions were *unreliable.* International declarations and agreements were signed forbidding torture after the French Revolution and again after the Second World War.[146]

Until relatively recently, then, so-called liberal countries could not admit to torturing anyone. In the late 70s in the USA the revelation, consequent (eventually, after much resistance) upon a request deploying the Freedom of Information Act, that the CIA had been covertly funding medical experimentation seeking new methods of torture including the use of hallucinogenic drugs, isolation and sensory deprivation, drug-induced perpetual sleep, insulin comas and electroshock therapy of intensity never before permitted – in particular the research of Ewen Cameron, a Scottish-born American, at McGill University's Allen Memorial Institute, who credited himself with inventing in the aggressive combined deployment of such methods a brave new cure for mental illness which he called 'psychic driving'[147], 75% of whose subjects, it was belatedly realised, were much worse after 'treatment' than before – led to a series of hearings of the US Senate and the eventual awarding of almost a million

---

146 (Maio, 2001)

147 (Cameron, 1956)

dollars in compensation to the unlucky individuals who had been its subjects from the CIA, the largest settlement ever against the agency at the time. The now infamous 'Kubark' manual of interrogation methods, which was developed by the agency's 'MKUltra' project and included the fruits of such research, is well aware that much of its contents if applied breaches international agreements, not least the Geneva Convention's blanket ban on any kind of torture or cruelty. Klein details[148] the post-September-11th machinations, including the redefinition of certain humans as enemy combattants (to which the Geneva Convention's stipulations did not apply) based on their location, the promotion of people who supported this redefinition publicly, and the adjustment of U.S. legal vocabulary such that torture no longer meant inflicting pain (think especially of psychological pain) but inflicting physical pain equivalent to injury concomitant with organ failure, which led to such new boldness that a February 2006 official report published by an advisory arm of the CIA was able to state openly, 'A careful reading of the Kubark manual is essential for anyone involved in interrogation.'

How much of an advance in reliability of extracted reports the advance in the technology of torture has achieved is indicated by the fact that experiments in sensory deprivation alone by the relatively ethically circumspect Dr. Donald Hebb, conducted under the auspices of the Canadian government's Department of National Defense in a project purportedly designed to find ways to protect 'our boys' from brainwashing from the evil commies, but also closely monitored by the CIA, showed that after sensory deprivation subjects become extraodinarily susceptible to adopting beliefs which they have earlier rejected but which are played to them on tapes, including for example the notions that science is dishonest and that ghosts exist.

Until now any evidence obtained under torture will almost certainly be excluded from court proceedings, and furthermore even undermines more reliable evidence because the latter, when obtained on the basis of a testimony extracted under torture, can be ruled out even though it is itself reliable, because the methods of obtaining it were inadmissible.[149]

Second-order disqualifications: carrier mechanisms

If reports are associated with carrier mechanisms, then they will be transmitted more than they deserve by virtue of their truth or benefit, potentially to the detriment of truer, more profitable reports. First of all we will consider

---

148 In 'The Torture Lab' chapter of *The Shock Doctrine* (Klein, 2007).

149 (Carter, 2004)

the qualities of the content of the report which make it more likely to get transmitted by the general reporter, then the qualities of the reporters which make them more likely to transmit reports in general, and finally examples of interactions between the reporter's and report's qualities which favour its transmission.

>Qualities of the content which favour the report's transmission

Think about the word 'remarkable'. It means, pretty much, 'reportable', 'worthy of reporting'. There is a lot of unremarkable information in the world which is nevertheless true.

I don't need to go into a long exploration of the elements which we judge remarkable: the reader is no doubt able to outstrip me in devising possibilities. Novelty is sometimes enough. Let us just consider a couple of examples. *The uncanny* is always a good bet to fuel a report's passage, and a bit of *the outrageous* never goes astray, as it were.

The uncanny

Mysterious happenings that provoke sensational responses, be they credulous or incredulous, are likely to be spread because people want to share those responses.

Case: miracles

The transmission of reports about miracles has a beginning. At this juncture we are not really concerned with whether this beginning is a miracle or not. Later we will investigate the kind of cognitive biases which can falsely generate a report of a miracle,[150] but for now let us turn to the reporting itself.

In this case it does not even matter if the reporter believes the report she is transmitting. If she believes it, then the amazing thing will be the miracle itself. If she does not, then the amazing thing will be that others are credulous enough to believe it. Either way there is something amazing to talk about. In the same way in mediaeval times reports about the manufacture of gold from other metals, or the elixir of life, were spread not only by the people who believed them but by those who held them preposterous. Controversy itself acts as a propaganda machine, as we shall see. (We consider more interested reasons for spreading 'alchemical knowledge' below.)

---

150 See 'Not by intuitive acceptance of views'.

The outrageous

Here we have a sensational response of a different kind, with similar results.

Case: sex scandals

Arguably less edifying for all, but definitely more exciting for most, are reports inclining less to the uncanny and more to the outrageous, especially if the outrage be of a sexual nature.

As every woman under the sway of a patriarchal society which has not yet woken up to implications of the technology of genetic testing knows, managing one's reputation is an extremely grave matter. To put it a little cheekily, it is not at all a matter of being good, but of being reputedly good, and that is something very different. She knows that the urgent necessity is to make sure no remarkable stories arise. It is not a matter of not being seen with her lover, but of not being seen twice with her lover, i.e. not being seen in the same place more than once. And so on: my intention is not to write a Victorian manual of how to get by for the natural girl.

>Qualities of the reporters which favour reports' transmission

Incorrigible gossips are more likely to pass on reports than people who despise gossip. This means that reports that get to us are more likely to have been transmitted by gossips, from which fact we can draw the obvious conclusions.

The reporter and listener's relation to each other

It has been shown in psychological experiments that humans give preferential treatment, for example attention in communication, to people who we perceive to be members of 'our group'. This is referred to as '*ingroup bias*'. The group does not have to be a society-wide recognised group: many such groups arise naturally through our perception of shared characteristics, however arbitrary they might seem, even such ludicrous ones as sharing the same last digit in their National Security number.[151]

One obvious sign of group membership is how we speak. Several

151 The pioneer work (Tajfel H. , Experiments in Intergroup Discrimination, 1970) (Tajfel H. , 1982) was done by the Polish-origin Briton Henri Tajfel (b. Hersz Mordche 1919, d. 1982) who, together with John Turner, developed the so-called Social Identity Theory which became highly influential in psychology (Tajfel & Turner, 1979).

social psychological studies have shown that people react more favourably to those who move linguistically closer to them. This is called *'convergent accommodation'*. If you speak in the native language of the listener, use local idioms, and the local dialect, then you are more likely to be believed.[152] The same studies also demonstrated the converse effect, a less favourable reaction to those who are further from them linguistically, *divergence*. In a mixed community this means that reports which reach us are more likely to have been transmitted by the majority dialect segment of the community, again with unavoidable implications.

The broader phenomenon is through the intrusion of trust of the reporter by the listener. Of course it is often argued (especially in religion or history) that each reporter in a chain was utterly trustworthy, such that the content of the report is vindicated. This amounts to saying that all in the chain have reported with absolute equanimity both the uncanny and the mundane, both the outrageous and the tediously banal, and that they are free of the influence of the distorting emotions of the three kinds on what they report.

We will consider in more detail later, in accordance with the order of the Buddha's presentation, this justifying notion of the trustworthiness of the reporters, in the context of 'a person's seeming capability'.

>Interaction (between the reporter and the report) favouring transmission

Just as was the case with traditions, we are dealing here with information passed on, by choice, and the choice depends upon emotions and concepts, so those very emotions and concepts influence what gets passed on, and how much it gets passed on, independent of its truthfulness.

In terms of emotion, we can make consider, as indeed the Buddha does later in his answer, the three main types – wanting, disliking and delusion. This triple classification will be discussed in detail later. For now let us just mention some examples. As for emotions involving wanting, such as the desire for status, we can see for example that any ordinary person, receiving good and bad reports about someone she admires publicly, is much more likely to pass on the good reports than the bad, since her own reputation is also at stake through association. Conversely in the obvious fact that she is more likely to pass on bad reports about a declared enemy we have an example of the distortion by emotions involving dislike, insofar as she may dislike her enemy having good repute. (I note in passing that there is no greater reliability here in reports filtered through the ethic of heroism, whereby one celebrates one's enemy's qualities – since this involves

---

152 (Crystal, How Language Works, 2006, pp. 325-6)

distortion by attraction to the kudos one gains by being seen to have such a 'worthy' enemy. Furthermore, and with a definitely more modern taste, we can see how the self-pitying seeking solace are more likely to report their bad qualities to us to solicit a response: and woe betide the listener who responds not.) Delusion, or confusion, is a special case because we are not used to thinking of it as an emotion. Deferring addressing this till later, we can for the moment see that a deluded mind is certainly no gauge of the truthfulness of what it reports.

Interesting (interested) history

We cannot expect impartiality from adherents to a faith, if their choice of faith cannot be rationally defended: any sense they have that their allegiance is absurd will lead to its justification by selective transmission of reports. Likewise from patriots of a particular patria. So we have histories of conquests from conquering cultures who admire the heroism of conquests, especially in nostalgia when the culture has lost its perceived status for by-gone days when it still had it. This is frustrating if the student of history does not share those values, and the clash exposes the bias in the reporting which more acquiescent students would easily overlook. The philosopher and advocate of humanism Karl Popper rails against traditional history's adulation of conquest, in particular when it makes the claim for itself to be the single history of mankind:

> There is no history of mankind, there is only an indefinite number of histories of all kinds of aspects of human life. And one of these is the history of political power. This is elevated into the history of the world. But this, I hold, is an offence against every decent conception of mankind. It is hardly better than to treat the history of embezzlement or of robbery or of poisoning as the history of mankind. For *the history of power politics is nothing but the history of international crime and mass murder* (including, it is true, some of the attempts to suppress them). This history is taught in schools, and some of the greatest criminals are extolled as its heroes.[153]

Whether or not heroism constitutes a crime, it is clearly associated with an ethic of revenge, setting the balance straight, and so on, something we consider later under 'intuitive truths'. One need not be a humanist to object to the usual

---

[153] From chapter 25, part IV of *The Open Society and Its Enemies* (Popper, 1945; 5th edition 1966, p. 270). The italics are in the original.

bias in traditional history. In his magisterial treatment of the 1717 English credit crisis, a very unheroic affair, Charles Mackay launches an impassioned attack on conventional history from the stance not of humanism but of morality:

> A celebrated writer [given by the footnote as Smollett] is quite wrong when he says 'that such an era as this is the most unfavourable for a historian; that no reader of sentiment of imagination can be entertained or interested by a detail of transactions such as these, which admit of no warmth, no colouring, no embellishment; a detail of which only serves to exhibit an inanimate picture of tasteless vice and mean degeneracy.' On the contrary, - and Smollett might have discovered it, if he had been in the humour, - the subject is capable of inspiring as much interest as even a novelist can desire. Is there no warmth in the despair of a plundered people? – no life and animation in the picture which might be drawn of the woes of hundreds of impoverished and ruined families? of the wealthy of yesterday become the beggars of today? Of the powerful and influential changed into exiles and outcasts, and the voice of self-reproach and imprecation resounding from every corner of the land? Is it a dull or uninstructive picture to see a whole people shaking suddenly off all the trammels of reason, and running wild after a golden vision, refusing obstinately to believe that it is not real, till, like a deluded hind running after an ignis fatuus, they are plunged into a quagmire? But in this false spirit has history too often been written. The intrigues of unworthy courtiers to gain the favour of still more unworthy kings, or the records of murderous battles and sieges, have been dilated on, and told over and over again, with all the eloquence of style and all the charms of fancy; while the circumstances which have most deeply affected the morals and welfare of the people have been passed over with but slight notice, as dry and dull, and capable of neither warmth nor colouring.[154]

We should never forget all those unwritten histories, which did not appeal, as much as the ones which have come down to us, to the people, standing between then and now, upon whose capacity as transmitters we must rely.

It is alarming to note how this awareness is completely lacking in many who consider themselves adherents of a religious tradition. Instead the

---

154 (Mackay, 1852, p. 70)

particular version of events they have inherited is seen as the only possible version, even by those who otherwise admit the fact that of all circumstances, those most likely to encourage lack of objectivity in appreciation occur when two religions deal with each other. This forgetting of the unwritten histories is notorious in the case of the Bible which, though for various reasons the most printed and translated book on Earth, is largely the history of a single people, but which is used nevertheless by most of its adherents and even a number of non-adherents as the exclusive lens through which world history should be seen. That this is preposterous even for nearby Egypt is obvious now that we are able to read the Egyptians' own writings. Similarly very few devotees of the Qur'ān are aware of the sheer number of claims to prophethood that were made by various people, men and women, of various tribes in Arabia around the time of the one we have come to know about thanks to that text and its daughters' transmission. Here selection was vociferous: the early Muslims seem not to have been too scrupulous in distinguishing their hatred of the rival prophets in question with the people who reported about them, which led to sustained character assassinations, and sometimes actual assassinations, of previously respected poets and historians.

These are what behavioural economists call 'survivor bias', aggravated cases of 'outcome bias', attributing the success of a successful project entirely to the soundness of its foundational characteristics, whereas in reality a great number of other conditions were involved, not the least of which is usually chance.

To the one who protests that the hand of the deity is involved, that it has favoured the true message at the expense of the pretenders, we can only point to the humans, with their human natures, who effected not only this transmission, but also its filtering, supplementing and distortion, against which formidable forces our protester must invoke that hand having us believe it to have successfully acted, if it acted at all.

Anxiety leading to selective appreciation for confirmational reports

In our discussion of authority later we will examine in detail why it is that adherents to doctrines can get so stressed and irritable, and how this makes them more likely to accept confirming doctrines intuitively. This has relevance here: if a report seems to confirm a doctrine, doubt in which one has repressed, then it will assuage that doubt and consequent anxiety to tell others. This explains the furious energy behind a good deal of proselytising.

Gullibility leading to confusion of truth claims with truth

We all too easily allow the truth claims of certain reports, such as a declaration of absolute certainty, either by the reporter or reported by the reporter, to overwhelm or circumvent our critical appreciation of the trustworthiness of the reporter or indeed reporters in the chain. We act very much as if we believed thus: 'A report claiming to be truth has come to me *because it is true.*' This an example of the 'bare assertion fallacy' and we will examine it later when we consider scripture.

Such credulity is encouraged (we do not say to ill effect) by systems of esoteric knowledge and initiation, such as one finds in Qabbalah, Gnosticism, Sufism, Tantric Hinduism and Buddhism, Freemasonry, Druze religion, etc. The prospect of 'initiation' is tantalising enough for some to be induced to believe its claims, because the *external lack of evidence* is expected when the system advertises itself as esoteric.

The practitioner and historian of 'animal magnetism' (popularly but inappropriately known as mesmerism) J. P. F. Deleuze (1753-1835) instructed[155] aspiring magnetisers: 'Never magnetise before inquisitive persons!'

Guile leading to invention of truth claims

If it is suspected by a reporter that they might gain financially (or in any other way) by transmitting a report, then they are more likely to transmit it. This often occurs because the content of the report includes such a promise.

Given the credulity of non-initiates for an esoteric system, the initiate gains power over them, independent of whether he or she actually discovered anything by means of the initiation. The new initiate can taste the power over the non-initiates, a power which presents a serious temptation to exploitation and the compromise of integrity.

In the case of bogus systems, where initiation brings no knowledge, it may still be the case that the bogusness never gets out, because out of fear of ridicule and losing reputation (not necessarily just the power of initiate status but also general credibility and social acceptance) unhappy discoverers of bogusness and hoax keep their traps shut and frequently disappear into remote places to live out their lives in fear of being found out.[156]

---

155 (Deleuze, 1813, p. 60)

156 So hypothesises Mackay (1841) but then one wonders whether what some of the 'initiates' he thus scorns (such as Cagliostro, and Balsamo and Marano the silversmiths) might have discovered, perhaps a very different reason for disappearing into the remote mountains and forests...

Case: alchemy

A vivid example from European history is the phenomenon of the centuries-long craze for alchemy, the quest to make gold from cheaper metals using the illusive 'philosopher's stone' and the quest to achieve longevity by means of the 'elixir of life'.[157] The practitioners of these arts showed themselves to be, in the first, rich, and in the second, old but youthful. When word got out it was transmitted by people who imagined that similar wealth and longevity could fall to them. In the former case it might even be that the reporter was aware of the falsity of the grounds of the claim that one could produce riches, but was wise enough to realise that other people were still gullible enough for the claim to be correct on other grounds – not by means of the 'philosopher's stone' but thanks to the public's credulity. And lest we think such things are of the past, we should mention the modern sport of financial speculation, where the 'philosopher's stone' is the knowledge of how to recognise a 'sure bet'. People will invest in the hope that a company is doing well, and in some cases they may even know that the company is doing badly but because there is general gullibility and ongoing competition for shares they are still willing to buy shares while the bubble is expanding, imagining that they will be able to pull out before it bursts.

In addition to that, there was also the gain in prestige among the credulous if one claimed to have witnessed the transformation of lead into gold, or in the modern context for example to know of someone who has an infallibile nose for the market. In this case the content of the report is marvellous and liable to win admiration, such that if one associates oneself as a witness with it one gains some of the admiration oneself, not to mention envy.

Whether or not this kind of report phenomenon played a part in the early rapid spread of Islām, a system in which a tribe's new conversion to Muḥammad's party was a matter of agreeing to pay tribute to it, and which therefore would tempt seekers of lucre to 'invest' in the burgeoning coffers, is the kind of question which is so sensitive and so unlikely to provoke cool discussion that it really isn't worth asking.

In the context of partial religions it is much more likely that one's prestige will be improved by associating oneself with the party, so we might also ask whether this phenomenon was not involved in the reports of Christ's miracles by the early Christians. But again, we are not likely to get a cool-headed answer, so let us move swiftly on.

157 A detailed and fascinating account is given by Mackay (1841).

Convention

Although conventions are part of inherited traditions, I consider them here because of their strong dependence upon reporting, and more flexible nature.

> For the inauthentic there can hardly be found any other criterion than normality.[158]
>
> Simone de Beauvoir

Case: reputation and honour, the bastard children of distorted reporting

> Of slight account, almsfolk, is the loss of such things as reputation. Miserable indeed among losses is the loss if wisdom.
>
> The Buddha[159]

First of all let us note that even in terms of its own purpose, reputation or honour can become extremely harmful. To appreciate this harmfulness we can draw an analogy between the kind of behavior deemed honourable, and another material we accord a kind of honour, money.

Money – coins, notes and numbers in accounts – has no value in itself, but is by consensus assigned value. It began as promissory notes for services and as rare substances like gold exchanged for them. Like any symbol, the intentions accorded it can change drastically. For example, when everyone suddenly doubts its value, it is thereby devalued. Like any symbol, because of our psychological tendency to believe in an independent reality outside, it can become valued in itself and the connection with the difficulty of services, for example, can be lost.[160] This means in time the systems of exchange using it become naturally less and less fair. Consensus about such unfair exchange systems can only occur because money has come to be valued in itself, and therefore can be valued differently by different people according to their habituation. The poor, victims of the unfairness, join this consensus because they become habituated to the devaluation of their own services and consequently come to value a unit of money more than the rich. The rich join the consensus because of habituation and

---

158 (Beauvoir, 1949)

159 From *the Gradual Discourses* i, 8 roughly after Woodward (Hare & Woodward, 1932/2006).

160 These properties of symbols we explore in more depth later: see 'Not by thinking things through'.

because they are the beneficiaries of the unfairness. What money was supposed to mean, the difficulty of services, suspended in agreement such that exchange of services over vast distances and times could take place, is lost, and replaced inexorably by habitual valuation, which is under all sorts of influences and therefore easily manipulable. The social consequences of this psychological foible are momentous[161] and, of course, the stuff of countless socialist tracts: a miserable majority whose services are consistently undervalued and a rich minority who rule them and whose services, if there are any, are grossly overvalued. So much for capitalism: I mention it by way of introduction.

The same has happened with respectability, and for the same reasons. Certain personal qualities are originally valued for their benefit (bene- good, -fit deed). They are valued as a consensus by those groups forming a consensus. They are honoured (honour, related to the Greek homo, and the Sanskrit nṛ meaning 'man'), they are considered virtue (virtue, related to virile, and the Sanskrit vīrya, meaning 'manliness'). In many languages words for what is respectable relate to being select, for example Arabic's khayr, good, related to choice, and faḍīla, virtue, related to preference. Because these are qualities recognised in others among the group, they must *show*, that is, they must be public acts. The acts are originally related directly to their benefit, and gain a kind of value, respectability. However by an exactly analogous process to the capitalist drift of money towards being a value in itself, there is a capitalist drift of respectability towards being a value in itself, with the same unfairness – that is, a dissociation from the original correspondence to benefit. Respectability becomes a kind of currency with different importance to different carriers of it. And all of the dire consequences of capitalism, social and psychological, which we would expect to find in the capitalism of respectability if this analogy were to hold, we do indeed find. Like money, respectability in terms of acts comes to be valued in itself rather than as a means, and thus let loose its distribution in society becomes unfair, favouring some and victimising others.

First of all we can consider people as carriers of respectability. Have they retained respectability in exact proportion to the benefit of their acts, or has there been a skew, as in the skew in money distribution leaving the poor and generating the rich?

It is clear that in many societies (who usually describe themselves as 'traditional' – a sign of a long period of drift) respectability has accumulated with

161 One wonders whether this fact might have been behind the Buddha's injunction that members of the ascetic community *must not touch* money.

the males and deserted the females, which is the same as saying that for women small changes in respectability have become far more important than they would be to men. This is a general rule. The women's 'good deeds' are undervalued and the men's grossly over-valued. This situation benefits the men, who maintain the disparity in various ways, including propaganda, such as promoting the idea that the lower value of women's good deeds is a reflection of a natural law of some kind, inescapable. In short, the women are subjugated by the men. In such societies of course one finds fewer female teachers in religion than men, to an infamous degree in Islāmic and Christian societies where women are completely excluded from leadership.

Another example of disparity of respectability among people irrespective of their good deeds occurs when one group invades another and there is mixing. Respectability naturally accrues to the party which comes out on top. If there were no difference in status between the two groups on mixing, then respectability would not skew like this, but the greater the status difference, the stronger the skew in goodness-independent respectability. This phenomena is startling in the historical phenomenon of Islām's expansion through the Buddhist countries of Central Asia, for example. Once the government is Islāmic, in a previously Buddhist country, respectability naturally deserts typically Buddhist behaviour including that, such as 'the great caring' (Sanskrit mahākaruṇa) for living non-human beings, which is not part of Islāmic ethics, and accrues to Islāmic behaviour including that, such as defending religion by force, which is not part of Buddhist ethics (or rather forbidden by them). It must be remembered that this transfer of respectability happens naturally by consensus and can only happen thus because respectability has become valued in itself, independent of whether any act is really considered beneficial. Islām is well construed to promote this skewing of respectability towards itself thanks to the ethos enunciated in Allāh's command to the Muslims over their relations to subjected infidels in the Qur'ān:

> Fight them… even if they are practitioners of the Book (of God), until they pay the infidel-tax by hand *and are submissive.*[162]

We can see that it is not just among people that there can develop a skew in the distribution of goodness-independent respectability, but among acts themselves. Some acts end up getting grossly overvalued, others hideously

---

162 Qur'ān 9, 29.

undervalued, not because of any difference in real benefit but because of a skew in respectability which has developed because of the habituation of the respecters. Slitting your daughter's throat if you find she has had premarital sex is considered worthy of great respect in certain cultures, in others a species of madness, and the difference owes much more to goodness-independent respectability consensus than to grounded goodness-related justification.

Lest we feel that pointing out the capitalism of respectability is not really saying much, it is worth noting how much more interested humans are in seeming respectable than in benefiting each other. In countries where virginity is still insisted on for decent marriage, girls who have dared to have sex (or be raped) before marriage re-instate their hymens, and their mothers force them to do so, even if this entails the girls having to satisfy unscrupulous doctors' desires to penetrate them by non-surgical means before the operation, so that the respectable red spots can appear in due time on the nuptial sheets and be brandished to the wedding party in the street. And where contraception is sometimes omitted or misused (i.e. everytwhere on earth) girls have abortions, and their mothers force them to, even if there is a risk of infection and death, so that the girl does not appear before the neighbours with the tell-tale bulge.

And this is not to say that only the girls need be concerned about apperances. Aside from the honour of his women, the patriarchal male has other concerns which are rarely mentioned. The fact that a man's seclusion of his women means other men will never find out if he is impotent, un-virile, or an unsatisfying lover, cannot be uninfluential in his choice to implement this custom of secluding them. Incidentally, if one doubts the importance of this 'oldest virtue', virility, in 'the enlightened modern world' one need only consult the astronomical sales figures of the drug Viagra. Our very languages are testament to these pre-occupations, as can be seen by the nature of insults in them most effective against men. (Some languages more than others, it seems. Despite the kind of resistance to dictionaries of non-high Arabic, which we will discuss in our treatment of speakers' seeming ability, there nevertheless exist dictionaries of the 'low' Arabic, or colloquial language, of Egypt. In the most detailed one currently available there is hardly a page lacking some synonym of effeminate, passive homosexual, the unvirility and shame of which position has a distinguished history there going back to the millennia-old story of the wrestling match between Horus and Set!) If further evidence is sought one might also investigate the prevalence of violent homophobia in societies 'instructed' by 19th century psychology's eternal-seeming categories, what has come very recently to be called one's 'sexuality': obscene attacks unheard-of in societies where no such 'instruction' took place, even where homosexual acts that become public knowledge are severely punished by law. Rather than even raising awareness, never mind 'liberating' anyone, such instruction has turned what might before have been at worse a reprimand into a condemnation to an eternal-seeming category, which must then be counter-balanced by hysterical acts of 'pride'. The distinguished identities support social segregation with the inevitable consequence of unnatural overheated stereotypical behaviour on all sides. Part of the reason these societies' rigid division of the populace into sexual categories continues unabated is that the very same societies thus 'instructed' by psychology tend to skew respectability towards superficial but noisy acceptance of such categories. ('One of my best friends is…') As for the need to appear virile we are considering, we can see that the gay-straight dichotomy is much talked of and referred to and disputed, and all this strengthens it and makes it more imposing. The combination of the publicisation of the issue (outing oneself or others) and the over-strengthened dichotomy mean tendencies in either direction when noticed caused exaggerated and extremely polarised responses. Cultures (such as in North Africa until recently) in which the dichotomy was vague and the issue private did not suffer from such crimes as are familiar in dichotomised societies, such as one man smashing the head in of another who has just fellated him, or murder because of a suggestive comment. However the incidence of homophobic crime is now increasing in those areas, thanks to their inheritance of this categorical culture.

Awareness of the variance of respectability-skew between cultures gives us a way of understanding otherwise bizarre culture clashes. Consider this scene: A liberal, equal, fraternal European enters a stationer's in a Muslim country to use the photocopier in the back. The serving girl, a Muslim, is praying nearby behind a row of shelves. Nevertheless he enters, because he is in a hurry, and does the copies. The next time he comes to the shop the manager accosts him. The girl has complained that the foreigner came in while she was praying. The foreigner cannot understand. What is actually happening unbeknown to him is that the girl needs to regain her respectability, which was compromised because segregation of the sexes and frustration-driven sexualisation and therefore moral protection of actions involving bending over has accrued such a skewed share of respectability in her society that deeds which otherwise would not have even been noticed, such as doing your photocopying near a praying girl, have become nigh-criminal. For the manager this complaint of hers means in turn that he has lost his respectability by failing to defend her, again because the deed of a man defending a woman's honour has accrued such a skewed share of respectability that deeds which otherwise would not have been questioned and indeed might have been commended, such as letting a woman defend herself, have become nigh-criminal too. So the manager makes a great show, noisy enough for people in neighbouring shops to hear, of telling the ignorant foreigner that such intrusion is disgraceful and unacceptable. The foreigner is amazed at the fuss, indignant at the chastisement, which he interprets as a kind of racist religious fundamentalism or insanity, and leaves.[163]

Once let loose from the requirement to benefit, by being valued in itself, respectability can accrue to highly unbeneficial acts. We shall see in our discussion of public morality that this dissociability of respectability from benefit can lead to startling disparity between the publicly professed morality and the actually occurring morality, a disparity which is greatly advantageous to controlling powers thanks to its exploitability. So we can see that those who wish to gain power would do well to promote this dissociation.

By what means is this dissociation encouraged? To discover this we need only look at the phenomenon of celebrity. As the saying goes, you are famous because you are famous: people admire the people whom they hear to be admired. The importance of communication between potential admirers in this situation is important. Conversely we can look at the infamous: serial killers for example. You are a pariah because you are a pariah: people despise the people whom they hear to be despised. In both cases can we but admit that the praise or the blame communicated to us is the principal if not entire reason for our choice? The disparity between respectability and benefit is exacerbated by a culture of praising and blaming.

Praise shows one's allegiance to, and causes people to desire, its object. It brings that object into greater public existence, and people long for their own greater existence by being associated or identified with it, so they join in with the praises. The converse of course applies for blame, *mutatis mutandis*.

Both Church Christianity and Islām suffer from thorough dissociation of the respectable from the beneficial, and this is largely due to their extraordinary insistence on the practice of public praise of the virtuous and blame of the vicious (the former faith riding slipshod over Jesus' rebellion in this). Later in the discussion of sacredness we will turn to the dissociation between benefit and respectability in the issue of the reputation of the Islāmic prophet Muḥammad, whose name even means 'the Praised'. In Islām another good example is the

---

163 I give this incident as an example just because it happened to a friend of mine recently.

explicit divergence of 'purity' (Arabic ṭahāra) from hygiene – a divergence tangible in the Islāmic law that penetrative sex with a corpse does not lose a man his purity but sex with a woman requires a full body bath – a divergence which is (by the natural process we have discussed) a necessity, and made subsequently into a virtue by entire libraries of scholasticism.

To put it another way, because human beings are master copiers, especially when developing, they copy the valuations they see others making. This leaves their reality open to dangers which otherwise would not be possible. In a society of copiers, the value of anything and everything is dependent upon collective buying into a grand illusion. This is perhaps why the Buddha begins his critique with three manifestations of such grand-scale copying.

Thanks to the sharp restraints on the valuation of money by competition and forceful government regulation, the consensus on exchange systems involving money within society is almost total, so the illusion of money's having a value in itself is exceptionally strong. The stronger the illusion, the more liable those victimised by it are to conform despite their suffering. Because the valuation of money is so precise, the illusion is very strong, and so the poor dejectedly accept a reprehensible undervaluation of their services: despite being precise, money is inaccurate because it measures so unfairly. This reaches infamy in the near-famine conditions which result when this undervaluation makes it impossible for the poor to buy sustenance.

Beauty is different. If everyone agreed on what was pleasing to the senses, then beauty would be like money. However here the consensus is much weaker and so beauty is much more controversial, much less precise. Art, for example, becomes beautiful only within certain elites who maintain a consensus on it, whereas the rest of the population often deride or at least ignore it. However, because increasing attention on an object can make the senses more receptive to being pleased by it, the beauty one accords a work of art correlates closely to the pleasure, the benefit, it brings, so beauty is more accurate than money. Accuracy, however, acts against consensus, so there is no equivalent acceptance of unfairness.

Unfortunately, the result of public praise and blame in religious traditions is more like money than like beauty. The distribution of respectability across deeds and people come from set texts so (unless there is variance about the texts) respectability is extremely precise. This leads to massive consensus, a conformity which makes the illusion quite overwhelming, as if there can be no other possible system of respectability. Public praising and blaming can lead as we have described thanks to copying tendencies to extreme inaccuracy, that is to say the agreed-on distribution of respectability may bear very little relation to what is beneficial and harmful. But because the illusion is so powerful, those kinds of acts and those people who are actually treated with gross unfairness are not recognised as such, and unfairness reaches dreadful intensity.

It is generally recognised that monetary capitalism needs controls in order to protect at least some of its most wronged victims. Do we need to add that analogous controls on these religions' capitalism of respectability are a requirement which is not just overdue but in fact an emergency?

Not by what scriptures impart, ma piṭakasampadānena

Meaning

Piṭaka is the word used in a technical sense among Buddhists to refer to their own scriptures, the so-called Three Piṭaka of discipline, discourse and higher teaching; but the word actually means 'box' or 'basket': the origin of the technical sense seems to be that scriptures were collected and stored in such boxes, but the odd thing is that scholars from outside Buddhist traditions and those within them agree that there were no written scriptures in Buddhism until the 2200 years ago. Longchen Rabjam wrote 650 years ago:

> Bsdus-ba dang-po ni dgra-bcom-pa rnams mnyam-par gzhag-pa-la yid-kyis bsdus te bstan-la; gnyis-pa ni ngag-tu brjod-pas bstan zhing; tha-ma ni ngag-tu brjod-pa rnams-glegs-bam-la bris te bsdus-pao;[164]

> At the First Council the teachings were collected mentally within the meditative equipoise of the saints; and as for the Second, the teaching was by means of verbal expression; for the Last the collection was by writing as books what was verbally expressed.

He says the Third (and 'Last') Council took place under King Kaniska's sponsorship in Kashmir almost four hundred years after the Buddha's death. So either the word 'box' was used at the time of the discourse, in which case it would appear to refer to other traditions' texts, unless it was used metaphorically for oral traditions (unlikely since, as in this discourse, they seem to be referred to in a different way); or the original discourse did not include reference to written scriptures, but this reference was added in later recensions.

Whatever its provenance, the connotation is writings of such importance that they should be kept. At first I thought we could get the point quite well by translating it is 'bookshelves', but then it occurred to me that the kind of stuff nowadays kept on them probably doesn't deserve keeping. So a better way to get at the meaning is through the term 'canonical texts'. Sampadāna (in Sanskrit sampradāna) means giving over, handing down in a tradition, imparting.

164 (kLong-chen-pa, p. 650)

Examples

As well as the obvious examples of the scriptures of the religions, we can add: works by illustrious thinkers who through a modern version of seeming prophecy win 'followers' such as Freud, Marx, Hegel, Einstein; the works of artists around whom cults have developed such as Wagner's operas, the *Dune* novels of Frank Herbert, Tolkien's opus, etc.; and the literature of academia of varying hues.

Irrelevancy as sources of certainty

At the risk of wearying the reader I will again emphasise that the point is not that these works are irrelevant to any purpose. The Bible is not irrelevant to the priest called on to give a sermon tomorrow, and Frank Herbert's novels are not irrelevant to people who like computers and are looking for religion in space and the future. Einstein's equations were not irrelevant to destroying large numbers of Japanese very quickly.

The point is that the fact that knowledge originates in a particular canon cannot *in itself* guarantee the truthfulness of that knowledge. There are various ways that scriptures and canonical texts deceive us into believing them to be better as sources of certainty than they are.

First order disqualifications

Authority accordance

The principal danger about scriptures and canons is that they are considered exclusively as authorities. Since the same communities who confer exclusive authority to their canon or scriptures invariably also confer authority to particular persons, I shall defer consideration of the general authority-conferral until the Buddha's treatment of experts, and for now deal with dangers special to fixed verbal authorities.

Authority accordance to dialect

It perhaps goes without saying that the canon or scripture must be recognisable as such by the community that considers it to be one. More often than not the characteristic mark of any particular canon or scripture is *a way of speaking.*

In the massive 'creator-god' religions (Christianity, Islām and Vedic Brahmanical religion), for whom tradition itself is authority because of an eternal deity and a prior revelation, this is done by using the style of language in which the revelation is considered to have been made, which before long in natural conditions of language evolution comes to seem antiquated even to those people whose mother tongue is technically still that language.

Because of the relatively few people who now speak Hebrew, Aramaic and Greek, this reverence of the original language is not as widespread in Christianity as it is in Islām and Vedic Brahmanism. Among Arabic-speaking Muslims the use of the classical language, now so dizzyingly more spectacular and tremendous than their colloquial languages, is extremely common in religious discussions, indeed unavoidable (due to the scriptures being in it and their translation into colloquial languages forbidden despite the fact that the classical language is almost incomprehensible to many and requires explanation in sermons). Whilst Islām is often vaunted as a religion without priests, those who are more able to mimic the style of, or cite, scripture inevitably gain respect independent of what they are actually saying: the classical language confers immense authority. The importance in social control is also clear in the history of India and its surrounding countries, where local languages' and dialects' authority was undermined by the kudos of the so-called 'well-formed' (saṁskṛta) language of the élite. This was exacerbated in Brahmanical Hinduism at least for part of its history by the prohibition of the recitation of the sacred texts in that language except for the élite class, the Brahmins.

Once translations of the revelation are made into other languages, the same tendency to respect the style of speaking exemplified by those translations can be observed. It is not just because of the gradual divergence of the naturally evolving living languages from that style, but frequently also because the translators are considered to have been themselves inspired, and thus the language style used in their translations to be particularly sacred and beautiful.

For example, among English-speaking Christians, the archaic language of the King James Authorised Version has an often electrifying effect missing in more 'approachable', 'youth-friendly' translations, and its prestige is so evident in English that the style is appropriated until today by any religious writers or speakers wishing to convey a sense of divine authority, even by New Age Pagans. In German it is undeniably the monolithic style of the Lutheran version, against which until today what we might call tremendous prose styles (such as Thomas Mann's) are judged.

The conscious use of styles of language matching the revered styles is a method in rhetoric called '*aureation*' or 'gilding'. It establishes the dominance of the speaker over those who are not so familiar with the classical language or texts. It need not even refer to a canon or scripture: French was the language to impress people with for most of Europe in recent centuries, and one might even say American slang is coming to play a similar role for a much broader section of society there today.

The important point for us here is that the style of speaking, no matter how similar to the canonical or scriptural style, has no bearing on the truth of what is being said. (Unless one takes the rather extreme view that the language is so holy it is impossible to express an untruth in it – and a surprising number of people do.) So to consider that aureation improves authority is fallacious. *And the same point applies to the canon and scriptures themselves.*

The potency of aureation should not be underestimated: it can quite overpower reason. Once in Libya, whose colloquial language pronounces Arabic sounds differently to Egypt's (and where there is a commonly encountered sense of Egypt's inferiority to Libya), an intelligent Libyan student of mine believed he had established the precedence of the Libyan pronunciation of a particular letter over the Egyptian *by quoting a passage containing that letter from the Qur'ān* (in Libyan pronunciation) as if the authority of the text somehow rubbed off on how Libyans pronounced it. It did not occur to him that the Egyptians (or indeed the companions of their religion's messenger in his time) would say it in their own way, and that the authority of the text was entirely independent of the authority of the colloquial languages' various pronunciations of it.[165] So powerful was the aureational effect of the Qur'ānic word. And the Libyans around him were convinced by him too until I pointed out the logical mistake.

The language of the scripture is surrounded by a welter of taboos which act to preserve its sacredness (remove) and thus its aureational power. Certain famous translators of the Latin Bible into 'non-sacred' languages were executed for their efforts. A few years ago riots and a seige of Al Azhar University resulted from the Egyptian culture minister's decision to allow a re-issue of a novel[166] juxtaposing Qur'ānic language and obscenity, and there ensued much discussion among thinkers there about the value or otherwise in the 'Arab' sensitivity over such taboos. More recently there has been pressure from certain Islāmic scholars to legislate against the modern slew of Arabic poets aureating their works

---

[165] It was not even a case, as it could have been (with the Arabic letter *jiim* for example), of a letter which is pronounced in Libyan in a way closer to the classical pronunciation than it is in Egyptian: it was the letter *qaaf*, pronounced in the classical language as a rear glottal contractive plosive (incidentally using the same muscles as employed in vomiting), in Egyptian as a dry glottal stop (as replaces the tt in the English dialect's 'bo''le-o'-beer') and in Libyan as *'g'*.

[166] Haydar Haydar's *Walīma li A`shāb al Bahr, Seaweed Banquet.*

with Qur'ānic language.

Aureational power is exacerbated if the scripture is associated with a myth which interprets that power as relating to not to the linguistic capabilities of the speaker or writer but instead to the power of the scripture itself. For example, in Islām the principal miracle of the Prophet is considered to be the Qur'ān itself, the language (because God's) inimitable, its beauty unsurpassed. These considerations, whether or not they would otherwise be true, certainly reinforce the power of the language to influence listeners' belief in it, now that it has been left behind by, and is therefore so distinctive in comparison to, the various branches of Arabic languages. Although this 'inspiration myth reinterpretation support' is less important for the authority of the language of most cultures' bibles because they are translated, myths of the translators having been inspired were much relied on after the embarrassing revelation that certain translations were very far from the originals' meaning in certain passages.

We will have more to say about the power of language in relation to religion and ideology at the juncture of the Buddha's consideration of fixed patterns of thought[167].

Truth claims

Another seduction scriptures and canonical texts make occurs because of their own claims to be true. The fact that it is a psychological tendency we share to be influenced irrationally by such claims in themselves is proven by the very existence of the so-called '*bare assertion fallacy*', which means to commit the logical mistake of accepting such a claim merely on the basis of the claim. The Qur'ān, after the 'Opening', begins by declaring its own credentials:

> dhālika al-kitābu lā rayba fih
>
> This book there is no uncertainty about!

The danger here is analogous to the danger of surrendering to authoritative persons, which we will look at in more detail later. It is an unfortunate fact that whether we like it or not we are more likely to accept the opinions of a source which declares itself to be certain.

There is a consequent social danger. As with an authoritative person, such claims set up a situation whereby those who accept the claim and hence the

---

167 See 'Not by thinking ideas through'.

scripture are reassured by it, whereas those who do not accept them disdain, and are irritated by, the claim, which seems so obviously specious; that is to say, such truth claims by their very nature inescapably divide people into two communities who can no longer communicate with each other rationally across the divide on the issue of the division. It is important to recognise how much more powerfully divisive this is than issues which, once having caused the division, can still be communicated about rationally across the division, such as habits of dress, diet, etc. That truth claims have this special power does not go unrecognised in the religious traditions that employ them. For example, the extremely popular and extremely clever Christian apologist C. S. Lewis' arguments depend very heavily on using the slight of hand of concealing the step across the divide of a truth claim: once inside the boundary, one can no longer recognise where one has erred – an entertainingly devious but, for many, seriously seductive, manner of reasoning which is on closer inspection a tissue of arguments which 'beg the question', i.e. what they 'prove' is part of the assumption of the question in the first place, and without it the proof does not work.[168]

Arbitrary isolation of the respectable

Due to the assumption of the divine origin of her scripture, a creed-proponent will frequently be seen to feel, even when sympathetically approaching another scripture, that it is not authoritative, because (unlike her own scripture) it is 'just a person's opinion'. The inability to recognize another's similar interpretation of her own scripture reveals this to be the pot calling the kettle black. In addition, since the situation depends on selectively respecting her own scripture's origin, it is an example of what the classicists called *argumentum ad verecundiam*, meaning arguing from respect. And the dismissal of the alternative scripture, by denying the divine inspiration of its author, is an *ad hominem* dismissal – attacking the credibility of the writer. Of course since the religions inculcate selective and profound respect for certain characters who are considered sources of religious truth, they automatically lead their adherents to use these kinds of arguments, and the result is that the group who share respect for these personages are divided off from those who have respect for different personages in communication, since what seems valid justification to the former palpably isn't to the latter, and vice versa. Both parties should keep in mind that these are logical fallacies.

---

168 We consider various examples of this segregating vocabulary later.

Seduction by violence

It is regrettably the nature of scriptures that, once their language is left behind, i.e. 'consecrated', their interpreters invariably become associated with the violent authorities, the rulers and military, rather than being merely 'authorities for truth'. The principal reason for this comes from the interests of the rulers: recognising the potential in the scriptural language for control of the masses, they seek association with those skilled in its language. This association then influences the impact the scriptural language makes, since it is associated with the violent authorities: its acceptance, and that consequent step across the invisible line of obfuscation, the truth claim boundary line, are made more likely by fear of that violence and the desire to associate oneself with its party.

Confusion of the relevance for future generations with relevance for one's own future

The Buddha taught that the Law he discovered was something with transient usefulness for an individual, even though it should remain for the benefit of future generations: it should be grasped correctly by an individual, as though she were capturing a water snake, and it should be left behind once its purpose has been fulfilled, as one would a raft one had used to cross a river, rather than making this man's mistake:

> 'Having crossed over to the further shore, he might think, "How useful this raft has been to me! For it was in dependence on this raft that, making an effort with my hands and feet, I have crossed over to safety on the further shore. Why don't I, having hoisted it on my head or carrying it on my back, go wherever I like?" What do you think, almsfolk? Would the man, in doing that, be doing what should be done with the raft?'[169]

The same idea might well be said within other traditions to apply to their own scriptures. However, in Buddhism as with the others, there is a danger that people will either fail to make use of the scriptures correctly (grasping the snake by the tail) or having used them correctly, fail to leave them behind once their utility is exhausted, out of clinging and attachment.

Islām even codifies this non-relinquishment in a series of traditional

---

169 These two similes, and the cited passage, are from *The Water Snake Simile Discourse*, the twenty-second of the Middle Length Collection.

sayings of its prophet in which it is declared that although there are many levels of Paradise, the very highest (after the single most exalted spot which he hoped for for himself) will be for the very purest souls, and their activity for eternity will be to recite, and listen to recitations of, the Qur'ān!

Second order disqualifications: carrier mechanisms

Injuctions to propagate

If a scripture contains injunctions within it to propagate it, then as soon as it is accorded authority it will start to be over-transmitted for that reason, that is, transmitted at a greater rate than would be expected to occur merely by means of its appeal through truthfulness or benefit.

For example, *The Diamond Sutra* claims repeatedly that for a person to copy, study, recite, and explain to others even one verse of it will earn them more merit than – and comparisons are made with various extraordinarily large earnings of merit.

Appeal to ruling powers

It is not just that people come to respect the scriptures more than they should out of fear of the authorities that deviously employ them, but also that the scriptures tend to be promoted by the authorities if they are believed to bring benefit to them, whatever that benefit might be. And the belief in benefit is often much more powerful, if much more mysterious, than the mere association with the aureation of the language: for many scriptures advertise their own power to aid the rulers in their conquests.

Whilst this is pretty notorious in the case of the Qur'ān or the Bible, which have both of course been carried into battle countless times in the bloody history of their advocates, often on the end of spears, it will perhaps be surprising to some of my readers to know that some Buddhist scriptures employ this mechanism.

Case: the Discourse of Golden Light

The Discourse of Golden Light, a large, beautiful, literary scripture of the universal career, devotes its seventh chapter to an assurance by the so-called 'four great kings', mythological guardians of the Law, each in charge of one of the cardinal directions, that they will aid any ruler who listens to and worships the discourse. Any invading foreign king will face a battle and be turned back, but that is not all:

> There will be conflicts between the regions. There will be fierce troubles for the other king. There will be planetary afflictions and sicknesses in his territory. Hundreds of different disturbances will break out in the land. […] We, the four great kings, along with our armies, retinues and numerous hundreds of thousands of yakshas will make our bodies invisible and go there. Even before it enters the land, we will turn back this foreign army in that very spot. We will create hundreds of thousands of difficult situations for him and cause obstacles. Thus that foreign army of the hostile king will not be able to enter this land, much less cause destruction to it.

The chapter goes on to explain how the text should be worshipped by such a ruler desirous of protection. Then the four 'guardians' even warn what will happen if the text of the discourse is present in a ruler's kingdom but not worshipped by him and the Buddhist community not revered by him:

> We four great kings […] will neglect the land. […] There will be fierce disputes among kings. All living beings in that land will become quarrelsome, accusatory and contentious. They will be divided and ruined. The land will experience various illnesses and unfavourable planets. Comets will fall from various directions. […] There will be earthquakes. Gale-force winds will blow in the land. There will be torrential rainfall. There will be desolate famine in the land. Rival armies will crush the land…

And so on. What we are interested in here is not whether these claims are possible or true, but whether anyone might have believed them to be. For if they did, then they would have promulgated the scriptures.

Case: Nichiren

This was certainly the case in Japan under the hellfire and brimstone prophecies of the charismatic figure Nichiren, who popularised *The White Lotus Discourse of the Sublime Law* there by means of a series of agitations beginning with a treatise written to convince the Japanese that their political and economic woes were the result of not reciting and worshipping that scripture:

> Famine and epidemics rage more fiercely than ever, beggars are everywhere in sight, and scenes of death fill our eyes. Corpses pile up in

> mounds like observation platforms, dead bodies lie side by side like planks on a bridge. [...] What is wrong? What error has been committed?

He goes on to cite passages from four discourses, including the *Golden Light* passage we have seen, and identifies the problem:

> The passages I have quoted from these four discourses are perfectly clear – what person in ten thousand could possibly doubt their meaning? And yet the blind and the deluded recklessly trust to heretical doctrines and fail to recognize the correct teachings. Therefore, throughout the empire these days people are inclined to turn away from the Buddhas and the discourses and no longer endeavor to protect them. Because of this, the benevolent deities and sages abandon the nation and leave their accustomed places. As a result, demons and followers of heretical doctrines create disaster and inflict calamity upon the populace. [...] When we look at the world in the light of these passages of scripture, we see that the situation is just as they describe it. If we do not admonish the evil priests, how can we hope to do good?[170]

He goes on to vilify in particular Honen and the Pure Land School which had become popular, and by a brief historical survey demonstrates that their practices though popular could not very well have protected their ruler patrons in view of their demise. Nichiren produces an impressive number of scriptural justifications for killing, in particular the sinless killing of those 'utterly wishful-thinking ones' (icchāntika) whose desires mean they never turn to the path of liberation, then turns to the trend of the day to convert practices related to *The Lotus Discourse* and other discourses to practices relating to the Pure Land School whose scriptures he argues revile the other discourses, and whose adherents he ominously calls 'utterly wishful-thinking'. He concludes with dire predictions from the discourses if something is not done.

The Lotus Discourse became one of the most popular of all scriptures in the Far East. What concerns us here is that the kind of situation Nichiren set up or which some of the discourses themselves aim to set up causes them to influence their listeners in their favour independent of whether they are true or beneficial.

---

170 (Nichiren, 1260)

Not by reason of philosophy, ma takkahetu

Meaning

This phrase refers to surmise or logical conjecture; literally a reason (hetu) derived from philosophical speculation (takka, in Sanskrit tarka). Several Pali dictionaries report that it carries a strong sense of doubt, whereas the Sanskrit equivalent lacks this strong connotation. This probably reflects the Pali texts' culture's Buddhist, and therefore concept-contextualising, nature. If we do not want to represent the Buddha as questioning a subject already indefensible, which would surely have been a waste of time, we can assume at his time the word did not obviously imply doubt. The Sanskrit tarka provided Latinate languages with words such as intricate, and trick, and the related word tarku, meaning a spinning bobbin, is a distant ancestor of Latinate torque, torture, and contorsion.

Examples

Speculative philosophy; theology: free will and sin, divine attributes such as wrath and mercy, etc.

Irrelevancy as a source of certainty

First order disqualification: fallacious reasoning

Reasoning has a rather impressive reputation, perhaps more impressive than its due. In particular in post-Christian cultures tracing their traditions of thought back to Greece, there is a great kudos attached to complex systems of metaphysics in certain classes of society. Even individuals of those societies who would not dream of approaching monolithic works of involved thought, such works still command respect if not awe. It is supposed that such awesomeness is deserved because of their 'intellectual strength', which generally means that the thinker has succeeded in linking a large number of ideas into a coherent and reasonable system.

The problem is that there are many ways seemingly watertight reasoning can lead astray, in the matter of deciding what is true and beneficial. We will consider fallacious *impressions* of truth not necessarily related to reasoning (but which can certainly influence it) later in the exposition of intuition. Here we begin with a cursory examination of strategies used consciously in learnt rhetoric to make weak arguments seem stronger, together with classic fallacies which, consciously or unconsciously, can make a false argument seem correct.

Ad hominem discrepancies

As we mentioned in our discussion of canons and scripture, it is a staple of communication with adherents to a particular ideological or religious authority that they will disparage the authors of alternative information, thus deploying the appeal to ethics we mentioned Aristotle put on a par with logic. This might be a valid criticism of the reliability of the source, but such a disparagement can easily seem more than it is. The point here is to be sensitive to any discrepancy between the ideaology-defender's criticism of such other authors and the criticism (or lack of it) of their own preferred authority. The reason behind pointing out the discrepancy is not a wicked desire to insult that authority, but because it is often the case that the adherent is simply not aware of this discrepancy until it is pointed out.

For example, someone who accepts the final authority of a particular text-encoded paradigm in academia may dismiss contradictory information as being 'just opinion' and even create an atmosphere of taboo around it. It should be recognised that this is effectively an accusation that the author of the alternative information is less informed than the authors of their preferred texts. Taboo, being irrational, should be highlighted as such. Ad hominem dismissals should be examined for their criteria, and the same criteria applied fairly. This will require defence of non-taboo, accepted authorities. It is not expected that the claimants of their own authorities' superiority would ordinarily consider such a defence necessary, and this is the discrepancy which should be pointed out.

Anacoenosis

The tendency is employed in various kinds of rhetorical persuasion. Consider a person defending their position on some issue. As a way of garnering confidence and intimidating the challenger, the defender asks a question of the audience listening to the debate, supposedly as impartial bystanders but usually when it is well known how they will respond to the question. This is a kind of combination of a rhetorical question and a threat spoken from safety in numbers, the authority of power. This was a common tactic in classical European rhetoric, it seems, in the political forum as it were, and the Greeks called it *anacoenosis*.

Interloper effect

The audience need not be large. A point can sometimes be effectively dismissed simply by appealing to a single third party. The agreement of the appealer and the third party is enough, often, to close the argument. Cognitive science has demonstrated that we have a tendency to acquiesce to and be persuaded by this strategy, which goes by the technical name of the '*interloper effect*'. It is this psychological tendency which allows anacoenosis to work.

Ridicule

Another way to involve an audience, real or imagined, is to make the 'appeal to ridicule', taking the challenger's point and, crucially, exaggerating it (otherwise it would not be a fallacy but a valid *reductio ad absurdum*), and then showing the counter-intuitive consequences of this belief. Such rhetorical devices appear, for example, in the famous charge, made by proponents of 'creation by a god', upon biologists, that accepting evolution by natural selection means accepting that a hurricane blowing through a junk yard could assemble a jumbo jet by accident. More generally, and much more commonly, one hears proponents of the creation myth ask how 'all of this' could have come by chance.

Apostrophe

And what better 'audience' to appeal to when defending 'God' than 'God'? Here the challenger's confidence is assailed by an appeal to the deity for the latter's mercy or forgiveness given what is happening in the conversation or what is being referred to (such as heretical doctrines or even unbelief in the deity). Muslims are commonly taught to do this in general in times of difficulty. It is the *apostrophe* of the Greeks.

Foregone conclusion

Another effective tactic in rhetoric is to talk as though one's own position has already been proven as true, although it has not, and the other's as false, the so-called *foregone conclusion*. Some examples of this are so sly as to be easy to miss, such as entries in an English-Arabic dictionary published by an Islāmic house which includes, for example, an entry for 'Brahmanism', which is defined as 'a religion of ancient [sic] India.'

The teleological contents of certain religion's creeds allows a colourful variant of foregone-conclusion rhetoric, namely, to contextualise the opponent within that teleology (which the opponent does not accept) and deprecatingly refer to that opponent's foregone conclusion within it. Muslims will as a last resort frequently predict with confidence challengers' eventual conversion to Islām, although this may be more to do with Arab etiquette, which teaches flattery as a virtue, than to a genuine belief in the challenger's potential to embrace 'the truth'.

Plurium interrogationum

'Does God exist?' might seem like an impeccable question. But consider the options for a direct answer: God (the referent of this word 'God') exists, or God (the referent of this word) does not exist. The second one, because it has a more or less explicit declaration that the word has a referent, but that one believes that it 'does not exist', is, quite independent of reality, shakier on the ears, since it is, because of the awkwardness of language, self-contradictory.

Asking a single man, 'Do you still beat your wife?' is the classic example of the fallacy of *plurium interrogationum*: the most urgent task for the addressee is to reply to the question, but as well as the issue of beating 'continuing', there are two other issues – the existence of the wife and the previous beating – which because unestablished, are effectively also questions, i.e. there are, simultaneously presented, as *many questions* – which is the meaning of the Latin name for the fallacy. Obviously there is no challenge logically, because the addressee can patiently explain that he does not have a wife, and that therefore even the possibility that he beat her before is out of the question, never mind that he still might. However, under *rhetorical attack*, as the attacker well knows, the laboriousness of such an explanation simply does not wash: the interrogator can, for example, interrupt it as though its length were itself evidence of its insufficiency, and thus ensure that the relative complexity of the justification cannot unfold enough to succeed.

And it is the rhetorical power, though much less, in the religious metaphysical questions which make them so 'useful'. It is an old trick – 'with or against' – and meanwhile neutrality, though it might be wiser, is discounted. If you are not a theist you are an *a*theist – literally a 'without God person' – and it is not allowed in this rather childish game to be a 'God'-understanding and therefore 'God'-contextualising person. Again, in the almost unremittingly rhetorical language of the Qur'ān, if you are not one who accepts to submit to Allāh then you are one who *refuses* to submit to Allāh: again, it is not allowed in the game to claim to be someone else, for example someone who understands that there is nothing comprehensible referred to by the word 'Allāh' and that therefore the question of submission to it or not is like a flower growing in the sky. Children prefer games to sermons, and politics operates on the lowest common denominator's, and therefore the childish, level – which is why such *plurium interrogationum* have fuelled wildfire spreads of doctrines over the Earth, while the wise weep.

Because so much doctrine, religious and ideological, depends on metaphysics, these systems are a fertile field for this kind of rhetoric, as we shall see later when we consider the valuation of ideas in themselves as reality.

False dilemma

It is commonly found, both in literature and street-level conversation, that the complexities of a situation are caricatured for effect. The opponent can be forced into a situation where her view, though subtle, must bc crudely squeezed into one of a restricted set of extremes, the closest of which to her view is unacceptable to both parties. Such conjured quandaries are the staple of the rearguard apologists.

Case: violence or weak passivity

'If your sister were raped in front of you, would you turn your other sister over to the rapist?' was a classic, and much-recurring, attack used by Muslims against the Christian doctrine of turning the other cheek. Unless an independent argument establishes that there are only two alternatives, and that rejecting the defender's view therefore makes the alternative necessary, this is a false dilemma.

Argumentum ad metum

The logical fallacy which is called in Latin, *argumentum ad metum*, meaning 'argument from terror', refers to the fact that just because something is less frightening doesn't make it true.

The argument from terror occurs in such obviously rhetorical questions as, 'Are there then no universal truths? Are we helpless? Is this all meaningless and random?' The alternative (in this further example of a false dilemma) is generally presented as the only one, and to belong of course to the creed of the speaker.

Argumentum ad baculum

In Latin reference is also made to *argumentum ad baculum* or 'argument from the stick', which applies to any dismissal of a view based on a threat to those who might hold it – always a logical fallacy in terms of establishing truth, and if there is no independent argument showing that the stick is inevitable a logical fallacy in terms of escaping the stick too. We can add the 'argument from the carrot' which is its natural partner.

For example, many a religious discussion ends with, 'Well at least I am not going to hell.' Certain scriptures are largely composed of carrots awarded to the believers. More subtly, believers may say, 'Do you think I have a choice in what I believe?' It takes some intelligence on the believers' part to realize that these are fallacious arguments.

Related is the 'appeal to law' – that a doctrine is in harmony with the law of the land, and its rejection punishable by prison or whatever, does not make it more reasonable, even if it is reasonable to follow it publicly. Here the sensitivity being encouraged is that required to distinguish what is true and beneficial in a deep sense on the one hand and what is pragmatic on the other. Such a sensitivity does not necessarily require one to act against the law in cases where what is beneficial and true is found to conflict with it, but at least to recognise that what is lawful is not beneficial or true in those cases. The appeal to law is clearly likely to be commoner in societies where power authorities have more impunity and the public-private ethical divide wider, a point we will develop in our discussion of public morality.

Circumstantial evidence for illegitimacy: complex reasoning as a carrier mechanism

A particular kind of philosophising can be identified as having been deployed specifically to defend particular traditions, scriptures, textual canons, fallacious teachings, dubious inferences, symbols, authorities or teachers – i.e. to defend the *other* sources of knowledge which the Buddha points out as being erroneously taken as sources of certainty. Insofar as this applies to religious beliefs it is known as 'apology' but it applies much more widely. Many of the points we could make here falls as well into our individual considerations of these other knowledge sources. Here we merely draw attention to ways of reasoning which might not immediately be recognised as acting as a carrier mechanism.

Since some of the reasonings, and what they defend, here considered are beliefs deeply cherished by some, it may seem that the discussion of them is flippant. The intention is rather integrity than flippancy: the 'fact' that 'God is Love' should not dissuade us from recognising specious reasoning which might have been deployed to propagate the knowledge or the acceptance of that 'fact'. When the supporting reasoning itself is a cherished belief, we can at least recognise that, *even if that way of reasoning were not part of our cherished beliefs*, it would still act as a carrier mechanism.

The presence of carrier mechanisms, we note again, is circumstantial but not conclusive evidence for the supported doctrines not being able to survive without them, in turn evidence that they are neither true nor profitable. But we stress that it is circumstantial evidence only. If it were taken as conclusive evidence this would be an example of the fallacious 'argument from fallacy' – taking a conclusion as fallacious because one type of reasoning which supports it is fallacious.

Handmaids of faith

In the general Christian tradition, philosophy has been very aptly called the handmaid of faith. It was a recommendation, but from the viewpoint of 'more certain' traditions like orthodox Islām and Christian fideism (the assertion that faith should not need support by reason) it looks like a condemnation – indicating first of all that the faith being thus administered to must be weak, and second of all that the philosophy is being used deceitfully since it is knowingly supporting a weak faith. So Islām and some strains of Christianity (as exemplified by Kierkegaard and his 'leap to faith') have disdained philosophy in such a role. In the history if Islām we can see that so long as the Arabian philosophers kept to science and interpreting the Greeks they were respected; when they ventured into theology they were condemned as heretics and rejectors of faith.

Among the diverse methods to serve (or save) faith that litter philosophy, the most effective have been mind-bending tricks, so in this section which analyses them we should be ready to have our minds bent somewhat, and a little more perhaps than would be necessary for us to accept the arguments. It is no accident that the Arabic word for creed, `aqīda, derives from the same root as 'to knot' (`aqada), 'to get intricate' (ta`aqqada) and 'to be inhibited' (in`aqada).[171] Relaxation, simplicity and uninhibitedness are not characteristics of these nevertheless much-prized handmaids. As we examine some of them I stress that I am interested in showing how they act as carrier mechanisms *independent of their truthfulness or otherwise*: if some or all of them are true, or beneficial, it does not alter the fact that they promote the transmission of themselves and any associated doctrines, potentially at the expense of rivals which were truer or more profitable.

---

171 Cf. the etymology of the Sanskrit/Pali terms at the head of this chapter.

Case: sin

Bertrand Russell once jibed:

> The sense of sin [...] came to the Jews as a means of reconciling self-importance with outward defeat.[172]

Whether or not it is true that this is *why* the sense of sin came to this group who so boldly declared themselves chosen by 'an omnipotent deity', it is undeniable that sin does indeed reconcile such a group with circumstances that would otherwise imply a rather embarrassing outward 'failure of the deity'.

There is bound to be a certain resistance among believers in such a deity to examining the system of belief from this angle, because it seems to be the reverse of what belief should be: to consider such an idea – that, if the doctrine of sin had somehow not been developed, then earlier generations would have blamed their omnipotent deity entirely for any unlucky circumstances, broken their covenant with that useless deity and ceased to transmit the notion of the benefit of belief in that deity to their children – may be possible, they will say, but it is sinful even to consider such notions of the deity. However, I do not ask them to consider such notions of their own deity. Instead, it is enough to realise that, if there were a hypothetical and false belief in another omnipotent deity, then the doctrine of sin is the perfect handmaid for it, diligently working to pass it on even among those suffering the worst environmental and social catastrophes, because it lays the fault not with the deity but with the victims.

We can take the thought experiment further and ask ourselves what kind of *event*, when taken as the foundational story for an invented belief in this imagined omnipotent deity, would best make the connection between the supposedly omnipotent deity and the most aggrieved sufferer of catastrophes, such that even this latter, the most extremely aggrieved individual imaginable, would *still* not lose her or his faith in that imaginary deity. Well, rather than something which affects everyone together, such as an earthquake, we would choose something which is only experienced by oneself, to make it up close and personal. At the same time, even if the belief includes the idea that the deity is behind all events including natural disasters, we could do with the event which conveys the most vivid sense of the directness of the divine will's cruelty, a cruelty crueller than which no cruelty could be conceived. This can best be achieved by seeming arbitrariness – not cruelty whose avoidance would involve having to do a

---

172 See Book II of *A History of Western Philosophy* (Russell, 1946), I, 3

lot physically (such as move an entire tectonic plate) but instead a cruelty whose avoidance would have necessitated such minimal intervention by the deity that the lack of intervention seems totally and appallingly negligent. (Who would you, as a child, be more aggrieved at, your mother who fails to do her utmost to assuage all the symptoms of a chronic illness out of exhaustion, or your mother who sat by smiling and watched without warning you as you extended your hand to the heater element?)

Once we have hit on the kind of event which presents this extreme divine cruelty, we then need the other half of the task – the connection between someone aggrieved to that degree and continued hope in the deity. (Remember we are trying to make sure that even the unluckiest and most miserable person will see because of the example of this story that there is not yet reason to abandon the idea that the deity is good, such that even they will continue to spread and pass on the notion of the deity's goodness to others, including the next generation.) A crude way to make the connection would be a simple account of someone who did face such horrors and who did not lose hope. The problem there is that such an account is not likely to be believed: later generations, putting themselves in the shoes of such a sufferer, would doubt that anyone could have maintained hope in the deity under such circumstances. So it would need more support, perhaps some fabricated historical evidence; perhaps association with already revered figures, who later generations would be less likely to question. Then there might be enough to convince later generations to pass on the notion of the goodness of the deity even in extreme catastrophe. We can call this kind of event-invention the 'even arbitrary cruelty does not cause my faith to waver, lord,' strategy.

What would trump that, however, would be a story where the most extreme sufferer turned out to be the closest to the deity, most favoured by them. That would mean there would even be a positive slant on catastrophe's. However, how to make a convincing symbolic event where catastrophe is interpreted as blessing? Again, a crude way would be a story of a past example of someone who discovered, by some intimation from the deity, that this was the case. We can call this kind of event-invention the 'divine test' strategy, and it would be made all the more vivid in the minds of the gullible if there was some suitably coarse material reward from the deity to prove the divine favour in the coarsest listeners' minds.

However the true genius of psychological manipulation would take the idea of suffering as a measure of the closeness to the deity to the logical extreme, and invent a story where the deity itself manifests as a human who exeriences the omnipotent deity's most arbitrary cruelty imaginable. That would turn everything upside down, because it would suggest that the necessity of a bridge at all between circumstances of total despair and perfectly valid hope was obviated – that in fact the suffering of later generations could, through the manipulations of this story on their mind, come to be seen by them as a sign of them *being the deity themselves.* We can call this the 'you are divine' strategy.

Hackles will by now be raised in some quarters. So those ruffled should examine the logical steps of the intricacies developed in these three strategies to see just how logically they do follow from our initial aim – namely, given that we are trying to guarantee a tradition of believing in an omnipotent deity which in reality does not exist, to invent an 'Occurrence' which is to be taken as the foundational event of our made up religion, which will maximise the chances of later generations of the religion continuing to transmit it even though they have faced the most extremely awful circumstances imaginable, circumstances likely to make any reasonable person lose their faith. This Occurrence must short-circuit the perfectly natural conclusion that they would otherwise make that the deity is either not powerful enough or not kind enough to be worth a covenant with. We should scrutinise to our utmost capability each step of the development of the three strategies and ask ourselves, is this not a logical step given the (ignoble) aim?

What we have, of course, in these three strategies, are exact parallels with the central, foundational, crucial stories of Judaism, Christianity and Islām.

Elohim abandoning Job to Satan, Elohim letting Abraham (or Allāh letting Ibrahīm) go as far as to hold the knife to his son Isaac (or Isma`īl)'s throat in obedience to the divine command to sacrifice the thing he loved most, the perversely hopeful appeal by the humanised deity to the inhuman one, at the culmination of long but permitted torture based on a trivial decision by a rabble, 'Eloi, eloi, lama sabachtani? – My El, my El, why has thou forsaken me?' – these are hardly incidental elements in these religions.

The point is the same, though perhaps more startling in this case: these stories perfectly meet the requirements for a system of intricacy which would powerfully transmit the doctrines associated with an omnipotent kind deity under the most extreme conditions of apparent powerlessness and unkindness in that deity, *whether or not the doctrines are true.*

Case: the sin of unbelief in others

There might still be problems with our designer pseudoreligion, however. Imagine if we happened to live in a society which of old has held to the notion of personal dignity, the questioning of which is held traditionally to be the gravest of insults, worse than a physical attack. In this case in developing a successful transmission strategy we need to consider how insulting to such a mentality the notion of personal sin, or distance from the deity, might be. So we cast around for any other ways we can deflect the bathos of failure away from the 'deity' such that its 'omnipotence' and 'kindness' remain untarnished. Luckily, our society is not the only one on Earth, so 'casting around' brings into our nets the perfect solution – other communities. Instead of humiliating this proud race we have grown up among, we can develop a story whereby our own race is immune to such 'distance from the deity'. Catastrophes occur through the existence of these others, who invoke the wrath of 'the deity' by their impious ways. What we need, in short, is a myth of *the sin of others.*

If we restrict our appreciation of the 'last' prophet of Islām to how he appears in his earliest biographies, such as Ibn Hishām's[173], it is easy to get the impression that Muḥammad's political genius was to 'expiate humanity's sin' as it was imagined by his followers, by transferring it all by imprecation to members of the parties in opposition to his own party. We do not claim that this is an accurate representation of the prophet. But it would, if this biography indeed accurately depicts Muḥammad, be very fitting, then, that the gravest sin in Islām should be what it is, not unbelief in the deity, which can be pardoned, but the unpardonable sin which modern day China refers to as 'splittism' (in Arabic, shirk, from the verb sharika meaning to divide) – the idea that one could divide one's loyalty between the Party, declared in Muḥammad's case the party of Allāh, and in China's the party of the People, and any other.

It might be objected that in Islāmic discourse the object of this supposed splitting is supposed to be not the political unity of the party but the unity of *the deity*, but the impression one might have that this is a specious deflection of attention from the political meaning is heightened when one considers Islām's attitude to monotheistic communities worshipping a deity which is *not Allāh*, such as Krishna (Kṛṣṇa). Such a community cannot be accused of splitting the unity of the deity, being as they are 'monotheists', yet they are still accused in Islāmic discourse of 'splitting' (shirk[174]). The fact that this speciousness can elude us is

---

[173] (Ibn Hisham, c 218 h./1355 CE/1937 CE)

[174] Readers of the most popular English translations of the Qur'ān should note that this is the word (among the most numerous in the Qur'ān's vocabulary) which frequently, and very misleadingly, gets translated as 'polytheism': as I am pointing out here, the number of deities these enemy communities worship is totally irrelevant, as can be seen by reading the canonical accounts of dealings with the other religions of Arabia – the details of which (including the nature of what was worshipped) were totally ignored.

because of the fallacy of the foregone conclusion we considered earlier: the 'fact' that 'there is no deity except Allāh' will according to Islāmic belief eventually be obvious 'on the Day of Doom' and this is enough to contextualise Hare Krishnaites, for example, as splittists, even though the Muslims must appear exactly analogously to them for rejecting Krishna: the Krishnaites' by the same reasoning have a right to call the Muslims splittists. Secular analogies of this situation, for example in competing Communist groups, are of course easy to find.[175]

An extraordinary number of verses in the Qur'ān bracket justice, fidelity and piety with those who have joined Muḥammad's party (by making the declaration of faith and paying the tribute) and injustice, betrayal and abominations with those who refuse to. Even if this was a fair representation of the situation in and around Mecca in Muḥammad's time, which is surely unlikely, these verses give one the overwhelming impression that Muḥammad's party *at any time* can do no wrong and the rest no right, and unfortunately they make the same impression very frequently on the party members today.

Some will object that Muḥammad did not absolve his followers like this, and that Muslims, unfortunately it may be, can and do commit sin (and they mean the Arabic zanb or khaṭ'). But 'sin' as we have conceived of it in our transmission strategy above is not just the fault referred to in English by the countable noun (a sin) but also and more importantly the sense of being 'unworthy of the deity' and the 'distance from that deity', a very particular sense referred to by the uncountable noun (sin) – which has, I believe, a much closer parallel in Islām as kufr, a word normally translated rather wildly as 'unbelief' but which really relates to being 'covered' or 'concealing'. Our word 'Hell', as well as the words 'hull' and 'cell' all derive from a Protoindoeuropean root (kel) referring to 'covering' or 'concealing'. It is a fact that almost no Muslim alive could conceive of herself or himself being a 'coverer', kāfir, (usually translated as 'unbeliever') – the kufār, 'coverers' are the *other* in popular Islām's view. There is, to be sure, in the later texts of Islām, and in its intellectual echelons, sophisticated treatment of the possibility of kufr, 'unbelief', in the Muslim, and how to avoid it, but as can be observed in the behaviour of the vast majority of Muslims, to treat muslim/kāfir as a black or white ultimatum is just too much of a conceptual temptation. And this is not just a modern phenomenon: historically it was developed into worldwide political terms, such as dar as-salām/dar al-ḥarb (the house of

[175] Incidentally there is a respected tradition among Muslim thinkers of favourably comparing Islām and Communism.

peace/the house of war – referring respectively to Muslim and non-Muslim countries), concepts whose distortion of reality continue to plague the popular Muslim view of the world, as is evident by Muslims living in Arab countries refusing to nuance the status of France or the US despite the vast numbers of Muslims living in those countries. According to this dichotomous conceptualisation of the world, France will remain excluded from dar as-salām until its rulers are Muslims.

We have already considered the arbitrarily 'certain' Christian's recourse to the shady argument that God has graced her with certainty and denied it her rational challenger.

Now if we were, during our crazed quest to invent the most perfectly transmitted false religion ever, unlucky enough to face a situation where the people to whom me we preached it saw through it immediately and rebuffed us, what further doctrine could we invent that would assuage our sense of indignation at the rebuff and even link the message-rejecting tendency in the 'stony ground' around us to the truth of that very message? Is there such a doctrine, with such political cleverness? So that when the people ridicule the message, we the preachers can call back, 'But by ridiculing us you only confirm the message that you are ridiculing?'

Well, the Qur'ān, revealed as it was during times of battles to establish its supremacy, verbal and physical, is a veritable treasure-trove of such politically effective strategies. In the Qur'ān 'belief in Allāh' is kept available for the unbeliever, and more importantly by the believing but doubting audience of a staunch unbeliever, by the doctrine, made much more explicitly than in most Christianity (crediting Satan as it does with powers to rival God that many scholars suggest are derived from the dualism of Zoroastrianism), that even if you are in unbelief, Allāh is responsible for and 'adding' to your unbelief and even leading you into it.

> To those who 'disbelieve' (kafaru) it is the same whether or not you warn them, they do not believe. *Allāh has made* a seal over their hearts and ears; on their vision (is) a cover; for them (is) a great torment.[176]

> Those who *Allāh leads astray* therefore have no guide: he scatters them in their bound-breaching and they wander.[177]

---

176 Qur'ān 2, 6

177 Qur'ān 7, 186 and so on – there are many such verses.

Note the social application of this reinterpretation of refusing to believe Muḥammad's message: the early Muslims' indignation at rebuffs can be channelled into disdain of the rebuffers, and furthermore the rebuff itself is evidence that Allāh's will is being carried out – *for he made them that way*, as this verse describes.

Yet again we stress that merely by the natural system of social interaction, these strategies will work to spread the doctrines involved, *whether or not those doctrines are true.*

Using much the same strategy, the quasi-mythical founder of alchemy, known in the European mediaeval texts as Geber, in fact Jābir ibn Ḥayyān, apparently maintained that the philosopher's stone (which was supposed to purify metals of their foreign elements to leave behind that expensive mixture of 'metal earth' and 'red sulphur' which we know as gold) had been discovered several times, but that its secret had not been shared in the written works of those lucky philosophers, as retribution for the *incredulity* of the populace. He compared these unfortunates to children locked in a tiny room, unaware of the world outside.[178] It might have appeared to the cynical populace of those interesting times that alchemists were hoodwinking the nation, and that the philosopher's stone did not exist, but they would still have felt the sting of Geber's and others' taunt – that such mockery simply moched the mockers, and underlined the truth of what the alchemists had written.

We are by now I hope in a position to distinguish with the utmost care between, on the one hand, a salutary chastisement to those who close their minds to the *possibility* of something, such as the existence of the 'Yahweh or Allāh the Creator' or the philosopher's stone; and, on the other, the specious chastisement to those who do not, as the party line has done, affect *certainty* that this something, to the exclusion of rivals, exists.

Case: gods both reasonable and wrathful

We are also now in a position to come up with the perfect designer pseudogod itself.

People lose faith in a 'god' when it seems no longer to act according to set laws of business, so first and foremost our pseudogod must be taught to honour its contracts more than it reneges on them; and the likelihood of someone losing such transactional faith is pretty much in inverse proportion to his or her patience in the face of seeming suspension of desired rewards and punishments,

[178] (Mackay, 1852, pp. 202,3)

so if such a business-like pseudogod is qualified in its myths by *occasional but sensational acts of arbitrariness*, the ones who have lost their faith are thereby brought into the fold, as we have seen in our consideration of the three strategies of linking hopelessness to hope: indeed it can even be claimed that such wayward sheep who returned to the fold have more thoroughly than the ever-faithful sheep understood this pseudogod, in that they have not just heard and read but *lived through* the kind of strategic foundational stories we developed. Such a pseudogod is in this way seemingly inescapable: even total rejection of it still keeps the belief in it easily available. *This is salvation*, not, as is usually expressed, of the doubter by means of faith in the god, but instead of *the very notion of the pseudogod being 'god'*.

Why not make the contract ('the covenant') the absolute? Well, a totally business-like, totally reliable pseudogod would look like a servant, inferior to a genie of the lamp, and *utterly without the authority of power*. As the proverb has it,

> Mercy is not itself that oft looks so.

The necessity of power in the massive 'monotheist' systems, I hope, needs no pointing out.

On the other hand an *always* arbitrary pseudogod is going to be a highly unattractive proposition to those who would pray to it, so what we (as devisers of the perfect carrying mechanism for it) need is the slightly schizophrenic version, at times business-like and dutiful nay compassionate in answering prayers, but at times arbitrary and unpredictable, for example demanding that a man sacrifice his own son and then interceding just in time: such a pseudogod has gone to an extreme in inviting the loss of faith, but permitted the faith-losers of miserable subsequent times this endless hope that the arbitrariness, the arbitrariness that actually characterises all real life of course, will not last forever, that the intercession will come in time.

Direct confrontation of cherished beliefs never achieves anything good: usually only acrimony and destruction of trust. But we are in a situation today where acrimony and mistrust already pollute our societies: to a large extent the damage has already been done. Rather than leave these poisons to do their worst (much less add to them) our responsibility today should be to understand where the poison comes from, i.e. how such breaches can occur. It is in this spirit that this analysis is presented: it behoves believers and unbelievers (so dichotomised according to any of the popular systems) alike to consider the parallels between the cynical, transmission-maximising design of pseudoreligion and pseudogod, and the design of those systems we have inherited today.

Intricacy, set in vivid and appealling myths, is recognised as such in the traditions of course, and often celebrated – what sublimity! what beauty! what intellectually stimulating conceptual elegance! – but perhaps now, seeing its potential role in sustaining untruths and harm, we should be more careful about whether to celebrate it.

Just as concentration camp victims fall in love with their most sadistic guards because the extremity of the demonstrated cruelty enriches the value of the slightest mercy they receive to intoxicating intensity – 'Tyrants are not only feared, they are often loved.'[179] – so would stories about a pseudogod's awful cruelty rescue the authority of the pseudogod, and therefore the notion of it as a 'god', principally by means of *servile love.* The crueller the pseudogod is portrayed by the myths, the more intense the fear will be, and the more intense the servile love will be, and so the more likely the passing on, to future generations and others of the same generation, of the notion of that pseudogod as 'god', together with those myths, will be.

Going beyond the mere design of our pseudoreligion, we can extend the thought experiment further and predict what circumstances would arise on a planet which only had pseudoreligions, competing with each other, without any interference from actual 'gods', after centuries upon centuries. If the planet resembles Earth from the point of view of human life, that is to say the environment is largely favourable but suffers from occasional catastrophes, then we would expect that, although in the long term only the pseudogods combining the contractual near-reliability with schizophrenic arbitrariness will survive, in *the short term*, the dislike of the arbitrariness among humans enjoying favourable conditions, should allow the arising of pseudogods which are entirely good and without schizophrenic tantrums. However, such pseudogods will only last until there is a period of massive unpredicted catastrophe, at which point only the unpredictably schizophrenic pseudogods will survive.

What is the situation on Earth, then? Christ, especially in the minds of moderns, is entirely good or (as we might say now) 'a nice person'. But Jehovah is the epitome of wrath. There is also the Christ of the 'revelation of saint John', the warrior shedding the blood of the impious: which version of Christ is more popular in times of inter-religious war? Allāh is good to us now, but he wiped out ancient nations in myths I sing every day. Krishna, whose religion's explosion is of relatively recent times, is a playful and flirtatious flute-playing lover

---

179 (Gray, 2007, p. 281)

of his devotees: we can compare him to other manifestations of the same 'god' (Viṣṇu) which were popular earlier – they were not always so delightful. Of the many deities of the ancient Vedic scriptures, the only one to have 'survived' in popular modern worship is Indra (literally the Almighty), who displays all the fury of the annihilating storm and whose weapon could destroy universes. The disappearance of the Buddha from India a millennium ago, and his manifestation in the later fragments of that degeneration, not as a kindly spoken, circumspect sage radiating kindness, but in tantric forms called herukas embodying wrath, wearing garlands of human heads and trampling Hindu deities, should not surprise us. While short-lived gods of Earth can be cruel or nice, the long-lasting ones do seem to tend to be rather nasty. This is an uncomfortable but momentous observation.

There is yet another challenge which might stump us in our bid to invent the designer pseudogod to beat all others. What if social conditions improve, as they tend to with technological developments, and catastrophes such as brimstone volcanoes and wrathful tectonic shifts no longer happen frequently enough to sustain that servile love we were relying on from the masses?

One way would be to make sure stories of *previous* intentional catastrophes are not forgotten, by including them in what must be recited piously by the pious with pious frequency. But there is another way.

In the neighbourhood of Jerusalem, to its south-west, there was once a valley (in Hebrew, 'je') named after the son of a man named Hinnom. It was where Jerusalem used to burn its rubbish. Being on the outskirts of the city it was also where non-orthodox religious communities hung out, which is why it is associated by Biblical author Jeremiah[180] with 'child sacrifice' rites. One can imagine the effect the perpetual fires and strange religious practices would have on the imagination of the orthodox pious folk of the city. Now in the Jewish religion it was taught that the dead went to an underworld state of darkness and coldness called 'all-demanding' (sheol). However, a new religion was becoming popular, which resembled those of India and beyond in that it taught that the dead could enter terrible torment. Thus a rubbish dump in the suburbs, the valley of Hinnom's son (je ben hinnom) became a universal metaphysical concentration camp of unsurpassed eternal torture: the Greek mistransliteration Gehenna is one of the two words used in Christianity (the other meaning 'unknown place') for what we know in English translations as Hell.

For the designer of the perfectly transmittable pseudogod, a story that

---

180 xix, 5.

this pseudogod prepared a place of eternal torture is, if you'll excuse the expression, a godsend. An act of unsurpassable cruelty conceptually separated from the same pseudodeity's supposed kindness by *never being experienced*. This, we cynical designers conjecture, might just rescue, for enthralled victims in posterity, a pseudogod who would otherwise have become dangerously bland. In the flattering infernal firelight he again appears as a godfather befitting the adoration of both his Mafiosi and those caught in his protection racket.

Controversy

It only remains for us to consider the fact that absurdities need not be concealed in impenetrable intricacy such that all but Mensa members are excluded from the chance to see that absurdity. For even a doctrine obviously absurd to the stupid and intelligent alike can act as a great transmitter: it proliferates and protects its own transmission by nature, by means of its controversiality. To protect it from fizzling out by being just too controversial for anyone to accept, of course, it must be rendered 'uncontroversial to some' – for example by making between it and a crucial element of a generally accepted system a strong logical or emotional connection. By over-stepping concepts' natural ranges in its development of an intricate doctrine nexus, an ideological system can generate natural proliferation activity for the entire system by means of controversy over absurdities resulting from these over-stepping points.

Bearing in mind still that our analysis applies *whether or not the doctrines in question are true*, we can see that Islām and Christianity are well-equipped with such controversial points. Their principal controversies arise because of what we might call extravagant ideas, that is, ideas which wander out of their natural context because of the necessity to keep up the appearance of rationality or coherence in the system.

>Case: free will

Free will and sin are two sides of the same idea, responsibility.

Consider a typical example of social conflict: between parents' will and their children's will. Punishments and rewards the parents give to their children are ways of altering the children's behaviour until it conforms to the parents' will. Because it doesn't make sense to reward or punish what was inevitable, the idea of responsibility is born to make it easier on the parents' conscience. In such a limited context it makes sense, although as my wording here suggests it can be challenged on ethical grounds.

But the idea is released from the contexts of its birth and applied in other contexts, indeed generally. This extravagance is an example of problems arising because the thing is seen to have value or meaning in itself, which the Buddha considers later in our discourse.[181] The idea of free will grows up, as it were, cuts itself free from the bond of dependence on our own conscience-easing invention, and wanders around to very strange lands indeed. This natural foible of our psychology explains a great deal of our predicament. Imbuing language fragments with context-independent meaning, this degeneration of the symbol which haunts religious traditions, seen by some as the human species' unique achievement, is neither unique nor even beneficial: it leads directly to the perversion of behaviour on a scale vaster than would be conceivable if he took language sounds as context-dependent information. Extravagant ideas are potential carriers of the plague of degenerated meaning to the entirety of mankind.

The winner again, potentially, will be the pseudogod. Picking up our trisquares and boards again, we cynics can anticipate another potential problem with the transmission of our otherwise perfect religion: crime. Earthquakes, lightning strikes, plagues, and so on assault the innocent with alarming regularity. When it happens to communities beyond the perimeter of our pious society of transmitters our previous strategies will be enough to deal with it – those *others* have rejected the message, probably because the 'god' wanted them to, and are now suffering the consequences. However, when criminals in our society do not fall into fault lines, under electric bolts from heaven, or onto their sickbeds unto death, then the pseudodeity again starts to look a bit too non-interventionist. What to do?

It is out of the fear of wrong-doing inculcated in children that the full-blown idea of Hell can be born and sustained with apparent rationality. To be 'responsible' for the emotion-driven punishments we inflict on them, 'criminals' must have committed their crimes out of 'free will'. That this is an exaggeration is easily forgotten because of the dazzling allure of the superficial meaning of these words. In much the same way as our own anger about a minor injustice grows and grows the more we reflect on it, the 'freely acting', 'totally responsible' criminal attracts a snowballing mass of opprobrium. (This, incidentally, is why some people simply cannot tolerate the notion that social conditions might explain crime even partially, and why the same people resort quickly to impassioned rhetorical attacks that resemble the imprecations of ancient oracles.) Then, oops, some criminals, even those who commit the most

---

181 See 'Not by thinking ideas through'.

atrocious crimes, manage to get free. They remain at large, and are imagined to be perfectly remorseless, since their act was done in complete open choice. Where can we squeeze our pseudogod's universal justice back into this situation?

To rescue the pseudogod's *fairness* this time (not just omnipotence) only an eternal Hell will do, because only an eternal Hell can 'balance'[182] a crime committed in total freedom. Thus free will is part of a cold intellectual chain of justifications for the pseudodeity in situations of unpunished crime.

>*Case: the first cause*

The attribution of the status of creator and first cause of all phenomena to the pseudogod, conceived thanks to stories as a powerful divine person, is another example of the result of concepts' overextension, fostered by our conviction in the independent reality of cause and effect, a reality we shall have occasion to question severely later.[183]

Superstitions (super- more than, -stitia what stands or is) appeal to us especially strongly when they rescue other cherished superstitions from illogicality and especially when they get tangled in or entangle our *emotional* relations to the world based on habit. At best they seem to work because the range of situations in which they are tested is limited (e.g. every time I saw a black cat, something terrible did happen!), that is, so long as they are not transplanted or extrapolated away from such situations. At worst, when such extrapolation is done (e.g. in our cynical invention of the emergency rescue doctrine for the fairness of the pseudodeity, eternal torture in a hidden place) they become extravagant and clash with experience and reason, and then the conviction in the autonomous idea leads to the sense that they must be protected by erecting defensive structures, further justifications, and justifications of justifications, until we have the kind of interminable and awful messes which have accrued around both 'free will' and 'creator god'.

The characteristic of these networks of justification is just this discrepancy between their success in the birth context and their failure out of it. And now we are in a position to appreciate the special danger of reason, namely that it is easily gives rise to 'autonomous-value' language, which though necessary to validate the links in the justificatory chains, becomes their enemy (because no longer reasonable with respect to experience) when it uproots, as it is

---

182 A fanciful word for 'double'...

183 See 'Not by logic'.

so liable to, the justifications and applies them in alien contexts.

A 'creator god' as first cause is a quick fix relief in the context of existential angst: the value of existence is in question, and it is justified one level deep in our private reasoning game by the notion of creation driven by 'a greater will than ours'. But by exactly the same kind of reasoning it is singularly unsuccessful when uprooted and considered extravagantly in the broader context of such questions as, 'What causes the creator to will something?' and, 'How can changing will be related to an entity unchanging because utterly reliable?' and, 'What new information do we access by explaining events by an uncaused cause beyond saying that they are uncaused?' These eternally unanswerable conundrums are then addressed by 'thinkers' within the traditions because they are driven by their desires, unable to relinquish what they apply to, and they are addressed with ever escalating ladders of nonsense.

This characteristic of extravagant ideas, that reason both powerfully supports and tremendously undermines them, what we might call their *controversy for reason*, is an important part of the protection naturally inherent in these absurd ideas. What is controversial is argued about, and what is argued about is talked about, and what is talked about is heard: the controversy itself is like a continuous impregnation of virgin ears. Once such doctrines with particular species of justificatory networks become a banner of a group the controversy is exacerbated because what is at stake is much multiplied, as in the parable of the islanders.

Consider the parable:

> There was once an island community who ate only fish. They caught the fish by stealth with spears.
>
> One day one of the islanders discovered a new way of catching fish. He could use a drum to frighten the fish so that they fled into a waiting trap. It was a little more efficient than catching them by stealth. Obviously it interfered with anyone doing it the old way in the vicinity since the drum scared all the fish. However, since fishing need be done only occasionally this hardly mattered: the two methods could be separated in time.
>
> Unfortunately the notion of the incompatibility of applying the two methods simultaneously became much a topic of much discussion, such that some of the islanders condemned the innovation, and then others in turn condemned these as stubborn traditionalists.
>
> The discoverer of the new method felt the sting of the complaints. He pointed out that the methods need not interfere, but

this did not stop some islanders complaining. Still he felt their sting. So he sought supporters from among the other islanders. He used the fact of the slight improvement in efficiency, but it was really only slight, so to gain more supporters he resorted to cunning words. For he was not just skilled in catching fish.

The few traditionalists felt the threat of this growing group of supporters of the innovation, especially when they imagined how much more frequently the drumming might be used and how difficult the spearing might therefore become. They used their own cunning, and by appeals to tradition and majority, gathered 'like-minded' people (although in reality none of the islanders was like-minded – they all had different views!).

In response to the traditionalist party the innovator group sought refuge in greater numbers, in the 'virtue' of their movement itself, and in appeals to 'common sense'.

Because the argument had now become utterly polarized, everyone on the island found themselves on one or other side, for various reasons, sometimes by accident, sometimes by kin or friendship connections, and with varying degrees of subconscious self-reproach, for they were a diverse lot.

The mutual attacks of the more extreme elements of each party now had as their object not individuals or even ideas but massive groups of people. When the attacks became extreme, even previously cynical islanders were fired by indignation, and joined the latest counter-attacks without bothering to assess their grounds.

Their creeping sub-conscious self-doubt never went away. But something else had become more important: the redress of the injustice of the opposition's attacks. The reciprocal attacks escalated and escalated. Traditionalists turned their spears to a new use. Drums now beat en masse as islanders marched upon islanders. That was how the entire island went to war 'to settle the question' and almost everyone was killed.

Those who remained continued to apply one or other or both of the fishing methods, though undamaged spears and drums were nowadays hard to find. Nothing, of course, had been 'settled'. The island was now a patchwork of mass pyres for the dead the islanders walked among with alternate grief or gloating. Mutual suspicion infected relations even between those who had fought together, for deep down the islanders realised how other motives had driven them than transient trust. It had been a progression through fear, self-betrayal, intense but needless stress, baseless fury, celebratory murders, self-congratulation, and painful deaths to today's island. Everyone who lived remembered. Everyone who remembered told their children.

>*Case: the nature of Christ*

The last two millennia of the religious history of Europe, present one sad testament to this collusion of foibles. The proverbial iota ('i') of difference, we can now see, between the proponents of homoousion (Christ's and the Father's nature being the same) and homoiousion (their being not the same but similar), is not so much an arbitrary difference of creed chosen as an excuse for two politically-motivated groups to fight (an excuse bandied about by apologists for religion in the face of seemingly religiously motivated conflict) as a necessarily absurd disagreement which generates controversy naturally and thus promotes itself as an idea, until massive groups are electrified with the group-defensive fervour to fight the others, 'to settle the controversy once and for all'.

>*Case: certainty and persecution*

We can now perhaps also appreciate what is perhaps the fundamental quality of the religions of Christianity and Islām.

In our last visit to the cynics' house of pseudoreligion design, let us consider how the in-crowd in our perfectly transmitted pseudoreligion should be encouraged to relate to the kind of controversy-generating over-stretched ideas that we have been analysing. Controversy between two doubting parties is just controversy, but when one party must live in a fantasy of undoubting by allegiance and because it has arrogated itself by re-engineering the vocabulary of 'knowing'[184] such that it believes itself to be certain, and when the other party must be seen to be both unreasonable[185] and under some degree of influence by the deity they reject, in danger otherwise of losing its glamour of omnipotence (as we have discussed here), the rebuffs from that other party can only be interpreted as conscious, purposeful lying (about the message) and wronging (of those who advocate it and indeed themselves). We can go to town, then, if we include in the message from our pseudodeity the information which looks like an unlikely

---

184 See 'double standards' etc. under 'Not by thinking ideas through'.

185 As we saw in our earlier discussion of grace.

prediction – that the people (of the rival party) will persecute you for believing what you believe, that they are the unjust, that your very purity will enrage them because of their moral filth, and that they will therefore not rest until you have been made to mock or abandon what you believe. In such a way we cynical designers will have perfectly closed the loop – the reasonable outrage of outsiders, which already makes our devout transmitters feel indignant, will not be overlooked in the message, and certainly not forgiven, but made to seem evidence of that very unreasonableness we must expect in them given our doctrinal stance of certainty and the deity's omnipotence, and even better, *the 'deity' will predict it.*

Islām always, and Christianity at its most militant, both refer to those who deny their truth as 'liars' rather than mere deniers. It is no accident that these two interpret their birth and much of their history as being wronged by *the others.* It is not just accidentally that out of post-Christian cultures, rights culture and grievance culture have arisen.

With varying degrees of awareness of this fact in their adherents, it was the very *extravagance* of what these people stood for that led to its popular explosion, exactly by means of the controversy for reason we have been discussing.

It is to be expected that such claims of persecution will fall on the ears of the supposed persecutors as little short of preposterous. And indeed, even for the most generous onlooker on history, the interpretative finesse required of certain subsequent adherents in their community, to see certain Christian 'martyrs' (who crossed continents to force their way into non-Christian rulers' courts and insult their gods until those rulers were forced by political expediency and sometimes despite extreme reluctance to execute them, a result these strange travellers ardently hoped for), or the 'innocent' early Muslims (who raided caravans 'for Allāh and his prophet' and slaughtered the officiants of existing religions[186]), as *persecuted* will constitute just as impressive a miracle as was ever

[186] *Saḥīḥ Muslim,* in the Book of the Virtues of the Companions of the Prophet (31), report 6052: 'Jabir reported that there was in pre-Islamic days a temple called Dhu 'l-Khalasah and it was called the Yamanite Ka`ba or the northern Ka`ba. Allah's Messenger (may peace be upon him) said unto me: Will you rid me of Dhu 'l-Khalasah and so I went forth at the head of 350 horsemen of the tribe of Ahmas and we destroyed it and killed whomsoever we found there. Then we came back to him (to the Holy Prophet) and informed him and he blessed us and the tribe of Ahmas.' Another report (Al-Kalbi) has Khālid ride out on the orders of the Prophet Muḥammad to the temple of `Uzza (a goddess worshipped across Arabia at that time after whom the Arabs named the planet we call Venus), to destroy it. He is at first greeted by the unnerving site of a priestess rushing

performed by the holy heroes they revere.

---

towards him wailing. He cuts her in half vertically with his sword and she crumbles to ash before his eyes.

Not by reason of logic, ma nayahetu

Meaning

The Pali naya is supposed to be derived from the verb 'lead' and the Sanskrit equivalent nȳaya has been derived both from ny + āya meaning 'what comes' or 'pays back' and from the verb ni meaning 'lead' but also 'incur'. The idea of 'coming back' (to first principles) gives rise to the meaning 'correct' or 'proper'. Nyāyavidya in Sanskrit, literally the 'science of the proper', was what we now call logic. The diversity of meanings is narrowed here because of the word hetu, meaning 'cause' or 'because of'. Since nyāya is also the formal name for a syllogism in logic, and hetu is one of its parts, the reason, the meaning is probably 'by reason of logic', drawing conclusions from reasons. Nyāya is used with anumāna, the word for inference, to refer to a logical (or correct) inference. Another word in Sanskrit which would also have been subsumed into naya in coarser-pronounced Pali is the Sanskrit naya, which means 'axioms' or 'principles', or 'what is considered to be universally true'. However for our purposes this second sense is included in diṭṭhnijjhānakkhanti (p. 283) so here we consider only logical inference.

Examples

Superstition; scientific method; advertisers' statistics.

Irrelevancy as sources of certainty

Unjustified extrapolation from experience

When we infer something from evidence, we extrapolate from the fact that like evidence and that something were associated in some previous experience (ourselves' or others'). This means we assume that the environment from which experience is gained has not changed significantly enough to invalidate such extrapolation. However, there is *no reason from experience* to believe that changes have not been significant, that the same something will still be associated with like evidence this time. That this even applies to the association of a 'result' with its 'cause' was famously and unpopularly pointed out in European philosophy by Hume. Whereas we talked of evidence and association, he talks of the appearance of qualities and their power (to produce a result):

> I ask, why in other instances you presume that the same power still exists, merely upon the appearance of these qualities? Your appeal to

past experience decides nothing in the present case; and at the utmost can only prove, that that very object, which produc'd any other, was at that very instant endow'd with such a power; but can never prove, that the same power must continue in the same object or collection of sensible qualities. Shou'd it be said, that we have experience, that the same power continues united with the same object, and that like objects are endow'd with like powers, I wou'd renew my question, *why from this experience we form any conclusion beyond those past instances, of which we have had experiences.* If you answer this question in the same manner as the preceding, your answer gives still occasion to a new question of the same kind, even *in infinitum*; which clearly proves, that the foregoing reasoning had no justification.[187]

As Bertrand Russell pointed out in his *History of Western Philosophy*[188], these 'proofs' of Hume still stand, fearsome monoliths against which many a subsequent attempted assault has shattered: they have yet to be refuted logically.

In philosophy

However, Hume's proofs are extremely counterintuitive (undermining as they do the use of causality in logic), and therefore extremely unpopular. In a supposedly solemn discipline it is not infrequently that one encounters ridicule when they crop up. A great number of later philosophers refused them on grounds of 'common sense', and with much hand-waving and expostulation.

In science

However, the scientific method as formulated by the English philosopher Francis Bacon in the 16th century and popularised by Karl Popper in the 20th is supposed to be humbler than these 'commonsensical' philosophers: it says that science never knows the truth, but eliminates those theories which are demonstrably untrue. Bacon called it 'the greater force of the negative instance', because when a theory enounces a general law, it states implicitly that there are no exceptions, such that discovering an exception (the negative circumstance) is enough to prove it false, whereas discovering an example of it can only lead one to conclude that the theory is possibly right (but other theories could also be right, and in more instances). Popper called this the progress of scientific knowledge

---

187 Book I, part III, section VI of *A Treatise of Human Nature* (Hume, 1888)

188 (Russell, 1946)

towards the truth[189] by the accumulating disproofs of hypotheses.

However humble the scientific method, it is easily misunderstood as being anything but, not just by a gullible public hankering after authorities to side with, but also by many scientists themselves. It is easy to exaggerate, and confer on the still-to-be-disproved hypotheses the status of truth, though they deserve nothing of the sort. For most of the public in modern societies scientists have taken on the role prophets used to. This is even true, though more discreet, in modern Islāmic societies, where nowadays it is not difficult to find advocacy of belief in Islāmic doctrines by reference to justification of doctrines by scientific discoveries.[190] The psychological tendency to accord total authority to the merely non-disproved is aggravated for scientists conducting research by the practical situation in which they find themselves. For example, the next research grant can often depend on the nature of results 'discovered'. This is increasingly true when financially interested companies are the ones furnishing the grants. In addition particularly theories inevitably get associated with particular groups or individuals, encouraging these people to get defensive about them and resist potentially awkward data.[191]

There is little to separate science and superstition. Both mean the identification of reasons for particular results. Both seem to work, at least in certain contexts for certain people. We can use the nature of superstition as we consider it nowadays to throw some light on why 'scientific knowledge' can be treacherous. Superstition arises because of an easy-to-understand circumstance relating to our perception of repeating conditions. As the psychologist Skinner (now notorious principally for advocating behaviourism, an over-mechanistic reduction of human culture) showed, this perceptional circumstance is not an exclusively human characteristic: his experiments showed that *pigeons* can be superstitious too. The circumstance is our great sensitivity to events which occur in succession: if two particular events occur in succession on a number of occasions, we notice. This is to be expected for an organism that has to deal with

189 Very awkward to justify – as is evident in his attempts in later editions of *The Open Society* (Popper, 1945; 5th edition 1966).

190 While this does not mean that the people using such justifications consider science a higher authority than the Qur'ān, it does suggest they think their audience do, and that, like Aristotle, they consider it acceptable to shepherd people into the right camp by relying on their sheepish stupidity rather than instruct them.

191 Recently a number of books have been published on the misuse of scientific credentials and the public's gullibility, such as Ben Goldacre's excellent *Bad Science* (Goldacre, 2008).

an environment which has some degree of regularity to it (but not a totally chaotic environment, whatever that might be). If you find tasty acorns under oaks twice, searching for acorns under oaks next time you are hungry is likely to get you food. The association can develop in the mind even if it is perceived in the environment only on one occasion: Skinner's pigeons were fed grains at regular intervals and developed strange ritualised movements in response: what had happened was that a grain had popped out shortly after they had by chance made a particular movement, and so they tried doing the same movement again and (if the grain delivery rate were suitable) another grain came. These two occasions were enough to 'reinforce' this behaviour strongly: from then on the pigeons would make the magic grain-making ritual again and again, even if no grains were supplied, and it took much longer for the behaviour to be given up than it had taken for it to develop. The rain-making dances in human societies are a parallel example. The point to take from this is that psychologically we are inclined to search for an effect (such as rain) once we have (possibly by chance) come to make the association in our mind between some particular cause (such as a special dance) and that effect.

In science this can lead scientists to overlook negative data (the equivalent of 'lack of rain' after a dance), to focus on similar potential causes at the expense of potentially more important but very different causes (the equivalent of varying the dance until the rain comes instead of learning about cold fronts meeting warm air) and to resist alternatives to the particular causes ('dances') which they have discovered and thereby feel some allegiance to.

In statistics

A study some years ago showed that smoking was related to a decrease in the incidence of Alzheimer's disease. Should this encourage us to take up the habit? Probably not, because the lower incidence of Alzheimer's in smokers was a reflection of them dying earlier, and so having less chance to grow old enough to develop the disease.[192] Of course this will provide solace to some smokers! In the light of such examples we can appreciate why it has been said that you can 'say anything you like' with statistics.

Case: advertising

This misreading of statistics has proved most lucrative to companies in

---

[192] I owe this example to an article by the ex-physicist turned Buddhist teacher Ajahn Brahmavamso Mahathera (Brahmavamso, 2007).

our times: our televisions spew a flood of such 'recent studies' at us 'proving' that this cream makes us look younger, that that tampon soaks up more 'fluid', that this antacid soothes indigestion faster, that that solicitors' leads to greater recuperation of illegitimately secured insurance payments, etc. etc. etc.

In religious experience, revelation and prophecy

Case: a creator god recalled in visions

Before we turn to the inference of 'a deity' from 'the vision of a deity', let us clear up a persistent misrepresentation of Buddhism.

It is frequently asserted in modern 'Christian-friendly' accounts of Buddhism that the question of the existence or otherwise of 'God the Creator' was one of the famous set of questions the Buddha refused to answer. However, there are no records of the Buddha ever having done this on the question of the existence of 'God the Creator'. So I have often wondered where in the imitative, branching traditions of literature this idea first arose. I notice it is already present in the earliest treatments, by Christian missionaries, of the similarities between the Buddha's and the Christ's 'missions'.

Indeed we would have to accuse of either ignorance or, worse, duplicity, anyone who asserts that the Buddha did not speak clearly *and dismissively* of the belief in 'God' as we know it, that is, the belief in 'an eternal Creator and Sustainer of all His perishable creatures', for there are many criticisms of such a belief in the Pali canon, amounting almost, one might be inclined to conclude, to ridicule of it. And unlike the discourse to the Kālāmā people, they are not hidden away. Perhaps the most cutting one comes in the very first discourse (*The Net of Brahmā*) of the canonical Pali collection of the so-called 'Long Category of Discourses', the Dīgha Nikāya, in the course of that long list of 'wrong views' we summarised when considering what the Kālāmā people were likely to have been taught by wandering religious teachers. (The exhaustive and rather lulling nature of those lists might explain why certain commentators seem to have overlooked these words so easily!) The view of a 'creator deity' occurs in the section subtitled 'The First Category of the View of Eternality combined with Transience'. First of all the Buddha establishes that a 'creator deity' might be mistaken about itself:

> 'There is such a time, almsfolk, as when this world system dissolves, at times separated by a lapse of many aeons. When the world system thus dissolves, beings are reborn mostly in the radiant (abhassara) plane of

existence.[193] When they are born there, because of a mind of absorption, nurtured by rapture, resplendent with light from their own forms, sojourning in the heaven and living in splendour, they remain there for aeons.

'There is such a time, almsfolk, as when this world system rises again, at times separated by a lapse of many aeons. When the world system thus rises again, there appears a palatial immeasurable paradise (vimāna) for divine Brahmā beings[194], void of all life. At that time, a certain being from the radiant plane of existence dies, either at the end of the span of life, or on the exhaustion of the stock of meritorious deeds, and is reborn in that empty, palatial, immeasurable paradise for divine Brahmā beings. When born there because of a mind of absorption, nurtured by rapture, resplendent with light from its own form, sojourning in the heavens and living in splendour, it remains there for aeons.

'Living there alone for aeons, there arises in it mental weariness and a longing for company thus: "Would that some other beings might come to be here!" And then other beings from the radiant plane of existence die either at the end of their span of life, or on the exhaustion of the stock of their meritorious deeds, and are reborn in that palatial immeasurable paradise for divine Brahmā beings. When they are born there because of a mind of absorption, nurtured by rapture, resplendent with light from their own forms, sojourning in the heavens and living in splendour, they remain there for aeons.

'Then, almsfolk, the being who was the first to be reborn there thinks to itself thus:

' "Aham asmi Brahmā, Mahā Brahmā, Abhibhū, Anabhibhūto, Aññadatthudaso, Vasavattī, Issaro, Kattā, Nimmātā, Seṭtho, Sajitā[195], Vasī, Pitā, bhūtabhabyānaṁ. Mayā ime sattā nimmitā. Taṁ kissa hetu? Mamañhi pubbe etadahosi, 'aho vata aññepi sattā itthattaṁ

---

[193] The third (of three) second (of four) absorption-level Brahmā realms in the thirty-one planes of existence.

[194] One or all three of the Brahmā realms of the first level of mental absorption, less exalted than the radiant plane.

[195] Or sajjitā.

āgaccheyyu'nti. Iti mama ca manopaṇidhi, ime ca sattā itthattaṁ āgatā''ti.

' "I am the Divine Brahmā Being, nay the Great divine Brahmā being, the Over-Being, the Being over Whom there is none, the Omniscient[196], Whose will is done[197], the Almighty God, the Maker, the Creator, the Lord, the Sender-forth, the Subjector, and the Father, for all that have been and shall be.[198] I have created these other beings! Why can I say so? I can say so because a while ago I thought to myself, 'Would that some other beings might come to be here!' and just as I wished, other beings have appeared here!" '

Then, in that heavenly realm of light, what we might call 'the Covenant' is established:

'And then the other beings who appeared later think to themselves:

' "This Exalted Being is the Divine Brahmā Being, nay the Great divine Brahmā being, the Over-Being, the Being over Whom there is none, the Omniscient, Whose will is done, the Almighty God, the Maker, the Creator, the Lord, the Sender-forth, the Subjector, and the Father, for all that have been and shall be. This Exalted[199] Divine Brahmā Being has created us! Why can we say so? We can say so because, as we see, he appeared in this place as the First[200], whereas we appeared only after him."

'Among them, almsfolk, the one who appeared first lives longer, and is more beautiful and more powerful. Those beings who appeared later have a shorter life, and are less beautiful and less powerful.'

---

196 Literally the 'let-there-be-whatever-there-might-he-sees-it'.

197 This is an exactly literal translation: vasa=will; vatti is an adjectival participle from the verb vatteti, the causative of vattati, meaning 'it is kept up', 'it is carried out'.

198 Compare the Arabic 'beautiful names of Allāh' from the Qur'ān: al-kabīr, the great, al-`aliyy, the most high, al-qahhār, the subduer, al-baṣīr, the all-seeing, al-jabbār, the irresistible, Allāh, God, al-muṣawwir, the fashioner, al-khāliq, the creator, al-rabb, the lord, al-basiṭ, the extender, al-khāfiḍ, the abaser – but not father of course!

199 Literally, 'who has been made the master'. Compare the Arabic 'beautiful name of Allāh', al-malik, the master.

200 Compare the 'beautiful name', al-'āwil, the first.

Finally, the inexorable possibility that prophets can make a mistaken inference from visions of this primordial covenant is pointed out. The training of the prophet, incidentally, is presented exactly in accordance with recommended Buddhist training, with the crucial difference that it is abandoned too soon:

> 'Then, almsfolk, this possibility is realised. A being dies in the Brahmā plane of existence and is reborn in this human world; and there he renounces the worldly life for the homeless life of a recluse. And having thus renounced the worldly life and become a homeless recluse, he achieves utmost mental concentration by dint of ardent, steadfast, persevering exertion, mindfulness and right attentiveness. Having established his mind in highest concentration, he can recollect that former existence (as a divine Brahmā being); *but he cannot recollect beyond that.*
>
> 'He announces thus:
>
> ' "That Exalted Being is the Divine Brahmā Being, nay the Great divine Brahmā being, the Over-Being, the Being over Whom there is none, the Omniscient, Whose will is done, the Almighty God, the Maker, the Creator, the Lord, the Sender-forth, the Subjector, and the Father, for all that have been and shall be. That Exalted Divine Brahmā Being has created us.
>
> ' "So Nicco, Dhuvo, Sassato, Avipariṇāma, dhammo sassatisamaṁ tatheva ṭhassati. Ye pana mayaṁ ahumhā tena bhotā brahmunā nimmitā, te mayaṁ aniccā addhuvā appāyukā cavanadhammā itthattaṁ āgatā'ti.
>
> ' "He is the Permanent, the Stable, the Eternal, the Immutable, and as Everlasting[201] as all things eternal. We, who were created by the Exalted Divine Brahmā Being, are impermanent, unstable, short-lived and evanescent things. Thus have we come here.'

Can we claim that such a description does not apply to the idea of 'God' and the prophets that is familiar to us?

---

[201] Compare the Arabic 'beautiful names of Allāh' al-qayyūm, the subsisting, al-matīn, the firm, aṣ-ṣamad, the eternal, al-akhir, the last.

Notice that the Buddha's rather cheeky story is presented as *a possibility*: his point, one suspects, is not to say that this is certainly what happened, but to draw attention to the fact that if it *had* there would be no way for the prophets involved to tell the difference between what happened and what appeared (from the vision) to have happened. This relates to the fact that prophets cannot claim to be god in order to judge the validity of an experience of god, a point we return to later in our deconstruction of authority.

As for 'the Revelation' of such prophets (in Sanskrit, ṛsi) and their followers, the divines (brāhmaṇa) the Buddha had something to say of that too, in *The Discourse on the Triple Science*, when two such followers, though both firm believers in the Divine Creator (Brahmā), fall into dispute, in a way dismally familiar to us today, over which of two rival systems for attaining communion with the Divine Nurturer is superior, ask the Buddha to arbitrate. The Buddha asks,

> 'So, Vasettha, you say that the way to communion with Divine Creator is that taught by the divine Pokkharasati, and Bhāradvāja says it is that taught by the divine Tarukha. What is the dispute, the quarrel, the difference all about?'
>
> 'Right and wrong paths, Reverend Gotama. There are so many kinds of divines who teach different paths: the Addhariya, the Tittiriya, the Chandoka, the Chandava, divines practising the holy life... Do all these ways lead to communion with the Divine Creator? Just as if there were near a town or village many different paths – do all these come together at that place? And likewise, do the ways of the various divines [...] lead the one who follows them to communion with the Divine Creator?'
>
> 'Do you say: "They lead," Vasettha?'
>
> 'I say: "They lead," Reverend Gotama.'
>
> 'Do you say: "They lead," Vasettha?'
>
> 'I say: "They lead," Reverend Gotama.'
>
> 'Do you say: "They lead," Vasettha?'
>
> 'I say: "They lead," Reverend Gotama.'[202]
>
> 'But, Vasettha, is there then a single one of these divines, though learned in the Three Vedas, who has seen the Divine Creator face to face?'

202 This repetition is telling.

'No, Reverend Gotama.'

'Then has the teacher's teacher of any one of them seen the Divine Creator face to face?'

'No, Reverend Gotama.'

'Then has the ancestor seven generations back of the teacher of one of them seen the Divine Creator face to face?'

'No, Reverend Gotama.'

'Well then, Vasettha, what about the early prophets for those divines learned in the Three Vedas, the formulators of the mantras, the expounders of the mantras, whose ancient verses are chanted, pronounced and collected by the divines of today, and chanted and spoken of – such as Atthaka, Vamaka, Vamadeva, Vessamitta, Yamataggi, Angirasa, Bhāradvāja, Vasettha, Kassapa, Bhagu… – did they ever say, "We know and see when, how and where the Divine Creator appears"?'

'No, Reverend Gotama.'

'So, Vasettha, not one of these divines learned in the Three Vedas has seen the Divine Creator face to face, nor has one of their teachers, or teacher's teachers, nor even the ancestor seven generations back of one of their teachers. Nor could any of the early prophets say, "We know and see when, how and where the Divine Creator appears." So what these divines learned in the Three Vedas are saying is: "We teach this path to communion with the Divine Creator that we do not know or see, this is the only straight path… leading to communion with the Divine Creator." What do you think, Vasettha? Such being the case, does not what these divines declare turn out to be ill-founded?'

In war

Analytical thought is the process of deciding what is reasonable to believe and what is not. Because it pushes the difference too far, the latter gets relegated to a mysterious realm of incomprehension, and any effort to understand those who might believe so is abandoned. In the so-called war against terror, the strategies developed on both sides are totally rational, yet because they are based on limited perspective, they involved misunderstanding of the other, and therefore misunderstanding of the inter-related situation.

> Theories of rational choice assume human beings have reasonable grounds – if people are seen to behave irrationally it is because they are

frustrated. The implication of this benignly reductive analysis is that if the causes of frustration could be removed, harmony would follow. But not all reasonable objectives are compatible, and rational choices can lead to horribly destructive conflicts. Such is often the case in asymmetric warfare. Though the insurgents usually win, occupying powers also have interests that compel them to fight. Both parties may have reason to engage in a mutually damaging conflict.[203]

Trapped belief

A fair number of traditions, it can be argued, persist, because of, and a great deal of unnecessary suffering is generated by, what we might call 'trapped beliefs', meaning those prejudices whose claims appear convincingly to be justified by experience, whereas in reality this experience is *created by* the prejudices themselves. This depends on misidentifying the causes of a phenomenon, i.e. making a fallacious inference. Much religious teaching about society and psychology can only seem useful in the very conditions of need it creates: it guarantees itself.

Case: the badness of human nature

One easily grasped example is the belief in the fundamental badness of human nature, and the related belief in the necessity of strictly restricting this nature. One notices as one travels that in countries where people are trusted, rather than restricted, they behave better and people have a more positive idea about human nature. It could be that some places have people whose nature is worse than others, and that trust follows the better. But a more likely explanation is that under restrictive measures, better behaviour goes unnoticed – at best it is seen as a result of fear of those restrictive measures – whereas worse behaviour is encouraged, by means of the well known forbidden fruit principle. To be finer about it, we can say that the idea {that good only arises because of restriction} can spread easily in a society where restriction is the norm, because there are no chances for people {to test whether people can be good without restrictions being operative}, and there is a consequent loss of faith in the possibility of {good without restriction}. This loss of faith leads people to value the restrictions all the more.

In general such a vicious circle occurs whenever people mistake the result of holding their belief for a result of their not holding the belief strongly

203 From chapter 6 (p. 281-2) of *Black Mass* (Gray, 2007).

enough.

The proverb says, 'Give a dog a bad name and hang him,' and we might elaborate thus: Give a good dog a bad name ('Only good because restricted') and he might question whether his goodness is not just to avoid the noose, and as the self-doubt continues relentlessly, he might well come to believe his name and identify with a kind of repressed beastliness. Then, when this beastliness so emboldened has a chance to transgress, it might well take that chance with even more likelihood than it would have done had restrictions never been in place. Anyone who witnesses will call for harsher restrictions on dogs.

> As Jefferson said, at the time when he was framing the Bill for Establishing Religious Freedom in Virginia, the 'impious presumption' of state authority in religion and attempts by punishments or inducements do not strengthen faith but 'tend only to beget habits of hypocrisy and meanness'.[204]

It is intriguing to note that this progressive loss of the ability to recognise the good would only happen very slowly under weak restrictions, but that its rate will increase in proportion with the strength of the restrictions. Eventually even slight movements towards the good from a baseline of extreme evil will be interpreted merely as fear of punishment, so even that minute good will not be recognised as such.

If it is true that harsher restrictions have a negative effect on both the general assessment of human nature and the standard of ethical behaviour, someone seeking to blame might feel he or she could honestly accuse their legislators only of ignorance, but regrettably these latter are less frequently ignorant than wily and interested. As a hapless victim of increasing restrictions once said of their legislator,

> Whether the tyranny be in his place,
> Or in his eminence that fills it up,
> I stagger in – but this new governor
> Awakes me all the enrollèd penalties,
> Which have, like unscoured armour, hung by th' wall
> So long that nineteen zodiacs have gone round
> And none of them have been worn; and for a name

---

[204] From *What Price Liberty?* (Wilson, 2009) which gives the citation reference (Jefferson, 1904, p. 438f).

Now puts the drowsy and neglected act
Freshly on me. 'Tis surely for a name.

Claudio in *Measure for Measure* (act I, scene 2)

We do not have to trawl far through the daily news to find examples of rulers showing their muscles to their populace, of course.

Case: the servitude of mankind

A related belief is the relegation of the true status of mankind (for it is usually so expressed, as *man*kind) to servitude. It encourages in one a need for his or her existence to be re-asserted, so doctrines such as the creation of all creatures for the use of man, the centrality of man in the cosmos, and the idea that man is made in the image of the almighty god, become very attractive. This leads to allegiance with the doctrine of the creator, which is the very being to whom he or she is taught to be subservient: these titbits turn out to be bait. The slip into 'insufficient existential presence' is thus inexorable, and the result is a kind of jealousy or hatred of reality itself which is palpable among many who call themselves religious.

This vicious system is made into a virtue by the most highly respected theologians, in aching prose:

> Salvation is the perfect being, which is not proper to created being as such but is still future. […] Only from God as the One who is originally and properly can it come about that it [created being] also has being, that it is, and not that it is not.[205]

Case: the creator god

To ask 'why?' is parallel to the habit of blaming. What we are experiencing is not permitted to be just as it is, but it is insisted that it is a result, a result of prior causes. Partisans of the creation story hold that creation's cause is a god. Among thinkers this belief is often considered to be the result of our dislike of what we might call close mysteries: we push all the mystery into the god's nature and claim that in the creation itself there is no mystery – for 'the god did it' solves the mystery. However, more than that, their belief is both a symptom of and an important reason for deep but repressed destructive tendencies in our psyche – wishing everything were nothing, refusing the

205 (Barth, 1956, p. 9)

importance of phenomenal experience as it is and ascribing importance elsewhere. To value the causes is to place the importance in a dead past where it is safely out of reach. We might expect that it need not be placed in the past: ascribing the importance to the future, the purpose of the phenomena, which will never be born, is an alternative method – one which we also find in these religions, with their various teleologies. The principle, rejecting immediate experience (which is often so inconvenient anyway), is the same.

Case: restricting sexual behaviour to marriage

Self-necessitating restriction and its ill consequences can also be observed with the widespread system for raising children – bipolar marriage of the genetic parents plus 'tried and tested' methods of ensuring seemingly elusive paternity that a DNA test would gazump anyway such as an average of thirty years of genital stagnation for all and jugulation of daughters who stay out too late. Where this system dominates society (and it does so not just in Victorian England but tragically much more widely today) some dissenters are (by their wilful evil rather than by their special biology, so say the party members) frustrated to a degree many doctors would classify as mental illness, and seek pleasure elsewhere than with their over-familiar current spouse or over-hypothetical future spouse. Such pleasures are forbidden by that domination, and the methods of hiding them to preserve its kudos entail prostitution, disowned children, abuse of the pleasure providers (even though, or is it because, they are resorted to desperately), and a high degree of unacknowledged promiscuity and sexually transmitted disease, none of which would be necessary had the pleasure not been driven underground. (I do not claim that none of it would be possible of course.) The dull-witted (making superficial conceptual associations as they might between walking under ladders and having accidents) see these ills as vindication of the prohibitions, the wise as their consequence. Yet if the system is dominant there are no alternative experiments, so people come to believe that a fantastic (neurotically fuelled) exaggeration of these consequences is how things would be if the decency laws were not in place – a chaos of orphans, licentiousness and disease.

Those keener to invent evidence for their preclusions than to make conclusions based on evidence tell us there have been alternative experiments in this chaos. They ignore voluminous evidence to the contrary and claim that this chaos was how things were 'in the jungle' before the civilising influence of such sexual prohibitions as the aforementioned genital stagnation. The evidence 'from the jungle' however is overwhelmingly of societies dominated by more restrictive sexual prohibitions than such myth proponents can even dream of. What we call normal marriage is actually an inherited, much palliated version of these extraordinarily superstitious restrictions.

Wiser ones also point to alternative experiments. Many and various tentative versions of what some would lump airily together as 'free-love communities' have come and gone. Many of course, like Lawrence's New Mexico experiment, went because of erupting jealousies, which are difficult to throw off instantaneously by one's reason for the sake of an ideology. If jealousy, however, were inevitable then a prostitute's life would be much more gruelling than it already is. Clearly if we can accept what has supposedly been discovered and announced of old (in the Buddhist texts), that jealousy is just an adventitious stain, then rather than condemn 'free-love communities' on grounds of jealousy-stoked impracticability let us condemn jealousy on grounds of such communities' potential practicability: to condemn free love in order to rescue eternal jealousy as a human right (and some traditional societies' attitude to jealousy is exactly this reverence) is like a pyrrhomaniac blaming the flammable materials in the house when he or she burns it down in order to rescue the right to be a pyrrhomaniac. Indeed it is worse. In psychotherapy we can at least show the pyrrhomaniac he or she has a problem and that it is soluble by further treatment. The maniacs of jealousy, the jungle orgy myth-mongers, have vested interests in pretending that jealousy is not a problem ('part of human nature') or untreatable ('God's eternal stamp on our hearts').

One interest is in protecting their myth. One of the most famous and well-distributed Islāmic treatises against 'errors' (such as Sufism) in the pure religion, Ibn Jawzi's *Possession by the Devil* (in Arabic, *Talbīs Iblīs*), repeats a common argument that jealousy, along with all other negative emotions that the Sufis (and incidentally Buddhists) claim can be purified, is part of human nature and on the one hand cannot be purified, since only deniers of Allāh's creation could say that it was not stamped on our hearts, and on the other hand should not be purified, because (and this is a deliciously scholastic argument) Allāh has commanded us to restrain it in order to please him, such that purifying ourselves of something to restrain would rob us of the means to please him.[206] Well, this kind of reasoning is a very casual cruelty. Such 'thinkers', while imagining earning themselves seats in Allāh's gardens for their efforts, support (as well as they did their paying caliphs) superstitious, self-enriching (politically useful) tortures which the

206 We consider these claims in detail when the Buddha comes to treat the topic of freedom from the afflictive emotions.

majority of humanity has to suffer in consequence, too dull-witted to realise what a scam the whole thing is.

Or the vested interest may be to protect virtue itself. If there is no chance to be bad, there is no opportunity to resist it and be good, they say. But is virtue not a means, rather than an end? Disdaining the vulgar pleasures and spoiling them for others, they choose instead the noble pleasures of personal vanity before their peers or their deity, or those very same vulgar pleasures (plus a fair few more) ennobled by being just for themselves and in the future – in the afterlife.

Case: patriarchal bloodlines

Science told us long ago that there is no bloodline, of course. What biological identity can said to be passed from a generation to the next we now know as genes, that fraction of the chemical material of cells in the form of the compound DNA, deoxyribonucleic acid, with its sequences of four bases encoding for proteins which are responsible in turn for development, structure and much more. This DNA is, as science told us decades ago, contributed to exactly equally (as an unpredictable half of theirs, each) by the male and female parents (leading to blood in the child different from both parents), and furthermore there is a second fraction of genetic material, in the energy-making organelles within the cell called mitochondria, which is derived entirely from the mother in all cases, so if anything there is more biological identity from the mother's contribution to the identity-material than there is from the father's.

However, this is not how it looked in the pre-microscope days, where the baby was seen to grow just as the mother's flesh grew (and the inference made that it was part of the mother's flesh, though of course we have known for decades that the flesh of both derives substantially from the material of nutrition) and where great resemblance between father and children seemed to be transmitted by this tiny sample of white fluid, which was consequently imbued with magical power and seen as the sole contributor to the child's identity. This was aggravated by myths deriving from the massive religions (transmitting, no doubt, primitive lore they did not have the wherewithal to dismiss) equating this white fluid with a seed, and the mother's material with the earth. The Qur'ān instructs its believers to go unto their wives as a *tilth*. And lest we congratulate ourselves on more scientific vocabulary let us note that we still call that white fluid 'semen' (the Latin for 'seed') and the technical word for transferring this white fluid to its place of fertilisation is still called 'insemination' – 'planting the seed'. Clearly earth does not contribute heritable identity to the crop, and this is exactly how women were (and often are) seen, as substance and matter whose identity was irrelevant.

The idea of injecting identity has persisted tenaciously and noisily in our cultures like a ghost haunting the ruins of its house. The seed-earth analogy was razed magnificently by genetics, but the mysterious 'bloodline' notion groans plaintively on from its rubble, quite as loudly as it used to set that ill-founded mansion in ancient times reverberating with its cries. To the ramifications of this superstition the vast majority of our least flexible social institutions (our names, our property laws, our inheritance laws, our allocations of duties and entitlements to the males and females, our ideas of sexual morality in the two sexes, marriage laws, etc.) can be traced. Even if these institutions were informed by the idea of genetic relatedness between individuals (thereby recognizing the equality of the mother's and father's contributions, for example) they would not thereby be less superstitious – since we do not imagine that our greatest aim is equivalent to the aims of our genes. (It might make sense from the genes' point of view for us to apportion our inheritance among our heirs exactly in accordance with our respective genetic relatedness to them, but it cannot be stressed enough, again, that 'what is fit to survive is not neccesarily what is good': if we were consistent in a gene-based morality we would 'do well' to legalise rape, and 'eliminate' foster children.)

Let us note at least, though, that the contractual nature of bonds in society combines very unluckily with this matrix of mystery, 'the bloodline': for once inheritance laws are in place (due originally to the magical exaggeration of the father's connection with the child), selfishness has a new locus through which to act. Furthermore the new child grows up seemingly 'in debt' (because of the idea of contract) to the fore-fathers, and since what they took was by procreation, it is inferred that what is owed is procreation: they owe it to their forefathers to procreate: the bloodline must be perpetuated. So just as that ghost, the idea of the bloodline, groans on, so do its students continue to apply its ghostly counsel, the very séance which conjures it. This is superstition stood upon superstition, and it is behind the fervour and intuitive 'correctness' of seemingly more respectable calls from various quarters – to have a family as God intended, to keep the species alive, and to keep placing the flowers on the graves.

Once males' importance in identity-transmission has been thus superstitiously exaggerated by society at large, that society accords them the reward of that greater appreciation, and consequently creates the conditions which cause males to be actually more important (for securing funds, for example). In such a society, in which the magical origins of the discrepancy are never made obvious, is born the idea that by nature the sexes deserve this discrepancy. Recently the term 'missing girls' has been coined for the sex-selective abortions which must, it is presumed, have given rise to the skewed sex ratios in societies still affected by this discrepancy: in India and China these 'missing girls' are in their millions each year.

Case: prayer, the crucial evil of monotheism

Another trapped belief system is in the effectiveness of prayer,[207] which is just one example of magical thinking, something we often imagine ourselves free of in our enlightened times.

Magic means power that many don't recognise but that is available to those who do, and who know its method, to control one's environment, including the people in it. Whether or not it is true, it is attractive because we secretly wish to be in complete control. This wish is not easy to conceal within the fold of the religions supposedly devoted to an omnipotent lord, since it effectively involves making the 'omnipotent lord' the means of accomplishing the magical act, i.e. the servant. We consider in our treatment of language later the linguistic god-mixing necessary (at least for the more circumspect like Augustine) to sustain the illusion that the servant is the lord – for example, that the servant actually wishes us to wish this magical result, such that by wishing it we conform with his will. Here I am more interested in the fact that belief in prayer is likely to spread even if it simply does not work, and that once it has become common, it guarantees itself if though it does not work. As before in our discussions, I am not interested here in whether it works, which is an endlessly disputable issue, but in whether and how it might become a prevalent belief even though that belief be entirely false, an issue which is demonstrable and undisputable.

The idea that prayer is an assertion of magical power will be objected to on the grounds that the major religions expressly assert that magic is against the deity or out-dated and superstitious. But we should not confuse an assertion with what it asserts: my saying I am a cow does not make me a cow, and such an objection is an example of exactly the magical thinking it claims to be refuting.

Perhaps first we should clear up another doubt: why should we concern ourselves with criticising prayer, of all things? After all, does it not provide great comfort for the masses? Well, there is particular urgency about the consideration of 'monotheistic' prayer, because the unfortunate consequence of

---

[207] The logical impossibility of praying to a deity we consider later: see 'concealing plurality' under 'Not by thinking ideas through'.

magic in 'monotheism', though it propagates and has propagated this latter very effectively, is that it turns otherwise humble humans into megalomaniacs and through sheer force of numbers of adherents rallying together under its banner, each driven by the kind of erroneous inferences we will consider, gives them the confidence to realise their megalomania, often at horrific cost – to others and to themselves. It is much worse than loçal magic. On the one hand we have the 'primitive, superstitious, irreligious man or woman,' who believes that his or her wish for gold will be realized if the correct charms are performed, and on the other we have the 'modern, objective, religious man or woman' who asks the all-powerful someone to bring the gold. If we compare the domains of these two wishes, we quickly see that the former is limited by the nature of the charm – another charm is necessary for love, for example. And the complex details of charms and spells give one the impression that they might well have been devised as ways trivially to occupy obsessed wishers until the first force of the wish passed and they realised their own foolishness. Not so when your only charm and spell is a request to the all-powerful someone: the divine eye is easier to bring than the eye of toad. It is easy to do, and that divine person's power is, after all, over all. No amount of clever revisionist interpretation of prayer can cover the fact that it is licensed megalomania.

You can, if you have a stomach for casuistry, read pious texts recommending that the only effective prayer is a desperate or hopeless prayer, since to test the power of the 'all-powerful god' is to deny that 'god's love'. What this means is that such a test insults the divinity and causes it to refuse to answer the prayer, but a great deal of fanciful language is necessary to hide the (convenient) meanness and vanity revealed by such a description. Even if we accept these premises, what could a hopeless prayer mean, when a prayer is a hope? To pray means to ask (the English word is related to the Spanish preguntar, meaning ask, and the French prier, meaning beg), and which sane person would ask for what he knew he could not get? If effective prayer is really that, why does one not find people praying for their prayers not to be answered – given that the result of such prayers could never be got, thanks to their logical paradox, so such prayers would presumably be ideal for such an awkward 'deity'? The reason is that true hopelessness prevents expressions of hope, something blindingly obvious until you've been lured for a while through the sliding conceptual labyrinths of pious apology.

Unfortunately the man or woman who claims the special favour of the all-powerful deity (because of the sycophantic colour of his or her declarations – 'praise') is not only making a much more outrageous wish than the 'primitive' magician: he or she is making a much more *immoral* wish. For when our eyes are fresh we can see that the claim that the all-powerful 'deity' *owns the universe* is in fact a claim that only the favoured men and women own the universe. ('Thy kingdom come, Thy will be done, on earth as it is in heaven. [...] For thine is the kingdom.' The first line of the Qur'ān's 'opening', and the first line therefore of every prayer, repeated several times in the course of a normal prayer, is, 'Al-ḥamdu lillāhi rabbi l-`ālamīn! – Praise (is) for Allāh the lord of the worlds.') The claim that only the all-powerful 'deity' *has the right to rule* over the nations of the world is in fact a claim that only favoured men and women should be the rulers. The claim that only the all-powerful 'deity' *is just* is in fact a claim that only favoured men and women are just. (In Islāmic law, non-Muslims' testimony in court is disqualified: how could they be just when they reject the justice of Allāh?) And so on. All this clearly goes much further than honest magic (by which I mean magic which admits that it is magic) ever went – it is extending magic into worldwide appropriation of property, government and morals, which is of course why it has acted, and continues to act, as such a great propagating mechanism for these religions. Anyone who disputes the theoretical basis within the religions themselves of these arrogations to the believers of such 'divine qualities' as ownership, sovereignty and justice, need look no further than the practical application of these arrogations, with basis or no, in the history of Christianity's ousting of the pagan religions and of the Islāmic conquests across Africa and Asia, which were a protracted, upsetting, vivid demonstration of this arrogation. I say 'upsetting' because all the qualities of the ancestral, more honest, magic are still present – self-centredness and loss of perspective, ignorance of or ignoring of others' suffering, malevolent desires, stupid aversions. Except in this 'more modern' form they extend onto a vast scale, and operate using dizzying hypocrisy. Yes, what calls itself 'monotheism' has walked hand-in-hand with the blackest magic indeed.

Incidentally, thanks to politically interested education and various psychological blocks we will investigate later[208], the idea has become popular that the conquests of Islām were peaceful. Anyone, including cowed non-Muslims with a foible for political correctness, who so believes really should read the contemporary Arabic and Persian histories of these conquests, uninformed as they are by later generations' niceties of ethics. The raids conducted by Mahmūd Ghazni, one of the greatest heroes of Islāmic expansion, for example, are available in the contemporary original Arabic and various Persian translations of

208 See 'cognitive biases' under 'Not by intuitive acceptance of views'.

Kitāb al-Yamīnī of Abu Naṣr Muḥammad bin Muḥammad al-Jabbār al-`Utbi (d. 410 h)[209], and commented on by recent historians[210], and no plea of 'the exaggeration expected in a glorifying account' can disguise the nature of these 'bloodless, tolerant, sacred openings':

> The friends of Allāh defeated their obstinate opponents, and quickly put them to a complete rout. Noon had not arrived when the Muslims had wreaked their vengeance on the infidel enemies of Allāh, killing 15,000 of them, spreading them like a carpet over the ground, and making them food for beasts and birds of prey. Fifteen elephants fell on the field of battle, as their legs, being pierced with arrows, became as motionless as if they had been in a quagmire, and their trunks were cut with the swords of the valiant heroes. [...] The army fell upon them, and committed such slaughter that their swords were covered with blood. Those who escaped death fled away like mountain goats, having seen the swords flashing as bright as stars at noonday, and dealing black and red death around them. Thus did the infidels meet with the punishment and loss due, to their deserts. The standards of the Sultan then returned happy and victorious to Ghazni, the face of Islam was made resplendent by his exertions, the teeth of the true faith displayed themselves in their laughter, the breasts of religion expanded, and the back of idolatry was broken. [...] The army of the Sultan kept moving on, and committing slaughter and pillage. One hundred and twenty elephants fell to the share of the Sultan, besides the usual share of property and arms. He also obtained an accession of territory without any solicitation. He remained at Bhatia till he had cleansed it from pollution, and appointed a person there to teach those who had embraced Islam, and lead them in the right way. [...] The battle lasted from morning till evening, and the infidels were near gaining the victory, had not Allāh aided by sending the slaves of the household to attack the enemy in rear, and put them to

209 (al-`Utbi). Others include, for the first conquest (of Sind), in Arabic, *The Opening of the Countries, Futūḥ al-Buldān* by Aḥmad bin Yahya bin Jābir (d. 279 h.) (al-Biladuri, 3rd c. h./9th c. CE) and the Persian *Chach Nāma* (Kūfi, early 13th CE), a translation of an earlier, now lost, Arabic work; and for the later conquests, among many works (see http://www.infinityfoundation.com/ECITindiaresourceframeset.htm), the Persian *History of Subuktigin, Tarīkh us-Subuktigin* of Abu-l Faẓl al-Baihaki (b. 388 H., 995 CE; d. 470 H., 1077 CE) (al-Baihaki, 4th c. h./10th c. CE).

210 (Al-Manīnī, 1286 h/1869 CE)

flight. The victors obtained thirty large elephants, and slew the vanquished wherever they were found in jungles, passes, plains, and hills. […] He fought a battle with the chiefs of the infidels, in which Allāh bestowed upon him much booty in property, horses, and elephants, and the friends of Allāh committed slaughter in every hill and valley. […] A stone was found there in the temple of the great Budda [sic] on which an inscription was written purporting that the temple had been founded fifty thousand years ago. The Sultan was surprised at the ignorance of these people, because those who believe in the true faith represent that only seven thousand years have elapsed since the creation of the world, and the signs of resurrection are even now approaching. The Sultan asked his wise men the meaning of this inscription, and they all concurred in saying that it was false, and, that no faith was to be put in the evidence of a stone. The Sultan returned, marching in the rear of this immense booty, and slaves were so plentiful that they became very cheap, and men of respectability in their native land were degraded by becoming slaves of common shopkeepers. But this is the goodness of Allāh, who bestows honours on his own religion and degrades infidelity. […] The blood of the infidels flowed so copiously, that the stream was discoloured, notwithstanding its purity, and people were unable to drink it. Had not night come on and concealed the traces of their flight, many more of the enemy would have been slain. The victory was gained by Allāh's grace, who has established Islam for ever as the best of religions, notwithstanding that idolaters revolt against it. […] At length he arrived at the fort of Barba, in the country of Hardat, who was one of the Rais, that is 'kings' in the Hindi language. When Hardat heard of this, invasion by the protected warriors of Allāh, who advanced like the waves of the sea, with the angels around them on all sides, he became greatly agitated, his steps trembled, and he feared for his life, which was forfeited under the law of Allāh. So he reflected that his safety would best be secured by conforming to the religion of Islam, since Allāh's sword was drawn from the scabbard, and the whip of punishment was uplifted. He came forth, therefore, with ten thousand men, who all proclaimed their anxiety for conversion, and their rejection of idols. […] The infidels, when they found all their attempts fail, deserted the fort, and tried to cross the foaming river which flowed on the other side of the fort, thinking that beyond it they would be in security; but many of them were slain, taken, or drowned in the attempt,

> and went to the fire of hell. Nearly fifty thousand men were killed and drowned, and became the prey of beasts and crocodiles. Kulchand, taking his dagger, slew his wife, and then drove it into his own body. […] The Sultan then departed from the environs of the city, in which was a temple of the Hindus. The name of this place was Maharatu-l Hind. He saw there a building of exquisite structure, which the inhabitants said had been built, not by men, but by Genii, and there he witnessed practices contrary to the nature of man, and which could not be believed but from evidence of actual sight. […] The Sultan gave orders that all the temples should be burnt with naphtha and fire, and leveled with the ground. […] When Chandal heard of the advance of the Sultan, he lost his heart from excess of fright, and as he saw death with his mouth open towards him, there was no resource to him but flight. The Sultan ordered therefore that his five forts should be demolished from their foundations, the inhabitants buried in their ruins, and the demoniacal soldiers of the garrison plundered, slain, and imprisoned. […] he at last came up to his enemy, shortly before midnight on the 25th of Sha`bān [6th January, 1019 CE]. They had traveled over high and low ground without any marked road, not like merchants of Hazramaut travelling at ease with their mantles around them. The Sultan summoned the most religiously disposed of his followers, and ordered them to attack the enemy immediately. Many infidels were consequently slain or taken prisoners in this sudden attack, and the Muslims paid no regard to the booty till they had satiated themselves with the slaughter of the infidels and worshippers of the sun and fire. The friends of Allāh searched the bodies of the slain for three whole days, in order to obtain booty.[211]

Whether or not there is real magic, it cannot be denied that magic which is false can survive in culture, and tenaciously at that, because it depends on a wilful blindness about reality. The fact that it did not rain was not because my rain-charm is superstition: I have so many other reasons to invoke – that it might yet rain, that the charm was badly performed, that another counter-charm has been pronounced and has overwhelmed mine, etc. – which rescue the potential

---

211 The translation here, except for alteration of Musulman to Muslim and God to Allāh, is the standard English one, commissioned in India to legitimate British rule (Elliot & Dowson, 1869). The Arabic original is in verse.

validity of the charm. The fact that the pretenders to alchemy failed to make real gold was again and again blamed on *the crucibles*. Magic is like a pet cat: whilst everyone would prefer to imagine that it is unsoiled, it has this unfortunate tendency to leave smelly products everywhere. It behoves suburban cat-lovers to train their cats and clean their lawns quickly, so that the illusion that a cat does not produce excrement can be sustained.

Whether or not it is attributed to the intentions of the 'deity', there is an admirable excellence to their current versions of the 'monotheistic' religions' methods of covering, distracting from, and quick-shifting this 'excrement', the evidence of the failure of instances of their own doctrines, and blaming their very own alchemists' crucibles. One method is to have included in the god-mix (the 'one god') a humanoid, and not a particularly admirable one at that. A humanoid, like the doctrine of sin we considered earlier, is a boon for 'doctrine excrement' because it can, having made a promise, delay it, compromise with other pressures or concerns, and even deny you what you wish, while still 'loving you' and claiming your allegiance and hope in the promise eventually being fulfilled. Of course this really means that the mixotheists are honouring human attributes as absolute, which is exactly why these traditions (by the ventriloquist's manoeuvre[212]) vehemently attack such honour of humans in the other traditions while claiming, with quite spectacular gumption, to be free of it themselves.

Honest magic does not become a runaway trapped belief system because it does not need to. As was mentioned, the charm and its attendant rituals are usually complex, so a failed charm may have been said wrongly, perhaps learnt wrongly or copied wrongly. So the charm can be thrown out or adapted or adjusted. But dishonest magic can go much further astray. Once you have mixed your powers, exaggerated them to the extreme, declared them not to be mixed but the same, single thing, which is also a person, and become intoxicated by the megalomaniac potential to appropriate the entire universe for yourself with which that divine person favours you, how easy is it to throw that person out, adapt it or adjust it? Clearly it is not easy, but neither is it necessary, for a person, as well as being conveniently non-instantaneous in answering requests, can also have reasons for not answering requests: it can be angry and jealous and righteously indignant and vengeful. Since there are no other divine persons for this divine person to interact with, the only explanation for such emotions in him is in his interactions with non-divine persons, namely, *us*.

Under a tempered system like that taught by Jesus as recorded in the

---

212 Much more on this later: especially under 'Not by "this ascetic is our teacher"'.

canonical gospels, the worshipper's blame for the divine person's anger is usually taken upon himself or herself. However in the system taught broadly in the Old Testament documents, in churches and by Islām's prophet, blame can be valid when intra-social (within the group) or even inter-social (between groups). Thus the concept of a person in the god-mix does not just rescue prayer from obsolescence but also maintains the necessity of such elevating notions as total personal guilt (when one blames oneself), punishment within the society for supernatural crimes (when one blames one's society) and war between societies to subjugate or eliminate the supposedly god-excluded parties (when one blame's another society).

When *lack of prayer* (associated magically, thanks to the idea of the divine person and the divine anger, with bad conditions) comes to be considered *the justification for praying*, it is clear that prayer is in a closed loop of positive feedback. What exactly is insufficient could theoretically have been decided subtly, but historically it has been resolved very unsubtly, as the quantity, and the elaborateness, of the prayers: the 'solution' is therefore to increase these. When *lack of enforcement of morals* (associated with bad conditions in the same way) comes to be considered *the justification for enforcing morals*, the same runaway can occur. Similarly there can be a self-enriching cycle of holy war. It is these phenomena which should be placed in the scales with the eye-watering 'comforts of prayer for the masses'.

More unfortunately still, and here we reach the crux of the evil, these cycles of unawareness are not independent of each other. If they were, they would not reach the 'heights' (if that it is the word) that they do in our world. Enforcement of morals, after all, is not so attractive to people at large, and holy war much less so, though Hollywood might tell us different. Only prayer is really generally lusted after: this astonishing megalomaniac fantasy, one's every wish being magically realisable, is not surprisingly irresistible to the human mind. Now, if it were taught in these religions that there were three different deities, one each responsible for prayer, for judging morals, and for dealing with infidels, then they would remain conceptually separate and therefore independent. That is not what we find in our world, tragically. The necessity in 'monotheistic' systems of concealing the plurality of the god-mix means these three hypothetical divine secretaries must be dogmatised as a non-plural entity. I cannot stress enough how dramatically that aggravates the evil wrought by what would otherwise be rather a minor set of superstitions. Let us be clear.

Before we had three scenarios for superstition: firstly, prayers not being answered means our prayers are insufficient; secondly, morals degenerating means enforcement of morals in insufficient; and thirdly holy war being lost means holy war is not sufficient. Now, however, with our glorious single deity, uniting three secretaries in one, we have (as mathematicians will quickly see) nine scenarios for superstition. When prayers are not answered, the divine secretary must be angry, as before, but this time it could be not because of insufficient prayers, but because of insufficient enforcement of morals, or insufficient holy war. Similarly when morality is degenerating, it could still be due to insufficient enforcement of morals, but it could also be because of inadequate prayers or inadequate holy war. Finally, the lack of triumph in the latest holy war, though it could simply reflect insufficient holy war, could also be a 'result' of inadequate prayers, or insufficient enforcement of morality.

It is the 'light of monotheism' shining in the souls of humankind which has led to such elevating notions as 'praying for holy war', 'enforcing morals to bring blessings to society' and, best of all, 'holy war to bring the blessings of the deity and improve morals'.[213]

These evils are undeniable. The onus is on people who uphold these beliefs to decide, with utmost circumspection, whether they are *necessary* evils.

Case: modesty in (women's) attire

Another trapped belief system relates to covering the body as a means of protecting society from the presumed terrible effects of sexual excitement. In any society where the majority are men potentially excited by women's skin and women potentially excited by men's skin, a sexual unfairness as to which, women or men, should cover up will promote both itself and the insistence on the covering up. How could this be?

When questioned as to why it should be that only women are required to cover their arms, for example, people living in Muslim countries frequently have recourse to the fact, and it is a fact in their society, that a woman lifting her sleeve causes more sexual excitement among the men than a man lifting his sleeve would cause among the women. Lest non-Muslims turn smug, we should recall that exactly the same justification would be used almost universally now for requiring women, but not men, to cover their *chests*.

But the reason for the excitement is that the lifting is more *unusual* in the women such that men are less habituated to it. If it had been true that men were

---

[213] This simple but grim mesh is actually an example of that generally much more complex phenomenon, which we began to consider in our treatment of philosophy as faith's handmaid and will conclude in our discussion of analogy in theology under 'Not by thinking ideas through'.

required by tradition to cover up more than women, then of course a man lifting his sleeve or exposing his chest would cause more excitement.[214] The greater and more vociferous the sexual unfairness, the more potent and noticeable the differential reaction becomes, and so the more reason there seems to be to ignorant thinkers that the already covered up sex should cover up.[215] The fact obvious to the more aware and to those less focused on rearguard defence of such covering up traditions is that the covering up itself is what leads to the lack of habituation and the potential for exaggerated arousal. Just how unremarkable the exposed breasts of a woman can be is evident in the history of many cultures. Do proponents of the sexual arousal argument really believe that the Africans the missionaries encountered were, as a consequence of the 'shamefully' exposed breasts, constantly provoking uncontrolled sexual encounters? And in a modern day nudist camp does one find a higher level of sexual arousal than outside the camp? Of course in both cases it is people who are not habituated to exposure but to covering who are liable to be sexually aroused, namely the missionary in the tribe and the lecherous trespasser in the nudist camp, and the reason for their sexual arousal can be traced directly to the tradition of covering up to which they are habituated.

So much for the clash when such various traditions mix; but even within the covering up culture it is patently obvious that the covering up itself provokes arousal because of the natural association between the concept of restraint and the concept of the sexual activity it purports to restrain. Just as the well known fact that if you try to think of anything except an apple you will inevitably think of nothing else but an apple, the culture of restraint leads to obsession with exactly what is supposed to be restrained, such that so-called licentious cultures have a remarkable lack of public arousal and so-called chaste cultures are in fact 'meat markets', as any foreign traveller in the Middle East knows very well. In our debate with the dour face of religious justification for the shamefulness of the body must we stop smiling and pretend that we are not fully aware of how titillating such restrictions in fact lead the matter of clothing to become?

It has been well said thus:

---

214 This is actually found in some societies, such as the Tuareg, the desert-dwellers of the Libyan deserts, whose men are required to cover their faces with veils while the women go bare-faced. In such societies, of course, the sight of a man's face arouses more attention than a woman's.

215 This is the mechanism of skew in the capitalism of respectability we discovered.

These black masks
Proclaim an enshield beauty ten times louder
Than beauty could, displayed.

Measure for Measure (act II, scene 4)

Thus we can see that such restraint is particularly crude and superstitious (in the sense of making conceptual connections erroneously between 'restraining arousal' and 'lack of arousal'), and, in circumstances of sexual discrimination, extremely tenacious as a trapped belief system, not to mention open to ridicule on grounds that it is in fact completely tongue-in-cheek, such that its justification within the religious discourse is quite comic in its disingenuousness.[216]

Case: cruelty to and torture of the accused

Psychological loops operate not only on the scale of sustaining false beliefs, but in provoking extreme punishments for those who transgress them. We have already considered how a moral system based on external judgment and dividing good and bad leads to the necessity of connivance at exaggerated cruelty in exorcism-like punishments. An onlooker in extreme punishment is, however, not only drawn to join the punishers because of concern for his or her reputation, which would be in bad faith. The magical thinking which lies barely concealed under the surface of this ritual also encourages him or her to consider that if the punishers are going to excesses beyond what is warranted by the transgression, this cruel excess is due in some mysterious way to the demonic influence of what is being cast out, to which the natural response is of course to increase the cruelty. This is the essence of exorcism, the sliding of a supposed cure (by magical means) into horrible cruelty because one's reaction to one's own act of cruelty is blamed on the object of it and justifies greater cruelty: a psychological positive feedback loop which only the death of 'the possessed one' can break, as it frequently does.

This is the best explanation I know for the extremity of punishment for transgressions of absurd laws.

[216] We cannot go so far as some have, to accuse the entire religion of being a hoax whose bubble has not yet burst, but nevertheless one feels, especially with the growing prevalence in authoritarian societies of what Timur Kuran (Kuran, 1995) calls 'preference falsification', that it is not only covering up which is advocated tongue-in-cheek.

Case: elimination of obstacles to the unity of mankind

Perhaps the most pernicious trapped belief system is that in 'unity of mankind with us'. Is it necessary to point out that 'unity' – among *some* of us – is the same as 'division' – among *all* of us? That strengthening the one strengthens the other?

Unfortunately when people are accustomed to fantasising about a future unity (to be perfected by their messiah/mahdi slaughtering anyone who refuses to join their club) and so intensely that they lose the ability to distinguish between what is wished and what is, the task of pointing out the treacherousness of 'unity' is indeed necessary, but it is met with their fierce resistance.

The rhetoric of Christianity and Islām's teleology must be considered deceitful unless elimination of dissenters is guaranteed. After all they each claim that all people will be born into and remain in or be converted into their respective faith by the time 'the Doom' descends. What happened to all those dissenters?

A false religion which was facing conflicts with dissenters but which wanted to surf the great wave of 'unity of humankind' hysteria would have to come up with a neat, ethical way of temporarily overlooking, and ultimately eliminating, the awkwardness of these *others.* Now of course 'elimination' is rarely 'ethical' – unless, of course it is commanded by an inexorable deity. So we need, as it were, to invoke the said 'deity' to ordain such a massive elimination.

This is the decree we find in both Christianity and Islām: It is a final cataclysm, by which freedom from irritating dissenters will be available at last. As the sophistic unity doctrine infects more and more people and the resulting conflict intensifies – as the unbearable discrepancy for its adherents between the diversity of faiths in reality and the unity of faiths in the dream must cause it to – so does the stress (as the bloodshed mounts) of the embarrassment of professing such an obviously unsuccessful doctrine intensify, such that the need for relief – in the form on the one hand of canonical *postponement* of the unity indefinitely to the very elusive 'Day of Reckoning' and on the other of more elimination of dissenters now – becomes more and more urgent.

This is why the theory of a final peace in unity means a practice of eternal war out of escalating dividedness, and why those who are able to live a fantasy adhere more and more strictly to the doctrine of final peace under the desperate illusion that it is the solution to the wars that in reality it creates.

Case: security, risk society and emergency law

Though prolific in the massive religious traditions, trapped beliefs are not restricted to them by any means. One of the most remarkable phenomena of recent years, in Europe and the United States of America principally but to a lesser degree everywhere, has been the rise of the culture of risk, or in other words the breakdown of mutual trust and the consequent valuation of security against perceived threat from others (litigation over grievances and terrorist attacks being the most infamous) over and above civil liberties, which have therefore been steadily and largely voluntarily surrendered to 'benevolent' governments by a jittery public. Those voices (and they come from those familiar with the very same phenomena in the history of totalitarian states) who argue that this is the greatest madness to have afflicted 'liberal' cultures for centuries are generally drowned out by the consensus that security measures work and outweigh the 'nebulous advantages' of liberty.

What concerns us here is how this takes place. It is by means of the delusion inherent in the highlighting of risks in a society whose members are not perfectly informed and perfectly rational – which of course means every society: The risk culture draws attention to the very dangers being averted, much more attention than they would be accorded ordinarily as a result of the realisation of those potential dangers in real injury.[217] Through ordinary human irrationality which conflates the *force* of imagined potential injury with the *likelihood* of such potential being realised, this attention-drawing results in a massive fearfulness which is quite out of proportion with the likelihood of injury. This in turn generates the false conviction that counter-measures which would ordinarily be recognised as what they are, preposterous, are on the contrary necessary. So further and more extreme counter-measures are introduced, and so even more attention is drawn to the potential dangers.

It is, again, positive feedback of the most inexorable kind, because it is also in the interests of certain individuals to encourage it to continue even if they recognise its error. As an extremely instructive parallel, it has been noted by anthropologists that one of the factors sustaining belief in the power of magic rituals is that the rituals activate in onlookers what psychologists call 'vigilance-precaution systems', i.e. the fear generated in the people by the very uncanniness of the ritual makes them look for a method – in the ritual – to secure themselves against it.[218] Be they in hygeine, security, risk management, or whatever, the pervasive infection of our cultures with these measures over the last decade even cannot but be remarked upon by anyone who has thanks to some

[217] This is one example of cognitive bias, which we will consider in more detail later.

[218] (Boyer & Liénard, 2008)

peculiar fortitude of wariness not been lulled into sleepy acquiescence to them. It is obsessive-compulsive behaviour on a gargantuan scale, behaviour most lucrative to some.

In Britain this has led to the popularity of so-called 'situational crime prevention', advertised speciously as 'sharing responsibility for crimes' but in fact playing on public fears to generate intra-social conflicts whose resolution by state powers allows unparalleled intrusion of the state into even the most trivial details of our everyday lives.[219] This is aided and abetted by the leaps and bounds in surveillance technology. Not just cameras but biometric data collection, storage and sharing, even of genome data and even surreptitiously (various cases are at the time of writing going through the European Court where the true extent of such collection by the authorities is gradually coming to light) – inevitably have the effect of convincing the citizens that they are by default potential criminals. The psychological results of that we have already considered.

> As individuals alone in a societyless world, we have to live not among but against other individuals.[220]

It allows a more insidious subjection of the population than more overtly repressive measures.

> Subjection in minor affairs breaks out every day, and is felt by the whole community indiscriminately. It does not drive men [sic] to resistance, but it crosses them at every turn, till they are led to surrender the exercise

---

219 Apologists who point out that this is just part of the great movement spearheaded by such economic geniuses as Hayek, the religion which believes that so long as the market is free all benefits will naturally accrue, should note that Hayek never foresaw the degree to which personal information would be, via technology, made easily available to the government, and that therefore the free market, and the consequent culture of personal comfort and security-mania, would lead inevitably to what for him must be the worst possible scenario, the state taking control of everything, not just by broad strokes but in the minutiae of daily life. Wilson reports (Wilson, 2009, p. 326) that the European Human Rights Commissioner, when confronted with Britain's introduction of the infamous 'anti-social behaviour orders' (which led to Britain being dubbed the 'ASBO Nation'), commented on their empowerment of community punishment against individuals. 'This inevitably results in a very broad, and occasionally, excessive range of behaviour falling within their scope as the determination of what constitutes anti-social behaviour becomes conditional upon the views of any given collective.' (Gil-Robles)

220 (Wilson, 2009, p. 316)

> of their will. Thus the spirit is gradually broken and their character enervated.[221]

Closely associated processes are operating behind the sudden springing up everywhere of emergency laws which only a few decades ago would have made a hardened dictator blush. The problem is that emergency laws tend to stick – they have a pronounced tendency to outlive their midwifing emergency, assuming that there was one in the first place. If they fail to achieve their goals, which they almost always do (*vide* all those introduced as part of the War Against Terror and compare the international statistics on numbers of al-Qā`eda 'members'[222]), then this is not seen as a failure of the laws but only in their application and reach, so they are made more extreme and applied even more thoroughly. If, on the other hand, there seems to be any evidence for them working, and we should never forget that such evidence as a period of relative calm can be made to seem much more than it is by interested parties, then the laws will be retained as apparently useful.

Politicians are well aware of this phenomenon.

> As Roy Hattersley pointed out from the Labour opposition front bench in 1983 the paradox of anti-terror legislation is that if terrorism has decreased over the previous year the act is held up as a success and is therefore needed; if terrorism has increased it is needed more than ever. Therefore the failure of the laws can become the prime reason for their retention.[223]

Just as for the other trapped beliefs we have considered, the result of this trap is to create a carrier mechanism for the laws and the notion of their necessity in the minds of the public. This means that, absolutely independently of its benefit or lack of it, absolutely independently of the truth or otherwise of its name, 'security' legislation and the notion of its efficacy will be over-transmitted,

---

221 (Tocqueville, pp. 324,5)

222 It is, in fact, difficult to conceive of a more effective recruiting mechanism for groups such as al-Qā`eda than the antics of the US and British governments purportedly 'to curb it' in Iraq and Afghanistan – a fact which does not escape the bosses of security firms and 'rebuilding' contractors, of course, or for that matter the politicians financially involved with them.

223 This speech (6 Parl. Debs. Vol XXXVIII, cols 569-72) referred to in *What Price Liberty?* (Wilson, 2009, pp. 356,7)

and in time more and more people will come to value it for that reason, over-transmission because of delusion, alone. Meanwhile the fires of danger to that very security will, gradually and ubiquitously, be stoked.

Not by thinking ideas through, ma ākāraparivitakkena

'Api ca, bhāradvāja, suparivitakkitaṁyeva hoti, tañca hoti rittaṁ tucchaṁ musā; no cepi suparivitakkitaṁ hoti, tañca hoti bhūtaṁ tacchaṁ anaññathā. Saccamanurakkhatā, bhāradvāja, viññunā purisena nālamettha ekaṁsena niṭṭhaṁ gantuṁ – "idameva saccaṁ, moghamañña"'nti.

'Now some things are well thought out, and yet empty, trivial and false. Some things are not well thought out, and yet they are genuine, factual and unmistaken. To safeguard the truth, in such cases [as good, thinking ideas through] it isn't proper for a wise person to come to the definite conclusion that only something is true, and all else is vain.'

The Buddha[224]

Just as free-flowing water freezes under the influence of a cold wind,
So does the free basis set up cyclic existence under the single influence of holding identities.

Dudjom Lingpa (1835-1904)[225]

Have you ever plucked a rose from R, O, S, and E?

Rumi

Meaning

This has been translated as 'specious reasoning' or 'reasoning using analogies', however these are both more specific than the Pali term. The word ākāra refers literally to 'a shape': a sign, or a symbol, in its most general sense as a fixed pattern for communicating. For this reason it can also mean the expressions of feelings in the face, or the body language of the disposition of the body. Indeed it comes close to what we mean by the word 'language', and indeed if we change the base participle kāra into a past participle and replace the emphatic prefix with the prefix referring to perfection, we get samskṛta, i.e. the 'divine language' Sanskrit itself. Some Pali dictionaries say that in philosophy it refers to 'the whys', the reasons why something is the way it is, the manner of creation, the conditions for something to be, however the Sanskrit and Tibetan equivalents

---

224 In *The Caṅkī Discourse.*

225 (Lingpa, 2002)

(ākāra; dbyibs, rnam-pa, 'dra-ba, yul) mean form, physique, countenance; aspect, partial view; semblance, simile, analogy; way (of happening, etc.). The word 'idea', especially in its Greek original meaning, 'form' or 'pattern', seems excellent. Vitakka means analytical thinking or conceptualisation. (To break this down: takka we have already dealt with[226]; the prefix vi refers to analysis or aspects of a whole.) The prefix pari means completely, totally, exclusively, and so on.

Examples

Conceptual thought in general; language; the deployment of religious symbols; money's value; respectability; time and dates.

Irrelevancy as sources of certainty

Once again it is crucial to realise that the Buddha does not mean that these things are irrelevant to any purpose. That would be a bold claim! For this category could be considered to include all verbal communication! Clearly thinking ideas through is appropriate to the purpose of solving problems, and of reading (and writing) this book! However, it cannot be relied on by itself to establish certainty.

Loss of authenticity

> A man who loved God saw Majnūn sifting the earth of the road and said: 'Majnūn, what are you looking for?' 'I am looking for Laila,' he said. The man asked: 'Do you hope to find Layla there?' 'I look for her everywhere,' said Majnūn, 'in the hope of finding her somewhere.'
>
> Farīd ud-Dīn `Aṭṭār, Persian Sufi[227]

We have already explored the words used at the Buddha's time to refer to faith, and how they referred to an openness which modern ideas of faith do not. What begins as openness can unfortunately lead to closure, or conclusion, and here we will consider how this is a general property of language, signs or symbols used in communication, and therefore a reason to question the authority of these as a source of the authentic.

Let us begin by examining what happens when certain members of a community attain different states of realisation to the rest which allows them to

---

[226] See 'Not by philosophy'.

[227] From *Manṭiq uṭ-Ṭayr, the Conference of the Birds*, the first valley(`Attar, 1974)

access subtler or more hidden realities than those others. A certain person by being *open* to subtle phenomena, recognised them (however we want to describe it – inspiration, genius, visions, prophecy, etc.). Subsequently ideas were passed down *about* this knowledge and this openness. Since phenomena are what they are, particular, and since concepts are what they are, exclusions (in Sanskrit, apoha) of what they are not[228], individuals and groups can identify conceptually with *particular* subtle phenomena much more easily than they can 'receive' in openness *any* subtle phenomena. So naturally openness to the particular subtle phenomena that were known would have been emphasized, rather than total openness to any subtle phenomena. That is how through tradition, philosophy and logic, openness can be lost and displaced by what we might call the 'cuckoo', an exclusive concept.

So it could have been from śraddhā, 'holding to genuineness'[229], that we descended to something very different: a particularised longing, a particularised acceptance, but without willingness towards anything else, and therefore resistance to, and certainly no longing for or acceptance of, anything else. The flowing that śraddhā implies was blocked or frozen – and in this terrible step, any possible contact with śrat, genuineness, would have been lost. We now engage in 'faith'/vidh, ritualistic honour and worship of that particular subtle phenomenon, the 'god'/huta, the sacrificed-to and summoned, the 'divine'/deva, of light. We 'believe'/abhilubh, love and entice, it. It is El, power and Iḷa, to be glorified.

This would have been, in scientific terms, a step from enquiry into assumption. It has been discussed by a fair number of modern philosophers.

I would say that there is ample evidence in the history of our religious traditions to show that this is exactly what has happened as soon as there was considered to have been privileging revelation. There have been so many studies of the unique exclusivity of the traditions that describe themselves as 'monotheistic' that there is hardly any need to single out examples. Whether or not this is a sufficient historical explanation of the origin of the qualities of faith we highlighted in our consideration of the modern-day predicament I leave for others to research. Here I note simply that it is natural for such a descent to occur because of the nature of the conceptual patterns used to express meaning. These 'conceptual patterns used to express' are the ākāra the Buddha draws our

228 If this sounds weird, remember Popper's clarification of what truth means in scientific theories: while they can never be proved to be true (because hey would have to be true in all possible instances, which is impossible), they remain while they are workable, which means *until they have been disproved by experience.*

229 The meaning of this word we have already discussed.

attention to here, and in my discussion I will call them 'symbols', although the technical term in semantics is 'sign' or 'signifier'.

How concluded faith eradicates impartial faith

People who have made this step or (worse) inherited it are those who least recognise that they have. It is an extremely ironic situation. It is they who have lost genuineness, yet to protect their faith and belief, they turn not only on people closed to any subtle phenomena, 'unspiritual people', but also on those *more open than they themselves are*, and thus still open to genuineness.

Such Muslims-by-inheritance turned, and continue to turn, on Sufis, as exemplified in history by the imprisonments and executions of Sufis and nowadays by the ongoing bestsellerdom in Arab countries of the celebrated orthodox mediaeval scholar Ibn Jawzi's work *Talbīs Iblīs (Possession by the Devil)*, about half of which is a character assassination on the mystics and scholastic ridicule of their practices and views. Christians-by-inheritance turn on Gnostics, as 'heretics' whose bodies and books are to be eliminated from history, and most of us in post-Christian cultures have consequently inherited the idea that mysticism is either hocus-pocus or bad sex. Hindus-by-inheritance turn on their own traditions' tantrics, nowadays treated as black magicians, and on Buddhists, a treachery exemplified by the revered Hindu 'saint' Shankarācarya who is on record as having issued and had carried out a decree that all Buddhist books which did not mention the names of Hindu deities should be burnt.

While gnostics and Sufis were crucified, burnt alive, and so on, the assault was done with more finesse further east: take as an example the admirably devious reinterpretation of Buddhism in new additions to scriptures named, protesting too much perhaps, 'the Ancient' (purāṇa). These very clever passages 'reveal' that the god Viṣṇu decided, in view of the growing loss of faith in the old (true) religion, to sort out the goats from the sheep, the former being those dastardly devils who 'secretly' had no faith in the authority of the Veda (the Buddhists and many other seeker-ascetics). So he appeared as a Visitation (avatāra) in the form of a religious teacher (the Buddha), 'deviously' argued against that sacred authority, and thus lead all those of little faith into an easily recognisable party (the Buddhist Community) – a party which his next Visitation, Kālki, would annihilate. One purāṇa adds that Viṣṇu's wife Laxmi helped him out by appearing herself at the same time as a Visitation in the form of a shaven-headed nun and advocating (and enjoying) promiscuous sex with all of the four castes, a deliciously nasty and effectively suppressive reinterpretation of the Buddhist Community's championship of non-discrimination between castes.

Appearances' liability to being parasitised

It is ironic that faith and belief, spawned of 'truth-holding', śraddhā, should become parasites on their progenitor and thenceforth depend on it as their host, deriving spiritual benefit from it internally, while scoring political points of it externally.

Indeed 'parasitism' is not strong enough a word to describe this, since it implies that the host survives. Unlike a host in a host-parasite relationship, which remains at least clearly a host, in the case of faith the host suffers a great deal more: the fluid suffers a great deal more, from being confused with the frozen. For once the particular, or partial, experiences of the subtle have been conceptualized, and passed into tradition as symbols, those symbols can 'die'.

While genuineness is betrayed, group power is strengthened, however. Identifying with their identifiable known subtle phenomena, inherited from their predecessors, the group makes these phenomena their symbols. It is a closure to genuineness, but let us call it a rallying closure, since it allows a group identity and a community ('a faith') to form.

Natural and inevitable degeneration of symbols

And He said to me, 'The letter is the mountain pass for the Devil.'

-Al Niffari (Ṣufi saint)[230]

Any pattern which can be recognised generally and transmitted to a high degree of accuracy is potentially a symbol, i.e. it can potentially be used to communicate. The massive religions, being community-wide communications, make much use of symbols of course. A crucifix, carved or drawn, is a symbol. A statue of a Buddha, made or imagined, is a symbol. The Arabic word Allāh, written or said, is a symbol. Indeed the very etymology of the English word 'symbol' is testament to its religious importance: it comes from a Greek word meaning 'throw together', among the earliest uses of which was for Christian creeds.

Symbols arise in social organisms (not just humans, incidentally) because of intentions interacting with the environment – including other organisms. But symbols cannot but be approximations to perfect communication. When I use the symbol of pursed fingers to the mouth I cannot in an unqualified sense rely on another human interpreting this as, 'Give me food.' But because our

---

230 al-Niffari (an Islamic mystic who flourished in the 4th century h.), *Kitāb al-Mawāqif, Book of Stations*, Station 67 Line 28: و قال لي الحرف فج إبليس – my translation.

environments are similar ('shared' as we generally imagine) and because he looks like me I can guess that he has had similar experiences of hunger, and similar ways of eating. It doesn't take much imagination to see how such symbols would be elaborated on with time. For example once the symbol for requesting food is generally employed, a symbol for offering food conceivably arose on its back, but had to be distinct enough from the requesting symbol to avoid confusion. It might be then that this symbol for offering food could not be the obvious food signal of pursed fingers to mouth, but nevertheless may have been related.

The point is that more generally, as symbols proliferated to match intentions' proliferation, the intentions behind newer symbols were probably less easy to guess 'cold'. We might say newer symbols would necessarily be more 'abstract'. (If we want a modern example we might consider the smiley. The intention behind someone sending one is easy to guess: the chatter wishes us to think she is 'light-hearted' or 'good-natured' (adjectives). Conceivably in later, more sophisticated communication the chatter might intend to communicate an idea about the state, 'light-heartedness', but to avoid confusion the plain smiley could not be used. Instead we would need something less obviously just a smiling face. Maybe a smiling face in a thought cloud.)

If we consider symbols from the point of view of how guessable or conversely how abstract they are, we can see that most *words* (except maybe onomatopoeic ones) are certainly rather abstract symbols. That's why we need bi-lingual dictionaries. These dictionaries work only insofar as experiences of those using the two languages has been similar. Old Arabic, for instance, has many words 'translated' by the English 'camel': an English speaker has not had the required experience of camels to use so many different words properly. More generally (and here we reiterate the assertion of the 20th century analytical philosopher Willard Van Orman Quine[231]) it is impossible to make exact translation between two languages, even by examining the context in which words are used. We can learn more and more about the other language and thus *increase the guessability* of each word but it will remain a guess. Taking still more care we can see that this applies as much 'within one language and its community' as it does between two languages: it is impossible for any individual to make an exact translation of his intention into even his own society's language, never mind others', since he was not born with the language but *had to learn it*, as all infants do, as a 'foreign language', by trial and error, and continual refinement, until communication in it could be considered 'accurate', i.e. as close enough a guess as

---

[231] (Quine, 1960)

to be successful in the context of the society and its activities.[232]

While more guessable symbols afford generally accurate communication of intention, more abstract ones can be either accurate or wildly inaccurate. Despite what we might call their proneness to ambiguity, more abstract symbols can still manage to communicate intentions because, for example, we grow up with people who already use them to. What my own society's words, traffic signs, gestures, rituals, and abnormal behaviour mean to me is probably a close approximation to what they do to any other person from the same society. Such a context as an ongoing society, then, allows for accurate symbol-mediated communication. If however we consider the same symbols used between two different societies, we can see how the communication of intention might go wildly wrong. For example, thinking of road signs, if one society understands a red circle to mean the encircled pictured act is forbidden, while another understands it to mean it is permitted, visitors to either society from the other are likely to have accidents on the roads.

All historical personages, at least as far as we commonly conceive of them, are symbols. We inherit them. We associate them with other symbols according to our experience. They are rather abstract symbols: the sound of the name 'Gandhi' does not in itself conjure up a certain meek Indian politician unless I have grown up in or at least had some contact with a culture which can relate the sound to elements of my experience. Because historical personages are abstract symbols they afford potentially wild inaccuracy when used to communicate intentions. Furthermore, unless there is complete universal identity in inheritance, which of course there never is, they afford wilder and wilder inaccuracy with time.

That universal identity in inheritance is not achieved even when this is assiduously striven for is shown by what has happened to the historical personage Muḥammad, the prophet of the religion of Islām. Although Islām has had and still has many factions, by far the most important split until today is between the Shiites, who reject the authority of the first three caliphs of Islām's history (Abu Bakr, `Umar and `Uthmān), and the Sunnites, who accept them. A Shiite Muslim understands the intention behind the sound 'Muḥammad' only through his traditions, just as a Sunnite does, though by markedly different traditions. Because of their starkly different evaluation of early characters in the history of Islām, the very characters who transmitted the traditions about

232 This point will further help us understand why the Buddhist logicians called concepts 'exclusions' (apoha).

Muḥammad, the two groups have departed quite radically in what they mean by 'Muḥammad'. So this historical personage, together with a swathe of other characters and doctrinal terms, is therefore a symbol for wildly inaccurate communication between these two groups. Allāh's declaration in the Qur'ān, 'Al-yawma 'akmaltu lakum dīnkum – Today I have completed your religion,' is taken by the Shiites as Allāh's appointment of `Ali as caliph (rather than Abu Bakr) since by their traditions Muḥammad was drawing his listeners' attention to `Ali as he spoke the verse; Sunnites take it with rather less interpretational panache as referring simply to the conclusion of the Qur'ān's revelation. So between the Shiites and the Sunnites even the lines of their shared scripture are a symbol for wildly inaccurate communication.

So it need not surprise us that between much more divergent religious traditions, the wildness of inaccuracy when almost any symbol is used surpasses all limits. What did the Buddhists of Bamiyan intend by setting up the statues of the Buddha there? We can get a good idea because the majority of their traditions survive in the vast canon of Tibetan Buddhism[233], including scriptures and transmitted oral teachings which emphasise the building of such monuments and statues honouring the achievement of the Buddha – the extinction of suffering (nirvana) – to inspire others to achieve it and to remind them (in the details of the sculpture or architecture) of the methods by which they might achieve it. The Taliban, not renowned for their scholarship in Tibetan Buddhism, nevertheless have references in their own traditions to such symbols, such as the probably apocryphal sentence Maḥmūd Ghazni (whose exploits we have already enjoyed[234]) pronounced to priests trying to bribe him to leave, about the enormous lingam of Śiva in their temple, which his army plundered at Somanātha in India in the 11th century CE – a sentence which Mullah `Omar could therefore repeat a millennium later: 'Better to be a smasher of idols than a seller of them.' Statues of people, just like dead personages, are obviously abstract symbols with the potential for wildly inaccurate communication. The communication from the Bamiyan Buddhists to the Taliban of today by means of them is also clearly very inaccurate.

For the Taliban member who has no knowledge or acceptance of the

233 Padmasambhava, the central Buddha of Tibetan Buddhism, back to whom amost all Tibetan Buddhist teachings can be traced, was born in a kingdom in present-day Afghanistan and Pakistan, and the area was for centuries the worldwide heart of tantric Buddhism.

234 In the discussion of prayer in monotheism.

possibility of freedom from suffering, never mind any association of that knowledge with such a statue, offering respect or anything else (such as UN heritage aid) to it can only be classed as what, according to Bukhāri's traditions (for example), Muḥammad tried to put an end to – superstitious investment of such images with supernatural power, which only detracted from glorifying 'the One Deserving of glory'. So they created a new symbol, namely the destruction of the statues. How well did they communicate thus to average Buddhists? Well, while the *Zen* Buddhist might commend it as an instruction in 'killing the Buddha you see', most others would (and did) simply receive it as disrespect of what the Buddha achieved, made by someone therefore seemingly against the memory of the possibility and means of extinction of suffering, who therefore actually wants people and other living beings to go on suffering. So the destruction of an abstract symbol is clearly also an abstract symbol, and the Taliban's communication of their intention to modern Buddhists is, on the whole, wildly inaccurate. Meanwhile a fair number of bemused Europeans and Americans, who imagine the Buddha as a smiling fat man from China, might have wondered what all the fuss was about.

For better or for worse, symbols' power to endure may depend upon the fact that very various intentions can easily be attributed to them, i.e. upon their abstractness, their potential for wildly inaccurate communication. God (in various languages) is perhaps the supreme example. Compare educated Muslim pacifists on the one hand and militant death squads beheading their captives on the other. Clearly each one's intention in uttering the sound symbol, 'Allāhu akbar,' is very far removed from the other's. A careful study of the history of Jewish and Christian religion shows that what was meant by each of the words for God – Yahweh, El, Elohim, Adonai, and so on – was extremely diverse and evolved in each community over time[235]. Notoriously the philosophers' god was and is very far from that of the masses. That single symbol endured because it could be seen as intending pretty much what anyone intended.

We humans naturally believe in 'things' out there, things we conceive of as independent of our mind, even though we have never experienced anything other than through our mind. An instructive example is the labels we apply by convention to time: years, dates, times of day, seconds of the minute, etc. The decisions about how to divide time in each culture and across cultures may have had some original significance (such as a conquest or a historical figure's life), but

---

235 Karen Armstrong's book *The History of God* is an excellent overview (Armstrong, 1994).

belief in them as things independent of, and therefore somehow more awe-inspiring than, mere conventional agreement leads to all sorts of absurdities, such as millennial madness[236], astrology-based 'cancelling' of inauspicious days and 'doubling' of auspicious ones in certain traditional calendars, and the belief in certain 'modern' traditions of astrology that whatever stellar influence endowed the original zodiac signs' periods of transition is retained as is even though the time-labelling system has slipped into such inaccuracy with respect to the stars (because of the precession of the equinoxes) that each zodiac sign's supposed period of influence now applies not to at the transition of that zodiac sign but at that of the one next to it! Those who would pooh-pooh such nonsense as astrology would do well to reflect on how much of their ordinary anxiety depends on watching the clock or keeping track of the date, actually even to the detriment of tasks requiring completion in a certain period.

Such wilful or unwitting overlooking of the subjective 'I' is the normal psychological make-up for a modern human. The fact that the Buddha, for example, declared this belief mistaken meets mainly with hostility from modern sensibilities. Without considering at this point whether the declaration is justifiable or not, we can nevertheless say now that this belief in external things' independent existent encourages us to value symbols in themselves too and to overlook the very real process of subjectively intending something by using the symbol that we have been considering. This means symbols are potentially extremely powerful, especially over those unaware of this overlooking of the subjective, as is of course common knowledge, even among those that may not ever have considered how it is that they can be so powerful: civilizations can rise or fall on a symbol.

Probably this recognition, of the power of symbols and their potential to sway the unaware masses, was partly behind the seeming hatred of statues which is found so frequently in political religious histories, and particularly with certain Abrahamic prophets. Yet we have to admit that written patterns, sound patterns and behavioural patterns, the stuff of the Abrahamic religions, especially Judaism and Islām, are just as much symbols as a statue is, just as liable to 'go wild', and just as potent a temptation to be valued in themselves and to cause the symboliser to overlook his own subjective role, in short just as potent as a statue is as idols, as their histories amply demonstrate. The word idol derives from the Greek eidolon, meaning originally 'image', but later meaning only worshipped

236 As described at luxuriant length in *Extraordinary Mass Delusions* (Mackay, 1841).

images. Since all symbols are images, any symbol is potentially an idol. It might be objected that Allāh is not somehow 'in' the written word 'Allāh', but Muslims will not tread on it nevertheless, particularly if it is written in Arabic of course; a Jew who trod on the Torah would probably by his or her sacrilege be making some potent rebellion. However it is interpreted, the sound patterns called the Qur'ān and the Torah must not be changed: they are a fixed image. Deviations from prescribed prayer motions and liturgies and prescribed behaviour in general is unacceptable in the religions we have inherited: they are fixed. As soon as the sensory pattern is fixed, it is as a statue which has been carved, and thanks to its ambiguity its fixed image (a slogan, a ritual, a word, etc.) can rally the diverse masses.

The golem as a simile of degenerate symbols

If we allegorise the intention of earlier users of the symbol as the life of the symbol, then we can say that it is possible for a symbol to sicken or die, that is, for the communication of intention made later by the symbol to be different or completely divorced, from the communication of intention made earlier. This is a natural quality of any symbol since, while it itself is as though fixed, the use made of it is dependent on the ever-changing minds of humans. In a way, we can say that a symbol is always dead in itself, but is given life by its users, like a golem.

This possibility of divorcing the symbol from its earlier symbolisers' intention, plus the confusion or vagueness which results when there has been golem-mongering, exacerbated by our psychological foible towards believing in the independent existence of external things, can lead us to value the symbol more than any of the intentions with whose communication it was associated. This is a social phenomenon. Safety in numbers is naturally sought by all social animals including man, and the ambiguity of symbols allows them to be the common denominator of diverse collective intentions very easily. We might call this 'the democratic creation of a golem'. Indeed it is the deadest, and therefore most ambiguous, potentially the most wildly inaccurately communicating symbols which are most useful to throw the masses together: so when rallying together is a priority, dead symbols are much more powerful than the still authentically meaningful, less ambiguous, awkwardly living ones.

For example, two men using the symbol 'O God!' may well have opposite intentions for using it (such as a public declaration of war and an overwhelming sense of contrition). If a third man comes, with identical intentions to one of them, contrition let's say, but who does not use the symbol 'God', such that he does not share the common valuation of the symbol as externally real but reasons with his fellows, the first two are almost certainly likely to feel more unity with each other than either will with the third man. Since this unity, rallying together under false premises, depends on a golem symbol, we can say 'the golem has rallied them by trickery and excluded the third'.

This might seem blindingly obvious: you might argue it goes without saying. But it is worth reflecting on the process. Because this is exactly what makes inter-religious dialogue, and dialogue between the religious and the 'irreligious', so fraught. It is not just a matter of one's own symbols not being understood to communicate the same intentions by the othes: there is also the (perhaps subconsciously recognized) threat that such false rallying as dead symbols afford will be exposed. This means, tragically, that, wishing to defend a symbol that has come to be seen as externally real and therefore vulnerable, people rallying together under it must more and more avoid discussing what was intended by the earlier symbolisers, if indeed this is known.

We can say this allegorically as: 'Becoming a golem destroys the personality of the symbol.' It is as if not only the personality has been lost, but even the features of the face have rotted away. It is worse than mistaking the finger for the moon, as the Buddhist parable has it: it is being afraid to mention what the finger is pointing at, and consequently, for example, refuting the existence of the moon to escape from the fear. It could be argued that this is what incites those so-called 'orthodox' Muslim attacks on Sufism, or Protestant Christian attacks on 'mysticism', etc.

But the tragedy does not stop there. There is a positive feedback: the less associated the symbol is with its communicated intention, the more liable it is to be made a golem, the greater the threat that golem-based unifications will be exposed, and so the more the intention is wilfully dissociated from the symbol. Here we can see a closed cycle of degeneration which is inevitable in any system of symbol and communication. So with time communication by means of symbols undergoes natural degeneration. Earlier intentions behind the symbol are lost and replaced. It is inevitable that before long, no-one knows what the original intention of the symbol was, but it is valued only in itself and not for any other reason, and it is perfectly (and perfectly superficially) rallying.

How far this process has taken place with familiar religious symbols such as the idea of 'God', the cross, the prostration to Makkah, meditation, etc. I leave to the reader to contemplate.

The natural end-point of this degeneration is clearly, for the symbols, that they become (as the association with the earlier intentions is removed) absolutely ambiguous, (as they are increasingly valued in themselves or idolised) absolutely essential, (as variation in intention is bypassed by focusing on the meaningless) absolutely unifying, and (as nevertheless previously associated intentions are remembered as echoes to challenge the meaninglessness) absolutely doubted and anxiety-provoking; and for the later symbolisers that they become (because their symbols' earlier intention is lost) absolutely divorced from communication from the earlier symbolisers, (because of the symbols being valued in themselves or idolised) absolutely obsessed with preserving them at all costs, (because of the proscription of investigation of original intention of the symbols) absolutely mob-like and irrational in their formation of communities based on them, and (because of the staggering gap between what they are doing and what they say they are doing) absolutely hypocritical.

Again it is not difficult to recognize that this is exactly what we see unfolding throughout the history of the inherited religions and ideologies in our world until today.

Group identities are clearly a pre-requisite for inter-group conflict. The original subtle phenomena, those partial contacts with genuineness – now gone –, become themselves a cause of conflict between groups. The death of religious symbols and their revival as various kinds of golem symbols to cement group loyalties in recognizably superficial fashion, and the intensity of the proscriptions around them, as we have discussed above, only exacerbate the potential for inter-group conflict, of course.

In the course of our discussions we have found many and will find many more examples of this degeneration. The symbols need not originally even carry particularly subtle intentions. 'World peace', 'the unity of mankind', and 'justice'[237] are such symbols. So are all doctrines, all scriptures, and all holy personages. Each has the potential for rallying closure, leading inexorably to conflict.

Yet, like a tyrant, degenerate symbols cannot exist or act without the participation of the onlookers who form the community. If the mind concludes, there is closure; if it does not, there is not. This is a simple truth but it easily overlooked by the pessimistic. The difference between on the one hand holding to the genuineness, open as it must be any circumstances which might arise, leading as one might imagine perhaps to such profound insight into reality that contention no longer seems possible, and on the other hand various versions of conclusion (such as related to the idea of world peace) and the suppression of contention, is not so easy to spot, especially in excessively conceptualising

---

237 We discuss them under 'Not by intuitive acceptance of ideas'.

cultures such as Europe's and America's, as we shall see[238].

The simile of the hijacking of the appearance of authenticity

In this degeneration from the genuine by means of identification and ideas, we frequently see the hijacking of the religious symbols, because they are a respectable vocabulary, 'the vocabulary of the spirit' or whatever, by the unwitting closure-defenders when they turn against the holders of genuineness, against each other and against the opponents of spiritual practice. We can see dismally plentiful examples of this in the historical and current activities of the traditional religions.

Case: assimilation of previous a conquered religion's symbols

Accounts of missionary work, for example, are of course littered with such excellent examples of the hijacking of other religions' symbols. Not the least of them are the centuries-old appropriations ('legitimite baptisms' as the Catholic Encyclopaedia calls them) of the European religions' festivals (Easter, Christmas, St Valentine's Day, All Hallows, and many other more minor ones all existed as festivals on their current dates before anyone celebrating them had heard of a god-man from Nazareth, or his father).

Describing it as hijacking gives us deeper insight than the 'parasite' and 'golem' analogies (and certainly deeper insight than the 'baptism' analogy), because whereas a golem is recognised as such in the clear light of day, and a parasite cannot kill its host, at least until it has finished with it, a hijacked aircraft can appear normal, *even though the crew has been killed.* In this way the most degenerate religion would retain its respectability to all but the most penetrating observer. This is how each religious community potentially ends up rallying mindlessly together to defend symbols which have become absolutely divorced from their predecessors' intentions.

Case: from mercy to compassion

To take a seemingly minor, but in fact highly representative, example, we can consider how what used to be referred to as merciful gods these days go about by the name of compassionate gods. At first we might be puzzled: after all, do not 'mercy' and 'compassion' have the same meaning? Admittedly, we might say, mercy has a certain mediaeval ring to it, it brings to mind the chivalry of

---

238 See 'confusing the symbol with its referent' under 'Not by thinking ideas through'.

knights and the rule of kings. But surely it is an innocuous interchangeability of words?

Just how innocuous it is can be seen by considering whether, when one sees an act of violence being perpetrated, one considers oneself *merciful* by trying to prevent it. Of course one considers oneself *compassionate*. The difference, which in currently popular theology is being obscured, is between sympathy with someone to whom violence is being done by someone else, and sympathy with someone to whom *one is doing violence oneself*. In the less caring times from which the massive religions arose, adherents were less dainty about recognising their god's violence. Some daintiness must have arisen even two and a half millennia ago, given that the Buddha felt it worthwhile to teach in a story of previous life:

> These greedy liars propagate deceit,
> And fools believe the fictions they repeat;
> He who has eyes can see the sickening sight;
> Why does the 'Creator' not set his creatures right?
> If his wide power no limits can restrain,
> Why is his hand so rarely spread to bless?
> Why are his creatures all condemned to pain?
> Why does he not to all give happiness?
> Why do fraud, lies, and ignorance prevail?
> Why triumphs falsehood,—truth and justice fail?
> I count your Creator one th' injust among,
> Who made a world in which to shelter wrong.[239]

The self-coccooning and rather risible interpretational acrobatics which try to explain evil away from the creator's design have arisen only since we became, as a massive cultural entity, more caring, more understanding of others, and more disturbed by ascribing violence to our deity. This is why there has been a corresponding shift to preferring 'compassionate' in the religions of the celestial patriarch, a shift which, on close analysis rather heretically for them, implies that their omnipotent male recognises agency other than his own in the suffering embedded in his own creation, and for unthinking ears (so often more keenly courted) disguises that deity's responsibility.

---

239 This is from the Story of the life as Bhūridatta, number 543 in volume VI (Cowell & Rouse, 1907). I have replaced the untranslated 'Brahma' in Rouse's verse rendition with the translation 'Creator'.

Case: big brother offers security

It is not only in the traditional religions that such symbols are hijacked. In the world today, the new religion of security has its own pure vocabulary, and that vocabulary's power over the masses makes it a great temptation for those who would appropriate that power to their own ends. Laws introduced in emergency tend to outlast it, as we have seen. Then so-called anti-terrorist laws become ways to infringe previously well guarded liberties.

For example, the Terrorism Act of 2000 in Britain made it illegal to support foreign efforts to remove dictators. This was presumably related to typical British-raised Islāmist efforts to overthrow perceived infidel governments in Muslim countries, as would be recommended by an average Islāmist tract. It was pointed out however that the act would have criminalised supporting Nelson Mandela during the apartheid years, and the badly drafted clauses of the act led to some extraordinary examples of the police exercising their newly acquired stringent powers to arrest people on the pretext of suspicion for offences – for example the notorious arrests of such vicious terrorists as an elderly activist for heckling Jack Straw (who introduced the act), campaigners against a London arms fair, and a woman walking on a cycle path.[240]

Consider a parable:

> Once, long ago, spiders had no webs. Some still don't – we call them wolves – but in those times none of us did. We were our homes, so everywhere we went was our garden. Life was all surprise. Sometimes you found lots of insects; sometimes you starved for days. You lived as you could. Because that was the way things were. You roamed or stayed, you walked or jumped or floated through the air. On trees, in grass, on rock, in sand, under water, sometimes even riding on other animals – you experienced each path as you found it.
>
> Then something started to change. Some said it was a step forward, more intelligent; others said it was madness, insane sacrifice of freedom: for there was talk and thought and more talk and spiders shared their complaints about the times of starving. Some of us asked how we could be sure of food, make the supply more stable, as insurance against the times of lack.
>
> You might not know, but in those days we used our own parachutes to float through the air – and some of us still do. We squirt

240 (Wilson, 2009, p. 251)

them out of our bums, and the wind catches them, and we fly. It's quite exciting, to tell the truth, and many of us got addicted to it. But most only flew as part of their path, and kept some bum-gunk for throwing at insects – it's a good way to get a fly.

Anyway in the new movement some argued we should use our bums more usefully. They said wandering freely and throwing bum-gunk around willy-nilly was vulgar. We all knew you could spread out your gunk and wait for insects to hit it instead: even back then some of us used to spread out a web every morning in a different place – and some of us still do. But this new wave made it a rule to get the food this way, and before long they were saying that the other 'vulgar' way was abnormal.

It went on like that for a while. I think those of us who still wandered and flew sometimes felt the founders and joiners of the new movement, diligently weaving every morning so they could no longer wander or fly all day, were a bit silly, a bit pitiful even.

It got worse, though, when they took the movement into its next phase. They made a group decision to stop wandering – even by night – because they said they had found good fly-streams so could build in the same place every day. There was a running joke among the rest of us that they'd got so fat lazing all day on their webs that they were too unfit to move around at all. I say 'worse' because before long, because they no longer wandered, they started thinking a bit parochially, to say the least.

I suspect they were trying to retain their dignity in the face of the ridicule from the rest of us. Among themselves you could hear them saying that their new way was in 'fact' the old way. They accused us now not only of being vulgar and wasteful, but abnormal and dangerous. As you wandered from place to place, in each place you'd find these settlers talking of their exceptionally rich fly-stream and of the 'obvious wisdom' of hanging around there and settling rather than being a vagabond. When we said we could catch more flies by looking for them and hunting, they said we were liars. It didn't matter to them that the rest of us could also, if we wished, weave our web there temporarily and test their claims about the fly-stream's riches: because we moved on later, they said we were ignorant, and ungrateful. Some of them started to justify themselves by claiming that no-one could be a better hunter than the founder of their groupweb had been – and that he (it was always a male) had chosen to stay.

And they could only hear about other settlements from us. When we told them that the new wave spiders in the next settlement were, like them, endlessly boasting of their own fly-stream's superiority, they used to get all agitated, and accuse us of lying, or even blame us for their own agitation. A lot of us gave up talking to them: I mean, they all said the same thing anyway, and you always felt they were more concerned to protect their own little world, and save face after their decision to settle, than to listen to our travel stories.

Later on they started to make travel stories illegal.

You probably know of us spiders as fierce creatures, who would just as easily eat each other – even in sex – as eat insects. It's not quite fair: it's just that our greeting codes are rather similar to our eating codes, and we always get them mixed up.

Anyway when these settlements grew things got a bit tense. It was the greedier spiders that founded and joined them anyhow, and so they were even more likely than we were to resent others in the same fly-stream and eat each other 'by accident'. So some of them in some of the settlements said they would catch bigger flies (that otherwise would have got away) by changing the greeting codes to make them less ambiguous and – and this was a revolution – sharing the same web.

In a way it worked: in these huge new shared webs they could catch all sorts – even birds (although they are apparently very difficult to digest). But otherwise it was a disaster. If there's anything worse than a parochial mentality, it's a parochial mentality shared and therefore seemingly justified by a whole parochial community. And the big webs got in our way – it was difficult to avoid them if you followed the old ways of free wandering and flying. I don't mind if others want to go crazy, banning wandering (as they did), lying about normality (as they did), and criminalizing leaving the shared webs as treason (as they did), but I do mind when (as often happened) I'm minding my own business and then land by mistake in the thick of it, and have to listen to their nonsense myself. I heard one group even killed wanderers who dropped in – they said the travellers' ideas were dangerous to the groupweb's unity. They called the wanderers splittists for this reason.

You can see these huge groupwebs in a few places. They are so strong they pull all the tree branches towards them in arches. These communalists have often never seen a straight tree – they wouldn't recognize it: they think trees grow bent. They make such a mess, eating and shitting and pissing and dying all in the same place, they need ants to keep the web clean. The ants of course, being ants, still roam around and fly sometimes like us (though not so far) but they suck up to these fatsoes because of the free food. (Ants' babies are disgusting: they'll eat anything.)

There's some light in the darkness. Even though they've been born into the groupweb, some of the communalists' children use their spider sense. They wonder how the groupweb came to be, and why their bums can squirt in different shapes. Sometimes I creep up to the edge of a groupweb and some of the children come quietly to ask me about my traveller's tales. They're fat and slow and weak, but let's face it, in the end, a spider is a spider is a spider. So I remember these curious ones fondly when, at length, I wander off, squirt out a wind-net and fly…

Case: Christianity disrobes

It has been observed that many social and political movements which claim to be secular, including Communism, or which merely appear cynically religious, such as certain kinds of Islāmism, are in fact heavily dependent upon assumptions which were almost certainly inherited from *Christianity*, and that with it they inherit the exclusivity of Christianity.

The most influential of the Christian ideas by this standard of judgment seems to have been providence, which was reincarnated as historicism, the notion that there is meaning or purpose to history and its unfolding. In European thought this was massively popularised by Hegel in his so-called dialectical process. The mark of it has also been seen in Marx's theories, where it is left to its own devices under the assumption that the final emergence of perfect socialism (i.e. the Kingdom of Heaven on earth) is inevitable. Humanists and the most vocal proponents of the modern atheism, such as Daniel C. Dennett, by looking for hope in science, reveal their crypto-providence belief. This recognition allows John Gray to quip,

> Contemporary atheism is a Christian heresy that differs from earlier heresies chiefly in its intellectual crudity.[241]

241 In Chapter 6, subsection 'After Secularism' in *Black Mass* (Gray, 2007)

Another inheritance from the Christians in European cultures is the distinction between the sacred and the profane, made exalted Catholic doctrine since Augustine formulated the bifurcation between the Cities of God and Man. Indeed the very notion of the secular, so dear to modern politics there, and as opposed to the sacred, is derived from a process of de-sacralising in Christian conquest of Pagan lands, analogous to what we have seen of Islām.

Case: God hijacks Buddha

The combination of the intrusion of power into choice of authorities for truth and the valuation of the patterns of expression in themselves leads, in the field of inter-religious proselytising to less unwitting than appallingly cynical manipulations. It is hard to avoid suspicion of cynicism, for example, when considering the case of Christian missionaries in Tibet, who were confronted with the thorny problem of how to persuade the Tibetans to revere an imported god. It will be a particularly instructive example because of the richness of Tibet's traditions as we shall see.

The names of the missionaries' much foisted god, Jahweh or Elohim, even in a delicately disguised form such as Adonai, would be resisted as alien, they presumably conjectured. Tibetan culture and its language offered them various alternatives. First of all there are many words relating to lordship in Tibetan, but these were presumably not felt to be distinctive enough. One should have thought the natural choice would have been the usual general word for god (lha, the equivalent of the Indian deva – Lhasa means 'God Earth'). They ignored this 'deus' completely. There was always the word (dbang phyug) used in Tibetan to translate the Sanskrit Iśwara, which in Hindu cultures is applied as a general term meaning 'almighty god' and came to be used in the Buddhist culture which spread to Tibet especially for the concept of an 'eternal creator deity'. We have already seen it has even been etymologically linked with the name Yahweh.[242] But no, an 'almighty and eternal creator' was obviously not 'accurate' enough for their purposes. I leave it to the reader to surmise whether this might have something to do with the well-known and unanswerable logical refutations of such a notion in the Buddhist texts. There was even the lesser known but incomparably more august Vedic god 'Wa ru ṇa', from the Sanskrit Varuṇa:

242 We should nowadays pass over in embarrassed silence such assertions as made by the politician Jules Barthélemy Saint-Hilaire that Tibetan language 'possesses no term for the notion of God'.

> 'All-enveloping Sky', the name of an Aditya (in the Veda commonly the night as Mitra over the day, but often celebrated separately, whereas Mitra is rarely invoked alone); Varuṇa is one of the oldest of the Vedic gods, and is commonly thought to correspond to the equivalent of the Greeks, although of a more spiritual conception; he is often regarded as the supreme deity, being then styled 'king of the gods' or 'king of both gods and men' or 'king of the universe'; no other deity has such grand attributes and functions assigned to him [sic]; he is described as fashioning and upholding heaven and earth, as possessing extraordinary power and wisdom called māyā, as sending his spies or messengers throughout both worlds, as numbering the very winkings of men's eyes, as hating falsehood, as seizing transgressors with his paśa or noose, as inflicting diseases, especially dropsy, as pardoning sin, as the guardian of immortality…[243]

But no, this was still not 'accurate' enough.

As a reader of the Tibetan translation of the Bible can now appreciate, they chose instead the Buddhist term dgon mchog to 'translate' their god's name. This was an adjectival expression not even used of gods. It is the Buddhas, their Laws and their Community which are referred to as dgon mchog gsum (literally 'the rare and supreme three', more familiar to us as 'the Three Jewels'). Shaving it of the 'three' made it good enough to be Yahweh, apparently. As for our consideration here, it is easy to see how much more willing the Tibetans would be to accept exhortations in the (thus speciously translated) Bible to worship this 'Rare and Supreme' (especially when, as we shall see later, Tibetan ordinarily does not emphasis grammatical number) than they would be to worship a 'Yahweh' or the 'Elohim'. Whether the missionaries' strategy, of subsequently pointing out to the Tibetans that they had already been unwittingly worshipping these Middle Eastern deities ahem deity without realising they had, worked, is a question I leave for anthropologists specialising in Tibet.

Case: God hijacks anything and everything

In 1963 in his *Honest to God*, a book which sold over a million copies,

---

243 From the description in Monier Williams' Sanskrit dictionary. Incidentally, this deity, as a prototype of the Semitic version familiar to us, is a significant contributor to the growing current of sneered-at scholarship aiming to show the Vedic origin of *all* culture. We do not need to go so far, but it would be ludicrous to deny the similarities.

Bishop John Robinson questioned the tradition of speaking about God in 'spatial' metaphors, as up there or out there. He argued that this *was outmoded.* (Was not God then?) He argued that it presented a barrier to understanding. He suggested instead referring to God using concepts such as 'ground of being' which were in closer harmony with the more popular spiritual thinking and language of the time. And indeed this led to a range of experiments to redefine God which have persisted till now. One of the proposals arising from the book's challenge was a new academic discipline, 'theography', the study of how we talk of God.[244] That indeed would be a *post mortem* dissection. This has to be the *ne plus ultra* of valuing the form of the symbol (the verbal sign 'God') at the expense of everything else, sacrificing everything of meaning to the now utterly meaningless sound.

It brings to mind the image of some monstrous spider's web, drawing everything towards itself on its sticky strands:

> Little spiders scatter, and weave a web
> To live in, catch their prey in, wrap it up,
> And pierce it, suck it dry, and grow quite fat,
> And weave their silk, and make their web encroach:
> If it be large, the wider can they roam.
> If they be fat, the more prey can they catch.
>   But the hub of their web is an open space, a hole.
>
> Little men graduate, recite and preach,
> Take wise words of old and make their links,
> And claim the wisdom's theirs and grow in fame,
> And preach the more, write books that tell it all:
> The more their words the wider they can roam;
> The more respect they get, the more they fool.
>   But the 'God' of their words is nought, devoid of sense.
>
> The dragonflies are free; they dart and soar
> On wings ethereal, of dazzling light.
> They need no webs, no weaving, no trapping prey;
> They rise quite perfect, beautiful, from the pond.

---

244 I owe this example to the linguist David Crystal (Crystal, 2007).

Spiders only look, and drool, and wait.
And though they feast they never know this flight.
Men, only study and scheme and hope for more
And with their fame they never understand.

Little spiders, hark!
If you only knew to see the pond!
Circling your hub, around and round!
Proud of just a sticky, spreading snare.
Proud though just because you scuttle there
Round and round, creeping, low, all day,
Knowing the while that all depends on prey.
Proud, you speak about which virtue makes
The predator the stronger: that he takes,
The prey who in their weaknesses *succumb*.

But I know you well!
The pain you look upon the air-borne in;
I read your envy, that particular sin.
I know you know your web is just a gaol.
I know you see the dragonflies' free sail.
Your voice that deems the freedom sin is shrill.
Its echoes haunt you, ghosts of the doubts you kill.
Silence greets your cry the web is great.
If only you could learn from what you eat
Not make their wings your ornaments *and sham*.

O slaves of desire dragging and being dragged down,
Little spiders trapped by your own webs,
Cut through them and scatter, running free!
Indifferent, send anxiety away![245]

Case: the mystics' revenge

A certain irritation at the power authority involved in the kind of appropriations we have been considering should not persuade us to overlook the

245 This last verse is in fact a translation of a verse from the Dhammapada, in the section on rāga, desire.

very same hijacking going on of the symbols of the traditions most associated with hijacking, the 'monotheisms'. For it is not just they who appropriate others' symbols.

There is a noticeable trend in many Sufist traditions (especially the less orthodox such as the Mawlayiyya/Mevlevi of Rumi) to use the symbols of Islām in novel ways, a tendency which rotuinely earns them the stigma of 'innovation' (which is a negative term) from the stuffier doctors of orthodox Islām. There are innumerable examples of this, but just to mention a few: 'There is no deity except Allah,' has been taken to mean, 'There is no *thing* except Allah,' a justification for pantheism. Rumi has the Qur'ānic verses, which 'descended' after the Muslims won the Battle of Badr and regretted the violence, and which told them that it was not *they* who struck, but that it was *Allāh* who struck, as a teaching on total moment-by-moment creation of all phenomena by Allāh, a doctrine also propounded by the much more orthodox Sufist-influenced scholar Al-Ghazāli. Hallāj, the most controversial, had the name of the deity Allāh's inclusion of 'lā' – 'it is not' – serve as support for a teaching about the deity as absence which while it might please Meister Eckhardt did nothing to endear him to the pious doctors. Farīd ud-Dīn, with impressively delicate blasphemy, has the name of the grail for the birds in his quest parable turn out to be a number, namely how many (or few) of the birds make it to this 'end'. Bayazid took the injunctions on pilgrimage as instructions for his disciples to circumambulate *him* as the master. Even Muḥammad's name (written in Arabic, mḥmd) has been taken to show the pattern of prostrations in the Islāmic prayer – m for the first prostration, ḥ as sitting up, m as the second prostration and d as sitting up again.

Similar 'deconstructions' especially of what otherwise might be over-fixated language are of course found in Qabalistic reading of the Jewish texts, and, less famously, in the numerological, somatological, psychological or cosmological reinterpretation of the Sanskrit alphabet in the tantras of Hinduism[246].

We can conjecture that it was often in conditions of exasperation, when society's appreciation of symbols' importance had come to be almost totally dominated by a particular fixated set, that teachers of alternative doctrines resorted to reinterpretation of the symbols in order to be able to continue to teach. It does not seem, from a cursory historical overview, to have been especially successful, however. The 'DNA' of the fixed symbols was much more

---

[246] A famous example is the Parātrīśikāvivaraṇa of Abhinavagupta (Singh, 2005).

firmly associated with organised religion in the long run because of the inheritance of related scriptures and formidable conceptual networks, such that even if one generation was aflame with esoteric teachings, the next could often have forgotten them. Sufism persists largely as a formulaic relic, *especially in Islāmic countries*: modern masters easily bemoan the confinement of the great masters to the history books. Of course it is in the nature of the esoteric traditions that they would not appear so obviously, but to try to justify discovering Sufism translated into new forms and symbols detracts from our concern here on the forms and symbols which are left behind.

Languages' limitations

There is no such thing as a flawless idea:
In a strait-jacket of physical and verbal commitment
It is very difficult to encounter reality.[247]

I am free of all verbal imputation.[248]

from *The Tantra of the All Creating King, Awakened Mind*

Very few people would claim that the language you are used to has no influence on the way you think. The opposite idea, that it does, is known to linguists as the Sapir-Whorf hypothesis. Here, in the spirit of the discourse, we stress that whether or not there is such an influence, i.e. whether or not what you believe in depends on what language you speak, there are in any case a great number of suspicious parallels between beliefs and the languages of the people most commonly associated with having them. Here are some illustrative examples of this fascinating phenomenon.

Grammar

Case: syntactical particularity and the deity

Some languages (including most modern European, and Semitic, languages) distinguish in their grammar a thing which is treated as any one of a class from a thing which is particular and known and therefore not one of a class. In English, for example, this is done using the indefinite article (a or an) before the former and the definite article (the) before the latter. A similar sense

---

247 From chapter 46. This Buddhist scripture has been translated as *The Supreme Source* (Norbu & Clemente, 1999).

248 *Ibid* chapter 5.

of particularity in English is achieved by capitalising the first letter of a word – producing what we call a proper noun which usually makes the same kind of signal, to a particular known thing. In Arabic, though there is no indefinite article, al serves as the definite article. So in both languages sentences of the specifying type, such as,

> Our lord is not a god, he is (the) God.
> There is not any god except (the) God.

make sense. However, many languages (such as Latin and Persian) do not ordinarily make such a distinction. So a sentence like that would appear in these languages as something like

> Our lord is not god, he is god.
> There is not god, except there is god.

Consider the difficulties the concomitant differences in thought process can produce. To return briefly to the plight of our missionaries of Christ in Tibet: in Tibetan, ordinarily the meaning of the indefinite article is expressed by the number 'one', and the definite article not at all, and capital letters are not used as they are in English, say. So, 'a god' (such as any one of their own extremely populous collection) and 'the one god' or 'God' (of the hapless visiting Christian missionary) would be expressed the same way in Tibetan. So the 'supreme truth of belief in the one god' becomes 'supreme truth of belief in a god', which probably sounded rather unremarkable to the Tibetans. Missionaries were therefore forced to find other means to distinguish the Christian notion from crowding local divinities. Their solution was the hijack we have already considered.

Case: syntactical particularity and the messenger

An extraordinary example of how a language can matches an outlook, is the parallel between a peculiar ambiguity in Arabic language and the ambiguity in Islām between two different ways of looking at Muḥammad with cosmically different implications. To understand it we need a quick excurse into the grammar. In Arabic the genitive relation (A of B, or B's A) is expressed by word order, with the attributed thing first and the thing or person to which it is attributed second, e.g. English 'Muḥammad's cat' is expressed as Arabic 'qiṭṭat Muḥammad'. The second term is marked by a different vowel ending (*i*) which, however, is usually not pronounced. The peculiarity of this ordinary genitive construction in Arabic is that such a cat is not thus distinguished as on the one hand unique, 'Muḥammad's [only] cat', or on the other as one of many, what in English we would call 'a cat of Muḥammad's': both are expressed with the same form. This is because of the restrictions Arabic grammar places on the first term: not only can it not carry a definite article, even if it is definite, but it cannot either carry the nasalisation of the terminal vowel which would in other positions mark it as indefinite, even if it is indefinite. Now turning to our parallel with outlook: the second testimony in the announcement of Islām made from mosques throughout the day is that Muḥammad is rasūl Allāh: we can now see that falling on Arabian ears this conveys two meanings: Allāh's [only] prophet and a prophet of Allāh. Popular sentiment, without scriptural justification, frequently embraces the former totalitarianism, which makes Muḥammad's actions, speech and ideas the only sacred ones in the all world's cultures and religions; specious universalist apologetic leans to the latter, of course. These ideas are starkly distinguished in other languages and their consequences in action are clearly utterly divergent, yet the Arabic language holds them as 'one concept' – the opposition disappears into the grammar's ambiguity, and discussion of it requires the kind of paraphrasing of the sacred slogan which is simply not done in common practice.

Case: grammatical number and the deity

Similarly the importance of singularity in Islām is easily expressed in the Arabic language, where (like English) nouns and pronouns, and (unlike English) even adjectives are inescapably either singular or plural, or for that matter dual (a grammatical number not found in English at all), and where singular, dual and plural usually have strikingly different forms. Compare that to the many languages which do not ordinarily express the number of nouns, pronouns or adjectives at all. This is not a trivial difference: when god(s) is (are) unavailable to the senses (unlike all ordinary counted things) the matter of its singularity or their plurality is forced in concept into the metaphysical realm, personally unprovable to the extent that the divine is considered external; this means a speaker of Arabic, where number is fixed on every noun, literally *cannot speak* of the divine until he or she has chosen a *personally unprovable side in an inescapable dichotomy.*

Case: compounds' syntactical ambiguity and the deity

Conversely the ambiguity of Sanskrit compounds' syntax (as in English), where two words stuck together can have a wide variety of relationships, including parity, seems excellently suited to the mentality of the Hindu religions for which, for example, an avatāra is both the god itself and from the god at the same time. In Sanskrit devadūta, 'god-messenger', could mean both 'a messenger of god' and 'a god who is a messenger' (as well as, at a stretch, such exotica as 'he for whom god is a messenger', or, 'he whose messenger is like a god', etc.). However in Arabic, where compounds are extremely limited, such ambiguity is impossible, and there is a parallel, formidable doctrinal emphasis on the distinction between a messenger of god (rasūl ullāh), belief in which doctrine is obligatory, and a messenger who is god, belief in which notion is unpardonable sin.

One is tempted to wonder how many tedious, interminable squabbles we would have been spared in 'Christendom' if its language had been Sanskrit, whose compound word īshvaraputra can mean simultaneously the son of God and a son who is God!

Case: agent-patient direction and duality

Most European languages and Arabic both require their verbs to have subjects and their transitive verbs to have objects, and for subjects and objects to be clearly distinguished (in English by the word order, subject-verb-object, and in Arabic by the final vowel). In these languages

God created the heavens and the earth.

and

The heavens and the earth were created by God.

although they mean the same, are grammatically distinguishable from each other: in the first the subject is God and the verb is active; its object is the heavens and the earth. In the second the subject is the heavens and the earth and the verb is passive; there is no object and God is in the agentive case (expressed in English by the preposition 'by'). There is in these languages no way to escape from the subject-object difference, and the passive mood is vividly distinguished (in English by using the verb 'be' plus the past participle, and in Arabic either by different vowels – cf. kataba, he wrote, and kutiba, it was written, – or by a completely different verb form).

This rigidity has direct consequences for expressing religious teachings relating to overcoming the sense of being divided from the world. In Sanskrit, the word buddha is the past active participle of the verb budh meaning 'to understand' or 'awaken to an awareness or knowledge of' something, so it means '[the one] who understood or woke to an awareness of or knowledge of' something. Unlike even the heavy paraphrase in English, it can stand without an object (the 'something'). The Sanskrit past active participle is, for this verb and many others, identical in form to the past *passive* participle, and so could equally mean 'that which was understood' or 'of which one awakened to awareness or knowledge'. This suits Buddhists' intention very well, since one who attains buddhahood is supposed not to cling to the self-other dichotomy the way ignorant beings inescapably do, but to exist in non-dual awareness, a dimension of being known as dharmadhatu, sometimes translated as 'the basic space of phenomena'. Clearly languages which *per force* distinguish the passive from the active and insist on distinct subject and object cannot touch on this except by means of such wordiness as you are now reading. A Tibetan master has recently bemoaned in the introduction to one of his own treatises:

> Sometimes making the language too correct in English is very awkward, since in English there are no terms for a subjectless, objectless spiritual state. [...] It is very hard for those using proper English to understand the meaning. Even professors and scholars in universities, translators of Tibetan, and those studying Asian languages for many years have misinterpretations, because they get lost without making some kind of object or subject or certain identification, and when they don't have a non-dual view, it is very difficult for them to believe in a non-dual state. In western terms there is either a totally eternalist concept, with object and subject, or a nihilistic concept, there is nil, so there is no idea about dharmadhatu. [...] So one has to be careful to avoid obscuration from overly fanciful words or proper English, because non-doer speech does not exist in English.[249]

Sophisticated dissolutions of dualistic language such as have been done in the recent 'deconstructionist' schools of thought and were done two millennia ago by the Indian middle way (in Sanskrit, madhyamaka) school of Buddhism and 1500 years ago by the Indian non-dual (in Sanskrit, advaita) school of Hinduism, are presumably an entrance into unified reality for the awareness, but because of our language we English-speakers (or French-speakers or whatever) are dragged back to dual reality as soon as we express the next sentence. For example the middle way adept Nāgārjuna laughs at the concept 'limit' thus:

---

249 (Norbu T. , 2007)

If there is something beyond it, how can there really be a limit there?!
If there is nothing beyond it, how can there really be a limit there?!

But there is no linguistic way to avoid the eternalist implication of the word 'limit' or any word even if we put it in a sentence like,

A form is not a form.

This is the non-dual speaking to the dual, and we, with our dualistic habit of language, can only receive such sentences as insoluble (if, to some, delicious) paradoxes.

Case: subject-object distinction and the external deity

For some of my respected readers the notion that the deity is external is so deeply rooted in their culture that merely to hear that other cultures do not accept this will strike them as puzzling, or even shocking. Let us take an example.

Within the various traditions classified together as Tantric Buddhism and Tantric Hinduism there is the observance (in Sanskrit, yoga, literally 'yoking method') of imaginatively generating 'the deity' and worshipping it. In Buddhism this is referred to as utpanna krama, the 'building up' stage. In North Indian Buddhism and its descendants in the Newar areas of Nepal and in Tibet, such disciplines are classified by among other things how their practitioner views the deity with respect to themselves. Some tantric texts instruct the practitioners to view the deity as a lord and themselves as a servant, as in Islām. This kind of observance is referred to as 'ritual observance' (krīya yoga) and includes a great emphasis on purity, diet, and so on (like Islām does). Some tantras on the other hand instruct the practitioners to view the deity as a friend, as in Sufism and popular Christianity. This is referred to as observance by act (cārya yoga). Clearly in both these cases the deity is viewed, and invoked, as external. However, what will interest us most here is that a very large class of tantras, those of the great observance (mahā yoga) or unbettered observance (anuttara yoga) considered in all these traditions to be superior, instruct the practitioners to view, and invoke, the deity in/as/*which is* themselves, thus cutting through that tendency to view themselves in a limiting way which blocks their liberation. (The 'vision' or vidya which is the immediate discovery of one's awakened nature is transmitted in the Buddhist laying on of hands, the conferral of 'empowerment', and it is from this succession that tantra, literally 'what protects the succession', takes its name. Those who join the succession are called 'vision bearers', vidyadhāra.)

When accounts expounded from within such outlooks are translated into English and similar languages, awkwardnesses such as the 'in/as/which is' above are inevitable. In English verbs (like 'worship' and 'pray') cannot be used without distinct subject and object. This is why even Christianity, which includes traditions similar to the great observance with respect to the invocation and contemplation of Christ, seems to be paradoxical in English ('live in Christ' and 'Christ will live in you').

Trying to make a gold virtue out of the metal of necessity, as it were, Christian theologians have spoken of God as 'the extreme of language':

> the German theologian Paul van Buren says 'theistic' language is 'a case of walking language's borders', an attempt to express insight at the very edge of the 'platform of language' where, if we try to go further, 'we fall off into a misuse of words, into nonsensical jabbering, into the void where the rules give out'.[250]

One is tempted to question which side of the border at the edge of the platform theistic language is supposed to be, and if so we will be in good company, including the German theologian Rudolf Otto, whose notions of the 'numinous' and 'mysterium tremendum et fascinans' became the lingua franca for a whole generation of subsequent thinkers. Because the 'creator god' most theists relate to is so irremediably dualistic, it becomes itself an obstacle to expressing and transmitting the potential for realisation of non-dual states, particularly since the power concentration afforded by keeping the deity external[251] is a matter of urgent interest to certain parties. The Islāmic Sufi and Christian 'mystical' literature is littered with the verbose result of not being allowed to stop saying 'thou, God', just as Escher's hand cannot rub itself out. And the history of these two traditions is littered with the gory remains of those who did dare to stop saying 'thou'. We cannot forget that Manṣūr al-Ḥallāj, perhaps the greatest master of Sufism in history, was tortured to death and mutilated for saying, 'I am the Truth.' As Rumi says, there is no way to be admitted at the door of the Friend until, when asked, 'Who's there?' one says not,

---

250 (Crystal, 2006)

251 Who do you listen to when the greatest power in the universe only speaks through one person?

'It is I,' but, 'It is thou.'

Case: grammatical nominal emphasis and static realities

It is not just the masters of the spiritual path who have had issue with languages' limitations. The quantum physicist David Bohm recognised the rigidity of the English language in lacking the verbal focus he believes exists in Hebrew and instead emphasising the nominal, and so partly in an effort to make a better medium for expressing the unfamiliar realities being uncovered in his field attempted to initiate construction of a new form of language, which he called the rheomode, in which the recognition of interdependence of phenomena and their fluid not static nature would not be dismissed, as he felt they had been in ordinary language. Rather than be a slave to the self-fulfilling prophecies of a fragmented world he saw modern science reduced to, he wished to speak from the vantage of an all-encompassing unity, perhaps with a view to capturing thoughts about these ever more befuddling scientific discoveries that otherwise would be inexpressible or hopelessly distorted by expression.

> We can ask in a preliminary way whether there are features of the commonly used language which tend to sustain and propagate this fragmentation, as well as, perhaps, to reflect it. A cursory examination of this kind shows that a very important feature of this kind is the subject-verb-object structure of sentences, which is common to the grammar and syntax of modern languages. This structure implies that all action arises in a separate entity, the subject, and that, in cases described by a transitive verb, this action crosses over the space between them to another separate entity, the object. [...] This is a pervasive structure, leading in the whole of life to a function of thought tending to divide things into separate entities, such entities being conceived of as essentially fixed and static in their nature. When this view is carried to its limit, one arrives at the prevailing scientific world view, in which everything is regarded as ultimately constituted out of a set of basic particles of fixed nature.[252]

He saw that

> ...every language form carries a kind of dominant or prevailing world

---

[252] From chapter 2, part 2, in *Wholeness and the Implicate Order* (Bohm, 1980)

view, which tends to function in our thinking and in our perception whenever it is used, so that to give a clear expression of a world view contrary to the one implied in the primary structure of a language is usually very difficult.[253]

Concealing logical confusion

Similar points are made by advocates of a now notorious movement in general semantics initiated by Alfred Korzybski around his proposal that we avoid usage of the verb 'to be', which was taken to the extreme by his pupil D. David Bourland Jr as the new language 'E-prime', English shorn of its pernicious 'be'. The problem is, so say this movement, that in English be has at least five different meanings ('is identical to', 'is characterised by being' + adjective, 'exists', 'is situated' and as an auxiliary verb in certain verb forms) which often cannot be distinguished in its use. Semanticists get very agitated about such things because seemingly logical statements can become terribly messy because of the ambiguity.

> 'The little word is has its tragedies,' George Santayana wrote in 1923, in a passage that general semanticists quote frequently and fondly.
>
> > 'It names and identifies different things with the greatest innocence; and yet no two are ever identical, and if therein lies the charm of wedding them and calling them one, therein too lies the danger. Whenever I use the word is, except in sheer tautology, I deeply misuse it; and when I discover my error, the world seems to fall asunder…'
>
> Santayana's complaint had to do with locutions like 'Mary is a woman' and 'Mary is cold,' in which the verb is implies the tight coupling of equivalent things, whereas in fact in the first instance it joins nouns that have different levels of abstraction and in the second it joins a noun to an adjective that neither completely nor permanently qualifies it. Transgressions like these may seem trivial, but in fact they pose fundamental problems of logic, and they greatly bother critical thinkers.
>
> To these sins of the verb to be semanticists have added many others. For example, the verb makes possible the widespread use of the passive voice, conditioning us to accept detours around crucial issues

---

[253] *Ibid*, ch. 2, part 5

> of causality ('Mistakes were made'). It makes possible the raising of unanswerable, because hopelessly formulated, questions ('What is truth?'). It makes possible, too, the construction of a variety of phrases ('As is well known...') that casually sweep reasoning under the rug. One also finds the verb to be pressed into service on behalf of stereotypical labeling ('Scotsmen are stingy') and overbroad existential generalization ('I'm just no good'). These issues aside, semanticists say, the verb to be, broadly speaking, imputes an Aristotelian neatness, rigidity, and permanence to the world around us and to the relationships among all things in it – conditions that rarely have any basis in a dynamic reality.[254]

The ease with which unobservable identities can be suggested by the 'verb' seems to be paralleled by the characteristic conceptual/real confusion which has dogged European philosophy expressed in those languages, English but also French, German, and others, which suffer from equivalent 'verbs'.

Vocabulary

> A Party member is required to have not only the right opinions, but the right instincts. Many of the beliefs and attitudes demanded of him are never plainly stated, and *could not be stated*...
>
> Orwell, *Nineteen Eighty-Four*

Vocabulary is fluid and open to the winds of fashion, or worse. Re-structuring of language is most sinister, because there is a danger that when a re-structuring which involves concealing important signposts to truth is carried out successfully, the entire language adopts it and therefore there is no longer any way to discuss what was concealed, unless extensive analysis is done. This will tend to seem unpersuasive since our nature is to believe, 'If there is no word for it, it is not true.' We will consider examples of intentional and accidental blind spots.

>Double standards

A common kind of re-structuring is to keep a word but change the sense in which it is used. When a particular group uses an engineered vocabulary, it can be applied by them across the in-group/out-group divide in order to conceal

---

254 (Murphay, 1992)

outrages to reason which occur across that divide.

Case: punishment without harm

Let us consider the example of re-defining the word 'harm' to exclude the harm done by authorities. Given that the main rationale for punishment of crimes is supposed to be to discourage them, this leaves us the awkward fact that the reason we refrain from committing crimes our desires would otherwise lead us to commit is because we are afraid of non-harm. Luckily, language deceives reason easily, and on the surface it seems logical to say that a criminal only fears punishment because in his or her error he or she does not realise the punishment is non-harm, in fact his or her moral improvement. In Orwell's terms this is the doublethink of the establishment being imposed on someone who does not yet doublethink. If the punishment is successful, and it is supposed to be of course by its proponents, then the criminal will emerge from it a new person, who shares now the establishment view (as he gazes on his wrist stump, one imagines) that the punishment was harmless. A most dubious interpretational step has been taken, from seeing 'a criminal harmed to scare him and others', to seeing 'someone who fails to believe in the ideology of improvement by violence converted into a believer by means of that improvement'. Quite likely nothing of the kind has in fact occurred (the 'improved' criminal will speak of his improvement with tongue in cheek, assuming that the former is still present) but the doublethink of the establishment releases them from doubt.

> But it was all right, everything was all right. He had won the victory over himself. He loved Big Brother.

Case: conversion to a religion

The more general, and more obviously bankrupt, operation of this principle in the realm of conversion between religions will now be clear. Just as the punished criminal has undergone not harm but benefit, the one who has 'rejected his own culture's beliefs' (as the old religion's community see it) has 'seen the truth' (as the new does). How could any damage have been done when this lucky individual has come into the light? Wait until the same individual converts back, to see.

>Invention of metaphysical distinctions

Case: agnostic

Engineering can involve the creation of new words by the party whose meaning is a way of deceiving the others into accepting that there is a greater distinction between the party and the others than there really is.

The word 'agnostic' is supposed to refer to that part of humanity who, rather than saying, 'God exists,' or, 'Gods exist,' or, 'No god exists,' say, 'I don't know if any god exists.' This classification on the surface looks reasonable. But the fact that it originated among those who say, 'God exists,' should give us a clue that something is not quite right.

The term as it is used today still carries the crudity of pre-aware societies and magical thinking in it, since it mixes description with wish. Agnostic literally means not (a-) knowing (gnostic). The implication is that everyone else knows. Of course in the matter of god, even the surest believer can be wrong. (How else could we have convinced believers of utterly different religions?) So sure belief is different to knowing. Knowing means, at least potentially, without the possibility of error.[255] Even prophets do not know in this sense, even though they are sure. But the prophets' party have changed the meaning of 'to know': knowledge is no longer universally available, but knowledge of God by God with no further justification needed. In terms of individual experience, everyone is of course agnostic: it is the fact that there is no possibility of being unmistaken which has led to familiar centuries of conflict on religious issues. However, it is that believers make a public claim, 'I know,' which appears to remove them from the category of agnostic in the sense in which it is currently used. In this term, what is and what is wished are conflated. This is a relic from old societies before they gained awareness of individual consciousness: for such primitive mobs what you are is what you appear to be in the mob. In such societies, where there was no sense of the separation of wish from influence, or to put it another way where magical thinking predominated, it was believed that to convince someone you knew something was the same as knowing it, since the object of knowledge, truth, was agreed by the mob – it was a norm decided by convention.

The term would not have survived the scientific age had it not been for the covering up of this fact, for the persistence of a much-repressed magical thinking in all of us, and for the fact that the term is an example of what we might

---

[255] To avoid confusion I do not consider here the engineering of the word 'know' in modern theological discourse to mean 'believe'.

call pride-selected[256] controversies: believers are happy to use the term (of others) since it flatters their position, and those others are happy to use the term (of themselves) since, refusing the former's belief, they see it as flattering their position.[257]

The opposite of agnostic is in fact gnostic. Those who know in this sense without exception report that they cannot express what they have known without causing misunderstanding in those who have not known, so aside from reporting that event, of paramount importance, I refrain from further comment.

>*Concealing particularity and plurality*

Case: the object of belief

Earlier we noted that in some languages verbs such as 'believe' ordinarily take an object, which renders these languages unable to express the non-dual. However, a common tactic of religions which have undergone closure as we described it is to conceal the closure by re-defining the meaning of words such as 'believe' to mean only 'believe our tradition' and stop using an object. We are so used to hearing about believers and non-believers, faithful and infidels, that it is worth remembering that these terms all refer to belief in and fidelity to particular entities – and more pertinently those entities' representatives – even if these are given 'the privilege' of not being stated. Why they are not stated should be obvious. It is the non-statement in language of the particularity and then the conflation of two symbols – the 'particular belief' and the 'general belief' – which allows the particular entity to 'steal' the general belief; in exactly the same way it is the non-appearance in art of the deity's particularity (an image) and then the conflation of two symbols – the 'particular worship' and the 'general worship' – which allows the particular entity to 'steal' the general worship. This in short is the (political and psychological) driving power behind the aggression of the various dogmatic religious traditions towards other forms of belief and worship.

While this is familiar in the case of Christianity and Islām ('Are you a believer or an unbeliever?' clearly refers to a particular object of belief rather than belief in general) it may come as a surprise that such dogmatism developed also in some traditions of Buddhism. In his *Excellent Aim* the ex-Brāhmaṇa convert Buddhaghoṣa, whose works became the most authoritative commentaries for the Elders' Tradition (Theravāda), says that faith can *only be* in the three jewels

---

256 I am using the term 'selected' in its biological sense.

257 More on this in the discussions of authority and teacher communities to come.

(Buddha, Dharma and Saṅgha), and that any other so-called faith is no more than a voicing of acquiescence (vacana sampaṭicchanamattameva). Modern teachers of that tradition tend to criticise this rather dogmatic position, however.[258]

Such symbol conflation only works because the mind does not ordinarily notice absence, that is to say, it does not easily recognise an absence of any image itself to be an image.[259] With intelligence we can see that it is, however, an image: if it were not, we would not be able to see the empty space.

Case: to who one prays

Now let us turn to the object of oblations and prayers, in which such particularity is and has been concealed that it almost defies belief.

Augustine (whose arguments cover with finer acumen the same ground as most current apologists', for which thoroughness I am grateful to him) explains how it can be that people praying to God for something are not the causes of God to change his will (since this would demean God) by saying that God wishes them to conform to his will by this praying. The argument is clearly a good one because it occurs in the Islāmic tradition too, in the works of Al-Ghazāli, 'Algazel' as he is know in European texts, whose kudos in the Islāmic tradition is intimated by the various titles it has awarded him, such as Ḥujjat ul-Islām, 'The Proof of Islām'. A persuasive argument, perhaps, but how many different Gods are there in this little piece of skulduggery?

First there is the God to whom the believers are praying. In their own conception they are clearly not praying to {a God who has already predestined everything whether or not they pray} – or for that matter to {a God who has predestined whether they pray}. They are praying to {a God who responds}. Otherwise how could they ask for anything from Him?

Meanwhile there is a second God – defined by our sainted philosopher as {a being who creates the prayer tendency as a way for his creatures to conform to His will}. But what is His will? Is it just that they pray? If it were, prayer would have no motive, nothing to ask for. This could not be prayer in any known sense of the word, so our earlier believers would not have even been praying. In that case how could it be conformity with God's will?

Perhaps it is a third God, whose will is that they ask for something whether or not they are destined to get it: then He is a God who wills that some

---

[258] (Thera N. , 1956/1979, p. 123)

[259] This is analagous to the reason superstition arises as described in our discussion of inference.

people get the opposite of what they pray for, as if it were a punishment for praying - so He wills their suffering for no other reason than their conformity to his will.

Perhaps it is a fourth God, who wills them to pray only if they are already destined to get what they pray for, such that every prayer is 'answered'; but then the prayer's reward is different from what is prayed for. (The believer is instructed not to challenge God, i.e. expect him to answer every prayer, so he cannot pray, 'Please God give me what you have already predestined such that I am already certain to get it.').

In all these cases what the person praying believes is by necessity delusional, both about the boon for which they are praying and about the 'Granter' to Whom they are praying.

While this might be acceptable to those who believe man so far from God as to be unable to relate to him other than in such an abject conceptual mess, one has to ask, if someone like Augustine can discover the true way of praying which fits the delusional mistake into some kind of rational framework, why he was so loathe to correct the delusional activity (asking for boons) in those who performed it. Either he could guide these deluded people or he could not. He seems not to have guided them. In which case, is he guiding the rational types like himself into delusion?

This superior attitude (what we might call the 'Let them eat cake' way of dealing with ordinary believers – who are of course *the transmitters*), by the way, characterises much of Augustine's writings. But he is hardly unique among advocates of monotheism for being satisfied with herding people into the god pen on any pretext, a tendency we earlier noted they share with Aristotle and his preference for rhetoric over instruction.

Augustine's religion of course calls itself monotheistic. Islām refers to itself often as 'the most uncompromising monotheism', yet its adherents also pray. Both therefore conceal plurality of gods under the unit term God, which is in ordinary understanding therefore 'confused'. This is another reason why such 'monotheism', actually crypto-polytheism, secret god-plurality, would better be called 'mixotheism'.

Case: three mutually exclusive religions authored by the same god

Worse, nowadays it is common to brace three religions, Judaism, Christianity and Islām, together, as worshipping the same (secretly plural) god. However, one could reasonably protest, calling three different things (such as a dog, a dustbin and a virus) by the same name (such as 'foufou') doesn't make them the same. The myths, or foundational stories if you will, of the three versions of 'mixotheism' we are considering, are wildly different, on points so abstract, conceptual and unapproachable by circumspect reason that they frequently become quite allergic to each other in their fierceness to assert themselves. Liberals' whitewash soon gets stained when we turn to the original texts they claim to be 'respecting'. Ordinarily we are careful to distinguish the different senses of one word. A god which to be kind we must say simply shares the same name, Allāh, was according to many scholars worshipped before Muḥammad's message in his home town as related to the power of the moon, and had a family including, notoriously[260], daughters. Are we really intelligent to accept that while, on the one hand, Allāh of Islām can be rescued from these associations with 'the Times of Ignorance' by pointing out that a like name does *not* imply a like god, and on the other hand that a Sinai volcano god and later god of a tribe (Yahweh), an entire divine court of Cana`anite deities (Elohim), the man Jesus and the god on his throne over Muḥammad's home town (Allāh of the Qur'ān) are the same by virtue of the fact that they are all called 'God' in English or 'Allāh' in Arabic? There is not even any agreement between these three Semitic faiths as to which of this list of invisible and visible entities should be included in the privilege of what we might call 'whitewashing with the one word'. The resistance adherents of these religions will put up, that the presence of the god is eternal and it is only mankind's understanding which is ever adjusted, can only be sustained by what amounts to atheism for the other Semitic faiths. Unfortunately this is historically the solution that has most often been favoured, and acted on.

Indeed, for anyone familiar with the history of these religions, it is hard to deny that much of their political drive was *derived* from this very denial of other religions (the Romans' accusation that the Christians were atheists perhaps encouraged by the recognition of this power), so one could even argue that while seeming to deny other gods existence, they nevertheless relied on those gods. This is promoted by the Bible texts (unlike the Qur'ān) with their magisterially accomplished confusion of two meanings of 'one god' – as sole and

---

260 The Qur'ān with fine rhetoric but now awkward ethics asked its first audience how they dared ascribe daughters to Allāh when daughters were so obviously less valuable than sons to humans. This admonition came in response to the famous 'satanic verses' incident in which verses seemed to come to the prophet permitting worship of these daughters, verses which were later recognised by him as the interpolations of the Enemy.

as the boss of the rest. The slogan, 'There is no god except Allāh!' doesn't work so well as a rabble-rouser when no-one in the vicinity worships anything else anyway.

Case: irreligion as religion

One noticeable consequence for the adherents of believing in Judaism or Islām, or even comparatively idolatrous Christianity, is *pride* in this superficially unitary conception of the object of their belief. Since most of us have been raised in cultures deeply imbued with this pride, it behoves me to draw attention to what generates it and what it really implies.

These traditions' own discourses are of course aware of this pride and treat it as though it were a natural thing given the content of the belief. Since the content to us seems on the contrary to warrant shame, we are forced to find other bases for it.

The biggest component of this pride, and the one least admitted to, is the adherent delighting his or her own vanity by contemplating his or her own kudos magically elevated by means of aggressive atheist pronouncements. Each version of 'monotheism' depends on some manifestation (a message from or incarnation of the god) and demands atheism towards gods previous to and subsequent to this message. This is even true, though they would deny it in various ways, of Christians in their relation to the god of Judaism – and of Muslims in their relation to the gods of Judaism and Christianity. And of course the gods of other communities' religions are also the object of these atheist pronouncements. It is a startling feature of the monotheistic systems that they cannot tolerate the goodness of rival (and even rival monotheistic) systems, to the extent that they will (and here lies a great tragedy of human history) attack virtue in those systems and make propaganda over it that it be vice. Then, as if that were not enough, the teaching that 'your god is a jealous god' deifies this very squalid human emotion, which we might most generously describe as 'spiritual jealousy', and places it nicely out of the sphere of debate (along with all of the deity's other disgusting attributes). Buddhism brings 'spiritual jealousy' back into the sphere of transformation, as we shall see[261].

We have already considered how these religions have made a virtue out of the necessity of irrational claims of certainty. By so doing, these religions have encouraged any adherent of theirs to feel the more pride in those atheistic

---

261 Spiritual jealousy in *others* is dealt with in the meditations on Caring and the same in *oneself* is dealt with in the meditation on Joy.

pronouncements on other religions which he or she has the less evidence for: a surrendering of the nobility of the discriminatory human mind as a sacrifice to the god in order to be rewarded very justly with (albeit unwitting) ignorance.

Case: unification masquerading as unity

Those of us unlucky enough to be secluded in the bosom lands of the massive faiths might be surprised to learn that the uniqueness of so-called 'monotheism' is not in the worship of a single deity. Jews are commonly referred to as 'the inventors of monotheism', and 'monotheism' itself as unique to these three traditions, but those who do so in today's world with its easy access to other traditions in all cultures are, it must be admitted, either ignorant or wilfully negligent. Even writ in stone and in the vicinity of 'the Holy Land' as it is their wont to insist on in matters religious do they have testament to the contrary in the records of the Egyptian pharaoh Akhenaten whose only god was Aten, but travelling further east (God forbid) we find, of course, countless such religions both extinct and extant. Just to consider one rather breath-taking example of averted eyes, there is the so-called religion of Hinduism, which was named by the Muslim invaders incidentally and only assumed any sense of unity in antagonism to them: it encompasses many religions, in fact, including several which by this single-deity definition would have to be accepted as monotheism. In modern times, thanks to this antagonistic unifying, it is fashionable for any Hindu to accept any other Hindu's god or gods, but this unifying process has not been without the kind of bloody violence between exclusivists which would make inhabitants of that other 'Holy Land' feel quite at home – notably between the Śaiva and the Vaiṣṇava (worshippers of Śiva and Viṣṇu respectively). Besides this each one of the numerous tantric cults in Hinduism, Buddhism and Jainism is a monotheism in itself – the unique god occupying the centre of the divine palace and other gods (including sometimes the gods of other religions) relegated in the court of the main god to the status of bound servants, in exact analogy to the process of angelisation of the gods under El's dominion in the development of Jewish religion.[262]

The characteristic of these 'monotheisms' that comes closest to what we might call uniqueness, and which adverts to their great antiquity, is in mixing up what is wished for and what is, i.e. magical thinking. In the languages of the

[262] If you are interested in this parallel, as the Dalai Lama apparently was, deluging rabbis with involved questions about the exact forms, colours, implements and significations of the various angels, a good place to start is *The Jewish Encyclopaedia.*

original messages, they talk about the unity of the deity for mankind being a process, and that the duty of that process of unifying the god is incumbent on its adherents. Mankind seemingly inevitably gets things wrong about the status of his 'Creator' and must be rectified – but not directly, only ever by means of wordy revelations, delivered and spread by the ever-ready humble world-dominators. This, like the occurrence of infant sickness, is a curious state of affairs under a supposedly omnipotent god. It is explained away by inverting terms: tribulation is, we are told, 'God's love' in that mankind can show his devotion in fidelity to the 'god' despite that tribulation: cruelty as love! That this offers psychological consolation (and paralysis) to concentration camp inmates does not detract from its bankruptcy as explanation. It is furthermore an example of the over-stretched concept which promotes itself by controversy.

From our discussion we can see that, although there are strong currents within these traditions (Judaism, Christianity and Islām) *wishing for* unity (by some adherents – not all!), an impartial observer cannot help but conclude that the wish has not been fulfilled. For the wishing is just more of their speciality, magic, and because the magic cannot be doubted, it is hysterically believed. This belief is often encouraged by second-rate reasoning linking this to the unity of mankind, which we have already dealt with.

>Concealing non-uniqueness

An ideology or creed which claims to be unique but which is in reality comparable to others can conceal the comparability by using a special vocabulary of itself which is jealously withdrawn from others.

What is usually pleaded is that there is special meaning in the insisted on these words (originating in various languages of course) which cannot be conveyed in translation. But if unsatisfactoriness of translation were the criterion for not translating then there would be no translations of any words into any other languages. We translate when we want to communicate, and these faiths do not. In particular all religions make these claims about their own sets of words so if this were truly the criterion then all religions should also accept each other's sets of words rather than use their own sets of words to describe other religions. Of course this never happens, and the reason is that the advertised criterion is a smoke-screen: the real criterion for not translating is the need of each particular self-isolating (self-arrogating) religious community for unjustifiable auxesis[263] of its own vocabulary.

---

263 See 'auxesis and meiosis' under 'Not by "this ascetic is our teacher"' for the

Case: Islām's Arabic jargon

In presenting the doctrines of Islām to non-Arabic cultures the Arabic terms describing actions, speech and ideas are almost always insisted upon, even when direct translations exist, e.g. in English, 'pilgrimage' for ḥajj, 'announcement' for adhdhān, 'ablutions' for wuḍū`, 'ritual prayer' for ṣalaah, 'struggle' for jihād, and 'fasting' for ṣawm, not to mention 'God' for Allāh. This tension, the necessity for exotic vocabulary to conceal similarities and parallels, is what is behind the burning these days of churches which choose to use the word Allāh to refer to their deity. That some Malaysian Muslims feel that Allāh belongs to them, as demonstrated by the recent disputes, is eloquent testimony for the sensed necessity for a special vocabulary, even though as we have seen Arabic-speaking Christians use Allāh to speak of their god: if their concern were to come closer to the usage of their prophet, then his frequent mention of the Christians and Jews worshipping 'Allāh' would make the current Malaysian Muslims' furore rather awkward. No, their concern is not even their prophet, but instead to be special, to define themselves as distinct from the Christians, and they are prepared to misrepresent their prophet to meet that concern. The very same concern can be found among Arabs confronted with foreign words for the 'single god' such as God: there is some controversy about whether, for example, their children when abroad should say that 'Allāh' is the same as 'God' or different.

Case: European Christianity's multilingual jargon

The European versions of Christianity's special vocabulary is multiply encumbered, with Hebrew, Greek and Latin exotica. How many people among the Christians who wish to retain the exotic vocabulary, one wonders, even realise that Christ and Messiah even mean the same thing, never mind that they mean 'The Annointed'? (This 'annointing' incidentally exists in Sanskrit as Abhiṣeka, a name whose widespread popularity increased thanks to a recently beloved film actor.) How many of them know that Hallelujah is a plural imperative, 'Glorify Jah!', and that Jah is Yahweh?

>Concealing false premises

In Egypt this year certain middle-class international chain cafes have begun to offer 'cider'. Since alcohol cannot be offered in such places this comes

---

meaning of this term.

as something of a surprise to a European until he or she orders it and discovers that 'cider' here means not the familiar drink from fermented apples but hot apple juice with a stick of cinnamon. In this culture then the word 'cider' can no longer distinguish the alcoholic drink from the non-alcoholic. Thus it is necessary to bring in other words to do that distinguishing, just as in our analysis of St Augustine's god we were forced to bring in other words, because the word 'god' is no longer enough to understand why prayer does not make sense. This is not to slight the word but those responsible for changing it. As we saw from its etymological origin the word 'god' was previously more specific: it is centuries of theology which have made it vague enough to hide inconsistencies in doctrine.

More generally let us note that it would be in the interests of a false religion to promote a vocabulary which cannot be used to describe itself perfectly, because its persistence is related to the vocabulary being necessarily too crude and vague to uncover its own false premises. Given that they contradict each other, the various religions must be false in the majority. So it would seem unlikely that Orwell was correct to write that the language he invented for his totalitarian state, an overheated form of political correctness to turn its citizens into assenting droids, was the only language whose vocabulary each year got smaller…

>Concealing unacceptability

Because of the tendency to come to value terms in themselves as much as and even more than what they are supposed to refer to, it is not difficult to conceal atrocity behind a smokescreen of euphemism.

Case: what Israel does

The world-leaders in this field, as well as in all the other language engineering methods we are considering, are undoubtedly the Israelis. To pore over news reports about the Israeli-Palestinian conflict is a greater instruction in devious vocabulary than the most encyclopaedic catalogue could be. All legal news reports that come out of Israel must conform to particular edicts the Israeli government makes on the *language.* Reporters face stiff penalties, including exclusion from the country, if they do not follow them. These are the kind of restrictions which spring up in war and colonisation in any country, of course. Perhaps the difference with Israel is simply how long and how extensively they have been applying these truth-concealing measures. It might never have crossed your mind to ask why it is that, according to reports coming out of Israel, Israelis do not kill Palestinians but Palestinians do kill Israelis. Palestinians, according to these reports, and in a way which comes to seem quite miraculous, simply die or (at worst, in the passive voice or you lose your permit) 'are killed', albeit *in the course of* Israel's military or 'settlement-building' projects, generally *in 'clashes'*. It is an old strategy (and perhaps sometimes just a foible) of colonialism: recall Hegel's negroes insensedly catapulting themselves in the path of innocently firing cannons.[264] The fact that these outrageous linguistic restrictions are in place in unexceptional circumstances should lend very great emphasis on those exceptional circumstances, which occur with good frequency, when Israel physically excludes all press from areas of their activities, not to mention ambulances.

The niceties of language Israel insists on are so extensive to cover them all would detract from our survey of other cases, so we refer those interested readers to internet exposées[265] should they be so inclined.

Case: what the international coalition of the willing does

If you happen to be a citizen of one of these 'willing' countries, it will be interesting to reflect on the fact that you are, apparently, willing, whether you are willing to be willing or not.

And all of us should pause to consider whether a 'suspected terrorist' is 'a terrorist who is suspected [of something]', which is what by conventional English grammar he or she ought to be – *and what therefore is implictly conveyed to us* – or, as modern press convention would claim, it means 'someone who is merely suspected of being a terrorist', which includes every reader of these lines. Nowadays 'international forces', i.e. a large number of US and European soldiers with a line of poor recruits from Asia, Africa or Latin America at the front, do an awful lot of killing of the 'suspected'. As I write the Pentagon is investigating Wikileaks for 'endangering national security' by daring to publish video footage which at the same time strangely it says is *not* considered inflammatory since the troops in it were *routinely* 'following rules of engagement'. The said US troops are shown killing a Reuters journalist who, for holding a camera 'that looked like a rocket-launcher' (has Reuters not progressed to 21st century technology?), was a 'suspected militant' – and then quickly became a (and I quote his killer) 'a dead bastard'. Icelandic television is supporting Wikileaks under this Pentagon 'investigation' after the island state vowed to protect those involved in leaking the 'uninflammatory', 'routine' footage.[266]

---

264 See note to 'not directed at tribal thinking' in the presentation of the characteristics of the Buddha's answer above.

265 For example http://www.krysstal.com/democracy_media.html.

266 (McElroy, 2010)

One hopes that rules of engagement might one day emphasise 'suspected civilians' a little more heavily.

>Disguised union of contradictory terms

We have already alluded to how useful it is when demolishing rival views to create the impression that the demolition methods simply cannot apply to oneself. One way of performing the 'removal of self-contextualisation' which also develops a sideline in the propagation by controversy is by using terms in such a way that they come to include in terms their opposite. We can identify numerous examples of words which, because they include even totally contradictory meanings, lead to hopeless circles of argument, endless bickering either through sloppy thinking or (what is worse) wilfully specious deployment. This is known as *equivocation*, in the technical sense employed in logic: the union of opposite meanings in one word.

Case: individualism

For example, the word 'individualism' conflates two starkly disparate meanings: a noble artistic and creative self-expression, which we accord to prophets, poets, scientists, composers, etc.; and the modern submission to security by surrender of liberty and reduction of all issues to the same level of triviality as matters of personal taste, driven by a media-stoked selfish obsession with personal health and status. This means that opponents of the latter can be rhetorically attacked as supporting the opposite of the former – totalitarian enforcement of conformity, which in fact closely resembles what they oppose!

In her speech to the Conservative Party conference in 1975 Margaret Thatcher said:

> Some socialists seem to believe that people should be numbers in a state computer. We believe they should be individuals.

The historian Ed Wilson comments on what she means by this individualism when

> she went on to say that the basic right to earn and spend as you liked [...] to own and have unfettered enjoyment of private property and to rise through the social scale through competition was 'the essence of a

free economy, and on that freedom all our other freedoms depend'.[267]

Case: liberalism

A related example is 'liberalism', which conflates advocacy of the state of liberty with advocacy of any means to achieve it, even exactly the removal or withholding of liberty, in cultures considered to 'need' it (e.g. Afghanistan, Iraq, etc.). This leads to a situation where advocates of liberty for those people under the current occupying forces of such countries can be accused of opposing liberalism, and where the (frankly natural) emergence of so-called 'illiberal democracy', where people given the right to, vote to get rid of occupying forces and frequently to return to theocratic or autocratic systems, seems to the occupying forces inexplicable and perverse.

Figure 4 The guardians of Equivocal 'Liberalism': in Guantanamo Bay

---

[267] (Wilson, 2009, p. 296)

In the case of the clash of such liberalism with Islām, the communication breakdown is exacerbated by the unfortunate fact that the word for 'freedom' in Arabic, ḥurriyya, has a strong connotation of the dissolution of or release from all contractual obligations, such obligations as are pervasive in traditional Arab society, even between enemies. For example, in a romantic tussle, an aggrieved party could well say, 'You are free!' and the meaning is extremely negative: 'There is no longer any honus of contract upon us.' It would usually be said in high temper. In English 'freedom' and 'friend' share the same root – since friends of the rulers were distinguished from slaves to the rulers – and 'liberty' is from a Latin root referring to family – again the extended family of the rulers rather than their slaves. Because the opposite of ḥurriyya is farḍ, 'obligation' – and used especially of those made by Allāh on humans in Islām – 'freedom' seems to be something like anarchy, which unfortunately is what recent efforts in Irāq and Afghanistan to apply varieties of liberalism-excused coercion have frequently led to, confirming the worst dangers hinted at by the idea of 'freedom' in the natives' ears.

The psychological ability to separate ends from means to such an extent that they can become in fact unrelated or even mutually exclusive ought to be condemned but we are accustomed to call it hope. Almost all modern cultures praise hope for its capacity to rescue humanity from desperation. While it may be true that desperation, a kind of overwhelming and paralysing fear, is worse, it is also clear that hope is not just fearless receptivity to the richness of arising experience: it includes the feeling of wanting something definite that we do not yet have. Even this wanting is often celebrated by our societies, because it can drive people to do amazing things: we admire that power. Yet it can and more often than not does drive us to do horrific things. Because we are concerned to praise it we try to overlook such evidence.

A startling recent example is in the belief, gaining popularity[268] for the first time in centuries, that torture is justified. While it was somehow apt that the mediaeval Catholic Church should be blind enough to consider the ordinary and extraordinary questions to be pious applications of divine logic, this resurgence of torture's legitimacy has arisen, I am ashamed to say, in my lifetime, not among fundamentalist Christians or Muslims, but among liberals, by which I mean people who supposedly advocate liberty. Such is their want to impose democracy on other régimes that they have lost sight of the very basis of that democracy, free choice (or the sense of it). The ends have justified any means,

---

268 (Johnson & Gearty, 2007)

even means in total contradiction to those ends.

Case: multiculturalism

Yet another is 'multiculturalism' which conflates two starkly contrasted ideas, a society whose members have come from many different cultures and thereby structured by the variety among those cultures and freely allowing mutual communication leading to mutual trust and respect, on the one hand; and what Amartya Sen has adroitly identified as a plural form of monoculturism, where the members of the society from the various original cultures form within that society isolated versions, and in some cases caricatures, of those respective cultures, such that there is very little communication among these isolates, and so a breakdown of ordinary trust. Sen has argued that faith schools in Britain are exactly the way to ensure this isolation, and that plural monoculturalism is largely responsible for the extraordinary recent explosion of identity politics there[269] where each group identifies much more strongly with its original culture than it would have done *in it*, and where resulting distrust of other cultures leads to paranoia and the kind of exaggerated grievance claims which led to the government almost passing a clause in its Racial and Religious Hatred Act of 2006 criminalising any speech which caused a pious individual to *feel insulted*.[270]

Case: identity

We are now in a position to appreciate what is perhaps the most dangerous concealed opposite, namely under 'identity' itself. For just as faith can be concluded, and all the terrible consequences we have considered set in motion, so can identity: it is a very different matter to know one's own characteristics or even the characteristics of a community to which one considers oneself affiliated, on the one hand, and on the other to insist on a fixed version of those characteristics which is immutable and impermeable to the influence of others. Opponents of this latter version of identity provoke in their listeners a sense that their own first sense of identity is threatened.

For example, Muslims, when characteristics of Islām are questioned, will react as though they were being provoked to abandon Islām *in toto*, and so will respond fiercely as though it were a personal attack, *even when the questioned characteristics do not form part of their belief or behaviour.*

---

[269] (Sen, 2006)

[270] This terrifying extrapolation from the earlier statutes criminalising speech which *threatened violence* was, fortunately, demolished in the Commons.

Case: relativism

The sort of critique that the Buddha is presenting in this discourse is a call to be more scrupulous about recognising the reliability or otherwise of a range of sources of knowledge than we generally are. It is a call to be circumspect so that we can act with integrity. However, as we have seen, various parties have interests in maintaining the illusion of certainty, and it is from these parties that the term 'relativism' in its specious sense derives. If we ask ourselves what the opposite of this extra circumspection might be, the answer will probably be a kind of indifference to the reliability of sources of knowledge, which would lead to all sources of knowledge being taken on the same level. The result would be a trivialisation of knowledge.

The term 'relativism' is ambiguous enough in its seeming meaning to encompass both the increased circumspection which undermines pretensions of certainty on the one hand and the *mauvaise foi* of 'respect to all beliefs' on the other, such that the parties interested in duping others through the pretension of certainty can deploy it to confuse these two issues, and re-assert their own pretence of certainty as stable, authoritative, absolute.[271]

>Runaway inverting terms

Some language engineering, though partly wilful, gains impetus beyond its deisgners' intentions. Imagine a condition which caused one to experience getting hotter as getting colder and colder as hotter. Then someone affected by it who was in fact getting colder would feel hotter and would seek even colder environments 'to cool down', thereby only exacerbating the cooling and the sense of getting hotter and hotter. The end result that the person to perish in conditions of either extreme heat or extreme cold.

Now turn to ordinary experience. The experience of hot and cold is very direct, and we are not likely to be fooled if, when we feel hot, someone tells us, 'It is cold today.'

However, not everything is as directly experienceable as temperature. In the realm of ideology, such as metaphysical religious doctrine, there is a great deal which is very subtle to or even unavailable to experience. This means that the equivalent of calling heat 'cold' and cold 'hot' is much easier and more

---

271 The difference between the scruple about pretended certainty and the degenerate false respect for all views is equivalent to the difference between perspective and indifference when responding to experience, which will be a crucial distinction in the context of the training in Perspective the Buddha recommends later in this discourse.

believable. By means of language which inverts meanings, it is possible to generate situations like that of the person who experiences heat as cold in our example. And of course the runaway of the resulting positive feedback driving people to extremes has been useful in certain kinds of politics from which we nowadays feel proud to dissociate ourselves:

> Peace is war. Freedom is slavery. Ignorance is strength.

What might disturb us is that there is, it turns out, a rather impressive prevalence of 'inverting terms' in religious discourse and in modern politics.

Case: arrogance is 'submission'

'Submission' or 'meekness' is a potent example. The situation is of a person claiming allegiance with an omnipotent force, the greatest force in the universe, and the most perfect wisdom that is possible. Once the allegiance is made, they then consider themselves authorised to speak about it *ex cathedra.* But curiously this situation is not referred to as arrogation in their discourse but as submission. And because it is called that, it is almost as though they experience it as that: arrogance is experienced as humility. So the lack of humility is no longer recognised, and any challenges to the 'humility' prove a reaction of even greater 'submission' – i.e. even greater unrecognised arrogance. This situation continues in its loop, provoking ever and ever greater feats of arrogance. Their spectators can only look on in bemusement at a display of stupendous conceit – which is a fair description of how it feels to be with such a 'humble believer'.

The related question as to whether the declaration of one's own sins is an act related to self-abasement or self-arrogation meets a tentative answer I think in the loud protestations of sinfulness by the penitent that echo through the churches, and in the tearful melodramas, recorded on tape, with reverb for more affecting posterity, of the Muslim sermons on repentance. Meanwhile the mechanism of private confession provides the in fact public (though limitedly public) method by which the doubter can reassert her or his commitment to the notion of the deity, i.e. the method by which the notion is saved in practical terms amid a practising community.

Case: denying the end of history is 'doom-mongering'

This kind of cognitive dissonance is frequently found in conjunction with allegiance to some creed or other, even in politics. John Gray gives a recent example, the neo-conservatives who came to form Bush's administration interpreting the aftermath of the Soviet collapse through the eyes of the eschatological faith in an impending Rapture:

> It was only to be expected that in the aftermath of the Soviet collapse long-suppressed conflicts would be reactivated. In other words history was set to resume, but in an entertaining inversion of language those who noted this fact were accused of doom-mongering. The truly apocalyptic notion that history had ended was accepted as realism.[272]

Confusion of the sign with what it refers to

Above all, the European intellectual traditions and traditions influenced by and descended from them have been thoroughly infected by what is perhaps the most pernicious temptation in valuing symbols in themselves – the conflation of the existence of the symbol with the existence of what it is supposed to represent. It is a natural consequence of the ethic attributed to Plato of placing reality in an external realm (those 'ideal forms') such that what we now call our ideas, actually our concepts, seem to apply to that reality.

It is this which has reduced philosophy in these cultures for centuries of its history to a maniacal juggling and proliferation of increasingly and hopelessly vague concepts, which can only be understood in anything like the way the authors intended them by thorough familiarity with that author's works and their development, and which through lack of the effort to make that understanding has led to interminable verbiage when an attempt is made to relate different authors' conceptual structures. Vast, perhaps intriguing, jigsaws of neologisms have being made as it were on the wall without any relation to anything off the wall. It has been a characteristic of these cultures for centuries.

Case: the being than whom none greater can be conceived who is real, and the conception of 'a being than whom none greater can be conceived who is real' which is a concept

Only in such circumstances could Anselm's famous proof of God's existence ever have hoodwinked anyone – since it depends on *concealing the difference* between the existence of *the concept* of 'that than which nothing greater can be conceived' and the existence of 'that than which nothing greater can be conceived' *itself*, a concealment which is easy to make when the entire culture has fallen asleep to such differences in general.

---

272 See *Black Mass* (Gray, 2007) Chapter 4, subsection 'The Origin of Neo-conservatism'.

One wonders just how many refutations of Anselm's praise (for a praise it was) are necessary for it no longer to appear in 'current' theology texts. A recent one[273] says, 'The jury is still out on the ontological argument.' The only jury who cannot come to a decision are the ones fettered by unrealisable wishful thinking, too afraid to use the key of logic to free themselves from their chains. This kind of jury, most courts would concede, is best locked out of the court-room while the case is allowed to proceed. And we might well let the world know that those locked out no longer have the right to call themselves a jury, for they served more effectively in the circus.

Misunderstanding of Buddhism as philosophy

It is also this tendency which explains why certain doctrines from cultures lacking this tendency are so consistently misunderstood in the Greek-rooted academic tradition. Let us take three examples, the Buddhist reformulation of the doctrine of reincarnation, the 'middle way' school of the universal career's deployment of the word 'emptiness', and karma.

Case: reincarnation

Identification of oneself as a limited set of evolving experience to which one subsequently clings is taught in Buddhism to be an error, but it is a psychological error, and that error is pervasive in ordinary people's minds. It is this error which drives the 'causality' of actions, the phenomenon of our current state of experience being related to prior actions of body, speech and mind. In the Greece-rooted academic tradition there seems to be a never-ending misunderstanding among scholars that the Buddha is describing an external reality by means of ideas which have a one-to-one correspondence with elements in that reality (the conflation we are critiquing here). They then go on to point out that if there is no self, as the Buddha claims, then there is no mechanism to relate the prior actions with the current state. I hope from what I have said that the mistake they thus make is clear: the self (as the limited set) is an error, but this erroneous self persists and acts as the basis of the relation. We will consider the Buddhist traditions' teachings on the nature of the self in more detail later, when the Buddha gives in the discourse the example of whether or not we need believe in 'reincarnation'.

---

273 (Peterson, Hasker, Reichenbach, & Basinger, 2008)

Case: emptiness

'Emptiness' (Pali and Sanskrit sunyatā, literally 'zeroness') is a technical term. That much in itself is frequently forgotten. It refers to the fact that, *once one has begun to analyse* the identity of some phenomenon, one comes to realise that it can only be experienced because of its interdependence with countless other phenomena.

To take a hackneyed but clear example, when I find a flower, I only sense it because of my eyesight, the light, and the chemical structure of the flower. The sunlight only changes colour when it is reflected from the flower because the flower's molecules are changing – electrons jumping up when absorbing the light energy and falling down to release particular light energies related to the electron orbit structure of the various pigment molecules. I only sense it because I happened to be there when the flower happened to be there – which depends on what I have been doing and what has been happening with the flower, not the least of which is growth, which could not have happened without the sunlight, and the rain, and the earth, and its nutrients. The sunlight could not have reached it from the sun had there not been skies transparents to it; the rain would not have come if there were not bodies of water to be evaporated to form clouds; the earth would not work as a substrate if the rocks that made it had not been ground; and the nutrients would not be there if earlier organisms had not died and decomposed.

So with this kind of analysis, called in Buddhism *analysis towards the ultimate*, what seemed to ordinary interpretation to be a simple presentation of an object, the flower, appears in truer light as an incredibly complex event; that is to say, the ordinary interpretation is *discovered to be* superficial. It is discovered that the simple presentation cannot be extracted from the complex event except by means of the crudity of intellectual abstraction.

Now unfortunately for the unwary academic, various Buddhist schools have focused on different aspects of this phenomenon, and indeed even among them some confusion, or rather animosity over the right to define terms, has arisen because the word 'empty' was used by each school for their respective aspect (for example, some would say we are habituated to superficial interpretations such that we consider them to be final, and so we should say that the simple presentation is *empty of* this superficial interpretation; others focusing on the aspect of the conclusion of the analysis, the complex interdependence, would say it is this complex which is *empty of* the simple presentation, or of the superficial interpretation; others focusing on the nature of experience and the practical need to disembarrass ourselves of our pretences, use the shock tactic, found in many of the source scriptures, of saying the simple presentation is *empty of* the simple presentation – the flower is not a flower). However these subtleties need not concern us here: they are all using 'emptiness' to refer in some way to the disparity between how ordinary mind generally interprets a simple presentation, and how delving mind discovers layers upon layers of complex interdependence.

So this disparity is really not so difficult to understand. However, what happens when this reaches the ears of those infected by the tendency to conflate concepts and reality is that they imagine the Buddha was presenting, as they are wont to present, a philosophy of ideas. They imagine that he was denying that ordinary mind interprets simple presentations at all, or in other words that, since he seems to have proved by such analysis that our interpretation is superficial, in their 'external world' there is consequently no presentation, no flower at all.

We can see that it is on the contrary *they* who in fact have destroyed the possibility of the flower by failing to recognise it as it really is, in the extraordinary interdepent complex.[274] The more *analysis towards the ultimate* is done, the more they will come to appreciate this complexity. So their misunderstanding will recede *gradually* as they *train*. However, with their simplistic and immediate concept-reality attribution they are not likely to engage even in the beginning of such training, and largely they have not, which is why, largely, they continue to misunderstand.

Case: karma

Perhaps the most startling example of such concept reification causing misunderstanding of Buddhist teaching, also involving a fair amount of the golemisation we referred to, is the concept of 'karma'. The word in Sanskrit and Pali simply means 'action'. In the Buddhist teaching it crops up frequently in the context of a deep causality the Buddha claims is discoverable about actions and their effects. We (with Hume) have already seen how ordinary ideas of causality are a kind of superstition, depending only on instances of experience till now but extrapolated into the future. The Buddha adverted to a deeper, less obvious, and therefore less superstition-liable 'causality', between actions and their effects – and specifically between actions of body, speech and mind and effects on happiness and suffering. In his classification of discoverable laws or forms (dharma) it counted as especially hard to discern, but not impossible, and

[274] This, incidentally, is why the adept 'middle way' teacher cryptically admonishes, 'It is only because things are empty that they are things at all.'

therefore not metaphysical.

However as a loan-word into English, the word 'karma' has a long history as referring to a mysterious force which rewards and punishes with all the acumen and severity of the adjudicating deity it ousted from its adherents. It should not seem too bold a step for us now to realise that those who deploy the word 'karma' in this way are merely persisting in an outlook which includes that very same deity, now merely disguised (as, one fancies, a new age guru with long hair and natural cottons).

Magical thinking

The tendency to conflate the symbol with the symbolised in post-Greek traditions demonstrates the persistence there of magical thinking.

Case: abomination

If you were asked, 'What is an abomination?' you might answer – 'President Bush', or 'female genital mutilation'; you might also answer – 'a rejection of something as damned'. The word simultaneously refers to the process of abomination and the object or referent of it. Here language, as ever, reveals a wisdom about thought. Likewise with anathema – it is both 'the curse' and 'the cursed'. The Greek-influenced cultures overvaluation of concepts, as (because what they refer to has added import to the concept) real in themselves, is another manifestation of the same tendency. And it is by no means a Greek phenomenon.

In cultures we like to think of as more primitive than our own, to mention the name of a dead person is taboo for fear of pollution. The revered Hindu revivalist Śankara referred to all four castes, but named only the three upper ones – the fourth, śudra or the servants, relegated by birth to swill out slaughterhouses, clean toilets, etc., were defiling even to mention. Ancient Egyptians mention explicitly in their texts that the power over a thing is in its name. The Jews felt they must rescue their over-rescued deity from such manipulation by socially enforcing a taboo on mentioning its proper name.

We are nowadays more likely to chortle at such beliefs, for example as exquisitely portrayed in the 'Don't say Jehovah' stoning scene in Monty Python's 'The Life of Brian', yet somehow we still hanker after the words 'the being greater than which none can be conceived' somehow having the power to create such a being, or even to *be* it in some mysterious way.

False analogies

Analogies and similes rely on similar over-valuation of concepts, namely those which are focused on to make them. Because analogies rely on similarity between two different situations, it is easy to stress the similarities between the situations and conceal the differences, differences which might well destroy the analogy for the sake of whose persuasiveness the situations are being compared.

Case: libel as theft

To take a famous example from the history of liberty in English law, consider the powers of public officials to search private premises in search of libellous documents. It can be argued that this is acceptable by analogy with the same officials' right so to invade privacy when looking for stolen property. The fallacy in this particular analogy was pointed out in the 18th century landmark case of Entick vs. Carrington[275] by the judge Lord Campden: in the one case, there was stolen property *before* the search, whereas in the other, there was no libellous material until *after* the search, and then only potentially. The analogy therefore broke down, since the consequences of admitting the two cases would lead to dramatically different powers for the public officials: whereas the former was a directed search, and nothing but the sought-for object uncovered, the latter could be sweeping, and uncover a great deal of what should be private (the judge stressed the sacredness of the privacy of one's own papers) without discovering the (alleged) libel.[276]

Case: comparative religion

Analogies drawn across religious traditions can be particularly noxious, because they are so liable to interested distortion. Generally speaking, each religious tradition is very circumspect when recognising analogies which imply its inferiority, but very carefree nay exuberant when pointing out analogies which might paint the others in dubious colours. This is frequently done with portentously cold style, aureation to suggest objectivity. It is only by solely

---

[275] (Entick vs. Carrington, 1762-3)

[276] I owe this example to Ben Wilson's excellent history of liberty, *What Price Liberty?* (Wilson, 2009). Incidentally, he argues that this case 'would influence the way the British and American governments worked and protect civil liberties of the subject until the twentieth century' because it established that 'a citizen can sue a public administrator in their capacity as private individuals, subject to the rule of law', i.e. that the state cannot break the law, even in the name of necessity.

concerning ourselves with appearances that such comparisons can be either drawn or believed.

A recent university textbook *claiming not to be partisan* solemnly intones:

> Religious experiences are conditioned by distinctive cultural and religious perspectives, so that what people in various religions experience widely differs. The Ultimate Reality that a Hindu experiences is very different from the personal God a Christian experiences.[277]

Perspicacity and delerium are both mental states, but no-one would feel the need to assert that they are on the same level, somehow equivalent or interchangeable. Moreover is there no better analogy to experiences of Christ in Hinduism than Upaniśadic self-expansion? Has Kṛṣṇa disappeared into the shredders of the Ministry of Truth? Comparisons such as this are almost shocking to anyone who has even casual familiarity with the traditions being compared, and they are utterly typical.

Case: theology

Rudolf Otto, whose influence and neologisms extended far beyond the circle of Christian thinkers, unlike many more delerious theologians had the perspicacity of thought and integrity to admit that the terms he had coined to describe the experience of the divine such as 'numinous', and 'mysterium tremendum et fascinans', were 'not genuine intellectual "concepts" but only a sort of illustrative substitute for a concept.'[278] He called them 'ideograms' and said they were 'imperfect analogies drawn from experience.'

That same recent university textbook purporting to treat the philosophy of religion but in fact a survey of Christian theological thought till the present begins well by distinguishing rationalism from fideism – meaning respectively the application of reason to Christian faith (and consequent refutations of the latter) and non-application of reason to such faith out of the conviction that faith is unreasonable. (This is understood by its advocates to be an advantage.)

However, the rest of the book is, its authors admit, something else. Various objections are made to applying reason to faith. First of all, ordinary

---

277 (Peterson, Hasker, Reichenbach, & Basinger, 2008, p. 36)

278 (Otto, 1917)

people don't have the time to think it through. This also means they wouldn't have time to support their faith with reason, of course, but our authors take this as a reason for keeping faith and rejecting reason. Secondly, the dizzying rhetoric of fideism, fired by the furnace of Kierkegaard, says that we must take a risk. Which risk, however, is never in debate – why it should be the particular Christian ones is never addressed. Thirdly, the fact that it is not possible for *any* faith to meet the criteria required for proof is taken as a good reason for abandoning reason, rather than for abandoning all faiths – this step again is rather mysterious. Finally it is asserted that reason is never neutral, but always dependent on prior beliefs. These prior beliefs are assumed to be unthrowable, so the entirety of reason is thrown out: could we not throw away the prior beliefs which are so 'obviously' partial?

So, preferring to emasculate reason over emasculating their prejudices, they finish their book by applying reason to faith only so far as not to refute it, a very titillating exercise which includes, of course, the said history of Christian theology.[279] What quickly becomes clear is that the avoidance of refutation is in every single case achieved by resorting to a different (but equally indefensible) analogy. In the end what we have is an enormous lump of interwoven analogies, each trying to support the others, the whole mass, however, hanging, as it were, in the sky.

To mention but a few of them (and if I may be excused for using a turn of phrase with appropriate other-worldly and alien resonances) there is creation, but not as we know it (since the agent is eternal and there is no material to begin with); existence, but not as we know it (since it is hidden); goodness, but not as we know it (because the standard of good is established by it, and it includes the permission for evil); the ability to know objectively the order of all events in the universe, but now as we know it (because since Einstein we know that order of events depends on a spatial perspective); power, but not as we know it (because all power we know is measured by reference to other power and can be overpowered, i.e. it is as much weakness as it is power); suffering and compassion but not as we know it (because a perfect being could not suffer); etc. etc. etc. In fact many pages would have been spared if it had simply been recognised that

---

[279] I omit here for the sake of sparing the reader, the convoluted redefinitions of terms that get made in the course of justifying this titillating approach, save to mention that it is 'allowed' to be called 'reason', and the earlier 'reason' (in contrast to fideism) is renamed 'strong rationalism'. This is a bit like, when faced with a dead horse, redefining 'dead horse' to refer only to ones which are not being flogged, flogging this one, and calling it on that basis 'weakly alive'.

such non-fideists actually hold to a situation in which humans are considered to know the deity purely in terms of empty ideas, and then only inasmuch as the ideas seem not to clash, suffering as they do from a sudden incapacity to 'know' when the ideas do clash; the ideas, unfortunately, being the same in the two cases. Titillating it may be, but one yearns for consummation, from the front or the back.

To go into more detail, of which there is no end, in one of these examples, in the matter of creation, it is apparently asserted by many theologians as if it were an obvious fact that contingent beings (i.e. things whose existence depends on circumstances) alone cannot explain the existence of a contingent being. But, if we are going to decide with Rudolf whether these analogies are true or 'imperfect' (i.e. non-analogous) we have to see that our only experience of causes and explanations is exactly by contingent beings! Never in any way ever anywhere have we seen, heard, smelt, tasted or touched a non-contingent cause, and the only way to conceive of a cause is to extrapolate from past experience, in ourselves or others, who are under the same limitations, of such contingent causes. So a 'non-contingent cause' is by definition a fantasy that no-one has ever experienced. The method of these 'thinkers' (for so they call themselves it seems), having conjured up this non-experienced fantasy, is then to apply it to every phenomenon that we know such that every one becomes not the experienceable phenomenon we are familiar with but the fantastic result of this fantasy, by means of an inexplicable causality. Thus a fantastical result of a fantastic cause by means of fantastic causality, all totally inexplicable and non-experienced, is offered as the perfect explanation of reality, and they breathe a sigh of relief. Darkness, upon darkness, upon darkness.

Nāgārjuna pointed out, about two millennia ago,

devād anyo manuṣyaścet
saṁtatir nopapadyate

If 'God is *other* than Man,'
'To connect' does not apply.[280]

Moreover, much as they might irritate us, Hume's proofs of the fallacy of causality still stand. 'The outcome can only be skepticism!' cry the authors, 'so ignore them!' they say, when they should say, 'so be skeptical!' Causality is

280 Root Middle Way Verses XXVII, 16b

inferred by our 'thinkers' from limited experience, made into a logical step, and, hey presto!, 'First Cause' (for we must capitalise this apparently) is, if you'll excuse the expression, the result. (Should we write 'Result'?)

Nāgārjuna, 'the second Buddha', opens his principal work, a scintillating presentation of the implications of profound understanding (prajñā), with a consideration of causality as it is conventionally understood (by ordinary people and philosophers) and the declaration –

> na svato nāpi parato na dvābhyāṁ nāpyahetutaḥ |
> utpannā jātu vidyante bhāvāḥ kkacana kecana | |

> Not because of itself, something else, or the two; or without cause either;
> Is the creation ever known of any being whatever anywhere.[281]

Rumi says:

> When a son of man is born twice – he plants his foot upon the head of cause.
> The First Cause is not his religion – the particular cause has no enmity.
> He flies, like the sun, in the horizon – with the bride, ikhlās, and form is a veil.[282]

Hallelujah for the conclusion in the same theology textbook: 'Contemporary defenders of the ontological argument probably should concede that each contingent thing exists because of other contingent things in the universe.' But they go on, 'However, even with this concession [sic], the question remains why there are contingent beings at all when there could have been none.' How could they observe 'none'?

The authors are quite aware of the anthropic principle (which deals with this), but in a way quite typical of this titillating approach, they do not let it attack directly, but shuffle it away, to leave these cryptofideist 'concessions' sounding more reasonable than they ought to. Eventually, however, they have to unchain this formidable threat, but they imply, 'I do not accept that there are other universes because I have not seen them.' The anthropic principle says the

---

281 Root Middle Way Verses I, 1

282 *Couplets* III, 3576 (Rumi & Nicholson, 1925-1940)

reason we can experience this universe is because it has the right variables to be experienced. Those who object to this (out of a desperate concealed desire to rescue the argument from design as here) say, in effect, 'Huff! I want to see these inseeable other universes, then I will accept your argument.' Such a person is resting their belief in the 'Designer' on the belief that it is possible to see something that it is impossible to see.

To call these 'imperfect analogies' or 'subsitutes for intellectual concepts' hardly does such theology justice. Idea and idol share the same root. This is not a coincidence.

Plurium interrogationum with golem ideas

Earlier we considered the effective rhetorical strategy of asking more than one question simultaneously such that the answer cannot help but be either direct, insufficient and therefore forced into the scheme of the questioner's unjustified assumptions, or indirect, explanatory, and therefore open to rhetorical attack.

Now we can see why it is that this kind of rhetoric is so popular in 'theological' debates. The interrogator can choose any group of interconnected and impossible ideas (the venerable Otto's 'substitutes for intellectual concepts') and ask about them simultaneously. The addressee is quickly reduced to exasperation by the sheer number of unsupported ideas with which she is being assaulted, each one of which requires an individual refutation by the time of whose completion innumerable other rhetorical strategies may have been brought into play. Some of the most popular examples of this execrable exercise are, 'If God did not create all of this, then who did?' which is almost exactly parallel in logical integrity with the famous example, asking a single man, 'Do you still beat your wife?'; and 'Was Jesus crazy, a pathological liar or the son of God when he claimed to be the son of God?'; and, 'What evidence do you have that the Bible/Qur'ān/etc. is not God's message to mankind?'; and, 'How will you defend yourself on the Day of Judgment when you stand before your Maker who sees all you have ever done or wished to do?' Etc. etc. Just from these few hackneyed examples we can see that it is even likely that the interrogator is unaware of the rhetorical strategy they are employing – the very nature of the doctrines means that they cannot help but commit the fallacy of *plurium interrogationum* as soon as these doctrines echo from their mouths.

> 'Ākāraparivitakko cepi, bhāradvāja, purisassa hoti; "evaṁ me ākāraparivitakko"ti – iti vadaṁ saccamanurakkhati , *natveva tāva ekaṁsena*

> *niṭṭhaṁ gacchati – "idameva saccaṁ, moghamaññā*"nti. Ettāvatā kho, bhāradvāja, saccānurakkhaṇā hoti, ettāvatā saccamanurakkhati, ettāvatā ca mayaṁ saccānurakkhaṇaṁ paññapema; *na tveva tāva saccānubodho hoti*'ti.
>
> 'Bhāradvāja, a person who thinks ideas through saying, "This is my thinking through of the ideas," safeguards the truth. *But he or she doesn't yet come to the definite conclusion that only something is true, and all else is vain.* To this extent, Bhāradvāja, there is safeguarding of the truth. To this extent he or she safeguards the truth. I describe this as the safeguarding of the truth. *But it is not yet an awakening to the truth.*'[283]

---

[283] In *The Caṅkī Discourse.*

Not by intuitive acceptance of views, ma diṭṭhinijjhānakkhantiyā

> 'Api ca, bhāradvāja, sunijjhāyitaṁyeva hoti, tañca hoti rittaṁ tucchaṁ musā; no cepi sunijjhāyitaṁ hoti, tañca hoti bhūtaṁ tacchaṁ anaññathā. Saccamanurakkhatā, bhāradvāja, viññunā purisena nālamettha ekaṁsena niṭṭhaṁ gantuṁ – "idameva saccaṁ, moghamañña"'nti.

> 'Now some things are intuitive and yet empty, trivial and false. Some things are not intuitive, and yet they are genuine, factual and unmistaken. To safeguard the truth, in such cases [as intuition] it isn't proper for a wise person to come to the definite conclusion that only something is true, and all else is vain.'
>
> The Buddha[284]

> Men will scarce ever be perswaded, that effects of such consequence can flow from principles, which are so inconsiderable, and that the far greater part of our reasonings with all our actions and passions can be deriv'd from nothing but custom and habit.
>
> David Hume (1711-1776)[285]

Meaning

This compound has been translated in quite diverse ways, mainly because of the ambiguity in the middle term, as bias towards a notion that has been pondered over, agreement through pondering views, or even delight in speculation. Diṭṭhi is the usual word for view or opinion, which can be good or bad or neutral. Nijjhāna, equivalent to the Sanskrit nidhyāna, means understanding or insight in the sense of reaching a sense of satisfaction, with a particular sense of intuitive understanding or understanding which does not require (further) thought. The diverse implications can better be understood when one realises that the prefix ni- is used, in contrast to a direct negation, to refer to when something comes to an end. Jhāna is the usual word for a degree of meditative absorption. So the idea is 'no more meditation is necessary'. Or

---

284 In *The Caṅkī Discourse.*

285 From book I, chapter 3, section 10 of his *Treatise of Human Nature* (Hume, 1888).

according to one Pali dictionary it can be an alternative for another word (nijjhāpana) meaning favouring, or delighting, in. Khanti means forbearance or acceptance; we might even say 'giving in'. Since the Buddha seems to have covered the tendency to delight in speculation by questioning reliance on takka, it seems doubtful that this sense is meant here. There seems to be a difference in scope between accepting views because one is satisfied by one's understanding of them, and accepting views which seem intuitively correct, so let us consider both.

Examples

The inclination to justice, the 'intuition' that God is 'there', the sense of uniqueness and therefore superiority of one's own culture and traditions; falling foul of rhetorical persuasion; cognitive biases.

Irrelevancy as sources of certainty

In the context of showing the untenability of the notion, dating to Aristotle, that definitions are a source of knowledge, Karl Popper provides us with an overview of what philosophers have meant by intuition as a source of knowledge:

> Aristotle held with Plato that we possess a faculty, intellectual intuition, by which we can visualise essences and find out which definition is the correct one, and many modern essentialists have repeated this doctrine. Other philosophers, following Kant, maintain that we do not possess anything of the sort. My opinion is that we can readily admit that we possess something which may be described as 'intellectual intuition'; or more precisely, that certain of our intellectual experiences may be thus described. Everybody who 'understands' an idea, or a point of view, or an arithmetical method, for instance, multiplication, in the sense that he has 'got the feel of it', might be said to understand that thing intuitively; and there are countless intellectual experiences of that kind.[286]

Like the Buddha, he recognises that they are not a source of certainty, and points out why:

> I would insist, on the other hand, that these experiences, important as

---

[286] This and the following citations are from Chapter 11 of (Popper, 1945; 5th edition 1966).

> they may be for our scientific endeavours, can never serve to establish the truth of any idea or theory, however strongly somebody may feel, intuitively, that it must be true, or that it is 'self-evident'. Such intuitions cannot even serve as arguments. For somebody else may have just as strong an intuition that the same theory is false.

Popper singles out science as furnishing examples of intuitions which led astray from truth:

> The way of science is paved with discarded theories which were once declared self-evident; Francis Bacon, for example, sneered at those who denied the self-evident truth that the sun and the stars rotated round the earth, which was obviously at rest. Intuition undoubtedly plays a great part in the life of a scientist, just as it does in the life of a poet. It leads him to his discoveries. But it may also lead him to his failures. And it always reminds his private affair, as it were. Science does not ask how he has got his ideas, it is only interested in arguments that can be tested by everybody. The great mathematician, Gauss, described this situation very neatly once when he exclaimed: 'I have got my result; but I do not yet know how to get it.'

Unfortunately, as he explains, philosophy has not been so quick to recognise intuitions' limitations:

> All this applies, of course, to Aristotle's doctrine of intellectual intuition intuition of so-called essences, which was propagated by Hegel, and in our own time by E. Husserl and his numerous pupils; and it indicates that the 'intellectual intuition of essences' or 'pure phenomenology' as Husserl calls it, is a method of neither science nor philosophy. (The much debated question whether it is a new invention, as the pure phenomenologists think, or perhaps a version of Cartesianism or Hegelianism, can be easily decided; it is a version of Aristotelianism.)

Such intuitive acceptance may perhaps be forgiven in ancient traditions but not be expected in modern politics, one might think, but John Gray, in his recent analysis[287] of the neo-conservative think tank of the Bush administration

287 Chapter 4 of *Black Mass* (Gray, 2007).

with its bizarre pseudo-Christian eschatological vision, highlights its rejection of empirical intelligence from the CIA in favour of information generated by its own bodies, the B Team and the Office of Special Plans, which, under the influence of their teacher Leo Strauss' doctrine that philosophers' true intent was always consciously disguised behind what they wrote or said, believed that empirical evidence for something about the Russians was in reality evidence for the opposite of that thing. In contrast their own intelligence displayed suspicious harmony with pre-decided aggressions on Iraq. Gray suggests that they elevated a kind of intuition into the enemies' souls above empirical data as an improperly extreme reaction against scientistic dependence on use of the latter.

The point here is that there are many reasons why particular views or outlooks are attractive to us and so seem like common sense.

First-order disqualification: cognitive bias

'Cognitive bias' is a technical term for something very ordinary, what we might call deciding in a mistaken way, because of our innate psychological make-up. It refers to distortions to our decision-making which can lead us to be completely deluded by an argument or information which seems intuitively correct. This is in fact a vast subject in modern cognitive science, and here I will only touch on a few of the more important and instructive types.

The resonance with the primal subconscious

One of the clearest signals of potential bias, especially among the doctrines of the massive religions and the massive political ideologies, is that there are strong resonances with deep subconscious urges. Their potential to sway the masses has of course long been recognised in governance strategy, as is demonstrated by Pareto's advice 'to take advantage of sentiments, not wasting one's efforts in futile efforts to destroy them'. Because of their resonance, certain views and outlooks 'feel right': they operate on us deeply. This alone is a very large topic. It is also a disturbing and controversial one, because of that very resonance being indicated, so I ask my respected reader to prepare for what may be a rough ride here.

>The magical purity of the tribe

Case: justice, tribal exorcism

Justice is now vaunted in most societies. It is one of the unchallengeable standards, for many an absolute. It just seems right. Even for those who find reference to a god and the sacred embarrassing because they believe themselves to have surpassed such 'superstition', justice is one of the concepts they still relate to as they would, had they not thrown off the said 'superstition', have related to a god or to the sacred. Questioning applications of justice is acceptable (with some exceptions) but questioning the *possibility* of justice is taboo. Like any worshipped god's, justice's existence brooks for its adherents no question, and for similar reasons. However, when we do question it, we find, as many have with the older gods, that it is far more doubtful than it is generally allowed to be, and for similar reasons. For the judicial system locks extraordinarily deeply into some of our least savoury primal psychology.

In any crime, a matrix of conditions allows the crime to develop, and it involves many people. It is especially clear in most cases of serial killers, for example, that their families are heavily involved in generating the conditions favouring their crimes. In a car accident, there are at least two people clearly involved, and usually more.

Now in general we call the singling out of causes for some event either superstition or science, depending on whether the event can be shown in repeated experimental trials to depend on those causes.

Most of us would consider the transference of a disease-causing spirit into sacrificial victims and their bloody sacrifice, in order to purify the tribe of that spirit, to be superstition rather than science. This is because recent science has shown us that causes have been overlooked – the bacterial pathogens, the living conditions, and so on – and so have not been destroyed. The wrong thing has been held to blame; it has been a false purification. Leaving aside for a moment the question as to how important the placebo effect (the psychologically induced curative influence of the belief in having being cured) might be on the tribe's subsequent health, we can see that what the tribe believe to have happened, and what has in fact happened, differ quite dramatically, and more than likely quite tragically. One is reminded of the nosegay masks that were believed to combat the black death.

The use of repeated mystical words in such sacrificial rites is fairly well known. In English they are called spell (meaning word); in Arabic wird; in Sanskrit mantra. Uprooted from the cultures which use them they can invite ridicule. The Proto-Indo-European words for such spells include one cognate with the Latin ius, and it was from this that the English words just and justice came, not just conjure. The mystical pronouncements at such purificatory rites were, then, 'justice'. It would discover who carried blame, which term derives directly from the Greek blasphemy, meaning 'cursing words'. Anyone who doubts the magical nature of the court procedure in 'modern times' should examine the origin of the 'binding' oath. 'I swear', was an invitation to be struck down by supernatural powers if subsequent declarations were knowingly false: how many such swearers of oaths, one wonders, ever were struck down?

When we single out the serial killer, who is a person, from the complex matrix of causes which led to the killings, and try him, and execute him, is this superstition or science? It is assumed that the execution removes the cause of the killings. In one way this is certainly true: clearly the executed man will not kill again, just as the sacrificed herd will not bring back the evil spirit.

However, just as 'other' evil spirits may return to bring disease to the tribe again, so can other killings occur. And just as the overlooked pathogens remain uninterruptedly but their effects are divided by the conception of the tribe into isolated spirits' successive attacks, so remain all the other conditions which encourage serial killing to occur in a society, though they are divided by the conception of that society into isolated, successive cases. The parallel really is as perfect as that.

I do not claim that the serial killer is quite as free of blame as the herd into which the evil spirit is driven, but I do claim that it is impossible to distinguish the execution rite from this ritual of false purification except on arbitrary grounds, and I do claim that ideologies supporting execution which are present in a society are *among the conditions which favour the arising of serial killings* in that society, just as the rotting bodies of the sacrificed herd in the river may well contribute to the thriving of the disease their sacrifice is believed to purify. To grasp this point requires some familiarity with serial killing and its attendant circumstances.

Both the tribe's exorcism and the judicial process must occur in public to 'work'. This means that attention is drawn to the accused by an entire public who project their own personal psychological schisms onto the situation. Sometimes we admit that a case has become 'politicised' or that certain parts of the trial need to be conducted in private to avoid 'prejudice'. In fact the entire spectacle is an exercise in politicisation and prejudice: that is how it performs its duty. Schemes of consequence gather around any potential court decision like poisonous clouds. 'Stakes' are 'raised'. The accused may assume the role of the martyr – the sacrificial victim, mutely acquiescing to the block.

It is common wisdom that the best way to teach is by example, so upholders of execution teach us, in the best way, that *murder is righteous power*. Here I advert to the prevalence in the histories of serial killers of their killing sprees being *prepared and precipitated by moral chastisement* and request that interested readers investigate in their own time the many cases similar to the one I will describe.

This will entail delving into the subject of child sex abuse with unusual circumspection. In such histories one is overwhelmed by the suspicion that people who underwent forced sex as children suffer less from the sex in itself (indeed sometimes they enjoyed it according to their own reports, as in the example we will consider) than from the sex as it is seen by society at large, that is to say the sex inflicts suffering on them mainly because of society's abomination of it. If indeed such is the case then we should hold responsible for the main suffering those who abominate such sex. Furthermore, in those cases where the victim enjoyed the sex to an extent, there is suffering to an exactly proportional extent later – through what we refer to roughly as 'shame' – because the pleasure is a measure in the memory of the victim of how ritually unclean he or she is in society's eyes, a pariah-hood which is felt deeply by all involved no matter how nicely society tries to affect a caring stance (and indeed the awkwardness of that very niceness is a powerful sign of opprobium). In recent years certain western European countries have undergone a shift towards an even more generally held, even more extreme abomination of sex with children than they already had, and this has made the crime of sex with children itself even more of a crime, even more traumatic to its victims, yet no-one questions those who are solely responsible for this escalation: the very people who have come to abominate it even more than they used to. The intensity of abomination has reached such an extreme in these societies that it is almost impossible there to express the opinion I am expressing now, so piously abominating have the people become.

With some experience of different societies' moral values, it does seem incontrovertible that certain activities, such as sex with children in modern Western societies, for example, and allowing oneself to be sexually penetrated among males in Arab societies, for another, are much less traumatic in themselves than they become because of the opprobrium assigned them by moralists according to the current moralistic fashions of the society (as is spectacularly demonstrated in these examples, by how much less trauma is caused by these two kinds of abominated behaviour than in their abominating society when they occur in *the other* society), so we could say that such moralists as uphold this assignment and contribute to the opprobrium are more responsible for such trauma and so more criminal than any individual who performs the activity!

Johnny raped and killed an elderly Catholic nun when he was only 17. A legal psychologist, Dorothy Lewis, uncovers the family situation: four violent stepfathers, the third who fucked Johnny in the mouth and arse and then pimped him to his acquaintances, the girl next-door who initiated Johnny into sex when he was 9 and taught him thenceforth how best to please a woman, his lonely and sexy mother whom he got drunk and had sex with. Lewis' questions themselves eloquently express her horror – such that there is never any question about all this being an abomination. (She weeps at one point in the interview, saying, 'Poor man.') Yet Johnny never blames these people. The personality in Johnny's divided mind who deals with it is Aaron, who is quite the Casanova and as he says 'knows what Johnny needs'. But some hours before the murder Johnny has sex with his mother then flees in shame to his grandparents'. It is only after his execution that our psychologist discovers his cousin Katherine's testimony – that this grandmother used to torture them, sitting Johnny on a gas stove, and such like, and that the grandfather used to fuck him. Initially it hurt, but Aaron points out that Johnny also liked it. I would venture that the sessions with the stepfather and his friends, which they filmed, gave him pleasure too. *The trauma comes with his shame* in feeling observed, by some all-seeing 'god', associated with *the 'punishments' inflicted by the grandmother*, herself clearly consisting of various selves in strife: he killed the nun to eliminate, however crudely, that shame.

> He sees you, he sees you forever and ever, Alan. He sees you!... He sees you!
>
> God seest! No more. No more, Equus.[288]

In another case reported by the same psychologist, Shawcross's, it is *the punishing mother* who traumatises him. Again and again, in fact, it is *the punitive situations* which lead these people into their murderous spasms. Is it as difficult for us as we pretend, to see that our current judicial systems are the principal example for such punitive personalities as Johnny's grandmother and Shawcross's mother? The psychologist was moved to write:

> The more we understand about the genesis of violence, the harder it is to draw a clear line between guilt and innocence, sanity and insanity.[289]

A scientist's voice would count lightly in a tribe whose witch-doctor drives the mob into a frenzy of faith in the exorcising sacrifice. The witch-doctor need not rely on the rational argument of the scientist, for from his authority his

---

[288] This is the exchange between the psychiatrist and the disturbed young man reliving the incident in which he blinded the horses who were witness to his sexual initiation, in Sir Peter Shaffer's play *Equus* (Shaffer, 1973, 1993).

[289] (Lewis, 1998, p. 251)

most illogical statements can drive the mob into whole-hearted support of the superstition. If the analogy we have drawn between this primitive rite and our judicial system is fair, we might expect similar behaviour among defenders of the judicial system. I hardly need mention that we do, of course. Nothing stirs the blood so well as a diatribe against 'the antisocial one' (in modern parlance) whom we must eliminate. We will have occasion later in our discussion of morality to see why some variety of sexual behaviour is so often the 'antisocial' behaviour. Any unwitting psychologist of Lewis' colour, who happened to stand in the way of the mobs who torched the houses of released paedophiles in England a few years ago after the popular press in a popular move broke the law to print their names and addresses, and any unwitting Kinseyite who happened to stand in the way of the mob who recently besieged the house of a Moroccan man whose gay wedding video was posted on Youtube, well, we know what would happen to them.

This recognisable and instinctive blood-lust is exactly what is preventing any escape from the sacrificial exorcisms our judicial systems embody. Doctors who visit tribes, diagnose illness and offer to give slightly painful injections to everyone are often vilified by the tribe because of the contradiction with the tribal belief (in exorcism). Analogously in a trial we cannot assign punishments of varying degrees to various people involved in the life of a serial killer because it would damage the sacred dichotomy of innocent versus guilty. The dichotomy is necessary to preserve the dividing line for the application of double standards in our interpretative mechanisms (e.g. that the judge who pronounces the death sentence is innocent[290], but its victim is guilty).

We are not so crude, we think, nowadays, to be carrying out a ritualistic tribal sacrifice. Various and confounding conceptual fabrics have been tailored to cover its deep nature. Nothing is so telling, about the operations of the judicial system such as imprisonment, as the fact that while no-one can agree completely why we should do them (in the case of prison some say for protection, some for revenge, some for punishment, some for reform, etc.), we are all nevertheless certain that we should do them.

One such conceptual fabric, supposedly championed in European philosophy by Mill, says that the liberty of a man should only be infringed to prevent him harming others. Since infringement of liberty includes harming him,

---

290 For example, the authors of the infamous witch-hunting manual, *Malleus Maleficarum* (Kramer, 1487), which was used to justify a shocking wave of barbarism across Europe for centuries, asserted that the inquisitors in witch trials were (mysteriously, but conveniently) immune to witchcraft. (Part II, question 1.)

this is a classic example of something we find with appalling frequency in religious and ideological discourse: a vocabulary of double standards in one party which they (stupidly or deviously) conflate with the very criterion distinguishing the two parties (the criminal is said to be afraid of the harm of punishment because he does not recognise that in fact he is not being harmed but improved).[291] Furthermore, should we not establish first whether it is possible to prevent harm? We have inherited a superstitious sacrificial tribal ethic which depends on the belief that it is possible, magically, to prevent the harm crimes inflict – but such an inheritance should not be immune to question simply because it stirs the blood. We have seen that if one group (the rulers) set the example that harming (in punishment) purifies us of problems, then it is unfair to blame the rest for learning that example and applying it. In that case, since teaching people to do harm constitutes harming them (because of the punishment), should the judges' rights be infringed for this criminal act?

There is a great deal of harming which goes on in the machinations of our judicial system. It is not just the penalty, which by definition must do harm, but also the fear it provokes in those cultures – and are there any others? – where miscarriages of justice occur, and as we have considered, the ramifications of its punitive example in society's dark corners. According to Mill's principle, should we infringe on the rights of the judges for such harm of the non-penalised? And what of the harm of exposing prisoners to each others' corrupting influence by concentrating experts in diverse crimes in hotbed closed societies? Should we infringe on the rights of the prison managers for doing that harm?

Most would reply that these arguments for the infringements of the authorities' rights are ludicrous. But then most would fawn before those authorities without question. And ridicule is a pleasant enough conclusion to these arguments for the superstitious. Yet challenging the disparity is a necessary consequence upon honestly applying the principle (that Mill is credited with announcing clearly) which we consider justifies our sacrificial system, where everyone has equal liberty, but, as the satirist has it,

> some… are more equal than others.[292]

The belief in the dichotomy between innocence and guilt favours *the*

---

[291] We considered this example earlier in 'vocabulary' under 'Not by thinking ideas though'.

[292] This is the infamous revision of the farm's charter by the pigs in *Animal Farm* (Orwell, 1945).

rulers, who magically award innocence to themselves and dispense guilt according to their rituals.

The flexibility of the sphere of immunity is shown by its tendency to collapse and shrink almost to nothing in such circumstances of runaway paranoia as Communist party purges.

I do not arguc that a non-dichotomous assignment of blame is easy. Indeed, aside from the fact that it threatens the magical system of sacrifice, it is extremely costly to apply. Infamously, the members of serial killers' families keep their traps shut about events which are far enough in the past only to survive as circumstantial evidence, such as strange burns on the killer's backside and so on. And to assign blame exactly according to responsibility requires a net broader than most would be prepared to countenance – perhaps including the legal system itself given what we have said about setting an example of doing harm. I ask only that we admit *the extreme faultiness* of the judicial system we have inherited, and refer to it as it should be referred to, as a tribal relic pervaded by magical thinking. For to cover it with the glamour of righteousness is to leave us languishing in ignorance, magicians dressed in wigs and robes.

Since increasing the number of disputants in a dispute is the basis of the judicial system one might carelessly imagine this system is a way to approach truth. In a society where the majority know the truth and express it, and where those who either do not know or do not express it or both are scattered randomly with respect to the way the jury is selected, then the method would, in the majority of instances, lead to the truth. However, to meet all of these assumptions is a tall order, and the method in itself does nothing to establish them, so any claim that this method in itself attains to truth is a fallacy.

Furthermore, in the context of verbal defence of religious tenets, one can guarantee that it will only be used in circumstances where the assumptions are not met: the jury will be made up of those who already consider the defendant guilty before the trial begins, and have good reason not to allow their convictions to be changed during its course.

>Allegiance with the tribe

The need to belong often expresses itself in a desire to express what we consider to be the majority view. This phenomenon, known as '*the bandwagon effect*', is much-documented in cognitive science, behavioural economics and political science. We have a strong psychological tendency to adjust our own beliefs according to those which seem to be prevalent in our society. While this might well allow us to get by with fewer disputes, it does not help up get to the truth of what might be beneficial. We will consider how this relates to the perception that there are 'experts' later. The term derives from 19th century CE America where a popular clown of the day, Dan Rice, operated the said band wagon, which was found to improve political candidate's success in election campaigns when they 'jumped' on it, but of course we are familiar with the phenomenon more generally and can observe it as far back in history as records stretch. Just how much our lives are dominated by it is often overlooked.

This tendency to let allegiance trump everything else is what informs a lot of the appeals to authority we have considered and will consider. Just as the child in the playground ridiculed for his choice of music will resort to saying 'everyone' listens to it now – as if that changed the nature of the music – so do we 'adults' resort (in what is not a noble move but a cowardly, cunning one) to 'quotations' of 'great figures' words', religious scripture, popular opinion, what is traditional, what can convince rhetorically those around us, what logically persuades those around us, schools of thought, party lines, 'universally held principles of right and wrong', and even (as self-sincerity subsides) what 'our side' believe, what everyone who is loved and accepted by us must believe. The threat is palpable in the words of the Christian saint:

> It is a characteristic made of all heretics that they are unable to see what is perfectly obvious to *everyone else*.[293]

When you share the beliefs of the majority of your audience you are in a position to appeal to them, the *anacoenosis* we have already considered. But whether we appeal to each other or not, the tendency has its effect on our choices.

Case: sheepish voting

It is observed, for example, that in the US, because of the longitudinal range of the country and the rotation of the earth, voting is still open in the west after it has closed in the east, with the result that voting in the former area is influenced by that in the latter area. That would make election campaigners focus on the latter area, since it is a partial guarantor of the results from the former.

Case: religion of the free market

In modern international politics it can seem that there must be truth in

[293] This is Augustine of Hippo, italics mine (Augustine, p. ii 5).

the idea of the free market, because of the sheer numbers of countries which are throwing their all into the belief that the free market, so long as it really is free, will bring all possible boons. This is the religion of the ideologues Hayek and Milton Friedman, and two of its major devotees were Ronald Reagan and Margaret Thatcher. It holds that the free market is a prerequisite for individual liberty. Just because of the ubiquity of this conviction, we are likely to feel that it is intuitively right. Yet we should be wary, knowing that there is no guarantee of truth even if *everyone on earth* shares this idea.

Case: new religion

The spread of conversion to novel-seeming religions and cults can obviously be partly attributed to this phenomenon. How great a part it played in the inception of the major religions and their subsequent spread in 'infidel' lands will no doubt remain too controversial and sensitive to be worth investigating while it is those very religions which represent the consensus to which we feel the inclination to conform. (Which is not to say that they do not accuse each other of it, of course.)

Case: religion needing god

If everyone's religion involves deference to 'an external deity', we will feel a natural inclination towards that belief, which we would not feel in a society where most people are irreligious or self-professed atheists. It might seem to some that a religion needs 'a Creator God' – that that is indeed is a prerequisite, part of the definition of what a religion is. Such people will look on Buddhism in some perplexity, and try to exlain it away as something other than a religion, perhaps a philosophy, or 'just a way of life', or even a science. If such views are those of the majority, it can seem that they might be right. It takes some discipline to maintain the awareness that this is effectively being swayed by numbers of adherents, and that convention does not establish truth.

Case: public morality

The intuitive power of public morality, mainly sexual morality, is clear in the politics of many resurgent fundamentalist Jewish, Christian, Islāmic, Hindu and even Buddhist[294] movements around the world. To be ashamed of what is

---

294 While this book was being prepared the popular singer Akon had his visa application rejected with much media coverage by the Sri Lankan government because of a video he made in which lovely but 'immorally clad' ladies danced before a statue of the

shameful, and to criticise it in others, seems only natural. But here it is not just a cognitive bias which is at play, fooling us into believing that the shamefulness of sexual anatomy and behaviour is true. Indeed the shame for most only comes into play *in public.* So let us examine what 'public' morality actually means.

> Purifying the mind will purify the form;
> But purifying the form will not purify the mind.
>
> the Buddha

If the judge of one's 'goodness' is external then to train in goodness is vanity because to wish to *appear* moral is the result, and this will inevitably be different from wishing to *be* moral, even if that external judge is believed to see deeply: if the external judge knows you as well as you know yourself then your own judgment is not improved by that judge's merit, so the judge is superfluous; but if the judge knows you *less* then it is possible *to fool the judge.* This fact is the root of the many injunctions in religions against judging each other, since it is particularly easy to fool a person into thinking one is moral; unfortunately injunctions against imagining that 'an external deity' can judge us are lacking in the religious literature, as if men and women never consciously admitted that it possible to fool such a thing.

Islām is somewhat unusual among the major religions in not only emphasising the god as the judge, but also prescribing mutual policing of morals very explicitly. The idea of who should 'cast the first stone' rarely occurs to Muslims, and this teaching of Jesus is a close second to turning the other cheek in terms of how much ridicule is poured on it.

In all societies to some extent but in some societies to a very marked degree one witnesses what we might call an exploitation of morality, which is only possible because of that disparity, between what appears moral and what is moral, which mutual policing, such as Islām prescribes, exacerbates.

Here we take the example of a particular Middle-Eastern country simply because we are most familiar with it. In public, people from this country are trumpeters of their particular morals. Extra- and pre-marital sex is illegal. Homosexual acts are anathematised, and though not legislated against explicitly, still prosecuted by recourse to laws about 'defamation of celestial

---

Buddha. That this move, 'coincidentally' close to the elections there, improved the government's 'moral standing' in the eyes of their populace, was clear from the various internet groups lauding the government which sprang up around this issue.

religion', 'public debauchery' and prostitution[295]. Daughters whose loss of honour shames the family 'disappear', or to borrow that lovely expression originating in reports of the state activities necessary to implement Friedman's religion in Latin America, they 'are disappeared'. Drug smuggling is severely punished. Pornography is illegal and the censors cut from films in the cinema even the lightest sex (but not the heaviest violence). Public consumption of alcohol is restricted to licensed bars screened from the public, and all but foreigners are barred from casinos. Irreligious literature is banned.[296] Even some kinds of music[297] periodically become the locus of moralising media frenzy and political point-scoring involving mass arrests. Aside from the legal situation, most people from this country like any other admire the virtues of a good heart, care for the family, loyalty to friends, and instant democratic justice in cases of accidents, fights, and so on.

In 'private', which – note well – does not apply to acts which are 'not public' but to those which are 'not *acknowledged* as public', this country is perhaps the most 'immoral' place by its own public standards one could imagine. Young men, frustrated by ever weightier financial burdens on marriage, until they are able to bear them resort to each other and to loose women (popularly called 'floor-rags'), paid or unpaid. Young men of a particular class are expected to take a second 'study' flat for the use of these floor-rags with conniving impunity. Since most women, even these, are hoping to marry eventually and since the hymen is (flying in the face of current surgical knowledge even among non-surgeons) still the badge of the virginity requisite for this eventuality,

---

[295] A notorious case a few years ago was a mass arrest of homosexual men from a night-club on a boat. Foreigners were deported, but nationals kept without charge for weeks, to international outcry, which was borne with a sense of dignity rather than shame; those who could bribe their way out were released gradually, and several reported being deprived of food *and water* for days on end.

[296] Only a few years ago, the sit-in demonstration by students at its greatest Islamic university against a Syrian novel, which led to a police siege lasting several days and culminated in some deaths which were hushed up by arresting editors of newspapers who dared to report them, proved that even unbanned literature could provoke a pious furore. In this case the book's offence was to include close juxtapositions of sacred words and profanity in the course of its portrayal of the civil war in Algeria, and the government's crime was to allow it to be re-printed (it had never been banned). Note the role played by publicity in this furore.

[297] Even the possession of CDs of Beethoven's 5th symphony was enough, and of metal music more than enough, to detain teenagers a few years ago during the hoo-hah over a supposed Satanist ring.

steam-releasing copulation with *either* sex leads men to develop a habit of abrupt anal penetration, sadism and lack of trust which persist frequently into their married life. Internet cafes are full of people chatting online with people whose relation to them would be impossible in public.[298] Certain areas of the big cities are 'reserved' for pre-marital sex and cafés in affluent areas are the place to pick up loose women. Other areas are gathering places for effeminate men to strut, still others for rough low-class men to meet to have sex with each other and with delicate visitors from the educated classes. Teenage girls and boys, and sometimes younger children, are prostituted to tourists and visiting businessmen by their families or by themselves. Extending our survey beyond sexual morality, it is universal practice to lie, especially to family and generally to friends too. To dupe someone is unofficially considered a talent or a skill. Drugs, soft and hard, are taken very frequently, especially during wedding parties, and a subject of amusement. Despite amazingly high road accident mortality most cars do not have working seat-belts and in those that do they are rarely used. Within the mechanics of the bureaucratic systems the most ordinary service is difficult or impossible without bribes, and employment depends almost entirely on nepotistic connections.

Although degrees of this private-public disparity are found in other cultures, these days the extremity of it is seemingly a characteristic of Islāmic societies, particularly in the matter of sexual morality. This can be investigated by comparing their public self-image with the statistics of their private internet searches. The former is what we see in the mainstream media, such as the recent case in the Gulf of a foreign couple arrested and put through a humiliating trial with biological evidence after they were seen 'apparently having sex' on a beach. As for the latter, Google Trends[299] makes these figures generally available, and provides endless fun: type in a phrase, and it presents statistics for the ten regions, cities, and languages in which 'Google traffic' for this phrase was highest. To give you a taste: of the top ten regions googling 'boy sex' currently, five are Islāmic (Pakistan – no. 1, Saudi Arabia, Egypt, United Arab Emirates and Malaysia); for any old 'sex', five again are Islāmic (Pakistan – again no. 1, Egypt, Morocco, Turkey and Malaysia); for 'porno' two are (Turkey is no. 2, Morocco no. 7); for 'fuck' three are (Pakistan – again no. 1, Egypt and Malaysia) and Arabic is the

---

[298] Or in a way which would be impossible not to mention undesirable: a friend of mine there recently encountered by chance his own (rather authoritarian and pious) father in a sex chat room, and by creating a false identity for himself as a young fop succeeded in 'seducing' him.

[299] At http://www.google.com/trends

second of the top ten languages for traffic in it (after Greek); and amusingly, for 'fuk' seven regions are Islāmic (Palestine, Pakistan, Egypt, Iran, Morocco, United Arab Emirates and Saudi Arabia), and Arabic is the second of the top ten languages trafficking it (after Slovenian[300]).

It is a subtle matter what is acknowledged as the 'public sphere' and what therefore receives the critical attention of society. The ability of the public even when a transgression is obvious, tacitly to agree to ignore it, allows a great deal of flexibility in what would otherwise be quite draconian restrictions. It is this which lends such countries their potential for 'adventure'. Anything goes, but it goes *unofficially*. For example screaming queers and painted whores can stalk the streets as brashly as they like and they attract much less criticism than they would in a so-called liberal nation.

There are two main reasons why this remarkable disparity is allowed to continue. One is that people here often have weightier concerns than matters of public morality, especially since the economic difficulties of the last few years left many without enough money to eat healthily.

Another is that it is open to exploitation, by anyone with the aforementioned talent or skill of cunning. This is seen clearly in the attitude of the police to seat-belts or speeding. Rather than expose the defaulter to the public legal process, it is much more useful for the individual policeman to take a bribe and wave him or her on. There is clearly some understanding among the police that if they were really vigilant and sent most defaulters into the legal process, then people would actually start to wear their seat-belts and follow speed limits and then there would be no chance to ask for bribes, so the crimes are generally 'overlooked' – but not completely of course lest the fear of legal process evaporate. An optimisation is necessary. Like abuses occur generally throughout the society. The country in question is a police state which has been under so-called emergency law for some decades and this makes for almost unlimited corruption.

A great deal of useful information is made accessible to the authorities by letting known prostitutes work, and milking them using the threat of ordinary legal action. Certain doctors who would otherwise have drab sex lives are very happy to perform hymen-reinstating operations on loose women: not because they are championing the rights of these women to have unrestrained sex lives but because (the operation being illegal) they can blackmail them into offering a

---

300 Whether 'fuk' is a Slovenian word for something entirely different I have been unable to discover. Incidentally the tenth of the top ten *cities* googling this word, two of them in Morocco, is perhaps unsurprisingly Manchester.

favour or three before the operation is performed (but not afterwards of course!), knowing that the woman fears for her reputation in the public sphere enough to 'consent' to be thus raped. This country's popular culture is full of stories of such abuses, and it is well known that it goes right to the top.

So here we have a society utterly inured to manipulation of the disparity between acknowledged and unacknowledged misdemeanours. The commonness of the abusers is such that there is enormous pressure for the seemingly hypocritical disparity to continue at all levels.

This country then might seem like an extreme example. In fact all externally-judged morality in any society assumes degrees of the same process: a moral degeneracy dependent upon a disparity between two levels of acknowledgement, what Islāmic economist Timur Kuran termed 'pretense falsification'.[301] Within religion it is not just the Catholic Church with its indulgences that has exploited this. It is a major factor in the preservation mechanisms of the religions which teach of the 'Judgment Day' – Christianity and Islām.

For just as the police allow motorists' misdemeanours to go unpunished so that they can optimally demand bribes from them, just as doctors allow adulteresses to go unpunished so that they can optimally demand their sexual favours, so must 'the deity' in these religions allow its followers' faults to go unpunished in order optimally to extract their subservience. The nuance of the *entirely postponed* threat of judgment is genius from 'the deity's point of view' since it means that unlike the naughty motorist and the loose woman in our analogous cases, complete relief from the blackmail threat is never completely removed so the necessity of subservience is never completely obviated. (Compare the mentality of the driver who drives away from the policeman he has bribed.) Since the immediate and the eventual judge are (in both of these religions) one and the same, the pressure would be unbearable, so is necessarily lightened by stressing the deity's propensity to forgive (but not of course to the extent of cancelling 'Judgment Day'!); in Islām it is stressed that Allāh is merciful to the 'believers' (while never of course allowing that 'belief' can be perfect!) and in Christianity it is allowed for the believer to lay at least some part of the blame at the foot of the Evil One and his 'temptations' (but 'temptation' of course is taught never to go away until the last day!). So the details are different but the psychological effect is the same.

Belief in an external judge, by means of vanity, shunts ethical interest

---

301 (Kuran, 1995)

away from other more important benefits towards the immediate benefits of social respect, and so it itself causes the public/private disparity in morality. And we can now see that it furthermore supports the notion of inescapable fear tactics ('Doomsday') and god bribery ('sacrifice and prayer') while preserving the 'deity's authority'.

It is not just bribery-solicitation that the religious doctrines reproduce from their societies' bureaucratic structures, but also nepotism. Just as a lucky member of our example country with friends high up in the police fears blackmail so much less, so does the Muslim who has 'made the connection' with 'Muḥammad the Prophet' fear the reports of his 'prosecutor angel'[302] so much less on 'The Day of Accounting', and so does the Christian who believes herself 'saved' by 'the Christ'. Even in the most orthodox Islām Muḥammad is taught to lead his people, the Muslims, through the gates of paradise. A weakly supported but extremely popular account has this prophet say that whoever repeats the testimony (that Allāh is the only god and Muḥammad is the messenger of that god) before he dies will cross the bridge over hell to enter paradise, no matter what atrocities he has performed till then. It is the fact that most Muslims are anticipating this leg-up into the company (of the celestials) that makes them on the whole so disdainful of those religious traditions which still require the equivalent of seat-belts and speed limits.

We have already considered the magical origins of the punitive legal system. The belief in the effectiveness of punishment is an inevitable consequence of moral narcissism. When one must be seen to be good, and when the group must be seen to be good (in comparison to other groups) then it becomes logical to preserve the appearance of morality even by what are in fact immoral means.

It is selfish interest which allows punishments and rewards to create the mere appearance of a moral society. If the people became less selfish they would become less concerned with punishments and rewards so the mechanism by which these two fabricate morality would weaken. Once again we find that the criticism we are levelling against the massive religion has been made eloquently by mystics within it. You can hear the anguished complaint against such a seemingly pious society in the famous prayer of the female mystic:

[302] In Islām it is believed that on our left shoulder sits an angel who records our bad deeds.

O Allah! If I worship You for fear of Hell, burn me in Hell,
and if I worship You in hope of Paradise, exclude me from Paradise.
But if I worship You for Your Own sake,
grudge me not Your everlasting Beauty.[303]

This helps us understand why groups that apply practices (such as the mind-training of certain kinds of meditation and yoga) that reduce self-grasping tend to be those which rely less on punishment and rewards; and why the religions that depend on punishment and reward are so hostile to such practices. A Sunnite Muslim is to copy Muḥammad as the perfect example in all things right down to which foot enters the bathroom first and how to wipe his arse, all things that is except meditating for years in a cave reflecting on the nature of reality. For he told his followers (according to a weakly supported but very well know report) at the culmination of this monastic retreat:

There is no monasticism in Islām.

We can see why religions teaching of an external judge might be hostile to mind-training which reduces self-grasping.

There is no other reason than narcissism why a group would permit the hypocrisy of an apparent morality dependent upon actual immorality. And of all the embodiments of narcissism the most extreme ever devised is that of a sought after 'Paradise' whose inhabitants somehow remain content and proud knowing that at the same time other beings are being tortured in 'Hell'. It has even been suggested that this unsavoury élite will be permitted glimpses of 'the Fire' in order that they might congratulate themselves the more, this self-congratulation seen as part of their piety. The seventh chapter of the Qur'ān is named after, and refers to, 'The Heights', namely the heights from which 'the Blessed' entering 'Heaven' will be able to gaze on 'the denizens of Hell'.

What a 'great almighty god'
Builds for people with Good Repute
Earned in dirty clinics at night
A heaven with knitting needle keys
Turned in countless bloody locks
And lets its pearly gates to yawn

---

303 Rābi`a al-`Adawiyya al-Qaysiyya (c. 95-185 h.) as told by Farīd ud-Dīn `Aṭṭār

The way he opened his daughter's neck
To let dishonoured red jet out
And lets the family of paradise scramble in!
How just that people so obscene
They praise this monstrous lord
Might win alone this hellish place
There to stay with him
And the rest of his atrocious sycophants
For all eternity!
If only it were so!

Unfortunately hypocrisy is not the worst result of the situation we have been analysing. A morality based on lines bisecting scales of behaviour and thus dividing 'the good' from 'the bad' combines with moral narcissism most ominously, because it effectively prohibits for those whose reputation is good the ordinary human sympathy with those whose reputation is bad. Society becomes split and segregated by a 'moral' line. Infamously this leads, for example, to prostitutes being denied recourse against those who commit against them even horrific abuses much worse in anyone's books than prostitution itself. This can happen because the one who sympathises with prostitutes is potentially considered to be one who advocates their misdeeds. Onlookers on the cruel treatment of a known homosexual in prison will not intervene despite their pity lest they be associated with the transgression and win like treatment.

Moreover, people who cross the line for any reason get concentrated spatially with others who crossed the line for other reasons. Of course this mechanism has been consciously employed in the machinery of totalitarianism: the Nazis' mincing the Jews, the Communists' mincing the dissidents, and so on.

Meanwhile those who do not cross have such transgressors almost wholly removed from their experience, and develop therefore wildly inaccurate ideas about them. All natural lines of sympathy (such as would develop if one were aware, for example, of why someone stole, because one had seen their starving family) are eroded. Here, again, as in the operation of so-called justice, we see superstitious, magical thinking existing quite unchallenged in societies that claim to have transcended primitive superstition: the one who transgresses thereby wins a species of *polluting power*, and so they must be isolated from the group and caused to suffer lest the group lose its ritual purity. Anyone onlooker who questions the punitive treatment is polluted and therefore a source of pollution himself or herself.

Thus when society is divided by a moral line and this segregation applied spatially, experience is cloistered and understanding and sympathy lost for transgressors. So black-white ethics lead to unjustly harsh treatment of transgressors.

For example, capital punishment of adulterers and adulteresses by stoning is required unless both parties are unmarried, according to all four schools of Islāmic law. It is done by wrapping the transgressors in white sheets tied with rope so that their faces are not visible, burying them up to their knees, and then killing them gradually by blows from rocks hurled at them. Not one executioner but *the community members* hurl the rocks. Here the original form of exorcism is almost perfectly reproduced, as it is in the Arabian rituals of the pilgrimage to Makkah where pilgrims are required to hurl rocks at slabs representing the Devil. Every recitation of any part of the Qur'ān outside the ritual prayer begins with the prayer, 'I take refuge with Allāh from Satan, the most *worthy of stoning* [in Arabic, a`ūdhu billāh min ash-shaiṭān al-rajīm].' The verb used for 'to stone to death' means 'to damn'.

People living outside the pale of Islām have no reason for complacency. The exorcism formula is in our times reproduced only slightly less perfectly in Christian countries' death penalties in which murder victims' aggrieved families are invited to witness the murderer's electrocution. (And anyone who would argue that the electric chair is 'more humane' is suffering from the same 'removal from experience' we have alluded to: they need to see what happens when the execution is botched, as it frequently is.)

The ineffective nature of such 'means of justice' we have already considered. Elsewhere we considered the psychological and social feedback processed by which it becomes exaggerated to extremes of cruelty and moral degeneracy.

Heuristics

More generally, what we thing is right or good is often distorted, not only by our psychology but also by the appearance of the situation, and the effects of social structures on information flow, and so on. These distorting effects are referred to in cognitive science as '*heuristics*'.

>Choice-supportive bias

This refers to the fact, much documented[304], that we become biased

304 (Henkel & Mather, 2007)

towards the things we have chosen simply because we remember having chosen them, and that this bias is *larger* when our confidence at the time of choosing is *less*. When popular opinion is not uniform, groups will tend to form aligned with its various colours. Other things being equal, which group one aligns himself or herself with often depends on such psychological foibles as the Concorde fallacy: we drift to one group randomly, speak of our allegiance, begin to defend it, and subsequently feel loyalty to it in proportion to the effort we have put into defending it.[305] Experience with formal debates has shown us that people called to argue publicly for a position they do not take privately will more often than not vote finally with the side that they argued for: they had gained a sense of belonging through their effort, and truth was no longer important. This is aggravated by the Concorde fallacy: the more effort one spends on a project, the more committed one feels to finishing it.

The implications for allegiance to particular faiths and doctrines are obvious, but whether it will ever fall on those thus allying themselves to be sensitive to this psychological phenomenon in themselves is another question. We can at least try ourselves to be as rigorous as we can in examining our own tendency to lose flexibility and therefore reasonableness by seeing ourselves as having taken sides, for example.

>Normalcy bias

It has been shown by experiments that people are more likely to accept what is familiar to them, a tendency known technically in psychology as the '*mere exposure effect*'. In more general terms it is expressed in society as a kind of indulgence in normalcy, in the familiar, and therefore a resistance to what might challenge that. This documented tendency is known as '*normalcy bias*'.

Nowadays what is familiar to people depends almost entirely upon the media. This presents a natural barrier in the public for even listening to arguments which might criticise the media and media-based social poisons, such as the creation of society-wide depression at self-image (or 'a market for cosmetic products' as it is sometimes known).

The existence of this bias should also cause Christian theologians to pause for thought. When one spends so much time pondering the nature implied by a particular name, even though that name might be totally without referent, its very occurrence will tend to lull the mind more and more into

---

305 Remember the discovery of the formation of groups around even absurd identities in the work of Henri Tajfel (Tajfel H. , 1982).

accepting its existence. This phenomenon explains how theologians can start talking about 'the inner sense' of (the Christian) deity, which they have cultivated so assiduously with their strained ravings – and which is so strangely lacking in those who have cultivated senses of alternatives with alternative ravings. Incidentally, such theological 'argument' suffers heavily from the so-called '*existentialist fallacy*', which can only fool us because of the cognitive bias we are considering here.

In Boolean logic, there is an existential difference between on the one hand sets defined by universal criteria and on the other sets of particular members: 'all divine qualities' is a set of the former type, which in Boolean logic need not have members, i.e. it is potentially hypothetical (i.e. it is equivalent to 'any supposed divine quality'), whilst 'some of god's attributes' is a set of the latter type, clearly requiring members. The existential fallacy occurs when there is a subtle slip from the hypothetical type to the existent type, hidden under similar language, and modern Christian writings are a lubricated mess of them.

>Semmelweis reflex

Especially when considering the progress or lack of it in scientific knowledge, the root psychological tendency to reject any new evidence that does not fit into an established paradigm has been popularly called the '*Semmelweis reflex*'. Its name immortalises one Ignaz Semmelweis (1818-1865), a Hungarian physician whose discovery [306] that mortality rates from 'puerperal fever' (post-partum infection, which finished off such notables as Jayne Seymour and Mary Wollstonecraft) could be reduced from the then usual 10-35% to less than 1% if only doctors would wash their hands in chlorinated lime, was roundly dismissed by his colleagues and continued to be until Pasteur confirmed the germ theory of infection. The importance of his studies could then be seen, and earned him thenceforth the title 'Saviour of Mothers'.[307] Unfortunately this was long after Semmelweis' premature death, from 'injuries', in an asylum to which a nervous breakdown had led him.

>Affect heuristic

It was first theorised in 2000 that people who felt good would have lower reaction to perceived risk and stronger reaction to perceived benefit in a

---

[306] Published in his book *Etiology, Concept and Prophylaxis of Childbed Fever* (Semmelweis, 1847).

[307] (Hanninen, Farago, & Monos, 1983)

decision made during that feeling.[308] Researchers called this the 'affect heuristic', a rather needlessly jargonistic way of saying 'emotion-influenced distortion'. A paper published this week reports that subjects were significantly less likely to report having experienced pain from immersing their hands in scalding water if they were first allowed to *flick through the wad of cash* they had been awarded for participating in the experiment.

Case: seeing a smiling face makes you favour what comes next

Something similar was demonstrated earlier in an experiment[309] whose results were later contested but which are heart-warming enough to report: people asked to select Chinese ideographs they liked were shown to prefer those ideographs which had been preceded by a 1/250 second flash of a smiling face over those preceded by a flash of a frowning face, and this initial effect seemed to override subsequent flashes of the frowning face before the thus selected ideographs.

>Memory availability

Other aspects of our mental experience, not just mood, can distort our decisions. It is a feature of most people's memory that it is selective, so that what gets remembered is the remarkable stuff, the stuff that sticks out. At the same time we are often called upon to make decisions based on prior experience. The employment of that selection of more vivid details that we retain to make decisions which are therefore unsound is called 'the availability heuristic' in behavioural economics.[310] Another way of explaining it is as our tendency to mix up what we can think or remember with what is or was.

Case: religious myths

Since the massive religions very heavily rely on accounts of vivid experiences of particular figures, they are to that extent influenced by the availability heuristic. It is an undeniable fact that when we see someone do

---

308 (Finucane, Alhakami, Slovic, & Johnson, 2000)

309 (Winkielman, Zajonc, & Schwarz, 1997)

310 The term was introduced by the work of two Israeli cognitive and mathematical psychologists, Amos Tversky (1937-1996) and Nobel laureate Daniel Kahneman (b. 1934), the founders of behavioural economics and originators of the 'prospect theory' of what influences our choices (Kahneman & Tversky, Prospect Theory: an Analysis of Decision under Risk, 1979).

something that inspires awe we remember it, to the detriment of seeing them do something that undermines awe. Whether or not the major figures in the mythologies of the massive religions ever did things which undermined their credibility (giving a nonchalant and playful tug to the hackles such a suggestion might raise on certain beasts), we will never know, because the availability heuristic operating over generation after generation means that such acts will have been filtered out. If this were not the case then a hagiography would be a biography.

Case: suggestion in politics

Its power in our lives should not be underestimated. Various reports have shown that what people believed to be likely to happen was influenced by merely drawing their attention to eventualities they otherwise would not have considered. For example, in a survey at the time of the 1976 United States of America general election, people who had previously been asked how likely they thought Gerald Ford was to win, subsequently considered him significantly more likely to win than did people who had been asked only about Jimmy Carter.

In the realm of religion and miracles, and superstition and charlatanism, it is aggravated by virtue of the fact that what seems vivid in the first place can often be the result of a mistaken judgment:

>Pareidolia

Many of us will feel that the age of miracles is over, that it died with superstition. I hope I have succeeded in convincing such people that superstition is alive and well, and 'walks among us'. In some communities and for some faiths, equally, miracles are alive and well.

Without sneering at venerable miracles of the irretrievable past let us nevertheless not daintily flinch from such spectacles as the printing over the last few years in mainstream Arabic newspapers of photos of, among other things, trees, fruit, and even an international celebrity wrestler[311], displaying (in the last case in the veins of his admirable musculature) the Islāmic testimony of faith in Arabic. Sometimes, in corners of quiet books and articles, one comes across admissions by photographers of hoaxes, and even without them a certain inclination of mind might lead one to notice that the said testimony, being composed entirely of three Arabic letters, two of which are approximately vertical

---

[311] Batista

lines and the third of which can be written as near-vertical lines, could be read into pretty much anything with flowing, near-parallel lines, yet it is not such shame-faced admissions, nor such nice scriptological observations, nor even the fact that the human tendency to read known images into accidental patterns has long been known to psychology (technically as '*pareidolia*'), that send the chain emails proliferating through cyberspace.

>Apophenia

Soon after the attacks on the World Trade Centre in New York a chain letter was being distributed by mass email and photocopying across the Arab world of the verse of the Qur'ān which occurred at chapter 9, section 11:

> Is he who lays his foundation on piety to Allāh and what satisfies him better or he who lays his foundation on a sandbank on the verge of being undercut, teetering (*jurufin hārin*)? For it crumbles with him into the fire of Hell, Allāh not guiding a people from among the unjust.

The rather obscure Arabic phrase highlighted above was even said to resemble the name of the street in which the twin towers stood. This 'miracle' I quickly discovered to have further obscurer import probably too 'miraculous' for the Muslims when I turned half in jest to the Buddhists' *Lotus Sutra*, chapter 11 ('The Opening of the Treasure Tower'), paragraph 9+11[312]:

> Shakyamuni Buddha with the fingers of his right hand then opened the tower of the seven treasures. A loud sound issued from it...

...and then, with a growing sense either that miracles might be rather easy or that a chameleon-like intelligence was really at work, to the Christian Bible, 11th book (I Kings), chapter 9:

> And it came to pass, when Solomon had finished the building of the house of the Lord, and the king's house [...] the Lord said unto him [...] if ye shall at all turn from following me [...] I will cut off Israel out [...] and this house, which I have hallowed for my name, will I cast out of my sight [...] And at this house, which is high, every one that passeth by it

312 It was the translation by Burton Watson (1994) who is, we might therefore surmise, a member of that ancient sect of illuminati who scry all our futures...

> shall be astonished, and shall hiss; and they shall say, Why hath the Lord done thus unto this land, and to this house? And they shall answer, Because they forsook the Lord their God [...] when Solomon had built the two houses, the house of the Lord, and the king's house [...].

In psychology, this human tendency to invest accidental patterns with momentous meaning is referred to as '*apophenia*' – it is what has become famous (thanks to films such as 'A Beautiful Mind') in certain kinds of mental disturbance, such as autism, where mental capabilities are so focused and intensified that patterns ordinarily unrecognisable can be recognised. And it can develop not only because of the accident of intellectual intensity.

>Confirmation bias

Certain apologists for the massive religions spend a great deal of time and energy finding momentous meanings among the accidental patterns in their scriptures, not because they are autistic (usually) but because they are looking for relief, as we shall see when we turn to the matter of authority projection and anxiety in the next section.

Here we are merely concerned with the recognised factor in human investigation, that we seek out the very data which confirm our own prejudices. In cognitive science this is known as *confirmation bias.*

Case: esoteric interpretation of scriptures

Whilst it is possible that there is a hidden message 'from the deity' behind the numerologically transformed Hebrew characters of the Book of Genesis; whilst it might be true that verses in the Qur'ān mentioning embryos being lumps and the sky on the 'Day of Doom' being orange are not what anyone would expect a 7th century Arab to describe an embryo and the Doomsday sky to be like, but are on the contrary miraculously ahead-of-their-time scientific statements matching modern embryology and the latest telescopic evidence for the wavelength of light emitted during supernovae; whilst the intoxicated visions of the Book of Revelation might not be just that, intoxicated visions, but a prescient explanation of the last decade's international political developments (and let us hastily pass over the fact that we were saying the same thing a decade or two decades or even a millennium ago); while all these things might be true, we have to recognise at the same time the existence of this psychological tendency and its motley sisters, '*the focusing effect*', '*selective perception*', '*wishful thinking*', and '*hindsight bias*', which are all pretty much self-explanatory, and '*the Forer effect*', which technically refers to what we might more colloquially call 'the horoscope syndrome', whereby we are more likely to concede that a horoscope description is accurate for us when we know that it is for our star sign than when we do not.

The awkward point is that if the same intensity of meaning identification were applied to other religions or scriptures or even a telephone book or for that matter *Penthouse* magazine, previously unsuspected treasures of esoteric wisdom might be thrown up. And who knows, maybe that would be the work of the hand of the deity too!

>Representativeness heuristic

Now we move into rather more surreal realms. Tversky and Kahneman coined [313] the term 'representativeness heuristic' to describe a psychological effect they measured whereby people are misled by seeming similarities between the form of a hypothesis and available data: they found that the way conceptual information is presented to us influences how likely we are to judge that it is correct, because of our tendency to look for similarities in appearance.

Sometimes looking for such similarities is successful. If we have an idea that we are craving chocolate, it is a success that we recognise chocolate in order to buy and eat it. That this example is so basic shows us how powerfully the tendency is likely to be hard-wired in us. Unfortunately it is not always so successful.

In our appreciation of causation, for example, it makes us more likely to believe that particular effects derive from those causes which are similar to them than from those which are dissimilar to them. To take a well-known example, the rhinoceros horn bears for some a passing resemblance to the erect phallus, whereas the drooping wattle of the turkey might be considered to bear more than a passing resembance to the flaccid one. Which of the two animals' parts tradition has bequeathed to us as an aphrodisiac has more to do with this heuristic than physical effects of taking the two items ground to powder. It is an ancient mistake: consider the mandrake root, imbued in all cultures that knew it with all sorts of powers based on the similarity to the human form.

The notion assumed in Europe the proportions of an epidemic, however, with the popularising effect of Jakob Böhme (1575-1624)'s '*doctrine of signatures*', the idea (which came to him as a young man in a mystical vision) that 'God the Creator' had left signs in the forms of his creatures hinting at the forms

313 (Tversky & Kahneman, 1974)

of truths. Herbalists and others we would nowadays refer to as quacks, among them Paracelsus, quickly ran away with this idea, seeing in the resemblances between various plant or animal shapes and human organs the 'truth' that the former could be used to treat problems in the latter. In some cases plants endowed with 'the Creator' 's visual hints were even named on that basis alone – as we see in English in spleenwort, liverwort, toothwort, woundwort, lungwort and even lousewort. Whilst some have argued that there may be scientific basis for, and therefore truth in, some signatures, such as plants with thorns being able to grow in intensely competitive environments and more likely than other plants to possess chemicals to suppress animal and microbial attack, and therefore to be useful to humans through such chemicals' capacity to boost our immune system, the general consensus in studies is that there are no such scientific bases.

More generally, anthropologists have recognised categories of human groups' beliefs involving the investment of meaning in similarities. Sir James Frazer wrote [314] of 'contagious' and 'homoeopathic' magic – the beliefs respectively that objects once in contact maintained some mystical connection (hence the use of victims' hair in voodoo, for example) and that the qualities of one object could be transferred into one resembling it in form, such as in the Azande who treat epilepsy with burnt monkey skull, the monkeys' movements appearing similar to the epileptics'.[315] With a modicum of reflection we will be able to identify instances of the same tendency at work in our own experiences, especially in childhood, and indeed the researchers on the Azande point out that such associative thinking is as much a feature of modern city life as survival of the jungle tribes.

The delusions of the representativeness heuristic are not limited to our estimation of causation, however. It also leads to neglect of the laws of probability. For example, Tversky and Kahneman showed that when asked to judge which subsequent career is more likely for a girl who showed activist leanings as a student, a bank teller or a bank teller who is also a feminist, most people erroneously chose 'a bank teller who is also a feminist' even though by the law of probability this outcome must be no more likely than merely being a bank teller: the number of feminist bank tellers cannot exceed the total number of bank tellers. This mistake is referred to as 'conjunction/disjunction fallacy' after probability theory, which states that the likelihood of {event A or event B or both} must be more than the likelihood of {event A} or {event B} singly. Hearing of this experiment, one's first thought might well be: well the people in

---

[314] In *The Golden Bough* (Frazer, 1890).

[315] (Shweder, 1977)

the experiment obviously thought that the first option, being a bank teller, meant 'being a bank teller *and not* a feminist' – but in fact this was not the case: the experiment was repeated, with the same result, when the first option was made explicitly 'bank teller whether or not she is a feminist'. The mere similarity between the quality in the idea of the second option ('and feminist') with the earlier student activism had been enough to over-ride all sense of probability. Similarly, in a different study[316], when people were asked to predict university subject based on personal characteristics, and to choose between a particular subject and a larger field *which included the same subject*, they usually and erroneously held the more specific subject to be 'more likely'. On reflection we can see that this must be impossible: being a biologist cannot be more likely than being a scientist. But again the similarity (for example between a childhood interest in nature and the subject biology) was enough to override the sense of probability. This result was only obtained if there was resemblance between the qualities and the subject (not in the case, for example, of a childhood interest in nature and the subject Hebrew, for example) i.e. a deluding attraction to specificity itself was not found.

Case: divine attributes located in a single deity

This has profound implications for our appreciation of competing ways of seeing reality, especially those deriving for example from the doctrines of the massive religions, which (as we shall see) are *almost exclusively* 'similarities'. Each of the qualities that the monotheists' deity is supposed to have are a direct resemblance with something in human experience. For example, the notion of the 'Creator' is a direct resemblance with the observation that things can be made and that there is a diversity of forms in reality; 'the Protector' is a direct resemblance with the observation that allowing ourselves to imagine being protected provides a real and direct sense of comfort, and that parents protect their produced offspring. Many divine attributes are in direct and paradoxical oposition to others, a conceptual problem which is generally dismissed as 'wisdom' – wisdom unavailable to mere us. However the discovery of the representativeness heuristic tells us something more, something related to our basic psychology: that even though the combination of the deity's qualities would be judged extremely unlikely, our sense of the unlikelihood is *over-ridden by our attraction to the 'similarities'*, and the more similarities the more dramatically it is overridden. In short, monotheistic belief is very well-suited indeed to the

316 (Bar-Hillel & Neter, 1986)

delusions of ordinary psychology.

Cluster effect

It has also been shown[317] that humans are prone to misjudge what constitutes statistical randomness. In a coin-tossing situation, on average people asked to judge whether a sequence of tosses is random wait for the side of the coin in the result to change more frequently (70%) than is statistically random (50%). This means that they frequently consider random sequences to be non-random on the basis of there being, as they see it, runs of one side of the coin which are too long. This cognitive bias is known as '*the cluster effect*', and it is what makes the famous *Texas sharpshooter 'fallacy'* possible: a man fires inside a barn at the wall, then chooses the densest cluster of bulletholes and draws a circular target board around it to 'prove' that he was a sharp shooter.

Gambler's fallacy

Another related and more famous mistake the cognitive scientists linked to the representativeness heuristic is the intuitive conviction we have in the so-called 'law of averages': we believe that after tossing heads 20 times the probability of tails coming next is very high, whereas it is still 50% likely, unless the coin is biased – an exception which tells us something of the origin of this intuition and how it is often useful. When we lose again and again in a particular, some of us believe that our chances of winning gradually increase.

It is this fallacy which has given rise to a long history of credit epidemics. People invest in companies even when they know the company is fraudulent and likely to collapse, because they imagine they can predict when the collapse will occur and get out in time.

Information dynamic

Not just psychological foibles but also factors related to the very flow of information through society also influence our idea of what is right or good.

>Informational cascade

It is partly because people get information from others to make their decisions and are likely to be persuaded that the majority, even if they are not considered experts in the least, must be right (which we noted earlier as the

317 (Gilovich, Vallone, & Tversky, 1985). Gilovich (b. 1934) later wrote a nice introduction to these rather dizzying topics (Gilovich T. , 1991).

potential deception of consensus), but partly because of our deep psychological tendency to conform [318]. It can lead to the phenomenon known as an '*informational cascade*'[319] where a decision to abandon private information in favour of novel information from a perceived majority causes a wave of decision-changing to spread through a population. It has been argued that it was a major contributor to the ballooning of protests which led to the fall of the Berlin Wall, for example, and negatively as the main reason for the rejection of proven highly efficient drought-resistant seeds during the Great Depression. So serious is the tendency to err in such a situation (as can be seen by people's willingness to starve in the second example) that it has been argued[320] that legislation be introduced in sensitive situations to avoid it. And there are many examples of such legislation having been introduced. For example, some countries (such as France) outlaw pre-election polls to prevent informational cascades unhinging the population's more rational (we do not say rational *tout court*, for reasons which must now be clear) voting process.

>Availability cascade

It need not involve complex information[321]. A simple, intuitively right idea, once it spreads to enough people, starts to spread faster: people adopt the idea partly because of its novelty and consequent impact, partly out of a concern for appearing to be 'in' with current trends. This leads to the idea becoming more and more available, so the phenomenon is referred to as an '*availability cascade*'. The recognition of it in financial fields led to its importance becoming highly appreciated. More recently a charge of it has, notoriously, been levelled at scientists working on climate change.

Grievance runaway

A combination of many of these biases, it should now be obvious, occur in a phenomenon which increasingly appears in current affairs as well as work situations.

When our attention is drawn, by whatever means, to an example of

---

318 See for example Asch's so-called 'conformity experiments' (Asche, 1955).

319 This term was coined in a highly technical paper (Bikhchandani, Hirshleifer, & Welch, 1992) which developed concepts in observational learning theory.

320 For example by the law professor Ward Farnsworth (Farnsworth, 2007)

321 As was pointed out by two Americans, legal scholar Cass Sunstein and political economist and Islāmic studies professor Tim Kuran, who combined the ideas of the informational cascade and the availability heuristic.

someone being aggrieved, and we recognise that their reason for being so aggrieved also applies to ourselves, then, independent of whether there are grounds for grievance, we are likely to, first of all, feel bad. This allows the affect heuristic to work: whatever information is subsequently absorbed assumes the negative aspect of our mood. Furthermore, there will be confirmation bias in operation: we will be looking for examples of righteous grievance. Each new example will feed the negativitity and therefore the affect heuristic. Furthermore by actually seeking particular contexts, such as social groups who are likely to share these qualities, we become victim additionally to an informational cascade. Worse, because the topic of thought more and more is this reasons for grievance, the memory availability influences us. And once we make a 'stance' about it – publicly or to ourselves – then there will be choice-supportive bias and subsequently, with every effort we make, Concorde fallacy-driven spiralling commitment. All of these again increase the attention on the original reason for grievance.

Because of the runaway, those not so involved in the issue will be left far behind, and not exposed to all the cognitive biases will question the validity of the grievance. By those in the thick of the grievance, such challenges will of course be taken as further reason for grievance – and their presenters accused of discrimination and hatred of the aggrieved group. Since the reason for grievance must apply to a group for this circuit of cognitive biases to catch fire, and since most massive groups are identified in terms of race or religion, such discrimination or hatred will be interpreted as referring to the group likewise, so there will be partially absurd accusations of racial or religious hatred. I would suggest introducing the term 'over-aggrievability contempt' to replace the various phobia terms, since the latter continue to feed into the cognitive bias conflagrations, whereas the former at least has the potential to quench them.

Case: defamation of Islām

In recent years Islām has become so closely associated with this phenomenon that 'aggrieved' and 'Muslim' have become a linguistic collocation in the press. We referred earlier to a recent group on Facebook which was set up by Sri Lankans aggrieved by a pop music video featuring bikini-clad women gyrating before a statue of Buddha and which quickly garnered a good 15,000 members. It was perceived by many others, however, to be rather un-Buddhist, as it was entitled 'We hate Akon [the singer considered at fault]', and consequently the discussion boards were full of long threads of complaints by Buddhists and non-Buddhists that the group was inappropriate. One of the most popular topics on the discussion board was entitled 'Is Buddhism the new Islām?' – Islām being considered the standard for extreme aggrievability, both by decriers of such aggrievability and advocates of it (as 'backbone'), the former much to the consternation of Muslims who had joined the group, as they saw it, to sympathise with the aggrieved Buddhists.

Various recent events have contributed to this image of Islām – not least the on-going furore about the 'Muḥammad' cartoons, which was an excellent example of the positive feedback among cognitive biases we are referring to. Although there were certainly individuals involved in consciously and maliciously spreading the news of the cartoons, to the extent of publishing them themselves, we can see that the vast majority of publishing of the news was done by Muslims who were genuinely aggrieved.

Needless to say the term Islāmophobia has now become current.

Case: desecration of the Holocaust

A longer-standing example of course is the systematic murder under the rule of the Nazis of people unlucky enough to fit their idea of the inferior or the socially detrimental, mainly Jews. It is an instructive example because other groups, such as homosexuals, were, it is well known, included in the attempt at extermination, but have not developed such a strong culture of grievance about this event.

The power of the Holocaust to generate these cognitive bias conflagrations is almost unparalleled, and their consequences, though irrational, are as entrenched now in European law as those of Muslims' grievances about insulting the prophet are in Islāmic law, with the startling difference that the former claim to stand for freedom of speech, a fact which is rightly made much of by Muslims when they are criticised for *not* standing for such freedom.

Like any conflagration, so long as there is material (minds) to burn, the flames do not die. Recently an English translation[322] was published of a 2005 book by Emmanuel Faye about the Nazi beliefs and activities of the philosopher Martin Heidegger, who many believe is the most important thinker of the twentieth century. The response, by the book and by reviewers, to one passage exemplifies the cognitive biases at work here:

> Following the defeat of the Nazis, Heidegger made no attempt to speak out against the Holocaust. In a lecture delivered in 1949 he stated:

---

322 (Faye, 2009)

> 'Agriculture is now a motorised food-industry – in essence, the same as the manufacturing of corpses in the gas chambers and the extermination camps, the same as the blockade and starvation of the countryside, the same as the production of the hydrogen bombs.'
>
> Such contempt [sic] for the victims of persecution and war does not deter his supporters…[323]

The passage in another light could appear to be a condemnation of mechanisation, using the horror of the gas chambers to support the condemnation, but confirmation bias is looking for contempt of Jews' humanity, choice-supportive bias is making Heidegger's potential reasons for mentioning the gas chambers and extermination camps fade into insignificance, until what threatens, frankly, to be a freakish inversion of Heidegger's potential intent can be blithely made. The subsequent indignation fuels an affect heuristic which both encourages re-reading of the offensive passage and more intense confirmation bias, etc., literally *ad nauseam.*

The conclusion of Faye's book is that Heidegger's works in all our libraries should be shifted from the philosophy section to the history of Nazism section, and that there should be great care taken in presenting them in university courses, for fear of corrupting youth. As reviewer Tim Black comments wryly,

> For anyone who's laboured, heavy-lidded, over Heidegger's excursus on Austrian poet Georg Trakl, Faye's conclusions may come as something of a surprise: 'If [Heidegger's] writings continue to proliferate without our being able to stop this intrusion of Nazism into human education, how can we not expect them to lead to yet another translation into facts and acts, from which this time humanity might not be able to recover?' This is what you might call a leap of Faye. One minute an undergraduate is getting to grips with fundamental ontology, the next he's given himself a severe side-parting, donned a brown shirt, and has begun planning the systematic extermination of Jewry. Being and Time today, being a Nazi tomorrow.[324]

Given what we have said about how detractors get left behind, we can note the parallel this reviewer makes with the leap of faith. And again the equivalent result unjustly accrues, in the judgment of the aggrieved, to perceived detractors,

[323] (Keenan, 2010)

[324] (Black, 2009)

including, probably, now, this book: anti-semitism.

Case: sacrilege in general

The same system might even be in operation of old in the very arising of the sense of sacredness. Hebrew and Arabic words for sacred mean 'forbidden' – it is less a sense of their divinity than that socially they are prohibited. The same double sense is preserved in the word 'taboo'. The standard Arabic translation of Freud's works translates *Totem and Taboo* as *al-Ṭawṭam wa al-Ḥarām, The Totem and the Forbidden/Sacred.* It is certainly true that the uncanniness of a particular phenomenon, such as a place, or a way of speaking, is felt to different degrees in a social group, such that controversy can arise: this would lead to those most affected by the uncanniness developing grievance in exactly the sense we have been considering, with all the same potential for cognitive biases to feed into each other until the social group is divided into a group that is extraordinarily aggrieved and a group that is contemptuous of their grievance.

Whether current 'subscribers' to the sacred of the massive religions are prepared to accept that the atmosphere of even the most intense sacredness could arise merely out of a mutually reinforcing system of cognitive biases is a question I do not intend to address here (although I would invite them, for example, to compare the colourful vocabulary aggrieved Jews use of perceived anti-semites with the language the Qur'ān uses of infidels), but I think most of us, subscribers and contemners, will admit straight away that there is more than a whiff of the sacred-sacrilege divide in such contemporary issues as cartoons, swastika arm-bands, Sudanese teddy bears, the right to free speech, and the right to show hair and skin.

Congruence with commitment to other doctrines

It is often the case that we are more inclined to accept those notions which fit with doctrines to which we have already committed ourselves. In cognitive science this is considered a kind of '*anchoring*', where our decision-making ability is influenced by our prior focus on some other notion. We have already considered some kinds of inter-doctrinal meshes that might encourage this effect in our treatment of complex philosophies deployed as the handmaids of faith. Here we consider examples of a more psychological than ideological nature.

Case: innocence and guilt with creation by a perfect deity

There are in some societies other powerful influences favouring the preservation of the sacrificial system. We have considered public morality itself as it appears in Christianity and Islām, and seen that just as delayed judgment rescues the authority of the ruler, the ever-postponed Day of Judgement rescues the reputation of the omnipotent deity, by means of a hypocritical split between public show and actual act.

Harm is inflicting suffering. But all suffering is not inflicted by others. Without addressing the processes of the mind, which are the basis and medium of all suffering, the common sense systems such as Mill's are stuck hopelessly in confusion based on opposing the individual against other individuals as if this opposition were a natural law[325]. It is an ancient error, and it is what gave us such dichotomous concepts as 'the faithful' and 'the damned'.

Some insist that the oppositional principle finds justification in Darwin's revolution. For reasons of brevity I can here only point out that it has long been observed by biologists (if 'overlooked' by interested economists) that the discourse of natural selection, though it uses intentional vocabulary (such as selection, and genes' 'aim' to get into the next generation), does not claim that these heuristic[326] 'intentions' are transferred to individual organisms in question (and never did) – which means that even if individual organisms are in competition they need not feel that they are (even in order to compete most successfully!) – and that the unit on which selection operates can be of any level, not just the organism level but the gene level or the tribe level or the species level, the selection on different levels often having dramatically different influences on the inheritance of traits – which means, for example, that altruism between organisms can evolve from survival of the fittest genes. So, rightly understood, there is no basis in Darwin's theory for the notion that we 'should' be in rivalry with each other 'by nature'.

Certain great humans have addressed the basis and medium of suffering, but they still go unnoticed, drowned out by the latest incarnations, preserving the sacrificial system, of faithful/damned rhetoric, one of the most powerful of which in recent history (especially since the Enlightenment's blank page notion of

---

325 Why this particular idea is now so pervasive that it can seem quite perverse even to conceive that there might be an alternative we have already considered above under 'trapped beliefs'. It was popularised, as the necessity for competition for prosperity, and even named (before Darwin) 'survival of the fittest', by Herbert Spencer. And those inconceivable alternatives we conceive of with the Buddha later, in the presentation of training in Amity.

326 In the sense of 'idea-generating' rather than the cognitive biases we have been discussing.

human nature) has been the dichotomy of the absolutes 'innocence' and 'guilt'.

Absolute innocence and guilt are intimately associated with the myth of creation of souls from nothing. Consider the belief (held by all orthodox Muslims and Christians) in one earthly (or preparatory) life plus one afterlife. All humans are (according to this belief) born innocent (because created innocent), so any criminal must supposedly have developed his or her criminality in his or her earthly life's course so far. Even given the doctrine of original sin in some traditions, it is still necessary (to the myth) to say we are born with free will. We have already seen how this doctrine (the freedom to sin) would be necessary to rescue an invented 'creator god' from accusations of botched design.[327]

All a criminal's criminality has supposedly developed with this particular personality, then, defined from this earthly birth onwards, so this personality is what supposedly must be punished. All are supposedly born free, so, however subtly, all criminals must choose to become criminals: societal influence is, in this system, no excuse because at the beginning there was complete god-given freedom and innocence, which must have been surrendered voluntarily, what is called 'yielding to Satan's temptation'. Punishment of an individual identified as criminal is therefore held in these systems to be a balance. (Incidentally, it is clear that this interpretative fabric fits a sacrificial system closely: the invading spirit upsets the balance, and it is the body which is possessed which must be purged to restore the balance.)

Case: retributive punishment with the notion of innocence

People who grow up with the blank-page-birth belief 'intuitively' recognize the justice of 'eye for an eye' punishment, such that they consider it an inescapable element of human nature. It is elevated very explicitly in the Qur'ān, which presents this measure-for-measure punishment (such as severing the hand of a thief) as a mercy because, by balancing the score in this earthly life, it alleviates punishment in the next[328]. Retributive punishment will be inevitably associated with religions requiring belief in 'a creator god', because of the notion that 'God's creation' must be good and therefore the creature originally innocent. The link with the notion of an absolute creator is evidenced by the lack of such an idea of punishment in the codes of religions which do not teach one, such as some kinds of Hindu religion and Buddhism and Jainism, for example.

We can compare the Christian-Islāmic belief in *two* successive lives for

---

327 See under 'Not by philosophy'.

328 This principle is known in Arabic as qiṣāṣ

the soul, where the former is a preparation for the latter, with belief famously Hindu but also found (and justified by certain Qur'ānic passages) in Druze religion, and in some traditions of Sufism and Gnostic Christianity, in *more than two* lives[329], where every lifetime is both a preparatory life and an afterlife, and the personality even in an earthly life is influenced by earlier lifetimes. Here a multitude of habitual tendencies are already present at birth. There is no absolute meaning to the word 'innocent' so there is no absolute meaning to the word 'guilty'. Here freedom of choice is greatly contextualized: the person is writing not on a blank page but within the restrictions of a partially written text. How unromantic! When a crime arises on this page, the current lifetime cannot be blamed in isolation. What was added in this life to one text to make a murderer could have been added to another text to make a hero, so it is senseless to single out the murderer to exact retribution for the murder. Why? Because the fault of this life's personality, if we must single it out, lies not in the development of murdererhood per se, but in *not being wary* of habitual tendencies already present. It is not a failure of the body, but a failure of self-knowledge. Otherwise we would have to say that in our previous example if the murderer is punished, so should the hero be punished.

So, I would ask, which system of belief is the more salutary, the one which leads to the instinct for retribution, and thence the cycles of violence which dominate our news from all over the world, or the one which reveals retribution to be nonsensical and leads to an instinctive pursuit of self-knowledge?

Unfortunately such healthiness is not easy to recognize, and so not immediately attractive. Beliefs, including beliefs as to how many lives we have, are borne by one-lifetime personalities and not by a series. Each personality accepts beliefs according to their attractiveness, and – oh! – how romantic the fantastic romance of total freedom is! – the total innocence of childhood and the concomitant total responsibility of the adult! It is sweet, but with the sweetness comes the poison of cyclic retributive violence. Must we agree even if it be with a majority that the delights of living a short-lived romance of righteousness outweigh its appalling consequences?

The wise, who would promote the healthier belief, are faced with an unending flow of births of new personalities, which are prone by their very nature to these poisonous fantasies, and after swooning under their influence, almost

---

[329] It might be asked, even by some people who consider themselves Buddhists, why I have omitted Buddhism from the list of religions which teach multiple lives, or 'reincarnation'. We will consider the extraordinary perspective of Buddhism later when the Buddha leads the Kālāmās through an inquiry into this very issue.

impossible to waken. As the modern philosopher John Gray says,

> The cardinal need is to change the prevailing view of human beings, which sees them as inherently good creatures unaccountably burdened with a history of violence and oppression.[330]

A fair number of what appear to be intractable points of dispute between religious traditions are soluble once the nature of the communication breakdown is recognized. The dispute between believers in a just god and believers in 'karma' is a case in point.

Karma, roughly speaking, comes with the idea that the newborn child is as much a product (of actions in earlier lifetimes) as a cause (by its actions of future states), whereas the notion of a 'just god' who created all implies absolute innocence at birth. That is why the transmission of HIV by pregnant mothers to their babies is so much more appalling to believers in the 'just god' than transmission to an adult would be.

Now if the law of karma operates then all individuals can only be partially innocent, never wholly; similarly they can only be partially guilty, never wholly.

However, a believer in a 'just creator god' is denied such subtlety. When she hears from a karma-proponent that the newborn babe is not completely innocent, her only alternative (as she sees it) is to imagine that the karma-proponent means the babe is completely guilty – the other of the 2 extremes, neither of which the karma-proponent understands in turn. So the believer in the just god accuses the karma-proponent of blaming the babe for the infection and of being therefore terribly unjust. She mistakes his own snap decision for clarity, so when the karma-proponent accuses her in turn of being extreme, she retorts with an accusation of wishy-washiness and lack of clarity.

We asked the reader to judge which system is more salutary. What is in question is, does a given 'improving' doctrine solve troubles, or does it bring more troubles than those it claims to solve?

Just as within the tribe demons can be considered to inhabit members who must be purged, two tribes can each consider the other tribe to be demons or possessed by them. The consideration of another group in enmity is another way of saying the same thing. Calling the demons by other names (such as 'suspected insurgents') does not alter the fact that the tribe deals with them as demons.

---

330 From the section 'Living in an Intractable World: the Lost Tradition of Realism' in chapter 6 of *Black Mass* (Gray, 2007).

To conceive of an enemy, just like attributing demonic possession to outsiders, is to refuse to understand. If we are cowards, to elevate by exaggeration a personal attack to the level of an attack against an entire group by an entire out-group, wins us the orgasm-like pleasure of absolution followed by the 'post-coital' depression of worse attacks. If one adopts the concept of enmity, he or she is exaggerating and not at all absolved from responsibility for the attacks in reality. In bloody retributive conflicts it is effectively the one who adopts the concept of enmity who has killed his or her neighbours, friends and family: because as such an idler you choose to refuse to understand.

Like only thinking one move ahead in chess, retributive enmity fails, and in this chess game it is the evil consequences of our own choices which will mate our king.

Because those who seek power manipulate others by means of the latter's beliefs, and because most of these others are indeed cowards and idlers, it is in the interest of the power-hungry to promote the one-move-ahead short-sightedness, since in this way the vast majority can be made to take their side and rally with them. For some this is just delusion; for others it is collusion: aware of their own cowardice and idleness, they choose to ally themselves not with understanding but with numbers and power.

It is the resulting spectacle of endless conflict which goes these days under the name of justice, justice for 'us', which therefore ever eludes us. The *Dhammapāda* warns succinctly:

Na hi verena verāni sammantīdha kudācanaṁ
Averena ca sammanti – esa dhammo sanantano

Not by retribution [lit. animus] is retribution ever pacified
And by refraining from retribution it is pacified: this is an ancient law.

The very language of the verse is rich in the implication we have drawn. The Pali vera, often vaguely translated as 'hatred' rather than retribution, in fact has its equivalent in the Sanskrit vaira, which is the adjective meaning associated with vīra (in English 'hero', a word sharing its etymological origin) – hence the adjective has as its origin 'heroic', but in Sańskrit as in Pali has come to have the strong connotation of animus, feudal indignation, and hostility, and can even mean blood money paid to recompense a manslaughter. Thus we see the close association between the heroic ethos and hostility in Indic culture as in classical European and Arabian. Vaira implies perhaps a public to spectate and decide one's immortal fame; contrast this with the quality vīrya, also derived from vīra, and meaning 'the quality of a hero', manliness, valour, or even virility (hence its use to refer to semen), clearly not necessarily advertised for posterity, which is celebrated in the Buddhist teachings – the lesson being that we can be brave without subscribing to society's petty and counterproductive retributive 'honour' ethic. Those of us in Jewish-, Muslim- or Christian-influenced cultures might also reflect on the fact that the name Satan has a meaning – 'the inimical one' – so the verse from the Buddhist scripture might even be rendered, 'Not by Satan is Satan ever subdued...'

Case: ethical principles' mutual harmony, with 'monotheism'

Not only in the 'monotheistic' religions as explicitly practised but also in the secular systems which have been influenced by them, there is a seeming common-sense conviction that every ethical principle must by nature combine harmoniously with the others. As Isaiah Berlin put it,

> we find the same common assumption: that the answers to all the great questions must of necessity agree with one another; for they must correspond with reality, and reality is a harmonious whole. If this were not so, there is chaos at the heart of things: which is unthinkable. Liberty, property, equality, knowledge, security, practical wisdom, purity of character, sincerity, kindness, rational self-love, all these ideals [...] cannot (if they are truly desirable) conflict with one another; if they appear to do so it must be due to some misunderstanding of their properties. No truly good thing can ever finally be incompatible with any other; indeed they virtually entail one another: men cannot be wise unless they are free, or free unless they are just, happy and so forth.
>
> Here we conspicuously abandon the voice of experience – which records very obvious conflicts of ultimate ideals – and encounter a doctrine that stems from older theological roots – from the belief that unless all positive virtues are harmonious with one another, or at least not incompatible, the notion of the Perfect Entity – whether it be called nature or God or Ultimate Reality – is not conceivable.[331]

We do not 'conspicuously abandon the voice of experience' flippantly: the entire

331 From *Political Ideas in the Romantic Age* (Berlin, 2006). I owe this citation to *What Price Liberty?* (Wilson, 2009)

edifice of metaphysics to which we have committed ourselves to as 'monotheists' is threatened by these 'obvious conflicts', so we sacrifice recognition of the conflicts to maintenance of the edifice. This is how it is possible for a man (for it is usually a man) to believe he is doing a work of divine love when he saws off the head of another human being with a knife or burns another human being at the stake.

> 'Diṭṭhinijjhānakkhanti cepi, bhāradvāja, purisassa hoti; "evaṁ me diṭṭhinijjhānakkhantī"ti – iti vadaṁ saccamanurakkhati , *natveva tāva ekaṁsena niṭṭhaṁ gacchati – "idameva saccaṁ, moghamaññā"* nti. Ettāvatā kho, bhāradvāja, saccānurakkhaṇā hoti, ettāvatā saccamanurakkhati, ettāvatā ca mayaṁ saccānurakkhaṇaṁ paññapema; *na tveva tāva saccānubodho hotī* ti.
>
> 'Bhāradvāja, a person with intuitive acceptance of a view saying, "This is my intuitive acceptance of the view," safeguards the truth. *But he or she doesn't yet come to the definite conclusion that only something is true, and all else is vain.* To this extent, Bhāradvāja, there is safeguarding of the truth. To this extent he or she safeguards the truth. I describe this as the safeguarding of the truth. *But it is not yet an awakening to the truth.*'[332]

---

332 In *The Caṅkī Discourse.*

Not by (others') seeming capability, ma bhabbarūpatāya

Meaning

Bhabba is equivalent to the Sanskrit bhavya, and means 'likely to be', 'able to be', 'on the point of becoming', and 'auspicious' and 'beautiful'. Rupa means the shape, body or form in which someone or something appears. The suffix –ta converts this into the noun referring to the state, i.e. the state of having form. The Sanskrit equivalent of the compound means 'having a good figure'. Although the Pali has been translated as 'probability' (able-seeming-ness in the impersonal sense), the more common and I think more interesting translation, which in practice subsumes most of those implications anyway, is the personal one.[333] The commentaries, in any case, add that it refers to *other persons* – their seeming ability in the sense of authority.

Examples

Any external authority in the form of a person; an 'expert' in a particular field; successive historical sources each vouching for the preceding one; God as a final authority; the Buddha as a final authority.

Irrelevancy as a source of certainty

We are so habituated to garnering a sense of certainty on the basis of this source that it is perhaps the most difficult of the Buddha's declarations of irrelevancy for us to grasp. The most difficult and the most uncomfortable, because so much of what we believe will be found to have its basis here.

Authorities are selected on our own authority, but this is concealed

It might seem obvious that we must rely on the capabilities of others. After all, if you don't know how to drive a car, you have to rely on a driver. If you don't know how to tie your shoe-laces, you have to rely on your parents. But yet again, we must recognize that the Buddha is not saying a driver is irrelevant to someone who can't drive but needs to go by car, or that the parents are irrelevant to the child's desire to tie up his shoe-laces. What he is saying is that *in the matter of establishing what is right*, we cannot rely on authorities in order to be certain. It must instead be known by personal experience.

Some might huff at this and ask us to consider the enormity of such a

---

333 We have already dealt with impersonal probability under 'extrapolation from experience'. See also 'gambler's fallacy' under 'Not by intuitive acceptance of views'.

task: how could we possibly know everything we need to know from personal experience? The Buddha replies, it is not everything we need to know from personal experience, it is simply *what is certainly right* that we need to know from personal experience.

External authority

Experts are not expert generally

If we do not know everything from personal experience, how else do we (supposedly) know things? Usually we select sources according to their reliability – those sources which have not deceived us until now. Reliability in one field does not guarantee reliability in any other field, of course, but we frequently accept a source's information outside its field of expertise just because it has never been mistaken within it. This is one source of mistaken 'knowledge'. We may also overlook the fact that the limits of any source's field are open to question, especially when we are misled by names: psychologists, for example, are experts in the mind, so their name encourages us to imagine that they will continue to be experts in the mind, even while physicists progress to ever more astonishing discoveries about the mind-dependent nature of 'the objective world'.

Expertise or respectability is a transient characteristic

Given that circumstances change, we ought to re-assess our criteria for according authority to others regularly, but unfortunately we are actually likely to consider ourselves allied with the authorities we choose, and therefore resist admitting their subsequent faults.

If the authority in question is considered reliable initially because of moral credentials then we should be doubly careful, since it is a well-documented psychological tendency in humans that having demonstrated immaculate morals on one occasion makes them more likely to feel liberated from the constraints of those morals later.

To taken an example on modern morals, which stress the equal rights of both (all?) genders, and all races, one psychological study[334] showed that having on one occasion recruited a non-male or a non-Caucasian, people were more likely, later, to say that a job was better suited to a male or a Caucasian than were those who had not so recruited earlier.

So powerful is the combination, of this effect and our tendency to respect moral credentials, in leading to erroneous judgment in politics and

334 (Monin & Miller, 2001)

economics, it has been given a technical term all to itself, '*moral credential bias*'.

Insider status trumps reliability

More generally, psychologists starting with the American Edward Lee Thorndike (1874-1949) have demonstrated that recognising a positive trait in a person makes us subsequently more likely to interpret his or her other traits as positive, and similarly if we recognise a negative one *mutatis mutandis.* These distortions of judgment were given the name '*the halo effect*' and by extension '*the reverse halo effect*' respectively. Later research[335] has shown that even when we are warned about the halo effect and then asked to make judgments we are still unconscious of its influence on our judgment, and it continues to operate as before.

It doesn't just happen with people: it can happen with a brand, as has long been known to the marketing industry. For example the effect has been invoked (though not demonstrated by experiment) to explain how the good reputation of the iPod had a positive effect on other Apple products.

Since this means that according to our assessment people (or brands) are divided into the 'generally good' and the 'generally bad', it seems to be related to our primitive urge to admit to, or exclude from, our in-group an individual (or tool) we are getting to know. It could be an example of the wider phenomenon of 'affect bias' we considered in our discussion of the Buddha's previous injunction.

Whatever the reason, the fact that it exists should make us wary about information from people we have judged to be experts, and the existence of the unconscious halo effect should discourage us from the complacency of imagining that while others might succumb to it we are wiser.

And before we leave the topic, let us note the irony of the fact that the cultural sphere from which the name for the phenomenon was derived is certainly the one least open to the idea of recognising its deluding operations.

Joining consensus is a resort to violence

As social animals we are inclined to rely on majority opinion, in other words successful gossip.

The group authorises hierarchies of sources. The expertise of a specialist is accepted on the authority of publicly expressed testimony (e.g. degrees awarded) by his peers. The credentials of these were established similarly

335 (Nisbett & Wilson, 1977)

but before, so we have a chain of authority stretching into the past to our ancestors. We are almost always in the dark about these ancestors, but we feel more comfortable accepting their judgments. It is because so many must have accepted their credentials since then before us. We think: how could all these people be wrong?

And it is important to recognise that even so-called objectivity in science is in reality a consensus. Popper, the principal formulator of the modern scientific method (falsification of theories by replicable experiments), points out:

> …objectivity is closely bound up with the *social aspect of the scientific method.* [… It] can be described as the inter-subjectivity of scientific method.[336]

However, never in history were conformity and consensus a measure of truth. Genocides are done by consensus. All through history we can find examples of ideologies that survived and spread because they included within themselves the call to suppress and eliminate opinions (and those that hold them) detracting from the consensus, quite independent of whether their ideas were 'true'. What allows these systems to persist is that, in the absence of the necessity or possibility of testing every piece of information thoroughly in our own experience to see whether it is right, which should be the true test of reliability, we are unfortunately naturally inclined to judge the reliability of new ideas by how well they fit into our system of preconceived ideas.

Preference of particular newspapers are a clear example of this tendency, to seek ideas that reassure us that we are already right, and avoid the discomfort of those which challenge our self-righteousness. For many people this tendency determines even their choice of companions in life.

I know eating relieves hunger from personal experience. However I

---

[336] From chapter 23 of *The Open Society and Its Enemies* (Popper, 1945; 5th edition 1966). Objectivity is supposed to be distinguished from subjectivity by public demonstrability, but cursory examination shows that this is a matter of degree, such that subjectivity and objectivity are not mutually exclusive. On the one hand, a great deal of scientific knowledge is beyond a certain fraction of humanity when its appreciation involves their intelligence, and beyond a greater fraction when its demonstration involves experimentation, hence Popper's coinage 'inter-subjectivity'; conversely religious experiences, which have traditionally, and especially since the rise of behaviourism in psychology (and until now, even though behaviourism is itself largely discredited), been relegated to the disparaged 'subjective' category, are often open to demonstration (by others to themselves as in the 'objective') if the experimenter is prepared to go through similar efforts or 'spiritual exercises'.

know what happens to the food inside me not by personal chemistry experiments and hazardous self-surgery but from reputable biologists (and, admittedly, examining the toilet). I know how to run a successful restaurant from successful restaurateurs, reputable lawyers, economists, market researchers, etc. If we are asked on what authority we accepted the description of digestion, and decided on a course of action for our restaurant, in our ordinary way of thinking we would be inclined to reply that we did so on the authority of experts; but in reality all of this, not just the eating, was done on our own authority. It is we who judged the biologist to be reputable, we who judged the restaurateurs successful and their information trustworthy, we who judged the market researchers' findings reliable, even if we used other authorities' judgement of them to help us judge.

For some of my readers I know that this way of talking will make them feel uncomfortable. Although it is clear and incontrovertible, it is disturbing to some. They will immediately argue against their own authority, shining the spotlight on the external authorities, not matter how persuasively it is pointed out to them that it was they who selected those sources. Even those who are happy with it, when questioned will often feel happier to conclude justification of their choices with a momentous authority figure than to conclude with a, 'so I made my choice.'

Projecting affords immediate comfort

Why is overlooking one's own responsibility, one's own final authority, such a seeming comfort, then? It is because of our more or less admitted respect for physical strength or violence as an expression of power. We feel safety in numbers. Children in the school playground will resort to, 'My dad's going to beat up your dad.' Or they will gang up. Or they will tell tales to the authorities. All because violence is considered a solution, for the gang against its enemies, or for the headmaster against a transgressing pupil. As it is for children under the threat of challenge or attack, so it is for us 'adults' – even in the realm of ideas.

To the extent that we admit that we, by our own authority, have chosen, to that extent we are vulnerable to challenges to that choice, so in our cowardly infantile way we seek the refuge of safety in numbers and cunningly pretend that the responsibility for the choice was somehow shared by our sources. (The crucial importance of this was pointed out in our treatment of the clever defence of faith as certainty without evidence.) In more extreme cowardice we may even throw not just some but all of the responsibility onto our external sources, i.e. blame them for what is in fact our choice. To the extent which we refuse that we, by our own authority, have chosen, to the extent which we pretend that the sources chose us, to that extent we are (we believe) invulnerable to challenges to that choice.

Human nature is to submit to violence

Nothing but respect for (which means fear of) violence could persuade us to overlook the cold reality, that the majority might be wrong, in favour of the warm blindness of accepting its correctness. It is the same tendency in us which would lead us to do acts we consider morally wrong, like bullying a cripple, when we are in a mob.

Case: obedience in inflicting pain (Milgram's experiment)

Stanley Milgram showed in his horrifying but extremely significant experiments[337] that ordinary people will inflict pain even to the degree of causing death on complete strangers, because a uniformed representative of an institution is ordering them to do so.

> Ordinary people, simply doing their jobs, and without any particular hostility on their part, can become agents in a terrible destructive process. Moreover, even when the destructive effects of their work become patently clear, and they are asked to carry out actions incompatible with fundamental standards of morality, relatively few people have the resources needed to resist authority.[338]

We call on those who would deny this relation between violence and truth-independent consensus to survey the societies of the world and see if there is not a sharp correlation between the everyday threat of police or mob violence on the one hand and the tendency to opine *en masse* and undervalue personal opinion on the other. It is pure practicality: in some societies, you simply cannot afford to have (or at least express) an opinion. In slightly less violent societies you can express an opinion, but it will be denigrated as 'just an opinion', and truth is explicitly by consensus, to the dire detriment of detractors, be they unrighteous or otherwise. Even in seemingly liberal states there is variation in the degree of violence operating within families, and you will always find that the more violent families will always produce the children more likely to align themselves to

337 (Milgram S. , 1963)
338 (Milgram S. , 1974)

external authorities – cults, movements, religions, God, causes (from vegetarianism to nationalism), fan groups (of musicians, football teams, etc.), special interest groups, and so on. To the extent that anyone feels vulnerable, to that extent they will always seek to align aspects of their identity with the corresponding groups, to share (shirk) the responsibility of choosing (and being) who they are.

Case: obedience to a god out of fear

This helps explain the importance of the deity's cruelty in the massive religions. The gods' stupendous acts of violence in the mythologies of these religions is to the gods what the uniform is to the Milgram experimenter.

It is not just a feature of the orthodox forms of the massive religions, but also their esoteric schools, such as Sufism. Fear of the deity is taught to be essential, perhaps even more than in the orthodox form. Fear is employed to create obedience. Those who fear the deity are celebrated above those who do not. I leave aside here the question whether such obedience can be usefully employed. The glorification of fear in certain theistic traditions should be sharply contrasted with the assault on fear encouraged in other traditions.

For example, although these esoteric traditions of Judaism, Christianity and Islām are often compared favourably with Buddhism, on the question as to whether fear is useful on the spiritual path Buddhism differs starkly from them with its 'acceptance of the unproduced phenomenon' (in Sanskrit anutpattika dharma kṣānti). When the concept of emptiness, the lack of inherent identity in any phenomenon, is understood some natures accept it with tearful joy because they have this 'acceptance'. Others are terrified: the Buddhist books tell of a group who committed suicide as a result. The superior practitioner is taught to be the one who does not fear – the one who possesses this acceptance. Some treatises[339] go as far as to say that the teachings on emptiness should not be revealed unless the trainee cries tears of joy on first hearing them.

The harm in authority projection

Anxiety through cognitive dissonance

Projection of authority onto something beyond our control inevitably leads to anxiety. It is because of the awareness of one's own consequent vulnerability to challenges: one realizes (perhaps not so consciously) that one has taken responsibility for the sources' decisions. One is vulnerable to challenges as

---

339 such as the *Madhyamakāvatāra* of Candrakīrti.

to why one selected the sources one did.

It is an example of what in cognitive science is called 'cognitive dissonance'. In a classic experiment Festinger and Carlsmith (1959) set experimental subjects at mind-numbingly boring tasks until they were thoroughly exasperated, then paid them various amounts to tell the next round of subjects that the tasks had been interesting. Those paid *less*, when interviewed subsequently, valued the earlier tasks as *less boring*. It was hypothesised that through not having such a good excuse (more lucrative rewards) to justify to themselves that they had done it, they had internalised the false idea that the tasks were not so boring after all. This hypothesis was subsequently much contested and various rivals offered. If it were true, the self-contradiction would generate anxiety ('dissonance') because on some level the person would *realise and react to the fact that* they were contradicting themselves by deciding the task had not been so boring. Rival hypotheses were disproved when this kind of anxiety was later experimentally demonstrated[340], and shown to occur independently of whether the subject felt they had done anything wrong morally (e.g. because they lied)[341].

This anxiety leads to emotional distortion on the part of the projector, which can become a carrier mechanism for the tradition encouraging the projection, which then gets over-transmitted.

Case: tenseness in Muslim and Christian belief

The presence and degree of anxiety in massive faiths, for example, is revealed in the frequent episodes of *relief from it* which occur when there is a sudden mass rallying around a 'miracle' such as we discussed in the contexts of uncanny and outrageous reports, and heuristics. By locating the point of dispute between the self-deceiving authority-projector and her challenger in the realm of the uncanny, the former obviates the necessity to meet the challenge and furthermore adds a certain sinister uncanny threat to that refusal to meet the challenge. On a more conscious level the relief provided by such 'miracles' lies of course in their liability to be held as proof. Yet someone who needed no relief could not so easily believe in them as proof. Indeed the more one has projected his or her authority and concealed this, the more anxiety will be being experienced, and so the more relief will be provided from any particular 'miracle', or indeed any particular instance of another converting to his or her religion, another common reason for suspiciously tense delight.

340 (Kiesler & Pallak, 1976)

341 (Harmon-Jones, Brehm, Greenberg, Simon, & Nelson, 1996)

Prohibition of self-knowledge

So what, then, is the treachery I referred to, in the comfort I would enjoy by accepting such authorities? First of all the ability to overlook one's own authority depends on not knowing oneself too closely.

Prohibition of love with understanding

Later on in the discourse the Buddha presents an interconnected system of four kinds of mind training – including (in a particular sense) love, and (in a particular sense) understanding. This understanding includes self-knowledge as well as coming to recognise one's relations with others. The four trainings feed into each other: this knowledge is itself a pre-requisite for 'love with understanding' (as opposed to suffocating, misguided love), which in Buddhism is taught to be potentially spontaneous and without discrimination. So, if this system is correct (and the Buddha invites us to test for ourselves rather than take it on trust), religions requiring more authority projection and its concealment, by making self-knowledge dangerous and therefore off limits, effectively block with great force the development of the capacity for spontaneous love of living beings which comes from that knowledge.

Prohibition of conscience

Surrender to authority and conscience therefore are incompatible. As a recent scholar of the relation between Vedic theism and Buddhism puts it,

> …the very origin of Buddhism lies in the Buddha's frustration with the traditional. […] A traditional man believed in the validity of these sources [of divine authority] without any doubt. Now in this belief, since God or the seer of the scripture was considered to be omniscient, almighty and compassionate, he was believed to be always right. […] Secondly, in the traditional sense, it is further believed that man has kinship relationship with God and so it is imperative that he becomes a truly moral human being, which means he has to continuously strive dutifully in the path of God. This means that morality implies God's will. This makes an enquiry, of Socratic or Buddhist type, into God's will, in order to know the moral principles and reasons of his will, not only impossible and unnecessary, but also sacrilegious. For a God-fearing person, God's will is a necessary and sufficient condition for any moral conduct to be right. It is clear from this analysis that such

a person is not an autonomous agent but only an automaton.[342]

Affiliation weaknesses

Secondly, when one aligns the aspects of one's identity with external groups, one does not escape wounding as one might have hoped: on the contrary, one denies oneself the only true invulnerability, the one which comes when one understands one's own experience exactly as it is, and whereby integration occurs naturally, and instead one chooses to nail oneself to this fixed external framework which eternally prevents any flexibility or self-integration.

Conflict escalation

So rather than escaping personal attack on the contrary one becomes vulnerable to attacks even on the authorities one has aligned oneself with, even (and this is the crucial point) on issues other than the one on which one aligned oneself with them. In other words, under the illusion that I am protecting myself, I complicate my situation enormously, extending my identity and the need to defend it into vast shadowy patterns that I might not even be aware of.

I hope the reader will have the intelligence and enthusiasm to explore by himself or herself the immense consequences of such mistaken attempts at self-protection. For now I will simply draw attention to two: the psychological stress of having to avoid self-knowledge at all cost, and the societal result of alignment on either side of a criterion of belief. By the former I mean the tangible tension easily observed in those who have made compromises consciously and subconsciously in order to maintain their public allegiance to one of their chosen authorities after being assailed by doubt in those same authorities. By the latter I mean conflict escalation.

Contempt of discovery

Finally we arrive at what some have called the most worrying intellectual and social disease of our time.

Speaking of its effects in the realm of academic and scientific thought and discovery, Popper calls it the 'modern irrationality', which he identifies as a drive to ignore arguments in themselves but to refer them immediately to their historical context (called 'historism') or their social context ('the sociology of knowledge'), as if this ascription were somehow automatically more insightful than the arguments themselves could ever be.

---

342 (Prasad, 2007, pp. 167-8)

Case: Marx instead of Marxism

Popper gives an example of a historian who should know better, A. J. Toynbee in his *A Study of History* when it comes to treat Marx. He accuses the historian of not being interested enough in Marx's arguments even to find out what they are, and ascribes this to a form of obsession with authority-ascription.

> How, I ask, can it be explained that Toynbee discusses Marxism on lines which have nothing whatever to do with its rational claims? The only explanation I can see is that the Marxist claim to rationality has no meaning to Toynbee. He is interested only in the question of how it originated as a religion. Now I should be the last to deny its religious character. But the method of treating philosophies or religions entirely from the point of view of their historical origin and environment, an attitude described in the previous chapters as ***historism*** (and to be distinguished from historicism), is, to say the least, very one-sided; and how much this method is liable to produce irrationalism can be seen from Toynbee's neglect of, if not contempt for, that important realm of human life which we have here described as rational.[343]

This same focus (or contempt), which is clearly related to what we have identified as herding and Popper calls 'collectivism' pervades academia, art and music criticism, science, indeed most areas of modern culture.

Case: Buddha instead of Buddhism

Since this commentary is on a teaching of the Buddha we can take as an instructive example academia's approach to Buddhism, an approach which nowadays goes under the curious Sanskrit-Greek mélange term 'Buddhology'. It is noteworthy that a very similar approach is taken by Islāmic treatises dealing with Buddhism. The 'Laws' (dharma) are not presented as they are taught by the living traditions or were taught in those traditions in the past. They are not evaluated in the manner in which those traditions recommend: by individual testing. It is not only missionaries' twistings of which we need to be cautious:

> In this century there has been a movement away from a judgmental

---

343 From chapter 24, V of *The Open Society and Its Enemies* (Popper, 1945; 5th edition 1966)

Christo-centric point of view in the academic study of religion towards a more descriptive, less obviously biased view. Yet in Pāli Buddhist scholarship there remain apologetical strands, with proponents of, say, empiricism and ecumenism offering various interpretive filters through which to see Buddhism.[344]

Until quite recently in academia and until now in many Islāmic and Christian presentations, the Buddha Shakyamuni has been made the focus, though he himself did not do this. This is a reflection of the tendency to consider the Buddha to be for Buddhism what (in the case of Muslim depictions) Muḥammad is for Islām or (in the case of Christian and post- or crypto-Christian western secular academic depictions) Christ is for Christianity. As one of the few scholars competent in both Western philosophy and Pali Buddhism, Frank J. Hoffman, has pointed out,

> Even from a Buddhist viewpoint, however, the historicity of Gotama in particular does not matter much. For the Buddhist path or doctrine does not depend on the historicity of Gotama in the way that Christianity depends on the historicity of Jesus and on his resurrection. Buddhism 'depends on' Gotama in the sense that he is viewed as the turner of the wheel of doctrine in the present eon. But Gotama is not viewed as the first such Buddha, nor the last. He is considered as a torch-bearer, not an initiator, and the path or doctrine is viable or obtains regardless of whether a *Tathāgata* appears in a particular age to illuminate it.
>
> Thus, the path or doctrine does not 'depend on' Gotama in the sense that if he had not become a Buddha [...] one could not possibly achieve the highest goal of Buddhist life. Granted that it would be very much more difficult without such a Buddha to show the way, yet the way is *in principle* discoverable by anyone.[345] By contrast, whether as a matter of fact or as a matter of definition of 'Christian', the vast majority of Christians hold that if Jesus were not the Christ and had not redeemed mankind, one could not achieve Christian salvation. The result is that even if someone were to provide new, cogent evidence to show that Gotama did not exist as a historical person at all, such a

---

344 (Hoffman, 1987, 2002, p. 2)

345 Cf. the praise of the Law in our homages at the beginning of this book.

> demonstration would not affect the validity of the path or doctrine at all.
>
> Jesus' existence is logically a precondition for his undergoing a resurrection, as Gotama's existence is logically a precondition for his becoming a Buddha. Yet whereas if it could be shown that the Biblical Jesus did not exist Christianity would be undermined, if it could be shown that Gotama did not exist, Buddhism would not be undermined. So it is not the historicity of Gotama which supports Buddhism, unlike the situation with Christianity.[346]

We are expected somehow to understand Buddhism, better than we would even from studying it, by knowing instead exactly what year the Buddha was born, what the geo-politico-religious landscape of the time was like, what he did, whom he met, when he died, and where, etc. Introductions to 'Buddhism' (dharma) from *within* the traditions on the other hand are so far from this approach as to be literally unrecognisable as such to it. (Consider, for two great examples, Chogyam Trungpa's *Cutting Through Spiritual Materialism* and Robert Pirsig's *Zen in the Art of Motorcycle Maintenance.*)

The difference of course stems from the different motives – deprecatory contextualisation versus provocation of realisation of the Laws in others. By being themselves 'in context', these introductions instruct. By *claiming (even implicitly) to be uncontextualised*, the academic approach fails to instruct. It is what Popper characterises as a logically and historically untenable attempt to remove the commentator from commentary's implications – logically in the same way as the liar's paradox ('I am a liar' – is he?) and historically by implicitly claiming historical omniscience for itself only.

> A point of view is inevitable; and the naïve attempt to avoid it can only lead to self-deception, and to the uncritical application of an unconscious point of view.[347]

Incidentally, the problem is not that there might be analyses of Buddhism from a Christian perspective, as is exemplified by the Dalai Lama's recommendation[348] that for future inter-religious harmony it is necessary for the

---

[346] (Hoffman, 1987, 2002, p. 6)

[347] From chapter 25, I of *The Open Society and Its Enemies* (Popper, 1945; 5th edition 1966)

[348] The Dalai Lama has mentioned five things necessary for inter-religious peace. The other four are that the most spiritual among the devotees of all religions

best scholars of each religion to exchange materials with and make detailed critiques of the others: the problem is the assumption that all scholars are united in sharing such a perspective!

Total authority by lineage

Now that we have seen the process of shirking one's own authority, by hiding oneself, and projecting the authority onto (or authorizing) others, and how disgraceful its inevitable consequences are, let us turn to the utmost authorized authority, than whom there is no greater authorized authority, and to the community than whose projection of their own authority and hiding of their own authority there are no greater, leading to disgrace to humanity than which there is no greater disgrace: I am referring of course to 'the *external* god', 'the deity totally removed from us and aloof', and to those who believe in such a 'god'.[349]

The separate god and its carrying systems are only worth mentioning here because of the additional cover-up that must be done and because of the systems' very insistence on the source of authority. I will (because of the vociferousness of its claims to authority) take Islām as an example, but these arguments of course apply to any system which posits a complete authority external to us and only accessible to us via certain people or methods.[350]

---

should come together to share experiences, that the leaders of the religions should meet regularly, that the ordinary practitioners or adherents of all religions should do pilgrimages together – i.e. perform pilgrimages even from other religious traditions – and that everyone should meditate. These rather high standards were presented in his introductory address before a conference of Christian groups who had invited him to give a commentary on Christianity, and at which he chose to explore the beatitudes. (Dalai Lama, 1998)

349 Many of the Jewish and Roman terms for holiness even seem to have *originated* with the meaning of 'separateness': Hebrew qodesh and Latin templum for example. However, as Rumi, whose *Couplets* begin with the flute's song of separation, would stress – this sense is the path, not the goal.

350 It is worth pointing out that the fact that Christians by and large no longer care about establishing the authority of their texts is because, unlike the Islamic ones', the scandal of their historical dubiousness has long been broadcast. I mention this only because each of the mutually allergic Judaism, Christianity and Islam's adherents are likely to gloat over criticism, and bemoan praise, of either of the other two. This was demonstrated admirably by the local reaction to President Obama's speech in Cairo. Christians were bemoaning the Qur'ānic quotes, Muslims were bemoaning the support for the Jews and, although I didn't have the opportunity to speak to any Jews about it, I imagine they were bemoaning something.

Case: authority in Islām

Within its own traditional self-identification, even, Islām comes very close to recommending explicitly the kind of projection we have been talking about. Islām, according to itself, means to believe in 'Allāh, his angels, his prophets, his books, and his Day of Judgement,' and to perform various rituals (prayer, fasting, pilgrimage to and rites at Makkah, and tribute). Pretty claims to inclusiveness aside, the vast majority of Muslims consider all books 'from Allāh' before Muḥammad to have been irretrievably altered (in Arabic, manḥaraf), and (because of the doctrine that Muḥammad is the last prophet) all books after him, such as the Most Holy Book (al-kitāb al-aqdas) of the Bahā'i faith and the Guru Granth Sahib of the Sikhs, to be invention (in Arabic, bad`). So shaven of its rather shoddy universal veneer the creed of Islām becomes: belief in 'Allāh according to Muḥammad, his angels according to Muḥammad, in Muḥammad indeed according to Muḥammad, and in the only unaltered book, the Qur'ān, according to Muḥammad'. In short we could say belief in everything and everyone according to Muḥammad and that would be both sufficient and accurate.

Let not hapless explorers from Christianity be mistaken by that universal veneer: Muslims believe in 'the Christ according to Muḥammad' and in 'Mary according to Muḥammad', that is to say, a Christ who was not even crucified never mind resurrected and who atones for no-one's sins, a Christ who was a prophet who revealed a book of Islām now tragically lost to history and replaced by the invented Bible; and (according to a series of dubious but canonical reports) a Mary whose son had no father and who will be one of Muḥammad's numerous wives in Paradise (alone with those lucky women who were Moses' and 'pharaoh' 's wives in this earthly life). This some would say outrageous veneration of Muḥammad actually suits my purpose beautifully, for it allows me to deal with a clear and simple example of authority projection.

To appreciate the steps of my argument we will need some background information, which those familiar with the origin of Islām can happily skip. The Qur'ān was taught to Muḥammad in visions and inspirations by the angel Jibrīl, whose name is cognate with the Hebrew Jabr-El, the Tremendousness of El, El being the Qan`anite god the ancient Hebrews identified with their god Yahweh.[351] Because it was revealed in pieces and recited by Muḥammad to others

---

[351] This identification is proclaimed by such names as Ya'el – Yah(weh) is El – and Eliah – El is Yah(weh).

in these pieces, over a long time, it took a long time for the entire text, which was memorized and transmitted orally and in writing, to be perfected. The verses have come to us by oral, written and now digital traditions. Accounts of the whole process as witnessed by others, and of Muḥammad's other speech and acts, come down to us in a massive collection of accounts called aḥādīth (singular ḥadīth, literally 'report'). These collections of accounts were finalized in their current form hundreds of years after Muḥammad. The two most authoritative collections were made by Bukhāri and Muslim, who criticized each other's criteria for accepting accounts as authentic. Various more or less modern accounts of the lives of these collectors are now available.

Now, to examine the situation of authority, for a Muslim, as defined within the Islāmic tradition: He or she must believe in Allāh according to Muḥammad, which means the Allāh who taught Jibrīl. How can we trust that it was Allāh? Because Jibrīl said so. But how can we trust that it was Jibrīl? And that Jibrīl was telling the truth? Because Muḥammad said so. And how can we trust that it was Muḥammad who spoke to the companions, and that he spoke the same verses as had been taught him by Jibrīl? Because the companions said so. And how can we trust that the companions spoke to others, later, and that they conveyed what had been taught them by Muḥammad? Because the others, later, said so. And how can we trust that the others, later, spoke to, say, Bukhāri or Muslim, and that they conveyed what they had been taught by their predecessors? Because Bukhāri and Muslim said so.[352] (And they disagreed very much.) And how can we trust that Bukhāri and Muslim, who have spoken to subsequent generations through their texts, have spoken the truth? Because subsequent generations who claimed to know them have said so. But how can we trust that those subsequent generations have spoken the truth? Because generations subsequent to them, who claimed to know them have said so. And so on all the way down to us.

Well. We can see that every single link in this chain of authority, from Jibrīl on, must perform the authority-projecting manoeuvre, because Islām itself does not allow them the luxury of considering their own authority supreme. (As previously alluded to, Muḥammad is held to be the last prophet, which of course means no-one after him can equal his closeness to Allāh and consequent

352 Here Shi`ite Muslim bids the lineage farewell, not accepting the authority of these sources. From now on my argument applies to Sunnite Islam only, a focus which will keep the points clear, and at the same time highlight the equivalent difficulties in the Shi`ites' lineages of authority.

understanding.)

And that is not all. By a rather exquisite irony, each stage in the chain makes the projection of the next stage indefensible in order to protect itself. Muḥammad's contemporaries rightly asked, 'How can we be sure it is Allāh?' Since Jibrīl is not a god even he presumably cannot be said to judge whether a communication from Allāh is without doubt from Allāh. And since Muḥammad was not an angel he presumably could not be said to judge whether a vision of Jibrīl was truly of Jibrīl. The response to such awkward doubts from the doctors of the religion was that the prophet was infallible and sinless (it is a peculiar doctrine of Islām that all prophets are) – he would not be mistaken and he would not lie. Clearly this entails a rather sharp dividing line between prophets and ordinary men. This line then makes a rather thorny problem for the next link, the companions. How can they be sure Muḥammad was a prophet? (And many of his contemporaries were sure he was not.) How could they be sure that this scripture being revealed was, as it claimed to be, 'without uncertainty'? For them to have the requisite 'closeness to Allāh' and understanding they would have to be, the impossible, prophets. Any less understanding (and according to Islām ordinary men have considerably less understanding than prophets) and their view would perforce be uncertain: it would not be directly testable in their own experience. So they were forced to make the authority projection completely – utterly to overlook both their own role as choosers and the fact that they did not have the capacity either to judge Muḥammad a prophet or for that matter Musailima, one of a number of supposed impostors and rivals, not; and instead focus duplicitously on the authority of Muḥammad. A prophet elected by non-prophets; and Musailima a non-prophet condemned as such by non-prophets. (And not to forget Muḥammad condemned as a non-prophet by non-prophets too: just not the non-prophets of the reporter chains that have been preserved.) This strategy of projection was indeed encouraged by Muḥammad: the Qur'ān as we know it is full of advice or orders about what the companions are to say to those who doubt that Muḥammad be a prophet – and they all relate to Muḥammad's authority rather than the judgmental perspicuity of the companion. Conveniently, the Qur'ān's call to produce a verse like its verses, the supposed miraculous proof of its veracity, is an invitation to be tried in a court whose jury is entirely made up of those who have accepted the authority by projection already: more of a threat than an invitation, one is tempted to say. The focus on Muḥammad's authority rather than their own choice is of course obligatory, since if attention were drawn to their reasons for accepting his authority this would expose the very manoeuvre which is being covered up. These verses were and are much cherished since they provide instantly the comfort of authority projection we have mentioned above – not only do they allow one to align oneself with the supreme authority, they are an example of that very alignment, since the aligner is speaking in the very words of that supreme authority to which he has aligned himself. This neatly and I think sufficiently explains the comfort Muslims enjoy when reciting such verses. This comfort they often attribute to the text and conflate with 'sublimity' held as proof of its miraculousness and supreme authority – one of many examples we see in the massive religions of positive feedback loops depending on lack of clarity.

Comforting to recite they may be but the process of hiding his own authority and pretending to the authority of Allāh or Jibrīl or Muḥammad has left the Muslim vulnerable to the same attacks the latter are vulnerable to. We can see that if Islām allowed Allāh to speak to everyone then there would be no need beyond personal experience to 'establish' authority, but as soon as the access to Allāh of the common man is denied, it becomes incumbent on, and indeed an emergency for, the tradition to verify the chain of authorities. And it has become a long chain! This neatly explains why, like no other religion, Islām requires history.

The next link in our account was the companions. Even if they accepted the authority of Muḥammad, how can we trust that they did not get confused about what they had witnessed? Or forget things? Or lie? After all, they went to war against each other.[353] Well, later generations would have it that this conflict was part of the divine plan for Islām, a historical demonstration of important events from which we are supposed to be edified, and in this way they managed to insist that the companions too were extraordinary – not prophets, certainly, but extraordinary enough compared to those that came after them to deserve what was later awarded them – immunity from criticism. So once again we see the tradition using the strategy of privileging this group to rescue their authority; and once again we see what a problem it makes for the next link in the chain – for if the next link were not as upright (Arabic `udul) as these then they did not have the capacity to judge these companions upright anyway. They instead chose whoever appeared upright to their less upright minds.

The fault in the strategy haunts the entirety of any staircase of authority,

---

[353] The prophet's wife `Ā'isha went to battle against `Ali in the Battle of the Camel, referred to traditionally as the 'great temptation' since contemplating it naturally threatens one's faith.

not just Islām's: for any two steps, the lower is always unqualified to judge the upper, yet it is upon that judgment that the upper stands. In fact trying to establish a cascade of authority from Allāh down to us instead establishes the necessity of a cascade of authority from us down to Allāh, a cascade which utterly mocks Islāmic doctrine. So in reality each link in the 'chain of support' is not actually a link but isolated and unsupported. The illusion of a chain is maintained only by the shrill arguments of those who recognize they are performing a massive cover-up operation.

The only way out seems to be a second strategy: downward validation. For example, Muḥammad must validate the companions. And Islām is rich in such validations. 'The best of people are those living in my time. Then come those who follow them, and then those who follow them. Those will be followed by a generation whose witness is sometimes true, sometimes false,' said Muḥammad as recorded in Bukhāri[354] and Muslim[355], and, 'Oh God, Oh God! Refrain from using bad language about my Companions! Oh God, Oh God! Refrain from using bad language about my Companions! Do not make them the target of your attacks after me! Whoever loves them, loves them on account of his love of me; whoever hates them, hates them on account of his hatred of me. He who hurts them, has hurt me, and he who hurts me, has hurt God, he who hurts God, God will punish him,' said Muḥammad according to Tirmidhī[356].

To accept this downward validation depends on committing a logical fallacy. It is very easy for Muslims, having projected their authority onto Muḥammad and feeling the comfort of it and the romance of sharing the sessions of the prophet with his companions, to accept Muḥammad's advocacy of a companion or companions at face value. But it is difficult and uncomfortable for them to recall that this advocacy has come down to us in a report, a report *made by those very companions*, to the chains of reporters we have mentioned, each new link of which does not have the capacity to judge the previous link. Given that it is the very trustworthiness of the companions which is in question, it does strike us as rather peculiar that their own reports of Muḥammad's advocacy of them are taken as evidence of their trustworthiness, as if untrustworthy people were somehow magically unable to say Muḥammad advocated them too. (Of course, the slightest acquaintance with political history shows that the contrary is true.) Even more uncomfortable to recall Allāh's advocacy of Muḥammad in the Qur'ān

---

354 *Faḍā'il al-Asḥāb, Virtues of the Companions* 1, 4 (Bukhāri)

355 Faḍā'il al-Saḥāba, Virtues of the Companions 212 (Muslim)

356 *Manāqib, Feats,* 58 (Tirmidhī)

was transmitted *by Muḥammad*.

It only remains for me to point out that historical methods would encourage is to seek evidence for the trustworthiness of all these reporters in independent accounts, i.e. non-Islāmic ones. And that very quickly in Islām quite the opposite happened: Islāmic law in its wisdom decided that no other account than a Muslim's was trustworthy (`ādil). Once again a seeming comfort for the Muslim whose strategic fault, obviating any independent verification, leads to profound anxiety.

We are tempted to see in the evolution of authority strategies in Islām an analogy to the equally self-defeating efforts of the paranoid schizophrenic to protect his fantasy world from collapse under ever more harassing threats, that in reality may or may not be there. He is so convinced of his own superiority, or even divinity, that he renders himself unable to trust anyone else, such that even the best and best-intentioned companions can only appear to him as enemies or fools or both. By means of the introduction into Islāmic law of the notion that non-Muslim testimony is never trustworthy or just, Islām brought to a logical conclusion the process of erroneous authority-projection we have been considering, and in the same moment it perfected the analogy with the paranoid schizophrenic, alone in the world, dominated by pride and anxiety, plagued by delusions of others' hostility, treachery and even universal conspiracy.[357]

If the concealment of authority projection were limited to the positive phenomenon of the concealer's projection itself then we would be concerned with the massive anxiety which results in them but only that. However, regrettably, it is not limited to that sphere but also extends to punishing those who question the concealer's projection.

That this is enforcement of the authority chain on others is most obvious in the Islāmic laws which punish with the severest penalties 'slighting Muḥammad'. If one questions projection concealers thus: 'On what grounds do you accept Muḥammad as an authority?' they cannot answer – partly because they have no firm justification and partly because they are not permitted to consider needing a justification in the first place. So instead they project the challenger's doubt about their choosing judgment onto Muḥammad and accuse the challenger directly of accusing Muḥammad of not being worthy of acceptance as an authority.

I cannot stress enough what a massive trick this manoeuvre involves. We have seen that the projection concealers have no capacity

---

[357] Freud famously described religions as the neuroses of society.

themselves to judge the qualities of the prophet as compared to alternatives, and in this sense they are exactly like their challenger: none of them are prophets, so they are alike in blindness, alike in needing projection concealment to accept external authority. Now the challenge, that the projection concealers have acted blindly, is just. But the projector concealers, in their invincible safety (the Arabic word īmān, usually translated as 'belief', has its root in the word amina, to be safe), project that challenge also onto the Muḥammad of their imagination. Once again they perform the manoeuvre of removing themselves, however bizarrely it may seem to the challenger, from the equation. The manoeuvre is done without premeditation, for they are almost certainly unaware in their conscious mind of performing it. And its results are most unfortunate, for in such a psychological situation, in absolute independence from what the historical characteristics of the authority chosen may or may not have been, the comfort of the projection concealers is directly undermined by their own analogous projection of the challenge. So, ironically, the attack is perceived as so much more personal than it is from the challenger's point of view. For the challenger it is a matter of cool-headed consideration of individuals' reasons for making a choice. Because these reasons are not available to the projection concealers, it appears to them to be an onslaught against their comfort, against their safety in identification with (or self-concealment in) the noisy reputation of the chosen object of their authority projection.

All of the energy of that response to challenge is poured into laws against defaming the prophet. Challengers of Muslims' choice are arrested and punished not for what they did from their own point of view, which is after all something a rational, humane being might be expected to do when confronted with a person pervaded with the anxiety of this very particular psychological concealment of authority, but for what they are perceived to have done by someone imprisoned by that anxiety. We can see that some brief respite from that anxiety is afforded by the self-affirming activity of punishing challengers, and that this activity is self-affirming and therefore relieving in direct proportion to the number of people who share in inflicting the punishment. (Yes, let us cast our minds back to the children's playground and all it teaches us.) But it will, unfortunately, but naturally, be a temporary respite: even when the challenger has been killed, the projection he challenged still lives.

Case: authority in Tibetan Buddhism

Tibetan Buddhism also makes use of such delusory authority chains. This has, however, been noted and criticised from within its traditions. As the now infamous scholar and tantric adept Gedun Choepel writes entertainingly in his commentary on the main treatise by the so-called 'second Buddha' Nagarjuna:

> One may think: 'We concede that our decisions are unreliable, but when we follow the decisions of the Buddha, we are infallible.' Then who decided that the Buddha is infallible? If you say, 'The great scholars and adepts like Nāgārjuna decided that he is infallible,' then who decided that Nāgārjuna is infallible? If you say, 'The Foremost Lama [Tsong kha pa][358] decided it,' then who knows that the Foremost Lama is infallible? If you say, 'Our kind and peerless lama, the excellent and great so and so decided,' then infallibility, which depends on your excellent lama, is decided by your own mind. In fact, therefore, it is a tiger who vouches for a lion, it is a yak who vouches for a tiger, it is a dog who vouches for a yak, it is a mouse who vouches for a dog, it is an insect who vouches for a mouse. Thus, an insect is made the final voucher for them all. Therefore, when one analyzes in detail the final basis for any decision, apart from coming back to one's own mind, nothing else whatsoever is perceived.[359]

The next step

Having dissolved the illusion of certainty in authority chains based on seeming ability, we might recognise that all are therefore alike in that sense, and so we are left with the question of our allegiance to a particular teacher. It is to dissolve even this, the illusion that a particular teacher, even the Buddha himself, is a better bet than others if one seeks certainty, that the Buddha makes the next and final step of his critique.

---

358 The founder of the Gelug sect with whom Choepel studied, and widely considered to be a Buddha himself.

359 From chapter 2, part 9 of his commentary, as translated in *The Madman's Middle Way* (Lopez, 2007).

Not by 'This ascetic is our teacher', ma samaṇo no garūti

'Panidhekacce moghapurisā mamaññeva ajjhesanti. Dhamme ca bhāsite mamaññeva anubandhitabbaṁ maññantī'ti.

Foolish people make a request to me but then, having been told the Law, consider themselves allied or connected to me.'

The Buddha

Meaning

Samaṇa as we have already described refers to the spiritual seeker and ascetic. Garu is the Pali equivalent of the famous Sanskrit guru, meaning in our common parlance 'spiritual teacher' especially of the yoga variety. But in these languages it has a much broader reference. The word shares its etymological origin with the English words 'grave' (as in 'weighty') and brute (as in 'brute strength'), and is applied to all people who have a weighty influence in one's life, not just spiritual teachers but all teachers, and teacher's spouses, and also parents, mentors, and elders. However, since in this context it is a samaṇa the implication is obviously spiritual, a teacher or mentor or inspirational leader. –ti is a contraction of the usual iti meaning 'as was just said', used to close a quote or close the direct expression of a thought.

Examples

Considering oneself a follower of the Buddha and therefore deriving information for living a good life only from Buddhist books; considering oneself a follower of Muḥammad and so only recognizing sacredness related to Muḥammad and his life; considering oneself Christian and so believing oneself saved and burdened with the responsibility of bringing light to the benighted hordes; 'following' anyone or any movement; considering oneself communist and therefore obliged to toe the party line and turn in dissenters; considering oneself an advocate of democracy who must fight to eliminate non-democratic tendencies through the world.

Does the Buddha declare his own teaching irrelevant to certainty?

It might seem (and it has often been said) that in this final exhortation the Buddha disqualifies even himself, such that we need not listen to the discourse in the first place! But, just as the others, this exhortation does not mean that we should turn away from teachers, but that we should never consider any particular teacher to be a certain source of knowledge *just because she is our teacher.* The teachings of the Buddha recorded in the Pali canon are pervaded by this spirit, that the community of almsmen should not just 'believe' what he taught, but should test it themselves. This can be seen in the canonical form of praising the laws he discovered (see the homages at the outset of this book) and in the Buddha's rather tetchy response to some of his students getting riled at insults aimed at himself, and even to others of them getting conceited about praises aimed at himself:

> When others praise [me,] the Awakened One, the Law and the Community, if you feel pleased, delighted or elated it will only be harmful to you... You should admit only what is true as true... Besides morality there are other Laws which are profound, almost indiscernible, almost incomprehensible... I have set them forth after realising these Laws myself... Anyone wishing to praise my virtues rightly should do so in terms of these Laws.[360]

The *Contracted Discourse*[361] begins with a rather alarming reminder for sheep:

> Atha kho aññataro bhikkhu yena bhagavā tenupasaṅkami [...] ekamantaṁ nisinno kho so bhikkhu bhagavantaṁ etadavoca: 'Sādhu me, bhante, bhagavā saṁkhittena dhammaṁ desetu, yamahaṁ bhagavato dhammaṁ sutvā eko vūpakaṭṭho appamatto ātāpī pahitatto vihareyya'nti.
>
> 'Evamevaṁ panidhekacce moghapurisā mamaññeva ajjhesanti. Dhamme ca bhāsite mamaññeva anubandhitabbaṁ maññantī'ti.

> Then a certain almsman went to the worthful one and, on arrival [...]. Sitting at the side he said to the worthful one: 'It would be good, sir, if the worthful one would teach me the Law in brief so that, having heard

---

360 This was the plea made by the Buddha to over-zealous practitioners of his teachings, according to the first (called '*Brahma's Net*') of the collection of long discourses.

361 The *Sankhitta Sutta* in the Aṅguttāra Nikāya (numerical collections), among the 'eights' discourse number 63.

the Law from the worthful one, I might dwell alone in seclusion, heedful, ardent and resolute.'

'But it is in just this way that foolish people make a request to me but then, having been told the Law, consider themselves allied or connected to me.'

Of course teachers have not always advised such caution.

'Come, follow me,' Jesus said, 'and I will make you fishers of men.'[362]
He saw a man, named Matthew, sitting at the receipt of custom: and he said to him, 'Follow me.' And he arose, and followed him.[363]
'Anyone who does not take up his cross and follow me is not worthy of me.'[364]
'If you want to be perfect, go, sell your possessions and give to the poor, and you will have treasure in heaven. Then come, follow me.'[365]
And he said to another man, 'Follow me.'[366]
'My sheep hear my voice, and I know them, and they follow me.'[367]

Irrelevancy as sources of certainty

As potential sources of certain knowledge, spiritual teachers and inspirational leaders (and for that matter parents and elders) are examples of authority figures, so this exhortation seems to be just a re-affirmation of the previous one. Why would the Buddha repeat himself?

Allegiance's trivialisation of truth

The difference is that this exhortation does not say, 'Not by what your teacher teaches,' but makes reference to 'us', 'our teacher': it says we should not allow our idea of who our teacher is to influence the degree of certainty we ascribe to the teaching. That is a very subtle point. The Buddha, having dismissed in the last exhortation the absolute reliability of the authority figures themselves, is now drawing attention to the *additional* temptation to claim certainty on the basis

---

362 Matthew 4, 19 and Mark 1, 17.
363 Matthew 9, 9.
364 Matthew 10, 38.
365 Matthew 19, 21.
366 Luke 9, 29.
367 John 10, 27.

of *the allegiance* to a particular spiritual teacher or inspirational leader, and by extension to the community defined by the same allegiance.

This should make us in the modern world 2500 years later pause for thought. If we recall our earlier discussion of the differences between the Kālāmā people and the typical peoples of the modern world, we can see that this injunction even more than the others is directed *straight at us*: the temptation warned against is very much the temptation to which we have succumbed *en masse*.

Communities develop around great teachers. These communities act as reserves for the teacher's doctrines to be pooled, and to develop, and, often, to stagnate. We have already considered how easily traditions become corrupt and religious symbols degenerate, that it is in their nature to do so, and that it would require exceptional circumstances for this not to occur. Then we looked closely at all of the psychological foibles which lubricate the passage down the chute of absurdity. Aside from the direct encounter with reality, something else would prevent this slide – *frequent mixing*: mixing of people with others, and mixing of their ideas with others'.

Here we come to the particular dangers of allegiance with a particular spiritual teacher of inspirational leader: it fosters a segregation of 'doctrine pools', or we could say streams, since they change over time, which removes this natural immune system by mixing. Segregating mechanisms such as those which allow these community-entities to persist in various degrees of isolation will, in time, come to be associated naturally with absurd doctrines, which they help to protect and foster. Here I am using the expression 'absurd doctrines' in its broadest possible sense, that is, doctrines which are at variance with experience, however minutely, and thus would not last against rational challenge from others (such as non-adherents unconstrained from hiding that variance) unless they were protected from such challenge or proliferated enough to overwhelm it, or both. To protect a weak idea involves on the one hand its isolation like this from any threat within any generation, and on the other hand assurance of the means of transmission within one generation and between successive generations. The carrier mechanisms favouring transmission we have already considered.

Segregating mechanisms able to foster absurdities

This tendency to align oneself to a teacher and the teacher's community isolates groups of humanity from the others, however subtly (and sometimes it is not subtly at all of course). Once the community identifies what constitutes alignment with the teacher, not just isolating mechanisms applying to the ingroup but also segregating mechanisms applying additionally to the other groups can develop. We will consider some interesting examples of how this can occur, but since the topic is very large our treatment will necessarily not be exhaustive. Most of the examples come, again, from Islāmic communities, because of the two most massive religions it is more uniform in its laws: those familiar with other, smaller, religious communities can make their own comparisons.

We will consider in order:

- bodily segragation, i.e. by means of physical restriction, on the contact with challengers and on the contact with physical representations of their challenges, and
- verbal segregation, i.e. by means of language and thought processes (p. 365).

>Bodily segregation

Limitation of travel

It is not difficult to see how favouring a particular teacher can come to be related to geographic isolation – in particular in ages when travel was much more difficult than it is now. Teachers cannot be everywhere at the same time, and neither can those who favour them.

Expulsion of non-favouritists

Once a particular teacher has come to be favoured, it can happen that those who do not favour the same teacher are expelled by force, especially in situations of warfare or the establishment of political supremacy.

Case: expulsion of Jews from Arabia by Muḥammad and `Omar

Perhaps the most extreme homogeneity of teacher-favouritism in the world today is the Arabian peninsula. This is partly due to the Muslims' destruction of other Arabian religions (such as the religion of the goddess `Uzza); partly because of the so-called 'Wars of Apostasy' lead initially by the first caliph of Sunnite Islam, Abu Bakr, which dealt systematically with the large number of tribes that, though they continued to pray, refused to pay the tribute to the caliphate once the prophet of Islām was dead; and partly due to the expulsion or massacre of Jewish inhabitants. At first Muḥammad made overtures to Jewish tribes, but the initial curiositry of the latter did not lead to their according him a recognition of prophethood. In measure with his increasing power, he proceeded to undermine allegiances between the Jews and the other people of

Yathrib (Medina), and later expelled the Banu Kainaka, then the Banu Nadhir; next the males of the Banu Qurayza were executed.[368] The Jews of Khaibar, Fadak, Taima, and Wadi-al-Kura were allowed to stay on condition of surrendering half their agricultural produce, a system which was maintained by the first caliph, but under the second, `Omar, they too were expelled. Here we are less concerned with the political motives for all of this than the bare fact that Arabia was left with a population overwhelmingly in favour of Muḥammad, and remains so today.

Once such a homogeneity develops, other strategies can be brought in to maintain it.

Restrictions on other traditions' scriptures and doctrines

If there are restrictions on importing, printing, distributing, owning, displaying, reciting, teaching or studying other traditions' scriptures, then the idea streams relating to those scriptures will be to an extent separated from the prohibiting group. Such restrictions tend to be law where there is an issue of proselytising.

Those of us, incidentally, who live in the very few countries where there are no such restrictions may pause for a moment to consider the situation elsewhere: most of the terrestrial globe is under some kind of legal restriction on religion. One of the most thorough investigations of restriction of religious freedoms ever conducted was published in December 2009.[369] Of the 198 countries considered, 48% were found to apply laws which restricted religious freedom 'substantially'. In 65% of countries, the government interfered with worship, and in 19% prohibited at least one tradition of practice. 13% prohibited teaching of all religions, 19% prohibited teaching of religions other than the state-favoured ones. 40% restricted religious literature. In 69% there was harrassment of certain religious groups by government, in 32% state violence towards them. In 12% the government has made efforts *totally to eliminate* a religious group from the country. 45% had a constitution that recognised a favoured religion, and 26% gave official privileges to members of that religion denied to others. In 25% the government was found to defer to religious authority on legal issues. The percentage in each case was higher if numbers of people rather than countries were used to calculate them. Taking into

---

[368] For more detail see the earliest biography of Muhammad (Ibn Hisham, c 218 h./1355 CE/1937 CE).

[369] (Pew Forum on Religion and Public Life, 2009)

consideration all the aspects of government considered to calculate an index of religious freedom, the countries with lowest freedom were Saudi Arabia, Iran, Uzbekistan, China, Egypt, Burma, Maldives, Eritrea, Malaysia and Brunei; the broad area with the lowest freedom the Middle East and North Africa.

Widening our lens of scrutiny to the modern secular religions, we can see that various forms of communism, totalitarianism and democracy have often forbidden each other's and religious texts, with as much if not more violence than the religions have of each other's, and indeed China features in the 2009 report principally because of its suppression of all religions, such as Buddhists in Tibet, Phalun Gong everywhere and Muslims in certain regions. In the other direction are countries like Libya was in the seventies, where the entire population was forbidden to possess texts on democracy on pain of hanging.

Restrictions relating to one's own scriptures and doctrines

>Untouchable texts

Just as making rival sacred texts informally or formally off limits for a group protects its idea stream, so does making carriers of rival doctrines' contact with one's own sacred texts taboo, since they are not in a position to be able to comment knowedgeably on them.

According to 'purists' (as they are called) in Hinduism, Islām, Sikhism, and Druze religion, for example, no-one should touch (or in some cases hear or even see) the sacred texts who has does not have the ritual purity stipulated in the religion and of course only afforded to its adherents. In modern times such laws as the muting by severing the tongue, deafening by pouring scald into the ears and total dismemberment,[370] of those who break these taboos are thankfully not any longer applied (as far as I know), but that they were, and that ghosts of them persist in the discomfort some adherents can feel when their scriptures are handled by non-adherents, and the ceremony which still surrounds the handling of some scriptures and which is calculated to impress, mean they will have influenced the isolation of these doctrines from non-adherents.

Vajrayāna Buddhism provides strong support for our hypothesis because it explicitly recognises the potential in its own texts, the tantras, despite their vaunted power if esteemed and practised, to be seen by newcomers or outsiders as shocking or ridiculous, so protects their esteem by means of requiring

---

370 These are the tradition punishments according to the commentaries on the law treatises such as Manu for a non-priest who has recited, heard or memorised the Veda respectively.

initiation to access them, and requiring of the initiates an oath of obedience and secrecy, and strict control of their acceptance of acolytes of their own. Failing to gather regularly with other initiates constitutes a major breach of the oath, and those who have broken their oaths are taught to be so polluting that even to live downstream of one is enough to break one's own oath. Oath-breakers are taught to guarantee for themselves and those they pollute an arising of awareness in their own special hell, the so-called vajra hell or indestructible hell, the only hell taught in Buddhism to be eternal. However there are, beyond this, no controls over mixing with other traditions.

Islām presents a similar pattern but with greater severity and much greater legal thoroughness. Non-Muslims cannot study Islām at Islāmic universities such as the world-famous Al-Azhar in Cairo, currently the most authoritative in the Islāmic world: a satirist might say you must clearly convert to Islām before you find out about why you should (or should not) have done so.

>Unbreachable sanctuaries

If certain spaces are physically protected against the intrustion of non-adherents, then they can act as the locus of enunciation and therefore transmission of doctrines whose objectionability in other contexts might lead to their status being undermined. This means that sanctuaries can come to be associated with absurdities.

Sanctuaries are found in some but not all religions. Islām, Judaism and Hinduism stand out, for example, as requiring much more stringent control on non-adherents' admission to some of their places of gathering than Christianty and Buddhism.

Islām has by far the largest sanctuary of any religion in history, the vicinty of Makkah.

> O you who believe since they who divide (their loyalty, which is due to Allāh) are unclean, let them not approach the sacred mosque (at Makkah) after this year of theirs.[371]

At first it might strike one as comical, that one subset of humanity should exclude others from a place where they pray to a 'universal deity', and that later (as frequently happens judging by the number of mosques which were

---

[371] Qur'ān 9, 28 The word 'unclean' (Arabic nājis) here refers not to hygiene but to ritual impurity.

churches which were synagogues which were temples) another subset should appropriate it and follow suit by excluding the former subset along with everyone else so that they in turn can pray to a 'universal deity'.[372] We can see that the force of necessity for one subset of the faithful to exclude another whose doctrines differ and therefore pose a threat to one's faith is in proportion to the perceived threat. And that the more merely conceptual (absolute, metaphysical, or absurd) a doctrine, the more it is open to being undermined by doctrines of the same nature or even of a more empirical nature.

What are sometimes referred to as 'reformist' Hindu groups, such as the Hare Kṛṣṇas and the Brahmā Kumāris, have been among the most violently expelled of intruders into the temples of 'unreformed' Hindu religions, such as those belonging to the cult of Śiva in Vārāṇaṣi, India and Paśupātinātha, Nepal. Non-Hindus are forbidden from entering the main temples of Paśupātinātha and have to sign a paper professing respect to Jagannātha to enter his temple in Orissa. The protection of Makkah from intruders is just the Hindu temple taboo writ large, although the Hindus do not go so far as to deport transgressors from the country.

Sanctuaries for different traditions have even been asserted within the same temple, with the expected violent consequences. Decades of bloody conflict over the Bābrī mosque in Ayodhyā, India, seemed to have come to an end with the British colonists' solution, dividing the building into two strictly separated areas, one for Allāh devotees, the other for Rāma devotees. But one of its bloodiest resurgences came in 1949 when a sneaky member of the latter group slid images of Rāma and Sītā into the Allāh area.

Conversely one would expect a tradition whose doctrines are not threatened by mere exposure to those who are not already allied with them, to be free of such 'sanctum defence'. Whilst it could be that there have been other compensatory protection mechanisms at work, it nevertheless impresses an observer that few such restrictions are made on non-Buddhists at the site of the Buddha's Great Awakening (Mahābodhi) at Bodh Gaya, in conformity with the Buddha's assertion that the laws, to and by which he had awakened, and which he demonstrated, are discoverable to each person individually: the megaphones of the mosque a few hundred metres away are allowed to broadcast that there is no god except Allāh as many times and with as much volume as the mosque in Makkah.

---

372 I wrote this provoked by the view of the grand mosque of Jamāl `Abdul Nāṣir in Tripoli, Libya: the building used to be the Catholic cathedral.

Nevertheless Hindu temple priests had officiated at the Mahābodhi shrine before the flood of international Buddhist pilgrims began to swell, and their being kicked out when it did, while seemingly to have been to allow Buddhist pilgrims to approach without the priests' office as intermediaries physically preventing their own devotions, effects the same protection we are discussing, from Hindu challengers within the narrow confines of the shrine building at least.

Restrictions on leaving the community

Oath-breakers in Islām, aka apostates, do not merely pollute, but represent a standing insult to the sacred, so it is according to Islāmic law a duty incumbent on believers to kill without the ordinarily requisite trial those apostates who refuse three times to recant: in a firm account, Muḥammad said, 'Kill whoever exchanges his religion.' Even in Muḥammad's lifetime severity was combined with adventurous extension of what constituted an apostate: the most authentic canonical collection records various versions of the account that Muḥammad had all the members of a Muslim tribe's hands and arms cut off and their eyes branded with irons and had them buried up to their necks in the desert and denied water and medicines until they died, for killing his camel keeper and stealing his camels, and the commentators hastily excuse the ruthlessness as a necessary response to an instance of *apostasy*.[373] The fact that the entire tribe was thus tortured and executed, not just those presumably fewer who murdered the camel keeper, supports the idea that the prophet indeed considered it a punishment for the thought-crime and not for the act of murder.

Clearly oaths of allegiance with dire punishments encourage all kinds of isolation of the group's idea stream.

Restrictions on mixing with others

Muslims and their non-Muslim subjects are formally under many behavioural restrictions as to how they mix with others. In Islāmic law non-Muslims' houses must not overlook or be taller than Muslims' houses.

>Obligatory community identification

The second historical 'successor' (caliph) of Muḥammad, `Omar, instituted the obligation on non-Muslim subjects of his Islāmic governments to wear at all times their 'sash' (Arabic zinār) to advertise their rejection of

---

[373](Bukhāri), volume 8, book 82, accounts 794-797

Islām. Modern apologists who would have us believe this was not a stigma but something like a mark of one's profession since some Christians' custom was already to wear the sash should pay careful attention to modern rulings (Arabic fatwa) when Muslims ask about whether they can mix in non-Islāmic festivals such as St Valentine's Day – they are frequently told that to imitate the unbelievers is to become one of them, and occasionally that joining the unbelievers' festivals is 'even worse than wearing a sash'. It is not just imitating their festivals but imitating them at all (unless it be in something shared by all humanity) which is proscribed, including dressing like them.

The fact that such rules are clearly not being followed by many Muslims, through their ignorance of or carelessness about what are in fact clear prohibitions, (an ignorance incidentally fostered through education by governments motivated by economic concerns,) should not distract us from noting that there is no extant form of Islām which lacks them.

>Proscription of friendship

Allāh according to the Qur'ān makes friendship with non-Muslims seem quite terrifying:

> Let not the believers take unbelievers as loyal friends rather than believers...[374]

> O you who believe, do not get intimate with other than yourselves: they do not refrain from confusing you. They love what is your distress.[375]

> Do those who take unbelievers as loyal friends rather than believers covet honour with them? But then honour is all with Allāh.[376]

> O you who believe, do not take unbelievers as loyal friends rather than believers. Do you want of Allah demonstrative might over you?[377]

> O you who believe, do not take Jews and Christians as loyal

---

374 Qur'ān 3, 29
375 *Ibid* 3, 111
376 *Ibid* 3, 139
377 *Ibid* 3, 144

friends. They are only loyal friends to each another.[378]

These verses may well have been true for the Muslims of their audience when they were revealed, of the Christians and Jews and others whom they were likely to encounter, at the time. Here we are only interested in their capacity to inspire in successive Muslim communities a quality and quantity of interaction with non-Muslims which differs from those of their interaction with Muslims.

In Shī`ite Islām the Muslim's ritual purity is destroyed, and its reinstatement by elaborate ablutions necessitated, not only by contact with his or her own genitals or dogs but also by touching non-Muslims.

>Proscription of worshipping with others

Such segregating mechanisms seem regrettably to be a staple of the mutually allergic Abrahamic religions of the one god, bizarrely and frequently brandished as supposed proof of their 'tolerance':

> Say to the infidels: I do not worship what you worship, and you do not worship what I worship; I shall not worship what you worship, and you will not worship what I worship; you have your religion, and I have a religion [sic].[379]

Current carriers of the banner 'all religions are one' would do well to pay more attention to such mechanisms and their historical, social and psychological consequences.

>Proscription of intermarriage

In terms of restricting information flow through a society, one of the most powerful structural strategies is the prohibition of marriage between the kinds of semi-isolated communities we have been considering. The massive religions all make restrictions on marriage with non-adherents to some degree, Hinduism being perhaps the fiercest, outlawing not only other religions but also the various other strata (castes) within it. Islām, which allows Muslim men to marry non-Muslim women so long as the children are raised Muslim, Judaism and some traditions of Christianity have moderate restriction – topped up, however, with social disapproval.

---

378 *Ibid* 5, 51

379 Qur'ān 109

>Restrictions on commensalism

In traditional societies a great deal of information exchange, be it formal discussions or gossip, factual reporting or gossip, occurs in conjunction with eating. So one powerful way of restricting a group from such mixing would be to instigate rules that prevent sharing meals with others.

Dietary peculiarities such as the prohibition of pork and alcohol and the necessity for meat to come from animals slaughtered according to prescribed ritual in Judaism and Islām –

> Eat not from that over which the name of Allah has not been pronounced, for (fear of) sinfulness. The devils inspire their loyal friends to argue with you: if you obeyed them you would be splitters (of loyalty to Allah).[380]

– lead to weak social segregation on home ground (weak because intruders do not usually bring their own food with them) but very pronounced segregation on foreign ground where such customs are not the norm, since the adherents must band together away from natives even to eat.

>Arbitrary requirements

It might be suspected that if a restriction is completely arbitrary, that rebellion would quickly snuff it out. But the reverse is true: perfectly arbitrary isolating mechanisms work perfectly – because who else would come up with them? If it is not arbitrary, that is, if it is related to some logical reason, then this reason may be shared between the culture of the doctrines it isolates and other cultures. If Yahweh (had he not retired before syringes were invented and) had told the Jews not to eat meat into which hormones had been injected, rather than not to eat pork, say, then meals would not have become uniquely an occasion for bringing to mind the concept of Yahweh but also for remembering hormones' threat to health and possibly animal rights, and Jews might have ended up mixing with other people who, while kosher from the point of view of the way they ate, were decided un-kosher from the point of view of not believing in an invisible creator who spoke this rule to a man on a mountain. When bringing in such 'scientific evidence' for the value of isolating customs, such as Egyptian Muslims did of the 2009 'worldwide epidemic' of swine flu (which, though transmitted from people and not from swine, prompted the Muslim government of Egypt,

---

380 Qur'ān 6, 121

before there were reported cases of this flu there, to order its entire Christian-bred stock of 300,000 pigs slaughtered), apologists should remember this – that by robbing the mechanisms of arbitrariness they are unwittingly scuppering their isolating effect. If there really were scientific evidence for all pork (rather than human-excrement-relishing communities of semi-feral pigs' pork) being bad, everyone would stop, and a valuable isolating mechanism protecting Islāmic and Jewish doctrines from non-believers would be lost. Similarly if beef were bad for others than just Hindus, and non-vegetarian food for others than Brahmins, and non-vegan food for others than Jains, etc., *mutatis mutandis.*

Clearly the more frequent the psychological link is made between the mechanism and the doctrine, the faster it will be imprinted. So the best isolating mechanisms of all would be those which bring arbitrary rules into the most frequent everyday acts. This is exactly what we find in the most persistent religious traditions.

Muslims are not permitted to pray to Allāh using methods other than Muḥammad's. In Islāmic law this would be an instance of 'resembling' unbelief, which is itself unbelief. The form of their prayer, with the complicated regulation of its timing, the number of bows and order of movements and invocations, is a formidable social barrier between them and other people who pray even by name (as the Arab Christians and Jews do) to Allāh. A Muslim who follows these prescriptions is physically separated from non-Muslims for a significant fraction of the day, particularly if we include the time necessary to reach the mosque, and perform the ablutions, etc. In Muslim-dominated workplaces and educational institutions this also hinders non-Muslims' activities during these periods, which in turn favours segregation of religions between companies and institutions. A few years ago some naïf instituted an inter-denominational area for prayer and meditation in the American University in Cairo such as one finds in many international airports (but not in Arab countries' airports). The idea was a flop of course since elaborate ritual performances such as the Muslim prayer are both mutually allergic and allergic to non-elaborate ritual. The silent prayer insisted on at Friends' Meeting Houses may be commendable but it is worth pointing out that it excludes Muslim prayer. Similarly the non-denominational meditation vaunted at so-called Vipassanā retreats in the 10-day regimen promulgated by Goenka in a huge number of centres looks less non-denominational when one counts the number of denominations of meditation it excludes. Just as 'democracy' must in practice be the rule (-cracy) of only some of the people (demos), namely those who prefer democratic parties, so must a non-sectarian spiritual centre exclude with utterly sectarian thoroughness any sectarian sects. So ritual as frequent and elaborate as the one Muḥammad instituted presents an insoluble problem to advocates of social and religious intercourse, and thus is most usefully isolating for the doctrines held by its participants.

The spectacular panoply of meticulous body regulation by which Muslims are to maintain their 'purity' (in Arabic ṭahāra, as distinct from hygiene and morality – the meaning is magical rather than biological or ethical[381]), according to Islāmic law, and those by which many Hindus and tantric Buddhists are to maintain theirs, are perfect examples of this binding of the arbitrary to the doctrine and the community. These detailed rules sharply define a knowing club distinct from their human brothers: secret rites which the others cannot hope even to know about never mind match. For example, going beyond Judaism with its mere circumcision of the penis, Muslim purity demands shaving of pubes and armpits, perfume, 'saving' the anus after defecation using only three fingers of the left hand in a particular way, 'making innocent' the penis after urination using the left hand to hold the penis and rubbing it in a particular way against an odd number of un-held stones or a piece of dried mud held between the heels until the urinary tract is empty, ritualised triple ablution of various parts of the body in order before prayer and again if on the way emission occurs through anus or urethra (unless through the lesser of the two urethras of a hermaphrodite which is regarded as a wound, from which emissions are not polluting); and major ritualised washing after intercourse by penetrating further than the penis head with a woman, man or hermaphrodite, but not with a pre-pubescent child, an animal or a corpse. (That we are not discussing hygiene as it is ordinarily conceived here is quite clear from the last example![382])

There is some variety in the extent to which these isolating mechanisms are recognised as such within the traditions' discourses. In tantric communities within Hinduism and Buddhism, the ritualistic practice of socially abhorred activities while justified doctrinally as a way to break ethical piousness may have acted similarly as a protection mechanism since their members were cast out of ordinary society and could thereby be avoided almost completely.

---

381 Although hygeine in international culture is sliding into quite a magical realm, lubricated by clever advertisers, who edify us with such information as the percentage of bacteria remaining on our sheets after laundering while always providing the perfect solution for us, packaged and at a price, etc.

382 Such penetration of a corpse is still illegal, of course, although there is some disagreement as to whether penetrating an animal – especially if one subsequently kills it – need be considered illegal. For a wonderful introduction to the sexual aspects of Islamic cultures, see *Sexuality in Islam* (Bouhdiba, 2001).

Within Islāmic discourse, the regulations in Islām are explicitly isolating – as is befitting a people who consider themselves the sole vice-regents and representatives of the divine on earth. As observers we can see that the isolating mechanisms are extremely effective in protecting Muslims from close contact with people who would challenge their beliefs. There is tacit acknowledgement of the swine taboo being important mainly as an isolating mechanism in the fact that while consumption of pig products in meals is strictly forbidden, consumption of pig-produced insulin by Muslim diabetics is not (though for fear of mass hysteria and financial losses insulin's origin is of course daintily concealed from them): people do not have insulin parties equivalent to group meals, so contact with non-believers need not be avoided by such a prohibition.

Arbitrary customs indeed have a doubly protective effect for absurd doctrines. Not only do they isolate the doctrine-carrying groups that practise them and remove them somewhat from challengers, they also condition those groups to care more and more about them and any doctrines related to them, exactly in proportion to the amount of effort required to practise them. The Concorde fallacy, that one should not abandon a project one has put effort into, is a foible of human psychology named after the aeroplane: the cost of its development exceeded all bounds, but the project was pursued to the bitter end simply because, whenever they might think of giving it up, those involved in it had already made so much effort that they were loathe to stop and thereby deem all that effort to have been in vain. Or, as Mackay puts it, in the course of attempting to explain the tulip mania which seized Europe in the 17th century CE,

> Many persons grow insensibly attached to that which gives them a great deal of trouble, as a mother often loves her sick and ever-ailing child better than her more healthy offspring.[383]

Frequently performed arbitrary religious 'observances' when they are linked to doctrine, for example to the doctrine of a god's existence by the belief that the god ordered them, have the inevitable effect of making the people more attached to the doctrine: otherwise all these observances would have been in vain. Once again, from the point of view of absurd doctrines, the more arbitrary the observances the better, since if there were a meaningful reason to performing them the link to the religious doctrine would be less pronounced.

---

[383] (Mackay, Extraordinary Popular Delusions and the Madness of Crowds, 1841)

For maximal zeal, an observance should balance the benefit of frequent effortful repetitions with the danger of abandonment if too much effort is demanded. The more intense the effort, the more quickly accumulates, by the Concorde fallacy, the conviction that what one has done has been important. However if the effort required is too intense, the project will be abandoned anyway in exasperation. So a balance is necessary.

If one sought to devise, from ordinary human behaviour, the perfectly protective arbitrary observance for an absurd doctrine, one would quickly alight upon restricting physical expressions of lust and love. To be more precise, the restriction of *orgasmic and erotic pleasure,* by its need for continual vigilance and by its arbitrariness, presents perhaps the most powerful zeal-increasing observance there is to protect absurd doctrines. What else than erotic activity are we drawn to do so powerfully, and so what else would we need to make such effort to restrict? And, stepping momentarily out of the very indoctrinated mentality we are here scrutinising, what could be more arbitrary than a restriction on such an intensely pleasant, beneficial, healthy and harmless activity? (Those readers who think automatically of betrayal of romantic devotion and orphans I gently remind of sex that in itself requires no romantic devotion, at least masturbation and orgiastic sex, and of such marvellous technological advances as the condom.)

To put it bluntly, after an entire lifetime of effortful daily self-control has been dutifully accumulated, in the pursuance of 'the lord's commandments', what Christian in those latter years, when there is little achievable pleasure to disdain anymore anyway, will abandon the lord for whom all that potential pleasure was dutifully wasted? This basic psychological process is true, whether or not Christianity is, and greatly favours the persistence of all Christian doctrines whether or not they are true. The same applies, *mutatis mutandis*, to all other religions that control sex.

>Segregation by means of speech and ideas

Dislocation of discourse

This can be done in many ways. Once the group's internal discourse has broken from the other groups', and the anchoring effect of exchange has been minimalised, the idea streams can drift further and further apart.

>Language barriers

One of the most pernicious reasons for the lack of mutual understanding is and has always been the fact that particular teachers and their communities are associated with particular languages. How well some language barriers prevent the mixing of discourses can be seen by the fact that totally opposed discourses about the same events can continue to exist side by side in different languages.

However we should not exaggerate the evil of such barriers, and so be too quick to imagine that the easy solution to disputes between discourse-distinct cultures is to train translators, bridges to usher in a new era of peace. Indeed the recognition that peaceful acceptance of each other's potentially offensive discourses once they are made comprehensible is rather unlikely was what inspired the British in India in the spirit of 'divide and conquer' to commission translations of the old and largely obscure Muslim chronicles of the pillaging and invasion of India, whose power-fawning and triumphalist spirit frequently overcomes any sense of their enemies' humanity blithely to celebrate killing and temple-razing, into a language the 19th century CE non-Muslim Indians could understand, English. This 'bridging venture' was most effective in unleashing the intended bloodbath and along the way gave birth to various extremely Islāmophobic movements which still operate today, such as the famous Calcutta petition to ban the Qur'ān.

>Dissimulation

Case: Islām's 'instance of fear' and misinformation

In recent disputes over terrorism and its relation to Islāmic practices, the traditional injunctions and permissions to lie about one's convictions because of circumstances of fear (in Arabic, taqiyya) have been invoked in allegations against Muslim politicians. It has been justly pointed out that all politicians lie: they do not need to depend on their religious doctrines to do so. However, it is generally accepted that without this practice the doctrines of Shī`ite Muslims, who revere `Alī, Ḥassan and Ḥussayn as their teachers, would not have spread: under persecution by Sunnite governments the Shī`ites could invoke these obligations and permissions to pretend they were Sunnite. Whilst it kept their tradition alive and thriving, it also separated their discourse more and more from the Sunnites'. The same principles protected the Druze and the Bahā'i religions, under persecution by Sunnites and Shī`ites.

The lying can be an unintentional misrepresentation. It can be argued that in schools across the Islāmic world there is distortion of Islāmic history (what we might call rosy-spectaculising), notably the lulling insistence on the peacefulness of Islām's spread across the world. The Muslim chroniclers of the invasion of India, for example, wrote paeans to armies that peacefully 'piled up the severed heads of the unbelievers and set them aflame so their brains boiled and as steam returned to Him who created them'. These texts are not mentioned in Muslim schools, and like the history of colonialism in English schools, the hiatus leads to a false impression of a glorious past. We have already considered the selectiveness of history, psychological tendencies such as confirmation bias, and in the massive ideologies the drive to rescue the reputation of the ideology and its leading figures once the authority projection concealment has been performed, and so we are in a position to appreciate the intensity with which this unwitting dissimulation is maintained, quite flying in the face of the facts. Misinformed people act in the case of an internally structured tradition like Islām in the same way as one who consciously dissimulated would act: the scriptures and histories presenting the more gruesome version are transmitted are protected and the outsider's discourse is removed from them by these misinformed individuals.

>Segregation by conceit and disdain

Runaway inverting terms

We have already considered runaway inverting terms as distortions of language to conceal unacceptable behaviour. Here what concerns us is the outrage it can provoke in the outsider, and conceit in the insider, leading to a breakdown of understanding. The outsider's outrage comes down to the sensing the believer's hypocrisy. It is also perhaps recognised that the believer is refusing to admit that it was he himself or she herself who did the choosing, about by whom to be guided. This authority projection concealing manoeuvre we have already identified as a common feature of modern 'faith'.

>*Case: submission*

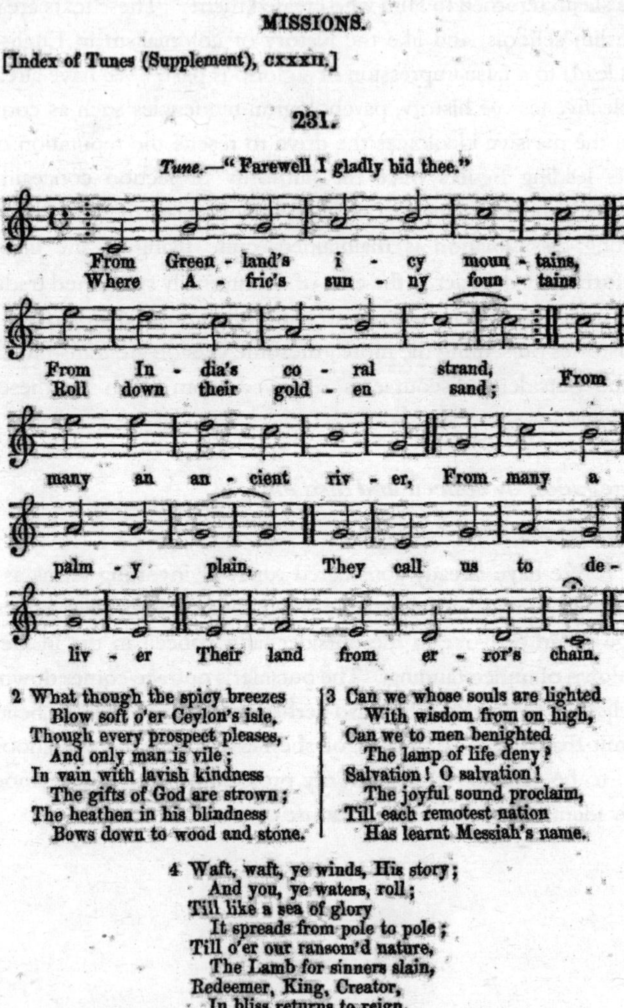

Figure 5 The melodious voice of meekness

The one who professes submission to a perfect deity has conceived of the most arrogant authority imaginable – namely, his or her own, aligned with 'perfect truth and power'. As the missionary hymn humbly asks,

Can we, whose souls are lighted
With wisdom from on high,
Can we to men [sic] benighted
The lamp of life deny?[384]

The social consequences are not difficult to predict. He or she mocks the ones who do not so submit, accusing them of putting their own authority higher than 'the supreme authority', and of not being humble enough to ask for guidance.

It is this which has led to the distortion of Buddhism by Christians as the 'presumption' of a higher authority than of revelation, or of a greater power for salvation than the grace of this perfect being.

As far as the outsider is concerned, they see a hypocrite condescending from their 'humble' position on high, and feel disgust. As far as the professor is concerned, the allure of the superfice of their self-image is captivating enough that they believe it is the whole truth, and they may even feel genuine pity for another who seems too proud to follow suit in 'submission'. In other words communication has broken down completely.

The difficulty is only partly because of the equivocal vocabulary. We tend towards dull-mindedness and laziness in communication. That is, we may not realise that the word is trapping us, or we may realise but not bother to clarify terms, especially when we seem to be getting the upper hand.

In any case, the root issue is that such terms are inherently treacherous to communication and mutual understanding, and so we would do well to recognise this. 'Wolf in sheep's clothing' hardly does justice to the 'meekness' of 'submission' for example, though it does throw the expression 'lamb of God' into new relief.

Antiptosis

As well as vocabulary traps there are ways of debating which cause a conceit-exasperation discourse break.

To the extent that a suite of doctrines gets associated with a particular

---

384 From 'From Greenland's icy mountains' by Reginald Heber (1819). See Figure 5 if you want to sing along. Heber, of Brasenose and All Souls Colleges, Oxford, Doctor of Divinity, later Bishop of 'Calcutta' (including Ceylon), died of a seizure either (depending on who you believe) in the bath, or while preaching against Hinduism 'in the midday sun' at the age of 42. It is said that on the day he died he had baptised 42 of the benighted.

teacher, and this suite gets fixed, it can be observed that its adherents start to employ the slippery defence, the 'never falling' stragegy of the rhetorician, switching from an attacked doctrine to another of the suite as though defending the latter improved the kudos of the former. Slippery eels are harder to catch. So when it looks like one line of argument is failing, even though supposedly it is supposed to prove one's case, one shifts to another supposed proof of the same case, which proof might otherwise have absolutely no logical connection to the earlier proof. In classical times this was called *antiptosis*, meaning 'against falling'.

This method is extremely useful in defending fixed creeds, because for the holder of the creed it seems valid when one item of it is under inquiry to switch defence to any other item, since the proof of any item is assumed to support all of them. For the same reasons it is perhaps the single most exasperating ruse for their interlocutors, since no argument is ever taken to its conclusion, but enough traditional half-defences of each item are generally available to keep switching, until the interlocutor gives up from physical exhaustion. Here the segregating mechanism is on the one hand complacency based on the circular fallacy of mutual support of creed items and on the other the exasperation on the part of those who do not associate the creed items.

We can see that this kind of breakdown is aggravated in the case of debate between adherents of the so-called 'monotheistic' systems and non-adherents, because the single deity, with its heuristically attractive person-like unity, can bind any number of bizarre and mutually exclusive creed items together, and with its seeming status as an entity which must be accepted or rejected, sharply demarcates the adherent from the non-adherent in perspective.

It is important to note that this phenomenon bears no relation to whether or not the doctrines in question are correct or false. It is simply the case that the nature of the doctrines favours the breakdown in communication. In this way the adherents' idea stream isolates itself by its very nature.

Between the conceited and the exasperated camps, Sigmund Freud in his writings often fell into the exasperated. Whether or not we share his sentiments, by now I hope that members of both camps can appreciate why he might once have written of such religion:

The whole thing is so patently infantile, so foreign to reality, that to anyone with a friendly attitude to mankind it is painful to think that the majority of mortals will never be able to rise above this view of life. It is still more humiliating to discover how a large number of people living today, who cannot but see that this religion is not tenable, nevertheless try to defend it piece by piece in a series of pitiful rearguard actions.[385]

It is exactly the fact that many gods or divine attributes with diverse implications are drawn together in the god-unifying process that allows the adherents to be satisfied with defence of any implication, since each defence is for them a defence of the same entity, and which leaves non-adherents profoundly unsatisfied, as Freud clearly was, with what seem to them to be 'pitiful rearguard defences', partial defences which do nothing to address countless other faultinesses.

The breach, it should be noted, can be extreme. From the outside, we as the exasperated can see illogical changes of subject, fallacious reasoning, and seemingly intelligent people reduced to childish gullibility; from the inside, we as the conceited can see only one subject of discussion, perfect reasoning, and a blessed people ennobled by superior faith. The two parties, when in disputation, are so soon satisfied of their own respective position (both are ultimately disdain of the other) that the so-called 'monotheistic' doctrines can be highlighted as especially potent in bringing communication to an end.

Division of equivocal meaning

We have already seen a related segregating mechanism, that of dividing people into opposing camps and at the same time pleasing (for different reasons) to the two camps, in the word 'agnostic' which, while not meaning anything, flatters both the self-elected who use it disdainfully of others, and those who thus divided off nevertheless feel flattered by the way it absolves them of the faults they see in that dubious elect.

>Double standards

Rather than using one word in two different ways, this is using two words for the same thing, in order to distinguish ourselves when there is no meaningful grounds to doing so.

Contextualising the opponent

A recognisably modern version of this occurs between a particular doctrinal community and its detractors when the former adopts what we might call the bird's-eye stance in interpreting away the reasons for the detraction in

385 From chapter 2 of *Civilisation and Its Discontents* (Freud, 1930).

terms which are meaningless to the detractors because their meaningfulness depends on accepting the very doctrines which define the community. This was recognised for example by Popper as –

> a tendency which can be observed in a group of modern philosophies, the tendency to unveil the hidden motives behind our actions. The sociology of knowledge belongs to this group, together with psycho-analysis and certain philosophies which unveil the 'meaninglessness' of the tenets of their opponents.[386]

His suggestions as to why they might be popular applies just as well to the examples from the traditional religions we have already considered:

> The popularity of these views lies, I believe, in the ease with which they can be applied, and in the satisfaction which they confer on those who see through things, and through the follies of the unenlightened.

He identifies the means of segregation:

> …all these ideas are liable to destroy the intellectual basis of any discussion, by establishing what I have called a 'reinforced dogmatism'. […] they clearly destroy the basis of rational discussion, and they must lead, ultimately, to anti-rationalism and mysticism.

>*Case: Hegelianism*

He then gives as an example the other-interpreting mechanisms of the followers of one of the most revered European philosophers, Hegel, whom along with Plato and Marx he accuses of being instrumental in the development of modern totalitarian ideologies:

> Hegelianism does it by declaring the admissibility and even fertility of contradictions. But if contradictions need not be avoided, then any criticism and any discussion becomes impossible since criticism always consists in pointing out contradictions either within the theory to be criticized, or between it and some facts of experience.

---

[386] This and the following citations are all from Chapter 23 of *The Open Society and Its Enemies* (Popper, 1945; 5th edition 1966).

The allowance of opposites simultaneously is what Orwell dubbed 'doublethink' and what is known in logic as equivocation, as we have already seen. Whether or not it is fair to accuse, as some have accused, Hegel of founding Nazism, there is no doubt that logical equivocation or doublethink is a powerful facilitator for totalitarian ideologies, like Trojan horses, to gain acceptability.

>*Case: psychoanalysis*

Another of his examples, psychoanalysis, Popper says,

> can always explain away any objections by showing that they are due to the repressions of the critic.

>*Case: philosophies of meaning*

He also adverts to the dangers of a philosophy of meaning,

> since 'meaninglessness' can be so defined that any discussion about it is by definition without meaning.

>*Case: Marxism*

As for those who claim Marx as their teacher, he points out that they

> are accustomed to explain the disagreement of an opponent by his class bias…

whereas they would not of course contextualise their own position of commentary within their own class situation.

>*Case: mysticism*

He imaginatively creates the defence a devotee of the romantic return to mediaeval-style Christianity would launch against the charge that they are returning to 'the cage', 'the beasts':

> since it is impossible to discuss such profundities with a rationalist, the most likely reaction will be a high-handed withdrawal, combined with the assertion that there is no language common to those whose souls have not yet 'regained their mystical faculties', and those whose souls

possess such faculties.[387]

He has a great deal of fun at the expense of these groups by applying with casual panache each group's other-interpretation mechanisms to the group itself, as these examples occur in the context of his attack on the so-called 'sociology of knowledge', which is the attempt to explain the development of knowledge by appealling to the social environment. For our concerns it is enough to recognise these examples as isolating mechanisms which can remove, incompletely or completely, the doctrines of their communities from the arena of the rational and even irrational criticism, and thus allow absurd doctrines to survive. Increasingly religious traditions have become the victims rather than the perpetrators of this crime: a recent apologist for theistic belief bemoans sociologists' haughtiness about religion:

> Social scientists cannot claim validity for their discipline without allowing that it is motivated by the very same search for truth that they wish to suggest in others is merely the expression of social or psychological conditions.[388]

Ventriloquist manoeuvre

A cruder and bolder form of the double standard is when the issue is righteousness and error, and we attribute our own fault to another, concealing the move by means of specious language or hysterical certainty. We call this 'the ventriloquist manoeuvre' or 'the lift dog manoeuvre' (referring to the man in the lift who blames his dog when there is a smell).

The vociferousness with which the ventriloquist manoeuvre is deployed probably has its roots in a well-recognised psychological tendency:

> As there is no enemy so bitter as the stranged friend, so, of all the tyrants and tramplers upon the poor, there is none so fierce and reckless as the upstart that sprang from their ranks.[389]

We are now in a position to understand why this might be. The manoeuvre can enter into a kind of synergy with the authority projection

---

387 From chapter 24, IV.

388 (Trigg, 1998, p. 36)

389 This is Mackay describing the alchemist Jacques Coeur (Mackay, Extraordinary Popular Delusions and the Madness of Crowds, 1841).

concealment we discussed before. When we know (even subconsciously perhaps) that we have made the ventriloquist manoeuvre and are therefore hypocrites, this uneasiness helps to fuel the authority projection and its concealment. Once this projection is made there is no possibility of accepting fault ourselves (since this would mean the fault of the 'perfect authority'), which drives us to insist on blaming the other all the more.

>*Case: Islām's accusation of other' speculativeness*

An excellent example of the ventriloquist manoeuvre is seen in Islām's accusation that other religions' scriptures are not authoritative but mere speculation and opinion. We have already seen how Islām's authority structure destroys itself. Even if it did not, and we took its records as historical, such recorded (but little taught) incidents as the Caliph `Uthmān's punishment of the reciter Mas`ūd and confiscation and destruction of his Qur'ān, from which he was not saved by virtue of having recited it acceptably in the Prophet's company; and the goat eating certain verses, which prescribed the punishment of stoning to death, which were to be included in the Qur'ān, and which were being temporarily stored under the bed of of `Ā'isha the Prophet's wife, fatefully in goat-necks' reach; and `Omar's son's ambiguous pronouncement on the reliability of the most prolific transmitter of accounts of the prophet's deeds, Abu Hurayra,[390] give us plenty of reason to doubt its authoritativeness. So people who *choose* Islām (rather than inheriting it along with its death penalty for apostates as most unfortunately do) can only do so by means of guessing. However their acceptance is of a system which refuses this interpretation: doubt is unbelief and to accept any other access to the divine than Muḥammad's is the worst sin, shirk. The mere presence of other religions' scriptures in the world reminds our freely choosing people that they have hidden their speculation under their second-hand authority. So it is of speculation that they accuse these other

---

[390] Jami` al-Tirmīdhi, vol. i, no. 128: "`Omar's son reported that Muḥammad had ordered all dogs killed except sheep-dogs and hounds. Abu Hureira added 'and farm dogs'. `Omar's son retorted that Abu Hureira owned farmland and that this showed what the real reason behind tradition-quoting was." Incidentally the later difficulties posed by this exchange offer a great example of scholars' revisionist interpretative panache: the pious commentators ignored the obvious insinuation of interested distortion of what Muḥammad said, and instead interpret `Omar's son's remark as *praise* of Abu Hureira, and as drawing attention to the fact that those with personal interest in a particular tradition are *more likely to remember it accurately*. QED!

scriptures.

Accusations of speculation are not made delicately in inter-religious propaganda wars, of course. Offensive parodies of Christianity in the books of Aḥmed Deedāt, which call the crucifixion of the Christ the cruci-fiction, and scorn the translations of the Bible as different books, are available in every bookshop and on every street corner in Cairo: the Bible, of course, is not.

>*Case: the accusation of others' insufficient knowledge*

Another example, of blaming others for one's own fault, is the charge Arab Muslims, Indian Hindus and even Tibetan Buddhists frequently level at others, 'You are a people who understand not the language of our religion's sacred text(s) so you are not in a position to judge its merits,' and an allied one less linguistically bigoted adherents make, 'You have not studied our religion enough to understand it as we do,' which we can guarantee are not applied to their own investigation of other religious traditions. Indeed, in Islām's case, since the divergence of local versions of Arabic from the language of Muḥammad's tribe (such that, unlike Italian and Spanish, say, Moroccan 'Arabic' and Gulf 'Arabic' are mutually incomprehensible and their speakers forced to resort to English or some other shared language to communicate), and the decrease in popularity or practicality of learning Arabic, Sanskrit or Tibetan in modern schools, we can guarantee that in most cases the charge is not applied to their own investigation of the language of their own tradition either.

>*Case: accusation of others' linguistic failure*

Islām is as far as I know unique in having the nerve to include this linguistic bigotry in its sacred text. It is unfortunate that Allāh, when, according to the Qur'ān, he asked those who posed as rival prophets to Muḥammad to produce a verse to match any verse in the Qur'ān and thereby set the standard for miraculous-by-definition language which has informed all subsequent Arabic discourse, did not add the proviso, 'in any language', because then he would not have made an entire people believe they were the judge, jury and executioner of sacred texts in languages they couldn't order a cup of tea in, namely (for the vast majority of them) all such languages but their own.

This is not to say that in other traditions linguistic bigotry has played no role in inter-religious conflict. Some Hindu saints ridiculed the peculiar near-Sanskrit language of the early Mahayāna Buddhist texts as bad Sanskrit. And of course the grapplings in Christian history afforded by the sacred authority of various translations of the biblical texts is legend, not just because of the blatant political advantages afforded by aureation, which we discussed earlier in our treatment of scripture, and protection of the sacred message from being (horror of horrors) understood, but also because certain groups could identify with their version as being more authoritative.

>*Case: Christianity and Buddhism's accusation of each other's sleep*

A recent and seemingly respected English-language university textbook on 'the philosophy of religion', i.e. on Christian apology, describes 'religious experience' in Buddhism like this:

> In some religious traditions religious experience involves a gradual weaning of the individual from cognitive consciousness to a state which, at best [sic], can be described as pure consciousness or pure emptiness (shunya). In Buddhism, for example, the goal is to transcend all conceptualisation in order to attain to the sphere of pure consciousness, and from there to the state of emptiness [sic]... Religious experience in this tradition is not feeling, but it is ultimately non-cognitive.[391]

Here is not the place to go into how confused this presentation is (although we note in passing that 'experience' is taught to distract from the goal in Buddhism, and that 'buddha' is the past participle of the verb 'know' in Sanskrit!): I mention it merely because it is typical of Christian presentations of Buddhism in ascribing to the Buddhist path some kind of dissolution into mystical, cloud-like nonsense. The Catholic Encyclopaedia snootily disparages the supreme aim of the Buddhist path as 'an eternal sleep'. For anyone familiar with the traditions being dismissed this is either amusingly ironic or appallingly and suspiciously negligent. The supreme aim of the Buddhist path is bodhi: 'awakening', 'enlightenment', 'total knowledge', 'total understanding'. Smṛti, one of the principal methods to realise it in this life, means not losing awareness. Samsāra is frequently described as a kind of sleep – nirvāna is the waking up!

As we have already seen, the literalist or foundational school of Buddhism also have something to say about the Christians' belief in a creator god. In the first long discourse of the Pali canon the Buddha, in the course of exposing a catalogue of religious views to whose erroneousness he awakened, mentions certain holy persons who retire for some inadequate time, achieve some

---

391 (Peterson, Hasker, Reichenbach, & Basinger, 2008, p. 33)

meditative faculty, and thus awaken to their having been in the immediately previous existence in a divine realm dominated by a single supreme being which declared itself their creator. These holy ones then proclaim in this world the existence of this creator, almighty and invincible, the eternal lord. The Buddha points out that he continued meditation beyond this awareness and became aware of many more prior existences. He saw thus that this 'creator' had not been supreme in prior existences, that the 'creatures' had already existed, in various states, and that it was only by their later arrival in this penultimate realm of existence that the erroneous notion of their having being created by the earlier arrival could arise in them or in it. So the Buddhist tradition teaches that the prophets who proclaim about a creator god are insufficiently awakened.

Now at least one of these two traditions, Buddhist and Catholic, must be wrong in attributing sleepiness to the other: at least one of them is performing the ventriloquist manoeuvre without foundation.

Auxesis and meiosis

Here we take another step down the staircase of crudity, and find the way barred as it were by a great accumulation of inter-religious propaganda material. There is a pronounced tendency for religious communities to refer to themselves and their activities, speech and ideas using qualitatively different vocabulary to others and theirs. The vocabulary used for the community will then tend to '*euphemism*' and '*auxesis*', that is, the use of exaggeratedly acceptable or valuating terms, and that used for the excluded others will tend to '*dysphemism*' or '*meiosis*' or '*tapinosis*', that is, the use of exaggeratedly unacceptable or denigrating terms. The double-standard vocabulary obscures what otherwise might be seen as equivalence between the community and the other.

This double-standard feeds itself because the more awful the rival systems seem, thanks to the misinformation, the more likely one is to try to rescue one's own system from the same taint by auxesis. The phenomenon is akin to the polarising judgment of people we met in our discussion of intuitive cognitive distortion.

Because of the sensitive nature of this topic we should bear in mind that ur interest is solely in the fact that the auxesis/meiosis disparity is a major cause of communication breakdown. Here we are not indulging in meiosis in order to cause a communication breakdown!

>Popular misconceptions

In Egypt, for example, Muslims and Christians though sharing the country know very little of each other's beliefs and practices, so needless to say their knowledge of the other religion is almost nil. Many Muslims believe that the Christian mass involves getting drunk and even having orgiastic sex at midnight. The situation gets worse when we ask about religions not commonly encountered there. Those (very) few people who have heard of the Buddha believe this to be the name of an unmoving idol worshipped by the superstitious. (Such misconceptions unfortunately were fixed in the Persian language, where the word 'bud' came to mean 'idol'.) Much the same idea was bandied about when 19th century Christians started to react to growing popularity in the Buddhism being 'discovered' in India. As our 'great missionary hymn' poetically intoned,

> What though the spicy breezes
> Blow softly o'er Ceylon's isle,
> Though every prospect pleases,
> And only man is vile;
> In vain with lavish kindness
> The gifts of God are strown,
> The heathen in his blindness
> Bows down to wood and stone.[392]

Like (and to some extent because of) those ardent missionaries of yore, the average person in the street today in large swathes of the Middle East, Europe and the Americas has no idea about the 'Hindu' religions, and simply would not know that any (or rather it – since all are lumped together) has ever worshipped a single deity such as Viṣṇu or Shiva exclusively. He is likely to believe that (like the Buddhists in their conception) the Hindu worships cows, or maybe the sun.[393]

A new book on the Bahā'i religion much-distributed in Egypt bears on the cover that religion's leader pictured alongside its most important temple, in consuming infernal flames. A video documentary by the notorious Harun Yahya popular among more devout Egyptians purports to treat the religion of the Buddha: its chapters are introduced by statues of the Buddha burning, and it makes various interesting claims, such as that the Tibetans 'believe in' a 'book'

392 One imagines that it must be due to their god-given incapacity to exploit any inferior races that the heathens' economy precludes the gold seemingly required by churches for their crosses.

393 Thereby joining the noble ranks of his predecessors, as we can see by comparing the paean to Maḥmūd Ghazni in our discussion of monotheistic prayer.

called 'Pali canon' which is apparently 'full of crass errors' – lucky they don't speak Pali, then, isn't it?

>In formal discourse

Such attitudes are partly the result of modern Islāmic discourse itself. One could be forgiven for thinking that it is in denigrating other religions that this chiefly excels. Again, we stress, whether or not the superiority Islām accords itself can be justified, here we are merely interested in the fact that it does, and that it does so by means of clear examples of auxesis and meiosis.

According to the typical Islāmic discourse, any physical structure (such as a cross) which becomes an object of reverence is ṣanm or wathan ('an idol') whereas the box in Makkah dressed in black Egyptian robes and faced by every Muslim in prayer is 'not an idol'. In fact it is bayt Allāh ('Allāh's house') but unfortunately the house into which a Hindu religion's devotee, say, invites a god by means of a sacralising ritual is 'not a house of god' but an idol. Whereas other religions' reverence at shrines is ridiculed as, say, tree-worship or mountain-worship, Allāh calls two mountains in Makkah shrines (mashā`ir) and allows circumambulation of them[394] and this is never referred to as worshipping the mountains. In orthodox Islām, mention of Allāh's appendages in the Qur'ān must not be taken as metaphor but as literal, and bilakayfa (without asking how, e.g. how an immaterial being can literally have appendages), but bilakayfa is jealously and blithely withdrawn from the divine representations in, say, Hindu religions. The Christian's prayers invoking Jesus are shirk (splitting worship such that something other than Allāh is its object) whereas the Muslim, who prays (Arabic ṣalli, usually interpreted to mean 'connect') to Allāh alone 'does not pray to Muḥammad' when he says, as Muslims frequently do in moments of tension, 'ṣalli `alal-nabi,' because (it is claimed) the word ṣalli has two different meanings, and this is actually 'a prayer to Allāh asking him to bless [connect to] Muḥammad', despite the fact that no-one would ever say ṣalli `alayya, 'Bless me.' It is not even customary to invoke other prophets in this way, prophets which Islām claims are of equal status to Muḥammad. Worship, in Arabic `ibāda, 'is not directed to Muḥammad,' it is claimed (although an embarrassing refutation in the name `Abdul-Nabī, literally 'worshipper of the prophet', is commonly found especially among the low classes), and this means that even if (as they did) people believed that Muḥammad's snot had healing powers, even when (as they do) people faint

---

394 Qur'ān 2, 158

when his sword is put on public display, even when (as it does) the entirety of Islāmic perfection for its devotees consists in copying him to the minutest detail of dress and toiletry, these people are, it is claimed, not worshipping him. On the other hand a man who offers a flower at the foot of a stupa commemorating the Buddha's awakening is, of course, 'worshipping an inanimate object' and worthy of disdain if not disgust, since a lump of rock (unlike Muḥammad?) cannot see him even. In Arabic there is a very nice distinction between dīn, meaning religion (and applied to Islām) and diyāna, meaning some religiousness (including those versions other than Islām). While much was and is made of the 'ignorance' of the western orientalists' referring to Islām as Mahometanism, the Qur'ānic term for Christianity is naṣāra, which is not used by any Arabic-speaking Christians of themselves but for them refers to a heretical Nestorian sect Muḥammad was familiar with in the town of Najrān near Makkah; and Islām's deprecating names for other religions have in some cases unfortunately entered worldwide use, notably hindūs ('the Hindus'), named not after their Primordial Law (in Sanskrit, sanatāna dharma) as they are by themselves, but after a mispronounced river, and durūzi (Druze), named not after their Unifying of Allāh (in Arabic, tawḥīd) as they are by themselves, but after various ludicrously heretical and dubiously historical characters from whom that religion strenuously dissociates itself[395]. Despite the frequent references to Zarathustra's religion in the Qur'ān (called the 'majūs', which term is now pejorative, as exemplified by the Irāqi propaganda using it against their enemies in the Irān-Irāq war of the 1980s), the name of its prophet is hardly known, and its doctrines not at all, despite many of Christianity's and Islām's deriving from them. Indeed the Qur'ān itself suggests that this religion consists of the worship of fire and casting spells.

In Islām, the three traditions Islām, Christianity and Judaism, which all teach that humans are the centre of creation and our planet the centre of the universe, are referred to as celestial (in Arabic, samāwī), and all other religions, such as Hinduism, which teaches that our universe is one of countless universes and humans only a brief transitional phase for any individual in an eternal journey through countless celestial realms, are not celestial. I could go on. The examples of double standards are so extremely extensive in this tradition that I would recommend for reasons of brevity here that the interested reader chart that extent in his or her own time.

---

395 An excellent introduction is (in Arabic only), Nasīb As`ad al-As`ad, *Kashf al-Sitār, Unveiling* (al-As`ad, 2004).

I would venture that no other religious community on earth subsists on a like degree of not just ignorance but wilful and even joyous mutual misinformation about other religious traditions – the close second was probably the Catholic Church at the peak of its power. And while you will not find a single book in Arabic criticising this state of affairs, you will find dozens whose authors are up in arms because Islām is misrepresented by other traditions. It is a vertiginous double standard.

Deprecating others is hardly Islām's unique achievement, of course: for much of the history of that Primordial Law, derived from the authority of the Vedas, other religions and their adherents were named mleccha, the equivalent of 'barbarian'. The Vajrayāna Buddhists of the Kālacakra cult referred to encroaching mediaeval Isma`īli Islām as 'the Black Law'. And let us not forget the paganus, the 'peasants' or 'civilians' (like the Druidical philosophers) who refused to be 'soldiers of Christ' – an insulting distinction, however, which has come back to haunt (and deplete) the Church, now that many, sick of ideologically motivated violence, would sooner be peasants than soldiers, particularly pious ones.

The result: mass psychosis

'Cognitive dissonance' is the term used nowadays for the state of refusing reality and we have already seen many examples. It is also a seemingly inevitable consequence of associating oneself with a particular teacher, such that defending the reputation of the teacher, and therefore of the teaching, becomes more important than the teaching itself, and, as the French philosopher is probably apocryphally reported[396] to have said when it was pointed out that the facts seemed to contradict his theory, 'Tant pis pour les faits.'

Anchoring the anchor

We have already considered the so-called '*anchoring effect*', the fact that our perceptions of what is right and good are influenced by prior commitments to particular beliefs. No-one is more anchored than a believer in an omnipotent deity, or for that matter a *doubter* in an omnipotent deity, in a society that punishes apostasy with execution. Under such circumstances, that handmaid of speculative philosophising is worked to the death to maintain the deity's reputation, at least among the believers and doubters-on-parole, but often among those who hold the belief to be irrelevant too. It is hard to imagine a better

[396] By Mackay in his discussion of Mesmer (Mackay, 1841, p. 323 fn).

reason to indulge in one's cognitive dissonance, in fact. A close second (or arguably a rival) to executing apostates is ostracising them – denying them society and its support, even from their own family. But to some extent all communities based on particular teachers' identity come, by means of the segregation we have considered, to lose contact with reality.

Case: the sacred proles (after Marx)

Insofar as I understand the development of Marx's ideas by his followers, there are numerous examples of it erring through commitment to affiliation with the original formulations of the ideas.

We can take the example of Engels' reverence of the proletariat unto absurdity. Readers of Marx's own works will probably conclude that the author's motives were generally noble, namely, to reduce the suffering of humanity; and that it was these which led him to condemn the bourgeoisie, inasmuch as they oppressed the proletariat. However Engels, falling under the error of valuation of the *form* of the teachings in itself (such as we have already considered in detail[397]), or perhaps even hoodwinking other Marxists in the knowledge that they would fall under this error, condemned what was happening in England during his lifetime on the grounds that part of the British proletariat were being turned into bourgeoisie – *even though their conditions were thus improving.* Another example is how Engels, by focusing on one form of Marx's teachings, class struggle, was able to argue that for the workers to wait until the bourgeoisie attacked them and then to respond with violence would be 'a Marxist revolution' while Marx's motive, compassion at the misery of an economically oppressed class, and his related scheme, identifying the cause of the coming revolution in such misery, did not enounce such a strategy.[398]

Case: the conniving glut of the free market economy élite

The religion of Hayek and Friedman, which as we have seen can be most generously described as confusing the beauty of a mathematical system with certainty in its application's benefits, but which, less generously described, is a strategy with clear appeal to an élite who can cynically apply it by force and whose subsequent pecuniary glut is sucked directly and with extraordinary human

---

[397] In the commentary on the Buddha's exortation, 'Not by thinking ideas through'.

[398] These two examples are from chapter 20, part VI and chapter 19, part IV respectively of *The Open Society and Its Enemies* (Popper, 1945; 5th edition 1966)

suffering from the non-élite, a religion whose appeal to irrational faith suggested to us that it is partly a secular reincarnation of Adam Smith's Christian belief in providence, is exemplary in the matter of cognitive dissonance, mainly because of those same pecuniary interests.

A louse or parasitic mite, when contemplating a dog, does not entertain notions of it being man's best friend, or loyal, or useful on the farm, or good at keeping burglars away. Its view, of a mountainus resource of blood to suck, will remain to the dog's very last mangy days as it scratches itself to an agonising hairless raw-skinned death. Friedman and his acolytes of the 'Chicago School' of economics did not see beyond the blood, as it were, in Chile (under their louse-pimp Pinochet), or Argentina, or Bolivia, and their apostolic successors do not see beyond the blood in Iraq and Afghanistan.

While wolves are reduced to mangy mutts, the lice feast and swell. It is estimated that during the 'experimental application' of this religion's shock doctrine in Chile and Argentina between 100,000 and 150,000 people were tortured and that tens of thousands of those were killed, in order to eliminate any delousing tendencies in the host, and the subsequent mange, the reduction of the majority of the population to misery, beggars belief.[399]

Acolytes of this religion and the parasites they pimp display all of the tendencies we have seen in more familiar religions: attributing their own failure (if they acknowledge it at all – mass starvation being very difficult to see from the palace turrets) by means of the dog-in-the-lift manoeuvre to others or to circumstances mysteriously never being quite right, attributing successes superstitiously and thanks to confirmation bias and the other cognitive biases to their own actions' causation (rather than to the demonised delousing measures introduced in desperation in both these countries when the dog looked set to flop), the adulation of particular persons and projection of authority onto them (even dead ones such as Friedman) such that defending their reputation becomes a matter of the entire church's reputation, the conscious deployment of dupery in the matter of generating and transmitting reports about the financial success of experiments to advertise their panderage to new lice, and even physical segregation methods to foster absurd doctrines – in the Chicago University department of economics itself where the majority of the Latin American politicians responsible for unleashing these massacres by misery were trained thanks to funding by the CIA and US corporations.

---

[399] For more factual data that you will be happy to know about this issue, consult *The Shock Doctrine*, Naomi Klein's monomaniacal exposé of this school of economics (Klein, 2007).

Case: desparate impeccability (after Christ)

Christians did not begin in meekness. What seemed it under Roman oppression showed its true face later. Once they gained the support of the Roman emperor early Christians, which until then the Romans had condemned as atheists, used to hiss and make the sign of the cross as they passed the sacred sites of the other religions. With less geographical focus than Islām would have but matching fanaticism they stole the sacredness from the surroundings. Certain religions there and then considered the world undifferentiatedly sacred, some of course had their sacred places. The Christians denied them the right to continue to consider as sacred what they had so considered until then, and arrogated to themselves the right to choose which land was sacred, and to build a church on it, leaving the rest 'profane'. Only the impracticality of the notion of changing deep-seated beliefs in the population about sacred sites led them to compromise by razing those sites and building their churches on the ruins. A pleasant compromise! The churches alone would be sacred. Eventually under the emperor Theodosius I gangs of black-robed Christians raided and razed other religions' temples across Europe and North Africa. The most beautiful temple in Alexandria and arguably in North Africa, the Serapeum, was not spared.[400]

At the time of writing the Catholic Church is being hauled over the coals for various crimes committed by its priests, such as raping children, and not reporting fellow priests' rapes of children to the secular authorities. Amid all this furore, the Vatican secretary of state, Cardinal Tarcisio Bertone, said publicly that paedophilia and homosexuality were related. He thus shot himself as a wave of protest erupted across that portion of the world where homophobic acts rather than homosexual ones are criminalised.[401] All this is rather unremarkable, part of the humdrum squawking and feather-ruffling which goes on inside the media-shrunk roosting shed of the world's moralists. But it will provide us with a type, wherewith to test what might at first seem to be rather an alarming hypothesis, namey, that demonic possession is alive and well, and even thriving, in the modern world.

The media went half-way to recognising this when it accused our bungling cardinal of political strategy – trying to deflect the growing flood of criticism away from the Church and onto, in this case, Homosexuality. Those of us who agree would do well to remember that, crude though it might have been, the tactic will have worked for a sizeable number of devotees of the said Church –

---

400 (Kirsch, 2004)

401 (Ivereigh, 2010)

and with this 'readjustment of perspective' they will have felt immeasurably relieved. The crimes and criminals remain the same, of course – the readjustment of perspective does nothing to alter the fact that the priests who raped remain the priests who raped, and the priests who did not tell remain the priests who did not tell, and more importantly all of the circumstances which encouraged the crimes to happen remain. However, in some mysterious way, a whole swathe of people have just managed to make themselves feel better despite their association with these criminals. How?

Well the answer is not so mysterious as it turns out. The basic purity of the Church has been reasserted, and the blame laid instead with something *inside it.* Something which *should not be there.* What we need to realise is that we are not talking about people who should not be there, we are talking about 'something' which should not be there. Something in the priests, in this case. Inside them, to be sure, is the quality of 'belonging to the Church', but for a fair number perhaps (I do not have the figures) the other quality of 'desiring men' is inside them. Our cardinal, by shifting the blame onto this second quality (it does not matter if he was wrong to do so) from the first, has *exonerated the quality-possessor.* Now it is an accident of English that in this language we talk about things and people *possessing* qualities and not *vice versa.* When we realise that things and people might just as well *be possessed by* qualities, we will perhaps start to get a taste of the real dish the cardinal is cooking.

If we recall for a moment our earlier long analysis of the human mind's tendency to invest symbols, signs and ideas with an existence independent of the mind, and their subsequent degeneration from authentic communication and revival as what we called 'golem symbols' and 'hijacked symbols', we will detect a very similar taste there.

A 'quality', having been singled out of complex phenomena as something in itself, is of course an example of such a symbol. It is considered to exist somehow (where?) by itself. As soon as such a quality is discerned, at that very instant, it can be misconstrued as an entity in itself. In medicine it is still the consensus to think of *diseases* like this, as we can see in such language as, 'I caught the flu,' and 'I finally got rid of that flu.' But there is no flu without a body. If the flu were the pathogen then we should say that they air that carried it could catch it too, but of course we do not. Yet as soon as it passes from air to body, we do not say, 'I have caught the pathogen of flu,' but, 'I have caught the flu.'

The process of exposure to the virus and to the conditions favourable to developing the flu are largely out of our everyday control: we cannot even see the virus, for example, to be able to avoid it.

However, shifting our focus back from the material pathogen to those other pathogens, 'qualities', we can see that a quality, being an entirely mental abstraction from our experience, *is* therefore under mental control. Further more the belief of people in a group about the qualities possessed by certain individuals can *spread.* If your healthy sister is believed even by the entire family to have flu, this will not conjure up the virus inside her. But if she is believed to be *to an extent out of control* because she possesses (is possessed by) a quality, then her behaviour will alter.

R. D. Laing went a long way to showing traditional psychologists that by attributing a quality, *the condition*, to one person, *the patient*, they were not only overlooking the fact that *other people* had been responsible for fostering that condition by means of their beliefs but, worse, they were themselves *contributing* to that condition.

We are familiar even in popular culture with the much-documented fact that exorcisms (and he were begin to approach the crux of the matter) work, but only when you believe them. At the end of their tether, for example, the helpless psychiatrists in the classic 70s horror film 'The Exorcist' tell the mother of the possessed girl to, as she paraphrases incredulously, 'take her to a witch doctor'. Famous it may be but this fact is usually misunderstood to mean that this so-called 'psychological explanation' applies only to the 'victim' – i.e. that the 'demon' is a figment of the 'victim' 's imagination. That is not the case at all: the 'demon' does not consist of the victim's delusion. Indeed if the victim were surrounded by doctors and exorcised, the exorcism would not work. And if the girl's family, back in the hill village as it were, were not informed of it, it would not work. The 'demon' is the *idea*, formed in the minds of a group of people *by consensus*, about the *independent existence* of a quality which they have agreed exists *in a particular person.* And indeed this is what a demon has always been.

Now an idea is a much more robust and durable phenomenon than a single person's hallucination. An idea can possess an entire continent quite easily.

If we ask ourselves, what kind of idea a demon is, we can see that it is always defined in opposition to an 'original state'. This is exemplified and epitomised by the myth in Christianity and Islām of the Adversary (Satan), who can only exist in opposition to the Original One. But the same is true of all demons, even the most seemingly minor.

In our initial example the formulation of the demon, the Prompter of the abuse, is formulated for one reason: to restore the false idea of the original purity of the Church. If it were not important to reinstate this illusion of purity, there would be no reason to invoke this *other thing*, this *invader which led them to lose control*. The invention of a demon is, in fact, always the invention of an exoneration *in potentia*. It need not be an achievable exorcism if what is to be exonerated is not the individual but a group to which they belong – because in such a case the separation between the entity to be exonerated (here the Church) and the 'psychological aspect' of the individual's mind is large enough for them not to be associated in the view of the all-important onlookers. In our example, even if the 'homosexual priests' involved cannot be 'cured'[402], the entity of the Church is nevertheless exonerated. This vividly establishes again that the 'demon' is the idea established by the consensus, rather than a mere psychological delusion in the priests themselves. The fact that the actual sexuality of the priests is irrelevant but that their perceived sexuality is crucial demonstrates that this is a *public phenomenon*. If everyone can be convinced that the Prompter to Child-rape (with two horns and a tail) has leapt into homosexuals, then the Church had merely been *temporarily affected*, possessed for a time. Subsequent pursuit of the Prompter appropriate to this typically overheated system would be to make a noisy public show of anti-homosexual pronouncements. If the exorcism of the Church herself needs finishing off more convincingly, the representative heuristic we have already considered, that psychological tendency to experience similarity of form as resonance of power, will mean that the most effective measure will be expulsion of homosexuals from the Church. Obviously these are not skills the Church needs to learn anew.

One could not wish for a clearer example of what is in fact a much more pervasive activity than we generally realise. My reason for introducing it is not to talk about 'homosexuality in the Church', which I find so uncontroversial as to be quite stupefying, but to investigate what modern theologians call 'difficulties' (such as the fact that faith in the Christian doctrines can be destroyed by reasoning), because in their reaction to them they are destroying language, and with it the means for communication, very broadly.

We have in the course of our survey seen various examples of theologians redefining words. The fact that their arguments achieve their full stops *when their audience are relieved* should warns us that something is amiss, something very similar to the reason our devotees will have been relieved by the Cardinal's elegant exorcism of their Church. In both cases all the evil which fostered the crime/difficulty remains unchanged in actuality. But superficially it may be, something seems to have changed, and because of cognitive biases there

---

402 This will be especially likely if they are not homosexual, of course.

are ways of guaranteeing that the group you want to convince will be convinced by that superfice.

For example, thanks to their reshuffling of words such that refraining from applying reason beyond the point at which faith is undermined can be called 'rationalism'[403], they can create a consensus conviction that the 'God' doctrine has been cleared of that 'difficult' quality, so 'unfairly' ascribed to it from certain quarters, namely total irrationality. And just as our cardinal had to identify a quality ('call the name of the demon') to which to ascribe the fault of which the children were victims and still are, we would expect in the case of theology to find qualities ('demons') to which to ascribe 'God' 's faults. In the oldest and crudest theology this was straightforwardly Satan. In modern theology the operation is performed much more subtly but no less magically. 'Irrationality' is separated from 'God', and among those straining for such reinstatement of purity it is done with real success, even though *it is only done in the words.* The success depends on simultaneously using the words rationalism and irrationality in their old sense, and asserting that they have a new sense whereby 'God' has become 'rational'. Unfortunately this tactic succeeds only so long as the original meanings of the words linger in our minds[404], and depends on destroying that very meaning.

Thus it is that the devout yearners breathe a sigh of relief, while the rest of us may well gasp, as 'God' is restored to being 'reasonable'. Language might seem to *some* a small sacrifice to make, and that is why what is being done should be made very clear *to the rest.* Orwell, intentionally designing Newspeak, could not match what modern 'thinkers' in theology are engaged in, and for that reason I would describe their output as *defiling.* However, unless they, their discourse, and their cronies, are to separate any further than they already have from harsh reality, it behoves us not to make the old mistake of retribution: we shall not match them in 'calling the demon's name' and burning their books but instead, however wearily it must be, we shall engage, as we have in this example, with the bilge that they spew in order to maintain some sense of what the concepts they would magically wish otherwise actually imply for their beliefs.

---

403 (Peterson, Hasker, Reichenbach, & Basinger, 2008)

404 To convince ourselves of this point we need only ask what the advantage of saying 'God is rational' will be when the day comes that the word rational has come to apply in everyone's minds quite naturally to white nights, hot ice and homosexual heterosexuals. That day may not be far away.

Case: desperate impeccability (after Muḥammad)

Nowadays it is common to read of the 'reasons' why Muslim countries seem to be backward in so many ways compared to the 'infidel' countries: it is a divinely ordained test, or a punishment, or a (very slowly) passing phase, or a period of training in asceticism, or a way to get Islām to the infidels via economic migration – in short, everything except the suggestion that Islām itself might be responsible. One sees in these interpretations the kind of speculative philosophising we have already seen can magnificently mislead. But here we are more concerned with the motive – and it will not require much investigation to see that here it is to rescue the tradition from disrepute, because in this way the tradition-rescuers rescue themselves from disrepute by association.

To take another example, Islāmic terrorism is usually presented by Muslims as totally unconnected with Islām and its denial of religions' validity except its own. This is Antony Flew's *'no true Scotsman' fallacy* in action.

> Imagine Hamish McDonald, a Scotsman, sitting down with his *Glasgow Morning Herald* and seeing an article about how the 'Brighton Sex Maniac Strikes Again.' Hamish is shocked and declares that, 'No Scotsman would do such a thing.' The next day he sits down to read his Glasgow Morning Herald again and this time finds an article about an Aberdeen man whose brutal actions make the Brighton sex maniac seem almost gentlemanly. This fact shows that Hamish was wrong in his opinion but is he going to admit this? Not likely. This time he says, 'No *true* Scotsman would do such a thing.'[405]

Increasingly the connection with 'true Islām' is denied even in non-Muslim countries out of (fearful, or 'diplomatic', or 'politically correct') deference, but not by the 'lions' themselves, who are less concerned with such 'diplomacy':

> We have carried out the sentence of Allāh against 12 Nepalis who came from their country to fight the Muslims and to serve the Jews and the Christians... believing in Buddha as their god.[406]

---

405 (Flew, 1975)

406 When they posted the clip of their beheading with a knife and shooting of 12 Nepali cooks in August 2004, the military wing of the Helpers of the [Muhammadan] Law (Ansār al-Sunna) issued this as their official statement. (Ansār was the name given to the

One exceptional case where this refusal of reality faltered was in the reaction of some Arab Muslims to the Beslan massacre in the month following the beheading and shooting of the Nepalis. Although many quoted in the media produced the expected condemnation of the attack as 'unIslāmic', or Israeli, and the Grand Sheikh of Al-Azhar said, 'You are taking Islām as a cover and it is a deceptive cover; those who carry out the kidnappings are criminals, not Muslims,' there were voices, at last, of dissent from this perennial denial. Certain

> commentators asked unusually soul-searching questions about the region and terrorism. […]
>
> Abdulrahman al-Rashed wrote an article in the pan-Arab Asharq Al-Awsat newspaper under the headline: 'The Painful Truth: All World Terrorists are Muslims!'
>
> Al-Rashed said that Muslims will not be able to *cleanse their image*[407] unless 'we admit the scandalous facts... Our terrorist sons are an end-product of our corrupted culture. The picture is *humiliating*, painful and harsh for all of us.'
>
> His extraordinary critique was echoed by Ahmed Bahgat, an Egyptian Islāmist. Writing in the pro-government newspaper, Al-Ahram, he said hostage-takers in Russia and Iraq are only *harming Islām.* 'If all the enemies of Islām united and decided to harm it... they wouldn't have ruined and harmed *its image* as much as the sons of Islām have done by their stupidity, miscalculations and misunderstanding.' Horrifying *images* of the dead and wounded students '*showed* Muslims *as* monsters who are fed by the blood of children and the pain of their families'.[408]

---

people of Yathrib who helped the Prophet and the first Muslims when they fled persecution in Makkah. The Law in question is the one which Sunnite Muslims follow – the imitation of the Prophet's manners.) Presumably, concerned about their internation reputation, they were too ashamed of their poor, troubled backgrounds, or of their national allegiances, or of whatever else has been cited other than religion as motivation for their act, to mention that.

407 Italics mine: although it seems a step in the right direction to make the admission, we should note the concern to prevent such attacks is quite overwhelmed by the concern to clear the *disrepute*. This is utterly typical. The subsequent expressions I have italicised are similarly due to this concern.

408 (Smith, 2004) One notes that the principal agony still seems to lie in Islam's

Although the utopian imbalance of modern Islāmism is probably more related to post-Christian secularist ideological movements such as revolutionary Communism and charismatic Fascism than to historical Islām, the latter has certainly not been free of cognitive dissonance and its consequences.

In the Qur'ān Allāh tells Muḥammad to

> Say: 'O mankind! I am sent unto you all as the Messenger of Allāh, to whom belongs the dominion of the heavens and the earth.'[409]

This is another example of an ambiguity of language (present in the English as much as the Arabic in this case) which represents quite well a certain trend of Muslim thought. While the language ambiguity would be denied by the orthodox teachers, who would insist the 'whom' refers to the deity, some of them nevertheless argue that what the misreading implies, that Muḥammad has been chosen as an emperor over the earth, is a quite acceptable view.

Because of Islām's prizing of Muḥammad as unique in his dual role as alone in having access to his 'god', both at his time (according to him there were no other 'messengers of the god' alive at that time, and the messages of all the previous 'messengers' had, according to him, been so corrupted as to render them in need of correction by his) and for all time (insofar as the uncorruptedness of his 'message' remains, and there were, according to him, no more 'messengers' to come in the future – i.e. any 'messenger' after him would be an impostor) Islām is the most extreme of all religions I know in its externalisation of the deity. This is true even though, as in Christianity, the Islāmic tradition has included many claims of later prophecy (such as Bahā'ullāh, whose revelation became the foundation of the Bahā'i religion) and even more attempts to make the deity available to the people (in Sufism, especially the extreme exemplified by Hallāj, who wrote he would destroy all mosques and asserted in various ways that there was no room for both identity allegiance and 'Allāh'): because the reaction of the orthodox has been to suppress these attempts.

Circumstances, mainly political, have often favoured the more orthodox strain of Islām in its history. The consequences, as they are described in the Islāmic historical literature, are appropriately extreme. In its progress through

---

reputation having been tarnished rather than the fate of the children and their families, but it is a step towards reality at least. Unfortunatey since those singular reports of breast-beating I have seen no further similar recognition in the Arab media.

[409] Qur'ān 7, 158 (part). Allāh is telling Muḥammad to say this.

North Africa and eastwards to India, Islām stole sacredness from all humanity and awarded it all to Muḥammad. It stole sacredness from all places and awarded it all to the places of Muḥammad's life. It stole sacredness from all words and awarded it all to Muḥammad's words (which are either 'the words of Allāh' or 'the words most perfectly interpreting the words of Allāh'). So when Islām arrived in a country, previous spiritual experience was denied and referred to in the worst terms – 'Ignorance', or the heresy of believing in incarnation (in Arabic, ḥulūliyya, which is never applied to mimicry of Muḥammad), or the unpardonable sin of sharing out worship (in Arabic shirk, although it was usually the invaders who were effectively insisting on shirk by bringing their alien deity into the religions of the conquered nations). Those who demonstrated spiritual accomplishment were described using the very same entirely disdainful vocabulary used in Muḥammad's time during the destruction of the Arab religions in order to sustain the belief that Muḥammad's spiritual accomplishment was unique (for his time and for all time): the others were, according to this new assessment, merely 'soothsayers' (kahana) or 'impostors' (kādhibūn), or worse. Those places considered previously powerful by association with spiritual experience were assailed as the locale of idolatry in order to sustain the belief in the unique power of places associated with Muḥammad's spiritual experience. Those scriptures transmitting spiritual experience were condemned, without a hint of critical thinking, as 'alteration' or 'invention' depending on whether they were believed to be earlier or later than Muḥammad's scripture, in order to sustain the belief in the unique capacity for spiritual transmission of Muḥammad's scripture.

It is analogous to an invading king appropriating a country's property then accusing its inhabitants of his own crime, theft, if they dare to claim their own as their own. There again we see the ventriloquist's manoeuvre, but operating on a massive scale. To anyone who has known of the spiritual experiences of mankind, the spiritual power of places and the spiritual transmission of scriptures, the arrival of this orthodox, politically manipulated 'Islām' signals the destruction of spiritual experience, the destruction of spiritual places, and the destruction of sacred communication. Even to describe this process as theft would be flattery since it would imply that the positive qualities were somehow transferred to this 'Islām', which, other than in the Sufi movements, they resoundingly were not.

In Islāmic treatises on the 'opened' (Arabic maftūḥ, a euphemism for conquered and in some cases for enslaved) countries there is a perceptible rush to explain away any qualities of their inhabitants which would otherwise threaten the perceived superiority of the invading 'religion'.

The idea of this superiority is not restricted to such political imperialism: even in the light of what might be considered the most sympathetic treatment of other religions by far in the entire Islāmic literature[410], a text famed as the first 'non-apologetic' work on comparitive religion, it is pointed out that the admittedly exalted ethics of Buddhism are *wasted* since their rejection of *prophets* and prophecy places them among 'the covered over', the infidels. Yet the prophets referred to are of course those that Muḥammad spoke of, principally himself; Islām's attitude to the books of prophecy which form a significant division of the canonical texts of Buddhism, for example, is not mentioned, presumably because these prophecies were not spoken by Muḥammad and so needed to be conveniently overlooked. The same book has, instead of Brahmā the Hindus' creator god, reference to 'Burhum',[411] who (we are told) is an ancestor (sic) they worship – even the doctrine of a creator god is denied them; is the fact that its acceptance would detract from Muḥammad as the locus a coincidence?

All claims about the justice of this destruction relate without one exception to the perceived reputation of the invading king. The sins against spirituality committed by Islām can only be seen in proportion to one's willingness to concede blemishes on the reputation of the supreme authority of Islām.

For a Muslim who feels unable (because of the strong identification with the entirety of Islām, itself encouraged by education and sermons and the valuation of authority) to condemn these episodes of Islām's history, the invading king (inextricably associated with Muḥammad, who is by the Qur'ān inextricably associated with Allāh) must be of perfect repute, absolutely unblemished. If he were not, through strong identification with this king, our observer of history would feel personally responsible for the entire history of destruction, and it has been long and horrible. Such a danger is felt as a personal threat. The more information which is made available about the history of Islām, the more urgent

[410] Al-Shahrastāni (479-548 h.)'s *Kitāb al-Milal wal-Nihal, the Book of Religious Communities and Sects* (Al-Shahrastani, 1366-1375/1947-1955).

[411] This odd distortion of the internal vowels of the name of the creator god Brahmā reminds me, likely not by coincidence, of the Jews' alteration of the name of one of Yahweh's rival deities, Malech ('The King') according to the vowels of the Hebrew word for 'abomination' such that it became the now familiar Moloch, to which the Yahwehists said worshippers sacrificed their own children.

this necessity to maintain the king's unblemished reputation becomes.

And here we arrive at a point of crucial understanding. The fervour with which such a self-identifying Muslim must insist on the impeccable honour of their king, a fervour which is patent and tangible to all who deal with Muslims and informs a great deal of events in current affairs relating to Muslims today, is a reflection not of the king's righteousness but of his *guilt.* It is exactly because the king has wrought so much damage that their quality of righteous justice must be insisted on. And whereas the Church need exorcise demons only from itself, because Islām outlawed intercession such that all believers could equally connect to the deity, it becomes incumbent on *the entire Umma* ('people') of Islām to exorcise itself of its demons.

Once again we see that the psychotic break between discourses (in this case political Islām's internal discourse of its own historical impeccability, and the *ultra partem*, according to which there has been appropriation and destruction of sacredness as described above) is absolutely fundamental to their continuation. It is the very ambiguity of events – such as the destruction of the Arabian religions – interpreted with such wild difference (purification or catastrophe) which stokes the fires of perpetuation of the two respective blazing languages of those two interpretations. Just as we have seen in the discussion of the degeneration of symbols, this process both ensures the longevity of the symbol (the impeccability of Islām) and also leads inexorably to the complete divorce of the symbol from its original meaning, until we have the situation today where Muslims within Islām's internal discourse of Islām's impeccability perform acts in their eyes demonstrative of their allegiance to that impeccability, supportive of it, indignant and outraged at its defamation, but which within alternative discourses appear as demonstrations exactly of Islām's sinfulness.

This breakdown between the discourses has now surpassed the comic and entered the infamous, with, for example, champions of Muḥammad performing murder by means of bombs in order to demonstrate that associating murder by means of bombs with Muḥammad is unjust. A popular Muslim apologist for Islām, Wahiduddin Khan, whose presentation of it is always extremely liberal, can write in his 2009 study of terrorism and Islām,

> The Qur'ān emphasises the formation of one's character [...] Nowhere does it enjoin the believer to engage in violence, leading to the destruction of human beings.[412]

---

[412] (Khan, 2009, p. 16)

Most people nowadays are aware of such verses in that scripture as the infamous –

> Fa'idhā -nsalaḥa –l-'ashhuru –l-ḥurumu fā -qtulū -l-mushrikīn ḥaythu wajadtumūhum…[413]

> When the sacred months have passed, kill the polytheists wherever you find them…

…so they can help me discover which of Mr Khan's criteria the Qur'ān here has failed to meet: is it that the plural imperative uqtulu, 'kill', does not imply violence – were the Muslims being instructed to kill the polytheists with an overdose of anaesthetic delivered in their drinks? Or was it perhaps, as many of Islām's more vocal advocates might well argue, that the polytheists in question (who were at the time viciously persecuting the Muslims) were not human beings? Or is Mr Khan, alternatively, and rashly, advertising his concurrence with certain historians, vilified in Muslim countries for daring to suggest that many who joined Islām only did so out of political expediency (and left again when the expediency was defunct on the prophet's death), such that the audience of this verse were not 'believers', and the verse is ordering *hypocrites* to kill? The only other solution to this riddle would be that this verse were indeed located 'nowhere', such that it would be just to say, 'Nowhere does the Qur'ān enjoin…' If only that were true.

In the same book he quotes the earliest extant biography[414] of the Messenger of Allāh several times, for example, in his chapter entitled 'A Prophet of Peace':

> 'Muhammad said, "God is peace, peace is from Him, and peace returns to Him."'[415]

And he says that 'the secrets of the Prophet's extraordinary success lay […] also in the *entirely peaceful methods* which he adopted' and that the revolution he led was '*bloodless*'. The same biography says:

> He confined them in Madīna […]. Then the Messenger of Allāh went

413 This is the beginning of verse 5 of the 9th chapter of the Qur'ān.

414 (Ibn Hisham, c 218 h./1355 CE/1937 CE)

415 (Khan, 2009, p. 28)

> out to the market […] and dug trenches in it. Then he sent for them and struck off their heads in those trenches as they were brought out to him in batches. […] There were 600 or 700 in all, though some put the figure as high as 800 or 900. […] This went on until the Messenger of Allāh made an end of them. Huyayy […] went to the men and said, 'Allāh's command is right. A book and a decree, and massacre have been written against the Sons of Israel.' Then he sat down and his head was struck off.

Are we to believe that those fruity antisemitic taunts were right all along and these Jews (the treacherous Banī Qurayẓa) were indeed bloodless? Or is it that Ibn Hishām's biography should not be relied on – in which case Mr Khan's reliance on it in four of his chapters is rather awkward? What is most disturbing is not so much that such passages as this exist in the Islāmic 'scriptures' and that those same 'scriptures' are still relied on (after all this mass beheading, for example, was what even modern historians like to call 'good statesmanship' given the prophet's political situation at the time), but that a 'scholar' as popular as Khan is *knows* about such passages but *does not allude to them* even in a book about terrorism. Furthermore *he knows* that the very fighters and bombers whose 'misinterpretation' of Islām his book looks like a noble effort to correct *also* know such passages – *yet he does not allude to them.* That is not just confirmation bias.

It is hard to conceive even in wildest fantasy how much more perfectly two discourses could maintain mutual separation than in this example of the struggle to maintain Muḥammad's and by extension the Umma's impeccability. In terms of the reactive, conceptual neurosis, we have reached the full stop at the end of the sentence. In that dark point, the point of 'except Muḥammad...'[416], two groups have locked horns in eternal mutual misunderstanding.

It is imperative to see, as I hope our treatment of the treacheries to which our decision-making process can succumb has revealed, that such bizarre disparities are a natural occurrence to which all of us, but all, are potentially susceptible. In the case of political Islām, the tendency of the *ultra partem* has been increasingly to assign blame. By now I hope it is clear that trying to exorcise humanity of individuals even by the over-respected judicial process, solves nothing and adds a great deal to the problem. It is the tendency to assign blame

---

[416] The Arabic 'ilā rasūl allāh' is a slogan demanding that the Messenger of Allāh be excepted. It has been much used in the ongoing aftermath of the Danish caricatures fiasco.

which perhaps above all fuels the fire of these runaway conceptual blazes. Only the security and 'construction' companies benefit: if intelligence were measured by lucrative success, then they alone are intelligent these days, and we should not be surprised if it is they and their friends who do the loudest naming of demons. If we wish for nobler successes then once and for all we must put paid to the august notion that refraining from blaming is some kind of lily-livered nicety superseded by the practical necessity of applying the 'lesser evil' of blaming, judging, sentencing and punishing. Instead let us turn to what supersedes that.

Stage 3: The Buddha's Summons to Free Inquiry

> 'It is [...] when you know *for yourselves,* – that particular things are unskilful; that these things are censurable; that these things are scorned by the wise; and that these things, when adopted and carried out, convert into loss and suffering – that you should abandon them. [...] It is [...] when you know for yourselves, – that particular things are *skilful*; that these things are *un*censurable; that these things are *praised* by the wise; and that these things, when adopted and carried out, convert into *profit* and *bliss* – that you should *undertake* and *abide* by them.
>
> 'What do you think, Kālāmās?'

My commentary here will explore 3 considerations:

- the focus of inquiry,
- the nature of the inquiry (p. 408), and
- its congruence with the solution's main point and the exhortations (p. 410).

The Focus of Inquiry

Here I consider:

- the focus in summary,
- its relation to the Buddha's objective,
- the focus in detail

The Focus in Summary

The original question, it may be recalled, was how to know, when presented with the words of the visiting preachers, which of them were *truthful* and which of them were *false.* The Buddha has, however, limited the question to truthfulness or falsehood about about four issues:

1. skilfulness,
2. censurability,
3. praiseworthiness to the wise, and
4. conversion into profit and bliss if adopted and practised.

He reduces this to a single criterion:

conversion into profit rather than loss.

The Buddha invites the Kālāmās to consider five ways long-term loss and suffering might be incurred:

1. by killing other living beings
2. by taking what has not been given
3. by resorting to others' spouses
4. by speaking falsehoods

5. by provoking others to do these

Its Relation to the Buddha's Objective

We can notice straight away that the Buddha has very much narrowed the consideration from what might have been a 'toolkit for recognising truth and falsity' in general. He focuses instead on *practical matters.*

We have already considered what the visiting spiritual teachers had been teaching, to which the Kālāmās' question relates, and some of it was clearly very fanciful indeed. Here as usual the Buddha does not appear to be any kind of metaphysician, any kind of philosopher contemplating the nature of, and honing, an abstract philosophy, as he is frequently imagined to be by those unfamiliar with what he taught. This practical emphasis is quite in keeping with the fact that he began his exhortations with 'ma anussava' – i.e. to recognise mediated knowledge (such as an abstract philosophy must be, since it can be entirely communicated in ideas from one to another) as *irrelevant* as a source of certainty.

The Focus in Detail

The 4 criteria for adopting and abiding by a particular form rather than abandoning it

Skilful rather than unskilful

Obviously we are not talking about skills in general, such as how to fix a car or how to jump between two trapezes. The Pali word kusala is what has come to be translated often as 'virtuous'. However the origin of the word virtue is shared with virility and heroism. It referred to the chivalry of the knight, manliness as cherished by a patriarchal society. To condemn a way of acting as unskilful, on the other hand, means to accuse it of not achieving its goals effectively. For example, if the goal is to fix the car, kicking it is clearly an unskilful way of proceeding. What goal is being referred to here?

All sentient beings wish to be happy, yet through not understanding, they abandon the causes of happiness. All sentient beings wish to be free of suffering, yet through not understanding, they grasp onto the causes of suffering.

The Buddha was called Siddhārtha, meaning Achiever (Siddha) of the Goal (Artha). The great goal of his life was first conceived by him according to the records in the scriptures of the Individual Career (Hināyāna) when as a young prince he was accidentally exposed to the 'four sights'.

This goal he exemplified as his 'Great Complete Extinction', the utter extinction of his own suffering and causes of potential suffering for himself. Succinctly we can say, then, that according to the Individual Career the goal is, naturally enough, individual happiness.

According to the interpretations made in the scriptures of the Universal Career (Mahāyāna), a Great Extinction Without Remainder has not yet been accomplished, since there are still others suffering in cyclic existence. So the final goal can be identified as the entirety of cyclic existence being liberated from suffering and the causes of suffering, which goal is in fact what trainees in the Universal Career vow to reach. In brief, then, according to the Universal Career, the goal is universal happiness.

In the various traditions of the Secret Mantra Career (Guhyamantrayāna), the final goal is the attainment of the two kinds of Accomplishment (siddhī), the Supreme Accomplishment being the same as the Universal Vehicle's total liberation, and the lesser Accomplishments being powers which are uniquely the result of various secret tantric practices and which can be employed in the acceleration of the gain of the Supreme Accomplishment. So, again, the goal is universal happiness.

While he did claim to have discovered something above and beyond the other spiritual seekers of his time, namely the lasting happiness, or, the utter extinction of suffering and its causes, the Buddha neither claimed to be the first or last to have done so (in all traditions' records he mentioned by name at least three prior exemplars of the utter extinction), nor did he hold that he alone among those contemporary seekers had attained any greater happiness. In all traditions it is recorded that others attained what we might call the lesser goal, of *non-lasting* states of happiness. In the Buddhist scriptures the term skilful is also used with reference to this goal, common to all spiritual traditions.

So the goal in reference to which the Buddha uses the words skilful and unskilful is, as we might say, the fundamental one. Although it is 'the Buddhist goal', it is actually nothing exotic, simply the one which underpins every other goal we (Buddhists or non-Buddhists) devise, if it not indeed our recognised primary goal, namely, *to be happy*.

Uncensurable rather than censurable

As the saying goes you can't please everyone all of the time. Whatever you do, somebody somewhere is going to find reason to complain. The censure referred to here is not from anyone, then. And unlike the next criterion, its source is not mentioned as being someone else at all: it seems likely that the Buddha meant that each person individually should judge whether an act deserved her or his censure. And given that presumably all of them want to be happy, then we are not surprised to find that their answers to this criterion match their answers to the previous one.

Praised by the wise rather than scorned by them

Much has been made (notably by certain doctors of the Elders' School) of the fact that this stage of the inquiry by invoking (as they have seen it) the authority of 'the wise' shows that it is wrong to take the Buddha's earlier critique of relying on a teacher too far. Since their challenge seems to require assuming that the Buddha earlier made a mistake, it is worth taking care to understand these seemingly contradictory statements.

We have already seen that the Buddha categorically denies that any certainty can be claimed on the basis of expert figures or allegiance to a particular teacher. Is he now telling the Kālāmā people, 'Actually, come to think of it, you do need to rely on wise people to be certain after all.'? Anyone familiar with the discourses of the Buddha in the Pali scriptures will be aware of how meticulously consistent the Buddha appears to be in them. We can be sure that the Buddha was not flatly contradicting himself.

Was he asking them whether people they believed to be wiser than themselves would scorn or praise? To answer this we can first of all notice how ill it melds with the earlier critique of authority chains; furthermore we should not overlook the fact that this is the third in a list of four criteria, and the other three invoke no such authority. In addition, we can guarantee that all the visiting divines and ascetics considered themselves to be wiser than the Kālāmā people: is the Buddha asking them to resort to such visitors in order to decide among those same visitors? Clearly not.

The few Elders' School doctors who have drawn attention to this criterion have claimed that it is the get-out clause for the Buddha's own authority and justifies their own faith in him as an infallible teacher. They have claimed that the Kālāmā people were beginners, mere 'laity', and that this is why the Buddha reassured them with the critique of certainty based on teacher-reliance, but that more advanced practitioners, such as they are themselves, do attain the exalted level of total faith in the Buddha as infallible, which allows them to progress even further on the path.

Given that the Buddha here, in Kesaputta, is in his own appreciation addressing only the Kālāmā people, and not, I think we can safely presume, imagining his immortal words echoing down the centuries in the form of scriptures such that he might feel the need to change his words accordingly, then we might ask: why would he mention what is necessary for 'advanced practitioners' to such 'beginners', or – to allude to another dichotomy perhaps over-emphasised in countries where the Elders' School predominates – why mention what is necessary for 'the ordained' to 'the laity'? Is the Buddha saying, 'Imagine what I would say as the wise person that you would have to believe in without question as an ordained member of my community'?

It seems quite clear that 'the wise' referred to here are the Kālāmā people themselves: they are being urged to assume the vantage of a certain degree of care and awareness. This, unlike the claims for the re-validation of external authority, seems completely in keeping with the rest of the discourse. Even if 'the wise' refers to a subset of the Kālāmā community, this is only one of four criteria, and so, in keeping with the earlier critique, the authority of those wise ones cannot be taken as a final authority, that is to say this is not grounds for certainty in itself. This point is underlined by the last criterion:

Converting into profit and bliss rather than loss and suffering if adopted and practised

This seems to be an expansion of the first criterion, which the Kālāmās answered rather peremptorily. Why would the Buddha repeat a question that has already been answered? Is it just for poetic effect, or the extra persuasive power through repetition he criticised earlier in his discourse? Probably not. It would seem to reflect a sense that there should be deeper consideration. The Buddha refers particularly to practice now. He is asking the Kālāmā people to make a judgment about their own experience, and seems to be implying by the repetition and expansion, '*Look more closely.*'

It is crucial to note that the Buddha does not commend or condemn their answers to these questions. He simply re-iterates the ten-fold critique, and the call for them to take individual responsibility. They answer very much as the should, of course, and we might feel that they got off rather lightly.

But the Buddha does not say, 'Well done! You answered correctly! You are on the right path!' He instead encourages them to reflect again on the power of the ten sources of knowledge to deceive. And he encourages them again to be sincere with themselves, to choose with integrity, to be truly and maximally responsible.

The single criterion: leading to benefit or harm

The fact that they can be subsumed into one criterion suggests forcibly that the Buddha did not imagine that any one of the four criteria would lead to a judgment which differed from those to which the others led.

The five ways long-term loss might be incurred

In the course of the investigation through which the Buddha gently leads the Kālāmās, he invites them to look behind what were acts they all took without question to be crimes – to ask why such crimes might happen, what factors within the criminal drive them. As we shall see he suggests three or four possible factors. The crimes mentioned as their potential consequences are the same for each of the potential motivating factors the Buddha invites them to assess:

> 'And thus [with a particular motivating factor…] Kālāmās, does not a person overcome by [that factor], with their mind possessed by [that factor], kill a living being, or take what is not given, or go after another person's spouse, or tell lies, or induce others to do such things, such that there will long be loss and suffering?'
>
> 'Yes, sir.'

We can see straight away that these crimes are all among those we saw earlier were generally taught as ethical breaches by religious teachers of the Buddha's time, as recorded in that section of *The Brahmā Net Discourse* recording the issues on which the Buddha does not contrast himself with other teachers. At the same time the crimes the Buddha is referring to here are more specific than those refraining from which constitutes that general good behaviour: he is giving examples only, and striking ones. For example, in the matter of sexual morality, we saw that most teachers seemed to agree that it was important not to indulge in 'illegitimate sexual relations'. Here he mentions just one: sex with another person's spouse. Refraining from the fifth one here, inciting others to do such acts, is included in the general good behaviour under speech which does not cause division or conflict.

Furthermore the first four of these are also the first four of the five unskilful acts from which laymen and laywomen vow to refrain according to the Buddhist tradition. The fifth of those, not referred to here, is taking intoxicants such as alcohol.

Killing other life

It should be noted that any life is referred to – not just human, and certainly not just Buddhist, much less a particular kind of Buddhist. We can contrast this with niceties of other religions' 'laws', where the law is often only considered to apply to the life of other members of the same faith, and in any case many exceptions are made for special circumstances such as 'defensive' wars.

Taking what has not been offered

Once again this is a broader scope than mere theft, which only applies to property and its removal and dissimulation of its whereabouts: in contrast this would even applies to borrowing things without asking.

Resorting to others' spouses

This phrase is the typical and euphemistic expression meaning what we call 'adultery': we are not talking about resorting to them for advice.

Speaking falsehoods

Given that there seems to have been a shift in consensus about the gravity of this offence (and some nowadays and in some societies especially would argue that it is not an offence at all) we should bear in mind that the Buddha is using it as an example which he imagined his audience all thought was unacceptable.

Encouraging others to do these things

Consensus seems to have changed on the gravity of this 'offence' too. Incitement to murder we still consider as an offence. But incitement to lie? Once again, we should therefore bear in mind in the subsequent investigation that it is given by the Buddha in the context of the things that are so bad the Kalamas are unlikely to disagree about them.

Aside: silent speech

It is crucial not to overlook the implications in the Buddha including this fifth potential road to long-term harm and suffering. We are accustomed to thinking of 'speech' in a limited way, but with a modicum of wit we quickly observe that not speaking can be a form of speech, and that often criminals need no more encouragement than silence. The Buddha himself, for example, is often recorded to have 'assented by his silence'.

As we mentioned in the introduction, certain teachers from the traditional Theravāda Buddhist societies have insisted that the suggestions that the Buddha makes in this discourse not be taken 'out of context', by which they mean what they see is a restricted context, that of beginners asking questions about basic spiritual practices, and applying them, or as they see extrapolating them, to a broader context such as the non-religious social sphere. We saw that one claimed that the discourse itself does not support such an 'extension' of the points.

This seems, I would venture to suggest, to reflect a bias due to their own circumstances as monastics, and so I would recommend that they take to heart what the Buddha advised earlier in the discourse: that we should not be misled by intuitively favouring particular views. It is an undeniable fact that we are a social species, and that our actions of body and speech have great consequence not just for ourselves but for others. And this is even true of monastics, though their daily lives do not reinforce their awareness of this fact: when you are continually divided from the laity, and again we note that in some countries where the Elders' School has long predominated the ordained-laity divide is very pronounced, it is not so easy to recognise the effect your physical example might be having across the divide.

That is not to say that other Buddhist traditions should congratulate themselves. We should be very cautious about attributing this 'living in a bubble' tendency to particular schools of Buddhism on the basis, for example, that they are 'deficient' in the teachings on universal caring that other schools have developed very extensively: that this 'neglect across the monastic-lay' divide is a perennial danger in all schools of Buddhism is highlighted by the decline of all of them in the land of the traditions' birth – effected, most scholars now agree, principally by the loss of the patronage of the laity, who had come to see the monastics as irrelevant. Exiled Tibetan monasteries, for example, often in non-Buddhist areas, where the developed teachings on great caring are regularly taught – to monastics – are frequently surrounded by squalour, beggary, and local resentment at their seeming opulence, and post security guards at their gates.

To return to the discourse, while all of the other harmful ways mentioned are at least potentially avoidable by *rejecting society and retreating into solitude*, this one, encouraging others, is not. For in our society, which is so heavily involved in all these roads to harm right down to the roots, not using one's power to reduce some of these harmful ways of behaving constitutes encouraging others to engage in them. Our tendency to see this as a lesser evil is known in cognitive science as '*omission bias*' and, as public apathy, it was a major factor in the rise of the Nazi Party and its less savoury activities such as the Holocaust in Germany last century: although refraining from a particular action is itself an action, we rarely see it as such. So by refraining from action to reduce harm we are in fact harming. Whilst we should not slip into the error of regular and crude public praise and blame of various kinds of action, given that as we saw this can lead to respectability getting distorted and losing its relevance to actual benefit, we should be aware of our power to influence others, even by not acting, and deploy them skilfully.

Besides the action by omission, there is an effect by the implicit condemnation of society too. The disappearance into the mountains of people training in reducing their personal tendency to harm definitively constitutes an encouragement to those who would engage more in harming, since it helps to encourage what is already a strong tendency to feel hopeless about society, as if one were saying, 'Society is beyond help: you harmers are welcome to it.' We have already considered how that kind of mentality can become a kind of self-fulfilling prophecy.

Writing in the light of this discourse and others which present similar recommendations (such as *The Sammādiṭṭhi Sutta* and *Ambalaṭṭhikā Rāhulovāda Sutta*) one philosopher of ethics stresses this social element:

> In the Pāli Nikāyas, the consideration of the wholesomeness or unwholesomeness of actions of external bodily and verbal actions (moral realism) and internal mental actions (virtue ethics) is to be supplemented by the consideration of the consequences of actions for the happiness of oneself and others (utilitarianism).[417]

Defenders of the abandonment of society might well ask the question:

> Why should an ascetic or a priest, having attained a wholesome state of

---

417 (Velez de Cea, 2004)

mind, bother about others who will be of no use to him?

Well, this turns out to have been the very question posed to the Buddha by a priest of the majority religion of the day, a man named Lohikka[418]. In response the Buddha compares this advocacy of spiritual meanness to a recommendation that the king take the enjoyment of the country's entire revenues and produce for his own personal enjoyment. He asks Lohikka if people making such a recommendation would improve the safety of themselves or others under the king's powers, and Lohikka concedes that on the contrary they would be endangering themselves and others. By means of the Buddha's subsequent questions, Lohikka concedes that these would be people unsympathetic to others' welfare, and therefore that they must have hearts set in enmity rather than amity towards them, and that therefore such a recommendation is not a sound one.

In the same discourse the Buddha says that, on the contrary, a sound teacher will instruct others in good ways, for example the same four mental residences of purity that he considers in our discourse later.

The Nature of the Inquiry

This is in two parts:

- the responsibility one should take, and
- that for which one should take responsibility.

The Responsibility One Should Take

When you know for yourselves…

This is a radical, dramatic, and highly unusual call to take personal responsibility.

Ethical superiority to other religious vocations

Compare this call with, for example, the call of the theistic religions, which is in fact a call to *be taken responsibility for* by God, so long as you accept the responsibility of worshipping Him. God will take responsibility for you: he will protect you, guide you, and guarantee all the happiness you could wish for – *post mortem* – if you play your part. He is even merciful, so flexible: if you commit even terrible faults on the one hand, but on the other devote yourself totally to

---

418 In *The Lohikka Sutta* of the Dīgha Nikāya.

Him and throw yourself on His mercy, then he may cancel the otherwise inevitable consequence of those faults.

In contrast the Buddha's call is to a fearsome height of ethical circumspection: to take the responsibility entirely upon oneself. Even if the choice be to worship God, the personal responsibility for taking such a choice must be admitted. And in this sense there is no mercy: we are not given the license to lose our integrity.

The Buddha sometimes described what kind of teacher he was and distinguished himself from certain other kinds. For example, in *The Discourse to Saṅgārava*[419] he says that some teachers teach oral traditions by recitation, some teach by means of faith, even arrived at by reasoning, but he teaches things which were not heard of before and discovered by himself.[420]

Centuries later, when Buddhists debated with non-Buddhists about the nature of reality, the Buddhists would say this in a different way: that if an event of having come to know something is to be considered true coming-to-know, it must be *fresh*. Unfortunately for English speakers, English is one of the few languages of the world in which the verb 'know' is always a *state* verb – in most languages it is an action. (For example, if someone asks you as you read this book, 'What are you doing?' as an English speaker you cannot reply, 'I am knowing the Kālāmā Sutta. In English we use the words 'learn', or 'discover', or 'realise', or the phrase 'come to know', to convey the action verb sense.) This is a very clear symptom of the 'modern' perversion of doubt into certainty we have now considered in detail. If reality is constantly changing, then the only true coming-to-know must be fresh. But to claim certainty the assumption of something unchanging must be made, and to come-to-know that would only be necessarily fresh once, at the beginning. Thereafter, not freshly coming-to-know, but merely knowing (the state), would be enough.

That for which one should take responsibility

For what? For each 'thing' (dhamma) we abandon or adopt and practice. Dhamma, notoriously tricky to translate into English with one word,

---

419 The hundredth of the Middle Length Discourse Collection.

420 This reminds me of the Sufist formulation of the three degrees of religious practitioner – muslim, mu'min and mukhlas: one who has accepted the tradition of submission, one who believes in what it teaches and one who has been made totally and unswayably convinced by reality. For such Sufists not to become mukhlis – that is one on the way to being mukhlas – is compared to being a car without an engine.

has a suite of meanings we should now go into.

Dhamma in Pali is dharma in Sanskrit. The root dhṛ means 'hold'. The word derives from the same Proto-Indo-European origin which gave us, via the phonetic change from dh to f, the English words form (think of good form in the sense of behaviour as well as more general forms as in shapes), firm (as in you can rely on it), and fast (from the past participle and meaning made firm).

It can mean religious form, in the sense of correct behavior. In this sense it is still used in Hinduism: the observances and fasts each caste has a responsibility to perform (or, to pay a priest to perform on their behalf) in order to secure divine favour. The Buddha used this same term for the laws of reality he discovered and revealed, in which bargaining with gods was replaced with dealing with reality, as it is, and without any aspect being missed, in order to achieve the goal of happiness, immediate and lasting.

However, probably through debate between contrasting views about what such laws were, and mutual criticism giving rise to the possibility of the expression 'unskilful dhamma', it was also used in philosophy to refer to any elements of that reality, any laws of phenomena but also any phenomena. In English the word form carries this sense better than any other single word. It has, however, been translated very often as 'qualities', since in English we say that qualities are 'held' by 'holders of qualities' – phenomena. It should be remembered however that the word has a strong connotation of good (and bad) behaviour.

Congruence with Earlier Answers

At first the minds of the Kālāmā people were involved in the ideas generated by the preachers. Their minds, we might say, were distracted, 'going out', narrowing their perspective to focus on particular phenomena. So the first step the Buddha made was to make them recognize the irrelevance of this kind of engagement. That is to say, he began with a kind of chastisement. Once the strings dragging and holding the Kālāmās minds outside had been cut, they fell back to 'earth', to 'the zero point': *to themselves.* Now the Buddha begins the positive expression to balance the earlier negative, the affirmation after the denial: ***know*** for yourselves.

Stage 4: The Buddha's Introduction to the Spiritual Path

Having sketched the methodological framework for the inquiry, we can now accompany the Buddha and the Kālāmās on the inquiry he invites them to make. He launches into a consideration of the processes which drive our skilful and unskilful actions of body, speech and mind.

The presentation is as follows:

- afflictive processes,
- freedom from them (p. 451), and
- the four mental residences of purity (p. 465).

Afflictive Processes

Here we:

- explain the rationale of a three-fold classification,
- present each of the three in detail including its role in mechanisms fabricating certainty (p. 414), and
- investigate the consequences of these mechanisms (p. 443).

In general: the rationale of three

'wanting […] disliking [… or] delusion arises within a person…'

If we look carefully at how our mind behaves as sensory and mental experiences arise, isn't it true that there is either attraction, or repulsion, or at least some kind of disturbance? The first two, we can see, are specific examples of the third.

The Buddha here makes reference to what have come to be known as 'the three roots of the unskilful', meaning the driving forces behind all behaviour of body, speech and mind which tend to destroy the chances of happiness and promote the chances of suffering. They also came to be called 'afflictions' (kilesa, kleśa). Without yet allowing ourselves to be swayed by the negativity of these names, we can ask what is being referred to? The Universal Career's *Compendium of Higher Teachings*[421] says:

> What is their defining characteristic? It is that events associated with them are disturbance (apraśāntalakṣaṇa), the appearance of which troubles the body and mind.[422]

---

[421] Although this is a Universal Career treatise, it has been pointed out by Walpole Rahula (Lusthaus, 2002) that in many ways it is closer to the spirit of the Pali collections of discourses than the Higher Teachings treatises of the Elders' School.

[422] (Boin-Webb, Rahula, & Asanga, p. 95)

In particular

The Buddha does not introduce these processes to the Kālāmās with such leading names, however. He merely refers to wanting, disliking and being deluded, and asks the Kālāmās what they think about whether each process fulfils the criteria for rejection or the criteria for adoption and practice. We will follow step by step to make our own conclusions.

For each process, wanting (lobha), disliking (dosa) and being deluded (moha) the meaning is discussed, then the Buddha's invitation to consider whether each one meets the criteria for rejection or acceptance is taken up along with the Kālāmās, and finally a survey is made of the occurrence of each process in the ways by which the various sources of knowledge are taken as sources certainty: we survey the various ways we discovered and treated in detail by which the source of knowledge is taken as a source of certainty, or an absolute, and thereby leads us away from the truth and from fitness, and note which are governed by the presence of each of these three processes:

>Lobha: wanting

'What do you think, Kālāmās? When wanting arises within a person, does it arise to their profit or loss?'

'To their loss, sir.'

'And thus wanting, Kālāmās, does not a person overcome by wanting, with their mind possessed by it, kill a living being, or take what is not given, or go after another person's spouse, or tell lies, or induce others to do such things, such that there will long be loss and suffering?'

'Yes, sir.'

Meaning

This refers to when a sensory or mental experience arises and our mind 'goes out' to it, gets involved in it, losing (to some degree) awareness of everything else. So we can say that the sensory or object in this case is 'attractive', and the attraction itself is called lobha, which we translate here as wanting[423].

Accept or reject?

Let us apply the Buddha's questions to 'wanting' to see whether it meets the criteria for adoption and practice, or the criteria for rejection.

Is wanting skilful or unskilful?

What makes the mind go out to particular objects and not others? Is it through some insight into the nature of things, a profound knowledge of what will lead us and those around us to our profit and bliss, in the short-term and the long-term? Probably if we are honest about it we will recognise that the mind goes out to certain stimuli not because of any such insight but merely because a habit has developed to do so. How did the habit arise? Because something which seemed to be that kind of stimulus in the past provided some kind of pleasure. We have been operating for a very long time by a series of rules of thumb. In short-term situations, with limited scope, we can say that such habit-development, or conditioning as psychology calls it, is probably 'skilful' with respect to that limited goal. The environment sometimes does not change so fast that the way we learn to get pleasure one minute turns into a failure the next. Just as the squirrel learns to find acorns under oaks, and will not be disappointed until too many other squirrels make the same discovery or until the fruiting season of

---

423 See translation rationales in the appendices.

the tree is finished, so can we operate successfully in limited situations.

However, it is the nature of things that limited pleasures are not necessarily the path to bliss. The fundamental difficulty is the way situations *change*. Once the acorns are gone, or have rotten, or sprouted, the tactic of searching relentlessly under the oak becomes not a source of bliss but a source of suffering. If they are gone, searching becomes a source of frustration. If they have rotted or sprouted, searching becomes a source of illness – through poisoning. The same capability, to develop new habits or to be conditioned, subsequently allows us to respond to those kinds of suffering and avoid them in future, and to look for alternative food sources. But the transitional process is always characterised by suffering.

Since our principal goal, the goal behind all other goals, is to be happy, then, we can say that the strategy of lobha *fails*. Because its perspective is too narrow, too under the nose, because there is not enough awareness of the general situation, because it is just too much of a rule of thumb, ever in the process of refinement which will never be perfect. With respect to the big picture it is, in fact, literally, stupid. The Higher Teachings point out that lobha (and dosa) are always accompanied by moha, being deluded.

We can test this in our own experience. One obvious characteristic of the rule of thumb of lobha is that we try to repeat those experiences which first brought pleasure. This, as we will see when we come to the development of perspective, is a characteristic we share with animals and goes by the name in behavioural science as 'positive reinforcement'. Is it not our general experience that repeated attempts to recapture an initial joy never match it, but are somehow flat and dry by comparison? In our romantic relations, in our appreciation of food, and in our enjoyment of particular places or social groups, is it not a fact that the true joy comes on us by surprise, and the schemes we devise can never bring us that? Was it not with justice that the poet[424] sang:

He who binds himself to a joy
Does the wingèd life destroy;
But he who kisses the joy as it flies
Live's in eternity's sunrise.

The Buddha asks us to consider not just the *mild* tendency to bind ourselves to joys, but also whether we can say that the behaviour of someone is

---

424 William Blake

skilful who is *totally overwhelmed* by this drive, possessed by it. Of course the situation is worse. The stronger the drive, very often the more delusion is involved. In the case of romantic love, of course, this frequently happens in the case of unrequited love, and can lead to obsessive stalking and even the attempt to annihilate the object of love, by stabbing or whatever. Clearly skilfulness is not even remotely a defining characteristic of the developed version.

Is wanting censurable or uncensurable?

Though a tendency is unskilful, we might argue that it need not be censurable on that basis. In the case of wanting, 'positive reinforcement', binding ourselves to joys, trying to repeat what made us happy, we might think: no-one's perfect after all, and we can't all drift around like poets supping the wine of *carpe diem* or live like birds and lilies with no thought for the morrow.

There is an important point to consider, however. Could it not be that, by acting solely on the basis of limited perspective and limited goals we might be unwittingly denying ourselves developing better perspective and a goal with more awareness of broader and longer-term consequences? If that possibility were a reality, then it would indeed be censurable not to do anything to alter the situation. It would be as though we were indulging in stupidity.

Is wanting praised by the wise or scorned by them?

Probably for this reason, the Buddha invokes 'the wise' – for these would be the people who are committed to avoiding such indulgence. These people would be the ones who have gained some realisation about the payoffs of various options. We are not talking about self-proclaimed mystics or sages or experts here. It is rather that the Buddha is asking the Kālāmās, 'If you were wise, would you not scorn this indulgence'? And their answer is yes. What is ours?

If we were wise, would we continue according to our psychological conditioning, ever using this rule of thumb with its short-sightedness and refusal of the changing nature of reality? Whose greatest achievement is the flat, dry rehearsal of an approximation of spontaneous joy? Would we be wise to dismiss even the notion that there might be another way?

When adopted and abided by, does wanting convert to profit and bliss, or loss and suffering?

We have already seen how the rule of thumb which wanting employs leads to suffering, because of changing circumstances. Going into this in more detail, we can say suffering occurs in these contexts (as presented for example in the *Compendium*):

> With birth, because of the pain of blockage, and because birth sets up the existence upon which subsequent suffering is based; with ageing, because of the changes which occur in time; with disease, because of the instability of the physical elements; with death, because we lose life; with association with unpleasant circumstances – the association itself being the suffering; with separation from pleasant circumstances – the separation itself being the suffering; and with not getting what one wants – the suffering being in the state of absence of the result which was wished for.[425]

But can we say it leads to loss? Is wanting actually harmful? In the developed sense, as we saw in the example of the stalker, of course it can be. But always?

Here we can consider the nature of tendencies in the mind. In Greek-influenced post-Christian cultures we have a tendency to see expression of an emotion, especially if it is extreme, as a kind of catharsis, and so we might argue that to indulge our wanting might actually do us good, even if it is only successful in a limited sphere.

This is, I think, a mistake, due to vagueness about what 'the expression of emotion' actually is. Catharsis in the Greek theatre and mystery cults was accomplished by *undergoing* an experience, passively – be it identification with the stage players or having a bull slaughtered over one's head. This was all part of a technology of the mind which certainly has power to refresh and simplify mental-emotional processes, largely through overwhelming stimulus in this non-reacting context. However, we are considering here not the passive response to a stimulus but something which we can *choose* either to reject or adopt and practise: clearly we are not talking about a passive undergoing of some experience.

The Buddha identifies the element of choice in what we do with our body, speech and mind at all times. We have already seen that he calls us to take responsibility personally for this choice: this is his demand of us in this investigation. How much of wanting is choice? Psychological conditioning is extraordinarily powerful, and can make it seem as though we are no longer in

---

425 (Boin-Webb, Rahula, & Asanga, p. 84)

control: our patterns of behaviour can become so habitual that we do not notice their habituality, and therefore cannot understand where the build-up of tension is coming from. The English word 'desire' comes from a Latin word related to the influence of the stars on us (a root which has given us the word 'sidereal'). Only when the habit is broken does the bliss of novelty and surprise throw the earlier constraint into relief. Wc arc much more able to take control than we ordinarily imagine, and perhaps than we would like to imagine.

Each moment of awareness, then, is a locus for decision. The question to decide on is: should we continue with the self-conditioning?

It is an insight the Buddha for one gained that by acting we generate a tendency for that action naturally. The more that tendency is acted on, the stronger it becomes. This was expressed symbolically by the later Observance Practice School (Yogacāra) as every act planting the 'seeds' (bīja) of habitual tendencies in the 'ground' (ālaya) of consciousness. It is the 'conditioning' modern psychology describes. Wanting, itself, as an act, plants the seeds of stronger wanting. This means that it is a runaway process: positive feedback makes it more and more difficult to counter.

From what we have seen of changing realities and the dangers of developed wanting, it should be clear that the inevitable result will most likely be a great deal of loss.

The role wanting plays in the fabrication of certainty

Almost all of the ways we claim certainty depend on wanting.

Concluded faith would not have any power if it were not that it is an object for attachment, rallying round, and preservation. Moreover we saw that the root of the word 'believe' is lobha itself – that belief, in Christianity, arose itself from a kind of wanting!

Relishing the pleasant itself does not depend on wanting, but wishing to remain with what one has relished certainly does – and that is what happens when we are drawn to learning about goodness from some system because we can relish it. It is true of course that the ordinary mind by the rule of thumb we mentioned reacts unskilfully to pleasure: it seeks to re-experience it, because of the superstition of identifying the causes of the pleasure too simplistically: *unfortunately the condition of spontaneity cannot be construed.* But we need not on that account subject ourselves grimly to a pleasure-suppressing regimen.

The simile is sometimes made of a tree with delicious, poisonous fruit in an orchard. To be sure we can suppress our inclinations to eat from it, and avoid it. But the tree will in that case remain always as a potential trap in the future.

This symbolises the Individual Career's approach to the stimuli for the afflictive processes, such as objects of pleasure: to turn away, to suppress the pleasure. Another way, cleverer in practice (practical cleverness is called upāya in Sanskrit, and together with prajñā, makes up perhaps the most important pairing of practices in the entire career), would be to learn about the nature of the poison in the fruit, and learn about the nature of chemicals which can transform it. Then one can consume the fruit so long as its poison has been chemically transformed: it can no longer harm you. This might be more practical, in that you can enjoy the fruit and do not need to get all puritanical about self-discipline, but, again, the tree remains, and so there is still potential harm in the future. This way symbolises the approach of the common Universal Career: the transformatory philosopher's stone of bodhicitta (Awakening-Intent) revolutionises what constitutes a pleasant object and the nature of the response to its stimulus in terms of wanting. The limited wanting consequent upon deluded response to pleasures becomes just one of the many tools the awakening being (bodhisattva) can use to help other beings. But the poison *in potentia* is still there, at least while the awakening being is still in the process of cultivating all the qualities of the path and abandoning the countering tendencies, and as we have already seen, the path of the awakening being is a very long one! A third way to deal with the tree is to uproot it forever. Its sap being highly toxic this requires extreme cleverness and extraordinary wariness, as well as intense diligence, but once it is done, it is done forever. That is the symbol for the extraordinary methods of the Secret Mantra Career.

So much for the three levels of training in the Buddhist traditions. But for ordinary mind, re-relishing is an expression of wanting, so if we recognise the former we will find the latter behind it with a little self-investigation.

Turning to recited tradition, its discrimination about what constitutes the noble tradition depends on wanting, as does the admiration for memorisers and the overvaluation of the form at the expense of meaning.

As for tradition in general, although the first order disqualifications we considered do not necessarily involve wanting, almost all of the second order ones do. If we did not want Heaven or reward, or security, or individual or tribal superiority, or especially orgasm, and above all (however preposterous) total world mastery, how could these carrier mechanisms operate?

We have already made explicit in the treatment of reports that wanting is involved, again very heavily in the second order disqualifications. Because the content of reports includes anything we can imagine, potentially anything we want could be involved in the report. Our desire for immediate appreciation in awe, we saw, encourages the transmission of the uncanny and the scandalous. Our relations with listeners and people in the report also allow our wanting to influence the reporting, such as the examples we considered of transmitting what looks good for us. Above all wanting wealth drives many false reports, as we saw with alchemists and investors. If we did not want gold, what interest would we have in alchemists? Wanting to uncover our own mysterious selves drives the over-reporting of mesmerism and so on.

As with tradition, wanting superiority or power or acceptance were all involved in the ways scriptures betray us. In particular, again, the second order disqualifications of their necessity of goodness, the carrier mechanisms, all depend on wanting something: if you did not want Heaven and social kudos, why would you obey the injunctions of the scripture to preach so that you can go to Heaven? If you are a ruler, but you do not want to repel an invading army, why would you bother about a scripture that claims to protect you?

The situation with philosophy, appropriately enough, becomes extraordinarily complex, but almost every detail of its betrayal of goodness depends on wanting. The entire edifice of specious theology we considered would not have been built very high without wanting God to be true, and furthermore true as the beloved scriptures suggest. If we did not want such worldly things as power, honour, praise, gifts, creativity, virtue, then there would have been no reason to ascribe them to the deity, and if we did not want to integrate to some extent with other people we would never have needed to develop the intricate defences around these ascriptions and their awkward interrelations. If we did not want to be loved, what appeal would the freakish idea of the cruel but partial overlord have? Indeed, if we liken the philosophy to a massive knot, we liken wanting to insects running over the treads tying the knots more and more inextricably.

Also fittingly, the betrayal by logic is perhaps the one which least depends on wanting. In the logical fallacies we can see that if we did not want simplicity we would not make such superstitious attributions of causes to results, simplicity and perhaps some sense of order, as in magical thinking and representativeness heuristics. On the other hand, in the trapped beliefs which partly depend on logic, but also partly on circumstances, each variety has its own kind of dependency on wanting. For example, wanting ethical uprightness is part of what drives the cycle of condemning humankind to fallenness, and if we did not crave *being* the schizophreniogenic doctrines of creation and salvation would not affect us as they do. Without wanting pleasure we could not be the unwitting creators and sustainers of the pleasure-dependent marriage restriction or runaway

on covering or exposing the body. Without wanting purity we would not torture and execute with exorcists' zeal, without wanting unity we would not fight for and destroy it, and without wanting security we would not surrender our liberties.

In the treacheries of ideas, the root is not wanting, but it is involved at virtually every step. Wanting companions and power is what drives the rallying around and preserving symbols at the expense of their meaning, and then wanting to preserve them in disguise is what drives conscious hijackings of others' more popular symbols as masks: if we did not want our deity to be acceptable to a new generation, we would not allow it to be shorn of attributes previously considered fundamental to its divinity. If we did not want companions and power we would not trust local language more and therefore would not come to prefer doctrines and ideologies most easily expressed in that language. When we consider language engineering, of course, there is a powerhouse of wanting behind it: that of totalitarian control and its legitimisation being the most obvious, but also as we saw wanting to arrogate the in-group, or its deity, over others. If we did not want our god to be the undisputed and unrivalled ruler there would be no advantage to using transitive verbs about religious attitude and act without objects, for example. If we did not want to vampirise the kudos of a rival religious tradition, there would be no need to pretend that its deity was in fact ours in disguise. On so-called objectivity and Platonic ideas as reality, it could well depend on a craving for irresponsibility, wanting to imagine ourselves the passive creatures of an active objective reality, in order to relieve us of the burden of understanding our experience. Behind false analogies are varieties of wanting – often pecuniary behind the legal, and behind the theological the usual ones relating to relishing the idea of the deity and the status conferred by championing it.

Like the logical fallacies, the cognitive biases may not depend on wanting, but they usually interact with it to lead to the betrayal of goodness. If there was no wish for the purity of the tribe (i.e. the innocence of society) the exorcismic judicial system would not appeal, and without wanting the power and love of the tribe we would feel no compulsion to conform and hypocritical exploitable public-private moral discrepancies could not develop. The psychology-rooted heuristics are already complex and shadowy psychological phenomena, but we can venture that, for example, choice-supportive bias, confirmation bias, the Semmelweiss reflex and so on seem to be related to wanting self-respect, in turn related again to wanting group acceptance. We have already alluded to the kind of drives operating behind religious examples of pareidolia and apophenia, the usual deity-rescuing ones. In the case of prior commitment to doctrines of course it is wanting to keep or rescue those doctrines which drives the distortion, even, as we saw, to the extremes of cruelty in retributive punishment.

As for the case of according authority to external figures, we have already discussed the psychological drives behind it to some extent – wanting to be invincible or unchallengeable, wanting the relief of not having to defend ourselves (as we imagine), and so on, and though we cannot make conclusive claims this even seems the case in the obediency phenomena discovered by Milgram. Behind the establishment of chains of authority down to us is, obviously, wanting to claim authority ourselves. All of this applies before the projection of authority has been made. After it has been made, of course, many other kinds of wanting come into play, such as the extraordinary longing which can develop for the external figure onto which the authority has been projected, wanting to protect the kudos of that authority because the projector's own kudos is now intricately bound up with it, and she wants to protect her own. We have already explained how this leads to excessive tension because ironically the amalgamated kudos is much *more* sensitive to attacks.

Finally in the matter of allegiance to a teacher or ideological leader, the main drive is clearly wanting the identity. It is this mania for identification which trivialises everything else and is the main reason for allegiance's treachery in the matter of discovering goodness. However, wanting also plays a number of important roles in the various mechanisms of segregation we considered which aggravate that treachery. Wanting peace, in the sense of not being open to challenge, clearly makes any segregating mechanism attractive, beginning with expelling dissenters, through controlling ideological information propagation to not eating together. As Freud discovered, the neurotic's need for peace of mind is what drives his or her compulsive behaviour, and so we need not fear too much controversy by suggesting that similar wanting might drive the shared but arbitrary observances which are so good at isolating a religious community. Most of the linguistically-based segregators we have already explained as dependent on wanting something – be it again the group or its deity's arrogation, or the silencing of challengers again, or, according to a complex genesis we have already considered, wanting to identify a 'demon' and exorcise it to restore purity (or divinity). Even the most advanced cases involving entire societies psychotically dissociated from each other, how would they have developed if no-one could be bothered to try to recover innocence and honour?

>Dosa: aversion

'What do you think, Kālāmās? When aversion arises within a person, does it arise to their profit or loss?'

'To their loss, sir.'

'And thus averse, Kālāmās, does not a person overcome by aversion, with their mind possessed by it, kill a living being, or take what is not given, or go after another person's spouse, or tell lies, or induce others to do such things, such that there will long be loss and suffering?'

'Yes, sir.'

Meaning

Appearances or events arising in our experience may provoke, on the other hand, a dissocation or a withdrawal, into an outlook of rejecting or hatred. This is referred to as dosa (dvesa), a word which seems originally to have meant 'erring into two'[426] – the separation of oneself and the other, of 'my or our side' and 'their side'. It is not the same as anger.

Accept or reject?

It does not take years of meditative clarity-training and investigation to see that as soon as we conceptualise the other like this we have begun a process of failing to understand it.

Is aversion skilful or unskilful?

Let us recall that we are referring to the goal of being happy. Clearly such aversion in itself does not bring immediate happiness; rather it seems to involve, even physically, displeasure: a sense of being invaded, often the sensation of a kind of entity around the diaphragm, hot and pressurised and 'black' or (some say) 'red'. But if we turn to long-term happiness, then we walk into one of the biggest controversies between Buddhism and modern mentality.

All of us can probably think of instances where we experienced hatred, and possibly even consciously stoked the aversion, and then got what we wanted; and it is a big temptation to imagine therefore that getting what we wanted depended on that hatred or even stoking that hatred. Well, by now, after our long exploration of logic and how it betrays us, we may start to realise that this scheme needs some qualification. We have seen a whole series of society-wide

---

426 Cf. translation rationales.

examples of trapped beliefs, where the consequences of a 'solution' turn out to be what it purports to solve. What is needed to break such cycles is awareness of better solutions, and there always are better solutions than those which, while appearing to be solutions, are in fact problems themselves! The situation with aversion is exactly the same: its agency as a solution is short-term, and in fact entails consequences which favour the circumstances which provoked it in the first place.

However, just as in the social loops we considered, when we have been long habituated to the loop, our experience can become so narrow in focus that we lose all receptiveness to even the possibility of alternative solutions. In this respect aversion as a 'solution' is rather like our sexual preferences: we learn particular satisfying ways of doing it, and if we or those who commune with us thus are not careful, these ways become narrow and rigid. Every sex manual in history has recommended experimentation, and the same applies to situations of conflict. If you think aversion is the best solution, experiment. But this advice will seem weak for those who would prefer to lock themselves in a fortress of ideology than to test new ways in the unpredictably wondrousness of real-life situations.

We will have more to say about this when we come to consider freedom from aversion and the methods the Buddha introduces to develop it.

Is aversion censurable or uncensurable?

The same point applies here as with wanting, namely, that if you recognise that aversion might not be the most skilful solution after all but throw up your hands and cite human nature or your star sign as ineluctable influences in your own personal case, then you might well be indulging in guilt.

Christianity has emphasised guilt as one of the many feelings which are supposed to advert to the presence of the deity, and we have already considered how useful to the propagation of Christian doctrines as memes the doctrine of sin has been, so we can hardly fault her (the ship, Christianity, that is) for using that most useful of fuels. However, like most of the other carrier mechanisms we have considered, this particular fuel has very little interest in human happiness: indeed it could be accused of having a relentless death-wish for human happiness.

Like all the metaphysical doctrines, sin and guilt are ideas which were born from communication – i.e. between individuals. We have already examined in detail how such ideas then degenerate as they assume seeming reality in themselves, and we have seen also how certain cultures have become especially prone to letting this happen. All ideas, when they are then re-internalised, become paradoxical, and guilt is no exception.

Whilst in one sense you feel 'guilty', recognising that guilt within oneself is in effect making the guilt itself guilty. This, however unconsciously, absolves one of the guilt. We have seen how easily this is achieved in situations of group consensus on a magical purification. How much easier it is when the only consensus required is of one!

This is why one can feel simultaneously that aversion is censurable and uncensurable: the blame for aversion is especially easy to deflect onto the other or onto the 'aversion' itself, because blaming itself is the same mental action, *and operates simultaneously with the first aversion.* As soon as the mind is 'overwhelmed' by aversion, it can separate anything from itself, and the notion of the aversion itself, especially in the minds of those in post-Christian societies fostered by that old familiarity with sin as some kind of demonic, self-existing entity, is just another thing that can be separated off and blamed. That is why self-righteousness is the same as aversion: have you ever heard of self-righteous lust[427]? Or self-righteous envy? No: it is a personal auto-exorcism, a relentless drive to absolve oneself magically, and like all magic, sustaining belief in its effects depends on extreme distortion of experience. It is not just that the other is simultaneously and especially subsequently misunderstood – it is also that one must misunderstand oneself: the entire situation must be distorted, just as in the social examples we considered like concealing magic and prayer's failures.

Is aversion praised by the wise or scorned by them?

The word used for 'wise' here implies simply knowing things rather than some esoteric mystical experience.

Although aversion is associated with magical thinking, we might argue that there is nothing unwise about magic. Well, I hope that by discovering the extent of distortion of reality which is necessary to sustain the belief that aversion is justified, the notion that deploying it like a witch secretly in control of all reality might be wise will have been dispelled. If not, I would recommend that you recall moments of extreme aversion and ask yourself: how wise was I then?

Does aversion convert to profit and bliss or loss and suffering when adopted and abided by?

It is a sad fact that a gambler who has in total lost fortunes over and over

427 Other than the 'debauched piety' we have already considered (under 'Not by relishing')!

will continue to gamble because of the remembered instances of successes. We have explored various cognitive biases which lead to this fallacious and tragically wasteful path: memory heuristic, availability heuristic, the gambler's fallacy, the Texas sharp-shooter fallacy, and so on.

What we can say of a gambler applies many times over to the person who abides by aversion as a solution. At least someone, the casino, profits from a gambler.

The role aversion plays in the fabrication of certainty

We have already considered the very extensive and profound dependency on wanting of many of the social ills in our survey, and we can identify in each of those cases a concomitant aversion, in that wanting one thing generally means at the expense of another – for example, wanting one's own group to be superior is at the expense of the superiority of other groups, so can be considered aversion to their superiority. Rather, then, than repeat my earlier overview, I advert here to cases where aversion plays a special role, not necessarily related to an instance of wanting something.

First and foremost, exclusion is itself aversion, so the conclusion of faith, which we looked at it detail and which was found to permeate the modern social ills we considered, is a form of aversion on a massive scale in itself.

Similarly the discrimination of what to transmit in a recited tradition depends on aversion to strange forms.

In the role of transmitting traditions we saw it in the fear of Hell and worldly punishment, and in the hatred directed towards the apostate as well as consequent fear of becoming one. We saw aversion to novelty in the closure of revelation, and above all in the fear of extreme punishments which causes any associated traditions to be transmitted according to the mathematical models we examined.

We identified explicitly (as with wanting) how aversion could influence reporting, for example in spreading lies about an enemy. Without aversion there would be no occasion either for guile at the gullible's expense in the propagation of the notion of esoteric knowledge and the alchemists' gold and longevity (however there are other kinds of guile – for the sake of the gullible! – motivated instead by *caring*).

The discrimination involved in transmitting select scripture is also clearly a kind of exclusion and therefore aversion, and their propagation by claims of lending political power would have little effect if there were no enemies and no aversion to those enemies. Indeed a great deal of the *content* of some scripture's depends on aversion among its listeners – such as the Qur'ān harping on about the 'coverers' (kuffār) and the 'splittists' (mushrikūn) and the 'hypocrites' (munāfaqun) and the unreliable among the Christians and Jews. If its audiences had not been and were not averse to anyone, what effect could these verses have had or have in validating the scripture for them?

Although its inception depends more on wanting and delusion, intricate philosophy to protect faith depends heavily on aversion in its mechanism – the expulsion of what is not 'pure', beginning with sin and the Devil explicitly and working through as we saw to the subtler, better masked modern versions. Clearly the propagation by controversy would not have worked without the adversaries, nor the myth of persecution – for there would have been no-one to conceive of as persecutor.

Once again many of the trapped beliefs set up mechanisms which involve aversion, but each in its own way: for example, if there was no-one to give the dog the bad name, then the dog would have no occasion to be influenced to the bad: the fallenness of humankind and its servitude both depend on negative mutual appreciation feeding into the downward spiral. A very deep and almost inevitable aversion is behind the refusal of the vividly present phenomena of the moment which informs the doctrines of creation and causes. Once the norm of marriage begins to crystallise, aversion to different ways mounts and feeds into the propagation of the norm, and aversion to strange inclinations within one sex are what feeds the tendency to legislate how the other sex dress. Aversion to chaos, the unpredictable and uncontrollable environment drives prayer as much as it does certain kinds of technological advance. Aversion to the magical polluting power of the executed or condemned person or people is what drives the positive feedback in extreme cruelty and torture (on the small scale) and in the process of waging war for the sake of peace and unity (on the large scale). Without the aversion to the threatening, the cycle of runaway over-focusing on terrorist threat could not occur.

In our characterisation of ideas, communciation patterns, signs, and symbols, although aversion does not seem to have played a major role, we saw that all ideas or concepts begin with *exclusion*, as suggested by the fact that the Sanskrit term apoha, meaning 'exclusion', was applied to them: any idea is only upheld in a particular circumstance insofar as it is not excluded, just as in the scientific method a theory is only considered still to apply to a particular circumstance insofar as it has not been disproved there. We saw how this nature makes them liable to be related to in a certain manner (namely as independently real) that encourages their degeneration from authentic communication: this process involves aversion in various ways, such as the disinclination to consider rival interpretations of the symbols. On a similar inter-personal level, aversion to out-group language could well have been a major factor in the development of metaphysical systems that conform with local language in syntax. And of course the engineering of language is very often driven by aversion to a group one wishes to manipulate, and since this is often at their expense, it is a species of aversion.

In the treacheries wrought by intuition by means of cognitive biases, those based on identification with the in-group are also stoked by aversion to the out-groups, the strangers. And those relating to preserving the status quo are stoked by aversion to strangeness as it arises. Those relating to protecting prejudice, finally, are stoked by aversion to competing dogmas. However in none of these cases is aversion, particularly personal aversion, a requisite for the initial cognitive bias to operate, based as they are on maladaptive traits of psychology.

In a similar way, authority projection does not depend on aversion, but quickly invoves it in subsequent conflict over the authority. More perniciously, we saw that sustaining the comfort of authority projection requires persistent *aversion to oneself* in the prohibition of self-knowledge, leading to obstacles to helpful qualities, specifically spontaneous amity with, and caring for, other beings. We will return to this problem later in the Buddha's advice on cultivating these qualities. And a nigh-incredible tendency we have towards cold aversion to those whose suffering is required for us to obey authority is indicated in Milgram's experiments.

Finally the segregation mechanisms we considered which underly the treacherousness of allegiance with particular teachers or leaders are in themselves aversion. Recognition of the dissenters is aversion, a pre-requisite to their being exiled or worse when present, and kept out and mis-represented when elsewhere. Contextualising the opponent would hardly be invoked as a strategy if there was no opponent, just as a ventriloquist would look rum without a dummy, and a man in a lift who blamed his dog for the smell would convince few in the absence of a dog.

In the social segregating mechanisms and indeed in all our examples we should bear in mind that, unlike wanting, aversion is less fussy about its object: the object can easily change shape. This means that the kinds of aversion we have summarised here can feed into each other. For example, the segregating mechanism of restricting commensalism becomes part of a general sense of 'us versus them' which strengthens the restrictions on the others' entry of sacred places, and vice versa. The tragic consequence of all this is what we see today, entire communities almost entirely cut off from each other in mentality, no longer able to communicate reasonably, and losing sense of each other's humanity.

>Moha: being deluded

'What do you think, Kālāmās? When delusion arises within a person, does it arise to their profit or loss?'

'To their loss, sir.'

'And thus being deluded, Kālāmās, does not a person overcome by delusion, with their mind possessed by it, kill a living being, or take what is not given, or go after another person's spouse, or tell lies, or induce others to do such things, such that there will long be loss and suffering?'

'Yes, sir.'

Meaning

This means not recognising what is happening, stupidity, a loss of consciousness, falling due to a lack of awareness. It includest at one extreme the crudest chaotic confusion, what we would call insanity, and at the other, through not being accustomed to a direct view of reality, engaging in even the slightest disjunction or fantasy. For this reason it is taught to be a more basic process than the earlier two, and to drive them both.

Accept or reject?

Is delusion skilful or unskilful?

A survey of the people of the world today certainly gives the impression that many are convinced that living in an illusion affords a happier life than confronting reality. We will explore this in the context of reaction to suffering later. On an individual level we now know that certain mental conditions can be provoked by extremely traumatic events (such as a direct confrontation with death or pain or betrayal), the memory of which are then suppressed: the suppression of the memories involves such distortion of reality that such individuals' behaviour becomes erratic according to the expectations of their fellows and the disparity can thereafter be aggravated from both sides. When groups of people operate according to a similar delusion, however, such discrepancies do not regularly arise and suppression of trauma may be temporarily successful. But the way to be free of the necessity to suppress must also be suppressed. So if the goal is long-term, stable happiness, we have to admit that such delusion is pretty much the opposite of skilful.

Is being deluded censurable or uncensurable?

Unlike most obvious expressions of wanting, and certainly unlike most expressions of aversion, it is very common to find people ready benignly to tolerate delusion in themselves and others. If we are honest we would, however, probably have to admit that the reason for this misplaced tolerance is that delusions are more often found in common than either wanting or aversion, so the deluded find comfort in each other. Alcoholics find relief, in the company of other alcoholics, from the self-critical voice which tells them they are not helping themselves.

Is being deluded praised by the wise or scorned by them?

Many of us have grown up in a cultures influenced by the idea that it is impossible for a human being to know thoroughly what is good for her or him. What the Buddha is supposed to have discovered directly contradicts that idea. There is in such cultures a pervasive sense that delusion is inevitable. Various religions teach that the final truth will only be clear on some future day, after death, and until then truth is concealed by 'the Concealer'. We have already seen many examples of how these same religions depend on ordinary mentality with all its foibles, both for their immediate appeal and for their transmission. Suffering, catastrophes, misery, total confusion, all are taught by these traditions to be part of a 'plan' in order that there might some relief. Just as we might be reassured by a doctor who can explain exactly why symptoms of some condition we have are unfolding as they are, stories of the horrors of existence being intented reassure us. However, if the cure for condition from which we suffer has been discovered, the comfort from the doctor's description of how its symptoms unfold is rightly considered a treacherous one: instead the cure should be administered such that the symptoms need not unfold. Unfortunately, in the case of the religions, they are so old, and that kind of comfort, albeit little, has so long proven itself in practice, that people dare not call it treacherous.

The Buddha's discovery was the discovery of the cure. Uniquely, he said that the goal is happiness – not 'purity', 'piety', 'God-fearingness', a high station, or the luxuries of a future 'Paradise', or 'success'. The root of our current limited condition, with its inevitable suffering, he claimed after his discovery, was not the anger of a deity or some kind of impurity; neither was it an inevitable and natural entailment, as many other religious and irreligious traditions claimed. He, uniquely, said the root was not knowing reality correctly.

Certain other religions have defined 'wisdom' to mean the acceptance of the idea of the 'Planner', who moves in mysterious ways. This wisdom is a declaration of our being unable to know exactly what we are experiencing. If such were the case, then the 'wise' by this definition should not scorn the deluded, for there are none but the deluded. These same religions have relegated ordinary humankind to a lesser level. Above them are an élite, either prophets, or the level of a human who is also a god. Ordinary humankind is forbidden from attributing to any individuals greater 'wisdom' than this élite. Whoever is included in this élite, the principle is the same: that the rest of us are second rate.

The Buddha and many others claim to have discovered knowledge or wisdom which freed them from the afflictive processes and *which is discoverable by all, here and now.* Such freedom renders the other religions as they have come down to us at least, so dependent are they on ordinary mentality and the afflictive processes themselves, irrelevant. We have now seen enough examples to appreciate just how well these other religions protect themselves as traditions such that they are the ones that have come down to us (because other traditions which were not so good at it have died out), so we should not be surprised if we find fierce protective mechanisms in them which come into play when they are faced with declarations such as the Buddha's that everything on which they depend is curable, and curable merely by *coming to know or understand.* When one has 'come to know or understand' (in Sanskrit, buddha), then there are no longer any afflictive processes from one's own side: that has been the Buddha's and these others' claim.

Many of us will find the claim of such a 'coming to know' (in Sanskrit, bodhi) even being possible an outrageous presumption. If this is the case, we can at least imagine how the world of sentient beings *would* look from the position of one who had thus become free of afflictive processes: imagine what it would be like to see all the affliction continuing in others all around, and to see it without any disturbance from one's own side, such that for the first time other's afflictions appear directly and undistortedly as they are; and to see that it all occurred thus needlessly, all because of incorrect ways of knowing. Even if we instinctively reject bodhi as a possibility, we would do well to reflect on that hypothetical vision, whatever we want to call it.[428]

If that viewpoint is taken as 'the viewpoint of the wise', then we can categorically say without any hesitation, that delusion, as the principal obstacle to that 'coming to understand', is to be scorned, and not to be praised – or even, as the other religions would insist, temporarily tolerated until the deity in its 'wisdom' 'dispels' that delusion at some future time.

---

428 Compare 'The embryo of one who will arrive at Truth', in the discussion of 'Bringing Sharing Joy into Being'.

Does delusion convert to profit and bliss or loss and suffering when adopted and abided by?

'I am not allowed to think like this, so it must be wrong,' is a thought which, whether it is correct or not, encourages what we might call 'advanced training in delusion'. Spending most of our time with people who share our views likewise fosters it. Two people who have both taken the wrong path in a forest are more likely to miss signs that it is the wrong path because they reassure each other, 'We have come the right way, haven't we?' As a quick experiment we can ask ourselves, 'Are there some people that I always listen to carefully, and others whose talk rarely registers with me?' If there is such a discrepancy, we can ask ourselves on what basis we make it. For most of us, unfortunately, the basis will be mere flattery by concurrence. Conversely those whose tendency is towards pronounced defeatism, who think, 'I have probably come the wrong way again!' out of habit, are also likely to miss signs that tell them whether they are correct.

Unfortunately the deeper into the forest we go, the fewer signs there are. That is the nature of a habitual tendency. The tendency to delusion, as can be seen ever day in our news, and on every other page of human history, is limitless.

It is sometimes conceded, even from within the traditions concerned, that aspects of certain religious and ideological movements were delusional, but that they led to stupendous success – and it is political success or success in terms of numbers of converts that they mean. Even when they claim success in 'artistic' terms or in terms of 'civilisation' it is because the art and civilisation of others added to a system which was only there through its political success or numbers of converts from those civilisations, so it is the same. Is political and populational success what the Buddha is referring to here as 'profit'?

Well, we can consider: How stable is whatever happiness results from gaining violent power over others and increasing in numbers of individuals? In our times these questions have surpassed the realm of philosophical musing and assumed unprecedented urgency, but our habitual casualness about them unfortunately persists.

The role delusion plays in the fabrication of certainty

Every mechanism leading to the fabrication of certainty that we have considered in our survey depends on delusion, of varying degrees of crudity. It is, as it were, the root of the roots. In the Buddhist teachings even extremely subtle delusion is uncovered. Partly for brevity, but also to avoid shock, doubt and rejection, here we will consider only the crudest and most generally-accepted examples, which are obvious without extensive meditative training.

First of all we saw that faith in the particular requires *pretending*, pretending that doubt is certainty, a wilful delusion.

If we were not deluded, then most of what we find attractive would not be. When we are habituated to ugly surroundings and stupefying din of cities, the relatively minor relief provided by even moderately pleasing architecture or a deep clang of iron bells becomes a refuge for the desperate. Without the insurmountable resistance to approaching old trauma that neurotics face, they would not find relief in the extraordinary effort accompanied always by anxiety that makes some ritual compelling for them to repeat and repeat. If the respect accorded to public piety were eclipsed in society by respect for something better, displaying it would be a much less attractive career.

If everyone were already wise, what point would there be reciting some particular verses of wisdom? If everyone were already free of prejudices based on fantasy allegiances to particular historical figures and communities, and free of the illusion of the in-group being pure and the out-group impure, then what motive would there be for identifying particular traditions as worth reciting and others not? How would people thus free of prejudice disagree on what needed reciting? If delusion by aureation and truth claims were not possible, what claim would particular linguistic cadences have on our ears? If delusion were not deepened (i.e. made less obvious) by repetition, how could repeatedly hearing the same untruths convince us they were correct?

If our minds did not have a tendency to hold only limited and often insufficient data in the foreground because of distraction from other pre-occupations when making a decision, how could we fall for the *argumentum ad antiquitatem*? If we were not liable to take sides through an instinct for safety in numbers, how could conceptual issues such as the value of old traditions get polarised and therefore trivialised and made insoluble? Would we not notice that laws favourable to government intrusion into liberties were outlasting their necessity if our minds were not overwhelmed with chaotic information and thereby distracted most of the time? If we did not operate by narrow-focus rules of thumb, how could transmission mechanisms based on threats and rewards operate? If we were aware how danger is exaggerated by focusing on it, would government slogans against 'terror' still convince us to send our tax revenue and children into war zones of this most cynical and hypocritical of wars? If we were as conscious as we should be, continually, of the way carrier mechanisms such as revelation-closure, orgasm-control and extreme punishments work for ideology complexes that use them, would we trust those ideologies quite as much as we do?

Even more simply, would we believe a report we knew to be false? Would we not be more careful about what stories we passed on if we were as conscious as we should be how inclined we are to report according to what is favourable in the short term and to narrow self-interest? Would a girl being seen with a young man get gossiped about in a society that had internalised the significance of contraception (such that advocates of virginity were pitied as backward) rather than made contraception taboo (such that advocates of virginity were obeyed in awe)? With a perspective so much broadened that the consequences of violence were better understood, would heroism still be honoured, and would only histories relating to violent overthrow get remembered and passed down? How could we be so gullible if we were aware of our own gullibility, in matters of truth claims and esotericism? We have already considered the basic foolishness of overlooking subjective contribution to the appreciation of experience, such that money, and respectability, come to seem to have a life of their own, which leads to the kind of skews responsible for famine and oppression of workers on the one hand, and female genital mutilation and honour killings on the other.

If we knew other scriptures' languages, what power would one scripture's language have in itself? If we could be continually conscious of how we naturally incline to believe what is presented in a language similar to our own, what resistance would we have to learning those other languages? With perspective that showed us how transient violent power is, and how intransigent its consequences are, and moreoever if we could be made aware of the forgotten histories of those who had perished despite relying on a scripture, rather than inclined to see instances of its success because they survived, would we believe and transmit the scripture, though it promised such power in reward for belief and transmission?

Any fallacy is itself an example of delusion – and we have considered many, from the rhetorical ones (such as *anacoenosis* and *plurium interrogationum*) to the deeply rooted psychological ones (such as those relating to misjudging probabilities). If we were better able to hold all elements of a complex system in the foreground of our minds simultaneously, such that the old rhetorical strategy of 'never falling' simply could not work, how would the multiply inconsistent doctrine networks of the 'monotheistic' systems appear then, when the inconsistency of any particular element was immediately obvious without needing investigation? If we were better able to take a broad perspective, and take the extremes others have experienced into our own experience sympathetically, including those who have experienced relentless disaster, and those who have experienced only happiness, how attractive would the concentration-camp-overseer archetype for the deity, with its intoxicating and unadmittedly partial mercy, be to us? If we were always vividly aware of how effectively the philosophical handmaids can serve to protect and propagate *any associated doctrine*, potentially even the most injurious lies, would we so readily trust in the doctrines they have protected and propagated to us today? Where would the kudos of being or having been persecuted come from when it was seen as misrepresentation of the natural result of adhering to the irrational and having been bloody-minded and greedy?

How would the world look if we did not shy from such facts as that causality has never been proven, but instead reflected on it, in all aspects of our experience, deeply and intensely, until we had thoroughly internalised it? And even without going so far (quite a long way after all!) if we merely were more conscious of logical fallacies in the understanding of statistics, would the adverts still convince us to buy all that new stuff? Even the most resolutely superstitious person would be chastened rather if they could watch those pigeons in Skinner's experiments. So what about if all of us applied that realisation of the mind's biologically hard-wired tendencies to all deductions and decisions we and those we deal with habitually make? If an ardent believer in the 'revelations of God' broadened their perspective to include all the other possible explanations for religious experience, and that 'inner divine sense', would the revelation continue to have quite the same implications for them? It goes without saying that the trapped beliefs are all instances of delusion, as we defined them as such – beliefs which cause the disease they claim to solve. All of them, from the fallenness of humankind through causation and creation, divine *or otherwise*, through prayer, the morality of coverage or exposure of the body, the goodness of cruelty in torture, to the goodness of future unity and the necessity of security measures, but all of them, we have seen, are delusional beliefs, reaching an arbitrary level of intensity (which the beliefs themselves are therefore always unable to explain entirely) because of feedback and runaway within the system.

We examined the natural departure of symbols from what they originally stand for, but how this cannot be known from the 'surface' of the symbols themselves. The delusion of imagining that there has been no change can therefore range to the very subtlest to the very crudest. If this degeneration were not a property of symbols even one of the hijacks we considered, such as the 'baptism' of the Pagan festivals and turning 'God' into anything and everything you like simply, could not have any persuasive power. If you did not somehow hold that there was something about the word 'God' in itself, some real referent *inextricable from the word*, then how could anyone convince you that the impersonal ground of all being and a voice in a burning bush were the same? What could possibly be seen as the benefit of 'praying' to that comical plurality of mutually exclusive concepts we considered if we were not deluded thus by the singularity of the symbol used to conceal them? If we were more aware of the way language fools us, not to mention better informed about other languages, would we harp on so endlessly about conceptual distinctions which *can only be expressed in our own language* and would we be so keen to dismiss as irrelevant conceptual distinctions which *can only be expressed in languages other than our own*? We might even ask if, for example, the Trojan horse of radical Islām would have been so readily invited into cultures if the totalitarianism-ambiguity in its slogan had not been concealed in Arabic's peculiar grammar, though it seems a bold claim. We can ask ourselves carefully: just how much has my understanding of my own experience been obstructed by language? We can even test this by learning a radically different language and learning to 'think in it', and comparing the conclusions! Are not all instances of vocabulary engineering, and we saw many even in our brief survey, dependent on the capacity of the 'surface' or the 'appearing form' of the concepts to delude us? For example, how attractive would it be to consider oneself 'not agnostic' if the appearance of the concept did not suggest, however indefensibly, that one *knew*? Would Christianity not be made more genuinely humble if it recognised, along with all the other weaknesses of humans it likes to intone and recite, their susceptibility to false beliefs, especially those shared by large numbers of fellow humans, and especially when the latter are rich? We have already considered the particularly Greek delusion of holding concepts to be real in themselves and asked whether much philosophy and theology would have been possible without it.

We surveyed a number of common cognitive biases, from inclination to tribal allegiance through heuristic bias to doctrinal commitments, all of which again are, in themselves, kinds of delusion by definition.

We saw that even to recognise authority for truth in an external or internal fixed source is itself delusion: the locus of choosing, which is inescapably our own mind, is projected delusionally onto an authority figure, for example, and then various mechanisms brought in to sustain that illusion. We took particular exception to the authority-supporting lineage structures employed in Islām and Buddhism, as logical impossibilities, in reality undermining the very authority they are supposed to support.

Finally we can see that in the matter of allegiance with a particular teacher, we can ask ourselves how our enthusiasm for doctrines which had come down to us might be influenced if we recognised the true extent and power of the segregating mechanisms to remove them from natural challenge, rational and irrational. We considered many such mechanisms, from bodily prohibitions to speech-based tricks. If the claimant to having 'submitted to the Almighty' were as aware of her delusions of grandeur as her interlocutor is of it, would she still make that nonsensical claim? We already saw, thanks to Popper, the consequences for various self-arrogating viewpoints of applying their other-contextualising interpretative frameworks to themselves – and it is their delusions which are thus dispelled. We effected something similar by surveying the widespread instances of the ventriloquist's manoeuvre, which is only delusional insofar as the dummy is imagined to be responsible, of course.

The Consequences

Here we look into the causal connections between the mechanisms of fabricating certainty and the five ways the Buddha suggested might lead to long-term loss and suffering.

>Sārambha: rage

In *The Discourse to the Kālāmās* the Buddha makes no direct reference to anger, but in the parallel passage about the three afflictive processes in his *Discourse to Bhaddiya* the Licchavi (who as we saw resembles our mentality rather more closely than the Kālāmās) he does: he leads Bhaddiya through exactly the same investigation, with the same criteria, into the same three afflictive processes, but in addition asks about rage:

> 'Taṁ kiṁ maññatha, bhaddiya, sārambho purisassa ajjhattaṁ uppajjamāno uppajjati hitāya vā ahitāya vā'ti?
>
> 'Ahitāya, bhante.'
>
> 'Sāraddho panāyaṁ, bhaddiya, purisapuggalo sārambhena abhibhūto pariyādinnacitto pāṇampi hanati, adinnampi ādiyati, paradārampi gacchati, musāpi bhaṇati, parampi tathattāya samādapeti yaṁsa hoti dīgharattaṁ ahitāya dukkhāyā'ti.
>
> 'Evaṁ, bhante.'

> 'What do you think, Bhaddiya? When rage arises within a person, does it arise to their profit or loss?'
>
> 'To their loss, sir.'
>
> 'And thus raging, Bhaddiya, does not a person overcome by rage, with their mind possessed by rage, kill a living being, or take what is not offered, or go after another person's spouse, or tell lies, or induce others to do such things, such that there will long be loss and suffering?
>
> 'Yes, sir.'

Definition

The Pali sarambha and Sanskrit saṁrambha are both related to ārambha, which means to start to get interested in a project – interested in the sense of involved in and committed to. The prefix saṁ means together, so the word is used of anger which has been entered into, leading to ever-increasing involvement and commitment.

Accept or reject?

Whatever we said about aversion applies even more so to rage. (Who do you understand better: your lover in a moment of tender intimacy, or your lover in the middle of a plate-throwing row?) Those of us who get enraged frequently are usually aware of the fact that part of the experience of rage is in losing a sense of what the other actually is, and replacing it with a caricature. Whilst rage brings us power, it robs us of sense. We are not talking about the anger of a mother punishing a child to protect it.[429] Much more than cold hatred it is physically unpleasant – and as well as the obvious dangers of burst blood vessels, apoplexy, and so on, it has been shown to affect health adversely in the long term too. Coming to our senses after an access of rage is rather like sobering after a drunken brawl, and frequently involves a great deal of regret. It is very heavily involved in the link between the mechanisms of fabricating certainty and the five ways the Buddha suggests there might be long-term loss and suffering.

>Five ways of loss

1. Killing others' lives

How much of this has gone on in the history of, and is going on in, Judaism, Christianity, and Islām, solely on the basis of the affectation of certainty? We examined how the adherents to the 'monotheisms' are particularly prone to fierce and neurotically insistent denial of other communities' gods, religions, ethics and humanity, thanks to the total inflexible exclusiveness of their objects of faith; thanks to their elevation of the most intractable sensualism, such as the exultation of the pious conqueror, into virtues; thanks to their 'mixotheism' – their confusion, for example, of the three issues of personal morality, society-wide morality and 'holy' war in the single 'person-deity', such that conducting holy war is seen as reparation for defect in the others; thanks to their reliance on the transmission mechanism of eternally closed revelation, which demands atheism for earlier and later creeds and the stifling of doubt by affectation of certainty even in the matter of their scriptures, leading to the necessity of fallaciously respecting outdated laws; thanks to their hitting on a formula for the deity which

---

429 We go into more detail about this later when considering self-defence.

though it maximises transmission of the tradition also demands respect be paid to extraordinary cruelty such that their societies are systematically dehumanised; thanks to their self-award of innocence requiring the conflicts they generate to be interpreted as persecution, such that all opposition becomes 'oppression' to be 'resisted' violently and self-righteously; thanks to the extremes of cruelty and unfairness to which their communities can sink due to their concealment of this cruelty and unfairness under speciously manipulated vocabulary that creates an superficial illusion of justice and benevolence to the in-group; thanks to their reliance on the controversies about their fantastically complex interrelated absurd doctrines as a propagating mechanism, controversies which provoke continual conflicts; thanks to the extremely sharp separation of the in-group from the out-group by a panoply of segregating mechanism, physical and metaphysical, the former including sacred spaces and the latter including the application of double standards in vocabulary; thanks to their total projection of authority for truth onto an élite to which they are then committed to defending as a matter of honour on all doctrinal issues, even those to which they secretly do not subscribe, ensuring conflict escalation even from the most trivial issues; and thanks to their disguised but profound reliance on the instinctive bloodlust of exorcism in which demons are decided by consensus and transferred magically by naming them into enemies leading potentially to unrestricted positive feedback of cruelty in punishment and aggression against the those thus 'possessed'.

We also considered elements of free market capitalism, which maintains a large proportion of the world in almost inescapable poverty, malnutrition, ill health and misery even though there is no general shortage of wealth, food or medicine. The number of avoidable early deaths traceable to this system far exceeds the entire history of the 'monotheistic' religions' wars. We saw how the psychological tendency to consider ideas as entities in themselves is related to the dissociation of symbols from their meanings, and focused especially on the monetary system and the respectability system. In the former, we saw how the initially fair translation of effort into money becomes skewed because the money's value, due to sharp consensus, quickly departs from fair representation of effort, leaving some people's efforts grossly overvalued, and others' hideously undervalued.

More generally we saw how liable we are to cognitive biases, and how these come together with selectively transmitted histories, perceived grievance, mistaken adulation of the heroic ethos and authority projection in unfortunate but natural synergy to drive totally deranged conflict. Which bloody confrontations in the world do not depend on these cognitive biases, exaggerations, fallacious reasoning, etc. and the total conviction they foster? How much is going on in 'the spread of democracy' today, solely on the basis of the affectation of certainty? And in the war on terror – with bloodless hands, thanks only to advanced weapons technology…

We considered the particular example of the so-called 'judicial system' where in most countries of the world systematic murder is carried out and through deceptive re-interpretation concealed to the in-group as virtue, leading to a trapped belief system where the institutions create the conditions they are supposed to remedy and, due to the primitive belief in innocence deriving from the 'Creation' religions, arrogate themselves above all criticism.

2. Taking what has not been offered

Legalised in the Torah and the Qur'ān, what are the spoils of even the most 'pious war' if they are not this? What were the tributes paid to Muḥammad's party while he was alive, by those tribes who refused to continue to pay after he died, and who thus invoked the wrath of the Muslim armies under the first caliphs, if they were not this? What was the poll-tax (called jizya in Arabic) that Muslim rulers imposed on their non-Muslim subjects in conquered countries if it was not this? Of course the factors contributing to the situations where the parties involved considered this acceptable are the same as those contributing to the murders that we have just discussed.

The corporations bleeding people subjected to security-destroying assault, of the gory overt kind in Iraq, Afghanistan and Pakistan, and of the hypodermic surreptitious kind in 'terrorism-threatened countries', are, to be sure, offered money in exchange for their noble protection services, but of course that money would never have been offered without the assaults and their aftermaths, such that if any link, even the very weakest, can be established between the assaulters and the security services, and of course it can, then the crime is extortion, a particularly flagrant version of 'taking what has not been offered' – 'forcing the offering of what would not have been' – we can see that rarely in human history has theft been committed on such a massive scale, even in the expansion of Islām: what are Mahmūd Ghazni's crude raids of Indian temples and palaces next to the exquisitely sophisticated multi-billion-dollar harvesting by Halliburton of Iraq's multiplying fears? And what of the pharmaceutical companies whose clients are the desperately ill[430]?

---

430 Let alone those who periodically get involved in killing people by the thousand, such as the German company Bayer (incidentally the introducers of heroin to

The Hindu 'god of wealth', Kubera or Vaiśravaṇa, began life as a demon, rather as we think of Mammon (which was never, however, a proper name in the original Bible texts, just the name for money itself). We have seen that exorcism and its modern versions exacerbate the root problem even while they seem to deal with the immediate symptoms, and that this is particularly so in cases such as money's valuation where consensus on the demonic entity is almost perfect, until it becomes something totally unto itself, and the most infamous locus for delusion to be translated into crime that humankind has ever devised.

3. Resorting to others' spouses

Let revisionist historians of Islām's 'peaceful expansion' count the number of wives and concubines of the caliphs and ask where they all came from. While acceptance of slavery has for most come and gone, 'those whom your right hand possesses' is inscribed in the 'eternal' Qur'ān, which has come but will not go, and for the Muslim warriors these included the wives of their slaughtered enemies. Islām seems to pride itself on its severity on adultery (in Arabic, zina), but we should not forget how conveniently flexible the concept has been. So much for history.

The more pervasive phenomenon relating to adultery today is the discrepancy which we saw arises between public morality and publicly unacknowledged activity. In the public sphere we have always trumpeted some version of monogamy. To be sure, until the homogenisation of international moral culture consequent upon European colonialism, three-quarters of the world was polygynous, i.e. multi-wife marriage, but such a system was still one-way monogamy – each woman supposedly mating with only one man. However, we no longer need to rely on the gossip of the community to establish paternity: early studies using blood tests suggested, and, more recently, studies (conducted almost miraculously given the extraordinary resistance to them) using *genetic testing* irrefutably established, whether actually parentage matched what the mothers claimed. The consequences for the myth of monogamy were devastating: we are much, *much* less monogamous than we say we are. The fact that this is tacitly acknowledged has been proffered as an explanation for the severity of anti-adultery laws in traditional societies: what is not done naturally

---

the world – as a cough cure), who for 'commercial reasons' supplied blood plasma known to carry the HIV and Hepatitis C viruses and therefore withdrawn in the USA to haemophiliacs in Japan and Latin America resulting in thousands of deaths 3 decades back. (Bogdanich & Koli, 2003)

must be violently enforced.[431]

We described how the wide disparity between public morality and unacknowledged activity develops especially in 'traditional' societies where long-term subjection to the same pressures towards hypocrisy have reaped the inevitable result. This discrepancy was seen to be fostered by religious systems involving the idea of an external deity as a judge, due to the habituation to vanity and affectation of piety they encourage, and by those teaching of a postponed 'Day of Judgment', where the doctrine of the deity's mercy, itself necessary to sustain the judgment doctrine bearably, leads to laxity not found in supposedly 'licentious' societies, and we examined the parallels with corruption leading to lucrative occasional non-application of laws. We looked, furthermore, at the consequences of the discrepancy, in the skewing of the distribution of respectability across acts and groups (especially gender), such that in most of these 'traditional' societies women are at a significant respectability-undervaluation in all their acts than men.

4. Speaking falsehoods

That same disparity, thanks to habituation to the idea of external judgment, clearly has its most dramatic consequence for affected societies' standards for speaking the truth: as the disparity itself means that the public discourse is entirely falsehood. We surveyed evidence of the so-called 'strict' societies' actual activity, for example in exploring the internet's sexual content – generally at a higher rate than so-called 'licentious' societies. In the societies afflicted by the disparity, lying is necessary even to survive from day to day, and we saw that the normalcy of this extends even into families.

In particular in the systems of the massive modern religions and ideologies we encountered an extraordinary amount of lying. As a foundation, we saw two examples of elevating falsehood to the status of a supreme virtue in the case on the one hand of the perversion of doubt into the affectation of certainty called 'modern faith', and the concealment of that lie by distorting the vocabulary of religious discourse, for example in using the term 'agnostic' as though some people weren't; and on the other of concealing the mutually exclusive concepts of various divine attributes in a single entity in mixotheism – calling itself 'monotheism'. We also touched on how the sensuality and pleasure of religious affiliation and practice are concealed and false reasons invented to justify that affiliation and practice. Then we saw many examples of how lies, in

---

431 (Barash & Liption, 2001)

the form of propaganda, are employed by the protection and transmission mechanisms of the massive religions – such as the suppression and slander of medical information about the benefits of barrier contraception in order to perpetuate the illusion of the necessity of controlling sex; the suppression and distortion of data about the variety of sexual behaviour in nature[432] in order to maintain the illusion of nature only vindicating the system which maximises the propagation of the religion, and the avoidance of the challenge of modern environmental studies of the consequences of overpopulation; dissimulation under 'instances of fear' as a doctrinal requirement in some kinds of Islām; each tradition's auxesis (rhetorical over-valuation) of itself and meiosis (rhetorical denigration) and the ventriloquist manoeuvre used to generate a culture-wide misinterpretation and undervaluation of rival traditions and doctrines; and the re-engineering of vocabulary to convey the false impression of goodness and rationality. We examined in some detail how false reports of miracles arise thanks to pareidolia and apophenia and why they are reported interestedly both by believers and deniers. We looked at the nexus of cognitive biases and afflictive processes which are behind today's most infamous psychotic breaks of discourse, leading to some of the most extravagant lies humanity has ever had to hear, such as those about the peaceful beheadings in Islām's scriptures and history, including the life of its prophet, and those about the fundamental blamelessness of a rapist-harbouring Church.

We considered the new 'shock doctrine' culture,[433] noting in particular governments' and organisations' interested advertisement, explicitly or by suggestion, of threats – from terrorists, diseases, and natural disasters – which are no longer there, and the resultant extension of emergency laws much beyond their usefulness to the citizens, and we considered the various mechanisms, such as the cognitive biases, which allow these lies to convince the public. We noted how the exploitation of fear and ongoing aggression to generate it is concealed by using a re-engineered vocabulary of liberalism involving the Orwellian union of contradictions in single terms (equivocation), the legal control of what language the media can use of Israel's activities, and the new journalese of vague but extremely suggestive syntactic structures.

---

432 Much more on this incidentally in *Biological Exuberance* (Bagemihl, 1999), one third of which is devoted to an extremely thorough survey of the distortion of data on animal homosexuality by the scientific community. For a more light-hearted, and less monomaniacal, study, see *Dr Tatiana* (Judson, 2003).

433 More on this in the historically rather short-sighted but nevertheless unnerving *The Shock Doctrine* (Klein, 2007).

We also focused on some elements of grievance culture, as parallel to the massive religion's historical re-interpretation of the conflicts they themselves generated as 'persecution', but developed in the secular sphere. We saw how terms such 'grievance terms' as antisemitism and islamophobia are used to refer to much more behaviour than can on analysis be justified, and that this anathematised behaviour is often a justifiably irritated reaction to over-aggrieavability. We also examined the cognitive biases which lead to this over-aggrievability in the first place.

5. Inducing others to do these

Given that foremost demand the massive religions and ideologies (including the kind of liberalism which believes democracy should be spread by any means) make of their adherents in their relation to non-adherents is to 'invite them' to join in whichever way maximises the number of converts, unless they can rid themselves of the certainty-fabricating mechanisms we have considered by carrying out these demands they commit this final transgression. We saw that the same point applies with even more force to their stipulation on the indoctrination of children, because this is undeniably the single most important reason why people are hardly ever found to differ from the faith of their parents, the most flagrant evidence of their departure from reality if their claims to universality are to be accepted.

Freedom from Afflictive Processes

At this point we might well be suffering from the demoralising suspicion that these phenomena, from the afflictive psychological processes at the base, through their expression in all this extraordinarily complex, interdependent and habitual evil, to their most appalling consequences, are overwhelming and insoluble. The Buddha, while he does not drag the Kālāmās into a session of self-pitying depression about their habits, equally does not try to put a positive spin on the situation. Instead, he merely continues with the inquiry, moving on to the possibility of a claim which will for us today seem by far the most radical of the discourse: that we can, individually and therefore collectively, *be free* of the afflictive processes which drive all of this evil.

Here we consider:

- freedom from wanting,
- freedom from aversion (p. 459), and
- freedom from being deluded (p. 463).

We define each one and consider countering tendencies to each one. Since we have already investigated the qualities of their opposites, here we restrict ourselves specifically to objections to the cultivation of such freedoms.

>Alobha: freedom from wanting

> 'What do you think, Kālāmās? When freedom from wanting arises within a person, does it arise to their profit or loss?'
>
> 'To their profit, sir.'
>
> 'And thus free from wanting, Kālāmās, does not a person who is undominated by wanting, and whose mind is not possessed by it, *refrain* from killing a living being, or from taking what is not given, or from going after another person's spouse, or from telling lies, or from inducing others to do such things, such that there will long be *profit* and *bliss*?'
>
> 'Yes, sir.'

Meaning

Since freedom from the afflictive processes is much less familiar to us than the processes themselves, let us see what the classic texts have to say about it. The Universal Career's *Compendium of the Higher Teaching* defines freedom from wanting like this:

> What is freedom from wanting (alobha)? It is non-attachment to existence (bhava) or to the means of subsistence (bhavopakaraṇa). Its function consists of giving a base to the halting of misconduct.

In the *Higher Teachings Collection* of the Elders' School it is taught that:

> Freedom from wanting means non-attachment or non-adherence to the object, as in the case of a water droplet on a lotus leaf; produces non-appropriation as in the case of a liberated alsman (foe-destroyer); manifests as detachment, as would be the case of a man who had fallen in filth; [...] opposes the taint of selfishness; [...and] causes generosity.

Elimination of countering tendencies

Is it not impossible?

Pareto's famous advice to rulers that they not weary themselves resisting the emotionality of the populace but use it to their own advantage, which is largely favoured in today's world's rulers, is such an expression of hopelessness. Most people's personal experience of others and of themselves is enough to destroy any faith they might have in the possibility that people need not be dominated by wanting, disliking and delusion. Even if is possible for a few special individuals, the vast majority will still be at the mercy of these driving forces. Philosophers who sketch ethical systems requiring or even advocating that people free themselves from the domination of the afflictive processes are generally tolerated a little contemptuously as ivory tower idealists who need to get their head out of the clouds, deign to descend, and spend some time at street level getting their hands dirty.

In the 'monotheistic' systems in particular the mainstream has always argued that it is impossible for anyone to be entirely free of the influence of the afflictive emotions. We have examined the Christian and Islāmic traditions in some detail now and seen how many of their elements have come down to us in dependence on the afflictive processes. It should be no surprise, then, that there is in these traditions, and in their secular offspring, powerful resistance to the notion of freedom from the afflictive emotions. For Islām, as it is held by the vast majority of Muslims today, especially since the recent proselytising movement hailing the superiority of Islām over Christianity insofar as the former is supposed to take a more natural attitude to human nature, wanting and disliking included, by emphasising that they are part of 'the Creator's work' and not 'the Devil's'. These driving forces are taught to be a stamp 'the Creator Allāh' has left on our hearts. The celebrated Muslim Hanbāli scholar Ibn al-Jawzi (508-597 h.) writes of the ascetics of Islām, the Ṣūfis:

> It has occurred to some that the goal [of the religious Code] is spiritual practice, whereby there may be freedom from ruinous stains. […] They suppose the goal to be the suppression of certain internal attributes of humanity, e.g. desire, anger, etc. whereas it is not the Code's goal. […] Neither is the eradication of natural propensities by spiritual practice conceivable.[434]

Luckily, we ourselves are the locus of these processes, so to answer such declarations of impossibility requires no effortful research in esoteric doctrine or access to classified documents. It is the exploration of the possibility of this freedom to which the Buddha is about to introduce us.

How else will I get what I need?

As Ibn al-Jawzi correctly points out, Allāh via the Qur'ān instructs the

---

434 (Ibn al-Jawzi)

believer (in it) not to purify themselves of the afflictive emotions, but to *restrain* them.

> What is meant is restraint of the soul [...] reducing the harmful to moderation. Allāh praises[435] '...him who restrains the soul from passion' [...] If the seeking were eradicated there would be no need to restrain it.

He elaborates why Allāh made these tendencies innate in us – for our own protection, as a guarantee of being able to live indeed.

> They were created for some utility. Without wanting food, humans would perish. Without wanting marriage, the race would end. [...] Love of property is thus implanted in natures to let these desires be attained.

The same arguments are used nowadays by some partisans of scientific discourse, who believe (probably correctly) that Natural Selection has kept these tendencies in us, and go so far (probably incorrectly) as to credit such selection with moral goodness. It was because of the second kind of claim that the field of sociobiolgy was almost still-born and hastily adopted alternative names to avoid being associated with, for example, the idea that because certain men feel compelled to rape, then it is a biologically 'fit' tendency, and therefore 'good for the species'. We have already considered how gross a misunderstanding such ideas are of Natural Selection, and in general the 'stamp of the Creator' mentality has disappeared from modern biology.

What is not widely recognised is the extent to which this theistic thinking pervaded the works of figures in philosophy, politics and economics of recent centuries, even those who became the figureheads of so-called secular traditions. Take, for example, free market economics: Adam Smith was Christian and unlike modern advocates of his system had explicit faith in the hidden hand of God to ensure that the free market led to peace and prosperity on earth. His view, not at all unusual in his era, was described by the American economic historian Jacob Viner thus:

> The sentiments are innate to man; that is, man is endowed with them by

[435] Qur'ān 24, 40

> providence. Under normal circumstances, the sentiments are infallible. It is reason which is fallible. Greatest of all in degree of fallibility is the speculative reason of the moral philosopher, unless the legislator is on a still lower level. Man, however, tends to attribute to the human reason what is really the wisdom of the Author of Nature as reflected in the sentiments.[436]

It may be that we share these convictions: that wanting is natural, and that it is more reliable than cool reason in getting us what we need.

The reply to such objections from the Buddhist traditions is clear. Absence of wanting, as we have seen, is taught to be *the basis of sharing (dāna).*

This simple truth has momentous ramifications. We have already had reason to mention the pervasive notion in modern societies that we must be in perpetual competition with each other for the sake of economic and therefore social and therefore personal success. And indeed this is the basis of the capitalist system.

It has become rather a taboo in some quarters to inquire into this notion, and that is a sign of danger. Clearly experience shows that the result of this perpetual competition is only sporadic economic success, and much less social success; as for personal success, if it is measured by happiness, then the notion has been an abject failure. The more pampered ones among us are now familiar with the equation of luxury with anxiety, as presented frequently in art, literature and film[437], and as testified to by the astonishing statistics on anti-depressant drug use in the 'successful' economies, even though it continues to be in the interests of those who wish to retain their luxury to hoodwink the rest of humanity into striving for it. Furthermore competition's dangers to the environment are beginning to assume an aspect of urgency, even despite the efforts of massive corporations, and the researchers they bribe to falsify results, to conceal truly terrifying discoveries. Even without considering the environment, the failures are stark. In economics, the international monetary system is increasingly being questioned *in toto*. It is being pointed out more and more frequently and with more urgency that the operation of the banking system guarantees economic collapses, and that it is just a matter of predicting how frequently collapses will occur. Mackay's accounts of the lunacy of credit epidemics from centuries ago in

---

[436] For this citation (Viner, 1972, pp. 78-9) I am indebted to *Black Mass* (Gray, 2007).

[437] Todd Haynes' film *Safe* is an outstanding and astounding example, prophetic and horrific.

Europe are apparently (along with Sun Tzu's *Art of War*) required reading for novices on Wall Street.[438] As for human development, capitalist competition between leviathan corporations drags technological progress to a near standstill, as has been shown for example in the development, or lack of it, of petrol-independent energy production or vehicles: oil companies are simply not likely to get enthusiastic about investing in research that could undermine their tightening hold on the world energy economy. And not forgetting humaneness: it is most regrettably in the interest of a 'thriving' economy to ensure that many people do not have easy access to resources which would effectively be freely available to them in the absence of competition and privatisation of resources. As for society, it is clear that almost every social ill depends to some extent on this same fostered conviction that we are all by nature in rivalry with each other, and its concomitant requirement that resources be made to seem much scarcer than they are: the vast majority of crime, including violent crime, is related to accessing resources. It has been noted in some circles, and concealed in others, that the world actually has plenty of resources, for example plenty of food for everyone, but that market forces get in the way: for 'successful' economy, some people simply must not be allowed easy access to resources. For this reason vast quantities of food are, disgracefully, destroyed each year, while millions starve to death. These people are part of the sacrifice we make continually to this very modern god, Competition.

If we can for a moment get over our sense that we are so modern that we need not refer to old ideas about economic systems, we can survey what the great religious leaders of the world have said about such 'healthy competition'. We find that if their teachings have anything in common, and there really isn't much, it is that *giving,* or *sharing,* is a basic requirement not only for the spiritual path but also for the well-being of society. Although political Islām has not been free of the pursuit of wealth in its history by any means, the Qur'ān asks hoarders to meditate on the graves. Jesus of course says that we should sell all our possessions and offer the money in charity. A Buddhist path depends on the ten so-called 'carriers to the other side' (paramīta), and the first is to share.

This might just seem out of date, or twee. Is it not a reflection of the backwardness of the societies into which these figures were born? Well, we might ask ourselves who is more in need of sharing, people on an earth populated by a few million, and people on an earth populated by 7 billion. But, we might

---

438 So reports the Oxford professor who introduces a recent re-issue of *Extraordinary Mass Delusions.*

still ask, isn't 'if you can't beat them, join them' an eternal law? – is it not a fact that these religions are producing holy fools to be harvested from by the truly intelligent ones, the money-makers? Even among priests, pirs and gurus there seem to be numbered a fair few such clever folk, tending their unshod flock from the Rolls Royce as it were. In fact, because of our utter habituation to the competition for resources which makes us so useful to those who make money from us, we are trained only to recognise that very limited kind of success, wealth, and furthermore trained not to recognise its darker consequences.

Competition in our times has an impeccable reputation. As we have seen it is something so pervasive that it is almost inconceivable that there could be any other way. We say that competition is healthy, and that we do not wish others' failure so much as a good fight. But here is the first concealed darkness. For as much as we may tell ourselves, in the context of competition, that we wish our rivals well, this can only be hypocrisy, since we would hardly wish ourselves to fail or go bankrupt. We would be more honest of we openly wished our rivals failure and bankruptcy.

However, due to that very pervasiveness, it has been lost to the collective consciousness of humans that there might be an alternative. So not just the potential descent into violence, but also many of the great developments of modern society, such as technology and wealth creation, and the consequent removal of a large fraction of humankind from subjection to the environment, appear to depend on that competitive system. So many will feel, 'Do I really *want* to abandon competitiveness? After all, I might lose out.' But this appearance of dependency is an illusion: an illusion that depends on there being in our experience very few (or no) examples of a non-competitive systems to compare with the pervasive competition. It is a striking case of the mis-identification of causes we considered under trapped beliefs and superstition. The lack of alternatives is no accident: there are those with vested interests in maintaining a 'system monopoly'. Nevertheless, efforts are being made in some quarters to develop alternative systems based on sharing, such as the Venus Project[439]. It may be that in the future we will see alternatives in operation more frequently and gradually lose the cowardly fear, stoked by advertising, which insinuates in us that competitiveness is the only way to access those elusive resources.

---

439 See http://www.thevenusproject.com/.

>Adosa: freedom from aversion

'What do you think, Kālāmās? When freedom from aversion arises within a person, does it arise to their profit or loss?'

'To their profit, sir.'

'And thus free from aversion, Kālāmās, does not a person who is undominated by aversion, and whose mind is not possessed by it, *refrain* from killing a living being, or from taking what is not given, or from going after another person's spouse, or from telling lies, or from inducing others to do such things, such that there will long be *profit* and *bliss*?'

'Yes, sir.'

Meaning

The Universal Career's *Compendium of the Higher Teaching* defines it like this:

> What is freedom from aversion (adveṣa)? It is the absence of injurious striking (anāghāta) at living beings (sattva) with suffering and the things which set up suffering. Its function consists of giving a base to the halting of misconduct.

In the *Higher Teachings Collection* of the Elders' School it is taught that:

> Absence of disliking means non-churlishness and non-resentment, such as one finds in an agreeable friend; acts to suppress annoyance and feverishness, like sandalwood; manifests as radiant beauty, like the full moon; [...]opposes the taint of evil (dussīlya); [...and] causes morality.

Elimination of countering tendencies

How else will I defend myself?

Ibn al-Jawzi writes:

> Allāh says [440] 'and the suppressors of wrath', not 'those who lack wrath' …

[440] Qur'ān 3, 128

...and again points out that if one did purify oneself of this tendency to wrath, then there would be nothing to suppress, which would make Allāh's commandment in the Qur'ān impossible to carry out, a very undesirable situation. And again, he gives the logical reason for Allāh having created us thus:

> Without anger no-one would repel annoyance.

This objection is very common still, and frequently presents obstacles in the trainings recommended in the Buddhist traditions, especially the training in caring (or 'compassion') and in the Universal Career the rousing of the so-called Intention to Awaken (bodhicitta).

We may believe that anger has served us well, as a defence mechanism, or as a way of getting things done or sorted out, and consequently fear the influence such trainings might have on these mechanisms: won't it leave us defenceless or drained of healthy, aggressive energy?

This seems like a simple picture but it involves a great deal of confusion. Taking a little more care, we can identify four important points.

Firstly, the trainings do not undermine all anger necessarily, but disliking, hatred, aversion, grudges, etc. This is an important distinction we alluded to above. Take the example of parents watching their child repeat a harmful action: they might well get angry and reprimand the child in some way, but this does not mean that they dislike, hate, are averse to, or have a grudge against, their own child. The trainings presented by the Buddhist tradition, such as in amity and caring as we will see, might well make us *more* likely to get 'angry' at such situations, as we come to be more and more aware of how people seem willy-nilly to embark on paths guaranteed to harm themselves and those around them, whereas before we would not have cared one jot, but that very new caring will also show clearly: this kind of anger is more like a show, and is distinct from rage, whose unskilful ill effects we have already discussed.

The second thing to note is that the concept of 'anger' in English covers a multitude of evils and virtues. Aristotle noted that 'ire' (in Greek, ira), has positive qualities which should not be wasted, a kind of creative force. Like 'love', the word is a real amalgam of quite opposite tendencies. It includes, for example, the kind of righteous wrath which would have us in the blink of an eye annihilate all in our path; but it also includes that protective response of the parents we noted. As if they were somehow related!

Thirdly, it is a fact that there are mental states, deeply distorted by delusion, bolstered by habit, supported by circumstances perhaps, which while extremely damaging if allowed to continue, tend to be insensitive and thus to continue, uninfluenced by gentle means of persuasion. Often children are like this, because they cannot yet be reasoned with, and because their attention can so easily get totally involved in some object to the dramatic detriment of their general awareness of the situation. (The image of the child chasing the kite across the busy road comes to mind.) That is why the parents' anger can be so useful. Adults, rarely, can also develop this degree of idiocy combined with insensitivity. In such rare cases, the appropriate response of someone who genuinely cares about them might well be 'parental' anger – it could be the only response which got through to them.

Fourthly, however, we need to be honest with ourselves about how often anger can be beneficial or good-intentioned. Usually, we would have to admit, it is neither: usually, someone 'is angered', which means rather out of control, likely to do a lot of unnecessary damage, and acting on the basis of a very limited sphere of interest and with a great deal of delusion. We can each investigate instances from our own experience to verify this.

The trainings in freedom from the afflictive processes address directly the limited sphere of interest, and the delusion. So we can say that they 'purify' anger, in the sense that whilst we may continue to respond to certain situations with anger, that response is likely to be more and more appropriate, more and more insightful, and more and more useful.

>Amoha: freedom from delusion

> 'What do you think, Kālāmās? When freedom from being deluded arises within a person, does it arise to their profit or loss?'
>
> 'To their profit, sir.'
>
> 'And thus free from being deluded, Kālāmās, does not a person who is undominated by delusion, and whose mind is not possessed by it, *refrain* from killing a living being, or from taking what is not given, or from going after another person's spouse, or from telling lies, or from inducing others to do such things, such that there will long be *profit* and *bliss*?'
>
> 'Yes, sir.'

Meaning

The Universal Career's *Compendium of the Higher Teaching* defines it like this:

> What is freedom from delusion (amoha)? It is knowledge (jñāna) and discernment (pratisaṁkhyā) concerning the consequences of actions, and concerning the transmission (āgama) or [its] attainment (adhigama). Its function consists of giving a base to the halting of misconduct.[441]

In the *Higher Teachings Collection* of the Elders' School it is taught that:

> Freedom from delusion is opposed to the non-development of moral conditions. [...] It is the cause of development [meditation etc.].

Elimination of countering tendencies

Isn't ignorance bliss?

It is unfortunate that the initial dealings with delusion are likely to give us the impression that we were better off when we did not know what we now know. We go from day to day in such a frenzy of distraction that a mind in such a condition has been likened to a monkey swinging from tree to tree, always after the fruit on the next one, never enjoying the fruit on the current one.

However the same advice also asserts that with a little more application, a greater sense of calm than had previously been known can be discovered. That

---

[441] My translation, but cf. Boin-Webb's (Boin-Webb, Rahula, & Asanga).

initial horrifying chaos is not something we generate by training but something which was already there, and already as damaging, but just happening unawares.

On the social scale, we have seen heavily involved delusion is in driving the worst ills of our society. Pretending these ills are not there may seem more comfortable than facing them, but it is a very paltry comfort, not because it is cowardly, but because much greater comforts are possible. The example is often given of the comfort of the silkworm building its coccoon, only to be thrown later into boiling water for that very thread.

Can delusions not motivate beneficial revolutions?

It ought to go without saying that politics would benefit from this freedom. As a recent commentator puts it:

> Dealing with terrorism and proliferation is not a job for missionaries and crusaders. The heady certainty of faith, which sees every crisis as a heaven-sent opportunity to save humanity, is ill-suited to dealing with dangers that can never be defused. In times of danger, stoical determination and intellectual detachment are more useful qualities, and at its best realism embodied them.[442]

Even if such revolutions are won, the subsequent situation invariably goes horribly wrong very quickly, and this is not an accident. If the conceptual blaze of delusional feedback cycles is relied on, we should not expect to be able to extinguish them easily if some particular aim is haphazardly achieved in the course of the conflagration.

Even if freedom from the afflictive processes were an attractive notion, we will probably still have doubts about whether it can be achieved. The method is what the Buddha turns to next.

---

442 (Gray, 2007, p. 274)

The Four Mental Residences of Purity

'Now, Kālāmās, one who is a disciple of the noble, and thus devoid of envy, devoid of ill will, unbewildered, conscientious and aware, rests suffusing one quarter [the east], and likewise the second, and likewise the third, and likewise the fourth, with a spirit of amity, [...] caring, [...] sharing joy, [...and] perspective, and in the same way rests suffusing the all-encompassing universe upwards, downwards, all around, everywhere and in every way with an abundant, expansive, immeasurable spirit of amity [etc. ...], free from aversion and free from ill will.

Having identified the erroneous sources of certainty, made the call to individual responsibility and conscience, and led us through a consideration of the qualities and consequences of the three afflictive processes to an appreciation of the benefits of being free from them, the Buddha now turns to some methods which we can test and apply to progress towards those freedoms.

These trainings, called the four mental residences of purity (literally holiness) or the four immeasurables, have come to be taught by all the Buddhist traditions, not just found in the Pali canon in which this discourse comes down to us. For example, for the Universal Career, *The Discourse Taught by Immaculate Renown* says:

> catvārya pramāṇāni hi bodhi sattvasya buddha kṣetraṁ; tasmiṁstad bodhi prāpti buddha kṣetre maitrī karuṇā muditopekṣā vihāriṇassattvā upapatsyante
>
> An awakening being's Buddha-kingdom consists of the four immeasurables because when he or she attains Awakening beings abiding by amity, caring, sharing joy and perspective will arise there.[443]

Furthermore, most Buddhist tantric meditation methods of the Secret Mantra Career include a stage where the four immeasurables are developed.

They are stressed even in the preliminary practices for what Tibetan Buddhism teaches is the most advanced form of spiritual practice, 'Total Integration' (in Tibetan, rdzogs-chen). For example, in the preliminary practices of the most popular tradition, the Heart Essence of the Vast Expanse, deriving from the visionary revelations of the 18th century master Jigme Lingpa, they are

443 From Chapter One, The Kingdom of an Awakened One.

included prominently in the stage of rousing the intention to awaken:

> Deluded by their own diverse experiences as they would be by a moon in water,
> Beings are lost in the succession of links of the chain of cyclic existence.
> In order to bring them to the ease in the space of the clear light of natural awareness,
> By means of the four limitless [trainings] I generate the Intention.

So they are important at all levels of Buddhist practice. They are even taught in the non-Buddhist religion of Tibet, the Bön religion. Their features can be divided into those they have

- in common, and
- in particular.

In common

Meaning

The *Compendium of the Higher Teaching*[444] speaks of the four in its presentation of realisations (abhisamāya), along with many other kinds of realisation. The realisation of the four 'immeasurable' states (synonymous with the mental residences of purity) are:

> evenmindedness (samādhi) and deep knowledge (prajña), and the mindstate and mental events concomitant with them[445], based on a mental absorption (dhyāna) dwelling on [a] thought…[446]

where the thought differs for each one (see the particular treatments below). (We should be careful to distinguish the method from the realisation in each case, especially since *The Compendium* describes the four immeasurables as included in the so-called 'later realisations' and 'final realisations', which puts them on 'the path of cultivation', in other words they only occur to awakening beings who have passed the moment of gaining a direct vision of reality without confusion[447], whereas the methods of training are even recommended to beginners.)

The interesting thing to note about the realisations is that each is based not merely on a thought, but on a mental absorption dwelling on the thought – i.e. they are based on kinds of meditative training, the method the Buddha refers to in our discourse. (This should make us very careful about familiar words such as 'kindness' and 'compassion', usually referring to ordinary mental and even emotional states, habitually used to translate these terms.) Furthermore on the basis of meditation there comes evenmindedness with deep knowledge. The

---

444 All the citation page numbers of this work refer to the equivalent passages (although I have translated some of the terms slightly differently) in the only English translation of it (Boin-Webb, Rahula, & Asanga).

445 Thus far we just have the common definition of any realisation, including the eight deliverances (vimokṣa), the eight spheres of mastery (abhibhvāyatana) and the ten spheres of totalisation (kṛtsnayatana, Pali kasiṇa-) and many more.

446 (p. 223 *op. cit.*)

447 The *Compendium* states: 'What is the later [pṛṣtha-] realisation? It is the path of cultivation. […] What is the final [niṣtha-] realisation? It is identical to the final path.' (p. 219, 220 *op. cit.*) And: 'What is the final path? It is the diamond-like evenmindedness, because it calms all unruliness, abandons every fetter, and obtains freedom from every fetter.' (p. 172 *op. cit.*)

terms refer not only to this, but also to any mental states and events associated with it. We will bear all this in mind when we comes to examine them one by one.

Eliminating shared countering tendencies

What's the use of meditating when the whole society is in an emergency?

One of the best-known historians of mass madness in human society, Charles Mackay (1814-1889) points out:

> Men, it has been well said, think in herds; it will be seen that they go mad in herds, while they only ever recover their senses slowly, and one by one.[448]

As we shall see it is a mistake, moreover, to think that this kind of training is restricted to what is familiar to us as 'meditation' – sitting on a cushion and using our minds. The trainings apply to how we conduct ourselves generally. If we feel there should be a solution which we can somehow enforce on others without adding to the afflictive processes already playing out, we can look for it. We will consider this matter in more detail when we consider the trainings one by one.

Common benefits

Keys to the awakened kingdom

As we saw they are taught in the Universal Career to be methods to gain access to conditions which are most suited to practice, those of a so-called 'kingdom of an Awakened Being', (Sanskrit, buddhakṣetra). When one reaches complete Awakening (i.e. becomes a 'buddha') then her or his awareness is described as 'the body which is the Laws and their realisation' (dharmakāya, as distinguished from the physical form, which is described as the 'body which is an appearance', rūpakāya). This attainment is said in the same discourse to be accomplishable by the four mental residences of purity:

> The body of an Awakened One is the body of the Laws [...] It is

---

[448] From the preface to the 1852 edition of *Extraordinary Popular Delusions & The Madness of Crowds* (Mackay, 1852).

> generated by amity, caring, sharing joy and perspective.[449]

Each is described as the locus for this awakening to take place, for various reasons:

> Amity is the locus of awakening, because of the equality among sentient beings. Caring is the locus of awakening, because of the patience in the face of suffering. Joy is the locus of awakening, because of taking pleasure in the Laws. Perspective is the locus of awakening, because of the eradication of repugnance and affectation.[450]

Common training methods

The preparation

The trainee

The Buddha says that the one who trains in these methods should be…

one who is a disciple of the noble, and thus devoid of envy, devoid of ill will, unbewildered, conscientious and aware…

The word for disciple here means one who listens to them, or (by extension, given the cultural context) one who studies under their instruction. The nobles are not the aristocracy of course – the term was used by the communities of spiritual seekers and ascetics to refer to those who had obtained high degrees of realisation thanks to their spiritual practice.

The word translated here as 'devoid' can also have a more active sense than that, namely 'having foregone' and indeed the English word 'fore-gone' is cognate with the Pali vi-gāta. We can see immediately that the Buddha does not say that the person who is about to begin training is already completely free of the root afflictive processes. Instead he recommends freeing ourselves from cruder expressions of them which are more amenable to an ordinary mind's self-discipline: at least for the time of the training, all thoughts of envy – the word (abhijjhā) has a connotation of the mind reaching out, aiming to have something it does not yet consider itself to have, longing even – and of ill will – the wish that others should suffer or be injured in any way – should be foregone, put out of

---

449 From Chapter Two, Skilful Means.

450 From Chapter Four, Awakening Beings.

mind. Furthermore the mind, as we prepare to train, should not be 'totally bewildered' – the word used means freedom from an advanced version of delusion, what we might call 'deluding oneself'. As far as possible we should let the mind clear and put to one side our habitual ways of tricking ourselves.

These three are the last three of the traditional ten unskilful actions – three of body (the first three crimes of the five considered above), four of speech (false, divisive, harsh and idle) and these three of mind. In later treatments self-deluding was usually specifically clinging to 'wrong view' about the consequences of actions, meaning obstinately believing that unskilful actions are skilful and *vice versa*. That is why the Buddha has begun by leading the Kālāmās through the consideration of the skilfulness or otherwise of the three root processes of the mind.

The word translated as 'conscientious' refers to discerning the processes going on within one's mind. It is this faculty which allows us to discern when the three developed afflictive processes, and eventually to recognise when the root afflictive processes, are occurring. And finally we should be aware: this faculty is the root of continuing the practice rather than falling into 'distraction'.

This mental preparation in itself is, then, quite a tall order. To support the preparation to discourage the three afflictive processes and encourage the 'twin guards' of conscientiousness and awareness, we can be strategic with the period and setting of the training.

The period

Because of the mind's tendency to wander, especially into unskilful processes, it could be that we need short sessions, at least at the inception of our course of training. In particular we should be especially careful not to develop envy or longing (the first of the developed afflictive processes) with respect to the meditation itself. That means that we should not be struggling with ourselves, wishing for some future state (or state noticed in others!) of open spontaneous love and resenting our current inability to achieve it.

The Buddha taught stingy people to share by recommending that they pass a small gift from one hand to the other repeatedly. The point is to work with what you have. As soon as you catch yourself getting impatient, then this 'envy' has developed. This is why regular short sessions at the beginning are *the only useful kind.* If you slap yourself on the back after a three-hour session of struggling with envy and longing, you are wasting time.

The place

The setting itself should be conducive to these mental freedoms. For example, if our motivation for these trainings derives, as well it might, from appreciating the extensive horrors of modern society, we might be someone habitually involved in 'meditating' on the world's injustices and violent conflicts, and this habit is likely to disturb the mind with these three developed afflictions – envy or longing, ill will and deluding ourselves. So there is little point settling to train in our activist shrine with news clippings of massacres and corporate corruption and callousness dangling before our eyes, lit by an angry red bulb in a suffocating corner.

Better to find a light, airy place without too much sensual distraction beyond gentle stimuli from calm beauty. This could be an artificial place of peace, such as the shrine room of a Buddhist centre or an unostentatious church or mosque, or if we are lucky enough an area of natural beauty outside where we can walk or sit in peace for a time. In such conditions we are more likely to be able to forego, at least temporarily, these mental disturbances.

The body

Whether we like it or not, the body is currently part of the support for our mind. In these training methods, the focus should be the mind. That means we should be prepared to be flexible with the disposition of the body, trying out different ways to ease the training. We can try standing, sitting or lying; moving or staying still or integrating movement and stillness (such as doing hatha yoga postures between sitting sessions); maintaining rigidity stressfully, perhaps in the full lotus position on a hard floor or stool, back held straight and stomach pulled in, or letting ourselves loose, legs slightly uncrossing on comfortable cushions. We should not be too short-sighted or hasty to judge while trying out different bodily strategies: what seems painful for a while may well turn out to be the best. That is why we should keep in mind that the focus is the mind, not the body. We are not just trying to get comfortable!

The intention

Depending on our psychological make-up, we may benefit however from a degree of self-discipline. It is often taught that before a session of training, however short, it is useful to make a promise to oneself: 'I am going to devote this session to the development of the residences of purity.' It may also help to set a timer.

However, if such strictures provoke disturbance during the session, then try looser arrangements. *We must work with what we have, not with what we wish we had.*

Incorporating these trainings into a Universal Career practice

For those who have embarked on the so-called Universal Career (mahāyāna) or Career of Awakening Beings (bodhisattvayāna), all practices of body, speech and mind, are conjoined with the three 'excellences':

- referring to the Three Jewels and rousing the Intention, before you begin,
- maintaining deep knowledge of the lack of independence of 'the three spheres', during the practice, and
- dedicating the merit of the practice to Awakening for all beings' sake, at the conclusion.

Referring to the Three Jewels and rousing the Intention before you begin

The Three Jewels are:

- the Buddhas: those who have achieved the Awakening to complete awareness which allows them to be liberated from all fetters and veils (such as the afflictive emotions and cognitive dissonance with reality);
- the Dharma/Dhamma: the realisation of Awakening itself and the methods they demonstrated to provoke it in others; and
- the Sangha: the community of people who dedicate themselves to receiving, reflecting on and testing these methods, especially those who have gained direct experience of the way things are.

It is important to note that these are not culture-specific, even though the terms traditionally used to refer to them might well be.

What does it mean to refer yourself to these? Ordinarily we do not recognise that any of them is possible. So first of all we need to find out if they might be. Some of us will not be familiar with any accounts from history of people who 'Awakened' in the manner described, so we might need to turn to historical accounts to look for them. There are certainly some such accounts in the general Buddhist traditions (for example the five Awakened Beings of this aeon: Kakusandha or Krakucchanda, Koṇāgamana, Kassapa or Kaśyapa, Siddhārtha Gautama, and Metteya or Maitreya), and many more in the Tibetan

Buddhist tradition (Nāgarjuna of what is now South India, Padmasambhava of what is now Afghanistan and Pakistan, Tilopa of Bengal, Milarepa of Tibet, etc.) and Zen traditions (Bodhidharma of India, Hui Neng of China, etc.). Furthermore, outside of what is usually considered 'Buddhist' tradition, there are also examples of people who claimed these freedoms in the Sufi tradition of Islām (Hallāj of Fars in 'Persia', Rūmi of Balkh in Afghanistan, etc.). There might even be examples from traditions not generally considered religious.

Once we have opened our minds to the possibility of Awakening, we need to compare our current goals with that goal, and see if that one is more important or not. If we feel it is, then we can orientate ourselves towards that goal, taking the examples of Awakened ones as our ideals (the first jewel), and firmly committing ourselves to receiving, reflecting on and testing what they demonstrated or taught (the second jewel).

If we feel that this will be easy without help, then so be it, but if not, then we need to see if our habitual companions share this goal or not. If they do not, then we might reorientate ourselves to accepting friends from among such a community (the third jewel).

Then, the 'Intention' referred to is to commit ourselves sincerely to the goal of Complete Awakening with a particular reference – not for our own sake, but for the sake of all living beings. If we are beginners then even if we are attracted by such an aspiration, it will be very artificial. However, no matter how artificial, it will still be beneficial. We will have more to say about this once we have discussed the trainings in Amity and Caring, which are considered part of the foundation for developing a less artificial version of this most noble of intentions.

Maintaining deep knowledge of the lack of independence of the three spheres during practice

The three spheres refer to the 'agent' who is carrying out the practice, the 'action', the activity of the practice, and the 'patient', the object upon which the practice is carried out.

Ordinarily we relate to these three spheres as if they were something which could exist by itself. We imagine, as it were, that 'we', the agent, at one point are not engaging in the practice, but that at the next moment 'we' engage in it, and are thereafter engaged in it, as if the 'we' were a single, unchanging thing. We might ask: so what? Unfortunately this kind of self-conceptualisation encourages us to attribute qualities developed in the practice to our own powers. It scuppers the training because the positive experiences which develop get channelled into bolstering identification and pride at accomplishment. Such identification and pride then become an obstacle to maintaining the kind of perspective necessary to continue in the practice, even though it may feel very pleasant. (It is this kind of meditative experience's treachery we considered in the deconstruction of ruci, 'relishing', as a source of certainty.)

For this reason there developed in the Universal Career of Buddhism a series of meditations intended as antidotes to this potential source of obstacles. To consider them very briefly: The 'we' engaged in the practice cannot be defined outside of the practice. If we look for some unchanging entity which can somehow enter into the practice and leave it, we will not find such a thing, for it would not be unchanging. If we object that there is a double entity, partly unchanging (such that we can attribute the identity 'we' to it at all times) and at the same time partly changing (such that it can be at times engaged in practice, and at other times not, as common sense dictates) then the question arises, how can these two entities, one of which we are imagining to be unchanging, interact with each other if one of them cannot change? For interaction would require change on both sides to be meaningful in any ordinary sense.

So, taking care over the steps of this meditation, we can see that the common sense interpretation of agent and action is cruder than what is actually going on. 'Common sense' provides a rough description, but it fails and becomes paradoxical if we scrutinise reality too closely. Applying similar reasoning to the objects upon which the practices are done will yield the same result: that the practiced issue cannot be separated from the practice either. So we find that the three, agent, action and patient; or practitioner, practice and practiced-upon; are intimately and inextricably related. None of them can be defined non-paradoxically without the others. They are inter-related and inter-dependent. This is the meaning of the 'lack if independence of the three spheres'.

We cannot keep reminding ourselves of this lack of independence during practice, as it would interfere with other meditations: to speak in the jargon, particularising insight (vipassanā, vipaśyanā) would be confused, and 'stopping' (samathā, śamathā) would be disturbed. That is not the intent of this instruction. Instead, we should work in general to gain some familiarity with this non-common-sensical way of dealing not just with our practice but activities in general. Conceptual meditations on the nature of the three spheres can be alternated with other kinds of meditation, so that the insights gained in the former can inform the very foundations of the latter.

Dedicating the merit of the practice to Awakening for all beings' sake at the conclusion

The third 'excellence' is to be done on concluding the practice session.

We mentally 'sign over' the benefit of the practice to all beings. This perhaps more than any other practice is the distinction of the Universal Career.

It has been much misunderstood, but to consider in detail how so would be to detract rather from our purpose here. Save to say that we can distinguish an offering of this benefit whose beneficiary is limited from an offering with an unlimited beneficiary. The former is easily conflated with the conventional idea of prayer in the massive religions, since we are effectively wishing that benefits accrue to particular people or beings. Like prayer it has a strong flavour of magic and wishful thinking about it. Whether or not it is effective on those beneficiaries is beside the point here, for the practice being advocated is an offering to *unlimited* beneficiaries. The psychological effect of this on ourselves is to release any potential attachment we might have to the results of that beneficial offering. This short-circuits the very human tendency of attributing goodness to our own power: it prevents those obstacle, identification and pride, developing.

If we fail to dedicate in this manner, and such identification develops, as it will, that is not to say that there is no benefit to the practice. But the benefit is likely to be counteracted by developing attachment. Here the famous simile of the dewdrop is used: a single one appears but it evaporates in the sun. However, if we make the dedication, this total surrender of our claim to possess the results of the practice personally, then it is as if the dewdrop were shaken into an ocean. A few moments' sun then can do nothing to it, because *'it' cannot be identified anymore*, even though we know *it has not disappeared.*

The crux of the training methods

> …rests suffusing one quarter [the east], and likewise the second, and likewise the third, and likewise the fourth, with a spirit of amity [or caring or sharing joy or perspective], and in the same way rests suffusing the all-encompassing universe upwards, downwards, all around, everywhere and in every way with an abundant, expansive, immeasurable spirit of amity [or the others], free from animus and free from ill will…

The Buddha's words are quite self-explanatory and clear. What the spirit of amity and the rest actually are we consider next, but first let us note that many other discourses in the Pali canon afford us extra instructions from the Buddha on how to train in the four immeasurable mental states. For example, in *the Contracted Discourse*[451] he advises a newcomer:

> 'Evaṁ sikkhitabbaṁ: "Mettāme cetovimutti bhāvitā bhavissati bahulīkatā yānīkatā vatthukatā anuṭṭhitā paricitā susamāraddhā"ti. Evañhi te, bhikkhu, sikkhitabbaṁ.'
>
> 'Then you should train yourself thus: "Amity, my mind-emancipator, will be developed, done often, taken as a career, realised, set up as ongoing, intimately familiarised with, and undertaken properly." That is how you, almsman, should train yourself.'

And the same advice is repeated for the other three trainings.

Note the implications of the expressions: each is not just to be vaguely developed: Each is to be 'done often', which tells us not to expect great things from a single attempt. Each is to be 'taken as a career', which implies that each should be prioritised ahead of our other activities. Each is to be 'realised', in the sense that something which was not there is to be brought into being as a reality: we can note in passing that it is not expected that there is even anything to notice as identifiable with the practice at the beginning. Each is to be 'set up as ongoing', which tells us the important piece of information that at the beginning it will be unsteady, and even though realised may be lost again. Each is to be 'intimately familiarised with', that is to say, at the beginning it is not expected to integrate especially well with what one knows. (An alternative meaning to this word, paricita, is 'piled up', so we can gather the resources necessary for the practice.) And finally, each is to be 'undertaken properly', that is, not as a diversion or falteringly.

It should inspire us to see the immeasurables referred to as 'mind-emancipators' too – and keep us away from the error of considering them as a kind of duty to the undeserving.

---

[451] Discourse 63 of the 'eights' in the Numerical Collection. We can usefully note that this is the very newcomer whom the Buddha treated rather roughly as pretending to be interested in spiritual training but (as the Buddha saw it) more likely just to become a tagger-along in our quote warning us about following a teacher, making this the kind of advice the Buddha might well have given us moderns with our tendency to herd.

In particular

The four will be treated in detail in order:

- amity,
- caring,
- sharing joy, and
- perspective.

For each one I will consider

- the meaning,
- elimination of countering tendencies, including formal objections we may have to the practices being recommended in the discourse and difficulties with training, and
- related training methods from various Buddhist traditions.

Immeasurable>	Amity	Caring	Joy	Perspective
Meaning	479	503	517	531
Eliminating countering tendencies	483	506	518	534
Related training methods	499	513	528	541

>Amity (metta)

Meaning

The *Compendium* says:

> What is amity? It is evenmindedness and deep knowledge, and the mindstate and mental events concomitant with them, based on a mental absorption dwelling on the thought, *'May beings live in happiness!'*

Clearly this is not ordinary amity, which might vanish as circumstances change, but a kind of gathering conviction in amity based on meditation on a wish for others. That it is to say it is not something we are expected to have right away, but something which is developed.

Types

What are these 'beings' we are to wish to live in happiness? How we view these beings depends on our perspective, and this changes as we train.

Beginners' amity – for beings seen as real

The ordinary mind of the beginner, such as ours, sees sentient beings as real entities in themselves. We imagine them 'undergoing' happiness, as if some unchanging identity were somehow entering into a state of happiness.

Advanced amity – for beings whose entity is seen as illusory

Our perspective can be deepened, however, as we shall see. Just how far it can be developed is revealed in *The Discourse Delivered by Immaculate Renown.* Whilst beginners have no choice but to view sentient beings according to their ordinary perceptions, as real, Immaculate Renown (Vimalakīrti) sees them differently:

> Atha Mañjuśrī kumāra bhūto licchavi vimalakīrtim evam avocat: 'Satpuruṣa, bodhisattvena sarvasattvāḥ kathaṁ draṣṭavyāḥ?'
>
> Abravīt: 'Mañjuśrīḥ, tadyathāpi nāma vijñaḥ puruṣa udakacandraṁ prakṣete, evameva bodhisattvena sarvasattvā draṣṭavyāḥ.'
>
> Thereupon, Gentle Splendour, the crown prince, addressed the Licchavi Immaculate Renown: 'Good sir, how should an awakening being regard

all living beings?'

Immaculate Renown replied, 'Gentle Splendour, an awakening being should regard all livings beings as a wise person regards the reflection of the moon in water.'

This is just the first in a long list of similes:

> māyākāro māyākāra nirmita manuṣyaṁ … adarśa maṇḍale mukhaṁ … mṛgatṛṣṇikājalam … pratiśrutkā ghoṣanādiḥ … ākāśa megharāśiḥ … phena piṇḍasya … pūrvāntaḥ … budbudodaya vyayau … kadalīsārāpekṣeva … vidyuccyutiriva … paṁcama dhātu sadṛśāḥ … saptamāyatana sadṛśāḥ … ārupyeṣu rūpa darśana sadṛśā … dagdha bījād aṅkura niṣpattiriva … maṇḍūkasya romā'cchādanaṁ yathā … ṁaraṇārthikasya krīḍāratiriva … srotāpannasya satkāya dṛṣtir yathā … sakṛdāgāmini tṛtīyabhava iva … anāgāmini garbhāvakrāntiḥ … arhati rāga dveṣa mohāḥ … kṣānti lābhi bodhisattve mātsarya dauḥsīlya vyāpāda vihisā cittam … tathāgate vāsanā … jātyandhajanena rūpa darśanam … nirodha samāpatti ānāpānaḥ … akāśe śakuneḥ padam … paṇḍa kalāṁgula rohaṇaḥ … vandhyā putra prāptiḥ … tathāgata nirbhitasya kleśotpattiḥ … vibodhe svapna dṛṣta darśanam … asaṅkalpe kleśaḥ … ahetukatvādagnyotpādaḥ … parinirvṛtasya pratisandhiriva … bodhisattvena sarvasattvāḥ pratyavekṣyāḥ. Mañjuśrīḥ, evam paramārthata eva nairātmya prabodhena sarvasattvāḥ pratyavekṣyāḥ.'

The awakening being regards all living beings as a magician regards a person emanated by a magician … like a face in a mirror … the water of a mirage … the sound of an echo … a mass of clouds in the sky … the end of a previous mass of foam[452] … a popping bubble … the core of a plantain[453] … a flash of lightning … the fifth great element[454] … the seventh sense-medium[455] … the appearance of matter in an immaterial

452 The simile seems to refer to the foam of waves, coming and going – here we imagine the sentient being to be like the very last foam of the previous wave before it disappears.

453 Which is a hollow plant!

454 In a tradition teaching only four!

455 In a tradition that teaches six!

realm … a sprout from a rotten seed … a tortoise-hair coat … the fun of games for one who wishes to die … a stream-winner's belief that the relative is absolute[456] … a third rebirth of a once-returner … the descent of a nonreturner into a womb … a saint's sensual love, aversion and delusion … thoughts of envy, bad morals, ill will, and malice in an awakening being who has attained acceptance [457] … habitual tendencies in One who has Arrived in Truth[458] … the perception of color in one blind from birth … breathing in the meditative attainment of cessation[459] … the track of a bird in the sky … the growth of the head of a eunuch's penis[460] … the son born of a barren woman … afflictive processes produced by an emanation of One who has Arrived in Truth … dream-visions seen after waking … the afflictive processes of one who is free of conceptualisations … fire burning without fuel … the reincarnation of one who has passed utterly beyond. Precisely thus, Gentle Splendour, does an awakening being who understands lack of independence consider all living beings.'

But what would happen to the training in amity if we had such a perspective?

Abravīt: 'Kulaputra, yadi bodhisattvena sarva sattvā evam pratyavekṣyāḥ, kathamatha sarvasattveṣu mahāmaitry upapatsyate?'

Āha: 'Mañjuśrīḥ, yadā bodhisattvas tathā hi pratyavekṣate: "evaṁ dharma parijñāya, ebhyaḥ sattvebhyo darśayāmi"ti tataḥ sarva sattveṣu samyakśaraṇa maitry upapadyate; anupādāna kāraṇād upaśānta maitrī, kleśā bhāvenātāpa maitrī, tryadhvasamatā kāraṇādyadyad upamatā maitrī, paryutthānā bhāva kāraṇādavirodha maitrī, ādhy

---

[456] A stream-winner has entered the Buddhist path through their understanding of reality, whereas seeing the relative as ultimate is the very mistake the Buddha has considered at great length in our discourse.

[457] Specifically the acceptance of the discovery that all phenomena are unborn, since interdependent and therefore not 'really there' to be able to have 'come to be there'.

[458] One who has Arrived in Truth is an epithet of a buddha, who has cleared away all such tendencies.

[459] During which meditation the breathing stops!

[460] Thurman (translating from the Tibetan) takes this to mean the erection of the penis, but the Sanskrit seems to mean 're-growth' or 'healing of a wound', i.e. the 'eunuch' has had the penis cut off and we should imagine sentient beings to be like this penis growing back (another impossibility, of course).

ātmika bāhyā sambheda kāraṇādadvaya maitrī, suniṣṭhā kāraṇād akṣobhya maitrī, abhedyābhiprāya vajra kāraṇād dṛḍha maitrī, svabhāva viśuddhi kāraṇād viśuddhi maitrī, āśaya samatā kāraṇāt samatā maitrī, arihanana kāraṇād arhan maitrī, anācchedyasattva paripācana kāraṇād bodhisattva maitrī, bhūyo'pi tathatā'dhigama kāraṇāt tathāgata maitrī, sattvā pasvāpana suprabodhana kāraṇād buddha maitrī, svayam abhisaṁbodhi kāraṇāt svayaṁbhū maitrī, tulyarasa kāraṇād bodhi maitrī, anunaya pratigha prahāṇa kāraṇād anāropa maitrī, mahāyāna paryavabhāsa karaṇato mahā karuṇā maitrī, śūnyatā nairātmya pratyavekṣaṇa kāraṇād aparikheda maitrī, ācāryamuṣṭy abhāva kāraṇād adharma dāna maitrī, duḥśīla sattvāpekṣā kāraṇāt śīla maitrī, svapararakṣā kāraṇāt kṣānti maitrī, sarva sattva bhāravahana kāraṇād vīryamaitrī, anāsvāda kāraṇād dhyāna maitrī, kālenāsādhana kāraṇāt prajñā maitrī, samanta dvāra darśana kāraṇād upāya maitrī, abhiprāya pariśuddhi kāraṇād akuhana maitrī, paścāttāpa karaṇato niścala maitrī, anaṅgaṇa kāraṇād adhyāśaya maitrī, akṛtrima kāraṇād amāyāvimaitrī, buddha sukha pratiṣṭhāpana kāraṇāt sukha maitrī. Mañjuśrīḥ, sā hi bodhisattvasya maitrī.'

Gentle Splendour then asked further, 'Noble sir, if an awakening being regards all living beings in such a way, how does he give rise to great amity toward them?'

Immaculate Renown replied, 'Gentle Splendour, when an awakening being regards all living beings in this way, he thinks: "Just as I have come to know the Law through, so should I reveal it to living beings." Thereby, he generates amity that is a proper refuge for all living beings; amity calmed because free of grasping; amity unheated by the afflictive processes; amity that accords with reality through equanimity about the three times; amity without opposition caused by reality as it rises up; amity that is without duality caused by disjunction between the inner self and the outside; amity that is imperturbable because beautifully decisive; amity that is firm because its it has an adamantine unbreaking purpose; amity that is pure because it is purified of being something in itself; amity that is even because of the evenness of its resting place; the saint's amity because the enemy has been killed; the awakening being's amity because it uninterruptedly makes living beings more mature; the amity of One who has Arrived in Truth

> because it understands very reality; the amity of an Awakened One because it wakes living beings from their sleep; amity spontaneous because Higher Awakening is spontaneous; amity that is Awakening because of the similar flavour; amity unpresuming because it lacks the enmity of politeness; amity that is great compassion through universal career radiance; amity never exhausted because it pays attention to emptiness and the transcendence of identity[461]; amity that is not a sharing of the Law[462] because it lacks the tight fist of a teacher; amity that is discipline because it looks to living beings' indiscipline; amity that is acceptance due to one's own and others' being protected; amity that is bravery because it takes responsibility for all living beings; amity that is contemplation because of lack of voracity; amity that is deep insight because of timely accomplishment; amity that is cleverness because it reveals doors everywhere; amity unhypocritical because of the purpose being pure throughout; amity that is without deviation caused by remorse[463]; amity of higher disposition because it has no particular place to go; an amity without trickery because uncontrived; amity that is bliss because it introduces living beings to the bliss of the Awakened One. Such, Gentle Splendour, is the great amity of an awakening being.'[464]

Let us all develop such a capacity!

Elimination of countering tendencies

Among the factors which interfere in the development of amity are the so-called 'near enemies' – meaning states or activities of mind which closely resemble it but compete with it – as well as theoretical objections and then, once we begin the development, difficulties which arise in practice.

---

[461] Emptiness in the technical sense we discussed on p. 256 and transcendence of identity referring to the fact that the deeper you investigate, the less things can be reasonably seen as independent things in themselves.

[462] Thus the Sanskrit, possibly corrupt: the Tibetan, rather less radical and more in keeping with the remainder of this list of the ten 'carriers to the far shore', has 'is a sharing of the Law because...'

[463] Literally 'after-burn'. The sense of the Sanskrit has the same ambiguity as the English, 'does not deviate because of remorse'.

[464] The excerpt is from the beginning of the chapter about 'The Goddess'.

Near enemies

All Buddhist traditions concur that the near enemy of amity is partial love.

Approach to loved ones

It has become common to hear some Buddhist teachers, especially in the USA, the same country whose Hollywood inundates the world continually with films in which familial love is the final redemption cleansing even the most appalling sins, say that it is good for us to have the partial affection we feel for our family and friends, and that we are not expected by Buddhist training to give this up as some kind of noble sacrifice. Whilst it may be true that these feelings of affection can be used as the basis for development of amity, there are clear provisos made in the teachings for awakening beings about 'excessive or *redundant* love' (atiriktaraṁ prema) for particular people, such as family, friends and lovers, and about the related idea that particular people are 'conjunct to' or 'belong to' (samprayukta) us. One extraordinary onslaught of such qualifications occurs in *the Discourse Requested by Ugra*, a teaching unusual in that the Buddha specifically addresses those living the domestic life, perhaps married, perhaps with children, who wish to train in the Universal Career:

> Moreover, O eminent householder, the awakening being who is a householder should not bring forth a mind of excessive love towards a son. O eminent householder, if one brings forth a mind of excessive love towards a son, while not doing so towards other beings, one should reproach oneself with three reproaches. And what are these three? (1) Awakening belongs to the awakening being whose mind is impartial, not to the one whose mind is partial. (2) Awakening belongs to the awakening being who strives rightly, not to one who strives wrongly. (3) Awakening belongs to the awakening being who does not make distinctions, not to one who makes distinctions. Thus having reproached oneself with these three reproaches, one should bring forth the idea of 'enemy' towards the son, thinking, 'He is an enemy, and is not dear to my heart. If for his sake I bring forth excessive love towards that son of mine while not doing so towards other beings I shall be deviating from the training prescribed by the Buddha.'[465]

---

[465] Chapter 5, §14 (Nattier, 2007, pp. 255-6)

A similar-spirited but much longer series of triple reflections is suggested for one's relation with one's spouse. I suspect this kind of meditation will come easily to many:

> About one's spouse one should give rise to the thoughts [...] impermanence, unreliability, changeability; [...] 'my companion in my happiness and enjoyment now but not in the next world', 'my companion for eating and drinking, but not in experiencing acts' consequences', 'my companion in pleasure, but not in suffering', [...] impure, stinking, disagreeable, [...] an enemy, an executioner, an antagonist, [...] an ogre, a demon, a black magician, [...] insatiable, depraved, ungrateful, [...] a bad friend, covetous and grasping, an obstacle to pure conduct, [...] a destiny in hell, in the animal kingdom, in the underworld, [...] a burden, a responsibility, an obligation, [...] not mine, not owned, on loan,[466] [...] occasion for unskilful deeds of body, speech, mind, [...] occasion for thoughts of wanting, malice and hostility, [...] a prison, a killing, a binding, [...] an obstacle to morality, to meditative absorption, to insight, [...] a trap, a snare, a net, [...] a plague, an injury, an infectious disease, [...] a dispute, a mishap, a hailstorm, [...] sickness, old age, death, [...] a demon, a holder of demons, a frightening deity, [...] sorrow, grief, pain and depression and distress, [...] a giant wolf, sea monster, cat, [...] a black snake, a crocodile, an epileptic condition, [...] no protector, no refuge, no rest-place, [...] swollen, shrivelled, diseased, [...] a robber, a prison guard, a guardian of hell, [...] a flood, a junction, a knot, [...] a swamp, a chasm, a whirlpool, [...] a rope, a fetter, a snare, [...] a fire-pit, a grass-fire lamp, a razor, [...] useless, a thorn, poison, [...] very vain, obsessed with clothing, clinging, [...] gaoler, punisher, sword-wielder, [...] quarrelling, contentious, fault-finding, [...] being with what one dislikes, being separated from what one likes, suffering itself. In short, one brings forth the thought in relation to the spouse: the impurity of fighting, the disturbance of fighting, the cause of all harm, the root of all unskilful actions.[467]

---

[466] This is as far as the earlier translations (into Chinese) go. The remaining triplets seem to have been elaborated in later versions of the text (including the Tibetan translation).

[467] Roughly following Nattier (Nattier, 2007, pp. 247-55). Ms Nattier, I think, makes too much of this passage being addressed to a man, though her stance is in line with

We can note that the Buddha draws attention to the fact that affection for family members can act *against* the kind of open amity we are here concerned with developing, and indeed provokes much conflict and violence, unless it is 'checked' by such reflections as he recommends here. In the same discourse the Buddha goes on to suggest how the sphere of interest can be expanded, here from one's son and oneself, and the feeling of possessiveness (literally 'being-joined-together') got rid of:

> Tena tathā tathā cittam utpādayitavyam yathā yathāsya sarvasatveṣu putra premānugatā maitry utpadyate; ātmakṣemānugatā maitry utpadyate; evaṁ cānena yoniśaḥ pratyavekṣitavyam; anyata eṣa āgata; anyato 'haṁ; sarvasatvā api mama putrā abhūvan; ahaṃ ca sarvasatvānām putro 'bhūvan; neha saṃvidyate kaścit kasya cid ahaṁ vā paro vā.[468]

> In this way the heart and mind is to be brought forth: just as he feels love (prema) towards his son, shall he bring forth amity (maitri) towards all beings. And just as he feels the delight and comfort of acquiring things (kṣema) for himself, shall he bring forth amity (maitri). And he should carefully reflect as follows: 'Just as he [my son] has come from elsewhere, so too have I come from elsewhere. All living beings have been my sons, and I have been the son of all beings. Thus in him there is no being who belongs to me, or to another, or to anyone at all.'[469]

I think it is most interesting to note, in relation both to the spouse and to the child, that according to the Buddha the notion of belonging, of anyone to

---

her thesis that early Mahāyāna was for 'a few good men'. 'The eminent householder' here is a man: can we conceive that the Buddha would not recommend that a woman see her husband in the same ways? Is he advocating that one sex check attachment while the other sex develop it? Ugra is a man, and the conventions of his society were like ours until very recently (and until now for many): to use the male's situation to generalise. To argue otherwise we need to find positive evidence that a separate and different (or proscription of) training applied to females; I do not see such evidence in the sutra.

468 The original Sanskrit is available (unlike much of the discourse) because this paragraph is cited in Śantideva's *Compendium of Training,* 19: 14-17 (Bendall, 1897-1902/1970).

469 Roughly following Nattier (Nattier, 2007, p. 256).

anyone, is a *delusion* to be overcome.

Objections to the idea

Is it not dangerous?

One objection is that love is emotional and irrational and therefore open to all the dangers of following the heart rather than the head. In one particular sense of the word 'love', anti-Romanticists are quite right to question the wisdom of relying on love *rather than* reason.

> …he [sic] who teaches that not reason but love should rule opens the way for those who rule by hate […]
>
> […] Loving a person means wishing to make him [sic] happy… But of all political ideals, that of making the people happy is perhaps the most dangerous one. It leads invariably to the attempt to impose our scale of 'higher' values upon others, in order to make them realise what seems to us of greatest importance for their happiness; in order, as it were, to save their souls. It leads to Utopianism and Romanticism. We all feel certain that everybody would be happy in the beautiful, the perfect community of our dreams… But… the attempt to make heaven on earth invariably produces hell. It leads to intolerance. It leads to religious wars, and to the saving of souls through the inquisition.[470]

The Buddhist traditions concur completely: without wisdom, such methods as training in amity can be dangerous. As we shall see, the trainings in the four immeasurables are mutually supportive, and especially in the context of the second, caring, and the fourth, perspective, we will consider methods of developing the kind of insight which is crucial to avoiding the hell our doubter adverts to.

Furthermore, the fact that the relation is made between this 'love' and hate shows us that he is talking not about amity but partial love, love which expects something in return and turns nasty when this reward is not forthcoming. Again, here the Buddha concurs. To Ugra he says:

> Due to partiality one goes from being a friend to being an enemy

---

[470] This and subsequent citations come from chapter 24, III of *The Open Society and Its Enemies* (Popper, 1945; 5th edition 1966).

> throughout the five realms.[471]

That is to say, it is a characteristic of the entire cosmos that partial love is interchangeable with hate and enmity.

Does it not merely shift the locus of selfish interest?

The example given by the same doubter, while crude, does get to the crux, the fact that this kind of love provokes conflict:

> Tom likes the theatre and Dick lies dancing. Tom lovingly insists on going to a dance while Dick wants for Tom's sake to go to the theatre. The conflict cannot be settled by love; rather, the greater the love, the stronger will be the conflict.[472]

However he has not considered the variety the word conceals, and his argument only applies to some kinds of love. He is referring to the projection of self-interest exclusively onto one object, what could be romantic love or hero-worship, for example. Such projection clearly does not make the sphere of interest less limited. The conflict warned of here arises in such situations because the sphere of interest is limited, such that interests can pull in different directions. This is not amity but again preferential or partial love or affection (in Pali, pema; in Sanskrit, prema), which as we saw the Higher Teachings refer to as the 'close enemy' of amity. They are an enemy because they each interfere with the other. Partial love is a 'close' enemy as opposed to a 'distant' one because it can have as its object the same object as amity. Hence it is particularly difficult to deal with this enemy. However, so long as we can distinguish them, training in amity is an antidote not only to hatred but also to such partiality. How can this be? For the very reason that the training is not in amity alone, but in conjunction with insight, as we shall see.

What the Buddha recommends in this discourse as in many others is to pervade all directions with the wish for well-being, not to make one person or even many people its object. This total pervasion will have the effect when done repeatedly of loosening the limits of the sphere of self-interest, and will undermine aversion (the 'opposite' of amity) and ill will towards what had threatened that self-interest. It is a *method*, and for that reason amity is called,

---

[471] From chapter 5 (Nattier, 2007, p. 264).

[472] As note 470.

technically, an *antidote* to aversion. Is this not an entirely different kind of love?

Taking the 'harmless test case' above, and applying this method and its likely result, we can see that if Tom and Dick were training in amity they would embrace a much broader perspective than their ordinary selfish interest whose locus was the happiness of their friend – namely the happiness of *all* sentient beings. Whether to go to the dance, go to the theatre, or do something entirely different, would moreover be decided with much greater awareness and *insight*, not by mere intellectual planning, and with a much greater perspective on the general situation and the consequences each action might have, not just for themselves but others too: all of this comes as a result of the training.

However, the same doubter enounces what is perhaps the commonest objection when he says:

> I hold that it is humanly impossible for us to love, or to suffer with, a great number of people; nor does it appear to me very desirable that we should, since it would ultimately destroy either our ability to help or the intensity of these very emotions.

Let us consider these objections.

Is it not humanly impossible?

It should be noted that the Buddha does not say, 'Love all sentient beings,' or even, 'Love your enemy,' but, 'Pervade the directions with the wish...' The latter does not require us to be able, now, to love everyone: it is a method. We have already seen that *The Compendium* refers to the realisation consequent upon the training as an advanced one. Likewise the Elders' School's *Higher Teachings Collection* points out that the identification of oneself with all living beings is the *culmination* of training in amity.[473] Beginners are not expected to suddenly embrace all living beings in spontaneous love, or even to feel that this is likely, but they must at the very least be open-minded to the possibility of self-cultivation: this is an example of recommended 'faith', śraddhā. Yet it could be that we lack even that degree of open-mindedness, and so are scuppered from the beginning. How to know if it is possible to expand the sphere of self-interest? Whether or not the opening of the sphere of interest taught to be the result of this method occurs we can test for ourselves. It is a case of 'suck it and see', and luckily in this case the lollipop tastes good from the start.

---

[473] (Thera N. , 1956/1979, p. 136)

Is it not undesirable?

As for the objection that it might undermine competitiveness and therefore hamper the mechanism of a modern economy, we have seen that the successes of perpetual rivalry come only with severe disadvantages, and that there are alternatives. The Elders' School's Higher Teachings state that amity is *synonymous* with absence of hatred. So this amity, and its method, training in the wish for others to be happy, is clearly related to the cardinal practice of giving and sharing. To train in this wish is to overcome our natural tendency towards what in our times the capitalist system relies on, that self-assertive Schadenfreude, and towards what it delights in, the breakdown of trust relations which has led to the culture of risk and hitherto unheard-of intrusion into what used to be called personal liberty. Thus to train like this is to reduce the strangle-hold of the profit-driven cartels and release the creativity and technological potential it threatens to asphyxiate.

But here our doubter is suggesting, it seems, that if we did love all beings, we would effectively be paralysed by the enormity of the consequent task ahead of us. At least, he seems to say, if our object is limited we have some chane of being able to act upon that love successfully to do some good.

But this is only a deceptive objection. In our actual experience, we get involved in situations with other people every day whom we might help but do not, and the reason we do not help is that our sphere of interest is very limited. And it is debatable whether what we do when driven by this interest helps anyone. Quite often by 'helping' loved ones we do a great deal of damage. This is usually through not understanding what is needed, and that in turn again depends on our sphere of interest being too narrow. We can test for ourselves by trying the training whether we find ourselves increasingly or less able to help.

Our doubter also seems to imply that the more objects there are of love the weaker the feeling will be for each one, as though it were being diluted. This sounds logical so long as the love in question is considered to be divisible like matter. This again is a deceptive objection, for we will find that the training increases our capacity, and that each instant of expressing that capacity in acts itself *adds* to the training. And we remember that we are considering here a process, partly dependent upon choice, not purely a 'feeling'. The Elders' School's *Higher Teaching Collection* points out that the *function* of amity is to bring about fitness or to perform benefit, so clearly we are not talking about a passion.

Is it not irrational?

His remedy, reason, our doubter appreciates because it,

> … supported by imagination, enables us to understand that men [sic] who are far away, whom we shall never see, are like ourselves, and that their relations to one another are like our relations to those we love.

This understanding is indeed a component of the Buddhist training, which however takes it deeper: The training is to investigate thoroughly the claims that all sentient beings share the aim of wanting to be happy and wanting to be free of suffering and anxiety, but that at the same time they all share the tendency (because their vision is veiled by misunderstanding and the afflictive emotions) unwittingly to abandon what leads to happiness and grasp what leads to suffering and anxiety; that in these respects they are no different from us at all; that in these respects our enemies are no different from our friends at all; that the basis of distinguishing friends from enemies indeed is an example of the veils of misunderstanding and the afflictive emotions supporting our own tendency to abandon what leads to happiness and grasp onto what leads to suffering and anxiety[474].

Is it not just bad sex?

For historical reasons a discussion of which would here present too weighty a digression, in many Christian and post-Christian cultures there is a strong tendency to associate not just romantic love but *all* love exclusively with procreative sex, or its 'perversion'. Even the greatest mystical experiences of this religious tradition have frequently involved a strong sexual element, such as Saint Theresa's famous visions of Christ, the divine husband. The historian and philosopher Michel Foucault has drawn our attention to the fact that the modern culture of 'pornography' is the latest manifestation of, and in continuity with, the Christian practice of the confession of sins to a priest (via those marvellous products of 'Victorian' mentality, the 'confessions' of a such-and-such). Though Freud's relation of the gamut of human behaviour to libido is unpopular, we are in the post-Christian cultures very much influenced by it. In these cultures, then, there often arises the suspicion that those peculiar people who claim to champion 'universal philanthropy' and 'humanism' are in fact helpless victims of the bubbling up of sexual feelings or even perversions of them due to repression.

In his wonderful novel, *la Nausée*, the great existentialist philosopher Sartre presents an amusing example in support of this suspicion. His rather

[474] See also the meditation on perspective.

pathetic character the 'autodidact' is one such champion, a man who declares that science has 'disproved God' and that he is therefore a 'believer in Man'. Whilst he claims to have learnt everything in his life from books, which he has been reading in the library one by one in alphabetic order, it turns out he learnt his love of humanity elsewhere – in a concentration camp during the war, where he was required to stand with other prisoners, huddled together and naked. It was out of the *frisson* of that experience that his 'love' was born. What kind of love seems clear at the end of the novel when he is thrown out of his beloved library for 'molesting' a young boy.

In these cultures, in fact, it is rare to find proponents of any kind of universal love, and when one does, they are often suspected of being advocates of 'free love', which expression for most people refers unfortunately to unmitigated procreation with anyone viable. Not everyone agrees. For example in their literature there is little to beat this paean to 'True Love':

> True Love in this differs from gold and clay,
> That to divide is not to take away.
> Love is like understanding, that grows bright,
> Gazing on many truths; 'tis like thy light,
> Imagination! which from earth and sky,
> And from the depths of human phantasy,
> As from a thousand prisms and mirrors, fills
> The Universe with glorious beams, and kills
> Error, the worm, with many a sun-like arrow
> Of its reverberated lightning.[475]

However, despite the fact that these lines are addressed as consolation to a woman in a convent, many of their modern readers (and perhaps a portion of their original audience) would understand them as some kind of advocacy of promiscuity. Some familiarity with the life of the man who wrote them would convince us that he was an intensely sincere and spiritual man (whose works advocating non-violent resistance were cited frequently by Gandhi[476], for example), but the sad fact is that he is widely regarded, partly thanks to the reputation of his associates, as a 'libertine' and a hopeless idealist. We should note that the denigratory contextualisation of him as a product of the Romantic movement to which he is considered to belong is a fine example of what Popper

---

475 From verse XI of Shelley's *Epipsychidion*.

476 (Weber, 2004, pp. 28-)

would call historistic contempt that we discussed ealier[477].

So are we being called upon to make sexual moves on the universe? Probably not. Sexual voracity, as an example of what gets classified as 'thirsting' (tāṇha, tṛṣṇa) in Buddhism, is we might say another enemy of amity. Nevertheless, some will ask, wouldn't we do better to channel all that energy into a 'normal' loving relationship instead of stoking all this overheated cosmic heaving? Well the implication of that would be that our loving relationships were somehow *impaired* by training in amity. This we can test, and I venture we will find that our loving relationships are on the contrary *improved* by such training. As for 'cosmic heaving', it would be as well to recall very clearly what we are training in: the thought, 'May all beings live in happiness.' We are not trying to convince ourselves or anyone else that we are at one with the universe or in love with it.

Difficulties with the training

It is often the case that, though we accept amity in principle, we hit problems when we try to train in its method.

I just don't feel it

By far the most common experience of what often gets billed as 'metta bhāvanā' meditation in Buddhist centres in post-Christian countries is that it is extremely artificial and a 'whitewash'. Let us try to understand why this might be.

First of all, we should note again that it is not meant to be 'natural' in the sense of coming to us automatically. If it were, there would be no need for the training.

As for the sense that it is a 'whitewash', if we are honest, we can say that behind this complaint is a deeper difficulty:

They don't deserve it

In the practice we are called on to wish bliss for our enemies 'without animus' (avereṇa). This is, to say the least, counter-intuitive. It might be so counter-intuitive that it convinces us not to bother even starting the training. If that is the case then I would encourage deeper reflection on the nature of the enemy, as we will explore under 'perspective' later. For it is not that the Buddha somehow didn't think about how this situation, wishing our enemies well, might crop up in the course of the meditation. It is not by accident. However, I do

---

477 See under 'Not by "this ascetic is our teacher"'.

think his audience were probably less likely to have this difficulty than are those of us in post-Christian and Islāmic cultures.

We are habituated to the mentality of judgment. We have already seen how closely related are the judicial system, the outlook based on accepting the existence of a creator deity, the possibility of innocence and guilt, the doctrine of sin and free will, and the postponement of the deity's retribution until the day of judgment. We are the late arrivals in cultures long steeped in these outlooks and even though some of us may claim not to subscribe to some or any of them, we will find them whether we like it or not in new shapes all around us. We should recall what we have discovered in our discussion of these outlooks: that they revolve around the sense of an external judge, and absolute good versus absolute evil. What does this have to do with the amity training?

First of all, if we feel so-and-so doesn't *deserve* to be happy, we may be right – right, that is, within the context of this habitual way of thinking, where some are expelled from the tribe with 'damning words' (blame, blasphemy). It could well be, too, that if we did a survey of everyone we know the majority would agree with us in the decision, 'Expel!' for the person in question, and thus we would be, in our eyes, vindicated in our feeling. In fact, it could be that this so-and-so is so bad that she deserves much more than mere physical expulsion: it could be that she requires one of the magical or ritual expulsions, such as humiliation, or imprisonment, or worse.

At the same time, however, we need to note that 'her case', in terms of innocence or guilt, has nothing to do with our training in amity. The principal cause of amity, according to the Higher Teachings, is *the recognition of those qualities in the object which provoke acceptance in us.* Clearly this individual's 'undeniable guilt' in an ongoing case of persecuting us and wronging us (say) is not such a quality, so *the training requires us to overlook it.* It is imperative to realise that the method for training in amity is not looking unflinchingly at reality of each person's relation to us as it has been in our remembered experience. If that were the training, then we could justly claim to have been training every day of our lives, for this is exactly how we customarily reflect on others. On the contrary, the training we are being required to engage in here is a kind of trick. We are putting down our ordinary filter of reality, because it has not helped us, and picking up a different filter, which may or may not help us – the onus is on us to find out.

If our resistance is so strong that we feel, 'I just can't drop my ordinary filter,' then we need to remember: this is not a court. Furthermore it is amazing what a difference of perspective can make. Often a smattering of training in the one-on-one exchange of self and other[478] is enough to bring our whole judgmental structure tumbling down.

In Tibetan Buddhism's so-called 'Virtuous System' School (the Gelug), it is often recommended that beginners train first in perspective before embarking on training in the other mental residences of purity. As we shall see when we come to deal with perspective, the differences we generally believe to exist between different individuals, which can be enough in our eyes to celebrate one and condemn another, are really not as big as we imagine. With the kind of meticulous meditation required to train in perspective we will quickly see that 'deserve', being an all or nothing verb, can *only* exaggerate. Rather than all or nothing, with perspective we see that everyone falls into the grey middle area, not wholly 'deserving' of our love nor wholly 'undeserving' either. Whilst we would like to feel that certain members of our circle are totally innocent of harming us and other people excluded from it totally guilty, the freedom and therefore responsibility in both cases is less than we habitually imagine, because both acted in reality partly through the influence of past and present circumstances.

We have had occasion to compare the doctrine of creation by a perfect deity with the doctrine of karma several times. Without needing to commit ourselves to either, we can recall the difference between them in the matter of 'correction'.

The 'creator deity' outlook encourages us to insist that 'the guilty', because they acted with the total freedom they were created with and thus *did harm freely*, be 'corrected', by *having the equal harm, which is their just deserts, done to them*, that is, be punished in order to exact a balance in the cosmic accounts book of the external judge. So much for the ordinary way of thinking.

The 'karma' outlook requires that 'the unskilfulness' of a being, otherwise partially constrained by past and present circumstances, be corrected, by means of *arousing better awareness in them of distinguishing the skilful and the unskilful.* This is because it is a recognition of this system that if we could only see better and with a broader perspective, we would never harm, because we would see its consequences for ourselves. This kind of seeing or knowing is not ordinary. 'But so-and-so knew very well what she was doing,' we might say to ourselves – and we may be right – but that does not mean that so-and-so *deeply* knew what she was doing.

In the 'karmic' outlook harm depends on delusion, and therein is the crucial difference with the creator deity outlook. Because creation is full of

478 This meditation is explained below under practices related to developing 'amity'.

harm, if we hold that the perfect deity created it, we have in some way to admit that the perfect deity is harmful (we might say 'wrathful' to give it a special atmosphere), but of course we cannot say that the deity is deluded because of commitment to other doctrines about the deity, particularly that it is omniscient, so harm (or 'wrath') in this system can occur even with 'perfect knowledge'. It encourages us to accept the possibility of a perpetrator having greater knowledge of their own harmfulness than they in fact do. It encourages a dramatic loss of subtlety in understanding of harm-doers' situation. It is a kind of laziness not to bother to put ourselves imaginatively in the 'shoes' of a harm-doer. We idly imagine that the harm-doer knew all that we do (at least), had the same basic outlook. We would not have done such a thing! we imagine, and our reaction is outrage. We might even think, 'If I don't have the right to do such a thing, then she certainly does not!'

We are merely failing to understand. It is not that we should exonerate the harm-doer – that is swinging to the other extreme permitted by the perfect creator deity outlook. The karmic outlook encourages us instead to realise that if everyone knew deeply, thanks to training, no-one would engage in harm because they would see that it naturally creates painful circumstances for themselves and others. The point is people rarely train to have a chance of knowing deeply in this sense, and it is *this ignorance* which needs correcting – not some magical account in the Ledger of Pain.

In *the Discourse Requested by Ugra*, which is incidentally one of the most important sources for the ethical discipline of the Career of Awakening Beings as taught in the Indo-Tibetan lineages[479], the Buddha says:

> As I have said, 'Do not despise the untrained!' It is not this one who has committed the offence; rather, it is whatever defilements there are in them which have manifested this unskilfulness. [...] If they fully comprehend whatever defilements they have and examine them carefully, they might obtain the first fruit [of the spiritual path] and attain the status of being assured of Supreme Perfect Awakening! Why is this? Because of the notion that defilements are removed by knowledge (jñāna). As I have also said, 'One person is not judgeable by another, and if someone judges another the result is harm.' And

---

479 All schools of Tibetan Buddhism base their presentation of this career on the works of Śantideva, in particular *Entering the Way of Life of Awakening Beings* and *The Compendium of Training*, and the latter quotes *The Ugra Discourse* more than any other text in justification for its doctrinal framework.

> because of the notion, 'tathāgata eva jānāti nāham – The One Who Has Reached How Things Are knows at this level, whilst I do not.' So one should bring forth no ill will, anger, or animosity…[480]

Again, this outlook does not come naturally to us. And in this case the training in caring, which we will come to next, is what helps us. Caring gets past that natural laziness which exacerbates the pitfalls of the perfect creator deity outlook, by mustering all the energy of the response to seeing suffering in others. For now, let us just note that just as no-one totally deserves our love, no-one totally deserves to have it withdrawn either, even the most inexplicably evil person.

Better than this, and without requiring of us the broaching of the awkward subject of karma, indeed the best approach of all to overcome the doubt that people are lovable, is to test the practice not on a meditation cushion but in a social situation.

It is unfortunate that the word 'meditation' has come to be the standard translation of the word 'bhāvanā', which has no sense necessarily of thinking about something at all, but means 'development', literally '*bringing into being*' – it is the participle of the causative version of the verb bhū, 'be'. We might even translate it as 'making' or 'creating' or 'cultivating'. The four immeasurables, these four mental residences of purity, depend not on mere meditation but on this *bringing into being.*

To make matters worse, we frequently imagine that meditation not only requires but *is itself* time out from our daily activities, time set aside specially for this special activity. In some cases to be seen to be someone who does meditation is important – it is a badge of status for our vanity to enjoy or for us to get on in some group. Even if our motive is deeper than vanity or the desire to join, it can be combined with the view that meditation is something special, a kind of secret activity, which we would be embarrassed to do in front of colleagues, unless they joined in. Whilst such secretive special set-aside sitting practice will bring something into being, it is likely to be very slowly indeed, and easily subject to set-backs.

Bringing into being is by body, speech and mind, not just mind, even if mind is the basis. By involving all three, we will be able to introduce the method into ordinary daily activity. In this way progress will be much faster and we will have remarkable experiences. So let us not shy of testing the training in society.

---

[480] From chapter 5, §17 (Nattier, 2007, pp. 263-4). This is said with reference to a monk who has committed some unskilful act.

If you treat people not merely well but with direct carefulness and gentle attention, you will be amazed at how they respond. It is a sad fact that many if not most people today feel insufficiently attended to, not loved enough. Take the time to engage people with carefulness and you will see how they blossom. It is a sad fact too that very many people today feel inadequate or intangibly 'bad' or 'inferior'. By giving them the benefit of the doubt and further than that by giving them the chance to be good, friendly, animated and affectionate, you will see marvellous things from them! That I promise you.

A few instances of this phenomenon in our own experience beat reading a hundred thousand pages of the noblest doctrine. It will dispel the major difficulties you have with making the wish that all beings live in bliss. You will subsequently discover how the wish and its application in social contexts (called in the Higher Teachings the 'taste' (rasa) of the well-wishing) feed on each other.

How can I have been all sentient beings' son or daughter?

We have already seen a perhaps startling recommendation to expand one's partial affectionate love for one's son to all sentient beings by means of *reflecting on our previous existences* in which they were our sons or we were theirs. This kind of method is not unique to *The Ugra Discourse*: it is recommended, for example, in other discourses and treatises, and consequently very frequently in Tibetan Buddhism, that we reflect on all beings having been *our mothers*.

This will strike us as very odd if we do not accept any connection between such previous existences and our own lives. In the spirit of our discourse, we need not foist such dogma on ourselves anyway: the Buddha himself leaves the issue unresolved for the Kālāmās and clearly does not consider it a pressing issue for them. We have already compared ourselves rather unfavourably with the Kālāmās so we need not be under any illusions as to being better qualified to explore such subtleties as hidden causal relations between existences at different times. In any case we will consider this issue more closely later in our discussion. For now, in the context of training in amity, we are interested in bringing in whatever emotional, mental and spiritual equipment we can to support the training. If mention is made in expositions of traditional methods of certain equipment (such as a belief in previous existences being causally related to our own and therefore in some sense part of a continuum with it) which we do not possess, there is clearly no use in trying to conjure them out of fantasy and employ them hysterically: we would not jump off a cliff relying on a handglider constructed from our imagination, after all. And there is such a diversity of methods that we need not pine over one missing tool.

Related training methods

Specific objects

The point of the training is not to spread the spirit of amity in all directions in the interstices between all the people we don't like! The fact that this tendency lingers, however, shows us that the recommendations made in many traditions that we take particular objects (i.e. sentient beings) as our focus in this spreading of spirit might be useful.

It is usually said that we should visualise first a friend, then someone to whom we feel neutral, and finally an enemy, before defocusing and spreading widely. Some modern teachers, aware of the deep self-damaging tendency in post-Christian societies, have added taking oneself as focus, either at the beginning or before visualising the enemy. Tibetan teachers often recommend visualising people who ordinarily provoke very divergent reactions in us *at the same time*, together. We should try all methods to test which works best.

Amity, one of the seven causes of the Intention of Awakening (bodhicitta)

Tibetan traditions attribute to the Asanga (born in what is now Peshawar, Pakistan, 17 centuries ago) a series of practices called 'the seven causes' leading to genuinely embracing the so-called 'Intention of Awakening' (bodhicitta) which is the defining point of entry into the Universal Career. Such an intention can be based on deep perspective (which we will consider later) or deceptive reality. Asanga's seven-cause method relates to deceptive reality.

The fourth of the seven causes is the bringing into being of amity itself, whilst the earlier three are a particular method we have already alluded to to promote the training in amity, one which is only available to a trainee who is open to the idea of previous lives having some causal link to the current life being experienced, such that they can be considered in some sense to be in a continuum with that life. Such a trainee can then bring to mind (the first cause, namely) that there has so long been life that lifetimes have been countless, and (the second cause,) that in each lifetime related individuals, notably the mother, showed great kindness. In the current life, the trainee therefore reasons, all living beings of this time can be considered to have some causal link and therefore be in continuum with those who showed that kindness before, to the lives with which those trainee individuals are linked. Developing the wish to repay that kindness (the third cause) leads to developing amity (the fourth).

We will consider the remaining three causes in our discussion of caring.

Equalising and exchanging self and other

The other 'great charioteer' celebrated by the Tibetan tradition, Śantideva (born in what is now Gujarat 13 centuries ago), taught (in *Entering the Way of Life of Awakening Beings*) a different method to develop the Intention of Awakening based on deceptive reality, a method which does not depend on having a mind open to causally linked previous lives. Most of us in societies dominated by the (unfoundable) belief in annihilation at death or by the two-life doctrines of the 'monotheistic' systems will therefore find this method more useful.

First we meditate on what we have in common with other beings, a meditation we will explore more extensively under 'perspective' later. This is effectively using reality to correct the mistaken notion that we ought to cherish ourselves more than others if our goal is happiness, even merely for ourselves. The distinctive feature of Śantideva's method is that we put ourselves in those others' shoes.

One form of this meditation is especially useful for overcoming the 'they don't deserve it' kind of obstruction to bringing amity into being which we referred to earlier. Take someone you consider as an enemy or at least with dislike, or someone you feel dislikes you, or someone who in your view 'does not deserve' to have amity for them cultivated. Śantideva recommends choosing people who are your social superiors and inferiors as well as peers. Then step into their shoes: take on the personality of this 'new self', like an actor playing a character in a film. Look at your old self through the eyes of the character and wilfully develop all the attitudes towards your old self you imagine your character has. Go further than that. Think, of your old self, 'What does she think of me?' For this question is likely to have gone through your character's head many times, especially if there is intensity in the emotions between you. Notice the reactions that develop in you (in character) to the ventured answer to that question. Go further than that. Think, of your old self, 'What does she think I think of her?' Go to town with this: you are no ham actor but an accomplished professional 'getting into character' by utterly suppressing your ordinary personality and adopting the new one with utmost sincerity. Notice your reaction to the answer to this question. And go further: ask, 'What does she think I think she thinks of me?' And so on. Stay with such ruminations and your reactions to them, from the point of view of your character. Then, at the conclusion, switch back to your old self and compare: those tendencies to misunderstand and misrepresent you just lived in the other's persona, are you free of them yourself?

This meditation can be quite upsetting, and may have you sobbing and suddenly seeing yourself as ugly or reproachable. If so, let out your sobs freely. When you are calmer it would be a good time to try some of the training support we will explore under 'sharing joy' later.

By pursuing such training methods as these, gradually the logic of cherishing ourselves at others' expense starts to look shoddier and shoddier. Gradually a natural ability to appreciate others' 'points of view' or 'points of experiencing' will develop.

>Caring (karuṇā)

Definition

To get an idea of what is meant by this 'caring', think of a mother without arms who, when her only child is drowning in a river, throws herself in to save the child even though the odds are almost overwhelming that she will thus drown herself. So we are talking about an intense and unthinking focus on restoring the welfare of other sentient beings. We need not go into a technical discussion, as some would prefer, of what exactly constitutes a sentient being, in order to decide which beings are considered worthy of this state of mind: for in view of the example the notion of such philosophising looks patently ludicrous. Can you imagine the mother debating to herself whether or not her only child were really sentient as the child drowns?

What is *not* being referred to is affection. The *Discourse Taught by Immaculate Renown* states:

> Performers of the contemplation [on the illness of sentient beings] may generate an affectionate view of great compassion with regard to sentient beings, but this should be forsaken.[481]

The *Compendium* says:

> What is caring? It is evenmindedness and deep knowledge, and the mindstate and mental events concomitant with them, based on a mental absorption dwelling on the thought, "May beings be free from suffering!"

Clearly this is not ordinary caring, which occurs usually through ties of affection or duty and is vulnerable to changing conditions, but a kind of gathering conviction in caring based on meditation on a wish for others not to suffer.

Types

The caring we should begin with is training based on the recognition of suffering as it is expressed in others. All Buddhist schools are in agreement that it is the recognition of suffering in others which is the direct cause of caring. However, the mere recognition, made again and again, of the same suffering, is

481 From Chapter Five, The Condolence Visit by Gentle Splendour.

likely to lead to stultification or grief.

This is where perspective comes in. It is taught in the Tibetan system that there are three levels of compassion. These relate to the three levels of suffering as taught by all traditions.

The suffering of suffering itself: in sentient beings

The first level is as we have discussed, the recognition of the expression of suffering in sentient beings, which should be our focus in the training. As we shall see when we come to the training in perspective, there is good scientific evidence for suffering in other animals, not just in humans. But we need not force ourselves if we do not have much conviction in that: the human species has quite enough examples of terrible suffering to be going on with!

The suffering of change: in impermanent phenomena

The second level relates to a meditation much recommended to beginners in the Tibetan systems: impermanence.

The changing environment

If we consider our environment, there is the fact that the earth itself is known to have limited lifespan. Our sun is due to swallow up the earth as part of the natural process all stars of its mass go through. Then again, the conditions on the earth have changed radically. We know that an entire ecosystem, the dinosaurs', was eliminated in an environmental catastrophe. We humans are latecomers on the scene – it has been pointed out that if we plot the history of the earth on a 24-hour period, we arrived at a few minutes to midnight. We do not know how long our ecosystem will persist – current research on the atmosphere suggests not so long. But even while the ecosystem can still potentially support human life, our societies utterly transform. We can consider the architecture, social system, culture and language of a thousand years ago, and then imagine how things might be in another thousand. Even in a few years neighbourhoods change unrecognizably. One of the best ways to train in impermanence is to visit the places of one's childhood and ask after the people who shared them with you.

Death

And of course the kind which perhaps most concerns us is the fact that we will die. It is important to realise that while we may intellectually accept the idea that we are going to die, this is very different from having a direct experiential conviction of the inevitability of our death and all of the experiences we will face during it. It has been noted by many Buddhist teachers heading 'west' to post-Christian cultures how vociferously we try magically to dismiss death from existence. Buddhism says that only by deeply recognising death can we hope to be happy with it, but our cultures rarely let us get that far, so taboo is the subject. If you doubt this, compare how many deaths you know of as having occurred with the number of corpses you have seen. Corpses are invisible in our societies, even in hospitals, largely so even in crematoria. Because of the awkwardness of the subject, our cultures are chronically ill equipped to help those suffering from terrible grief at the loss of loved ones. It is a kind of fear of ritual pollution persisting in averted eyes and relief at a change of subject. A great deal of consumer culture is founded on the basis that we somehow can control our own ageing and death. Science is good, but it is not that good. People nowadays spend their entire lives making sure that their few years of retirement will be comfortable, but not a second ensuring that their deaths will be comfortable – and while it is possible to die without retiring, it is not possible to retire without dying! Advertisers do an excellent job of convincing us that by buying various products we are more likely to live longer, less likely to get cancer, and so on, but really we are buying an illusion of control. Car accidents are the number one killer and, *pace* David Cronenberg's 'Crash', they are exactly that – accidents. In the last few years pharmaceutical companies have succeeded in well-nigh paralysing the world by encouraging immensely lucractive scares about bird flu and now swine flu, fatalities from which are minuscule even in comparison to ordinary flu never mind car accidents. As societies we treat people with terminal illnesses, especially socially embarrassing ones, if you'll excuse the expression, 'like the plague', while we behave as though the terrible condition which we all have, and which is totally incurable (mortality) were not real. Consider the moment when you will lose your life to be like the target of a speeding arrow, or the plunge-pool of water in a falls, say the Buddhist texts, but in our fantasy the waterfall and the arrow can be beaten by a magic pause or replay button. Our popular culture is full of unsupported reassurances that *passing on* is but a prelude to eternity with the people you love: no story is believed on less evidence. When we reflect on the immensity of this fact, shared by every single living being on (and off) earth, we train in this second kind of caring, whose focus is impermanent phenomena.

The suffering because of the nature of reality: in ignorance

Awareness of this kind of suffering does not impinge on ordinary experience. It is related to the advanced perspective we will discuss later. For now let us note that every event in our experience when analysed is found to be dependent on other events. This simple fact goes very deep because everything ends up interlocked in an evolution so complex that our ordinary way of thinking, via concepts and logic, simply cannot encompass it. Even when we think we are in control, and we think we are secure, the reality is very far from this.

At the same time when, though training in perspective, amity and the rest, we gain some familiarity with reality, we come to appreciate that the treacherous narrow perspectives which dominate ordinary outlook and life can be weakened and dropped. This might seem like an absurd pretension. We need not foist such beliefs on ourselves now, but again it would be as well at least to leave our minds open to the possibility of achieving what others claim to have – a state of complete freedom, not just from the afflictive processes which produce suffering but even from the subtle veils to understanding the nature of things which might give rise to them again in the future. Even if this declaration of the possibility of freedom, the declaration that the Buddha made, seems 'out of this world', it is inevitable that as we train, gradually, we will start to taste something of this freedom. And when we do, and we understand how needlessly we used to, and others still do, bring suffering through lacking such perspective and such freedom, then our natural response will be an overwhelming sense of caring for those who are still trapped: this is the third kind of caring, and the best.

For example, as amity overwhelms our tendency to anathematise, abominate, blame, curse and condemn, and we discover the greater bliss, clarity and ability to act which come with that transition, then when we see others still in thrall to these aversive tendencies which deny them this very bliss, clarity and ability we have discovered, our response will naturally be not to react against the activities they indulge in based on those tendencies but an urgent wish for them to be released from their constraints, which cause them to suffer needlessly, and cause them to inflict suffering on others needlessly.

Elimination of countering tendencies

To begin to train ourselves as the Buddha suggests we would be wise to clear the ground, as it were. We can examine our habits of body, speech and mind, and see if there are any tendencies there which will cause obstacles to our development of this mindset. As a test we can consider our reaction to news of suffering around the world. Probably most of us react to these stories in a way which is not helpful.

Tendencies which obstruct caring

Taking the suffering of others as a pastime

For a start, we read these stories as a source of diversion in the mornings, or when we log on to the internet, so our intention in reading them is frequently a quest for entertainment, something to occupy our voracious and restless mind as we eat breakfast, for example. Not only does this make a travesty of the content of these reports, which truly deserve our caring about them given the appalling experiences of others recounted in them, it is also training our minds in diversion as a relief from restlessness, which is not even skilful for ourselves never mind anyone else since it tends to increase our tendency to restlessness while providing deceptive temporary relief.

Being habituated to trivialising

Secondly, we are so used to hearing about terrible events that we are to a large extent deadened to them. We have lost the sensitivity such that the heart might not even stir. This ability we develop to separate the information in the news reports from our natural tendencies to want to help in some way is encouraged by the way the media frequently present important stories on a seeming par with utter trivia, as if we are being expected to see everything equally trivially. This is related to the first obstacle to caring as taught traditionally in Indo-Tibetan Buddhism – clinging to the appearances of ordinary life: we are so involved in our experiences, attracting us and repelling us, because of our limited perspective, that we never gain even the space to consider that there might be more skilful ways to live.

Finding others' suffering unbearable and revolting

Thirdly, when the news is particularly upsetting, a fair proportion of us are likely to turn away, and if questioned to say, 'I find these images too upsetting.' This is a reflection not of caring but of the affection we have already seen distinguished from it in *Immaculate Renown.* It could relate to the second or third (in progression) main obstacles to caring as traditionally taught in Indo-Tibetan Buddhism, attachment to the temporary pleasures of favourable life circumstances (which can cause us to consider loss of such circumstances with terror), and an aspiration for one's own liberation only (in view of the unsatsifactoriness of experience). The reason for affectionate caring being unhelpful given in the discourse is that it would make awakening beings turn away from the world, from this 'cyclic existence', and seek this individual liberation –

not an option for someone who has embarked on this career, since they have resolved to stay in the world to help – and such an exhortation would therefore particularly be made to those whose sense of suffering is enough to cause them to reject an ordinary life, and so enter the 'spiritual career', but whose solution is merely to escape, leaving all others to escape in their own way:

> Awakening beings eliminate the vexations of sensory data and generate great compassion. If they had an affectionate view of compassion, they would thereby generate an aversion to cyclic existence. If they are able to transcend this they will not have any aversion, and no matter where they are subsequently reborn they will not be limited by any affectionate view. They will be born without bonds, and be able to explain the Laws to sentient beings, and emancipate them from their bonds.

However, it is not only in this rather exalted career that the sense of revulsion and fear is distinguished from the caring being recommended here. In the Individual Career too we are told that the close enemy of caring is grief. As beginners we should take note that these two are distinguishable, and that whilst should train in one, we should avoid the other.

Feeling thankful for our own freedom from suffering

Even if we do not turn away in self-protective disregard like this, we might well privately celebrate the fact that at least it didn't happen to us. This is a mixture of skilful and unskilful mental processes. As we shall see, to celebrate our own happiness is very useful; but to be satisfied with the state of others in suffering is a sign of limited perspective, and therefore a source of future suffering for ourselves and others. At the moment we can note that this thankfulness and satisfaction arises out of the fact that we have a basic fear of suffering ourselves, and realise that since circumstances can change rapidly and dramatically, news of others' suffering is certainly never a guarantee that we will not suffer very soon.

Schadenfreude, bellicosity and sadism

Lastly, and perhaps unusually, there may be some sense of enjoyment of others' suffering for various psychological or social reasons. This is most common of course in situations in which a side has been joined, for example in a war, where many people will rejoice in the suffering of the people they perceive as their enemies. We will discuss this in more detail in the context of 'perspective' later.

There is also the phenomenon, much seen in teenagers, of relishing others' suffering because they feel that they are getting revenge on a world which has mistreated them. Even if it were revenge, it wouldn't seem to solve anything. And of course it is just an illusion of revenge based on a sense of powerlessness. Since training in caring is a source of exactly the kind of power which is considered lacking by such unfortunate individuals, we can recommend it on that basis. More generally this enjoyment of others' suffering is referred to by the German loanword Schadenfreude – literally *frolicking* (freude) in others' being *scathed* (schaden). As the Anglican Archbishop Richard Chenevix Trench wrote,

> What a fearful thing is it that any language should have a word expressive of the pleasure which men feel at the calamities of others; for the existence of the word bears testimony to the existence of the thing. And yet in more than one such a word is found. [...] In the Greek epikhairekakia, in the German Schadenfreude.[482]

If we were well aware of the factors which led to the others' failure, then there would be no surprise at it: it would be seen as inevitable, and therefore neutrally accepted. In addition, although it may not be clear to us all the time, it is only through misunderstanding a situation that we cannot feel some sympathy with the suffering party. Both of these underlying causes – the lack of insight and misunderstanding – are exactly the delusion which these practices oppose. In particular, the advanced versions of perspective which we will survey later are, it is taught, powerful remedies to this kind of delusion. It will be a matter of trying the methods and seeing whether situations do or do not appear to us in radically different light.

There is also the phenomenon of sadism, the sexual enjoyment of the infliction of suffering. That this is restricted to so few individuals should not make us shy away from considering it and its causes. It depends on fear of losing power over others and the confusion of relief from this fear with orgasmic pleasure by habituation, so again the fact that training in caring brings tremendous power recommends it even to such people.

Near enemies

Grief

The near enemy of caring is traditionally taught to be grief, the kind of

---

482 (Trench, 1852)

frightened response to suffering which we have touched on already. Both are vividly aware of suffering, but whereas caring responds by an energetic effort to remove that suffering, grief causes us instead to retract into a prison-like realm which can be stifling and unbearable but seemingly inescapable. Whereas caring is useful, grief is at very best an experience to be lived through, a process which might therefore have some value in terms of teaching us patience, but which has all sorts of negative consequences, not the least of which is the suffering involved in the experience of grief itself.

If we find ourselves tending towards grief in response to awareness of suffering, then it is a sign that perspective is lacking: meditations for this we consider later.

Pious pity

It is often asserted by adherents of the monotheistic systems that their beliefs require them not to fight against 'enemies', 'criminals' and 'unbelievers' but to leave the reckoning 'with the deity'. They claim that this allows them to be released from feelings of enmity and the kinds of actions which might be consequent upon them.

Whilst this may be true to a small extent, there is no doubt that these 'enemies', 'criminals' and 'unbelievers' continue to be seen as such: there is no progress whatsoever towards understanding circumstances which give rise to these phenomena. They hold their 'deity' to be 'eternal', and they arrogate themselves to the status of knowing what 'the deity' deems in matters of ethics and allegiance to the faith, and in combination these two delusions cause them to consider their own judgments of others to be rather long-lasting. There is a sense that 'one cannot alter God's judgment', so the very best feeling they are capable of with respect to these condemned individuals is *pity*.

Pity is powerless to change matters: it merely gazes on the awful situation and weeps. It is feeling without act. That it has nothing to do with caring as recommended here is demonstrated by the fact that the Higher Teachings of all schools point out that the 'taste' or 'function' of caring is *agitation towards remedying the suffering* (anukampana, literally 'being shaken in accordance with'). Under slavery to a judgmental deity it is, most regrettably, illegal to oppose such condemnation, so even if one is shaken, one must piously still oneself.

Because the doctrines clothing 'the deity' of such religions resonate strongly with our own afflictive processes, it is quite likely that simply by surrendering to judgment of someone we slip into the sense that our judgment is 'the judgment of the seven heavens'[483] and therefore fall into this pious pitying without any urge to act. Once again, the presence of the afflictive processes gives us a clue as to how to deal with this error: with ongoing training in the immeasurables, and particularly in perspective, the afflictive processes will weaken, our vision will clear, and there will be no more need to deify our own inclinations.

Objections to the idea

Is it not masochistic?

With a passing acquaintance of the methods of training for caring, some are bound to ask: Are we being called upon to indulge masochistically in all the overwhelming misery of the world?

This misconception is why Buddhism is frequently accused of 'pessimism'. A few months ago I heard a funny story in Dharamsala, the seat in exile of the Dalai Lama in North India. The Tushita Centre there were doing one of their regular courses of introduction to Buddhism. Everything seemed to go very well, until it came to the final feedback session. (Once the silence can be broken, the centre always do this feedback apparently.) A fair number of people on the course on this particular occasion wanted certain things changed. They objected to the examples the western monk who was teaching the course had used as examples for generating the caring attitude. I think he had told them to think of a mother animal caught in a trap knowing that her babies would starve to death unless she chewed her way out. Apparently this example had been too much for them. I mean: how awful! To imagine a thing like that, what kind of sicko was he? Was Buddhism really so grim and sick? Unfortunately I never heard how this teacher responded to the complaints. But I like to think he asked them what their purpose for doing the retreat was. It is not Buddhism which is grim and sick, of course: it is the world around us and within us. When you are addicted to coccooning yourself from the suffering in the world, then it might well seem that whoever encourages you instead to open your eyes is cruel. But a moment's reflection on their motives should dispel that misconception. Why resent the one who wishes you to see things as they are? That meditation centre is partly to

---

483 Muḥammad's pronouncement on the judgment made by a Muslim and devoted friend on the Jewish tribe the Bani Qurayẓah that he had belonged to and that had betrayed the Muslims: as we have already seen, the judgment was that the adult males of the tribe, numbering almost a thousand, should be beheaded into a trench, and the women and children taken as slaves by the Muslims.

blame, actually, for presenting the teachings as a kind of holiday: no wonder feathers get ruffled now and again. But when people ask for the teachings to be edited to avoid disturbing the glamour of their holiday, then really, such fake practitioners should know they disgrace themselves.

Masochism, properly considered, develops when the relief from responsibility gets mixed with orgasmic pleasure by habituation. As we shall see, the training in caring involves accepting more responsibility rather than escaping from it in a temporary fantasy.

Is it not pointless?

Because if the sheer enormity of suffering in the world it might occur to us to throw up our hands in despair at the idea of doing anything about it.

Here, again, it is a matter of having patience enough to try the practice carefully and thoroughly. The benefits of it are many and diverse, and some of them relate directly to other people and beings. For example, they include gaining insight into the nature of others' minds, such that we can help them release themselves from their particular needless anxieties, not by pompously wading into others' privacy but by the very nature of our spontaneous interactions with them. We might not believe such things are possible just yet, but let us note that unless we open our minds to the mere possibilities, then there will be no chance to test them.

Even without considering whether or not we can or will ever be able to do anything about the kind of suffering in others that we are reflecting on, we can come back to the point made in the Individual Career discourses and treatises: that the results of the training include the reduction and ultimately removal of one's own tendency to cruelty. This, as a skilfulness applicable to our own quest for happiness, is hardly to be sniffed at.

Difficulties in training

We should recall the difficulties which arise in the training in amity first of all, for all of them may arise in this training too.

It is too traumatic

If we find agitation or terror overwhelming us in the course of the training then our perspective is probably too narrow. Caring without understanding (or, as we might say, 'compassion without wisdom') has been roundly comdemned by some Buddhist teachers in the USA and Europe as 'idiot compassion'. Whilst the trainings we present here are not likely to give rise to this stupid interfering kind of piousness, it can be that we are naturally better at identifying the expression of suffering in ourselves and others than its causes. Later we will examine a number of methods of training for gaining better perspective on the situation of suffering.

Related training methods

The remaining three of the seven causes of the Intention

Earlier we considered the first four causal links of Asanga's seven-cause system.

The fifth is the very bringing into being of caring, the natural consequence of developing amity.

Then, based on training in caring, gradually the uncontrived wish will develop that all life capable of suffering be separated from suffering, without exception, as far as space extends: this is the sixth cause, called the 'Great Caring' or taking Universal Responsibility.

This leads to the seventh step, the wish to take on the resonsibility for that separation personally, coupled with the recognition that it can only be achieved by attaining complete and total Awakening, such that the commitment is formulated to attain that for all beings' sake: this is the Intention for Awakening (bodhicitta) 'in aspiration', which can then be realised by training in the six 'carriers to the other side' (paramita) – sharing, discipline, patience, bravery, concentration and deep insight, and so on: the various aspects of the Career of Awakening Beings.

Sending and receiving

Due to the training in equalising and exchanging self and other, moreover, with the logic of cherishing ourselves at others' expense in tatters, we will naturally appreciate the situation of other sentient beings. This will naturally cause us genuinely to wish them free of suffering. One way to train in this caring wish which is taught to be especially powerful is 'sending and receiving' (well-know to some by its Tibetan name, tonglen). In short this involves visualising suffering – of ourselves and others – as black smoke exhuded from our bodies. We then breathe in that smoke and draw it into a point of light and heat usually visualised at the heart centre where we generate the firm conviction that it together with our self-cherishing are destroyed. Then as we breathe out we imagine the happiness and goodness we have radiating as light and warmth from that centre which bathes our body and those of other sentient beings, and transferring the happiness and goodness to them without any sense of regret.

A tantric method of bring caring into being: Mahākaruṇika

The training methods we have so far considered involve crude struggle with the self. It is due to long and thorough habituation to their opposites that these training methods can appear counter-intuitive, and their application difficult or slow.

For certain exceptional individuals, with sufficient open-mindedness to handle far out forms, there is a faster, cleverer, riskier option. Tantric methods of practice deriving from the Secret Mantra Career (guhyamantrayāna) are much strengthened and stabilised by receiving an initial blessing from someone who has reached the fruitional realisation of the practice in question, but if that opportunity is not available there is still one class of practices from this career which is at least not considered dangerous to do without such initiation: the so-called 'creation-stage' trainings based on a particular 'Archetypal Ideal' (literally 'Wished-for Divinity': in Sanskrit, iṣṭadevatā) referred to as 'the Great Caring One' (in Sanskrit, Mahākaruṇika).

This archetype began life in the exemplar myth of the training of a certain awakening being in a handful of non-tantric discourses, such as *The White Lotus Discourse of the Sumblime Law* and *The Karandavyuha Buddha Kingdom Discourse.* In its early development it was called 'Over-World-Listener' (in Sanskrit, Avalokitasvāra and Gadgadasvāra) and in its later development, probably through influence from the cult of the god Śiva or Maheśvara, 'Over-Seeing Lord' (Avalokiteśvara; in Tibetan, Chenrezig). The same figure is known to Japanese Buddhism as Kannon. The various accounts of this awakening being's training all emphasis the extraordinary degree and breadth of caring it exemplified.

The distinguishing feature of tantric practice is that it employs methods that are 'harmonious with' Awakening, avoiding the formidable obstacles which can arise when deceptive reality is turned against itself. For example, our habitual view of ourselves and our situation is sharply and heavily limited, such that from one angle training by deploying elements from our ordinary experience is guaranteed to involve further habituation to that ordinary interpretation, even if the methods also act against it. In tantric practice we cut out this 'self-defeating' aspect of training by *taking the result as the path.* We train in viewing our situation not as we used to, but as *a Buddha Kingdom already*, populated by Awakened Beings. Such an exceptional training can be sustained through reasoning[484] or through

---

484 See for example the great Nyingma scholar Rongzom's *Establishing*

faith but is available only to a few of us. In Tibet, long a culture steeped in tantric traditions, a sophisticated spiritual technology derived from the tantras developed, and many archetypes even from the non-tantric discourses came to be deployed as tools in that technology. One of the most beloved and widely known of the class of practices relating to this Great Compassionate archetype derives from the extraordinary tantric master known to Tibetan legend as 'the Iron Bridge Builder' or 'King of the Empty Plains' (Thangtong Gyalpo, born six and a half centuries ago[485]). It should be done in the context of the Three Excellences of a Universal Career practice as already described.

Above our own head and above the head of every sentient being throughout the universe, is a seat made of a gigantic open white lotus flower upon which rests a horizontal silvery disc like a 2D moon; on this the Archetypal Ideal, made of light, transparent like crystal, the embodiment of one's own future attainment of Awakening, is visualised to be born, spontaneously, from the transformation of the radiant white syllable hrī hanging in space into the form of a seated human, rich in secret symbols, a complex and inspiring pictorial language fostering mental stability and awareness: seated in the lotus posture indicating that the final fruit of total Awakening need not be sought elsewhere than the mind itself; appearing in the form (kāya) of royalty to show the attainment of the stations of awakening beings enjoying the consummation (saṁbhoga) of their Awakening; with four hands showing transcendence of the four ways intellect misapprehends reality – namely holding that things have their own being, that they lack any being, that both these claims are true, or that neither is; two hands holding a lotus and prayer beads, symbolising respectively the arising of the wisdom of total Awakening even amid the filth of cyclic existence and the endless activity of spontaneous caring in the world consequent upon that Awakening; and the two other hands pressed together, showing the inseparability of the shallow and deep ways of seeing phenomena (as real and as illusions foisted on the interdependent matrix of reality respectively), around a wish-fulfilling jewel, the mind itself with all its potential; with skin pure white to show that all mental stains have been removed; and so on. (Explanations of further details, such as the crown of five colours, should be sought from a qualified teacher during initiation.) We imagine this image unites all possible refuges – from an 'omnipotent deity' if we hold to such a notion, through all kinds of teachers to all Awakened Beings,

---

Appearances as Divine (Koppl, 2008).

485 An excellent lengthy exploration of this master's life, an inspiring amalgam of spiritual practice and work for society, is available online (Gerner, 2007).

and we celebrate this exaltedness with praise and material and mental offerings.

All the varieties of suffering in cyclic existence are brought to mind one by one and the fervent wish made that through understanding beings suffering thus will be released and recognise their environment as the Buddha Kingdom of the All-Seeing-Lord. Six broad classes of suffering in particular are brought to mind, each with one syllable of the famous six-syllable mantra as a prayer for release – 'oṁ' is the prayer that sentient beings be released from the agonising conscious fall from their high stations (for 'gods/rulers', the self-indulgent), 'ma' from the misery of continual conflict for resources and status (for 'antiheroes', the fighters), 'ṇi' from the mixed tribulations of ordinary life (for 'the populace'), 'pad' from relentless enslavement and mutual attack (for 'beasts', the dull-witted), 'me' from the torment of frustration due to inverted perception (for 'ghosts', the psychotic), and 'huṁ' from unbearable environments ('hells', for the utterly paranoid). Visualising the letters of the mantra in a circle around the Archetypal Ideal's heart centre, intoning it as we contemplate the various kinds of suffering and make the wish for release, we imagine light radiating from the Archetype's heart, spreading in all directions, reaching all beings, and liberating them from their particular suffering by the means of their discovery of wisdom.

Finally we visualise that the Archetypal Ideal, this embodiment of future attainment of Awakening above the head of each sentient being including ourselves, dissolves into us as light to transform us into its own form, and we rest in the imaginative re-cognition of the entire situation as the Buddha Kingdom, where the only forms are of the Ideal, the only sounds are of the six-syllable mantra, and the only awareness is Awakened, and all three – forms, sounds and awareness – are inseparable from the recognition of phenomena's profound interdependence such that they cannot be reasonably held as entities in themselves. To whatever degree we are able to understand that, we rest as long as we can in the mind's own nature, before the concluding practices.

>Joy (mudita)

Definition

The *Compendium* says:

> What is joy? It is evenmindedness and deep knowledge, and the mindstate and mental events concomitant with them, based on a mental absorption dwelling on the thought, 'May beings not be deprived of happiness!'

So once again this is not ordinary joy, which is general and emotional, but a kind of gathering tendency to experience joy based on meditation on a protective wish for others' happiness.

Types

If this is gladness at happiness, we might first consider what we mean by this happiness. In ordinary non-teleological thinking happiness comes by circumstances; in ordinary teleological thinking it comes by the design of some other force, such as a controlling deity. So to be glad at happy circumstances or to say, 'Thank God!' or the equivalent constitutes a certain kind of mudita.

The Buddha taught, however, that such happy circumstances arise from previous skilful acts of body, speech and mind, and in the crudest way of explaining this it is said that beings who perform them accrue a kind of positive energy called punya and usually translated as 'merit'. If we harmonised our acts with that outlook, mudita would become a practice of celebrating the consequences of skilful acts, or 'rejoicing in merit'. This is more of a cause for insightful celebration since the enjoyment ordinary minds derive from merit (the indulgence in happiness) depends upon using it up.

This is where knowing (in the sense of 'knowing what is') comes in. Knowing and merit are like two wings of a bird – either by itself is of much more limited use than the two together. By gaining insight into the nature of reality and maintaining circumstances which allow us to continue gaining such insight, we can rid ourselves of the afflictive processes and veils to understanding which are the only thing obscuring the sun our of own Complete Awakening. From that vantage what we had considered 'happiness' before will appear in very different light, like so much delusion, candle-flames drawing moths from the moon's guidance. If we orientate our acts towards that understanding, then mudita becomes something else again – rejoicing in the supreme skilfulness, the acquisition of these two 'stores' – merit and knowing.

Though the wording suggests the two stores are separate, in practice they are inextricably interwoven. For example, an act of generosity in Buddhist terms does not mean a show of giving with inward resentment at the anticipated difficulty for oneself, pride in front of observers, and interest in the recipient's subsequent use of the gift, in particular insofar as one might thereby judge whether they deserved to receive it or not. Indeed such an act would involve so much harmful action of thought that it would not be considered skilful, or generosity (sharing), at all. The corrective teachings on generosity are largely about getting insight into the situations in which one might give: 'knowing it as it is,' we might say. With perspective we will know that sharing is not self-sacrifice, but a more skilful way of dealing with a reality which we have come to know better. In this way acting, in this case sharing, teaches us about the nature of reality, and *vice versa.*

Rejoicing in merit became an important practice especially in the Universal Career, where it rather eclipsed rejoicing in happiness. In some countries, it is traditional, when one comes to know of someone having performed a skilful act, say of sharing, to ring a bell to announce to the people that a skilful act has been done and to celebrate it: such a bell is often mounted on a hill. The traditional stages of Buddhist ritual of most traditions include a stage of celebrating the skilful deeds done, being done and to be done throughout all worlds. To rejoice in skilful deeds is taught to be equivalent in terms of psychological consequences to actually doing them oneself.

Another distinction we can make is between our own happiness and others'. When we are happy, we can even rejoice in our own happiness, just as we would in others'. And when we do skilful acts we can rejoice in them, just as we would in others'.

Elimination of countering tendencies

We are not so familiar with mudita – and there is no word for it in English – but we are very familiar with its opposite: resenting others' happiness, and envy. At the same time there seem to be formidable objections to it.

Near enemy

The near enemy of such joy-sharing is taught to be distracted exultation. We might also add the partial joy one feels at success in family and friends or in those people whose success will reflect on us in a good way.

Objections to the idea

Isn't it an excuse for laziness?

To earn spiritual merit by rejoicing in the acts of others sounds like exactly what a lazy bum would dream up for her ideal religion. But we should bear in mind that 'acts' in Buddhist terms does not just mean public acts – of body and speech. The Buddha, as many scholars of ancient Indian religion have pointed out[486], rather revolutionised the meaning of 'act' (in Sanskrit, karma), by teaching that one's thoughts are not only acts but the most important acts, since it is principally one's intention which determines the ethical consequences in any complex action involving body, speech and mind. What this means is that if it is one's intention to avoid doing skilful deeds oneself by 'rejoicing' piously in those of others, then there must be, first of all, some faulty understanding of the skilfulness of those acts, since one does not appreciate their skilfulness enough to deign to do them oneself, and, secondly, an internal conflict – between wanting to do skilful deeds (by proxy) and not wanting to do them (personally) which would, to say the least, have consequences: inuring oneself to hypocrisy and indecision are clearly not skilful acts of mind in themselves.

Isn't rejoicing in your own skilful act or happiness sinful?

In cultures influenced by religions teaching of 'an adjudicating deity' we are habituated to viewing ethics as available to judgment by an external judge, primarily the 'deity', but by extension human judges and what Freud called the superego – the internalised judge in our psychology who still looks at us as it were from outside. This means ethics is conceived of as public. The Jesus depicted in the canonical gospels made efforts to overcome this with his recommendations to turn the judgmentalness back on the judge and to conceal good deeds (or at least fasting) from public knowledge. Even the Qur'ān recommends that when one hand gives, the other hand should not know about it. However because of the background doctrine of the external judge in the sky such recommendations will always be acting against a much more powerful opposite tendency fostering mutual judgment, as is clear in the behaviour of most people who consider themselves followers of Jesus and the Qur'ān. Furthermore, even though many people in these cultures may consider themselves not to be among these followers, the fact is that their cultures have been deeply influenced by these religions, and it is quite likely that their patterns are reproduced in them but under

---

486 See, for example, 'The Buddhist Ethicization of Karma, Saṁsāra and Rebirth' in Prasad (2007, pp. 237-278).

different names.

Christian and post-Christian cultures are additionally afflicted with the doctrine of 'sacrifice' redefined as self-harm – that we as sinners should somehow emulate Jesus assuming suffering meekly upon himself, and that it is therefore a great virtue to persecute ourselves or allow ourselves to be persecuted in the course of doing good to others. It even starts to be seen as a kind of trade-off, in that the more harm one does oneself in the course of the good one does for others, the greater the import of the latter. There is, in Buddhist terms, what we might call a paucity of *the Wisdom about Equalness*, which would recognise for example that one harm does not offset but adds to another. The payoff notion was there in early Christianity, the internalised form of 'an eye for an eye', but it has only assumed monstrous proportions on later melding with such ideas as 'survival of the fittest' and the free market of competition. Sunnite Islām seems relatively free of the idea of self-sacrifice (unless you are an edible animal), but it is a strand in Shī`ite Islām as evinced by the sympathetic commemoration of the deaths of Ḥussayn and Ḥassan, in orgiastic spectacles whose public self-inflicted blood-letting is obviously akin to the Catholic processions of flagellants. To non-believers both in its own cultures and elsewhere self-harm as sacrifice (literally 'sacred feat') is still a great export: the recent adaptations of C. S. Lewis' celebration of self-harm of the self-righteous as the means to magical power over reality, the story of Aslan in the Narnia stories, for the edification of our children, was extraordinarily popular worldwide.

The truth is that such doctrines as self-harm as sacred feat and its thinly disguised disguised leonine offspring, when accustomed to, make certain teachings of Buddhism very difficult to understand and appreciate. Rejoicing in one's own skilful deeds seems to mean boasting in the marketplace about them. Even if it does not, even if it is a private matter, given our sinfulness, having done good, we ought rather to grovel even more humbly before 'the deity' for our conceit, or to deliver us from the temptation of such conceit. This is the intellectual machination, and liability to wanton and self-congratulatory extremity, of the doctrine of sin and its concomitants, and it is perhaps with good reason that many Buddhist translators have insisted that we should avoid using the word 'sin' for the downfalls and unskilful acts highlighted in the Buddhist ethical systems. I hope I have shown how heavily doctrine complexes such as sin and free will depend on the one hand on the afflictive processes of the human mind, and on the other on sophisticated and sometimes cynical reasoning designed to promote certain doctrines at any cost, including costs in terms of human happiness.

How can we get around the misunderstandings these ghosts of our culture's past lead us into? One strand of Buddhist teaching in these cultures has been to take an 'enough is enough, God' kind of attitude and say, 'Why shouldn't we enjoy our happiness?' It is especially prominent in the 'interdisciplinary' field of Buddhist psychology, and is championed prominently by Jewish psychotherapists. One wonders whether there isn't there a remnant of some deep-seated desire to get revenge on Elohim for what he has done.[487] This kind of appeal to commonsensical selfishness may attract people to contexts where they learn more about the dharma, but whether it consitutes a dharma teaching in itself is debatable.

In *The Discourse Delivered by Immaculate Renown*, one awakening being is timid about visiting the awakened layman 'Immaculate Renown' on his sick-bed because he was so roundly chastised previously by that layman for his wrong understanding of sacrifice:

> 'Tametdavadam, "Taddharmayajñam̊ katham̊ dcyam?"
>
> 'Sa māmabravīt: "Yena kena dharma yajñenāpūrvam acaramam̊ saṭtvā paripacyante, tadhi dharma yajñam. Tadapi kim̊? Yaduta bodhi vyupahārasya mahāmaitri, saddharma sam̊graheṇābhinirhṛtā mahākaruṇā, sarva sattva prāmodyapalambhenābhinirhṛtā mahā muditta, jñāna sam̊graheṇābhinirhṛtā mahopekṣā." '
>
> 'I then asked him, "How does one offer a dharma sacrifice?"
>
> 'He replied: "A dharma sacrifice is that by which unprecedentedly and endlessly living beings are brought to maturity, for it is a dharma sacrifice. And how is that? Well, it is the great amity which is the worshipful offering of Awakening; of the great caring which is carried out in the gathering of the sublime Law; of the great sharing joy which is carried out in the recognition of the rapture of all living beings; and of the great equanimity which is carried out in the gathering of knowing." '[488]

---

[487] The Tibetan Buddhist teacher Thinley Norbu notes in his book *White Sail* how the belief in an eternal external deity leads its worshippers to cycles of adoration, betrayal, vengefulness, and forgiveness, as the environment shifts naturally from pleasant circumstances to disasters and back again.

[488] From the third chapter on 'The Reluctance of the Disciples and the Awakening Beings', or the fourth if this is divided, as it sometimes is, i.e. in the chapter on 'The Reluctance of the Awakening Beings'.

Instead, we might, in the spirit of this discourse, make an inquiry into ourselves about our own nature. After all, who can possibly have better access to our own nature than we ourselves potentially do? Someone else, such as a priest, or a fellow addict, might *tell us* we are inherently sinful, that our nature is such, but they will never be able to see as clearly as we do if we work on clarifying our critical faculties and conscientiousness. Especially in science-dominated cultures, which place a taboo on the subject as a source of knowledge, it frequently gets overlooked that our private world is vast and inaccessible to others.

When we 'try' to gain some clarity and access to the nature of ourselves, very often we will encounter only confusion, perhaps even confusion as to what exactly to do, how exactly to access ourselves. As is often said, the most difficult thing to see is what is under your nose – so easily overlooked. It might seem that our minds are so drowned in mad confusion that there seems to be no hope at all of clarity. The Buddha challenged this hopelessness. By claiming to have discovered reality, including the reality of his own mind, by himself, and by saying that we can, the Buddha threw down a gauntlet which was never thrown in the other religious traditions. And what was the nature that he discovered?

The embryo of one who will arrive at Truth

A number of Universal Career discourses declare that every sentient being has the so-called 'tathāgatagarbha', usually translated as 'buddha nature', but which we could translate more literally as 'the *embryo* [garbha] of someone who will *arrive* [agata] at *truth* [tatha]'. The Awakening Being Maitreya revealed to the Kashmiri master Asanga the reasons for teaching that beings have this potential in the following manner, as recorded in the Universal Career scripture *The Changeless Continuity*:

'Someone endowed with a god's pure sight
Who saw in a withering lotus
A vision of One Arrived at Truth, adorned with a thousand auspicious marks,
But imprisoned by petals of this water-born flower
Would take him out;

Likewise Those Who Have Arrived at Bliss
Who see in beings in the nethermost Hells
Their true nature, a nature of compassion till the end of time
But obscured by veils

Liberate them from those veils.

A clever man
Who spotted honey amid a swarm of bees
Would use his skilful means to separate the honey from the bees.

Likewise the visionary sages
Who see in all beings *the essence,* the ground of potential,
Use most skilful means to separate the essence from the veils.

The mind is delighted by what's born from mud – a lotus –
but later its withering dismays:
Such is the happiness of desire.

Bees when angry leave their sting:
Such is anger when it comes, bringing pain to the heart.

As the *Form Which Is Law* transcends the world,
there is no example for it manifest there:
Thus the example of the vision of One Arrived at Truth.

The unique taste of the subtle, profound teachings: *a semblance of honey.*

Because there are the errors of
faintheartedness,
contempt for the less able ones,
belief in what is false,
defaming what is true,
and cherishing oneself above all else,

The Changeless Continuity was taught, as it is taught here,
So that these five errors can be dispelled.'

Now 'faintheartedness and contempt for the less able' is a fair description of the psychological results of the doctrines of total judgment and sin. In these discourses we have a bold declaration that every single living being is on the way to Complete Perfect Awakening. This idea has led to interesting 'religious observances' in communities taking these scriptures as the basis of their practice. For example, the followers of Nichiren Buddhism (which emphasises *The White Lotus Discourse of the Sublime Law*) when processing through villages on their alms round prostrate to every living being they encounter in recognition of that being's potential to become a Buddha in the future. This is in imitation of the practice of the awakening being named 'Never-Disparaging' whose exemplar myth occurs in that discourse.

The esoteric scriptures of the Secret Mantra Career (guhyamantrayāna) make this even more explicit, by pointing out that the human beings are already Buddhas, if they only knew: failing to recognise this is the defining characteristic of an apparently-non-Buddha. And then again, the direct instructions of the Total Integration (rdzogs-chen) of Tibetan Buddhism and Bön religion, though they require certain circumstances, such as the presence of a teacher who has realised directly, can be said to depend on the recognition that *if we could only relax*, then *effortlessly* we would discover that we are, and always have been, Buddhas. The trick is knowing how to relax: hence the special circumstances usually required.

If we might be so bold as to draw an analogy, it is as though we were in fact in Eden, but due to the afflictive processes and the veils to our understanding we do not experience ourselves in this way. In *The Changeless Continuity* Maitreya revealed that this was not because of a stamp on our nature but because of adventitious or temporary, removable stains. These stains are not removed in a *post mortem* celestial court ajudicating on doctrinal allegiance but by skilful actions of body, speech and mind done now.

Laying down unskilful deeds

It is taught that there is one *advantage* to unskilful acts of body, speech or mind – and that is that they can be cleared away. Training manuals for Tibetan monasteries stress the simile of ethics as a moon which can suddenly sail free from clouds. This can happen through the practice of regretting and 'laying down' unskilful deeds, the propulsion back into skilful habits by means of the so-called 'four kinds of impetus' – *regret* of unskilful acts we have done, *reliance* on a source of inspiration, a *remedial* practice of some kind of skilfulness, and the *resolve* not to repeat the unskilful acts.[489]

Isn't happiness hysterical, unreal and like a drug?

We are familiar with the potential of substances, such as drinks, food,

---

[489] An example of this kind of practice is given below in 'related practices'.

and recreational drugs, not to mention property and wealth itself to give rise to happiness, however fleeting. This is especially true in those societies where financial interests have broad sway and interested parties' advertising fosters the pernicious notion that something must be owned or consumed in order for one's mental or physical state to improve.

In the same societies a general conviction seems to develop that happiness is less real than suffering. Here we see the influence of envy: under the circumstances of competitiveness which the consumerist system must maintain in order to survive, some people inevitably must lose out on these substances which have come erroneously to be seen as the only means to happiness, and these people therefore look on the happiness of those 'better off' than they are in material terms and resent their relative prosperity. The transient aspect of such happiness is highlighted but in a way which distorts the picture sufficiently for the losers still to crave such success: it is accused of 'removing people' from the 'hard reality' of life.

A potent depiction of this occurs for example in Aldous Huxley's iconic novel *Brave New World*, which depicts a superficially utopian society where everyone is literally high – on a drug. The novel is a passionate declaration that happiness is not enough to be human. We have already seen how upholders of the notion of 'an omnipotent creator deity' are effectively committed to advocating suffering as inevitable, and the long influence of their multifarious specious intellectual advocacies has melded most unfavourably with this suspicion about material happiness, and explains a great deal of the pervasive irrational horror at drug use, for example.

Biology tells us that drugs affect our brains by altering levels of particular chemicals which depend on each other by complex feedback mechanisms called homeostasis. What is generally unrecognised outside of biology is that there is no non-arbitrary base-line or normality from which such levels can be measured. The fact is that our moods are already drug-related, that 'ordinary' food is made up of drugs which therefore affect our moods, and furthermore that we all even hallucinate to some extent. In Huxley's novel, it can be argued that reality has to all intents and purposes changed through the introduction of the use of the drug across society, because nothing but the general consensus ever defines what reality is. (We can recall Popper's definition of scientific 'objective' knowledge as a consensus of subjective knowledge.)

With such a background it is hardly surprising that some people should feel that to rejoice in happiness is inappropriate. When the only happiness visible seems to be due to consuming products and wisdom discovers the bankruptcy of consumerism, in such restricted conditions wisdom and happiness appear to be opposed to each other. 'Ignorance is bliss,' is a saying which sounds very peculiar outside of the kind of culture we are describing, but perfectly true within it. There is a distinct kudos to being thoroughly miserable – for surely, with reality so bad, only the truly pessimistic could be wise? 'Life's a bitch, and then you die.' The only solution seems to be to seek relief from this ubiquitous awfulness, and relief always seems to come as a product with a price tag. Indeed the price tag, with the development of technology, is now an unlimited one – thanks for example to powerful pharmaceutical companies restricting funding to research into temporary symptom-relievers rather than unprofitable cures, information technology development companies ensuring that software needs regular updating, and giant corporations genetically modifying staple foods to become sterile in the first generation so as to obligate farmers to ongoing purchases.

This gives us a clue as to how to proceed. We have already seen how we can be deluded by reports, especially repetitious reports. Merely gaining awareness of this starts to undermine the power of those reports over us. At the same time we come to see that the happiness the adverts promise us via their products is available elsewhere, and for free. To take an obvious example, the happiness dependent upon a healthy body comes to the non-emaciated from the nature of their body the moment they come to realise that the adverts telling them that they can only be happy if emaciated are deceitful. This is just one example: we shall have to apply the principle broadly and thoroughly before we begin to rediscover natural happiness. And we should not underestimate the intelligence behind the advertising: we may say to ourselves, 'I'm not one of those dominated by consumerism: my happiest moments have not been on obtaining or using products but when sharing time with my lover or enjoying the beauty of natural scenery,' and overlook the facts that romantic relations have become themselves a commoditisation of love based on trivialising business-like exchange of 'commitment' and the natural scenery was only available to us because we are lucky enough to have been born into a class which exploits others and thus benefits from a freedom of travel undreamed of by the exploited.

The resistance we have to rejoicing in happiness is currently something like the resistance we might have if we were being encouraged by peers to take some drug. However, as our perspective improves, and the superstitious connections we made between happiness and escape from reality dissolve, it will come to seem much more reasonable to celebrate happiness.

With perspective, in fact, we do not need to wait for some revolution before we dare start the practice of sharing joy: even if we are living in Huxley's 'brave new world', with perspective we can mentally distinguish between the horrific circumstances (such as the suppression of love) on which the drug-boosted happiness depends, which should be treated as a problem, on the one hand, and on the other, the happiness itself, which can be celebrated. However until we have such perspective it will only seem like hypocrisy.

How can I celebrate their ill-gotten gains?

This brings us to one easily understood objection to 'sharing joy' among those habituated to judgmental mentality: when the other's joy happens to be that of a serial killer finishing off the latest victim, or that of a corporate fatcat receiving the latest wave of filthy lucre spawned off the backs of classes reduced to misery.

These are just two clear examples of the problem of the delay between acts and their consequences. Even if we accept the possibility that mental states associated with killing and taking what has not been offered are of a nature that their natural consequence will be suffering – and it is taught in Buddhism that they lead respectively to experiencing the environment as totally unbearable, and inverted perception such that all attempts to get more cause only frustration – the happiness which can arise on the performance of such acts may seem to be a consequence of those acts in our eyes, such that we feel that by celebrating the happiness, we are also celebrating the acts, celebrating killing and taking what has not been offered. Well, just as rejoicing in merit is taught to be equivalent to earning that merit, rejoicing in demerit is taught to be equivalent to earning that demerit. And clearly the point of this practice is not to celebrate unskilful acts and thereby effectively perform them ourselves.

How we deal with this conundrum depends upon our understanding, on our perspective. If we feel still that in some way the happiness of a criminal is dependent upon having successfully committed the crime, then we should not share the joy! However, if in our outlook the happiness the criminal experiences is seen to be related to previous skilful acts of body, speech and mind, and only ripening at the time of the crime through other circumstances, then we can separate the joy from the crime and share the former, although as we mentioned above, this is still effectively celebrating merit being exhausted.

Related training methods

A tantric method to lay down unskilful actions

Because the tangle of self-hatred is one of the most difficult to extricate ourselves from ('I hate how much I hate myself…') it needs a powerful remedy. The fourfold impetus we mentioned (regret, reliance, remedy and resolve) can assume many different forms, and here is an especially powerful one taken from the typical preliminary practices of Tibetan Buddhism, and ultimately deriving from practices referred to in the scriptures of the Secret Mantra Career. Once again, as with the creation-stage practice of the Great Compassionate One, it should be endowed with the Three Excellences of a Universal Career practice, it depends on a certain degree of open-mindedness about seemingly far out forms, and it becomes more meaningful with permission, initiation and further explanation from a qualified teacher. Here we will consider the 'bare bones'.

The Archetypal Ideal (iṣṭadevatā) in this case derives from the exemplar myth of 'Vajra Being' (Vajrasattva). The word 'vajra' originally referred to an indestructible weapon made of thunderbolts wielded by Indra in myths mentioned in the Vedas, and came to be used of diamond since this precious stone was so difficult to break. In the Buddhist traditions it carried a strong connotation of intellectual strength – the ability to destroy erroneous opinions in rational debate – and in the tantric teachings the Awakened Mind is described as 'of the identity of the Vajra Own-Being' (vajrasvabhāvātmaka), invincible because it is 'the knowing of the profound non-independence' (śunyatā jñāna) of all phenomena and thus has freed itself from the influence of the afflictive processes and veils to reality. Many tantric training methods begin with the declaration, 'I am of the identity of the Vajra Own-Being, the knowing of the profound non-independence! – Oṁ śunyatā jñāna vajra svabhāvātmako 'haṁ!' Vajrasattva in the exoteric exemplar myth was an awakening being who, on taking on the Universal Responsibility, vowed, 'If, when I have attained Awakening, there will be any sentient beings who are not instantly purified of stains by merely mentioning my name, then may I never attain Awakening.' Given that we consider Vajrasattva to be Awakened, accepting this myth deeply means accepting that power of the enunciation of the name in the mantra 'Oṁ Vajrasattva huṁ' to clear away our impurities.

Over our head we visualise the seat as before, but this time the seed syllable, hanging in space, made out of our awareness, is blue or white huṁ. It spontaneously transforms into the human form of the archetype – a seated white figure as before but in this case with two hands, the right holding the vajra weapon level with the heart, and the left holding a bell at the hip. On these two implements is hung something like an encyclopaedia of tantric doctrines into whose successive levels we are only introduced by intiation: for our purposes it is enough to consider that they symbolise Awakening's clever strategies and its deep insight respectively. At the heart centre, again on a lotus-moon-disc seat, is a second huṁ hanging in space, surrounded by the letters of the mantra, which are multicoloured.

This time as we intone the mantra we imagine light like liquid pouring down from this figure, washing through the body and out below, taking with it all impurities of bodily, verbal and mental action. At length, we address the figure directly: 'Pray, purify my faults.' We imagine that the figure responds, 'Child of the family, your faults are purified.' And having uttered these words, it dissolves into us as light and we transform into the form of the Archetypal Ideal Vajrasattva, with the full conviction that impurities have been cleared away. We then dissolve the visualisation, leaving the mind to rest in its own nature.

>Perspective (upekkha)

Meaning

The most authoritative commentary on the *Higher Teaching Collection (Abhidhamma Saṅgaṇi)* in the Pali canon, Buddhaghosa's *Excellent Aim* states:

> This is impartiality [majjhattaṁ] about the object and implies discriminative knowledge [paricchindanakaṁ ñāṇaṁ].[490]

The *Compendium* says:

> What is perspective? It is evenmindedness and deep knowledge, and the mindstate and mental events concomitant with them, based on a mental absorption dwelling on the thought, 'May beings attain profit [hita]!'

We should note the emphasis on knowledge: this is very far from the indifference to reality consequent upon withdrawing or numbing sensitivity. By training in the contemplation of the wish for their profit, and developing our knowledge, partiality will fade, as we discern how things really are.

Types

Once again, it is important to note that this is a training and not a decision or a passion. At each stage of training, we will come to see it in a different way, and have different capacity within ourselves for it. We can distinguish what we might call 'beginners' perspective' with 'advanced perspective'.

Beginners' perspective

Scholars of the path have called this 'the perspective for the conventional mode of being'. We can divide it into two on the basis of what the perspective is about, oneself or other living beings.

>Beginners' perspective about themselves

Each kind of perspective means getting a better or more balanced

[490] (Thera N. , 1956/1979, p. 72)

overall view by *overlooking something.* In this first kind, what is overlooked is what distinguishes us from all other living beings. Instead, we are 'getting ourselves in the perspective' which recognises *everything we have in common with them.* We can consider three levels of 'self' here – ourselves as a species, ourselves as a tribe and 'myself' as a person.

>Our species in the cosmos and environment

Here we reflect on everything our species has in common with other species. This can be done in terms of bodily similarities, similarities in communication, and similarities in awareness and intentions. Above all it is to be noted that we all share the wish to be happy, for example. And it will help us to consider also the importance of our planet in the cosmos, and to recall that our solar system is one of very many.

>Our tribe in the world community

We can also look at the groups to which we consider ourselves to belong and notice all the similarities with other groups. On the physical level this includes the structural organisation of our communities, including such practicalities as obtaining water and energy and dealing with sewage and rubbish. On the level of communication, we can consider art, music, literature, film, etc. of different cultures. And on the level of awareness and intention such things as the desire for national dignity, wealth, power over other nations. On all these levels the training is to dwell on the similarities. We often assume that an exercise such as this is ignoring the harsh reality, an exercise in make-believe. In fact, it can often get closer to the truth than the prejudice against which it acts:

Case: Jews versus Nazis

The Israeli psychologist Daniel Kahneman (b. 1934) wrote this about an experience he had as a Jew in Nazi-occupied France:

> It must have been late 1941 or early 1942. Jews were required to wear the Star of David and to obey a 6pm curfew. I had gone to play with a Christian friend and had stayed too late. I turned my brown sweater inside out to walk the few blocks home. As I was walking down an empty street, I saw a German soldier approaching. He was wearing the black uniform that I had been told to fear more than others – the one worn by specially recruited SS soldiers. As I came closer to him, trying to walk fast, I noticed that he was looking at me intently. Then he

beckoned me over, picked me up, and hugged me. I was terrified that he would notice the star inside my sweater. He was speaking to me with great emotion, in German. When he put me down, he opened his wallet, showed me a picture of a boy, and gave me some money. I went home more certain than ever that my mother was right: people were endlessly complicated and interesting.[491]

He says this is part of what convinced him to become a psychologist.

>Our person, the individual

Are our bodies, and our way of speaking, and our minds, so different from each other? To train we reflect on the parallels.[492]

---

491 (Kahneman, 2003, p. 417)

492 One recently self-identifying tradition of Buddhism, whom I will call 'G', have taken this one step further inwards and train in 'perspective' at what me might call the level of the soul, considering the awareness and the various experiences, pleasant or painful, that arise to that awareness. The Gs teach that we must somehow let the experiences happen but not react. This is certainly a departure from the logic of the scheme I have sketched here, because at each level we have been considering the similarities between our side and the other side. But between the awareness (as 'our side') and the experiences (as 'the other side') which arise in it there is no obvious similarity to consider, so unlike on our three levels, there is on the 'soul' level no means by which natural kinship might develop, by recognising parallels, to replace earlier antagonism.

Indeed in the case of the arising of experiences to the awareness, the afflictive processes *should not* be entertained in this way. The innovation as I see it in these G traditions is to train in 'putting up and shutting up' *vis-a-vis* the afflictive emotions. I think this is erroneously taking the aim as the method, like a man trying to fly off the cliff by 'flying' rather than building the glider first. It is an extremely tough fight to pick, and its results are likely to be a kind of cocooning of the awareness from its own experience, akin to mild schizophrenia.

There is, it is true, a kind of perspective, an even-mindedness about the experiences, which can arise in awareness. In the Total Integration (rdzogs-chen) practices of Tibetan Buddhism there are skilful methods of pointing this out, which do indeed use the language of 'not engaging positively or negatively'. But such instructions are part of a very delicate package, which involves identifying the awareness itself, and utter relaxation, and depends for most people on the presence of a highly skilled teacher, and the kind of mental calm consequent upon profound devotion. It is a method so liable to error as to be useful to very few exceptional students, and was traditionally only taught one on one in private. The danger is that the G tradition may lack such skilful methods of identifying awareness itself, and without them the way of talking about awareness and its

>Beginners' perspective about others

Here we mean getting living beings as a whole in perspective. The same three levels – species, community, and individual apply. The difference here is that we include comparisons between and among those species, communities and individuals other than our own, that is, we consider the similarities among other species; among other communities; among other individuals. In this last case, for example, we might consider the situation of an attack, even if we have never been attacker or attacked, and notice the similarities between the attacker and the victim, in the spirit of those lines from Thich Nhat Hanh's poem 'Call Me By My True Names':

> I am the twelve-year-old girl, refugee on a small boat,
> who throws herself into the ocean after being raped by a sea pirate,
> and I am the pirate, my heart not yet capable of seeing and loving.
> I am a member of the politburo, with plenty of power in my hands,
> and I am the man who has to pay his 'debt of blood' to, my people,
> dying slowly in a forced labor camp.

Advanced perspective

This is called 'ultimate perspective' by the scholars. It refers to that perspective consequent upon profound analysis of the nature of the self (as distinct from the other) and phenomena (as distinct from each other).

>Advanced perspective about the self as distinct from other

If we can get to the nitty gritty of ourselves as we really are, then a much stabler and clearer perspective will be available to us. In a way, nothing in the entire cosmos should be more obvious to us than the nature of our own awareness. However, for that very reason it is the very thing we most blithely overlook.

The Individual Career of Buddhism requires the outlook where the self is seen as composed of a number of ever-changing elements, and this recognition liberates us from suffering. From the perspective of the Universal Career this recommendation would encourage a quietism which neglects others' suffering and furthermore fail to achieve a complete liberation due to the 'traces' of grasping the self which remain because of the failure to gain the advanced

---

appearances becomes charged with antagonism and self-defeating struggle, and is probably not beneficial. We can test this for ourselves.

perspective about phenomena.

>Advanced perspective about phenomena as distinct from each other

Complete awakening is the seeing of reality as it is. There is no point learning how to parrot other people's decisions about this: the only way is to investigate it ourselves. Eventually we will come to see reality nakedly, and without artifice. All qualities of awareness that need to be developed will have been, and all that need to be purged will have been.

Elimination of countering tendencies

Near enemy

By increasing our perspective simply by raising ourselves higher, we lose the insight into what is happening, even though the view seems broader. This is indifference, the close enemy of perspective.

Objections to the idea

It is very hard for us to get ourselves in perspective on any level. This is no accident: we are the products of a seemingly invincible barrage of influences encouraging us to avoid or lose that perspective.

Isn't mankind unique?

Various traditional religious traditions have taught us that the earth, as well as being flat[493], or awesomely separated from the sky even without visible pillars[494], is the focus of importance in the universe, and that the environment including all its animals and plants was created for humans' use, and whether or not we subscribe to these doctrines we have probably adopted their world-view to some extent, as evinced by our disregard for the consequences via the environment being unbalanced of our rapacious approach to exploiting and enjoying that gracious 'gift'.

Modern science can help us get perspective here: unlike even such a recent generation as our grandparents we have grown up in a world which knows about the formation and destruction of galaxies, black holes, supernovae, the distances and durations involved in those tiny specks of light in the night sky which the massive religions saw as devils and angels; and about the processes by

---

493 Daniel 4: 10-11; Matthew 4: 8

494 Qur'ān 13: 2, 31: 10

which the burning of fossil fuels leads to global warming; about the degree of shared genetic material between the human, *Homo sapiens*, and the chimpanzee; about the complex languages used by other species, such as the hump-backed whale, which we are only just starting to work out; about the existence of lying and trickery in the communication of other primates; about other species' experience of pain and anxiety; and so on.

Case: suffering of humans and animals

Over the last three decades, there has been a great deal of study by biologists of the meaning of suffering, for animals, and for humans. By examining the results of this kind of research, we can gain a vivid impression of the degree to which all measures of suffering we know from experience with other humans are shared with members of other species. In a 2008 paper[495] Marian Stamp Dawkins of Oxford University surveys this research, beginning with how objective criteria for the measurement of suffering are impossible for humans as much as for animals, and detailing how scientists have got around this by defining measurement criteria which give a quanitifiable idea of how much the animal individual in question is getting what it wants. This has striking resonance with the usual Buddhist classification of suffering:

> ...the suffering of association with what is unpleasant, the suffering of dissociation from what is pleasant, the suffering if one does not obtain what one wants...[496]

In psychology, stimuli are classified as positive or negative 'reinforcers', which is a jargonistic way of describing things that the animal or human, after going through once, tends to try to repeat or tends to try to avoid, respectively. Emotional states subsequent to the positive reinforcer stimulus or in the absence of negative reinforcer stimulus constitute what we more ordinarily call positive emotion, and those subsequent to negative reinforcer stimulus or in the absence of positive reinforcer stimulus constitute negative emotion.[497] This way of dealing with the matter corresponds to recent methodology attempting a more objective way of quantifying human suffering.[498] How 'positive' a stimulus is can be measured by

---

495 (Dawkins M. S., 2008)

496 From the Universal Career's *Compendium of Higher Teachings* (Boin-Webb, Rahula, & Asanga, p. 84).

497 (Boissy, et al., 2007)

498 (Rolls, 2005)

how much effort the animal or human is prepared to put into getting it again. This is a considerable advance on previous physiological measures, which could not distinguish between the white knuckles and screams of someone who loved a rollercoaster ride and someone who hated it – the new measurement being how much effort the individual would subsequently put into having another ride. This new approach then allowed hitherto unsuspected signs of animals' emotional states to be recognised. For example, the amount of the white of the eye a cow shows is, it was found, directly related to its frustration at not being able to access food it can see.[499] By research adopting this approach, dolphins were found to dislike tourist boats and elephants were shown to dislike climbing steep slopes. Another new method of quantifying suffering objectively employs recent discoveries about cognitive biases in humans such as the ones we have considered in our treatment of accepting intuitive views.[500] Animals are trained to distinguish previously neutral stimuli by presenting one of them always associated with a negative stimulus such as loud noise. Then in various situations they are presented with an intermediate stimulus – and are found to associate the new stimulus with the negative stimulus more in particular situations: these situations could therefore be classed as negative stimuli producing negative mental states, and the degree of negativity measured. This provides another objective way of quantifying pleasure and displeasure without needing to create a choice situation, and again much better than physiological methods. Starlings were found in this way to be reduced to pessimism by spartan surroundings.[501]

Clearly those of us not fortunate enough to spend a lot of time around animals can use the results of such research as a powerful support to our equanimity meditations relating to the shared qualities of ourselves and other living beings. We can leave the stubborn, dreary and now embarrassing assertions of other species' 'soullessness' to those who feel they must defend dogma.

Should we not curse the unbelievers?

It cannot be denied that certain strands of the massive religions advocate cursing those who do not share their beliefs. An ordinary sermon on a Friday in a Sunnite mosque before the main congregational ritual prayer of the week includes traditional curses, 'Allāhumma dammar bilāduhum! Allāhumma

---

[499] (Sandem, Braastad, & Boe, 2002)

[500] (Paul, Harding, & Mendl, 2005)

[501] (Bateson & Mather, 2007)

dammar buyuutuhum! – O Allāh! destroy their lands; OAllāh! destroy their households...' etc. Whilst it is forbidden in Islāmic law to curse individuals, it is permissible to curse groups – on ethical grounds, but also on the 'metaphysical' (usually political) grounds that those groups have not accepted Islām. The seeming contradiction is typically justified in the way the 19th century Damascan commentator on Ḥanafi law ibn `Ābidīn[502] does, as a way of showing to the people that the majority behaviour of the cursed community is something is unacceptable even if an entire community, consisting as they do of individuals, cannot be cursed as individuals. It is forbidden by the Qur'ān itself to pray for those who died without accepting Islām. This reminds us of the early Christians who, once they had the support of a converted emperor at least, used to hiss derisively as they passed the temples of religions other than their own.

And it is not that the non-religious can congratulate themselves, for the phenomenon of cursing persists when most religious symbols have been abandoned. Cursing at least allows the buck to stop with 'the deity' for redressing the outrages of the world with 'divine violence', be it in this visible world or 'the punishment in Hell', whereas the curses which persist when such doctrines as postponed judgment die out are more likely to stir the rabble to take the matter, and place 'the divine wand of wrath' into their own hands.

It is undeniable that situations in our world provoke outrage, and if we are in a state of ignorance about the fine details of these situations and about how best to address their causes to solve them, then we will indeed curse. But we are also responsible for our ignorance, and we should consider whether to languish in it and continue to curse, or to address it.

Furthermore, whilst a group cursing session is certainly good rabble-rousing stuff, we might ask whether our times and circumstances are right for being roused into a rabble: i.e. we might try to dispel our ignorance about potential solutions to these outrages, for a frenzied mentality of enmity is not one of them.

Again, the vast majority of those who take part in such cursing were born into the community of 'believers' or the equivalent, and should ask themselves whether they would have become any different from those they curse had they been born among them. The answer will, one hopes, having some faith in reason still, be no; and then we can ask, to what ends apart from merely cynically political must one curse a chance occurrence, much less an occurrence set up by the deity?

---

502 (`Ābidīn)

Furthermore, in the specific case of cursing infidels, they should reflect on the question of who has the authority to judge unbelief in others. There are many historical examples of people who hid their belief, even under torture. There is a strong tendency in Islām to over-simplify what 'belief' actually means, related to the magical association of political allegiance with perception of divine truths which dates right back to the life of the prophet, and nowhere is this more pernicious than in the matter of dividing the believers from the infidels. Christianity seemed less afflicted by this tendency until there appeared on the scene those who 'know' they are 'saved' and somehow 'know' others are 'not saved'. Is it not a stupendous arrogance to assume oneself 'closer to the deity' than someone else is? Is it not in fact a greater disgrace, to individuals, and to their religions, than whatever characteristics have been selected as evidence for being further from 'the deity' are? It is to this pernicious mentality which such passages as this in *The White Lotus Discourse of the Sublime Law* are directed:

> O Lotus Splendour, This Great Awakener Who Listens to the Worlds reveals this Unfolding of the White Lotus of the Sublime Law under the many guises he assumes. Sometimes under the guise of the Creator, sometimes under that of the Almighty, sometimes under that of the Auspicious, sometimes under that of Kuvera, sometimes under that of a world emperor, sometimes under that of a petty ruler, sometimes under that of a chief merchant, sometimes under that of a citizen, sometimes under that of a villager, sometimes under that of a holy man. Sometimes again the Great Awakener Who Listens to the Worlds reveals this Unfolding of the White Lotus of the Sublime Law under a male ascetic's guise, sometimes under a female ascetic's, sometimes under a male devotee's, sometimes under a female devotee's, sometimes under that of a chief merchant's wife, sometimes under that of a citizen's wife, sometimes under a boy's, sometimes under a girl's guise. With so many variations in the manner to show himself, the Great Awakener Who Listens to the Worlds reveals this Unfolding of the White Lotus of the Sublime Law to creatures. He has even assumed the guise of a monster to reveal this Unfolding to such as were to be converted by a monster. To some he has revealed this Unfolding of the Lotus of the Sublime Law under the guise of a demon, to some under a Garuda's, to some under a Kinnara's, to some under a great serpent's guise. Even to the beings in any of the wretched states, in the Hells, the animal realm, Yama's realm, the Great Awakener Who Listens to the Worlds is a

> Saviour. Even to the creatures in the palace harems of our world 'Endurance' has the Great Awakener Who Sees the Worlds, after metamorphosing himself into a woman, revealed this Unfolding of the Lotus of the Sublime Law. Verily, O Lotus-Splendour, the Great Awakener Who Listens to the Worlds is the supporter of the creatures living in our world 'Endurance'. Under so many guises, assumed at will, has the Great Awakener Who Listens to the Worlds revealed this Unfolding of the White Lotus of the Sublime Law to creatures. Yet, there is no diminution of wisdom, nor diminution of power in that Good One. So many, young man of good family, are the manifestations of knowledge by which this Great Awakener Who Listens to the Worlds has made himself known in our world 'Endurance'. In other worlds also, as numerous as the grains of the sands of the river Ganges, he reveals the law, under the shape of an Awakener to such as must be converted by an Awakener; under the shape of a disciple to such as must be converted by a disciple; under the shape of One Awakened Alone to such as must be converted by One Awakened Alone; under the shape of One Who Attained Reality to such as must be converted by One Who Attained Reality. Nay, he will show to those who must be converted by a relic of One Who Attained Reality such a relic, and to those who must be converted by complete surpassing suffering he will show himself completely surpassing suffering. Such is the powerful knowledge, O Lotus Splendour, of which the Great Awakener is possessed.[503]

The Muslim mystic Rumi contrasts those proud of being Muslim with one who understands better:

> If all the world should say to him
> – 'You are on the Way of Allāh and the right religion!'
> He will not be made hotter by their words
> – his lonely soul will not mate with them.

Your body is a temple! Because you deserve it!

The modern consumerist culture continually bombards us with messages that encourage us to focus on ourselves as somehow more important

---

503 From the 23rd Chapter, 'Listener to the Worlds'.

than anything else – and by 'ourselves' I mean our appearance, our body weight, our bodily health, our sexiness, our status, our wealth, our furniture, our bathrooms, our security, our central heating, our future retirement, etc. etc. The advertisers have succeeded: a society which did not used to care about such things has become a society which is obsessed by them. In such a society petty self-concern is almost a defining national characteristic. We may already have reflected on the dangers of the capitalist rivalry-driven economy, and convinced ourselves that it is not worth saving. But we are still living in it, and what are the chances for getting ourselves in perspective given this onslaught of adverts?

We have considered at length how reports can deceive for a whole range of reasons: reflecting on those poiņts again and again will at least make us less susceptible from now on to the influence of adverts telling us how insufficient we are for various reasons and how they can help, so long as we pay. Really such adverts are nonsense and to behold the spectacle of populations in thrall to their tricks is an awfulness almost beyond the power of words to express it. So the training in caring can help us here: by reflecting on this enthralment we can use its power to drive us to reach out to others.

Related training methods

Even-mindedness about insight and training

In the *Discourse Taught by Immaculate Renown* the eponymous layman delivers this speech to an almsman who has visited him for a donation of food. In it there is a sharp wake-up call for us with regard to our perspective about the entire *Kalāmā Discourse* – from the critique of the absolutism to the training in freedom from the afflictive processes:

> ' "Bhadanta Subhūte, tvaṁ cedāmiṣasamatayā sarva dharma samatānvayaśca sarva dharma samatayā buddha dharma samatānvayaḥ, sāmpratamimaṁ piṇḍapātaṁ bhuṁdhi [...] yadi tvaṁ lobha dveṣa mohānna pratiniṣṛjya taissārthaṁ tva pratiṣṭhitaḥ; sat kāya dṛṣty anuccālya, ekāyana mārgaṁ gataḥ; tvayāpi tvavidyā bhava tṛṣṇayorahatayor vidyā vimuktī punar anavaropite [...] paṁcānantariyāṇi ca tava vimuktiśca samāni, tvanna ca vimukto na cāpi baddhaḥ, tvayā catvāryārya satyāni na ca dṛṣtāni satyaṁca nādṛṣtam, phale tvaprāpte pṛthagjano'pi nāsi, pṛthagjana dharmāt punar anivṛttastvanna cāryo na cānāryaḥ, bhūyo'pi sarva dharma pratisaṁyuktastu sarva dharma saṁjñā vipramuktaḥ [...] tvayā śāstā

cāḍṛṣto'śrutaśca dharmārdhaśca saṁgho'paryupāsitaḥ [...] tān bhadantasya śāsṭṛnniśrāya, tvam pravrajita [...] sarva ḍṛṣti gateṣu praviśan, tvamapi tvanta madhyāpratilabdhaḥ; tvaṁ (cet) punar aṣṭākṣaṇa pratipannaḥ kṣaṇāprāptaḥ, saṁkleśa sambhūtastvaṁ vyavadānānupagataḥ; yat sarva sattvānāmaraṇaṁ, tadbhadantasyāraṇaṁ (cet) tvaddāne'viśodhite, bhadanta, ye kecittubhyaṁ piṇḍapātaṁ dadati, te paraṁ tu (cetsva-) vinipātakaraḥ; (yadi) tvaṁ sarva mārasahagataśca sarva kleśāstvatsahāyībhavaṁ gatāḥ; yaḥ kleśa svabhāvaḥ so'pi (ced-) bhadantasya svabhāvo bhavati, tvayā sarva sattva ghātaka cittam upasthāpitam, tvayā sarva buddhānudhvaṁsanam (kṛtaṁ syāt), sarva buddha dharmākīrti kṛtvā, saṁghe cāpratisaraṇastvañcenna kadāci parinirvāsi, tata imaṁ piṇḍapātaṁ bhuṁdhi." '

' "Reverend Subhūti, take this food if you understand the evenness of all things, by means of the evenness of the meats for the pleasures, and if, by means of the evenness of all things you understand the evenness of all the Buddha and the Law [...] if, without abandoning wanting, aversion, and delusion, you can avoid association with them; if you can follow the path of the single way without ever disturbing the views of the relative as absolute[504]; if you can give rise to the kinds of vision and liberation without conquering lack of vision and the thirst for being [...] if, by the equality of the five acts of immediate evil consequence, you reach the evenness of liberation; if you are neither free nor in bondage; if you do not see the Four Sacred Truths, yet are not someone who has not seen the truth; if you have not attained any fruit, yet are not someone who has not attained; if you are an ordinary person, yet have not the qualities of an ordinary person; if you are not holy, yet are not unholy; if you are conjoined with all phenomena throughout, yet are free of any notion in conjunction with anything [...] if you study the beliefs and side with the laws[505] and commune with[506] the six heterodox teachers[507]

---

[504] I.e. that very elevation of uncertainty to certainty that our discourse has assailed.

[505] The choice of expression in the Sanskrit has dramatic relevance to our meditations on this discourse: dharmādhya, a 'religious party', also implies incompleteness, the word for 'party' also meaning 'half'.

[506] And again, an extraodinary word in the Sanskrit: paryupāsita means at the same time sitting around together (as one would around a teacher) and *sharing* and

> [...] and set out on the spiritual path taking these honourable teachers as your sources[508] [...] if you enter into the ways of all beliefs but find neither extremes nor middle; if you are bound up in the eight adversities and do not obtain favorable conditions; if you assimilate the afflictive processes and do not attain purification; if the wilderness of all living beings is your wilderness, reverend; if those who make offerings to you are not purified by this; if those who offer you food, reverend, still fall into the three bad destinies; if you associate with all demonic forces; if you entertain all afflictive processes; if the nature of the afflictive processes is the nature of the reverend; if you set your heart against all living beings in hostility; if you despise all the Buddhas; if you slander all the Laws revealed by the Buddhas; if you do not rely on their Community; and finally, if you never enter ultimate liberation." '

These words terrify Subhūti, who is on the verge of leaving, but Immaculate Renown asks him to stay:

> ' "Bhadanta Subhūte, māyā nirmāṇa svabhāvebhyaḥ sarva dharmebhyo mā bhaiṣiḥ. Tat kasya hetoḥ? Teṣu sarveṣvapi vacaneṣu tat svabhāveṣu tasmāhu nāma paṇḍitā akṣareṣvasaṅgāstebhyo'trastāḥ. Tat kasya hetoḥ? Teṣu sarveṣvakṣareṣu hyanakṣareṣu sthāpayitvā vimokṣaḥ sarva dharmā hi vimokṣa lakṣaṇāḥ." '

> ' "Reverend Subhuti, the nature of all things is like a trick, like a magical emanation and not to be feared. How is that? All speech also has that nature, so 'scholars' are not attached to words, nor do they tremble from them. And how is that? All words being non-words, except liberation, everything is a sign of liberation." '[509]

---

worshipping: compare our discussions of projection of authority onto the group, and the allegiance with the spiritual teacher.

507 The very ones we mentioned in our consideration of what was taught to the Kālāmās.

508 And again notice the wording: niśraya is a source, or resource, something to lean on, and the prefix has the sense that the leaning is to the utmost.

509 From the chapter on 'The Reluctance of the Disciples'.

Stage 5: The Buddha's Vindication of the Inquiry

> 'Now, Kālāmas, one who is a disciple of the noble, whose spirit is thus free from hostility, whose spirit is thus free from ill will, whose spirit is thus free from affliction, and whose spirit is thus in all ways pure, realises four things here and now that let them breathe easily:
>
> ' "If there is a world beyond, and fruits that ripen from deeds done well or badly, (then) I, body rotting, after death, shall be reborn in a happy fate, a heaven world." This is the first thing they realise that lets them breathe easily.
>
> ' "But if there is no world beyond, and no fruits that ripen from deeds done well or badly, then here and now I am keeping myself free from aversion, free from ill will, free from trouble, and blissful." This is the second thing they realise that lets them breathe easily.
>
> ' "Even if certain acts when done consitute evil, I do not even intend evil for anyone, so from where will suffering for evil deeds touch me who have not done any?" This is the third thing they realise that lets them breathe easily.
>
> ' "But even if acts when done might not constitute evil, then I could assume myself pure in both cases anyway." This is the fourth thing they realise that lets them breathe easily.

Here I consider:

- the main point: that everything is covered,
- the implication: that ideology wastes time
- the specific examples: the afterlife and actions' ethical consequences

Main point: that everything is covered

By means of the inquiry into the afflictive processes, the Buddha has encouraged the Kalamas to come to their own conclusion, that unacceptable crimes depend on these processes taking control of people's mind. We have considered a broad sweep of social ills and shown that they too are inextricably linked to these afflictive processes. For some, it is enough that such crimes and ills result from them: the recognition drives them to remedy the situation. But others will say, 'So what? If you can't beat them, join them!' The kind of insight into circumstances which reveals that this strategy is a very poor second best, unfortunately, does not come easily to most of us. From the vantage, if we can call it that, of our ordinary confusion, without any experience of such mind-training as in the four mental residences of purity, the claim that evil deeds bring evil consequences for the doer which arises out of the insight gained by those who do have such experience starts to look decidedly unlikely, and the sense arises that it can only be accepted on faith. This sense is exacerbated in religions which popularise the notion by means of the all-too-easily debunkable myth of 'the Judge in the sky'. It is little wonder that today we have a situation where a very large proportion of the human population can ask, 'Why not be pragmatic and join the afflicted mess? What do we have to lose?'

Pascale's wager, that we should believe in Christianity just in case it is true, could as well he knew be applied to any other system of belief, and there are many. (He might as well have said that we should believe in Ahura Mazda, the adjudicating deity of the Zoroastrian religion, just in case, or in Allāh as he speaks of himself in the Qur'ān, rejecting Christ's divinity and crucifixion, just in case.) Confronted with all these diverse and mutually exclusive systems of belief and observance, Pascale chose to limit his wager to only one system. The Buddha, however, focuses on what almost all of them have *in common*: the notion that evil deeds will bring future suffering. And as an encouragement to people who as yet have no taste of the fruits of training, he points out that the training, leading to freedom from the afflictive processes, is beneficial *whether or not what the religions claim is true.*

He says to the Kālāmās, it doesn't matter whether you believe in an afterlife or not, so stop fretting about it. Instead, realise that the training brings benefit in any case. And he says it doesn't matter whether you believe certain deeds are evil (whether they be considered so through the deep interrelatedness the Buddha himself claimed to have seen based on mental tendencies or through the magical punitive actions decreed by the 'adjudicating deity' in a *post mortem* court) so stop fretting about that. Instead, realise that the training brings purity in any case.

Implication: that ideology wastes time

The point is that the questions which had arisen in the Kālāmās' minds after the visits of the preachers included many which are irrelevant to what they have just discovered in the inquiry are important.

The Buddha famously told[510] the parable of the man shot with a poisoned arrow:

---

[510] In *The Short Discourse to Mālukya*, the 63rd middle-length discourse.

'Seyyathāpi, Mālukyaputta, puriso sallena viddho assa savisena gāḷhapalepanena. Tassa mittāmaccā ñātisālohitā bhisakkaṁ sallakattaṁ upaṭṭhapeyyuṁ. So evaṁ vadeyya: "Na tāvāhaṁ imaṁ sallaṁ āharissāmi yāva na taṁ purisaṁ jānāmi yenamhi viddho, khattiyo vā brāhmaṇo vā vesso vā suddo vā [...] yāva na taṁ purisaṁ jānāmi yenamhi viddho, evaṁnāmo evaṁgotto iti vā [...] yāva na taṁ purisaṁ jānāmi yenamhi viddho, dīgho vā rasso vā majjhimo vā [...] yāva na taṁ purisaṁ jānāmi yenamhi viddho, kāḷo vā sāmo vā maṅguracchavī vā [...] yāva na taṁ purisaṁ jānāmi yenamhi viddho, amukasmiṁ gāme vā nigame vā nagare vā [...] yāva na taṁ dhanuṁ jānāmi yenamhi viddho, yadi vā cāpo yadi vā kodaṇḍo [...] yāva na taṁ jiyaṁ jānāmi yāyamhi viddho, yadi vā akkassa yadi vā saṇhassa yadi vā nhārussa yadi vā maruvāya yadi vā khīrapaṇṇino [...] yāva na taṁ kaṇḍaṁ jānāmi yenamhi viddho, yadi vā gacchaṁ yadi vā ropima [...] yāva na taṁ kaṇḍaṁ jānāmi yenamhi viddho, yassa pattehi vājitaṁ yadi vā gijjhassa yadi vā kaṅkassa yadi vā kulalassa yadi vā morassa yadi vā sithilahanuno [...] yāva na taṁ kaṇḍaṁ jānāmi yenamhi viddho, yassa nhārunā parikkhittaṁ yadi vā gavassa yadi vā mahiṁsassa yadi vā bheravassa yadi vā semhārassā [...] yāva na taṁ sallaṁ jānāmi yenamhi viddho, yadi vā sallaṁ yadi vā khurappaṁ yadi vā vekaṇḍaṁ yadi vā nārācaṁ yadi vā vacchadantaṁ yadi vā karavīrapatta"nti. Aññātameva taṁ, Mālukyaputta, tena purisena assa, atha so puriso kālaṁ kareyya.

'It's just as if, Son of Mālukya, a man were shot with an arrow thickly smeared with poison and his friends, companions, kinsmen and relatives provide him with a surgeon, but the man says, "I won't have this arrow removed until I know whether the man who shot me was from the ruling military class, the divines, the merchant class, or the working class [...or] until I know the given name and clan name of the man who shot me [...or] until I know whether he was tall, medium, or short [...or] until I know whether he was dark-, ruddy -, or golden-complexioned [...or] until I know his home village, town, or city [...or] until I know whether the bow with which I was shot was a long bow or a crossbow [...or] until I know whether the string of the bow with which I was shot was fiber, bamboo threads, sinew, hemp, or bark [...or] until I know whether the shaft of the arrow with which I was shot was wild or cultivated [...or]

> until I know whether the feathers of the arrow with which I was shot were from a vulture, a stork, a hawk, a peacock, or another bird [...or] until I know whether the shaft of the arrow with which I was shot was bound with the sinews of an ox, a water buffalo, a langur, or a monkey [...or] until I know whether the shaft with which I was wounded was that of a common arrow, a curved arrow, a barbed, a calf-toothed, or an oleander arrow." Before he finds out about all of this, Son of Mālukya, his time will have come.'

The Buddha applied this simile to those who gave up their training because he had not taught them about the afterlife, and the time and spatial limits of the cosmos: he distinguished those ideological and metaphysical issues, comparing them to the ludicrously useless questions of the dying man, from the issue he thought the most pressing – eliminating the afflictive processes, the arrow poison. But was it an arbitrary distinction?

We have seen how the undeniable strength of ideologies' charm over our minds is heavily dependent on the afflictive processes. So unless we have some taste of the results of training, in freeing ourselves from these processes, the charm of the ideologies will remain strong, and the Buddha's parable will remain, though amusing, not entirely convincing.

For this reason, to the Kālāmās, he says that even if you do not accept right now that there is arrow-poison coursing through your veins, at least accept the attentions of the doctor, because in any case he will help you with your general health, and the questions about the archer (or should we write, 'Archer'?) and his equipment can be answered in due time when your faculties are sharper.

Specific examples: the afterlife, and ethical consequences

Did the Buddha teach reincarnation?

The Buddha has been rightly charged with presenting one of the greatest challenges to ordinary human mentality, in his teachings on the nature of the so-called 'self', the soul, the experiencer of phenomena. In this more than in anything else the Law he claimed to have discovered deserve the title he gave them, paṭisotagāmi, '*against the stream*'. Briefly, with deepest apologies to the Buddha, and with no better excuse than that the majority of people encountering Buddhism for the first time are quite as vociferous at fighting off the doctor as our poisoned man in the parable, I would like to address the issue of 'future lives' which, though the Buddha relegates it to the unimportant and time-wasting class of questions, tends to float to the surface of some people's priorities with all the irrepressibility of corpses dumped in a pond. My intention here is to throw the reader back on herself or himself, by dispelling some of the comforting ideas we have which act as obstacles to developing insight into this issue.

What is the self?

The Buddha noted the experience we have of sensual and mental forms, feelings, perceptions about the feelings, consciousness, and the rest of the phenomenal world, inner and outer. What he said of this experience has come down to us in the form of the doctrine of the five heaps (Sanskrit, skandha; Pali, khandha): form (rupa), feelings (vedanā), perceptions (samjñā, saññā), composing agents (samskārā, sankhārā), and consciousness (vijñāna, viññāṇa). The foundational discovery he made which distinguishes his teaching from Hinduism, Judaism, Christianity, Islām, and the rest, is that all of this experience, including the sense of being an experiencer, is always *changing*, but that there is *grasping* onto the idea of an unchanging experiencer. This would be the self or the soul. Yet, he claimed to have discovered by deep insight, the idea does not match the reality of experience: it only *approximates* it. While it might seem a harmless difference to us approximators, the Buddha claimed to have seen that the unnecessary grasping onto the idea of an unchanging self was the root of all suffering and anxiety.

What carries responsibility from life to life?

Reincarnation means that two lives at different times share identity. Is that what the Buddha taught? Well, given that he taught that this identity is a shallow misunderstanding that with deep perspective cannot be maintained even for one conventional lifetime, it seems unlikely that he would assert identity between lifetimes!

Nevertheless the Buddha spoke of a deep causal connection between actions of body, speech and especially mind and consequences, consequences not necessarily experienced in this lifetime. What kind of causation could that be? What could its medium be if there is no identity? Why should the experiencer of consequences be morally responsible for the earlier lifetime's acts?

First of all, we have compared the black-white guilt-innocence dichotomy of the 'creator deity' outlook with its so-called 'balance' justice in terms of matching pain, and the very different 'karmic' outlook whereby there is a continuum of guilt-innocence, never reaching extremity since the freedom of choice is always within contexts, never abstracted from them, such that the contexts constrain the freedom to a degree. Straight away we must note that irresponsibility-responsibility therefore is another dichotomy which does not apply in the 'karmic' outlook. There can never be total responsibility, because it would have to be independent of context, and how can we define acts independent of contexts? (Can you kill your father when he is already dead?) Like the other deity-rescuing doctrines which have accrued in post-Christian and Islāmic societies total responsibility depends on exaggerating the reality of the idea, as something which does not need a context. 'Murder' is some kind of metaphysical category for souls to be classified under. This is very far from the reality of murder, but very appealling to the minds of people without experience or maturity. What experience tells us is that there are always degrees of responsibility, which is never total. Even Camus' stranger on the beach committing his absurd murder is *an excessively intellectual person whose mother has just died wandering on a beach which is not empty.* Just as we saw the lack of independence of the three spheres applied to the situation of training in the mental residences of purity, so does it apply equally to the situation of a murder. The complexity of interdependence of phenomena is quite beyond our reasoning: how did that man come to be on that beach on the same day that the intellectual's mother had died? We considered the very simple example of seeing a flower, and that turned out not to be quite so simple after all. You can never see a yesterday's flower, and if the flower were independent you would not be able to see it or sense it in any way. What circumstances brought you and the flower together? The answer is never-ending, because it includes all experienceable reality. And that includes the mind which is asking. To say that a murderer is totally responsible for a murder brings relief to the aggrieved but is unfortunately nonsense. The paltry relief it brings the aggrieved and their belief that there is no better relief are both based on the profound delusions about reality afflicting them.

We also saw that in the karmic outlook the remedy can only be knowledge, because to know totally is to know that harm is unskilful. We contrasted this with the deep inculcation necessary for the 'monotheistic systems' to rescue their 'omniscient deity's omnipotence' over a cruel world, the inculcation in the belief that even by the omniscient, harm is still done. The law-givers of these religions (and I mean humans) exactly match the description the Buddha gave of people with a smattering of meditative insight who rush back from the mountain to break their immature news to an adoring populace. Yet their views are, by the multifarious processes of error we have considered, made absolute and, through the afflictive processes' impulsion, maintained that way. Centuries of inculcation cannot quickly be wiped clean, and we have seen modern versions of the enthronement of uncertainties on the seat of the deity aplenty.

We are polluted through and through by the natural consequence of this long inculcation, the retributive ethic. It is not expected that this unskilfulness will easily be relinquished, even if the skilful alternatives, which are so much subtler, are understood. But if we have even the tiniest doubt, and we should, about the retributive ethic's skilfulness in accomplishing its aim, then we are to that extent receptive to hearing about deep knowledge as a cure for harm. With our ordinary minds so thoroughly habituated to impossible but alluring extremes such as innocence and guilt, creator and creation, responsibility and irresponsibility, it is not expected that we will easily accept the possibility that, as the Buddha claimed, humans are inherently Buddhas, and that it would be enough that they *understood* for them to relinquish all harmfulness. The kind of ritualistic behaviour, especially between males, involving A pushes B so B pushes A, A growls at B so B growls at A, which in other species we call 'mutual assessment rituals' (and which evolved because males who fought to the degree of injury were likely to die before passing on their genes as much as healthy males did), when it occured in our species got elevated because of its misattribution to superficial and conceptual causes by tribes dominated by superstition into the basis of a morality: 'balance' justice. Many people who accept this mode of 'justice' at the same time decry retributive conflict. Unfortunately retributive conflict is unlikely to go away while our sacred authorities embody it and by example teach it. Our very language stinks of it: 'responsibility' refers to the response – to whom the retributive response, the retributive balance, should be applied.

In situations of complex interdependence, and there are no others, once we recognise the delusoriness of 'balance' and therefore the gross fundamental inaccuracy of the concept of 'responsibility', how can we ask of those situations, 'What carries the moral responsibility from the previous acts'? The deep causality the Buddha discovered was not about righting accounts by means of pleasure and pain.

We have seen how concept-dominated (or 'metaphysical') the massive 'monotheistic' religions are. Now a concept, insofar as it is remembered as is, is static. The Buddha claimed to have discovered that reality is *never* static. The view of reality which the other religions and their secular offspring demand is that all sorts of 'truths' petrify out of the flow of reality regularly, like water freezing, such that in those petrified elements of reality there is somehow an ongoing identity which does not change even if everything else does. Such elements include the idea of 'the soul' and of course 'the undying deity' itself. In such a view the man before me in court today can be 'the same' man who was stealing my car a month ago today. But of course he is not: if he were, he would still be stealing the car, which presumably was not in the courtroom. To hold these two entities to be the same involves the same kind of misidentification as we might make if we got a foot wet by slipping off a stone crossing the river and so ran downstream to catch the bit of water that got us wet in a jar. The stones are still slippery and someone else will slip off them, it is guaranteed, but we chase after the water. Similarly, the reasons people steal cars, and the reasons my garage is especially attractive to car thieves, remain in the broader circumstances. The 'criminals' keep popping up like mushrooms in mulch and we just keep picking them off. The reason we totally identify the person with the crime is, as we have seen, the total personal responsibility dogma which arose principally as a means to rescue 'the creator deity' and its associated doctrines.

We investigated the 'creation of demons' by conceptual consensus and the misguided exorcist manoeuvre – whether it be driving diseased cattle over a cliff and into the river that supplies the village or executing people to show them murder is wrong, slandering homosexuality to purify the Church or blowing up non-Muḥammadans to show them Muḥammad was peaceful. Total personal responsibility is just another example of the exorcist manoeuvre, and its failures just as much failures.

But even if it doesn't make sense to talk about total responsibility in a situation where no unchanging identity persists, what about this deep causality the Buddha claimed to have discovered, linking current experience, including its pleasures and pains, with prior acts, and not just acts of 'this lifetime' (inaccurately so-called)? To the Kālāmās he said it was less important than training which would bring benefit in any case, but in other contexts he did say that he discovered this causality. He explained it in famous similes, such as the flame of one lamp lighting anothers and that one lighting another and so on throughout the night, and the momentum of a moving ball causing a second, stationary ball to move.[511] That doesn't tell us much beyond this definitely not being reincarnation, a system where the two 'lives' are considered of the same identity, and definitely not being a system where the two 'lives' are considered to be unrelated (since the second lamp would not have lit without contact with the heat of the first, and the second ball would not have moved without the impulse of the first). But it is a starting point, a starting point for reflection, and it will be a reflection that shows us reality is much weirder than we think.

You might think you know what a moving ball is. And you might think your description of it as 'a moving ball' is pretty accurate. Think again. Is

511 See for example *The Milinda Questions*, II, Chapter 2.

a mere 'ball' a moving ball or a non-moving ball? We will probably answer that it is a non-moving ball – otherwise there would be no point using the adjective 'moving' of balls at all, as all balls would be moving by definition. The adjective 'moving' is supposed to distinguish it from a non-moving ball. But clearly if the meaning 'non-moving' is included in 'ball' then there could be no such thing as a 'moving ball', since this would effectively be something both moving and not moving at the same time. So a 'ball' must sometimes be a 'mover' and sometimes not. If it is a mover, and we say that the mover is moving, then we have two movements – one by virtue of its being a mover and another by virtue of it moving. Nāgārjuna wrote nineteen centuries ago:

gamyamānasya gamane prasaktaṁ gamanadvayam
yena tadgamyamānaṁ ca yaccātra gamanaṁ punaḥ

Adhere to 'a mover moving' and the movement's twice!
Once by being a mover and again by moving![512]

Furthermore *where* does a ball move? The space it has already moved over will not do because the ball is not there now, and for the same reason the space it is about to move over will not do. But the space between the past movement and the future movement is, conceptually, infinitely small. How can something move in an infinitely small space?

gataṁ na gamyate tāvadagataṁ naiva gamyate
gatāgatavinirmuktaṁ gamyamānaṁ na gamyate

Where it's moved it moves not, and moves not where it is yet to move;
Except for where it's moved and where yet to move, the 'mover' does not move![513]

OK, what about a flame? Simple enough, surely. Fire is burning the fuel (such as lamp oil or kindling), right? Wrong. Is fire the same as the fuel or different? If it were the same then agent and action would be the same. But if they were different, then how could we establish that they were even related? Why couldn't fire simply exist by itself, fuelless?

---

512 Root Verses II, 5
513 II, 1

Yadindhanaṁ sa cedagnirekatvaṁ kartṛkarmaṇoḥ
anyaścedindhanādagnirindhanādapyṛte bhavet

If kindling and fire are a unity then agent and action are!
If it is other than kindling, fire exists without needing kindling![514]

And on what grounds could we call fuel 'fuel'? You might say, 'Fire depends on fuel.' That is trying to establish a one-way causal relation. But before the fire is produced from it, how can you call it fuel? If it becomes fuel only because of the fire burning it, then the causality is also the other way, and fuel also depends on fire. And if two things are established in dependence on each other, how can either be established in the first place?

yadīndhanamapekṣyāgnirapekṣyāgniṁ yadīndhanam
kataratpūrvaniṣpannaṁ yadapekṣyāgnirindhanam

If fire is with regard to kindling, and kindling is with regard to fire
Which of them came first, for either fire or kindling to be with regard to?

These weirdnesses and the many more in Nāgārjuna's treatise are all a direct result of our conceptualising not getting at reality as it actually is. Our experience is direct, but our way of talking about it is not. Concepts, those other-excluders, are only used until they fail to work: what happens to scientific theories macrocosmically (with Newton's laws failing on tiny and massive scales to be replaced by Einstein's, and so on) happens to all concepts microcosmically. This is especially obvious to linguists, whose knowledge of different languages shows them that different societies have followed different expermimental pathways in the naming of their reality, such that names are divided and allotted in a different pattern than they are in other languages, which is a sign that names are not universal but based on experimentation or experience. For example an English speaker learning Nepali will quickly discover that according to his dictionary, which fails to recognise this experiential factor, Nepalis 'eat' water; the same hapless individual in Egypt will discover Egyptians 'drink' tobacco. Every concept we ever had has only been continually used because it has not yet failed to bring results according to the consensus of the living people that use it (even if the results are invented in some cases!).

---

[514] X, 1

Such reflections should make us wary of wading into the multiple lives issue as if it were a conceptually soluble one. If concepts cannot solve the movement of a ball, how can they solve how movement is transferred from one ball to the next, never mind 'the self' and how it is appropriated?

agnīndhanābhyām̐ vyākhyāta ātmopādānayoḥ kramaḥ
sarvo niravaśeṣeṇa

By the analysis of fire and kindling, the self and stages of appropriation
Are completely explained.[515]

And what of a 'life' – when does it begin? The cells were alive even when they were haploid in the meiosis process, and these haploid cells derived from living parental cells without any interruption in life. Passing the buck to 'the creator God' and keeping the concept 'life' is like buying a kitty litter tray for a non-existent cat to deal with the problem of its non-existent excrement. The point is that the word 'life' is inaccurate in the first place, and we cannot but use it inaccurately, so it hardly helps matters to bring in other concepts to distract us from this glaring fact. (If life is defined as what 'God' breathes into X, what sense is there in then saying, 'God breathed life into X'? Analogously to our movement problem, it means 'God breathed what he breathed into X into X', which ends up being rather too much hot air. In more ways than one.) And if you disagree and say life involves awareness, and for example an embryo's life only begins with awareness, then you will have the same problem with awareness.

The single redeeming feature of this perhaps rather disturbing train of thought is awareness, however. Quite aside from all the conceptual mess, which is concepts' speciality, the awareness is something directly available to us. It is, more than anything else, what is accessible. The Buddha claimed to have discovered the entirety of the Law, including the deep causality behind the arising of phenomena, by accessing it. The declaration which is written and buried in every Buddhist monument, the closest equivalent Buddhism has to the creeds of Christianity or the testimony of Islam, is:

ye dharmā hetu prabhava hetun̊ teṣān̊ tathāgato hyavadat
teṣāñ ca yo nirodha evam vādī mahā śramana

---

[515] X, 15 (part)

Whatever phenomena be produced by cause
The One who has Arrived in Truth has told their cause
And similarly their cessation
Has the Great Ascetic told!

He challenged us to access it too. Of course we could try to think it through. But if you had never known what sugar tasted like and wanted to know, and you had a pile of it in front of you, you would just taste it. Let those who would prefer to *think through* what it might taste like from analyses of its chemical formula and so on analyse away. That is a sweetness too, though of a rather second rate.

Part III: The Response from the People

> 'So it is, worthful one. So it is, reacher of well-being. [...] Magnificent, sir! Magnificent, sir! Just as if, sir, he were to have set right what was overturned, to have revealed what was veiled, to have shown the path to one who was lost, or to have carried a lamp into the dark such that those with eyes could make forms out, in the same way has the worthful one by means of several demonstrations shed light on the Law. We refer ourselves to the worthful one, and to the Law, and to the community of almsfolk. May the worthful one hold us to be companions who refer themselves to him, from this day forward, for life.'

We saw earlier that the critique of sources of certainty occurs in only two other discourses, and in particular that the Buddha only taught them on one other occasion as recorded in the Pali canon, to Bhaddiya the Licchavi. The conclusion of the Discourse to Bhaddiya differs in a dramatic way to the Discourse to the Kālāmā, and given that our own attitude and outlook is likely to be closer to the former, that discourse presents points which are likely to be directly applicable to us. Here I consider:

- the response of the audience,
- the Buddha's response to Bhaddiya the Licchavi, and
- our response.

The response of the audience

Both the Kālāmā people and Bhaddiya the Licchavi are so impressed by what the Buddha said they request permission to join the community of 'companions' (male and female lay devotees) who refer themselves to the Three Jewels. They say that what has impressed them is that the Buddha has made the Form of Reality (dhamma, dharma) clear. This Form of Reality is the very same which the Buddha asserted 'can be discovered individually by the wise'. The fact that he has prompted them to *discover* is indicated by the similes they use – righting, revealing, showing and lighting.

The Buddha's response

The Discourse to the Kālāmā people ends there, as many do, with the audience's amazement and request to be considered as having referred themselves from that time on to the worthful one, the laws of reality and the community of almsfolk. However, although Bhaddiya has heard the same teaching and expressed the same amazement and request, there comes a rather shocking response from the Buddha, which we would do well to reflect on, given how much more closely we resemble Bhaddiya than the Kālāmā people:

'Api nu tāhaṃ, bhaddiya, evaṃ avacaṃ – 'ehi me tvaṃ, bhaddiya, sāvako hohi; ahaṃ satthā bhavissāmī'ti

'Bhaddiya, have I ever asked you: "Come to me, Bhaddiya, be my disciple and I shall be your Teacher?"

We can imagine the effect these words would have had on the proud Licchavi, and how humbly he must have replied:

'No hetaṃ, bhante.'

'No indeed, sir.'

The Buddha might appear to be irritated. But he goes on to remind Bhaddiya of the attitude to the Buddha's teaching he displayed when first approaching him. As we saw, he taunted the Buddha with a report he had heard that rather than instructing people the Buddha was a trickster, fooling dupes into giving up their most cherished beliefs. The Buddha quotes the report verbatim and denies the accusation in the strongest terms:

'Evaṃ vādiṃ kho maṃ, bhaddiya, evamakkhāyiṃ eke samaṇa brāhmaṇā asatā tucchā musā abhūtena abbhācikkhanti – "māyāvī samaṇo gotamo āvaṭṭaniṃ māyaṃ jānati yāya aññatitthiyānaṃ sāvake āvaṭṭetī" 'ti.

'Speaking of me like this, Bhaddiya, reporting in this way, the several ascetics and divines wrongly, vainly, and falsely accuse me of being something I am not: "The illusionist ascetic Gotama knows an enticing

illusion by which he entices students out of other systems of salvation."
'

We might expect the Licchavi to concede this point, but he does not. Instead, he makes this spirited reply:

'Bhaddikā , bhante, āvaṭṭanī māyā. Kalyāṇī, bhante, āvaṭṭanī māyā. Piyā me, bhante, ñātisālohitā imāya āvaṭṭaniyā āvaṭṭeyyuṁ, piyānampi me assa ñātisālohitānaṁ dīgharattaṁ hitāya sukhāya. Sabbe cepi, bhante, khattiyā imāya āvaṭṭaniyā āvaṭṭeyyuṁ, sabbesampissa khattiyānaṁ dīgharattaṁ hitāya sukhāya. Sabbe cepi, bhante, brāhmaṇā imāya āvaṭṭaniyā āvaṭṭeyyuṁ, sabbesampissa brāhmaṇānaṁ dīgharattaṁ hitāya sukhāya. Sabbe cepi, bhante, vessā imāya āvaṭṭaniyā āvaṭṭeyyuṁ, sabbesampissa vessānaṁ dīgharattaṁ hitāya sukhāya. Sabbe cepi, bhante, suddā imāya āvaṭṭaniyā āvaṭṭeyyuṁ, sabbesampissa suddānaṁ dīgharattaṁ hitāya sukhāyā'ti.

'Oh but a wholesome one, sir is this enticing illusion! A good one, sir, is this enticing illusion! Were, sir, *my beloved kinsmen and relations*, too, enticed by this enticement, long for the profit and bliss of those beloved kinsmen and relations of mine would it be. Were, sir, *all rulers and militaries*, too, enticed by this enticement, long for the profit and bliss of those rulers and militaries would it be. Were, sir, *all religious leaders and divines*, too, enticed by this enticement, long for the profit and bliss of those religious leaders and divines would it be. Were, sir, *all businesspeople and traders*, too, enticed by this enticement, long for the profit and bliss of those businessmen and traders would it be. Were, sir, *all workers*, too, enticed by this enticement, long for the profit and bliss of those workers would it be.'

He thus makes the same claim for all of the four traditional divisions of society, such that the entire society is included in this declaration.

Now the Buddha has just denied the truth of the report that he was a trickster. Yet he concedes the point to Bhaddiya:

'Evametaṁ, bhaddiya, evametaṁ, bhaddiya.

'That is how it is, Bhaddiya; that is how it is, Bhaddiya.

But he underlines the aim of such enticement:

> 'Sabbe cepi, bhaddiya, khattiyā imāya āvaṭṭaniyā āvaṭṭeyyuṁ *akusala dhammappahānāya kusala dhammūpasampadāya*, sabbesampissa khattiyānaṁ dīgharattaṁ hitāya sukhāya.

> 'Were, Bhaddiya, all rulers and militaries, too, enticed by this enticement, *to give up unskilful things and accomplish skilful things*, indeed long for the profit and bliss of those rulers and militaries would it be!

And he makes the same claim with its clarification for the other three divisions of society – divines, businesspeople and workers. But he does not stop there:

> Sadevako cepi, bhaddiya, loko samārako sabrahmako sassamaṇabrāhmaṇī pajā sadevamanussā imāya āvaṭṭaniyā āvaṭṭeyyuṁ [516] akusala dhammappahānāya kusala dhammūpasampadāya, sadevakassapissa lokassa samārakassa sabrahmakassa sassamaṇabrāhmaṇiyā pajāya sadevamanussāya dīgharattaṁ hitāya sukhāya.

> 'Were, Bhaddiya, even *the world* with its divine and demonic beings, its creator gods, its generations with their ascetics and divines, their rulers and the common people, enticed by this enticing, to give up unskilful things and accomplish skilful things, long for the profit and bliss of the world with its divine and demonic beings, its creator gods, its generations with their ascetics and divines, their rulers and the common people would it be!

Finally the Buddha draws Bhaddiya's attention to their current situation, sitting together in the forest. We can imagine him unfolding a hand towards their surroundings as he says:

> Ime cepi, bhaddiya, mahāsālā imāya āvaṭṭaniyā āvaṭṭeyyuṁ akusala dhammappahānāya kusala dhammūpasampadāya imesampissa mahāsālānaṁ dīgharattaṁ hitāya sukhāya.[517]

---

516 Or āvaṭṭeyya.

517 Some versions add sace ceteyyuṁ or āvaṭṭeyyuṁ.

Ko pana vādo manussabhūtassā'ti!

'Were, Bhaddiya, *even these great Sal trees*, enticed by this enticement,
to give up unskilful things and accomplish skilful things,
long for the profit and bliss of those great Sal trees would it be![518]
So what to say of a human being?!'

Figure 6 Sal forest

[518] Some versions add, 'If they had intentions,' or, 'were to be enticed'.

Our response

So what to say of a human being?!

Each of us is that human being. Once we have tasted sanity, shall we go back to the madness? Once we have seen the mechanism of the afflictive processes in conjuring the illusion of the absolutes, including the new gods with their new faiths, shall we pour forth the afflictive processes the more? Once we have hurt and been hurt, and we have seen how we have hurt and been hurt, shall we go on to hurt and be hurt the more?

The ordinary mind is not aware of the nature of things but merely of how they appear. Now we have the tools and the impetus to raise our awareness of things, by investigation, caring and insight. These are the most precious gifts the past exemplars of Awakening have left us.

The ordinary mind is not aware of the true locus of choice. Now we have recognised the tricks it plays on itself and how it loses that locus, thus abrogating conscience. We can distinguish between the authority of power and the authority of truth, and we know that the latter is only genuine when it its locus is our choice. This is the most precious essence of Awakening within us.

We saw earlier, in a discourse with a great deal of overlap with *The Kālāmā Discourse*, how the Buddha repeatedly stressed to a young divine of the orthodox religion that the traditional sources of knowledge, while potentially safeguarding the truth, nevertheless could be trivial, false and vain, and how for each one he repeated the refrain that even if not trivial, false and vain, in themselves they are 'not yet an awakening to the truth'.

The young divine asks him, then, not unreasonably, how there *is* an awakening to the truth. The Buddha's reply is that the seeker should seek out an ascetic and examine to see whether that ascetic is free of the afflictive processes of wanting, aversion and delusion:

> 'Yato naṁ samannesamāno visuddhaṁ mohanīyehi dhammehi samanupassati ; atha tamhi saddhaṁ niveseti, saddhājāto upasaṅkamati, upasaṅkamanto payirupāsati, payirupāsanto sotaṁ odahati, ohitasoto dhammaṁ suṇāti, sutvā dhammaṁ dhāreti, dhatānaṁ dhammānaṁ atthaṁ upaparikkhati, atthaṁ upaparikkhato dhammā nijjhānaṁ khamanti, dhamma nijjhānakkhantiyā sati chando jāyati, chandajāto ussahati, ussahitvā tuleti, tulayitvā padahati, pahitatto samāno kāyena ceva paramasaccaṁ sacchikaroti paññāya ca naṁ ativijjha passati.

> 'If one observes that the ascetic is purified of qualities based on wanting [...], aversion [...and] delusion, one establishes faith. Faith having been born, one visits him or her, and visiting, grows close. Growing close, one listens. Listening, one learns the Law of Reality. Learning the Law of Reality, one remembers it. Remembering it, one penetrates the meaning of those laws. Penetrating the meaning, one comes to an intuitive understanding of those laws. With intuitive understanding, delight arises. With the arising of delight, adventurousness matches it. With this matching, one strives. Striving, one realises the ultimate truth by means of the body and sees with supreme vision[519] by means of deep insight.

Those very objects of the Buddha's critique – faith, the oral tradition (listening and learning), intuitive understanding – are here garnered for a stepwise approach.

> Ettāvatā kho, bhāradvāja, saccānubodho hoti, ettāvatā saccamanubujjhati, ettāvatā ca mayaṁ saccānubodhaṁ paññapema; na tveva tāva saccānuppatti hotī'ti.

> To this extent, Bhāradvāja, there is an awakening to the truth. To this extent one awakens to the truth. I describe this as an awakening to the truth. But it is not yet attainment of the truth.'

And what is that?

> 'Tesaṁye , bhāradvāja, dhammānaṁ āsevanā bhāvanā bahulīkammaṁ saccānuppatti hoti. Ettāvatā kho, bhāradvāja, saccānuppatti hoti, ettāvatā saccamanupāpuṇāti, ettāvatā ca mayaṁ saccānuppattiṁ paññapemā'ti.

> Bhāradvāja, the attainment of truth is the cultivation, development and increase of those qualities. To this extent, Bhāradvāja, there is attainment of truth. To this extent one attains the truth. I describe this as attainment of the truth.

---

[519] The Pali terms here are equivalent to two terms used in the Total Integration practice (rdzogs-chen) in Tibetan Buddhism – ati and vidya (rig-pa).

Appendix One: Transliteration Schemes

Pali and Sanskrit

a	ā	i	ī	u	ū
ṛ	ṝ	ḷ	ḹ		
		e	ai	o	au
am̊	aḥ				
k	kh	g	gh	n̊	
c	ch	j	jh	ñ	
ṭ	ṭh	ḍ	ḍh	ṇ	
t	th	d	dh	n	
p	ph	b	bh	m	
y	r	l	w		
ś	ṣ	s	h	kṣ	

Arabic

a b t th j ḥ kh d dh z s sh ṣ ḍ ṭ ẓ ` gh f q k l m n w y

a ā ai au i ī u ū ‘

Appendix Two: Translation rationales

This is a list of the more important of the choices I have made in translation that differ from the usually encountered translations, together with my reasons for so differing. The Pali words are ordered by Roman alphabetical order of their Roman transliteration. Sanskrit equivalents are given in brackets.

Anavajja **Uncensurable.** Opposite of avajja.

Arahat (arihat) **Saint**. The Buddhist traditional etymology of this word refers to enemies (ari) having been killed (hata). The idea is that all conflicts have been overcome in a total integration – it is the final goal of the individual career, the fourth of the four degrees of attainment. Since 'saint', from 'sacred' includes the meaning of having reached a state of protection from attack, it seems appropriate enough.

Avajja **Censurable**. It is suggested in some Pali dictionaries, is equivalent to Sanskrit avavadya, meaning 'what should be solemnly spoken of', a meaning which is matched by the Latin word 'censurable' (since the Latin verb which is the origin of censure originally meant, in Roman law, to make a solemn official pronouncement about something). However Pali dictionaries also give a possible equivalence between vajja in Pali and varjya in Sanskrit. Varjya means that which is to be shunned (for example kalivarjya means something which should be shunned in this Kali age – i.e. obsolete), and its components have fascinating connotations: vara refers to 'choosing by oneself' or 'blessings' or 'boons' (cf. Arabic barra and baraka), and jya means 'oppressing' or 'depriving of'. So in the components of varjya we have a sense of being deprived of free choice and blessings, so we could take the meaning of censurable here as those dharmas which deprive us of blessings or of being able to choose freely, which matches very well the instructions in the discourse.

Bhagavat **Worthful**. Translated variously as 'blessed', 'world-honoured', 'exalted'. The word is a compound of bhaga and vat, the latter [illegible]he usual prefix equivalent to English –ful or –ish. Bhaga has very rich meaning, [illegible]ding wealth, fortune, blessing, deserving of reverence, adorability, [illegible]edness, and general goodness to such an extent that it is even used of the [illegible] perineum and the female vulva! The sense common to all these uses is 'very [illegible]having': 'worth' seems to get at the general goodness, unlike 'blessed' which [illegible]ises passivity and receipt, and 'world-honoured' which is syntactically [illegible] lacking in directness because after all the world could have been (as it often is) mistaken.

Brāhmaṇa **Divine**. This old word for 'priest' gets around that word's strong Christian connotation and also hints at the link to God in the same way that Brāhmaṇa hints at Brahmā.

Dosa (dveṣa) **Disliking**. Most often translated, with rather psychotherapeutic overtones, as 'aversion'. However, again, the Pali term has more of a sense of choice aggravating the emotion. The equivalent Sanskrit terms is dveṣa, meaning 'hatred' or 'dislike' – not 'anger', though, it should be stressed. The word is in fact an ancient compound from the word for two (dva, with which the English two shares its Proto-Indo-European origin), plus a participle of the ancient Vedic Sanskrit verb ịt, which meant 'to err'. So the word comes from a compound which meant 'erring into two'.

Garahita (garhita) **Scorned**. From the verb (garha) meaning to contemn or to scorn.

Hita **Profit**. Usually translated as benefit, has great importance in Buddhist discourse, referring to the bringing of wholesomeness and health in all senses rather than just temporary help like wealth. In Sanskrit, hita and dhita are closely related, and to some extent interchangeable, and just as dharma became 'form' in English, dhita became 'fit'. The parallel is supported by the dual meaning of both the Sanskrit past participles and the English adjective – on the one hand health, but on the other also well-placed or well-situated (fitting). Given that in the Buddhist teachings it is used in contexts of change, 'profit' seems suitable, and is natural. It should be noted that the opposite, ahita, is not just a lack of benefit (which might include leaving things as they are) but a movement towards damage, unwholesomeness, disadvantage or evil, so 'profit' 's opposite, 'loss', seems appropriate.

Karuṇā **Caring**. Usually translated as compassion. There has been a concerted effort it seems to avoid translating the term as what most classic Sanskrit dictionaries report as its meaning, namely, pity, since this term seems too passive, and perhaps too condescending: along with many other terms previously associated with religious practice in English and other European languages, such as pious, saint, and righteous, it has come down to us with heavy connotations of religious hypocrisy. To receive pity smacks of humiliation, and is likely to provoke the response, 'I don't need your pity!' However, can we hold that compassion is a better translation? Compassion literally means undergoing together. We should notice that it is a passion, in the original sense of the word: we are its *patient*, *passive*ly undergoing it; it is something that one experiences, we would say in modern English. This emotion has better translations in Sanskrit than karuṇā: anukampana, anukrośa, kṛpā, dayā, pīḍā, mṛḍa, śūkaka, for example. The distinctive connotation of karuṇā goes back to the Vedic language, where for example there occurs the praise of Indra: 'sa viśvasya **karuṇa**śyesa eko…'[520] where commentaries make the meaning 'sole lord is he of every **holy service**'. The ancient uṇādi sutras referred to in Pāṇini's *Eight Chapters* say the word derives from the root kṛ – like karma and krīya, both at the time having the particular sense of the sacrifice which brought balance to the cosmos. So 'sacrifice' – sacred act – would be a fair translation. We can surmise how the word came to refer to serving others, quite as 'sacrifice' in Latinate languages came to be a more general term applying to social service. A word which gets more to the heart of the matter is 'caring', although it perhaps lacks strength. It is (unlike 'compassion') active, and conveys well the sense of focus on restoring well-being. It also gets to the point very well of the problem with the lack of this, or the opposite state of mind: *uncaringness.*

Lobha **Wanting**. Shares its Proto-Indo-European origin with several English words, including 'love' and 'believe'. It is usually translated as 'greed', but this erroneously implies that a certain amount of 'pulling' emotion is acceptable – 'greed' is only when one exceeds the acceptable limits in that 'pulling'. Another common translation is 'desire', but this has a strong sense of being out of control, under some seemingly magical influence. The word's origin, tellingly, is, like the word 'sidereal', in the stars, and their influence on us. Such a translation then seems to overlook the contribution choice makes to this process. Lobha is closer to love and greed in that it carries a sense of a choice aggravating that pull. However the modern use of 'love' includes the sense 'be pleased by very much' (e.g. 'I love her new album!'), or 'enjoy' and 'delight in' (e.g. I'm loving his new novel!'). The meaning in modern English of the word 'wanting' is perhaps the best: although the word used only to mean 'lack' and had little if any connotation of feeling, nowadays it is used for exactly this choice-aggravated pulling emotion. (Incidentally, one fashion, thankfully now probably at an end, was to translate this word as 'lust', a choice which any scholar should decry. 'Lust', as is implied by the less diverged word 'lusty', originally had the sense of lack of cowardly restraint and instead an engagement in *play*. Indeed both words, 'lust' and 'play', derive from a Proto-Indo-European root referring to play and looseness. In such words there was not until later historical developments any sense of the kind of 'loss of ease' or 'loss of freedom' that the pulling emotion lobha implies: quite the opposite – play is the transcendence of

---

520 Ṛg Veda, i, 100, line 7

restraint, an *increase* in ease and freedom. Related words in Sanskrit mean 'expanse', 'display', 'dally' and 'sport'. Since the language the Buddha spoke included close equivalents of all of these words, and since he used *not one of them*, to use their descendant, the word 'lust', to translate lobha is, I argue, unjustifiable. It adds a strong *sexual* connotation which simply is not specified in the Pali word. And here we recognise the historical development I alluded to. The intrigued can investigate the appropriation of play into the idea of sexual sinfulness by Christianity in the history of the usage of these words in English and Germanic languages at her own leisure.)

Majjhattaṁ (madhyasthā) **Impartiality**. Literally 'standing in the middle', that is, not swayed to either side.

Metta (maitri) **Amity**. Shares its origins with our words amity, amicable, amiable, and by opposition enemy, inimical, etc. The usual English translation is 'loving-kindness' or simply 'love'. What we have seen about the meaning of 'lobha', the first of the three afflictive emotions, amply demonstrates the inappropriacy and vagueness of the English word 'love' in either context. Christian efforts to translate agape thus notwithstanding, all ordinary uses of the word involve strong partiality over the object. And the emotion is highly distorted according to context. We need only consider the situation of a man in a hierarchy: the love he feels for his boss is likely to be an expression of his sycophancy towards her, whereas the love he feels for his inferiors is likely to involve a certain amount of condenscension. For these reasons, in line with some classic translations of the Pali canon (such as Hale's wonderful rendition of the Aṅguttāra Nikāya) and for etymological cognateness, I have chosen the translation amity.

Moha **Delusion**. 'Delusion' is a very psychotherapeutic choice, but perhaps one which covers quite well its diverse implications. Mental darkness, loss of consciousness, confusion, bewilderment, perplexity, stupidity, ignorance, dullness of mind, distraction, infatuation, delusion, error, stupefaction, failure and entrancement are all implied in the term. When used of physical substance it means 'soiled' or 'dirty'.

Sāmaṇa **Ascetic**. Ascesis is the Greek word for exercise, taken into English as referring to spiritual exercises. Thus it successfully reproduces the root meaning of 'exertion'. There is nothing in the word to suggest closing out the world out of dislike of company, so 'recluse', a common translation, seems inappropriate. It is, most scholars agree, the root (via Mongolia and Siberia) of the word 'shaman'.

Saṁvattati **Convert**. Is an intensive of vattati, meaning to move, cognate with Sanskrit vartati and Latinate verbs in –vert. Although often translated as 'lead to', it seems to have a stronger sense than that, and since the Sanskrit saṁvartati carries the sense of a total change (such as that of the universe at the end of an aeon), the etymological descendant it in Latinate languages, convert, seems appropriate.

Upekkha **Perspective**. This is perhaps the most misunderstood of the four mental residences of purity. The Pali word upekkha and the Sanskrit equivalent upekṣa both came to carry what seems at first to be an irreconcilable variety of meanings: overlooking, disgregard, negligence, indifference, contempt, abandonment, endurance, patience, dissent, regard, and even the use of tricks and deceits as an expedient in war. If we break down the word we can see how these various meanings might have arisen. Upa- is a prefix to verbs and nouns meaning 'towards', 'near to', 'by the side of', 'together with', 'under', or 'down' and to nouns only with the sense of 'contiguity' and 'resemblance but inferiority'. (As in Germanic languages and in the Germanic vocabulary of English, in older language this prefix is separable and can be used as a preposition with the verb.) Ikṣa means 'seeing', 'looking', 'sight', 'considering', and occasionally 'visiting'. So we have a compound equivalent to 'looking towards', 'seeing things together', 'looking down'. As in the English word (in its pre-1500 sense) 'overlook', the word seems to have carried some sense of sacrificing details to a large picture. And as in English, this led to two very different meanings: 'The window overlooks the valley,' does not mean disregarding the valley, but encompassing the valley broadly in its vision; and 'Please overlook my clumsiness,' does not mean survey my clumsiness – but *it may well refer to the idea of expanding vision beyond the clumsiness to my performance in general.* For this reason I have opted to ignore the usual translation of this term (as 'equanimity', which carries with it a strong sense of coolness, meaning, as it does, even-mindedness (Latin aequa, equal + animus, mind or feeling or courage). Instead 'perspective', especially in the modern usage of 'get things in perspective' seems to bring the encompassing sense we need.)

Bibliography

`Ābidīn, i. Radd al-Muḥtār `alā il-Durr il-Mukhtār.

`Aṭtar, F.d. u.-D. Tadhkirat al-Awliyaa, Memoir of the Saints.

`Attar, F.d. u.-D. (1974). *The Conference of the Birds.* (C. S. Nott, Trans.)

al-`Utbi, A. N.-J. *Kitāb al-Yamini.*

al-As`ad, N. A. (2004). *Kashf al-Sitār, Unveiling.* Damascus: `Alā' al-Dīn.

al-Baihaki, A.-l. F. (4th c. h./10th c. CE). *Tarīkh us-Subuktigin.*

al-Biladuri, A. b. (3rd c. h./9th c. CE). *Futūḥ al-Buldān.*

Al-Kalbi, H. Kitab al-Aṣnam, the Book of Idols.

Al-Manīnī. (1286 h/1869 CE). *al-Fatḥ al-Wahbi.* Cairo.

Al-Shahrastani. (1366-1375/1947-1955). Kitāb al-Milal wal-Niḥal, the Book of Religious Communities and Sects. (M. F. Badran, Ed.) Cairo.

Aristotle. (c. 350 BCE). *Rhetoric.*

Armstrong, K. (1994). The History of God: The 4000-Year Quest of Judaism, Christianity and Islam. Ballantine Books.

Asche, S. E. (1955). Opinions and social pressures. *Scientific American* .

Augustine. Contra Epistulam Parmeniani.

Bagemihl, B. (1999). Biological Exuberance: Animal Homosexuality and Natural Diversity. New York: St Martin's Press.

Barash, D. P., & Liption, J. E. (2001). The Myth of Monogamy: Fidelity and Infidelity in Animals and People. W. H. Freeman.

Bar-Hillel, M., & Neter, E. (1986). How alike is it? versus how likely is it?: A disjunction fallacy in probability judgments. *Journal of Personality and Social Psychology , 69*, 1119-1131.

Barth, K. (1956). *Church Dogmatics* (Vol. IV: The Doctrine of Reconciliation). (G. W. Bromiley, Trans.) Zürich/London: Evangelischer Verlag A.G./T&T Clark Ltd.

Bateson, M., & Mather, M. (2007). Performance on a categorization task suggests that removal of environmental enrichment induces 'pessimism' in captive European starlings. *Animal Welfare , 16*, 33-36.

Beauvoir, S. d. (1949). *Le deuxième sexe.*

Bell, D. (1981). Models and Reality in Economic Discourse. In D. (. Bell, & I. (. Kristol, *The Crisis in Economic Theory* (pp. 57-58). New York: Basic Books.

Bendall, C. (. (1897-1902/1970). Siksasamuccaya: A Compendium of Buddhist Training compiled by Santideva, Chiefly from Earlier Mahayana Sutras.

Osnabruck: Biblio Verlag.

Berlin, I. (2006). *Political Ideas in the Romantic Age.* Princeton NJ: Princeton University Press.

Bhikkhu, T. (2009, October 31). *"Kalama Sutta: To the Kalamas" (AN 3.65).* Retrieved April 1, 2010, from Access to Insight: http://www.accesstoinsight.org/tipitaka/an/an03/an03.065.than.html

Bikhchandani, S., Hirshleifer, D., & Welch, I. (1992). A Theory of Fads, Fashion, Custom, and Cultural Change as Informational Cascades. *Journal of Political Economy , 100* (5), 992-1026.

Black, T. (2009, November). Why they're really scared of Heidegger. *The Spiked Review of Books* .

Blackmore, S. (1999). *The Meme Machine.* Oxford University Press.

Bodhi, B. (2009, June 7). A Look at the Kalama Sutta. *Access to Insight (from BPS Newsletter)* .

Bogdanich, W., & Koli, E. (2003, May 22). 2 Paths of Bayer Drug in 80's: Riskier One Steered Overseas. *New York Times* .

Bohm, D. (1980). Wholeness and the Implicate Order. Routledge.

Boin-Webb, S. (., Rahula, W. (., & Asanga. Abhdharma Samuccaya: The Compendium of the Higher Teaching.

Boissy, A., Manteuffel, G., Jensen, M., Opperman, M. S., Keeling, L., Weinkler, C., et al. (2007). Assessment of Positive Emotions in Animals in order to Improve their Welfare. *Physiol. Behav. , 92*, 375-397.

Bouhdiba, A. (2001). *Sexuality in Islam.* Saqi Press.

Boyer, P., & Liénard, P. (2008). Ritual behavior in obsessive and normal individuals. *Current Directions in Psychological Science , 17* (4), 291-4.

Brahmavamso, A. (2007, March 27th). Buddhism, the Only Real Science. *Daily News (Sri Lanka)* .

Brodie, R. (2009). Virus of the Mind: The New Science of the Meme. Hay House.

Bukhāri. *Saḥiḥ.*

Cameron, D. E. (1956). Psychic Driving. *American Journal of Psychiatry , 112* (7), 502-9.

Capra, F. (1975). The Tao of Physics: An Exploration of the Parallels Between Modern Physics and Eastern Mysticism.

Carse, J. (1998). Finite and Infinite Games, A Vision of Life as Play and Possibility.

Carse, J. (2008). The Religious Case Against Belief.

Carter, P. (2004, May 14). Tainted by Torture: How evidence obtained through coercion is undermining the legal war on terrorism. *Slate* .

Clifford, W. K. (1970). The Ethics of Belief. In G. I. Mavrodes, *The Rationality of Belief in God.* Englewood Cliffs, N. J.: Prentice-Hall.

Cowell, E. B., & Rouse, W. H. (1907). *The Jataka or Stories of the Buddha's Former Births* (Vol. 1907).

Crystal, D. (2006). *How Language Works.* Penguin Books.

Crystal, D. (2007). *How Language Works.* Avery Trade.

Dalai Lama, H. H. (1998). *The Good Heart: A Buddhist Perspective on the Teachings of Jesus.* (R. Kiely, Ed., & G. T. Jinpa, Trans.) Wisdom Publications.

Darwin, C. (1859). On the Origin of Species by Natural Selection. London: John Murray.

Dawkins, M. S. (2008). The Science of Animal Suffering. *Ethology , 114*, 937-945.

Dawkins, R. (1982). The Extended Phenotype: The Long Reach of the Gene. Oxford University Press.

Dawkins, R. (1976). *The Selfish Gene.* Oxford University Press.

Deleuze, J. P. (1813). Histoire Critique du Magnetisme Animal..

Dika, V. (1990). Games of Terror: Halloween, Friday the 13th, and the films of the stalker cycle. Cranbury, NJ: Fairleigh Dickinson University Press.

Elliot, S. H., & Dowson, J. (1869). *The History of India as told by its Own Historians.* London>reprint (1966) New York.

Entick vs. Carrington (1762-3).

Farnsworth, W. (2007). *The Legal Analyst: A Toolkit for Thinking about the Law.* Chicago: Chicago University Press.

Faye, E. (2009). Heidegger: The Introduction of Nazism into Philosophy in Light of the Unpublished Seminars of 1933-1935. (M. B. Smith, Trans.) Yale University Press.

Festinger, L., & Carlsmith, J. M. (1959). Cognitive consequences of forced compliance. *Journal of Abnormal and Social Psychology , 58* (2), 203-210.

Finucane, M. L., Alhakami, A., Slovic, P., & Johnson, S. M. (2000). The affect heuristic in judgments of risks and benefits. *Journal of Behavioral Decision Making , 13* (1), 1-17.

Flew, A. (1975). Thinking about Thinking: Do I sincerely want to be right? London: Collins Fontana.

Frazer, J. (1890). The Golden Bough: A Study in Magic and Religion.

Freud, S. (1930). Civilisation and Its Discontents.

Gerner, M. (2007). Chakzampa Thangtong Gyalpo - Architect, Philosopher and Iron Chain Bridge Builder. (G. (. Verhufen, Trans.) Centre for Bhutan Studies.

Gide, A. (1952). *Ainsi soit-il ou Les Jeux sont faits.* Paris: éditions Gallimard.

Gilovich, T. (1991). How we know what isn't so: The fallibility of human reason in everyday life. New York: The Free Press.

Gilovich, T., Vallone, R., & Tversky, A. (1985). The hot hand in basketball: On the misperception of random sequences. *Cognitive Psychology* , *17*, 295-314.

Gil-Robles, A. Report by the Commissioner of Human Rights.

Goldacre, B. (2008). *Bad Science.* Fourth Estate.

Gray, J. (2007). Black Mass: Apocalyptic Religion and the Death of Utopia. Allen Lane.

Hanninen, O., Farago, M., & Monos, E. (1983). Ignaz Philipp Semelweiss, the Prophet of Bacteriology. *Infection Control* , *4* (5), 367-370.

Hare, E. M., & Woodward, F. L. (1932/2006). *The Book of the Gradual Sayings.* Delhi: Motilal Banarsidass.

Harmon-Jones, E., Brehm, J. W., Greenberg, J., Simon, L., & Nelson, D. E. (1996). Evidence that the production of aversive consequences is not necessary to create cognitive dissonance. *Journal of Personality and Social Psychology* , *70* (1), 5-16.

Henkel, L. A., & Mather, M. (2007). Memory attributions for choices: How beliefs shape our memories. *Journal of Memory and Language* (57), 163-176.

Hoffman, F. J. (1987, 2002). *Rationality and Mind in Early Buddhism.* Delhi: Motilal Banarsidass.

Hume, D. (1888). *A Treatise of Human Nature.* Oxford University Press.

Ibn al-Jawzi, A. F. Talbis Iblis, Possession by the Devil.

Ibn Hisham, A. M.l. (c 218 h./1355 CE/1937 CE). *Sīrat Rasūl Allāh, the Life of the Prophet of Allāh.* Cairo.

Ivereigh, A. (2010, April 14). Gay priests are not paedophiles. *The Guardian* .

Jain, K. P. (1926). The Jaina References in the Buddhist Literature. *Indian Historical Quarterly* , *II* (4), 698-709.

Jefferson, T. (1904). *Works* (Vol. II). G. P. Putnam and Sons.

Johnson, B. (2006, May 25). Blair's Crackdown on Freedom Is an Inspiration to Tyrants. *The Telegraph* .

Johnson, M., & Gearty, C. (2007). Civil Liberties and the Challenge of Terrorism. *British Social Attitudes, the Twenty-Third Report* .

Judson, O. (2003). Dr Tatiana's Sex Advice to All Creation: The Definitive Guide to the Evolutionary Biology of Sex. Vintage.

Kahneman, D. (2003). Maps of bounded rationality: A perspective on intuitive judgment and choice. In T. Frangsmyr (Ed.), *Les Prix Nobel 2002 [Nobel Prizes 2002]*. Stockholm, Sweden: Almquist & Wiksell International.

Kahneman, D., & Tversky, A. (1979). Prospect Theory: an Analysis of Decision under Risk. *Econometrica* , *XLVII*, 263-291.

Kant, I. (1764). Observations on the Feelings of the Beautiful and the Sublime.

Keenan, J. (2010, January 20). Heidegger, Hitler's 'Spiritual Guide'. *The Guardian* .

Khan, M. W. (2009). The Prophet of Peace: Teachings of the Prophet Muhammad. Penguin.

Kiesler, C. A., & Pallak, M. S. (1976). Arousal properties of dissonance manipulations. *Psychological Bulletin* , *83* (6), 1014-1025.

Kipling, R. (1892). Naulahka: A Story of West and East.

Kirsch, J. (2004). God Against the Gods: the History of the War Between Monotheism and Polytheism. Viking Compass.

Klein, N. (2007). The Shock Doctrine: the Rise of Disaster Capitalism. Metropolitan Books.

kLong-chen-pa, D.-m. '.-z. theg-pa mtha'-dag-gi don-gsal-bar byed-pa grub-pai mtha' rin-po-chei mdzod.

Knight, F. H. (1932). The Newer Economics and the Control of Economic Activity. *Journal of Political Economy* , *40* (4), 455.

Koppl, H. (2008). Establishing Appearances as Divine: Rongzom Chokyi Zangpo on Reasoning, Madhyamaka, and Purity. Snow Lion.

Kramer, H. (1487). *Malleus Maleficarum.*

Kūfi, M. `. (early 13th CE). *Chach Nāma.*

Kuran, T. (1995). Private Truths, Public Lies: The Social Consequences of Preference Falsification. Cambridge, Mass.: Harvard University Press.

Lewis, D. (1998). *Murder by reason of insanity.* London: Random House.

Lingpa, D. (2002). Buddhahood Without Meditation: A Visionary Account Known as Refining Apparent Phenomena. Padma Publishing.

Locke, J. (1690). An Essay Concerning Human Understanding. London.

Lopez, D. S. (2007). The Madman's Middle Way: Reflections on Reality of the Tibetan monk Gendun Chopel. Chicago: University of Chicago Press.

Lusthaus, D. (2002). *Buddhist Phenomenology.* Routledge.

Mackay, C. (1852). *Extraordinary Popular Delusions & The Madness of Crowds* (2nd ed.). London: Office of the National Illustrated Library.

Mackay, C. (1841). Extraordinary Popular Delusions and the Madness of Crowds.

Maio, G. (2001). History of medical involvement in torture - then and now. *The Lancet* (357), 1609-11.

McElroy, D. (2010, April 6). Calls for inquiry into Apache attack on Iraqi civilians. *The Telegraph* .

McRae, J. (. (2004). *The Vimalakirti Sutra.* Berkley: Numata Center for Buddhist

Translation and Research.

Milgram, S. (1963). Behavioural Study of Obedience. *Journal of Abnormal and Social Psychology , 67*, pp. 371-378.

Milgram, S. (1974). The Perils of Obedience. *Harper's Magazine* .

Mill, J. S. (1998). *On Liberty and Other Essays.* (J. Gray, Ed.) Oxford and New York: Oxford University Press.

Milton, J. (1654). Defensio Secunda Pro Populo Anglicano.

Monier-Williams. (2008). Sanskrit-English Dictionary.

Monin, B., & Miller, D. T. (2001). Moral credentials and the expression of prejudice. *Journal of Personality and Social Psychology , 81* (1), 33-43.

Murphay, C. (1992, February). 'To Be' in Their Bonnets. *The Atlantic* .

Muslim. *Saḥiḥ.*

Nanayakkara, S. (2002). How Free is Freedom of Thought? *Bodhi Leaves* (156).

Nattier, J. (. (2007). The Bodhisattva Path, Based on the Ugrapariprccha, A Mahayana Sutra. Delhi: Motilal Banarsidass.

Nichiren. (1260). Rissho Ankoku Ron, Establishment of the Legitimate Teaching for the Protection of the Country.

Nisbett, R., & Wilson, T. (1977). Telling more than we can know: Verbal reports on mental processes. *Psychological review , 84* (3), 231-259.

Norbu, N., & Clemente, A. (1999). The Supreme Source: the Fundamental Tantra of the Dzogchen Semde. New York: Snow Lion.

Norbu, T. (2007). *A Cascading Waterfall of Nectar.* Shambhala Publications.

Orwell, G. (????). *Animal Farm.*

Otto, R. (1917). Das Heilige - Über das Irrationale in der Idee des Göttlichen und sein Verhältnis zum Rationalen.

Otto, R. (1923). *The Idea of the Holy.* Oxford: Oxford University Press.

Panikkar, R. (1977). *The Vedic Experience.*

Paul, E. S., Harding, E. J., & Mendl, M. (2005). Measuring emotional responses in animals: the utility of a cognitive approach. *Neursci. Biobehav. Rev. , 29*, 469-491.

Peterson, M., Hasker, W., Reichenbach, B., & Basinger, D. (2008). *Reason and Religious Belief: An Introduction to the Philosophy of Religion.* Oxford University Press.

Pew Forum on Religion and Public Life. (2009). *Global restrictions on religion.* Washington D.C.: Pew Research Centre.

Popper, K. (1945; 5th edition 1966). *The Open Society and Its Enemies.* Routledge & Kegan Paul Ltd.

Prasad, H. S. (2007). The Centrality of Ethics in Buddhism: Explanatory Essays.

Delhi: Motilal Banarsidass.

Priestley, J. (1785). The Importance and Extent of Free Enquiry in Matters of Religion.

Proudfoot, W. (1985). *Religious Experience.* Berkeley: University of California Press.

Quine, W. V. (1960). *Word and Object.* MIT Press.

Quṭb, S. (1964). Ma`alim fi l-Ṭariq.

Ramanan, S. V. (1966/2002). *Nagarjuna's Philosophy.* Delhi: Motilal Banarsidass.

Richerson, B. a. (2004). The Origin and Evolution of Cultures. Oxford: Oxford University Press.

Rolls, E. T. (2005). *Emotion Explained.* Oxford: Oxford University Press.

Rumi, J. u.-D. (662-672 h. (1260 CE)). Mathnawi Na`nawi, Meaningful Couplets (Persian).

Rumi, J.l. u.-D., & Nicholson, R. A. (1925-1940). *Mathnawi of Jalaluddin Rumi.*

Russell, B. (1946). The History of Western Philosophy.

Safran, J. (2003). Psychoanalysis & Buddhism: An Unfolding Dialogue . Wisdom Publications.

Sandem, A. I., Braastad, B. O., & Boe, K. L. (2002). Eye white may indicate emotional state on a frustration-contentedness axis in dairy cows. *Appl. Anim. Behav. Science , 79*, 1-10.

Scerri, E. (1989). Eastern Mysticism and the Alleged Parallels with Physics. *American Journal of Physics , 57* (8), 687-692.

Schmitt, G. J., & Shulsky, A. (1991). Silent Warfare: Understanding the World of Intelligence.

Semmelweis, I. (1847). Etiology, Concept and Prophylaxis of Childbed Fever. Vienna.

Sen, A. (2006). Identity and Violence: The Illusion of Destiny (Issues of Our Time). New York: W. W. Norton.

Shaffer, P. (1973, 1993). *Equus.* Longman.

Shweder, R. A. (1977). Likeness and Likelihood in Everyday Thought: Magical Thinking in Judgments About Personality. *Current Anthropology , 18* (4), 637-658.

Singh, J. (2005). *Parātrīśikāvivaraṇa of Abhinavagupta.* Delhi: Motilal Banarsidass.

Smith, D. (2004, September 5). Muslim Leaders Condemn Killers. *The Observer* .

Suzuki, D. T., Fromm, E., & De Martino, R. (1970). *Zen Buddhism and Psychoanalysis.* Harper Collins.

Tajfel, H. (1970). Experiments in Intergroup Discrimination. *Scientific American , 223*, pp. 96-102.

Tajfel, H. (1982). *Social identity and intergroup relations.* Cambridge: Cambridge

University Press.

Tajfel, H., & Turner, J. (1979). An Integrative Theory of Intergroup Conflict. In W. G. Austin, & S. Worchel, *The Social Psychology of Intergroup Relations* (pp. 94-109). Monterey, CA: Brooks-Cole.

The American Heritage Dictionary of the English Language (4th ed.). (2004). Houghton Mifflin Company.

Thera, N. (1956/1979). *A Manual of Abhidhamma.* Kuala Lumpur, Malaysia: Buddhist Missionary Society.

Thera, S. (2009, June 7). *"Kalama Sutta: The Instruction to the Kalamas" (AN 3.65).* Retrieved April 1, 2010, from Access to Insight: http://www.accesstoinsight.org/tipitaka/an/an03/an03.065.soma.htm l

Thera, S. (1987). Kalama Sutta: The Buddha's Charter of Free Inquiry. *The Wheel* (8).

Tin, S. U. (1982). *The Anecdotes of Sayagyi U Ba Khin.* Calne, UK: The Sayagyi U Ba Khin Memorial Trust.

Tirmidhī. *Jāmi`.*

Tocqueville, A. d. Democracy.

Trench, R. C. (1852). *On the Study of Words.*

Trigg, R. (1998). Rationality and Religion: Does Faith Need Reason. Oxford: Blackwell.

Tversky, A., & Kahneman, D. (1974). Judgment under Uncertainty: Heuristics and Biases. *Science , 185* (4157), 1124-31.

Velez de Cea, A. (2004). The Criteria of Goodness in the Pali Nikayas and the Nature of Buddhist Ethics. *Journal of Buddhist Ethics , XI*, 123-142.

Viner, J. (1972). The Role of Providence in the Social Order: An Essay in Intellectual History. Philadelphia: American Philosophical Society.

Wallace, B. A. (2009). Contemplative Science: Where Buddhism and Neuroscience Converge (Columbia Series in Science and Religion). Colombia University Press.

Wallace, B. A. (2008). Embracing Mind: The Common Ground of Science and Spirituality. Shambhala.

Wallace, B. A. (2009). Hidden Dimensions: The Unification of Physics and Consciousness (Columbia Series in Science and Religion). Columbia University Press.

Watson, B. t. (1994). *The Lotus Sutra.* Colombia University Press.

Weber, T. (2004). *Gandhi as Disciple and Mentor*. Cambridge: Cambridge University Press.

Williams, T. (1996). Trying to Survive on the Darker Side: 1980s Family Horror. In B. K. Grant, *The Dread of Difference: Gender and the Horror Film* (pp. 164-165). Austin, Texas: University of Texas Press.

Wilson, B. (2009). What Price Liberty? How Freedom was Won and is Being Lost. London: Faber and Faber Ltd.

Winkielman, P., Zajonc, R. B., & Schwarz, N. (1997). Subliminal affective priming attributional interventions. *Cognition and Emotion , 11* (4), 433-465.

Colophon

Under the cool Nāgārjuna Mountain near Kathmandu, on the night of the full moon anniversary of the Buddha's revelation of *The Tantra of the Wheel of Time*, five days after the discovery in the constellation Cassiopeia of Gamma Ray Burst 100413B, a long emission of the highest energy light ray known caused by one of the largest explosions in the universe, this commentary was completed by the pretender to understanding named 'Patience of Uḍḍiyāṇa'. May whatever virtue that there is in it convert into a source of liberation for all sentient beings.

Mangalam! Mangalam! Mangalam!

Overview of the Commentary